THE A.
STRIKES AGAIN

COLLECTED WRITINGS OF THE ANIMAL LIBERATION FRONT IN NORTH AMERICA

Rights Group Claims Credit

Animals Stolen From Scientists

By PETER M. WARREN, *Times Staff Writer*

More than 100 animals being used in medical research at the City of Hope National Medical Center were stolen early Sunday morning. The building in which the animals were kept was defaced with animal rights slogans.

A group calling itself the Animal Liberation Front claimed responsibility for the theft Sunday, saying it "freed" the dogs, cats, mice and rabbits because they were being sacrificed in what the group called unnecessary medical experiments. A spokesman said the animals were being kept in "inhumane, immoral conditions."

Charles Mathews, a City of Hope spokesman, said the loss of the animals would seriously affect about $400,000 in cancer and emphysema research work being done at the center's large-animal facility.

"We will not be responding to their allegations point by point until we've had a chance to thoroughly assess the situation . . . including talking with all the (scientists) involved to assess how much damage has been done to these vital research projects by this illegal act," he said.

Dr. Joseph Holden, associate director for research, said the facility's inventory of animals showed stolen animals included 36 dogs, 12 cats, 12 rabbits, 28 mice and 18 rats.

'First-Class Facility'

"We run a first-class facility here," he said. City of Hope officials refused repeated requests from the media to view the interior of the cinder-block building that housed all the dogs and cats taken by the intruders. Dogs had access to the outside through ramps.

The thefts were discovered by Thomas Amaral, who supervises the care of the animals there. Los Angeles Sheriff's Department investigators, who have called the crime a burglary, were called to the research area about 7 a.m., said sheriff's spokesman David Tellez.

Ingrid Newkirk, a director of the Washington-based People for the Ethical Treatment of Animals, said the animals were removed from a cinder-block

CRAIG T. MATHEW / Los Angeles Times

Thomas Amaral, supervisor of animal facility, beside cages that were broken into.

building and a trailer at the research facility in Duarte by about a dozen persons in the early morning hours Sunday, then given immediate veterinary care, special food, vitamins and antibiotic therapy. New homes have been found for the animals, she said.

In a telephone interview, Newkirk said the facility had "peeling paint, soiled floors, rusted cages with broken wiring and fetid air."

"Dogs were lying with bloated bellies, multiple tumors. They were standing in water from the rain," she added.

She said she was acting as a spokesperson for the Animal Liberation Front, which took responsibility in a similar announcement for a theft last Christmas Day of 12 dogs from Harbor-UCLA Medical Center.

Please see ANIMALS, Page 10

The A.L.F. Strikes Again: Collected Writings Of The Animal Liberation Front In North America

This collection first published in 2021 by Warcry.

ISBN 978-1732709690

For information, submission guidelines, bulk requests, or general inquiries, please contact:

peter@peteryoung.me

Also published by Warcry:

Liberate: Stories & Lessons On Animal Liberation Above The Law (Peter Young)

Flaming Arrows: Collected Writings of Animal Liberation Front Activist Rod Coronado (Rod Coronado)

From Dusk 'til Dawn: An Insider's View of the Growth of the Animal Liberation Movement (Keith Mann)

Underground. The Animal Liberation Front in the 1990s (Various)

Cover image: Animal Liberation Front raid at University of Arizona, 1989.

"Let this message be clear to all who victimize the innocent: We're watching.

And by axe, drill, or crowbar—we're coming through your door."

A.L.F. statement after 2004 liberation of 401 animals from the University Of Iowa.

ANIMAL LIBERATION FRONT GUIDELINES

- To liberate animals from places of abuse, i.e. fur farms, laboratories, factory farms, etc. and place them in good homes where they may live out their natural lives free from suffering.

- To inflict economic damage to those who profit from the misery and exploitation of animals; and

- To reveal the horror and atrocities committed against animals behind locked doors by performing non-violent direct actions and liberations.

CONTENTS

The ALF is non elitist, relatively easy to join, and innately secure. Because of its decentralized structure (small, independent cells), it has become a large and effective terrorist group.

THE A.L.F. IN THEIR OWN WORDS

This is the definitive record of the Animal Liberation Front—their history as told by those who made it.

The A.L.F. Strikes Again ties together over 40 years of documents with one goal: A complete collection of all writing by members of the Animal Liberation Front (and A.L.F.-adjacent groups) in North America.

The A.L.F. breaks into buildings, rescues animals, and destroys property of animal abusers. That's what they do. They work outside the law, and, unless caught, their identities are never known. They are not an organization, you don't join, and you are not invited. You carry out an action in accordance with the A.L.F. guidelines, and you can claim your work as the A.L.F..

For the purpose of this book, that's all the reader has to know. This book is a platform for the A.L.F. to tell their story—without the filter of editors, narrators, critics, or historians.

The Lost Chicken Heist

Twelve years ago, a journalist requested the communique for my first significant A.L.F. action. After fast-forwarding through a blurry memory-lane of small-scale sabotage (for which writing a statement is neither standard nor sensical), I landed at my first action of any strategy or skill: the break-in at a chicken slaughterhouse in downtown Seattle. Friends and I entered a fenced-off loading dock through the roof, trashed an office, and rescued three chickens.

It was a blip in A.L.F. history, but to us (and three chickens), significant. This marked an escalation in our tactics, our first live liberation, and the execution of something they said couldn't be done—a break-in and burglary of a building in downtown Seattle.

As such, I placed a lot of weight on the statement (aka communique) we would release to the media. To me, our short statement had a twofold purpose: A "coming out" to animal abusers that a new threat had risen and nowhere was safe, and a call to action for a new generation of 1990s activists—the 1990s movement was too comfortable with small-scale symbolic sabotage, and it was time to inherit the tactics of the previous generation. It was time to start breaking into buildings again.

The next day, my search for an untraceable typewriter on which to compose the communique took me to the Value Village thrift store. Rather than purchase a typewriter that, for security reasons, I would be forced to immediately discard; I found a dusty 1980s model, walked it to the used furniture room, took over a couch, and—surrounded by shoppers—typed the communique.

I mailed four photocopies: One to the *Seattle Times*, one to the *Seattle Post Intelligencer*, one to *No Compromise*, and one to *Underground.*

And 13 years after this action, when asked to produce the communique—it was gone. There was no digital record, no archive to turn to, no evidence it existed. The editorial collectives at *No Compromise* and *Underground* had long since disbanded, and penetrating layers of corporate lattice to reach the *Seattle Times* archives seemed improbable—if the original document survived at all. The typed statement had simply been erased from history.

The communique for my next action of consequence—a break-in at a pig slaughterhouse in Burlington, Washington (in which we removed every killing instrument from the building)—had also vanished. And communiques for the next several month's actions—which may be confessed to at a later time—were all gone.

(The chicken slaughterhouse communique later surfaced, and is included on page 390.)

SEATTLE - An animal-rights organization is claiming credit for a break-in at Acme Poultry last weekend.

In an unsigned letter to the media, the Animal Liberation Front took responsibility for the raid early Sunday. The letter claimed the group had raided the plant, at 1024 S.King Street, destroying paperwork in an office, sabotaging machinery and taking three chickens. The letter indicated the break-in was done to protest the killing of animals.

This incident 12 years ago was the impetus for this book, and preserving what history remains is its guiding premise.

With few blindspots, this book compiles that history—settling the score on what the A.L.F. is, what they believe, and exactly how they do what they do.

Actions To Ashes, Justice To Dust

The material here was compiled across decades of sources—most of it in print format, and most of it (nearly) lost to history. Approximately 70% of the entries are not available anywhere on the internet (and the digital deterioration of what remains accelerates daily).

A collective belief the internet adequately records and preserves history has had disastrous consequences for below-the-radar historical niches. A small publication in the print era might have 1,000 copies in existence. It then follows that 1,000 individual documents have to be lost or destroyed before that history is erased. Online, it requires only a single site owner to lapse on a hosting payment for that history to vanish.

The early material for this book was first compiled 12 years ago. More recently, when comparing the internet-sourced portion from that era, I found well over half of it had vanished. It has become clear the internet accelerates—rather than prevents—the erosion of history.

This book offers an indelible record of what remains.

Preserve The History, Destroy The Evidence

The anonymity of the A.L.F. makes its history inherently fragile. Animal liberators suffer the same vulnerability of other clandestine groups: relying on those outside its ranks to be custodians of its message and archivists of its history. This happens with very mixed results.

Basic security dictates A.L.F. operatives purge themselves of all evidence. Post-raid success hinges in part on how quickly and thoroughly the guilty can create maximum distance between themselves and all video, photographic, and/or written documentation. Once the communique email is sent or the package hits the mailbox—the liberator abandons all control over the preservation of their work. Whether it's recorded into history—or erased from it—

is left to the whims of those on the safe side of the legal line.

If the greatest way to honor the A.L.F. is to become them, and the second is to support them if arrested; perhaps third is to preserve the history they have no ability to preserve themselves.

Scope Of Inclusion: The Three-Part Test

Every entry here had to meet several guidelines.

The first threshold for inclusion was geographical: The actions represented had to occur in North America. Documenting Europe (and beyond) is another (and much larger) book.

The second threshold was having an overt association with a larger movement to save animals. Writings from the A.L.F. or A.L.F.-adjacent groups passed this threshold—including offshoot (and sometimes one-off) groups such as the Animal Rights Militia. Orchestrated actions that were *not* claimed (such as unclaimed lab or fur-industry supplier break-ins) were still included . Excluded were opportunistic actions which were not claimed, such as rescuing a dog from a backyard (however admirable), and actions carried out by non-vegans or vegetarians.

The third and most restrictive threshold was "significance." Any writings related to, or from a person imprisoned for, any small scale property damage were not included. The threshold for "significance" was undefined, but in filtering content for publication, ambiguity was rare. Most actions fall clearly on one side of the line. E.g. broken windows and spraypainting = not significant. Arson = significant.

These standards insured this book as a quality-dense, deep-dive into the highest levels of A.L.F. activity—containing the words of those who have delivered the biggest impact, made the most history, and saved the most animals.

Dispatches From The Underground: The A.L.F.'s Writing In Five Forms

The significance of this book's existence is that, unless arrested, the A.L.F. are rarely free to speak. Every dispatch, communique, or broadcast introduces risk of arrest. Every anonymously-authored piece is written under the looming shadow of federal investigations and prison. For the effort alone required to safely transmit from the underground, it is remarkable this book exists at all.

The book is broken down into the five forms A.L.F. writings take:

How It Was Done: In these first-hand accounts, the A.L.F. gives a step-by-step account of some of their most spectacular actions.
Interviews: Whether granted in anonymity while underground, or after their arrest, rare tell-all interviews with the A.L.F.
Essays: Any writing outside the scope of the other four sections is here. From anonymous bulletins for the A.L.F. to communicate between cells, to overt calls to action, to prison writings, to critiques of the above ground movement—it's all here.
Communiques: When the A.L.F. carries out an action, there is but one chance to declare it as the work of animal liberators: the communique. The communique is the only vehicle for liberators to declare the what, where, when and why of their actions.
How To Guides: Literal manuals on carrying out A.L.F. actions—large to small.

The material here shares minimal overlap with other books, with very little ever seeing an audience beyond small publications and even smaller corners of the internet. Among the content currently available elsewhere are excerpts from *Flaming Arrows* (Coronado), *Underground: The A.L.F. in the 1990s* (various), *Liberate* (myself), and *Terrorists Or Freedom Fighters?* (Best).

On Forming A Complete A.L.F. Bibliography

The mission of this book was to capture all A.L.F. writings that don't already exist in book form. And it comes very close.

To the historian or voyeur looking to go even deeper into the writings of the A.L.F.—what would a complete collection look like? What's missing? I'll come as close as possible to answering that question.

How it was done

There are no known first-hand accounts omitted here, save for an alternate account of sinking two Icelandic whaling ships titled the "Raid on Reykjavik," found in *Flaming Arrows* (Coronado).

Interviews

Two notable A.L.F. interviews did not surface for the publication of this book. One, an interview with one of the activists behind the raid at City of Hope in 1984 printed in an early issue of *PETA News*. Two, a short pamphlet titled *Interviews With California A.L.F. Activists.*

Interviews with former prisoners could fill volumes. From Rod Coronado to David Barbarash to Gary Yourofsky to Jonthan Paul and several others, ex-prisoner interviews are too voluminous to track. While the mission of compiling unpublished anonymous A.L.F. writings was accomplished within 90%, once caught, A.L.F. activists no longer have the constraints of anonymity, and their output becomes prohibitively spacious. Most former-prisoners occupy a position under the radar after their release, while some reconfigure their arrest record into a soapbox. As such, many hundreds of interviews have resulted. Included here are a deliberately chosen "best of."

Essays

All known anonymous (pre-arrest) A.L.F. writings are included.

Writings from former prisoners face the same more-material-than-space issues explained above, but the following books bring us close to a complete essay collection: *Always Looking Forward* (Bond), *Flaming Arrows* (Coronado), and *Liberate* (myself) add another 600 pages of writing to the A.L.F.'s record.

Communiques

The older the action—or the further it predates the internet—the less likely it's communique was preserved. Notably absent are all but a few 1980s communiques—the period of the A.L.F.'s most legendary raids. Did these actions have communiques? Or were the official press statements left to PETA, LCA, and (later) the A.L.F. Supporter's Group (the three most common conduits between the A.L.F. and the aboveground)? And if communiques do exist, who has them? And how do the answers to these questions differ for the 1990s, during which many dozens of communiques are either unknown to exist or are MIA? History has faded to the point that these questions became difficult to answer.

Evidence of lost 1980s communiques is revealed in media coverage, which occasionally included references such as "In a statement, the A.L.F. said…." Leaving us with excerpts, but no intact communiques. (Only a few intact statements from the 1980s exist, including the A.L.F.'s statement on their raid of the University of Oregon in 1986, which only surfaced when a student contacted me after finding an original copy in a student newspaper file cabinet). Any surviving copies are likely resting in the archives of PETA, Last

Chance For Animals, and (later) the A.L.F. Supporter's Group, along with any media they distributed them to.

Lost 1990s communiques may be even more elusive for two reasons. One, unlike PETA and LCA, the 1990s organizations that received and disseminated communiques (The A.L.F. Supporter's Group in Canada, and later, a press office in Minnesota) were less structured and stable, and far less likely to have an "archive" in any formal sense (were you even able to track down their organizers). Two, the A.L.F. in the 90s all but abandoned media strategy. Media-oriented components to actions that were almost obligatory in the 1980s —video of the raid and rescued animals, the confiscation and release of documents— became sparse. Claims of responsibility took an emphasis on a call to action for activists, and threats to abusers, over anything optimized for media.

As such, the "diary of actions" in publications such as *Underground* and *No Compromise* are laden with brief communique excerpts, while the full statement remained unpublished. Whatever the editor's motives for these omissions, we have been deprived of crucial history.

In cases of partial communiques where at least one paragraph was salvaged, the excerpt was included here (or in the instance of the Fur Breeders Agricultural Co-Op bombing—an action too significant to leave out—three salvaged sentences sufficed).

I was fortunate to turn up communiques for the majority of "significant" actions for the 90s and beyond.

How-to guides

Only three notable how-to guides are missing.

First (and regrettably), those seeking A.L.F.-authored writing on constructing incendiary devices will have to reference this book's source material. Content on constructing such devices was redacted—and one guide dedicated entirely to this subject (*Arson Around With Auntie A.L.F.*) was omitted entirely.

This was done not for legal concerns, but reasons more banal: preserving this book's distribution. The recent trend of online booksellers and distributors (including the one distributing this book) banning books which contain material on arson drove this capitulation. Had the threat been assessed as something short of "almost 100% imminent," I would have erred on the side of inclusion.

If *The Final Nail #1* has not vanished from history, it has vanished from my personal archives and those of my sources. If memory serves, the changes in content from #1 to #2 were negligible, and the reader is deprived of very little. A *Final Nail #1* "supplement" is included.

Lastly, also omitted is a rare untitled guide to carrying out lab raids, unofficially dubbed "*The Final Nail for labs.*" A rough draft circulated among activists in the early-to-mid 2000s, and was never formally released. This draft (ostensibly written by those with experience on this subject) contained instructions ranging from lock picking to identifying labs and campus buildings imprisoning animals, side-by-side with a state-by-state guide to known research labs. While copies were preserved and considered for inclusion here, the document appears partially incomplete, and the reasons it was never formally released are unknown. With its author(s) unavailable to grant permission, it is not included.

(Submissions of missing material can be sent to peter@peteryoung.me)

Status By Insinuation: Full Clout, Hold The Risk

The aforementioned passive threat of historical atrophy is accelerated by a more active one—"supporters" exploiting the A.L.F.'s work in diabolical ways, spinning history, and attempting to remake the A.L.F. in their own self-serving image.

There is a historical vacuum this book intends to eliminate, one that has opened space for this mini-plague of "direct action commentators." The most insidious of which commit a form of "status by insinuation," building a personal brand hinting at a role in the direct action they champion (spoiler: they never had one).

The FBI knocking at your door does not make you a participant, your friends getting arrested does not make you an expert, and professing academic knowledge of history doesn't write you into it as a frontline fighter.

For every activist who risks their freedom for animals, there are 100 using their image to sell t-shirts or drive website traffic. For every A.L.F. member who went to sleep fearing a SWAT team at their door, there are 10 in the safety zone, once briefly inconvenienced by an FBI visit, now doing speaking tours like they were active participants. And for every raider for whom merely telling their story is a jailable offense, there are thousands who lack the courage to break laws while pontificating on "toxic masculinity in the A.L.F." from their parent's basement.

These people will find this preservation of the A.L.F.'s words uncomfortably inconvenient. In this book, many liars are exposed, many revisionists laid bare, many motives and attributes revealed as irrelevant to—or uncorrelated with—A.L.F. participation. This record will come as problematic to current or future attempts at imprinting A.L.F. history from ideological or status-seeking sidelines.

This collection settles the historical record on many fronts, forcing all hanger-ons, idealogues, and groupies into obsolescence; and returning the stage to those who earned it.

Poison Fills The Void

How would the A.L.F. be recorded by history were their words not preserved? What distortions has this void allowed?

To start, media distortions. In the absence of the A.L.F.'s words, painting them as "terrorists" (assigning a motive of "terror") is an easy sell. No amount of evidence will stop journalists from ignoring the A.L.F.'s driving motive of saving animals, but this book lays bare the lie that the A.L.F. is motivated by anything else.

Similarly, the media myth of the A.L.F. as "opportunistic vandals" is dispelled. Stories of staking out labs for weeks and large teams emptying multiple buildings of animals undetected tells a much more deliberate and methodical story.

And what of distortions by academics and historians? A clandestine group unavailable to challenge any brush they are painted with creates room for endless distortions. The anarchist academic, "social justice scholar," and "counter terrorism expert" all have free reign to exploit anonymous groups as props to bolster the credibility of whatever thesis they peddle.

No single document obligates those with an agenda to yield to its facts. But this book offers a counter to future distortions, and tethers outside commentators to the truth.

Forced To A Side

With the erasure of any lingering ambiguities to hide behind, this collection forces the reader to take a side.

For those not sold on the philosophical underpinnings of the A.L.F.'s work, all such ambiguities are removed. For those unconvinced of the A.L.F.'s efficacy, innumerable victories are showcased. And most importantly, for the activist on the threshold of action and lacking a "how," nearly every tactical secret is revealed.

With no stone unturned, no excuses left, and no blindspots left to hide in, this collection forces the reader off the precipice of indecision.

One-Stop Plotting

To capture how dispirate these writings have been to date, consider the journey of a young activist wishing to learn how the A.L.F. carries out a raid of a laboratory.

Internet research would be almost entirely futile, but may bring up grainy VHS-sourced footage of activists raiding the University of Minnesota or UC-Riverside, leaving nearly every question unresolved (How did they get in? How did they evade alarms? Do labs have alarms? How did they find the lab? How did they know where to go once inside?).

They might move deeper into the internet-depths and find an old PDF: *An Animal Liberation Primer*. The info here is cursory, still leaving more questions than answers.

Had they the rare persistence to forge onward, they wouldn't come close to a well-rounded "how to" guide without making several more stops, among them "Raiding Arizona" (in the book *Underground: The A.L.F. in the 1990s*), *Memories of Freedom* (a PDF and print zine), and old hard copies of *No Compromise*. Only then could one assemble a patchwork of tactical crumbs that come moderately close to a workable model for breaking into a lab.

And even then, the aspiring raider would be best served filling remaining holes by wading through dozens of communiques, interviews, and more—an unmanageable task with no clear road map.

Without following this convoluted path, the only alternative courses of action are abandoning the mission, or reinventing the wheel without the hard-fought knowledge of generations before them.

The A.L.F. Strikes Again brings all these resources (and more) together. If the A.L.F. in North America said it or wrote it, it's probably here.

Homage To The Co-Conspirators

To most readers, it will be unapparent how close history came to the majority of these writings never existing. Were it not for a handful of publications, the A.L.F. would have had no platform to disseminate their writing, and history would have been robbed of it all. *Militant Vegan, Underground, No Compromise*, and *Bite Back* alone published the majority of pre-internet North American A.L.F. writing. Had a handful of people not launched these publications, the A.L.F. would have had nowhere to submit their "how it was done" articles, no one to publish their communiques, and no one to cheerlead their work.

Prior to the internet, the world came far too close to a nearly 25-year black-out of A.L.F. history.

Digital preservation has been only marginally less spotty. The transience of internet content became glaring in the research for this book, with the majority of digital-age writing having vanished from their original sources, found only in the dark recesses of internet archives, and snapshots of long-vanished websites.

Outside of these publications, the broader world of A.L.F. supporters have been poor custodians of their history, and we are grateful for those who gave the A.L.F. a platform—however briefly—and made this book possible.

The Honor Of Thievery

Opinions are just words until you take a risk for them. Convictions are just theater until stress-tested under the weight of social or legal consequences.

The words in this book come from a place of credibility, forged in sleepless nights and first-degree felonies. The integrity of the authors cannot be questioned, because by virtue of their risks, their credibility is bulletproof.

For Every Story, A Hundred Untold

The stories here can be read as engaging narratives, the essays as historical insights, the communiques as periscopes into a secret world. This is the book's face value, and it delivers.

Yet this book has a hidden layer, where its greatest impact is felt.

Most "true crime" stories are written after the culprits have served their time. The stories here are written in secrecy by fugitives. Most interviews are given conversationally across a table. The interviews here are done behind masks in hotel rooms. Most essays are written at home in slippers. The essays here were typed on public computers in partial disguise with two layers of gloves.

To experience the depth of these writings, consider the stories behind the story, the parts that can't be told.

The menagerie of crowbars and sledgehammers abandoned at the scene unused, because the morning of the raid, the lab tech left the master keys in an unlocked office. The action unclaimed so as to not bring in the DNA resources of federal investigators after a conspirator cut themselves on broken glass. The floor of animals that couldn't be emptied after months of planning because the stolen key card permissions changed the day of the raid. The building blueprints ordered from the campus facilities department in crude disguise. The room of pigeons discovered minutes after the animal transport vehicle left. The lookout brought to fill in last-minute, who threw away boxes of damming files confiscated from the lab because they "got scared." The communique sent the morning after, one state away and bleary-eyed, from a display computer in an Apple store. The nights hiding out under stairs inside a locked building, taking notes on overnight basement activity. The lonely and unsuspecting lab worker who gave a well-acted "suitor" a full tour at 12am.

These words are the echoes of calculated risks, hasty flight, and close calls. And their full weight cannot be felt without affection for the tomes of history that hide between each line.

Voice Of The Voice Of The Voiceless

Forty years into the A.L.F.'s history in North America, despite over 1,000 actions, being the subject of multiple congressional hearings, and surviving the label of "America's number one domestic terrorist threat"—their history has been largely untold.

Academics, journalists, internal opposition and external opposition—many have taken small shots at the full story. Among it all, the A.L.F.'s voice in its own history is the one pushed furthest to the back. In being the saviors of the voiceless, one also becomes the voiceless.

In this collection, the A.L.F.'s voice is restored.

Not Guilty

Regarded by many as heroes today, yet regarded by all as heroes tomorrow—history will vindicate the Animal Liberation Front.

-Peter Young

Special thanks to all the publications that made these writings possible: *Bite Back, No Compromise, Militant Vegan, Animal's Agenda, Underground, PETA News,* and more.

And thanks especially to the Animal Liberation Front.

HOW IT WAS DONE

How the A.L.F. carried out some of its biggest raids.

CONTENTS

HOW IT WAS DONE

Arguably the quintessential form of A.L.F. writing is the "how it was done" piece—first-hand accounts of spectacular A.L.F. raids.

You've seen the A.L.F.'s video of taking crowbars to doors inside UC-Riverside—how did they get in? You've read the communique for 14,000 mink released in Iowa – how is that possible? You've heard 14 beagles were rescued from HLS—how does a group of activists get in, transport 14 dogs from a lab, and escape undetected? Answers like these are revealed here.

This section opens with the first documented animal liberation in US history—the 1977 rescue of two dolphins from a University of Hawaii marine lab. This entry strays from the book's guidelines in that it wasn't written in first-person, but rather "as told to." Yet it was too significant to not include.

A short (very short) write up follows, by one of the rescuers behind the 1982 heist of 35 cats from Howard University. Lifted from a periodical covering academia titled *Campus Voice*, the brevity and disjointed continuity indicates this is an excerpt from a longer story. Yet the source of the original (if it exists) is not known.

The elusive and prolific A.L.F. organizer "Joseph" breaks his silence for the next entry, the story of rescuing 12 dogs from UC-Harbor in 1983. This action set off a small wave of high-profile lab break-ins across the west coast in the 80s, many of which Joseph helped organize. While the writing style is a little scattered and the story low on specifics, it is significant by way of documenting the earliest recorded animal liberation on the west coast.

Rod Coronado's 1986 tale of sinking half of Iceland's whaling fleet is next, giving a more detailed account of the "Raid On Reykjavik" story found in the book *Flaming Arrows*.

Also from 1986, an unusual story of a (mostly) failed break-in at the University of Toronto's School of Dentistry.

Among this book's highlights is the next account, of one California cell carrying out numerous raids (by the end of the story, you'll lose count) in the late 1980s. Remarkable in that it ties together several well-known actions, revealing them all as the work of one small group.

The University of Arizona is the crown jewel of this section, a scene-by-scene action piece on the largest lab raid in US history. In terms of detail, no other account comes close.

Another tale of significant historical value: how the Western Wildlife Unit shut down the Oregon State University experimental fur farm. (An alternate, less detailed account of this action can be found in the next story…)

"Operation Bite Back" chronicles the entire OBB campaign, taken from the widely-circulated *Memories of Freedom* zine from the late-1990s. Written by Rod Coronado in prison, it is the largest piece in this section for a reason—it details six separate actions over two years, and a multi-state effort to destroy the fur industry. (An even more detailed look at Operation Bite Back, including stories of failed actions left out of *Memories of Freedom*, is included in Dean Kuiper's book *Operation Bite Back*).

A first-hand account of an early fur farm raid follows. The location of the farm is not revealed, however at the time of its writing, only a couple dozen such actions had been carried out in North America.

Next, a previously unknown and unclaimed laboratory liberation gets written into history for the first time, with the story of 250 mice rescued from a small Silicon Valley college in 2000, wiping out over 70 years of research.

The legendary 2001 rescue of 14 beagles from Huntingdon Life Sciences follows, giving new details behind this raid heard around the world.

Then another mink release account, this one notable in the way it shattered the mold for fur farm releases. In this action, one small group released every mink from a farm, then returned six days later to re-release the animals that were recaptured. The second visit shut the farm down forever.

The next story takes place, coincidentally (or perhaps not) just two miles south, at the Hawkeye Mink Cooperative, a pelt processor and mink feed supplier. Here, the author details how a team of two broke in to confiscate addresses of previously unknown fur farms (some of which would go on to be raided soon after).

Lastly, the rescue of 115 chickens from pharmaceutical manufacturer and HLS client, Merial Select Laboratories. This is the last known "how it was done" article before the long dry spell that brings us to the time of this writing.

How It Wasn't Done

With the A.L.F. claiming well over 1,000 actions, and over 100 of them significant enough to be worthy of a first-hand account, why have only 15 surfaced?

As possible explanations—and to better appreciate how fortunate we are that any of these writings exist at all—what follows are a few barriers the A.L.F. faces in writing and disseminating any "how it was done" piece.

Trade secrets: By making details public, the A.L.F. risks inviting obsolescence of its investigative and entry methods. In revealing a trade secret to activists, it is also revealed to their targets. Any exploited security hole or intelligence leak can be quickly patched, and that "engaging how-to story" suddenly comes at a high price: sacrificing the lives that could have been saved had their methods been kept secret. This cost, weighed against the distant benefit (i.e. other cells applying the tactic before the loophole is closed), usually leaves full-disclosure on the losing end of the ledger.

Security: Every time the door is opened on a past action, it introduces risks. Either a risk of revealing identifying details in the writing (through revealing phrases or other tells), or an (albeit easily avoidable) forensic or digital-forensic risk of the dispatch being traceable.

Consensus: Some cells may feel the need for every participant to either contribute or sign off on any "how it was done" piece. Depending on the group, this challenge will fall somewhere between inconvenient-to-impossible.

Compartmentalization: While remote and relevant only to highly complex actions, there are likely examples where no single person sees the entire picture, and no one knows enough to write a thorough account.

Futility: Unfortunate but legitimate, the author must weigh the risk of an article against the probability it will be acted on. Anonymous pieces bring no personal reward—they are written to incite. They are written to inspire others to take their lead, learn their tactics, and take action. To those on the front lines, it's apparent how few others there are by their side, and how limited the likelihood their work will provoke real action. Regrettably, the A.L.F. knows the impact is more likely limited to vicarious spectatorship.

On Forming A Complete A.L.F. Playbook

These stories are the A.L.F. at their most transparent, yet they don't reveal everything. To those looking for a total A.L.F. tactical blueprint, where else would they turn? If every "how it was done" story and how-to guide is included here, are readers who have unanswered questions forced to fend for themselves?

Here is a list of additional writings to supplement this section:

Free The Animals (Newkirk). This history of the US A.L.F. gives a narrative look at the planning and execution of multiple lab break-ins on the east coast. While some of the actions depended on inside help and aren't entirely relevant as how-to material, these stories remain insightful and mandatory reading.

The balance of tactical guidance (excepting many small or international resources) comes from the strictly criminal realm. *Art of Deception* and *Art Of Intrusion* (Mitnick) cover unconventional research and physical entry techniques. *Access All Areas* (Ninjalicious) guides the reader through accessing and navigating off-limits physical spaces, the implications of which should be clear. *Burglar's Guide To The City* (Managuh) tells the story of our man-made environment through the eyes of burglars. While the A.L.F. works to remove contraband from physical structures in a more righteous context, their work is just as illegal as classic "burglars," and their tactics are often identical. *Confessions Of A Master Jewel Thief* (Mason) is the story of how one man working alone became the most prolific jewel thief in history. The book removes any excuse for inaction by showcasing the possibilities of working alone with no skills and few tools.

Elsewhere in this book, the "how" finds its way to all five sections, with this and "How To Guides" being the most direct. Several passages straddle the line between "interviews" or "essays" and "how it was done" pieces. Refer to Darren Thurston's interview on the University of Alberta, or my interview on fur farms.

Even communiques can be mined for how-to guidance (can doors be bypassed by drilling through walls? See Genesis Labs, 8-28-00 for the story and photo).

Big Shortcuts To Bigger Felonies

The A.L.F. imparts many lessons in these stories both explicit and implicit. Let's take a short look at the less overt lessons, for the benefit of the A.L.F.'s current and future generations…

Everything starts with finding a way in: The three biggest impediments to live liberations are:

1. People to work with.
2. Homes for animals.
3. Getting in.

But "getting in" is the Big Domino—the one that knocks over the rest. When you have a way in, the #1 and #2 are more likely to resolve themselves by way of the obligation #3 brings. Everything from finding people to work with, finding homes for animals, logistics, equipment, and the motivation to carry it through to execution—all these resolve themselves more quickly when the Big Domino of physical access is resolved.

There is always a way in: There is *always* a way in.

Know your outcome: No one runs into a lab without a plan. The A.L.F. rarely acts opportunistically. Big actions have specific intentions. Having a defined outcome (liberating animals, maximum damage, maximum media exposure, documenting abuse, etc.) resolves the dozens of small decisions that go into planning an action. Clarity brings simplicity, and simplicity brings execution.

Simplicity is success: Alternately, "complexity is the enemy of completion." If a reader's response to these stories is "that sounds too easy," they might ask themselves if this is less likely to be true than it is an emotionally convenient bias to justify inaction. Complexity and yield are not correlated, as these stories show, and overthinking can have casualties.

The "how" is situational: Successful actions frequently depend on site-specific features that make them possible. The all-applicable "A.L.F. action blueprint" doesn't exist, because so much is situational. Showing up, as they say, is 80%

of success. Only then will the opportunities that are the runway to victory present themselves.

Throughout this section (and elsewhere) are stories of going through windows, air vents, scaling walls, lifting keys from unlocked offices, and more. What worked at the University of Alberta may not work at University of Nebraska. The A.L.F. knows that while opportunity always exists, it assumes many forms.

The Black Mask Award

Once the "how" is settled, this A.L.F. adage offers the next step:

"Be so good they call it an inside job."

University Of Hawaii

1977

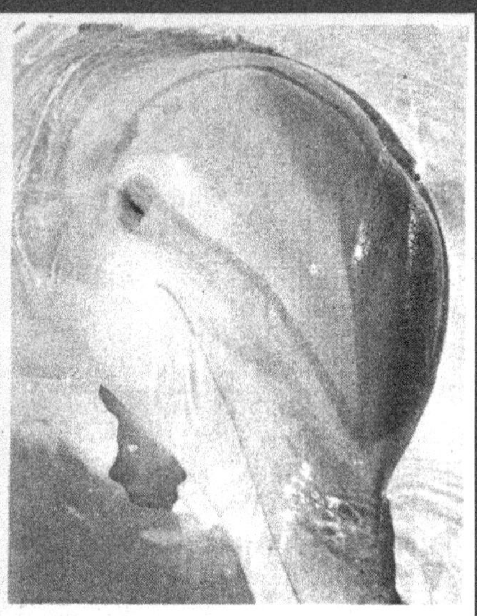

Kea Kiko was one of the dolphins released by two UH graduate students who have questioned man's right to keep intelligent animals in captivity.

How two scientists carried out the first documented North American animal liberation.

Before many of us in the current generation of animal rights freedom fighters were born, before *Free the Animals*, and long before the term "open rescue" had been coined, a couple of students at the University of Hawaii had an idea. Cetacean liberation, they called it. A simple idea really, that keeping intelligent, sentient animals captive for entertainment and research was unacceptable and should be stopped. Dubbing themselves "The Undersea Railroad" they put this idea into practice on the night of May 29, 1977. Steve Sipman and Ken Le Vasseur, the two founding spokespeople for The Undersea Railroad, were unconventional scientists and animal liberationists. They were hippie surfers who were helping Dr. Louis Herman study dolphin communication ability at the Kewalo Basin Marine Animal Research Laboratory, and spending their off hours wondering what the animals were thinking as they rode the waves in ways the researchers could only imagine. As Herman, who kept his dolphin subjects, Puka and Kea, in small, cement isolation tanks constantly, attempted to induce better cooperation from Puka by depriving her of toys, Steve began to rebel against the scientist.

At first, Steve filled Puka's tank with Frisbees, defying Herman's direct order. Herman called Steve into the main office and told him he was becoming too attached to the dolphins and to get in line with the research or find another job. The lab was both Steve's office and home, and the threat was real. Still, at night, listening to Puka and Kea cry out in loneliness for the life they had lost when they were abducted from the Gulf of Mexico to become prisoners of science, it was not enough to keep his real loyalties from coming to the surface.

One evening, after Steve unsuccessfully attempted to calm the dolphin cries, he realized toys and company would never be enough. For months, employees of the lab had joked that one morning they would come in and find Puka and Kea liberated by Steve and his cohort Kenny. Steve called a like-minded friend and told him it was time to prove them right.

The logistics of releasing two captive dolphins into the ocean were complicated. First, Steve and Kenny had to teach the dolphins how to procure their own food. This was doubly challenging since the dolphins were used to being hand fed frozen fish and the cement tanks were too small to simulate the ocean conditions anyway. Still after weeks of extra feedings, and exercises in which the dolphins natural instincts were honed, Puka and Kea had convinced the team it was time.

The next question was how to actually transport the two dolphins from the laboratory to the open ocean. Steve and Kenny knew that even moving the dolphins from their tanks was often an all-day production, since moving them and cleaning the tanks was part of the mens' job descriptions.

Fortunately, that experience had taught them tricks to make the process go a bit faster. The plan for the liberation was simple. It would be like cleaning the tanks, except instead of placing Puka and Kea into their holding tank, the dolphins would be placed in Steve's VW van and driven to freedom. Working from the culture of aloha rather than the culture of security, the team asked a friendly seeming boater if he would help out by transporting the dolphins into open water on the night chosen. The boater agreed.

Unfortunately, the actual liberation was not to be that simple. For the weekly tank cleaning, the dolphins were lifted by winch and moved into their holding tank. The evening before the liberation, the team attempted a practice run. During the run, the winch broke.

However, the team had made a promise to Puka and Kea that they would be free, and time was running out. The liberation was planned for a Thursday evening of a holiday weekend, and on the next Monday, a new employee was set to move into the lab. The liberation had to go on as scheduled.

The team met at a local Woolworth's to think. In the end, they decided to drain the tanks, and lift the dolphins out using their own strength and determination. They hoped that the kinship Steve and Kenny had developed with the dolphins would keep Puka and Kea calm enough to go along with the effort. However, draining the tanks would take hours, and they would not be able to drive the dolphins to the marina, move them into a boat, and release them into open water all before sunrise. Instead, they would have to pick a nearby protected bay and release them there, hoping the dolphins would swim away to safety.

Nervous, they all looked around at each other and checked their resolve. Out of the corner of his eye one man saw something and began to laugh. Next to them, in the aisle, was a shelf of inflatable dolphins. This was a good sign for the team. They purchased two, walked out, and knew everything was going to work out.

That evening, the laboratory staff left for the long weekend. Steve and Kenny waved them goodbye and quickly began to drain the cages, all the while trying to calm Puka and Kea. The rest of the team arrived with supplies. Foam to place under the dolphins for transport, ropes to help lift them out of the tanks, wet sheets to keep their sensitive skin moist and cool, and treats for the two animals.

The hard work of hoisting and moving the animals went remarkably easily. The team was running on adrenaline and Puka and Kea seemed to know they were heading for a better life. The hours flew by, and soon enough, it was time to say a final goodbye to the laboratory. The team blew up the inflatable dolphins, placed them and Frisbees in the drained tanks, and executed their final task. On the employee blackboard, they wrote "gone surfing. Puka, Kea, Kenny and Steve." The blackboard would be found by a very confused lab manager called into work by Steve the next day.

The team took off and drove to shore. Dressed for surfing, they carefully carried the dolphins on their padding into the water. Steve and Kenny paddled out on surfboards away from shore with the treats.

It was now time to coax Puka and Kea into open water and introduce them to their life of freedom. Before they had the chance Puka took off into the ocean, and they watched her disappear into the blue horizon. But Kea, always the more gentle of the two, stayed near the only two humans she could call friends. When they had brought her out what they deemed a pretty safe distance from shore, they returned to land ready to turn themselves in to the authorities and hold a press conference.

Though Kea swam near shore for days, and was the delight of Hawaiian families and surfers alike, she eluded recapture by Herman and his team.

Both Puka and Kea were often spotted in the waters off Hawaii, swimming free and healthy. After saying goodbye to their friends, and before their press conference, the undersea railroad released the following statement to the press:

"Early this morning two slaves were freed in Honolulu. They had been kept in a circular enclosure five ft. high for the last six years, during which time they were kept in total isolation while undergoing remorseless experiments.

These innocent prisoners were Bottlenose dolphins, the same species as the famed 'Flipper'. These dolphins possess a highly developed language and intelligence compared to that of a human.

The dolphins were safely transported to a carefully chosen location where they will start a new life of freedom. They will never again know the nets of a captor or the relentless probing of scientific research.

A statement of our feelings was left at the Kewalo Basin Marine Animal Research Lab."

Though the names Steve Sipman and Ken Le Vasseur have faded into relative obscurity, the aftermath of the daring liberation of Puka and Kea by the Undersea Railroad was overwhelming. The event garnered international media and was the focus of a popular Hawaiian song. The two men were tried and convicted of felony theft, over international protest by the growing throngs of animal rights activists. Their story is far from over as they continue to oppose Herman's laboratory and his enslavement of dolphin after dolphin.

Whatever they do, their actions the night of May 27, 1977 should continue to remind generations of activists that animal liberation can and should happen in the least likely of places.

Police investigate dolphin abduction

By JOHN C. GIVEN
Advertiser Staff Writer

A daylong air and sea search yesterday failed to turn up any sign of Puka or Kea, the two valuable dolphins abducted last weekend from the University of Hawaii's marine animal research lab at Kewalo Basin.

A specially chartered fishing boat left Kewalo Basin at 4 a.m. yesterday morning for the waters off Makua Beach, where the dolphins had last been seen. While the chartered boat searched, a Coast Guard helicopter flew overhead and private boats also combed the area.

Attempts to net Kea failed three times Monday, according to Dr. Louis Herman, an animal psychologist who had been running the research projects on the dolphins.

He said at that time that Kea was injured, with one eye closed, that she was very nervous and eating very little.

The attempts to get a net around Kea failed Monday apparently because the net itself was too small. Yesterday's plan, then, was to use a larger net to drape it in the water to keep her close to shore. The idea might have worked, except for one problem. After two days in the area, Kea headed out to sea at about 8:30 p.m. Monday night — and hasn't been seen since.

The search was given up yesterday but was to resume today. Officials at the Kewalo Basin lab put out a plea for members of the public sighting dolphins close to shore to call the lab at 537-2402.

Meanwhile, the case is being investigated by the Honolulu Police Department. "So far, it stands as a theft, a felony-type offense," said Police Lt. Jeremy Postmus.

"The University has filed a complaint on the theft of two porpoises valued at $30,000 — that's $15,000 each," he said.

What kinds of experiments were performed with Puka and Kea? See Page A-18.

Two former employes of the marine lab, Steve Sipman and Ken Le Vasseur, have already admitted responsibility for removing the animals and releasing them into the sea.

A letter to the local news media Sunday morning said "2 slaves" (the dolphins) had been "freed" after six years of "total isolation" and "remorseless experiments." It was signed "The Undersea Railroad," a reference to the "Underground Railroad," a network of abolitionists who smuggled black slaves to freedom in the North during the Civil War.

Yesterday, Postmus said that Sipman and Le Vasseur "have expressed willingness to come in and talk with us," and that "we would like to talk to them to see what their side of the story is."

Howard University

1982

A short story of the break-in and rescue of 35 cats from Howard University.

We gathered in Washington a couple of days before the raid. We agreed not to resist arrest if we were caught and to remain silent while we waited for the bond to be posted. Everyone realized we could serve time for this.

There were five or six of us from different parts of the country—it's harder to track people when they scatter afterwards. We didn't know exactly what work was being done in the lab because another group had researched that, and we weren't responsible for where the creatures were going once we released them. In case we were caught, it was better for us not to know much.

A driver dropped us off at the lab on Christmas Eve night, and we went in through a window. I was wearing dark clothes with a dark cap and gloves. It was nerve-racking. We went into the researcher's offices first, looking for keys and notebooks or videotapes documenting their experiments. The last thing we did was get the animals since they might make noise. We found one cat dead in a cage. The rest—maybe 20 cats and a couple dogs—we slipped into knapsacks and loaded into a van, which took them to a truck. The truck driver delivered the animals to a veterinarian who checked them before they went to their new homes all over the country. It felt great to get out of there.

We left behind a gift-wrapped copy of Peter Singer's book *Animal Liberation*. It was Christmas, you know.

Cat Liberation

Night Squad Whisks Doomed Kitties from Medical School

WASHINGTON (UPI) — A group calling itself the Animal Liberation Front said yesterday it freed more than two dozen cats who had been doomed to death at Howard University's School of Medicine.

The group said many cats rescued Christmas night were lost pets brought from dog pounds in Virginia, Pennsylvania and North and South Carolina.

University spokesman Alan Hermesch said that he didn't know if the cats were to be killed, but that they were "used for medical research." The school lab "is accredited by the American Association for the Accreditation of Laboratory Animal Care," which sets standards for the treatment of research animals, he said.

The group did not say how the rescue was carried out but said it left a copy of Peter Singer's book, "Animal Liberation," in the animals' place.

"Several have respiratory infections; others have spinal lesions; all are starved for affection and the companionship they once knew," the statement said.

A group spokesman said, "This is not a sentimental appeal for cute animals. It is an appeal to thinking people to examine the prejudices that lie behind animal experimentation. There cannot be peace on earth until we respect all God's creation. This Christmas we must try to 'unlearn' our acceptance of this abhorrent treatment of our fellow animals."

Cats requiring no extensive medical care would go to "pre-screened, loving, safe homes 48 hours after veterinary examination" while some would stay under medical care indefinitely, the group said.

University of California - Harbor

1983

One of the first documented animal liberations in the US, by a founder of the west coast A.L.F. - Joseph.

Inspired by the recent surge in ALF raids, especially those against laboratories, I have decided to share my own experiences. I feel that my fellow brothers and sisters now leading the fight against vivisection and exploitation of all beings should know what the struggle was like in the early eighties.

When I was doing what was most important in my life, my close inner circle and the FBI knew me as Joseph. We were the West Coast cell of the ALF. We pulled off some of the most precise, well-thought-out, and expertly executed raids known to the animal rights movement in this country.

Our first raid (the largest on the US West Coast at the time) was at UC Harbor Medical in Torrance, California. On Christmas, 1983 we liberated 12 medium-large dogs, even though the facility had their own police department about 300 feet away from where the animals were kept. But after several weeks of surveillance, we knew their schedule better than they did.

In 1983, the animal rights community did not have the ALF support base or militant minded faction that exists today. When I made the decision that I would break into the UC medical center and rescue the animals inside, recruiting other activists willing to cross the line proved a difficult task. No one had ever even heard of this timely and effective method of directly saving animals' lives.

We had no selection process to put out feelers for willing activists or carefully gauge the opinions of others concerning direct action and the ALF. No one had opinions on the ALF because no one knew what it was. I asked a few friends for a favor and we carried out the first raid by a west coast ALF cell. It was a huge risk, but maybe the best decision I ever made. What grew from those tentative beginnings evolved into what was arguably the most effective ALF cell in this country to date.

I had been in many labs before the one at UC Harbor Medical, but our first illegal forced entry felt very eerie. When we entered this particular vivarium and began carrying most of the dogs out they were so quiet. All I could hear was my heart beating and the pattering of my comrades' feet.

The dogs knew why we were there. There is no question in my mind. We had specially constructed cages in two vans for the long haul to make it as comfortable as possible for them. While driving, one young fella chewed his way out of the cage through the makeshift wall to sit up front on my lap. To be in the front was not enough; he sat on my lap and would not move. And they say animals can't think or feel. People who say this are the ones who can't think or feel.

So for seven hours, we drove—my partner, my new loyal and appreciative friend and myself. He lived to be 19 1/2 years old and was still going strong until the very end. Times like that made it all worthwhile.

While security may have been less sophisticated back then, it was still very strong. Our skills evolved, and we later employed a variety of techniques to get in and get the animals out. It is my belief that almost any facility could be raided and every animal liberated with enough careful planning and expertise. This theory has been proven by the latest handful of lab raids.

Avoid sloppiness in surveilling, planning and executing a raid. It's important that good dedicated activists don't go to jail. You are of more help to the animals out here. It is equally important that activists not be too paranoid or over-zealous in their security precautions—this can impede the progress of an action, and far too often stand in the way of a raid being carried out at all. Being security conscious and getting the job done are both equally important.

Some factors to consider when planning a successful liberation include media and public opinion. It is vital to get maximum media coverage. Only very few types of A.L.F. actions can be carried out without regard for public opinion. The Animal Liberation Front operates outside the law and strikes without public permission, but it is nonetheless vital to win the favor of public opinion when possible. This will give the vivisectors millions of opponents, not just a handful of angry activists.

One of the best ways is to film and document the conditions in the lab before the raid to send this video to the media immediately after completion. It is also vital to video and document the raid itself so this can be released a few days later to the media for more coverage. Keep the action in the public eye for as long as possible.

Once an action is big news, anything that you can give the public and news media will be picked up and broadcast to millions. Ride the wave. Seize and release documents and video to the media detailing the specifics of lab experiments, animals used, feeding and veterinary logs, anything that will shine a negative light on the researchers and their animal experiments. Even the most seemingly insignificant documents and bits of information can reveal the cruelty of the vivisectors.

Remember, don't take for granted that everyone knows the horrors of animal experimentation. Most people will be shocked when they receive their first glimpse behind laboratory doors. As activists, we know the facts and are reminded every day through graphic photos on AR flyers and anti-vivisection videos. We forget that others are not so aware. What is old news to you will have a powerful impact on the public.

It is also very important to make sure the video footage is well shot and well thought out. Know what you're going to film ahead of time. Showing the horrific conditions of the animals and the cruelty inflicted on them in the labs should be a top priority.

I personally don't believe in random graffiti or vandalism — you should send a very clear message. A well thought out slogan on a wall makes your motivation unmistakable to the public and unalterable by the media. Just throwing books, desks and other things over may make the ALF look bad in the eyes of the public. Remember, it is the public we are trying to educate so we can ultimately outlaw these barbaric practices.

In my mind we want to create an image of Robin Hood or of David and Goliath. Americans and the British can relate to this, and will root for the good guys. It is crucial to present yourselves as the good guys. So, again, know what you want the media to see and how the public will construe this information and footage. One has to look at the big picture in order to accomplish our ultimate goal: liberation for all animals.

I will in further articles explain the other raids and what we went through. I am so proud of everyone who puts his or her life on the line.

One last thing. If you are not ready to give up your freedom or life then maybe you should ask yourself if you are ready for the Animal Liberation Front. There is always as important work in the support groups you may want to consider because there is nothing worse than someone that rolls over and gives up his comrades to save himself.

Recently I've noticed a new batch of young activists ready to go the distance. You are the best! Keep up the fight and be safe. We all need you and love you.

Reykjavik Harbor

1986

Rod Coronado describes how he and David Howitt sunk half of Iceland's whaling fleet.

David Howitt and I spent the whole Summer of 1986 working to raise the money for our mission to infiltrate Iceland with the sole purpose of causing maximum economic sabotage to their whaling industry. I waited tables in a nightclub in London's Chelsea district during the nights, and I refinished antiques on Kings Road during the day. David went to southern England where he picked hops. Every few weeks we would meet to discuss our plans and go over intelligence we had gathered on Iceland. When our work was complete, we would make a batch of paint-filled light bulbs and ride out on our bikes to redecorate London fur shops.

Finally, the day arrived when we rode the London Underground Subway to Heathrow Airport to catch our Iceland Air flight to Reykjavik. As we rode to the airport, I removed a patch from my jacket that read "Save the Whales, Save the Earth" with a picture of a fin whale. All we carried with us was our cameras, clothes and raingear, underwater flashlights, knives and a couple of maps. All the tools necessary for any action would be acquired in Iceland.

When we arrived in October, only the hardcore tourists were still around. We got beds in the local youth hostel, and one of our first tasks was to buy a pair of bolt cutters and a large adjustable wrench from a hardware store. We wanted as much time as possible between the purchase of our tools and the action, in case anyone might remember the purchase.

On one of the first nights in the capital city of Reykjavik we snuck out of the hostel late at night and into a scrap yard from where we could view the four, 175- foot Icelandic ships that comprised the nation's entire whaling fleet. Hvalur ("whaleship") 5, 6, 7 and 8 bobbed in the harbor, alongside each other like four Riders of the Apocalypse waiting to unleash their evil on the natural world. The ships' superstructures were painted white with the bridge windows and portholes dark and imposing, resembling the eye sockets of a skull.

Needless to say, we were a little intimidated. The reality of what was so simple to discuss in England but was now staring us in the face in the freezing fall weather of a Reykjavik night was more than a little daunting. But we had known it would not be easy, so we began a series of late night observations of the harbor. Within two weeks of surveillance, a definite routine began to emerge. Every Friday night, a watchman would relieve the day watch, carrying with him two bottles of Brenivin, a strong Icelandic vodka. No activity could be seen on three of the ships, the watchman staying on the fourth ship, the one furthest from the dock. A weekend night emerged as the best night for action.

In Reykjavik we saw photos from the whaling station, which was 45 miles from town. Tours were offered for the station, so David and I hitchhiked to the desolate station and were dropped off near the entrance. As we approached, not a soul was visible. The whaling season was over, and with it the demand for tours. David and I began to walk throughout the premises in broad daylight, gazing through windows at offices, machinery and workshops, and it quickly became evident to both of us that we might be able to strike the whaling station also. We knew we would have only one shot at the Icelandic whaling industry, and any risk to ourselves did not matter. Already we felt the chances were high that we would not get off the island once our sabotage was discovered.

Iceland in November 1986 was not a country that expected or even remembered the threats of a militant anti-whaling organization. Only one watchman was aboard all four ships. It was the off-season and the crews were ashore, with work on the ships restricted to daylight hours. The week of our planned attack, the whaling ships were taken into drydock. One by one, they were pulled out of the water for repairs and cleaning, which is a major operation. David and I had planned on attempting to sink all three ships minus the one that housed the watchman. Now we were forced to sacrifice our third target. Our money was running low, and the fear of discovery still haunted us. Maybe we were already under surveillance ourselves, and the police were waiting for us to act before they could legitimately arrest us?

Already David and I had read up on the Icelandic penal system and learned that the longest sentence given to any crime was eleven years. We also learned that Icelandic prisoners were employed making cement sidewalk blocks. From that day on, the jokes never stopped of how good we might become at building Iceandic sidewalks

Finally surrendering to our fate to the whale spirits, we decided to act. We chose the night of November 7th for our task of vengeance. We said goodbye to our European friends and told them David and I were going to rent a car for our last day to do a little sightseeing.

We drove to the airport the morning of the 7th to pre-check our luggage for the 6 a.m. flight out of the country the following morning. It was to Luxembourg, but we did not care where it went, as long as it was not Scandinavia. Next, we drove to Iceland's only vegetarian restaurant for what might be our last supper. We had been saving our money for this last luxury but found the restaurant closed. Not to be disappointed, we bought food from a supermarket and drove to a clearing above the whaling station to eat our meal and await the early winter darkness.

While eating, we listened to the car radio and after our meal discovered we had drained the battery dead. Here our mission might have ended, had not a vanload of Icelandic locals, probably employed by the whaling station, came to our rescue. They towed our car until we could jump start it, and then we waved goodbye and drove to our prearranged hiding place for the car, as night was fast approaching.

A rainstorm began to fall, adding a brilliant cover as David and I pulled on our dark rain gear, gloves and ski masks and strapped on fanny-packs filled with flashlights and tools. I then placed the car keys on the top of the rear tire, and we began the long walk to the whaling station in complete darkness, bending into the wind and increasing rain.

As we approached the whaling station, we were surprised by the sight and sound of a front-end excavator that was digging a trench at the station. We dropped to the ground and spent the next hour lying in the freezing rain until the workman and his machine headed off to the local town. As the lights of the machine disappeared, we leapt into action.

After this task, we found the computer control room that kept the entire station's machinery fully automated. We smashed the computer panels until sparks flew and LEDs flashed and the beautiful music of machines dying all around us could be heard. There was no time to waste, so we moved next to the ship's store, where the spare parts for the four whaling ships were kept. Taking the most expensive pieces, we walked to the edge of the docks and tossed them into the waters.

Finally, we reached the offices where record books detailing the illegal catches were confiscated and cyanic acid was poured throughout the building. Windows were smashed, and anything that looked expensive met the business end of our wrenches and bolt cutters.

Our first task was the sabotage of the six huge diesel generators that provided power for the station. David and I were both experienced diesel engineers, and we knew what was good for an engine, as well as what was bad. Before long we were stripping off our outer clothing and sweating profusely in our handiwork.

Next, we moved onto the centrifuges that processed whale blubber into a high-grade lubricating oil that was used in missiles. Smashing the delicate gear, we next located what we could not find at the meatpacking plant: the Whalemeat Mountain. David had attempted to move the many crates of whale meat, housed in huge refrigeration units beneath the station, but the forklift he drove ran out of propane gas. We were forced to wedge open the refrigeration units and then sabotage the refrigeration units themselves so that hopefully the meat would thaw and spoil.

Watching World News a few days later, we would hear the station's foreman recount with shock how it appeared that the whole whaling station had been the target of an air raid.

We could have spent all night sabotaging the station, but the ships were waiting, so David and I signalled a retreat and returned tired and sweating to our car. Once there I experienced a frantic moment as I reached for the keys on the tire and found them not there. The high winds had been so strong as to blow them some feet away, where I found them with my flashlight. Now covered in grease and drenched in sweat, we drove back to Reykjavik. The weather made the roads treacherous, and often the car would start to slide when it hit ice.

I am convinced that many of my premature grey hairs were earned that night. An hour later we reached Reykjavik Harbor, where three ships lay bobbing in the water, the fourth in dry dock. Resting, David and I ate some quick energy food and stashed our confiscated record books from the whaling station in the backseat. Taking a deep breath, we opened our car doors and stepped back into the pounding rainstorm that made our ski masks and rain gear not just a disguise but a necessity. With hands in our pockets like two cold fishermen, we walked down the dead-end dock towards Hvalur 5, 6 and 7.

The tides in the harbor were such that we were level with the ships' decks; so to board, all we had to do was hop a few feet from the dock to the steel-plated decks. Moving quickly to Hvalur 5, David pulled out our bolt cutters and cut the hasp on the lock that shut the engine room hatch. Moving into the fully-lit engine rooms, David searched the ship for any sleeping watchman while I moved into the engine room and began lifting deck plates, looking for the saltwater cooling valve that regulated the seawater that cooled the ships' engines at sea. By the time I found it, David had returned to announce that the ship was indeed empty.

We began to wrestle off the sixteen or more nuts that held the valve cover in place, and when most were removed water began to shoot out from the bolt holes. I tasted it, and it was salty. When the cover was fully removed, the ocean water would flood first the engine room and then the rest of the ship's compartments, dragging it to a watery grave in Reykjavik's deep harbor. Leaving the cover partially removed, we moved to Hvalur 6, where we repeated the process, quickly locating removing that ship's salt-water cooling valves.

Finally, with all the nuts and bolts removed, we took a pry bar to the valve, and with a little persuasion the valve quickly popped free, releasing a flood of seawater that drenched both David and me. Quickly returning to Hvalur 5, we removed the last of that ship's cover bolts, and again the ocean began to rush in.

Now it was time to execute our escape. The whaling station had been demolished, and two 175-foot whaling ships were sinking. The time was just before 5 a.m., and the airport was almost an hour away. Walking away from the two sinking ships, we tossed our tools into the icy waters and pulled our ski masks off just as we reached the car. Hopping into the driver's seat, I started the car and pulled onto the road. Less than two minutes later, we were pulled over by a Reykjavik Police Car.

My first thought was, "No, they can't be that good; they can't have been watching us this whole time ..." possibly leaving us for the next eleven years to fine tune our masonry skills at the local prison. And a police officer was walking to my window while David and I sat soaked in water, with grease from engines all over our clothes.

The officer asked me to get into his car. Looking at David as he sat with eyes forward, I got out of the car and into the back seat of the police cruiser. The officers ignored me and spoke to each other in Icelandic before finally turning around and asking me in plain English, "Have you drinken any alcohol tonight?"

Almost laughing, I said, "No, I do not even drink!" which was a lie, and he then asked if he could smell my breath. It was tempting to utter a joke, but hot coffee on an IcelandAir jet was calling. So I breathed on him, and he wished me a safe trip to the airport, knowing that was where we were probably headed because of the early morning departure. That police officer is probably still cursing himself today after having the nation's only saboteur since the second World War into his police car and then letting him go.

Returning to the car, David told me he had almost bolted but thought it best that he wait for another moment for some signal from me. The zoo liberation was now out of the question as we sped towards the airport to catch our 6 a.m. flight.

Pulling into the airport we grabbed our daypacks and quickly changed our clothes, dumping the grease-covered ones in the airport garbage can. We next went through Icelandic Customs without any incident, checked in and grabbed our boarding passes.

The polite ticket agent told us the flight was delayed due to the harsh weather. The words were what we least wanted to hear, and David and I spent the next 30 minutes staring at the clock, imagining the chaos erupting at Reykjavik harbor just about now. Finally, our flight was called, and we quickly boarded, still not feeling safe until we landed in Luxembourg.

Hours later we did just that, David and I gazing out the window half expecting to see Interpol agents waiting for our arrival. They were not. We collected our luggage and walked out of the airport after making an anonymous call to the Sea Shepherd offices in the U.K. saying only, "We got the station, and two are on the bottom ... " We hitchhiked to Belgium, where we caught a ferry to England and then a bus to London. Getting off the bus now 36 hours after our action, I walked to a news agent and picked up a copy of the morning paper. A story on the front page said only, "SABOTEURS SINK WHALERS, photo page six ..." Flipping to the page, I saw one of the most beautiful sights in the world. There was Hvalur 5 and 6 resting gently on the bottom of Reykjavik harbor, only their skeletal superstructure peeking above the waves. Paul Watson was quoted as accepting responsibility for the attack, which he said was an enforcement action of the IWC's moratorium on commercial whaling that Iceland had violated.

David and I embraced in the streets, laughing with the elation that only a realized dream can bring.

University Of Toronto

1986

The break-in and attempted liberation at the University of Toronto's Dentistry building.

In the early morning hours of Sunday, February 16, 1986, a group of ALF activists entered the University of Toronto's Faculty of Dentistry building, in an attempt to liberate some of the imprisoned animals who were being tortured in pain experiments.

Surveillance of the building had taken many months and all of us had been inside at night on at least two or three occasions, so we had put together extremely detailed maps of the upper floors .

The target research laboratory was a major problem! First, we knew that the time between guard rounds was very short. Secondly, the response time by police had been estimated at approximately two minutes, which meant we'd be trapped in the building if we accidentally triggered an alarm. Third, the doors and the inside of the lab were under 24-hour video coverage.

Despite all these obstacles the lab was felt to be such a hell-hole that those involved in the planning voted unanimously to go ahead with the raid!

So, that Sunday morning, as soon as it was felt safe, we made our way in ones and twos to the point of entry. Those who were on watch outside would remain in close contact via the CB radio.

Once inside, we made our way to Sessle's (the bastard in charge of the pain studies) office, intending to get documentation on the research. Unfortunately, our tools were not strong enough to break the lock and so, as time was running short, we decided to go to the fifth floor where an attempt would be made to enter the lab via the window of an adjacent meeting room and then, from there, across the roof.

We discovered very quickly that the window glass was shatterproof , which naturally increased our determination to smash through it! Once that was done we discovered a second shatterproof pane behind the first one! Again determination enabled us to break the window—but it cost us an enormous amount of time (again lack of proper tools—damn!) and the noise was incredible! We were so concerned we chanced breaking radio silence to check with the activists outside to see if the sounds of crashing glass could be heard from the street!

Once through the window there was an 8-foot drop to the roof and a 10-yard sprint across to the lab wall. Two of us stayed in the main building, manning the radio, handing out tools to those on the roof and watching and listening for both guards or movement from the three main elevators. The rest of the group made their way across to the laboratory.

A quick examination of the laboratory roof and walls made us realize that we would have to try going in through the wall. Several layers of material were ripped away with more brute force than finesse, but when our time-keeper noted that we had been inside the building for more than three hours it became apparent that we were not equipped to complete the break-in to the lab in the time we had left.

THE FRUSTRATION AND RAGE ONE FELT AT BEING SO CLOSE TO THE ANIMALS AND UNABLE TO GET TO THEM WAS INDESCRIBABLE! THE THOUGHT OF GOING OUT WITHOUT THEM TORE US ALL APART!

With some difficulty, and by lowering chairs onto the roof, we managed to get the group back through the jagged hole in the window without injury. Then we all decided to return to Sessle's office where we daubed the area with ALF slogans. After this we wandered into some adjacent areas and smashed some equipment and defaced the walls with slogans. Economic sabotage is hardly as satisfying as liberating animals, but we were to feel much more satisfied several days later when we learned the damage amounted to at least $10,000!

By now we had been inside the Dentistry building for over four hours and our time-keeper was getting really edgy, to say the least, and so we decided to get out while we could. We made our way to the exit point where we left, again in twos and threes, after checking with our outside contacts that all was clear.

It may have been four months since this action, but all the activists involved are spiritually still inside that building. How can we find peace when we still think of those we left behind!

Loma Linda University (+ more)

1987-1989

How one anonymous activist formed a prolific A.L.F. cell, raiding numerous labs and farms in the late 1980s.

In the early 1980s, I first heard of the Animal Liberation Front (ALF) when they raided the University of California at Riverside. Nearly 1,000 animals were rescued from laboratories, and I immediately knew that this was the kind of animal rights activity I wanted to become involved with. It wasn't until a later trip to England that I learned of the autonomous cell-like structure of the ALF which allows any group of individuals to call themselves "ALF" if they follow the group's basic guidelines.

When I returned to the U.S., I began to privately evaluate the few animal rights activists I had met to determine who might be most willing to accept my offer to start an ALF cell. I didn't want to ask people who would only decline and then be aware that I was recruiting for illegal direct action. At a regional animal rights conference, I had met a few young, like-minded activists who I felt were inclined to direct action and proposed to them my idea which they readily agreed was similar to their own.

Having been exposed to the effectiveness of the A.L.F.'s direct action campaigns in Britain, where not just animal liberations, but fire bombings, were employed to thwart animal abuse, it was decided that we would take the ALF down a new road in the U.S.-a road where our prime objective would be maximum destruction of the property used to exploit animals and the Earth, not minimum damage. We knew that other ALF cells focused on live animal liberations that often were aimed at attracting public attention to particular abuse, but we were more determined to have our actions impact the profitability involved in animal abuse rather than simply gather public support.

Though most of us had already engaged in individual direct action, such as inflicting economic sabotage against local fur and butcher shops, our first initiation as an ALF cell came in the spring of 1987, when it was decided that we would target a laboratory animal supplier in southern California. The rabbit breeding operation was located in a rural area that would allow us to drive our vehicle close enough to pick up the rabbits we would be rescuing. We entered the premises from neighboring fields and within minutes were shuttling wet burlap bags with rabbits into the awaiting vehicle. By the end of the night, 116 rabbits had been spared from the horrors of vivisection.

Next we targeted a battery egg farm where security was nearly non-existent. With cardboard animal carriers in arm, we moved into the long barns housing literally thousands of hens. What quickly became evident was the frustration and depression encountered by animal liberators who are forced to choose between which animals live and, by not rescuing more, which animals will be left to die. The euphoria felt when one successfully drives away in a vehicle loaded with liberated animals quickly wears off when you remember the thousands you were forced to leave behind.

Of course, it is impossible to rescue all animals living in abusive conditions, but once you have crossed that threshold where you accept individual responsibility for intervening to save animals' lives, you feel an even greater obligation to rescue victims of animal abuse.

Animal liberation becomes more of a realistic practice than an abstract philosophical theory, and direct action only becomes more of a personal necessity than a moral obligation to preserve one's peace of heart and mind in our overwhelmingly cruel world.

Our cell's strategy to remain empowered rather than powerless against the tide of animal abuse was to escalate to tactics that would target the property of animal abusers, rather than just aim to rescue a few victims. It was theorized that more animals can be spared abuse when the machines and buildings used to torture them are destroyed. In many situations, live animal liberations were easily recovered from when a vivisector or factory farmer replaced rescued animals at a minimum of costs. It was decided that we would begin to use arson.

Watching *The Animal's Film* one night, two members of our cell were upset after having been exposed to the conditions veal calves endure on factory farms. What normally might have led to depression, instead fueled action.

That very same night, the two ALF activists visited a veal processor in the San Francisco Bay Area where they were able to jar a door open into a warehouse. Gasoline was liberally spread throughout, and a crude cigarette timer was used to ignite the building which suffered tens of thousands of dollars in damages. Before the year was out, a slaughterhouse, livestock auction yard and fur shop all went up in flames without any injuries.

In the summer of 1988, our cell targeted its first vivisection laboratory. Previously, we had mistakenly believed that animal research labs were impenetrable due to increased security as a result of earlier ALF raids, yet a veteran ALF activist assured us that even the most secure lab always has a weak security link. We began to survey the laboratory of baboon heart transplant researcher

Leonard Bailey at Loma Linda University (LLU) in southern California.

By August we had discovered that the field station where Bailey operated, just off campus, lacked a security system. By the night of the raid, we had already entered the laboratory repeatedly, removing documents to photocopy before returning them the same night. The night of the action, we were not only able to smash tools of vivisection, but were delightedly surprised to find five recently-arrived puppies accompanying the two full-grown Labrador retrievers we had planned on liberating. By the end of the night, hundreds of thousands of dollars in damage had been done to the lab and seven dogs were on their way to new, loving homes.

Before the LLU raid, animal rights activists dismissed lab raids as no longer possible. Our cell found this to be a self-defeating excuse to avoid the serious work and responsibility necessary to carry out lab raids.

As opposed to attacks on property, lab raids require an incredible amount of surveillance and planning. One must spend endless hours observing targeted buildings until a cycle of activity reveals itself whereby the liberator can then determine a window of opportunity within to act. It may only be 30 minutes or an hour when no one is in the target building, but a well-disciplined ALF cell needs little more.

Our next major action was to be a raid on the University of Arizona at Tucson. After more than two years of working together, our cell had developed a working dynamic whereby we could identify each member's strong points and assign him or her roles in an action accordingly.

Our intelligence gathering members had spent months surveilling the U of A and had identified numerous weak links in the security of its animal research facilities.

Disguised as students, cell members had identified animal holding rooms to be targeted and entry points for the team of rescuers to gain access to the actual labs.

By sifting through the garbage of the targeted buildings, we were able to find rough drafts of research protocols, unpublished notes, invoices and a discarded set of blueprints for the entire microbiology building.

On the night of the action, our surveillance had paid off and rewarded us with a window of 50 minutes between security patrols. As soon as the patrol passed, our team entered the building and rode the elevator to the fifth floor where we quickly began to smash through the doors of four separate animal rooms. In less than 30 minutes, we were riding the elevator back down with more than 900 rabbits, guinea pigs, rats, mice and frogs.

Our animal transport team met us at the doors of the building where we quickly loaded the animals for their getaway. Within three minutes of our departure, the security patrol passed harmlessly by, unaware of the activity since their last pass.

At another basement level lab on campus, cell members removed an extractor ventilation fan to gain entry to the building where an additional 100 rats were rescued from psychology experiments. In a third research building, 120 mice were emptied from their cages and an incendiary device was placed in the vacant laboratory under construction.

Our last course of action was to plant incendiary devices in the basement of the off-campus residence offices for the U of A's animal research department· where computer records of all experiments were stored. The ensuing fires at the two buildings injured no living being and destroyed irreplaceable files and records as two vehicles with over 1,000 animals safely made their getaway. It was the largest liberation raid on an animal research facility in the ALF's U.S. history.

After these successful raids, our small ALF cell had proven that a handful of people can truly wage an effective guerrilla campaign against an otherwise immense industry. In true ALF fashion, we had employed tactics that exploit advantages that only anonymous hit-and-run activists can benefit from. We didn't attack the vivisection and factory farm industries head-on, but bit at their flanks and other weak points where their security was weak.

In this way, our small group of committed activists with very limited resources was able to rescue hundreds of animals while costing their abusers millions in not only destroyed buildings and equipment, but increased security costs. In traditional guerrilla fashion, we struck when our opponents were least expecting it and then melted away into the shadows to evade the net thrown by federal and state law enforcement determined to capture us.

Following the U of A raid, a law enforcement publication reported that of

150 leads in the U of A raid criminal investigation, not a single one led to any credible evidence.

Now it is 1999 and raiding animal abuse facilities is a federal crime punishable with years in prison, but the ALF survives. Recent raids—including the University of Minnesota raid—have proven that there are still weak links in the vivisection industry awaiting the strength of committed activists willing to break them.

The ALF is not a highly organized, militarily-structured terrorist organization. It is people like you and me who are fed up with the ineffectiveness of a political process that favors big business and profit before human and animal welfare. The ALF is the people's response to governments' lack of responsibility to eliminate institutionalized animal abuse and cruelty. As animal liberationists, we must not be intimidated by the consequences of our convictions. No amount of prison faced by an ALF member can compare to what the victims we have rescued endured in their forced captivity.

We must prove our love for our animal relations with actions not words. Don't just say you believe in animal liberation, with individual direct action, show it.

Underground group defaces lab

Red paint splashed, animals taken in Loma Linda

By STEPHAN STERN
Sun Staff Writer

LOMA LINDA — An underground animal rights group took credit Monday for a predawn raid on a Loma Linda University Medical Center laboratory, confiscating 18 animals it claimed were victims of painful experimentation.

Sheriff's officials said the intruders poured red paint over telephones, typewriters, clothing, a microwave oven and a television, and scrawled slogans on the walls such as "murderers" and "torturers."

"Everything possible felt the wrath of the red paint. It was splashed all over," said Jim Bryant, spokesman for the San Bernardino County Sheriff's Department.

The Animal Liberation Front, an extremist group opposed to animal vivisection, claimed responsibility for the raid through Margo Tannenbaum, an San Bernardino animal rights activist.

In a strongly worded press release, the group also crit-

See RAID/Back page

UNIVERSITY OF ARIZONA

1989

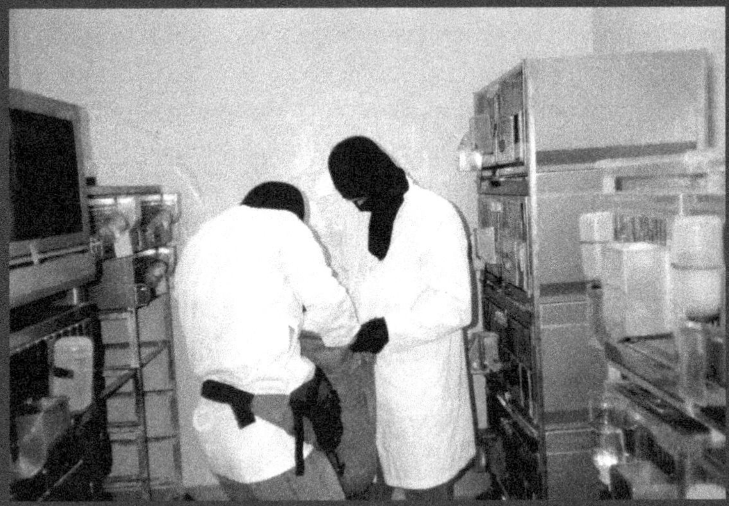

Perhaps the most detailed "how it was done" piece to date: How the A.L.F. carried out the largest laboratory liberation in US history.

In the summer of 1988 we were alerted to animal experimentation conducted at the University of Arizona in Tucson. We were told that pound-seized dogs from the Sierra Vista Animal Shelter and greyhounds from local racetracks were only a few of the thousands of animals used in vivisection on campus. Other animals including rabbits, rats, guinea pigs, frogs and primates were used in primarily cancer and diet research with the majority of the experiments being a variety of grant-funded disease research and basic repetitive vivisection such as skin irritancy experiments to teach the medical students, and of course, the notorious LD-50 test.

Whereas many Animal Liberation Front actions are chosen to target specific experiments of the work of a controversial vivisector, the U of A was chosen simply because it was one of the nations top 10 animal research campuses funded by both the federal government and the pharmaceutical industry. Annually, thousands of animals were ground up in the institutional mechanism of animal research that generates millions of dollars for universities in this country and billions for the pharmaceutical corporations that use educational institutions to develop the drugs that will make them filthy rich. All at the expense of innocent animal life while animal-based diets, environmental contamination, substance abuse, and the true causes of most deadly illness and disease remain unaddressed by the same people who profit from vivisection on one hand while the other encourages the lifestyle that created the illness and disease.

We began our reconnaissance by disguising our members as college students who would walk the halls of university buildings searching out the vivariums where the laboratory animals were housed between and during experiments. Campus maps detailed the biological and psychological sciences buildings where we knew we would find animal research; while the rest of our search was focused on the research wing of the nearby university hospital, renowned as one of the best in the world. Once it was determined where vivisection was conducted, the next goal was simply using our noses to lead us to the animal rooms themselves, which are usually kept either at the basement or rooftop level. The scent of pine shavings and urine emitting from underneath doors and through extractor fans and vents led us to our targets.

Once it was established what buildings we would target, we began nighttime surveillance of the outside areas surrounding the labs. This meant spending countless hours hunched low in cars parked in filled parking lots where all comings and goings by staff, students, and security patrols were recorded in our notebooks. After the first few weeks an obvious routine began to become apparent. Before long we could correlate the late-night activity with the lights that were turned on and off, visible from the parking lot. Custodial activities were very predictable as these employees followed a meticulous routine. Security patrols were equally predictable, and we learned the times of shift changes for the nearby university police by surveilling their campus station. Of course, there were completely unpredictable events, which are always a factor, but the majority of activity was the day-in day-out mundane habits of a university during a school year. We chose the school year as our time for action, as it was expected that there would be late night activity on campus and in the targeted buildings and "students" coming and going would not draw unwanted attention.

Next, we obtained the frequencies of university police and began to monitor their transmissions with police scanners to gather intelligence on the periods of greatest police activity and their appropriate responses. This way we were able to learn response times and familiarize ourselves to common police communications and codes. The equipment and frequencies are frequently available from Radio Shack-type electronic stores.

Now it was time for us to begin physical infiltration. Our first actions were simple walks around the target buildings, visibly inspecting doors and windows for possible entry. During daylight hours the target building's exterior doors remained unlocked, which allowed us the opportunity to inspect locks on doors and windows. This gave us an idea what kind of tools we would need to obtain late-night entry. Our next objective was to search the trash bins and wastepaper receptacles outside the targeted buildings where we discovered a wealth of information on what type of animals were housed in the buildings and the names of researchers and their individual experiments. This allowed us to reference the index Medicus at the campus library for more information on particular published works by the targeted vivisectors. What was more important to us was when we struck a goldmine by finding in the trash physical descriptions of the building's construction. This saved us having to draw our own maps for the different units of A.L.F. members that would be called in for the raid.

The night finally came when we began to enter the targeted buildings at night, surveying firsthand the interior traffic and conditions we would encounter on the night of our action. By this time we felt fairly confident the targeted vivariums and labs would be empty due to our exterior surveillance, and interior observations confirmed this. Our only problems would be encountered should we run into anyone in halls, stairways, or elevators the night of the action. We would only be able to liberate rabbits, rats, mice, guinea pigs, and frogs from the biological sciences, psychology, and microbiology labs, and the off-campus headquarters of the animal sciences department which was located in a house in a residential area.

We did everything but enter the targeted rooms during our reconnaissance mission and recorded the times it took to enter and leave the buildings. Once we knew how long it would take to carry out the action, we then took on a task of choosing a window of opportunity that would correlate with our outside recon. We needed not only enough time to enter, break-in to the individual rooms, load the animals and transport them to the ground floor, but also a safe time to literally drive a vehicle to the door and load the animals without any witnesses whatsoever. Here lay our greatest risk. No amount of preparation could help us deal with having to explain to anyone why we were taking animals out of the buildings late at night on a weekend.

Finally, the word went out to the individual specialists that would be required for an action we knew would be North America's largest laboratory animal liberation ever. All unit members would have to fit into the visible role of students, should they encounter another person, as well as have the skills to carry out the raid. Homes had to be arranged for the rescued victims of vivisection and a safe house established where a sympathetic veterinarian could inspect the animals before they could go on to safe homes to live out their natural lives. We also had to prepare for the unfortunate circumstance should any be deemed too far gone to survive, whereby they would be humanely euthanized. No healthy animals or any with a fighting chance would be killed. Vehicles for transportation of both the animals and the A.L.F. members had to be tuned up and inspected for no signs of mechanical or legal failure, and cages constructed for transportation. Most of the animals would be transported in the cages they were already in. Tools were purchased far away that would be needed for the break-in, and our technological division had to develop and build incendiary devices that would allow enough time to escape, while at the same time ignite at a synchronized time. Disguises were constructed for each individual member including wigs, false beards, eyewear and clothing that would be expected of college students.

Shoes to be worn during the action would be either too small or large, depending on the wearer, so that any footprints would not match the feet of A.L.F. members. All tools, clothing, and equipment for the raid were kept in plastic bags where it could not collect even the minutest fragment of forensic evidence such as hair or lint. This precaution was taken in case any item should be inadvertently left behind during the operation.

A day was chosen for the action that would fit the safest window of inactivity for the four targeted buildings: April 4th, which also happened to be the anniversary of Martin Luther King's assassination. All unit members were assembled and some told for the first time what their target was. The next 48 hours were spent meticulously going over each individual unit member's role and conducting final surveillance on the campus. Meanwhile the "handlers"—that is the people charged with caring for and transporting the rescued animals once they were safely out of the labs—prepared cages, water bottles, boxes, and feed in the transport vehicles. Now all that remained to be done was perhaps the hardest part of any A.L.F. action: the waiting.

On the day of April 3rd, while the majority of the A.L.F.'s active service unit tested and recharged radios and the incendiary devices to be used in the microbiology laboratories and the Animal Sciences Department offices, another team was on campus where they walked out a "dry run" of the action ensuring that all doors and windows were just as they were supposed to be. This team was also charged with the responsibility of estimating just how many animals could be safely liberated in the time allotted for the action. The break-in unit would be given a cut-off time after which they would have to be out of the building to ensure that their entry and exit would not coincide with one of the regular police patrols or cut into the time needed to allow the demolition unit entry and exit to plant the incendiary devices.

As dusk turned to darkness, over eight A.L.F. members began to load their daypacks with tools, radios, ski masks and spray paint which would be worn once inside the buildings. Lastly, the whole operation was reviewed with each team repeating its role and objective and the time they would take to carry it out. If all went well, not only would hundreds of lab animals be rescued, but also two animal research facilities would be set ablaze thereby destroying the equipment used to torture animals and countless records for research experiments that were kept in the off-campus offices of the Animal Sciences Department.

At approximately 2100 hours, a man and woman holding hands passed two male students walking towards the Biological Sciences Building. Neither couples were students and while the two men headed one direction the man and woman approached the bottom floor doors of the Microbiology Building.

Not far away in a campus parking lot, a surveillance member watched carefully the surrounding area should the need arise to radio either team to alert them to the occurrence of anything out of the ordinary. The man and woman reached the door and quickly gained entry with the aid of a few small hand tools which left no telltale sign of forced entry. Next, they climbed the stairwell to the top floor where they pulled on their ski masks before swinging open the doors that led to the vivarium where it was known over 100 mice were being used in cryptosporidium experiments. While one member stood watch, the other carefully transferred the mice into small boxes that were then placed in two separate long duffel bags. With this completed, the two A.L.F. members each picked up a bag and exited separately out of different doors minutes apart. Before they left the Microbiology Building there had been no radio transmissions which translated into everything appearing normal to the surveillance unit. The two team members walked towards a van where waiting inside for both of them was a driver and handler to receive and transfer the mice to larger cages for their journey to freedom. The two A.L.F. members then returned to their own vehicle and drove away, their role completed with total success.

At about the same time as the Microbiology Building was being entered, the A.L.F. team that passed the other A.L.F. members reached the basement loading dock of the Psychology Building. Here they were somewhat hidden, as only a pedestrian walkway passed the adjacent doorway where the unit members would gain entry through an extractor fan that led to the vivarium of the Psychology Building where hundreds of rats used in experiments were housed. While one member stood watch, the other began cutting through the sheet metal ventilation cover with tin snips. Next came the removal of the fan itself, which took all of the 20 minutes allowed for this stage of the action. With precious minutes ticking away (which would translate into more lives saved, should any time be saved) the break-in team member entered the vivarium while the watchperson replaced the slightly bent and cut vent cover which would only appear tampered with at close inspection.

Next the A.L.F. member on the inside opened the adjacent door allowing in the other team member. Quickly the two began to remove individual rat cages from their tall racks and place them on rolling tables which could then be rolled to the loading area. Once 150 rats were ready for transport, the two-person team called in the transport vehicle which was awaiting their call with anticipation. In the time it took for the vehicle to arrive, one of the A.L.F. members began to smash the small electroshock boxes that were used in the psychology experiments and spray-painting demands that all vivisection be ceased. With the transport vehicle now at the loading area, and the driver serving as a lookout, the two A.L.F. members began wheeling out the carts full of rat cages. Unfortunately, there was limited space in the vehicle allowing only a certain amount of rats, all of which were standing on their hind legs sniffing at the cool night air as they were taken away from the sterile smells of the vivarium. Looking back at the hundreds of rats that would be left behind to a certain painful death, both team members rushed back to grab one cage each which they carried on their laps as the transport vehicle ferried the animals to freedom.

Phase two of the operation was now complete with no unexpected developments. With radio-communicated word that both the mice and rats were safely off campus and both strike teams equally safe and secure, now came the most dangerous and largest stage of the five-pronged attack. Between timed police patrols a vehicle drove up to the five-story Biological Sciences Building and dropped off one unit member who was to gain entry through a bottom floor door. Once that was accomplished, two separate teams entered the building bringing the number of A.L.F. members in the building to five. Meeting in a stairwell, the unit members donned ski masks and white lab coats and, pulling a five-pound sledgehammer from one of their packs, charged to the fifth floor where hundreds of animals awaited their freedom.

Days later, police and media would still be talking about the brazen attitude of the A.L.F. commandos who not only carried out the lightning strike raid, but also video taped their crime. In the video, A.L.F. members, many of whom were obviously women, were seen smashing through vivarium doors and rushing in to spirit the animals away. When the team reached the fifth floor, one member approached each locked animal room and with a sledgehammer smashed a hole through the reinforced glass, then reaching in and unlocking the door from the inside. Immediately after, each room was entered where a small colony of guinea pigs were transferred to smaller cages.

Many of the animals were without food and water and sank to the back of their cages, many with shaved fur awaiting exposure to toxic substances which would inflame their skin. The A.L.F. had arrived in time to prevent such cruelty. Slowly, rolling carts were filled with guinea pigs, more rats, hundreds of mice, and finally six African frogs used for breeding, their offspring to be sacrificed for dissection. A separate cart was filled with over a dozen rabbits in cloth sacks. Now, the elevator was brought to the floor by an A.L.F. member who was in it. The carts full of animals were carefully rolled into the elevator with two unit members while another two spray-painted our greetings to the animal's executioners.

Now traveling downward in the elevator, the A.L.F. team held their breath, hoping no one else in the building would call the elevator. If they did, the doors would open to reveal not only two masked members but also hundreds of mice, rats, frogs, guinea pigs and rabbits. When the elevator full of animals left the fifth floor, a radio call was made to the pick up vehicle which was to receive the over 900 animals. At the ground floor the two A.L.F. members wheeled to the double doors where the transport vehicle was reversed directly to the building. Any student or police officer who saw this would immediately become suspicious, but here the weeks of nighttime surveillance paid off. The unit knew that as long as it stayed in the window of opportunity they would evade the regular police cruiser patrols.

Backing up to the Biological Sciences Building, a handler swung open the rear doors of the vehicle and was met immediately with the break in team who quickly began to load the many cages. Within minutes the animals were safely loaded and the vehicle drove away at a normal pace. The break in team rendezvoused with the other unit members in the stairwell where clothes and tools were neatly packed into their daypacks and the team split up to leave the campus on foot. The surveillance watchperson would later report that literally three minutes after the vehicle full of animals departed from the doorway, a student would exit through the very same doors.

When the A.L.F. watchperson received word that all animals and unit members were safely out of the buildings, a radio call was made and with a one-word pre-arranged message called in the demolitions unit.

Minutes later a solitary "student" entered the Microbiology Building carrying in their daypacks an incendiary device. Climbing the stairs to the rooftop laboratory where the cryptosporidium mice had been liberated earlier, the demolition member pulled on their ski masks and set the device in the center of the laboratory. Carefully setting the timer for 0400 hours, the A.L.F. member then built a pyramid of dissection boards and desk drawers around the device to fuel the fire once it ignited. As the member left the building, they took one last look at the torture chamber where literally thousands of animals had lost their lives, their eyes being the last to ever see it standing.

Exiting the building the demolition member met with their driver who next drove them to the quiet residential neighborhood where the Animal Sciences Department headquarters was located. Previous reconnaissance had revealed a weakly constructed basement vent which entered into a crawlspace beneath the house filled with computers and file records which contained vital information and data necessary to every animal experiment on the U of A campus. The same unit member now walked casually to the basement, crawled beneath the building, and set the second device also for 0400 hours. Completing this, they returned to the vehicle and departed towards the interstate, their mission completed.

At approximately 0438 hours residents were awakened to the sounds of multiple sirens responding to a blaze on the rooftop of the Microbiology Building. Before the fire could be brought under control it had destroyed not only the complete animal research laboratory, but water doused on the flames had caused hundreds of thousands of dollars of damage to the labs beneath the targeted lab.

No sooner had the fire at the Microbiology Building been brought under control when the Tucson Fire Department received the call the Animal Sciences Department headquarters was also ablaze.

Though damage caused by the fire at the residential offices was first thought to be minimal, later news reports would detail that the heat had caused irreparable damage to the complete systems, and since the fire caused serious structural damage to the very foundation of the building, it would later have to be demolished.

Meanwhile, in the network of safe homes established as the A.L.F.'s Underground Railroad, the 1,231 rescued lab animals were beginning a new life—one that would quickly erase the nightmarish memories of the laboratories at the University of Arizona. Though federal investigators and local police pursued over 150 leads in the A.L.F.'s raid at the U of A, investigators would later report in law enforcement journals the virtual lack of evidence that might lead to any arrests. Michael Cusonivich, head of research for the U of A, later conceded that not only had the A.L.F.'s raid caused the cessation of over a dozen experiments, but also the university was forced to spend over half a million dollars on an improved security system for all animal research buildings on campus. University officials would also admit how the raid had placed such attention on their animal research program, that they were left with no alternative but to clean up their act to ensure that not even the slightest violation of weak federal animal welfare guidelines were violated. While the attention was focused on the U of A's animal research, a small A.L.F. active service unit infiltrated Tucson once again that year. This time the Veteran's Administration Hospital was targeted where four former racing greyhounds were liberated from outdoor kennels. The message was painfully clear to vivisectors in Arizona: Wherever you are, no matter how hidden, if animals were sacrificed in the name of science at your hands, the A.L.F. will find you.

Now it is up to you. The A.L.F. active service unit which carried out the raid at the University of Arizona may not have been caught, but without the young blood of the next generation they may not survive. Though this action was highly organized, it was carried out by simple people who never imagined they would be labeled as domestic terrorists by the U.S. government. They are people just like you and me, men and women, young and old. They were not career criminals, veterans of military operations, but simply people who cared enough to stand by their beliefs even when it meant breaking the law. For many, the U of A raid was their first laboratory action. But as the U of A proved, with vigilant surveillance, a lot of common sense, and most importantly the self confidence that you can achieve anything you set your mind and heart into, anything is possible and no target of animal abuse is impregnable. Now it is time for you to charge forward and deliver freedom to the millions of victims of vivisection.

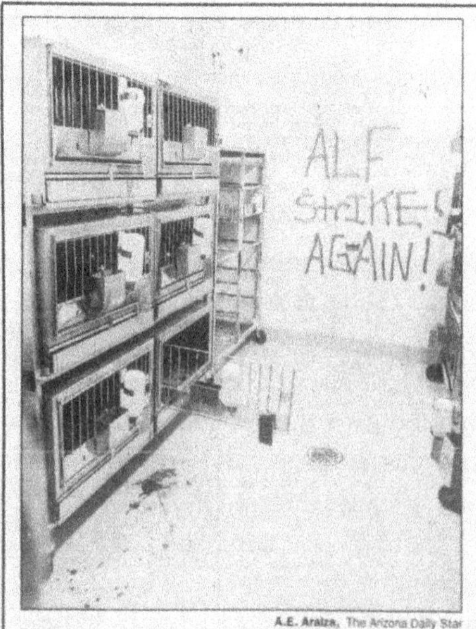

A.E. Araiza, The Arizona Daily Star

Splattered red paint and empty lab cages at Bio West

Rights group 'liberated' over 1,200 UA animals

By C.T. Revere
The Arizona Daily Star

An animal rights group has claimed responsibility for setting fire to two UA buildings early yesterday and "liberating" more than 1,200 research animals — including 30 mice said to carry a parasite that causes a potentially dangerous form of dysentery.

The fires caused an estimated $90,000 damage to a rooftop research area on the UA's pharmacy and microbiology building and another $10,000 to a residential office north of the campus, a Tucson fire spokesman said.

Forty-six firefighters took an hour to put out the fire, which was set with an incendiary device inside the penthouse laboratory of the pharmacy and microbiology building, said fire Capt. Keith Richter.

Second fire at office

About the time the first fire was put out, a second blaze was set at a home in the 1500 block of East Mabel Street where the offices for the Division of Animal Research are located, Richter said.

In a letter distributed yesterday to the Tucson media, the Animal Liberation Front (ALF) claimed the 1,231 animals were freed to protect them from "certain torture and death at the hands of UofA students and researchers."

But a University of Arizona professor researching a treatment for a strain of dysentery caused by a parasitic organism said the members of the animal rights group and others may be endangered by the mice.

Chuck Sterling, a professor of veterinary science, said during a news conference 30 young mice taken from the fifth floor of the Microbiology West building were injected with cryptosporidium, a parasite that endangers young children in Third World nations.

"If the people are caring for the animals and directly handling them, it is likely they could get feces on their hands and then it could come in contact with their mouths," Sterling said.

The parasite will cause severe diarrhea in most people who are subjected to it, but can be fatal for those whose immune systems are

See ANIMALS, Page 2A

Oregon State University Experimental Fur Farm

1991

How Rod Coronado and a small group shut down a fur farm research facility forever.

In Spring of 1991 some friends and I decided it was time for a direct action campaign against the U.S. fur farm industry. We had been contacted about animal research being conducted at Oregon State University that was funded by the Mink Farmers Research Foundation, an organization that collects a tax on mink pelts at the auction house and funds research to benefit fur farmers.

An undercover investigation funded by Friends of Animals had exposed the vulnerable links in the fur farm industry, specifically in research and development. Through only a handful of universities the MFRF financed research that was aimed at lowering the overhead costs to raise mink and prevent the spread of disease among mink in captivity. By the end of February 1992 all but one recipient of MFRF funds had felt the bite of the A.L.F. Besides OSU, Washington State University in Pullman. Michigan State University in East Lansing, the Fur-Breeders Cooperative in Edmonds, Washington and Malecky Mink Ranch in Oregon had been raided. This is the story of the first raid of what would become known as Operation Bite Back.

We rode up to Corvallis, Oregon on our mountain bikes surveying the outlying areas of campus until we located the long barns of the Experimental Fur Farm. Ditching our bikes in the brush we approached along Oak Creek, a waterway that wound along the fur farm right up to its property boundary. Everywhere were the tracks of mink that had escaped from the farm. Having never been the target of even protests, let alone a direct action attack, the farm's security consisted of little more than outdoor lighting, fences and a caretaker's quarters.

After a few hours in the brush watching for security activity, we ventured over the fence onto the property where we surveyed each building until we felt we had identified the general layout of the station. Besides the mink barns there were storage buildings for farm equipment, a workshop, the experimental feed building, a laboratory, the caretaker's house, and offices of the head researcher, Ron Scott.

Next we hopped over the five-foot fence surrounding the mink barns which was topped with an electric wire, the type used to pen in horses, choosing not to open the gate should it be alarmed. A few of the sheds were empty of mink and one small female roamed freely within the confines of the actual farm. Checking the gate for an alarm, we wedged the door open and watched as the female who had followed us bolted to freedom. Just then, we looked above the gate to the adjoining research laboratory and noticed a window to a bathroom that was left unlatched.

We opened the window and then closed it again and retreated off the property to the creek to watch for any response should the window be alarmed. There was no noticeable activity. Next we ventured onto the roof where we could view the entire field station. It was an extreme rarity to conduct a first time reconnaissance and feel confident enough to conclude that an action was possible, but that is exactly what we did.

We knew that the type of action we planned would bring down a wave of repression on animal rights activists, but we believed it was time the fur farm industry was targeted by the A.L.F. and OSU, as the number one recipient of MFRF funds seemed the logical first strike. If successful, in one attack we could neutralize over six research projects that, if concluded, would result in innovative developments in captive mink raising. OSU's Experimental Fur Farm had been established by the US Department of Agriculture in 1926. At 65 years of age it was high time for its retirement. Now came the recruitment stage of the action. Rather than draw from already suspected A.L.F. activists, it was decided to approach people completely unknown to law enforcement authorities. A handful of trusted activists who had proved their commitment in other campaigns were contacted, only in person and talked to only outside of their homes. Not one declined the invitation to become a member of what would be called the Western Wildlife Unit of the A.L.F.

On our second recon mission we were armed with topographical, county and state maps for the entire region. Roads were driven to establish escape paths should we be detected during the raid and drop-off and pick-up points were established. We avoided stopping at any shops and stores in the area and filled up on gas far from the target. When the raid happened and if we became suspects because of our above-ground activism, we knew our pictures would be shown to local merchants so it was wise to not be seen in the area.

Our group began to get to know the strengths and weaknesses of one another and crafted our roles for the raid based on them. Some people were better drivers, others more observant and vigilant. In that way we delegated who was to drive, be lookouts and lead the entry team. We conducted all night surveillance on the day of the week we planned the raid and became intimately familiar with the normal activity during that time. With the confidence that only competent A.L.F. operatives and thorough planning can create, we next discussed tactics. We wanted to shut the farm down, not necessarily win public support. Arson became the logical tactic as well as confiscation and destruction of vital research documentation and genetic records for the mink.

The primary experiments being conducted at the time involved tests of experimental feeds. We decided that the experimental feed building where the feed was mixed and stored would be targeted for an incendiary device attack. The building was a safe distance from the mink barns and downwind from the caretaker's home. Next we decided on removing all the identification cards from the mink cages and seizing all records of the mink in the head researcher's office.

With the open bathroom window we were able to enter the main laboratory numerous times before the raid which aided in not only locating vital records, it also afforded us the opportunity to read letters and memos that detailed the relationship the station had to area fur farms and the MFRF. We were even able to remove documents on recon missions, photocopy them and return them the same night. By the night of the action we already had our own records of every research project at the station and the names and addresses of literally every fur farm and supplier in the Northwest.

The long awaited day finally came when justice would be done for the Mink Nation. Operatives gathered in a not so distant city and from the morning onward we rehearsed our roles and reviewed surveillance maps, photos, videos and notes until even those who did not participate in surveillance missions were familiar with our target. No one was allowed to wear their own shoes or clothing and everything we intended to use on the raid would be disposable. New tools had been purchased and incendiary devices assembled and tested. The routes we would take were driven and checked for unusual activity and the vehicles gassed up and checked for burnt out lights or other signs that would attract police. The previous night a final reconnaissance mission was con-ducted and the conclusion made that all was a go for action.

Finally came that time when anticipation was the hardest part of an action. Plans had been reviewed, batteries in flashlights checked, day packs loaded. Darkness is all we awaited. Two separate vehicles were loaded with operatives and gear and we broke off into two groups. In the first group one operative set out on bike to establish the look-out position. This person would monitor a police scanner programmed with the frequencies for city, state and county police and should they respond to any suspicious activity at the station. Their job was to identify the police codes and inform the rest of the team immediately. Radio silence was to be maintained unless something was amiss. This way any communication would be deemed urgent instead of frequent radio communication, which eventually becomes distracting.

One team approached from the creek and immediately entered the fenced in mink barn area and began stripping identification cards from cages. Another two-person team climbed through the bathroom window and moved directly into offices and labs with targeted documents and began loading empty packs with the material. All other research material was spilled out onto the floor and a water line broken to flood the building. Any equipment of value was taken into a sound-insulated room and smashed. With the main laboratory trashed and flooded and all documents either destroyed or seized, the trademark red spray-paint was pulled out and messages for the researchers left in three-foot letters. Of them all the most telling would be, "A.L.F., MORE TO COME...THIS IS ONLY THE BEGINNING."

Every tool and paint can used in the lab was wrapped in plastic garbage bags and loaded back into the packs. By now the amount of documents seized was easily over 75 pounds. One operative's sole duty would be to carry them out. A more direct escape route than that taken into the station was chosen and the break from our original plan revealed immediately an overlooked hole in our security. As the operative crossed in front of the caretaker's house a motion detecting light was activated and their presence revealed. Luckily they were able to take cover before anyone could see them but to the lookout it appeared that we had been detected.

At that very moment two other operatives inside the experimental feed barn were setting up incendiary devices. When the alert came over the radio an evacuation from the property commenced and all operatives were called off the action. From the lookout's vantage point the two joined the third and surmised that, though the light had been triggered, detection had not occurred. With the knowledge that without the destruction of the experimental feed building the station and research projects might be able to continue, the two operatives opted to return. All other operatives were withdrawn, except the lookout and the incendiary devices left behind were set up and activated with a 50 minute timed delay. The two warriors piled nesting boxes and skinning boards around the devices, which were placed centrally in the wood building, and then called in over the radio for pick-up.

Once in the vehicles, with all seized documents off in a separate vehicle where they would be taken for review, the remainder of the Western Wildlife Unit stripped off all clothing worn during the raid and wrapped it in more plastic garbage bags. These and all other disposable items were deposited by separate individuals in separate garbage receptacles. No tools were disposed of with clothing and we chose dumpsters and trash cans where it was unlikely anyone would be rummaging through. With the adrenaline rush fading with the evening darkness, exhaustion crept over the team members. As we headed south on the interstate at the speed limit, the sun began to rise over the horizon.

Today would be a new day for the Mink Nation. Never again would fur farmers feel secure in their bloody business. It would still be hours before news reports would confirm that a fire had swept OSU's Experimental Fur Farm, destroying its feed building, but still those of us on this action knew our efforts had been successful. We didn't need anyone to tell us our actions were justified. The look in the mink's eyes the previous night said enough. Already documents seized in the raid were being reviewed by still action-ready warriors. Of particular interest was letters stating that the Northwest Fur-Breeders Cooperative in Edmonds, Washington was making feed donations that made experiments at the station possible. Without such support, the station would not be able to conclude its feed experiments. Before the week would end a fire would rip through the Cooperative causing $400,000 in damages and destroying half of the facility. Six months later OSU would announce the permanent closure of its Experimental Fur Farm citing in part the lack of state and private funds to continue research. An A.L.F. press release issued on the fur farm's own letterhead accepting responsibility for the raid promised more attacks and ended with the vow that Operation Bite Back would not end... "Until the last fur farm is burned to the ground."

In the name of all fur farm prisoners, this was and is only the beginning.

Operation Bite Back

1991-1993

How one A.L.F. cell targeted multiple fur industry targets in a two year campaign to cripple the fur industry's infrastructure.

(Excerpt from *Memories Of Freedom*)

In the darkened New Moon of May 1991, we found ourselves on the roof of Oregon State University's Experimental Fur Animal Research Station. The headlights from passing cars bounced off of the five long barns containing 1,100 mink and the sounds of their scratching and the unforgettable scent of their musk was in the night air. Below, we could just make out the outlined shape of a black-clad woman whose long black hair shielded her face, a radio antenna extending from her hand. Receiving an "all-clear" a warrior lowered themself into the mink barn compound and circled the rows of cages. This was one of many reconnaissance missions whose sole purpose was to familiarize our unit with the layout and night activity of the research station.

The target buildings had been located and all that we lacked was an entry point. All doors were avoided as they are the obvious and most common place for alarms. Walking amongst the mink in their cages, it wasn't long before it was discovered that a few mink were outside their cages, yet still prevented from freedom by a surrounding five foot fence topped with electric wire. As one mink approached, the warrior stood still as she sniffed their scent, then continued on in search of an opening to the nearby creek that flowed past the station. Walking to a gate in the yard and after checking it for alarms, the warrior opened it and stood back. The solitary mink approached slowly and as she crossed the threshold to freedom, bolted in a sprint to the nearby river and disappeared. Shutting the gate the warrior glanced above her to a small window and upon testing it, discovered it wasn't locked.

Through the windows it became plainly obvious that this was the building that housed the archives of research records from the last 70 years of fur farm research, as well as laboratory equipment for the research performed at the station. The offices of the head researcher, Ron Scott, also adjoined the lab. This would be one of two targets of the first raid on a fur farm research station by the Western Wildlife Unit of the ALF. The other was to be a barn containing all the experimental feed and mixing equipment that stood a safe distance and downwind from where any animals were caged.

Already preliminary investigations had proven that the experimental feeds were the backbone of all research currently in progress on diets for the mink that would ensure optimum pelt quality and yet remain economically feasible. We also knew the already high cost of these feeds was being covered by the Northwest Fur Breeders Cooperative and without this donation the research station would have to cut into its research budget to provide feed for its research animals. Drawing back from the station that night we felt elated, not sad, knowing the next visit would be the last and one the researchers would never forget.

The following days were spent choosing a night for the raid that would offer adequate darkness and minimal activity on the premises and neighboring campus and houses. In late May we received word that state charges against three accused ALF activists of a raid on University of Oregon labs in 1986 were dropped and decided what better way to celebrate this, then with another ALF raid in Oregon.

As the sun lowered itself on the day of June 10, 1991 six ALF warriors found themselves gathered around a campfire on nearby forest lands checking battery power on radios, reviewing hand drawn and topographical maps, and dressing down in bright college attire to hide the dark clothes they wore underneath. A joy that rarely inhabits our ranks was in the air as we readied ourselves for a night that would bring long-awaited justice to the nation's largest fur farm research station.

Fanny packs were organized with the assorted equipment necessary to each individual member and cash was distributed to each warrior who would be on foot in case of separation, as well as maps with predetermined routes out of the area. Easy retreat plans were reviewed, roles were discussed and each warrior would repeat their responsibilities until everyone was assured that they understood every action that would comprise the raid.

With darkness among us as our greatest friend, we gathered for a last vocal moment and each expressed our reasons for being there that night and spoke of what we hoped to achieve for our mink relations. Never have I seen a finer group of warriors and as we piled into our separate vehicles, it was hard to hide my pride in this handful of people who were about to risk all for our Mother Earth.

Within an hour, lookouts were in place and four warriors on mountain bikes descended into the nearby creeks that led to the station. Without a spoken word, only hand signals, we deployed ourselves to our various positions and hearing no radio warning (silence meant the all-clear) we began the night's work.

While one warrior busied themselves with removing breeding identification cards from the mink cages (to confuse the researchers as there was no other way to identify the animals), two others slipped through the still unlocked bathroom window into the main records building. Research photos, slides and documents were loaded into backpacks along with the vivisector phone books, address books and other material that would reveal supporters and financiers to the station's dirty work. After this, every single file, research paper and archive in the station was spilled onto the floor and every available liquid poured onto them until a water line from the bathroom was broken that would flood the entire floor.

Following this the most expensive laboratory equipment was quietly smashed and test tube samples were dumped down the drain. Veterinary medicines that might come in handy in the future were loaded into a fanny pack and lastly, the red-spray paint came out and the WWU's calling card and suggested advice to vivisectors left behind, that and the tell tale "ALF." Exiting the research building the same way we entered, our forces began their withdrawal as the demolitions warrior and one watch person stayed behind.

With a one-hour delay incendiary device the "demo" entered the experimental feed barn after the official ALF key (boltcutters) was used to obtain entry. Placing the device near the structural center of the building, the warrior then piled wooden fur farm equipment around the device, set it, and fled. Within minutes all team members regrouped carrying plastic trash bags in their fanny packs containing all tools and evidence of our presence. In a few more minutes with mountain bikes loaded and all confiscated research documents and photos in a safe car, we drove the speed limit across county lines to the nearby interstate where all clothes worn during the action were distributed in various dumpsters. Shoes worn during the action also were thrown away and all tools although new were deposited in the nearest river. At about this same time a fire erupted in the experimental feed barn and demolished the feed supply and all equipment in the barn, as well as the barn itself. Over 1,100 mink watched from their cages as the fur farm researchers arrived to survey the damage. Within minutes T.V. cameras were on the scene as federal and local authorities waded through years of fur farm research, down the drain.

Morale among the Northwest's fur farmers was at an all time low as they now wrestled with the uncomfortable fact that not only had virtually every research project at O.S.U.'s fur Animal Research Station been destroyed, but also every name and number of theirs was now in the hands of the ALF. Genetic logbooks for the research mink were also missing along with vital research records necessary for the continuation of research.

The blow was too much for the tight budgeted research lab to endure. When 1991 ended and O.S.U.'s mink herd was killed, O.S.U.'s animal research department decided to cut funds to the fur farm and within six months the Oregon State University Experimental Fur Animal Research Station closed its doors forever.

In its first stage, Operation Bite Back had shut down the nations largest Fur Farm research facility.

Biting the Hand That Feeds You: Northwest Furbreeders Cooperative

Before the dust could settle on the still smoldering ruins of O.S.U.'s research station, a small WWU-ALF war party was dispatched to Edmonds, Washington, home of the Northwest Fur-Breeders Cooperative. NW Co-op provided annual support to O.S.U.'s research station, not out of the goodness of its cold heart, but because its members represented the majority of fur farmers in Washington, Oregon, Idaho, and Montana, who served to benefit from O.S.U.'s research.

Located on the docks of Edmonds, the NW Co-Op serves as a feed manufacturer, processing tons of factory-farm and fish by-products into the food that will keep Northwest fur farms operational. Operating as a hub, the NW Co-Op sends out diesel tractor-trailers weekly to its member fur farmers, distributing feed, nesting materials and other equipment to the fur farm industry.

On the night of June 15th, four warriors stood above the docks of Edmonds watching the 11 o'clock p.m. shift end its business for the night at the co-op from a nearby hillside. In each one of the warriors' nightpacks (to others known as daypacks) were radios with microphone and earphone extensions extending out to the raiders' shoulders much like bike cops in nearby Seattle. Once again, the trusted mountain bike war ponies were used and if anyone saw them that night, they would remember four warriors riding down from the hills above Edmonds to the docks where the four riders broke into separate directions to establish lookout points at all road entry ways. One of the warriors carried a police scanner and through previous reconnaissance, had already become familiar with the "normal" radio traffic and was familiar with codes used by the police.

Two warriors went on foot, casually walking along the docks like two star-struck lovers, holding hands and stopping intermittently to survey the scene that lay before them. When they passed into the shadows behind the NW Co-Op, the two warriors quickly darted behind two tractor trailers whose refrigeration units buzzed loudly over the surrounding sounds of the docks. The smell of fish entrails permeated the air and the warriors quickly donned their dark disposable coveralls they could use to crawl through the mess.

Locating an access window for feed products to enter through, they crawled into it, carefully lifting their nightpacks into the building. With continued radio silence signalling the all-clear, the two warriors quickly surveyed the empty building to ensure that no late night employees or watchman remained. Upon confirmation of an empty building, the two warriors entered the warehouse portion of the building where dry feed and nesting materials were stacked to the ceiling on wooden forklift pallets. Opening a ceiling vent to allow a little air circulation to fuel the fire, one warrior set to work assembling the incendiary device while the other left the ALF calling card accompanied with a mink paw encircled within the female symbol for the mink mothers at O.S.U., whose young the ALF were unable to rescue.

A security patrol circled the building, but the warriors knew as long as everything appeared normal, there would be no reason for the guard to stop and investigate. Once the incendiary device was set and the patrol truck had passed, the two warriors exited quickly and quietly, stripping off their coveralls and continuing their stroll through the harbor back to their mountain bikes and the friendly dark night.

Within 90 minutes firefighters were responding to the four alarm blaze that injured no one, but effectively destroyed 75% of the NW fur breeders warehouse causing an estimated $750,000 in damages. Phase two of Operation Bite Back was complete.

Following the O.S.U. and NW furbreeders raids the fur farm industry went ballistic. A $35,000 reward was offered for the capture and conviction of ALF warriors, and fur farmers had announced in the media that they were now arming themselves against further attacks.

The fur farm industry mouthpiece, the Fur Farm Animal Welfare Coalition held a press conference in Seattle asking animal rights groups to denounce the ALF. Granted, none publicly did at this time, but neither did one ever come forward to support the ALF except the small grassroots group Coalition Against Fur Farms who distributed press releases and attempted to organize mainstream follow-up campaigns to continue the pressure on fur farm research stations. And so the summer of '91 began with the Western Wildlife Unit back in action. Training continued, and confiscated research papers and fur farm trade journals were reviewed to determine the next link in fur farm animal abuse that could be broken. ALF moles followed up on leads of other potential targets, and searched veterinary medicine files for possible future actions.

In July, a newspaper article arrived from CAFF from Spokane, Washington describing the impact the ALF was causing on Washington State University's fur animal research. At this same time confiscated documents from O.S.U. revealed how research programs of W.S.U. vivisector John Gorham were groundbreaking in searching for a remedy to diseases suffered by mink on fur farms due to their intensive confinement. Within days ALF warriors were on their way to W.S.U., in Pullman, Washington.

The Night of Stars Falling: Washington State University

As Animal Liberation Front moles busied themselves in researching all they could about the research of John Gorham, the foot soldiers began reconnaissance missions on the Washington State University campus that spread out across the rolling hills surrounding Pullman, Washington. Like most of southeastern Washington the Pullman area is grass covered plains devoid of trees having been mostly deforested by the timber industry. We already knew the location of the U.S. Department of Agriculture's Experimental Fur Farm at W.S.U. was hidden from the public, but how difficult could it be to find unmistakable mink barns? Our first step was the now tried and true tactic of riding mountain bikes like casual bicyclists on every road, trail and path that crisscrossed the W.S.U. campus. Checking outlying buildings and keeping our noses to the wind for the easily recognizable scent of mink musk.

Meanwhile, the moles had discovered that W.S.U. is a nerve center of animal research on native American wildlife. Grizzly and black bears, mule deer, elk and bighorn sheep were just a few of the animals we soon discovered wallowing in the misery of concrete pens and corrals. Serving as a prostitute to the livestock industry, W.S.U. vivisectors were busying themselves in studying bacterial and competitive grazing threats native wildlife posed to cattle and sheep grazed on public lands. Never before had the ALF discovered vivisection on America's wildlife outside of O.S.U.'s mink farm and now our strategist and logistics experts were discussing ways to transport these larger animals. Unfortunately, our resources and warrior shortages would prohibit us spiriting away bears or deer this time. . . Our focus remained the mink.

The newspaper article we had received had also discussed a furbearer research facility also on campus, where vivisector Fred Gilbert tested underwater traps on beavers. His lab also housed wolverine, fishers, badgers, and martens. We would also attempt to locate Gilbert's laboratory and liberate the wildlife prisoners there. Gilbert's research was funded by the Canadian fur industry. John Gorham's research was not only funded by the Mink Farmers Research Foundation, but also by the U.S. Department of Agriculture. Gorham targeted Aluetian Disease, Encephalopathy (known in cattle as Mad Cow Disease) and other diseases that could economically wipe out a fur farmer should mink become affected. To conduct his research, Gorham would grind up infected mink brains and force-feed them to healthy mink until they contracted the chosen disease. Animals in his laboratory often died slow deaths as the paralysis of their disease slowly developed in their bodies, causing nervous disorders and hemorrhaging. Fur farmers across the world had identified John Gorham as "one of the world's leading researchers in fur farm diseases," according to an article in *Fur Rancher Magazine*, in 1991.

After locating the fur farm on W.S.U.'s campus, hidden in plain sight off a road to the local airport, a nighttime recon was planned. In the early evening of a full moon before the lunar rising, two warriors hiked to the fur farm where they scaled a chain-link fence topped with barbed-wire to reach the mink barns. The perimeter was walked until it was determined that no infra-red or motion detector alarms surrounded the facility. Being a federally funded research station, we expected as much. There wasn't any electronic security.

The warriors surveyed the area and quickly located the control group mink who had not been infected with any disease. Once the layout of the facility became familiar and no premise watchmen or watchdogs were located, the warriors pulled back to the chain-link fence. From a distance a car could be heard approaching so the two warriors quickly climbed the fence when one warrior was snagged by barbed-wire. As the headlights of the oncoming car became visible, the trapped warrior wrestled with their pant leg, finally freeing themselves and jumping from the fence and sprinting across the road to cover just as the car approached and passed. It was a police car.

As the two warriors walked in the pre-moon darkness, they noticed the headlight beams of the police car had made a 360 turn and then went out. As the two warriors walked the shoulder of the road they became suspicious.

Pulling out a pair of binoculars the warriors sighted in the distance the outline of a car parked on the shoulder of the road with its lights off, on a crash-course with the warriors. Quickly the two darted into the surrounding bare hillside, just as another police cruiser came speeding from the opposite direction on the same road. The first police cruiser gunned its engine and turned on its headlights in an attempt to sandwich in the two warriors. As the warriors scrambled into the knee-high grass the two police cars came together at the fur farm and began to shine spotlights into the facility, then the surrounding hillsides. This fur farm research facility was obviously expecting a visit from the ALF.

As the two warriors lay on their bellies in the sparse hills surrounding the fur farm, the moon rose clear and bright, illuminating the whole area. One police cruiser inched with its lights off just feet past the two hiding warriors and parked on a ridge overlooking the entire fur farm compound. As the warriors remained motionless, coyotes began to howl as the moon lifted itself into the sky. Something sounded out of place, as most of the coyote cries were concentrated, and coming from the direction of a small building above the fur farm. Still other coyotes could be heard howling from the distant hills. It became plainly evident that in one of the buildings above the fur farm coyotes were held captive. With little to do but wait it out, the two warriors cursed themselves for being trapped under the moon's bright light. Finally the police cruiser gave up the hunt and drove away and the warriors hiked the long way back to their hidden mountain bikes. The element for a surprise attack was gone. Not only had Washington State University's animal researchers had the O.S.U. and NW furbreeders raid as a warning, but now university police had spotted trespassers near the hidden fur farm. Within days, security was increased and when Fred Gilbert's lab was finally located nestled in a grove of pine trees, an infra-red perimeter security system was seen in place. The beaver sheds were clearly visible just beyond it.

Despite the increased security, cautious reconnaissance continued and soon a kennel was located on a hill containing 12 coyotes, the subjects of sarcocystis research. Sarcocystis is a disease that is not fatal to coyotes or sheep, the disease passes through a coyote's system in a few short weeks, while the parasites contain themselves within sheep, destroying the economic value of their meat and wool. Coyotes commonly spread the parasite in their feces where it is transmitted to sheep who are grazed on public lands in coyote country. The coyotes for these experiments were conveniently provided by the U.S.

Department of Agriculture's Animal Damage Control Program. Survivors of aerial gunning and gassed out dens where their families perished.

A strategy session was called to discuss the future of any actions at W.S.U.'s fur research stations and it was decided that in order for any successful attack, warriors with various degrees of experience would be needed. By mid-August, seven ALF warriors confirmed their willingness to risk an attack on the already on-guard fur animal research departments of W.S.U. Moles informed the Operation Bite Back team that John Gorham had been chosen as the U.S.D.A.'s "Researcher of the Year" for 1991, and would be out of town the week of August 21st to receive his award. It was time to act. The raid would be a three-pronged attack. One team would enter the Veterinary Building on W.S.U.'s downtown Pullman campus where Gorham's office was located, another would strike the fur farm and a third would release the coyotes from their hilltop kennel.

In a motel room miles from Pullman, ALF warriors gathered around maps while others scanned local police frequencies. Except for the designated drivers, the remaining warriors divided heavy gloves to the mink handlers, forced entry tools to the Veterinary Building team and boltcutters and red spraypaint to the coyote liberators. A medium of communication was agreed upon for necessary radio transmissions and pick up-points and times were finalized. Already all the team members had been driven through the area pointing out spots near the road where warriors would be dropped off and animals picked up. This time there would be no full moon, but there would be meteor showers according to weather forecasters. When the final emergency contingency plan was understood should the police become aware of our raid, the warriors drove away in the direction to Washington State University.

The first team arrived at the Veterinary Building just as a late night student exited the bottom level. One warrior moved to a lookout position while another located a door latch that had earlier been tampered with so that all that was needed was an aggressive pull to detach the lockplate that held the pin of the door lock. Climbing the stairwell to the 3rd floor level where Gorham's office was located, ALF warriors entered the lit hallway and removed a ceiling tile in the hallway outside Gorham's office. In the ceiling crawl space only thin sheetrock separated the hallway from Gorham's office on the other side of the wall partition. With a small key-hole saw, a hole was punched through and ALF warriors were in "one of the world's leading fur farm researchers" office.

Computer discs, photo slides and address books were removed and a brand new computer for Johnny Boy lay still in the box beside his desk. Lifting the computer over her head a warrior smashed it to the ground and proceeded to do the same to every piece of research and computer equipment in the room, the ALF version of therapy. Meanwhile another warrior dumped every file of Gorham's on the floor until the pile was over a foot thick across the office. As a final touch two gallons of muriatic acid was poured over the complete mess until fumes forced the warriors out of the office. As the warriors exited down the hallway, they passed a gurney with a plexiglass box filled with white mice with a label reading "irradiated 8/21/91" grabbing the box under one arm the warriors fled the building, completing phase one of the attack on W.S.U. At about the same time as the Veterinary Building was being entered, four ALF warriors were dropped off out of sight of the mink barns and coyote kennels. Splitting into two groups, one approached the mink barns, the other the coyote kennels. At the mink barns a watchman was now living on the premises, but would go to sleep after an 11 p.m. check on the mink barns.

Approaching the watchman's window, an ALF warrior peered in to hear the sweet sound of loud snoring. Returning to the mink barns, the official ALF key was used to cut the small padlock on the barn door and two warriors entered the control animal barn with a wire cage with six separate compartments. One by one mink were coaxed into the cage until it was full.

Leaving the barn one raider replaced the cut lock with a similar duplicate in case the watchman decided to conduct a visual inspection later that night he would see nothing out of place. Each warrior carrying one handle of the mink cage, the two figures disappeared into the darkness. Back on the hilltop coyote kennel, one warrior busied themselves clearing low fencing surrounding the kennel with boltcutters to provide an escape from the area for the coyotes, while the other cut the lock leading to the kennel and entered. Moving down the cages the coyotes became anxious as they anticipated this late night visit as a friendly one. The coyotes had been visited regularly by the ALF so were accustomed to the strangers with covered faces. One by one, cage doors were opened and coyotes leapt out towards the door of the kennel.

While most of the coyotes fled the area immediately, others could be heard in the distance, howling from the dark shadows of the wild as we had heard them before. Meanwhile, one coyote hung back attempting to sneak past the liberator to the last cage. The warrior then noticed the last caged coyote to be a young female who eyed the hesitant coyote with anticipation. As the liberator swung open the last cage, the two coyotes bolted off together into the darkness as stars shot across the sky in a magical brilliance. Tears soaked the liberator's face mask as they realized the love these last two coyotes had for one another, so strong that one refused to leave this hell until the other was also free. As coyote shapes disappeared across the plains, the masked coyote warriors took a spraypaint can and painted in large letters across the back of the now empty coyote kennel: "AMERICAN WILDLIFE, LOVE IT OR LEAVE IT ALONE — freedom for fur animals now!!!"

As the sun rose the following day, the evidence of the raid was quickly discovered by veterinary students who normally fed the now-free coyotes. As the authorities were alerted, both vivisectors and W.S.U. administrators were furious that they had had the wool pulled over their eyes by the cagey ALF. Fur animal researchers attempted to deny that research projects were funded by the fur industry, only to be dispelled by ALF released documents stating the contrary. Though Fred Gilbert's laboratory escaped the attack, his experiments did not. A Seattle T.V. station had filed a legal action against Gilbert and Washington State University for the release of his videotaped underwater trap experiments on beavers. Citing that the videotapes were the property of the funder, the Fur Institute of Canada, Gilbert refused to release the tapes, while Washington residents were shocked that their university was being used to benefit the Canadian fur industry. Within a year Fred Gilbert quit his post as the head of the Fur Bearer Research Facility and retreated to a British Columbia University to continue his work, out of the U.S. For Gorham, his selection as Researcher of the Year was tarnished by the destruction of his ongoing research which was rendered useless by stolen computer records and acid-damaged files, slides and records. Gorham attempted to distance himself from fur farm research only to later be featured on the cover of Fur Rancher Magazine in late 1991 as an honored guest on tour of Russian fur farms overseas. While the fur farm industry mourned the loss of the second largest recipient of Mink Farmer Research Foundation funded research, six mink began their new lives on the banks of the Lochsa River on the nearby Nez Perce Reservation. As summer turned to fall, a coyote family began its preparations for the coming winter, their tattooed ears covered over by thickening fur, never would they forget the

Night of Stars Falling and their human relations who freed them. Down on the Farm. . . Malecky Mink Ranch

By September of 1991 U.S. fur farm and Federal law enforcement forces began to anticipate an all out war by the ALF. Photographs of known fur farm activists were being circulated among fur farmers and caution was being exercised when hiring farm help. The '91 pelting season was drawing near and with it the anxiety among fur farmers that they would be the next target of the ALF. Fears were justified, when in the end of September an unsuccessful attempt was made to burn down the Utah Fur Breeders Cooperative in Sandy, Utah where feeds for the state with the largest amount of fur farms were produced. The rural cooperative also housed a mink farm on its premises which was also used for experimentation in fur farm research.

Not to be discouraged, the ALF activists returned to the Northwest where once again vigilant security forces almost discovered ALF raiders on their farms and the fur farmers were poised to attack. The war party then travelled to a mink farm outside of Olympia,Washington where a four-person party was deployed on the perimeter of the mink farms guard fence surrounding the mink barns. While others stood watch, one warrior began surveying the farm searching out the breeder mink, the most valuable part of the herd. Crouched in the darkness the warrior watched as another human form approached casually with a flashlight in hand. Thinking the approaching human to be one of the other members of the war party, the lone warrior remained crouched in the open while the human form approached. When the figure retreated before seeing the warrior, the ALF warrior returned to the waiting party. "What's up?", "Nothing, why?" "Wasn't that you that just came near me?" "We've been right here." There was a watchman patrolling the barns. In a slow retreat the raiders were forced to abandon their attack, once again escaping confrontation with fur farmers.

At this time, an ALF mole alerted the Operation Bite Back team to a fur farm up for sale near Salem, Oregon just down the road from O.S.U. The fur farmer, Hynek Malecky, was interested in not just selling his mink operation, but maintaining a partnership in a joint venture. Benefiting directly from O.S.U's research, Malecky had developed a state-of-the-art mink operation and now with the declining market in mink pelts, he needed additional financing to keep his business alive. No bank would dare loan a fur farmer money not only because of the instability of the fur market, but also because of the recent attacks by the ALF. Malecky Mink Farm was only one of many fur farms teetering on the edge of bankruptcy. The Western Wildlife Unit of the ALF decided to give it a little push.

In early December, long cold rainy nights of reconnaissance had revealed almost no security on the mink farm surrounded by adjoining ranches. What was difficult was approaching the fur farm through the patchwork of private residences that surrounded it. It was decided that a three-person team would be adequate on this action. One driver and two mountain bike riding warriors launched the attack. On December 10th on a still evening the ALF driver dropped off two warriors and their trusty steeds on the narrow country road leading towards Malecky Mink Farm. Donning dark blue rain gear and hooded sweaters the two warriors swooped towards their target, their small nightpacks on their backs carrying the tools necessary to carry out the action.

One warrior monitored an open radio channel with the ALF driver who sat in their truck a few miles away monitoring the police scanner. The local Radio Shack had provided radio frequencies for law enforcement in the area as they normally do for scanner-buffs. The "demo" warrior remained radioless so that she could keep her senses attuned to every sound around her, with her long black hair braided behind her neck to prevent loose hairs from not only snagging on fences, but also to insure no DNA traceable clues would be left behind.

With the radio-warrior in place within sight of both the Malecky home and the target building and the advancing demo warrior, the two exchanged a thumbs-up in the darkness and the demo warrior disappeared into the pelt processing and feed mixing building which served as the heart of the operation. Separate from the mink barns, the nerve center of the operation housed feed mixing equipment, refrigeration units, drying drums for the mink pelts, skinning racks and the assorted supplies necessary to keep a mink farm operational. Standing in the darkened processing building the warrior imagined the farm in full operation, the mobile gas chambers unloading still quivering mink to the waiting skinners, the smells of musk while the pelts are stripped from the minks' warm bodies like banana peels. Returning to the present the warrior was glad that would be a scene never experienced again at Malecky Mink Ranch.

First locating the structural center of the building, the warrior then identified it to be of wooden framework. Gathering mink nesting boxes, pelt-stretching boards and other flammable available materials, the warrior built a pyramid of combustible materials and then placed the one-hour kitchen-timer delayed incendiary device beneath the whole mess. Setting a series of flammable liquids in open plastic containers surrounding the device the warrior twisted the dial on the timer, connected the nine-volt battery and slowly fled the building mentally noting on her watch when the device should trigger. By the time the warriors rendezvoused with their pick-up driver, there were still 36 minutes left before the device ignited. Thirty-two minutes later the device ignited and before fire trucks could reach the scene the heart of Malecky Mink Farm lay in ruins. One fur farm down, 600 to go. The action was clean and smooth and by the time Federal investigators arrived on the scene, the only evidence they found was a burned down fur farm. Not even the telltale "ALF" was spray painted anywhere. The warriors had decided that to do so would only leave evidence that might narrow the scope of suspects. Spray painting would only help law enforcement to conclude that the fire was arson and not accidental or an insurance scam.

This action which took place after the pelting season ensured that there was not only a minimal risk of harming animals on the farm since most had already been killed, but also cost the fur farmer expensive pelts which were still in the processing building.

The Michigan Mink Militia: Michigan State University

Before 1991 came to an end an attempt was made to destroy the pelt processing operation of Huggan's Rocky Mountain Fur Company outside of Hamilton, Montana. The fur company, which also operated its own mink and fox farm, processes pelts for most mink farms in Western Montana. Montana is also home to many of the U.S.'s lynx and bobcat farms, with Fraser Fur Farm in Ronan, Montana boasting the largest wildcat fur farm in the country. As the 1991 pelting season came to a close, after being on the alert since the June ALF attacks, many fur farmers breathed a sigh of relief hoping the brunt of Operation Bite Back was over. Nothing could be further from the truth. In January of 1992, People for the Ethical Treatment of Animals ran a series of radio announcements in western Michigan drawing attention to Michigan State University's animal experiments by Richard Aulerich whose primary laboratory animal "models" were mink. Unbeknownst to PETA, Richard Aulerich was also the second largest recipient of annual grants by the Mink Farmers Research Foundation and had for the past 32 years provided vital research developments to the U.S. mink industry.

Any discussion of mink farm disease research never omitted Aulerich from the conversation. ALF moles repeatedly found his research developments cited in correspondence seized from O.S.U. and W.S.U. Through his service to the U.S. Government and the mink industry, Aulerich had been awarded federal grants to also use his mink farm for toxic experiments involving the force-feeding of PCP's, dioxins and other industrial pollutants to captive mink. Published research records detailed how poisoned mink died violent deaths in Aulerich's laboratory suffering severe internal hemorrhaging before vomiting blood and finally dying after being fed only feeds laced with contaminants, in the infamous Lethal Dose 50% (LD50) test.

Students at M.S.U. had informed ALF moles that a 39-mile stretch of the lower Fox River which feeds Lake Michigan, is home to the largest concentration of paper mills in the world. Despite PCP production having been banned almost 20 years ago, these pollutants still remain from early discharges in the mud and sediment along the river and lake causing high levels of PCP in fish and other wildlife. Another area situated at the mouth of the Grand Calumet River at the southern end of Lake Michigan, has the largest accumulation of industry contaminated sediments in the Great Lakes. Students were frustrated that despite all dioxin in the Great Lakes being traced to less than 200 factory stacks and all PCP traceable to five industries, the only remedies were to entrust these corporations to voluntarily clean up, or continue animal testing of the contaminants to determine its danger. A 1990 "study" showed 100% mortality among test animals exposed to sediment samples from the Grand Calumet River. Rather than study contamination in wild mink and otters in the Great Lakes region, Aulerich chose to cause further suffering by using mink and otters from his fur farm in experiments. ALF moles had also been given information by students about Aulerich making keychains for his students out of the severed paws of vivisected mink. One of Aulerich's research associates was Karen Chou who herself conducted toxicology experiments in rabbits, rats and mice for chemical manufacturers, industrial polluters and the U.S. Government.

To the American mink industry, Richard Aulerich represented the last hope for the conquering of diseases commonly found on fur farms. O.S.U.'s Experimental Research Station was out of the game, and John Gorham's research was in tatters. The Fur Animal Research Station at Michigan State University was on alert against attacks by the ALF following the raids in Oregon and Washington. When PETA radio spots fingered Aulerich, M.S.U. increased its already strengthened security. In the midst of fur farmer and research hysteria, a council of ALF warriors was formed on behalf of the Lake Michigan Ecosystem to stop the suffering to mink at the hands of Aulerich and to draw attention to the real threat: industrial polluters.

As a light rain fell on the February night on the mink barns at M.S.U. three figures lay crouched low to the earth in woodland camouflage. As cars rumbled by on a nearby highway, the warriors cut through chain link fences and entered the perimeter of the Experimental Fur Farm. At this same time another ALF cell from the newly formed Great Lakes Unit was walking towards Anthony Hall on the Michigan State University campus like three college students returning home from a late night drinking session. One of the warriors had an earphone beneath his hooded sweatshirt that kept the team in contact with a lookout parked in a car nearby monitoring a police scanner. With no signal, the three activists cut across the lawn in front of the building and dropped into a storm drain depression below a bottom story window. The latch on the window was ajar and with a long thin strip of metal a warrior slid the latch open and opened the window and two warriors slipped into the building landing on the desk of an M.S.U. researcher. Closing the window behind them, the third warrior removed his bright college sweater and replaced it with a black hooded rain jacket and kept watch.

Inside the building the other two warriors walked the lit hallway to a stairway and up one level to the office of Richard Aulerich. During early daytime reconnaissance in the building, the warriors had viewed the open office door, not noticing any type of entry way alarm system in place. While one warrior stood watch against late night students in the building, the other broke through three wooden vent slats on the door and reached through and opened the door and ducked in. Aulerich and Chou's office lay before them with a receptionist area, complete with a glass case filled with mink pelts for display. Opening all the file drawers in every office and dumping their contents on the floor, the warrior removed his pack and opened a tupperware container that contained a one-hour time delay incendiary device cushioned with toilet paper. Suddenly, flashing red and blue lights could be seen through the windows. The warrior knew if it was cause for alarm, he would have been alerted by one of their two lookouts. Continuing in his task, the warrior filled his nightpack with computer discs, color slides and selected research documents describing grants for continued vivisection. In a few short minutes the patrol car drove away as did the motorist he had pulled over, and the warrior set the incendiary device and gathering his lookout, returned to the basement level office.

Before the warriors exited the window they glanced at the office of the researcher they had entered in through. The nameplate outside the door had said "dairy research." The warriors, both vegans, looked at each other then slid all the computers and office equipment on his desk onto the floor with a crash. Then the two rolled out the window into the storm drain and with a quick clothing adjustment returned on their path walking off campus. The pick-up driver pulled up to them a short distance away and in minutes they were safely off campus.

Back at the fur farm neighboring the poultry research farm, one warrior stationed himself with a clear view of all incoming roads and the occupied quarters of the sleeping caretaker. One warrior ascended the roof of the field laboratory and removed a portion of sheet metal roofing and dropped into the lab through the ceiling. Without any exposed windows to the outdoors, two warriors switched on headlamps tinted red to preserve their night vision and began to remove hinges on a door leading into a laboratory. Upon entering, one warrior began to quietly destroy all the research equipment, while the other searched files and research records. Muriatic acid was poured over feed mixing machinery for the experimental mink farm as well as over all the research equipment and documents that were in the offices. In a freezer the warriors found the severed heads of over 30 otters wrapped in aluminum foil. When the laboratory feed mixing room and a research office were wrecked, spray-painted messages were left for Aulerich and other researchers, including "WE WILL BE BACK FOR THE OTTERS," meaning Alice, the sole surviving experimental otter prisoner who watched attentively as ALF warriors raided the fur farm. Exiting the lab through the ceiling, the two warriors entered the perimeter of the mink farm itself and began to remove every identification card from the mink cages, first locating two minks slated for contamination, yet still healthy. Borrowing two nestboxes the mink were loaded into the boxes separately for their journey to freedom. The close busy highway prohibited the liberators from opening all the cages and releasing all the mink. Night began to give way to dawn's early light. The hardest part was leaving behind the hundreds of other mink as well as ferrets and otters that we knew would soon be poisoned. Hours later on the shores of a remote lake the two liberated mink were given their last meal by human hands, a road-killed rabbit and protein rich wet cat food before being released into their native habitat where they quickly disappeared into the lakes underbrush.

Back on the M.S.U. campus, within the hour, a fire erupted in Anthony Hall that totally destroyed 32 years of fur animal research by Richard Aulerich and over ten years of unpublished research by Karen Chou. With this final attack, all major recipients of Mink Farmer Research Foundation funding were effectively neutralized leaving the U.S. fur farm industry struggling more than ever to survive. Never before had the ALF successfully eliminated the research and development arm of an animal and earth abuse industry as it did with the MFRF. As the ALF earned its title, of an effective threat to animal and earth abuse industry research, warriors from across the nation began to feel the oncoming wave of federal police repression as joint law enforcement task forces accelerated their hunt for the ALF renegades.

The Last Bite: Animal Damaged Control

Most people would think with four grand juries and a multi-divisional task force of FBI, ATF, state, university and county police forces investigating the ALF, that the warriors were hunkered in hiding from the law. The ALF was hiding, but not only from the law.

The sun was setting on a warm autumn day as three figures passed binoculars back and forth, gazing from a ridge on national forest lands in Utah at the U.S. Department of Agriculture's Animal Damage Control Predator Research Facility located in Millville, just south of the University of Utah campus in Logan; the ADC field station is the largest research station in the U.S. that performs vivisection on coyotes, the objective being not saving lives, but destroying them.

For 65 years ADC has waged with full taxpayer support, a war on America's wildlife. In 1931 Congress passed the Animal Damage Control Act which plainly states: "The Secretary of Agriculture is hereby authorized to promulgate the best methods of eradication, suppression, or bringing under control on . . . areas of public domain or private lands, of wolves, lions, coyotes, bobcats, prairie dogs. . . injurious to agriculture and animal husbandry, for the protection of stock and other domestic animals . . . and to conduct campaigns for the destruction of control of such animals." Since its beginnings, ADC has been responsible for the murder of hundreds of thousands of grizzly and black bears, grey, red, swift and kit foxes, grey and timber wolves, mountain lions, bobcats, lynx, jaguars, mink, moose, elk, pronghorn antelope, bighorn sheep, blacktail, whitetail and mule deer, buffalo and coyotes.

Their tactics include M-44 sodium cyanide charges, steel-jaw traps, aerial shooting, neck snares, cage traps, burning and smoking out dens, spotlight shooting, shotgunning, leg and foot snares and a variety of poisons which frequently kill thousands of "non-target" species. All for the benefit of the livestock industry.

The ADC's chief eradication researcher on coyotes is Frederick Knowlton who heads the Millville Predator Research Facility and whose headquarters is an office at the University of Utah. The primary goal of Knowlton's research work is to develop techniques to totally control predator populations with poisons, traps and even tracking and eradication using radioactive isotopes. Knowlton has spent the last 30 years contributing directly to the killing of literally tens of thousands of coyotes.

In a 1960's book on coyotes Knowlton is described on an aerial gunning campaign which downed two running coyotes. Upon landing and collecting the animals Knowlton comments with surprise at one of the coyotes which had only two legs, the other two having been ripped away in leghold traps. In the minds and hearts of the coyote nation there is a devil and his name is Fredrick Knowlton. Known to the environmental and animal movements for years the ADC has remained a bastillion of environmental and animal destruction in the U.S. What manifest destiny has done to indigenous peoples in this country, ADC is doing to its indigenous wildlife.

As the fur farm wars raged with federal authorities and fur farmers on extreme red alert, an ALF council gathered in the Rocky Mountain wilderness to discuss the prospects of future guerilla campaigns. Warriors from three different bands expressed the need to escalate the defense of America's wildlife in the face of major repression and not to run and hide. Gathered around the council fire, federal documents detailing Knowlton's research were passed around in the firelight. With Federal police on all sides, any future attacks would have to be lightning fast, already our numbers were too reduced to risk the loss of even one warrior. As a full moon rose over the encampment each warrior voiced his or her opinions on the path of war or retreat.

When each had spoken, a final voice recounted the generations of death and destruction waged by ADC, and its impact on the nations of animals that had once roamed freely on these lands. In the distance a coyote's voice sang out, echoing in the warriors' hearts sending shivers down their backs. It was decided the path would be war. As the old British ALF adage goes: "once it's decided, it's as good as done."

The next month, ALF moles were sent in the four directions recruiting warriors for this massive attack. While in Utah camouflage-clad "hikers" camped out above the Predator Research Facility spending long nights watching the movements of students and researchers on the compound. It was on one of these first nights that the raiders heard what would become a familiar sound.

Each night wild coyotes from the nearby hills would sing their evening songs, in response most of the eighty captives would answer in unison in lonely heartfelt cries. The first time these songs penetrated the hearts of the hidden warriors, tears of sadness and rage would cloud their vision through binoculars as they pledged to avenge the dying coyotes in the pens below.

Back on the campus of the University of Utah at Logan (U of U), warriors dressed as college students were studying the courtyard office of Knowlton which stood just 50 yards from the University Police station in a dead end cul-de-sac. By October, the warriors were poised to strike. Gathered in a canyon far away from the Research Facility, ten warriors stood in a circle, each in their own uniforms for the night. For some university sweatshirts and daypacks and running shoes, while others wore thin ski-masks rolled above their eyes, camouflage shirts and pants and disposable hiking boots. Two others were dressed in nice dinner clothes. These were to be the drivers.

Topographical and highway street maps were given to the warriors in waterproof ziploc bags and enough unhandled cash in case of emergency, should separation be necessary for a fast escape. The drivers would be monitoring police scanners and each team would have radio-contact and hand relay signals between the warriors in each team should a call come in.

In one warrior's pack was a suction glass remover and incendiary device for Knowlton's office. In another, boltcutters, wire cutters and thick gloves for the many holes that would need to cut in fences and coyote pens. One warrior, the lookout, held binoculars, spotting scope and an astronomy book; should this warrior be discovered, a stargazer was their alibi. The last warrior's pack was filled with another incendiary device, mini-mag flashlight with red lens and an assortment of tools that would be used to gain entry into the Predator Research Facility.

There was something very different about this raid. It was not seen as an offensive action, but a defensive one, not only on the coyotes behalf, but also for the warriors. Our movement was under attack, with human freedom as well as animal freedom at risk. Such an action was necessary to prove to our enemies that the ALF's back would not be broken.

Far away in downtown high-rises ATF and FBI agents worked feverishly around the clock attempting to eradicate the threat of an action like this one about to take place. Also, the long nights of recon had led the warriors to feel personally connected to the coyotes in the outdoor pens of the PRF. Many of these animals were born in the wild and knew the freedom others never had experienced. Each night the warriors would hear their cries and on some days would see coyotes in pens that had been intentionally starved for four days and then given poison-tainted feed knowing the coyote could not refuse food after this period of intentional starvation.

Throughout the compound improvements could be seen being made as researchers attempted to expend their budgeted funding before their fiscal year was up. If a government agency did not spend its allotted funds, its budget might be reduced the next year rather than increased. On one day Knowlton himself could be seen directing construction, while coyotes circled in pens surrounding him.

Our attack would be focused on the Predator Research Facility building itself and the large outdoor enclosures that held over 40 coyotes. Another chain-link kennel building held at least 40 more coyotes but their location was too near the night watchman's house to risk liberation. Maybe if the facility was not on alert due to recent ALF raids the risk might be worth it, but to endanger the whole action most importantly the destruction of the Predator Research Facility for animals that sadly could be easily replaced, could not be justified.

In most ALF actions the feelings of victory are often offset by the rage and frustration for having to leave animals behind. But if our action was successful, the destruction of the lab and Knowlton's research would mean the preservation of innumerable lives that would otherwise be extinguished by the benefits of ADC research.

Back on the U of U campus we would also attempt to strike Knowlton's office right beneath the University police's nose. On the evening of October 24th, two bicyclists pulled into a parking area on the U of U campus next to the Natural Resources Building, locked their bikes and walked arm in arm towards the police station near the courtyard that led to Knowlton's office. One of the cyclist's daypacks held a radio which was tuned to a channel monitored by a lookout with a police scanner. Establishing themselves with a clear view of the cop shop one warrior flashed the thumbs up while the other entered the dead end courtyard and approached the exterior window leading into Knowlton's office.

Pulling on a dark pair of coveralls, the warrior then removed the aluminum trim on the window holding the glass against its frame and used the suction cup device to remove the glass. On an earlier recon mission a "student" had banged on the glass hard enough to set off any alarm that might be connected to it, then withdrew to watch for any response. There wasn't one. The window was not alarmed. Setting the glass aside, the warrior rolled into the opening after lifting his daypack gingerly in. Emptying his pack of firestarting equipment and the incendiary device, he next filled the empty space with all of Knowlton's computer discs and other vital documents. Next he gathered books, desk drawers and other combustible materials and laid them around Knowlton's desk where the incendiary device was then placed setting the timer for shortly before dawn. The warrior then connected the 9-volt battery to the device thereby engaging it and gazing around him, took one last look at the office of a man whose career was based on the annihilation of a species.

No radio transmissions had been made which indicated the all-clear. Just minutes after having entered the office, the warrior fled, gathering the computer discs and other bounty. Stripping off his coveralls, the warrior then walked past the lookout's location just 100 feet from the police station. The two then walked back to their locked mountain bikes and rode away into the night.

At about the same time as Knowlton's office was being visited, a single file line of six warriors jogged along a path in the forest lands that led to the boundary fence of the Predator Research Facility and outlying coyote pens. The sky was magnificently filled with stars, and as the warriors approached the furthest fence, the lookout broke off to climb a rise where contact would be established with another lookout in the drop-off and pick-up vehicle. Climbing the ridge the lookout could see all roads entering into the ADC compound as well as the watchman's house and coyote pens.

At the fence the remaining five warriors followed the lead warrior who began to cut a hole in the boundary fence in which to enter through. Once inside the fenceline, the warriors broke into two groups, one which would free the coyotes while the others would raid the lab.

Crawling on their bellies, two warriors approached the Predator Research Facility. Climbing one last chain-link fence the warriors were now deep within the ADC compound and only a stone's throw from the sleeping watchman's window. An alarm test had been made on a small bathroom window with success and now the warriors approached the window and began to remove the screen and frame.

At this point too much noise was being made to continue, so the warriors contemplated other points of entry that would create less noise as precious minutes ticked by. Finally as if on cue, the coyotes in the nearby kennel building began to howl and cry offering enough noise cover to rip the window from its frame.

Entering the PRF, the warriors were immediately faced with dozens of coyote skulls, leghold traps and "do not feed" signs outside the laboratory bathroom. Crawling on hands and knees, one warrior went straight for the structural center of the laboratory while the other gathered more computer discs and photo slides. The two warriors could have spent hours leafing through the files of predator research, but time was not something they had a lot of. After the stolen records in Michigan were recovered and their shipment used as a lead to a safe house, the decision was made to destroy the research at the PRF, not just seize it.

Setting the incendiary device amidst a pile of traps and desk drawers and other wooden materials the warriors activated the device and quickly exited the building. The incendiary device in the PRF was scheduled to go off at the exact time as the device in Knowlton's office.

Retreating quietly back to the outlying coyote pens the two warriors regrouped with the three warriors cutting gaping holes in coyote pens. The warriors were each carrying a pair of boltcutters and excitedly described how coyotes were approaching the fence and digging opposite the warriors as they cut through the fence only inches away from the coyotes in an obvious attempt to speed their release. Stepping back, the coyotes were quick to follow each other out the pens and toward the mountains where wild coyotes could be heard calling to them.

As the five warriors cut fence after fence, coyotes in groups of twos and threes could be seen escaping the pens and racing to freedom. When the last pen was emptied the warriors retreated single file back towards the hills themselves. By the time they regrouped with the lookout on the ridge the warriors had already called for the rendezvous pick-up driver to come, so the six warriors quietly padded down the same path they had entered as the star-filled sky was filled with the songs of coyotes disappearing into the mountain wilderness.

As the first signs of dawn shone grey in the night sky, the incendiary devices triggered in both the U of U office of Fred Knowlton and at the Predator Research Facility. On the campus, it wasn't long before the police noticed smoke billowing from the Natural Resources Building and quickly extinguished the fire but not before years of research went up in smoke. The firefighters' own water had caused much of the damage. As the firefighters on campus doused the flames of Knowlton's office the call came in from the watchman that the PRF was ablaze. By the time firefighters reached the facility over half of the laboratory had been completely destroyed. A week later, the whole structure would be determined unsafe and the entire lab was demolished. In January of 1993 Fred Knowlton was still pleading with county planning commissioners to grant him a temporary building permit to construct a new lab. All research at the U.S.D.A.'s Predator Research Facility had ground to a halt.

To add further insult to injury, the ALF accused Knowlton of illegally dumping tons of radioactive contaminated coyote carcasses from field experiments in New Mexico and when he denied the allegation the ALF provided an investigative reporter with his own memo to another researcher admitting his knowledge of not having obtained the necessary permits before burying his dead research subjects.

Thirty-three coyotes meanwhile were never recovered and the researchers were quick to express their concerns that the animals could not survive in the wild, but we know better don't we? Running from the torture chambers of Knowlton's lab that night the escaping coyotes saw not six human figures trotting down a mountain path, but six wild coyote warriors who had not forgotten their fourlegged brothers and sisters.

Days later at a remote hideout victory campfires blazed as Knowlton's computer discs were fed to the flames by the ALF warriors who had confiscated them from his office. Once more the ALF had proven that what could not be accomplished with years of protest, could be achieved with a handful of bravehearted warriors. Now it was time to wait for others to follow our lead.

Unknown U.S. Fur Farm

1997

An anonymous account of a raid on an unnamed mink farm — one of the dozens raided by the A.L.F. in the mid-1990s.

Late one night, I sat on a small patch of grass under the stars, listening to the dried leaves rustle in the wind. A few moments had passed when I saw the headlights of a small vehicle turn the corner and head towards me. After loading my gear into the trunk, I climbed into the front seat and exchanged anxious smiles with the driver. She gave my hand a quick squeeze before steering the car (rented in an untraceable manner) back onto the road. We were on our way.

As we drove, the sun came up. Stopping only to eat and refuel the car, we continued driving all day. A few hours after the sun had disappeared, we met up with another man, well known to us and trusted wholeheartedly. Together we headed to a dark clearing near a small lake and sat and discussed our plans.

Afterwards, taking special care to be sure we didn't have unwelcome company, we hit the road and headed for our final destination. Using detailed maps, we made many, many turns off the main road. We found the address we were looking for and quickly found some thick brush where we hid the car from sight.

We had brought with us a radio scanner which had already been programmed to monitor all the local and state law enforcement frequencies. One of my comrades double-checked that it was working and that the controls were set appropriately, secured it in her jacket pocket, and inserted the small earphone in her left ear, leaving the other ear unobstructed. Throughout the reconnaissance and the raid, she would listen carefully in case the farmer or a neighbor reported any suspicious activity or in case an undetected alarm caused an officer to be dispatched to the farm.

We also made sure that no one was carrying any loose articles, wearing jewelry or anything else that could inadvertently be left behind. The last thing we did was hide the door key near the car so no one person would be carrying it. (If that person should run into trouble, the others would have no mode of transportation.) Our pockets were empty except for the scanner, flashlight, and gloves. We were ready to go.

RECONNAISSANCE

Our team knew how important it was to be familiar with the area, so we scouted around on foot for about an hour. Of course, while on or near roads, anytime we saw or heard a car in the distance we hit the ground or bush and made ourselves invisible. We located a creek which ran through the area nearby and out to open, wilder spaces. We also made note of the darkest areas for hiding and which side of the country road was least lit. We set up an emergency rendezvous point in case we were separated.

When the wind was just right, it carried the stench of the fur farm to us—an overwhelming assault on our senses. When I inhaled I could taste the blood and filth, I could hear the cries of pain, I could see the suffering, and I could feel the terror of this place. It was (and is) pure evil.

We cut across several large fields to get to the back fence of the mink farm. When walking in open spaces, we hunched over and let our arms hang down so that, if anyone was watching, we wouldn't look human. As we travelled, we often had to pull strands of barbed wire apart and squeeze through to get past perimeter fences. We made friends with the many cows and other animals we passed on our way towards the farm.

After checking for alarms, trip wires, and video cameras, we easily climbed the back fence and entered the concentration camp. Still watching carefully for alarms, etc., we hurried through the many sheds. Our presence brought the many thousands of mink to attention. They became very excited, rustling around in their tiny cages and "talking" to each other with short, high-pitched squeaks. With our small flashlights, we could see their curious little faces and inquisitive eyes—truly beautiful animals! I imagined the fate that would have awaited them if we had not come to intervene: their necks snapped or their lungs filled with gas after a few more months of enduring the psychological and physical torture of being imprisoned in this hell.

We took note of the cages: four rows in each shed. Filthy, corroded cages which provided no bedding for mink who normally nest in the wild. Simple latches held most cages shut, but some (the breeders) had a piece of heavy-gauge wire twisted around the wires of the cage, securing the doors.

Our reconnaissance told us what we needed to know and we retreated to the back of the field that ran behind this farm. We sat under an old willow tree for a few hours, watching the compound to see if anyone was aware of our intrusion. On this evening we would leave the animals behind, but we would return. We hiked through the fields and creeks, back to the vehicle, and drove for about an hour. We then camped for the remainder of the morning.

At mid-morning we rose and began to further discuss a plan of action, detailing tools we would need and delegating duties. We had brought with us a radio scanner, dark disposable clothing, flashlights, wire cutters, gloves, spray paint, and ski masks. We would need to purchase packaged envelopes, paper, and stamps (to send a communiqué after the action), as well as back-up batteries. We fueled up the car and drove by our target once (and only once) during the daylight to further familiarize ourselves with the surroundings.

The rest of the afternoon and evening was spent taking apart all our equipment and wiping it down inside and out. We went over every detail of the plan in our heads and prepared ourselves mentally for whatever we might encounter, including any consequences we might face.

It began to rain. We double-checked our inventory of equipment and then set out. We made our way back to the concentration camp, again making sure we were not followed. Just like the night before, we checked and secured the scanner, emptied our pockets, and hid the key to the vehicle. Again, we followed the road part way, diving to the ground with the coming of headlights, and then crept through the dark, still fields, towards the many mink awaiting their freedom.

LIBERATION

We opened the cages. After opening roughly one dozen cages in the dark, I paused for a brief moment to shine my flashlight across them and caught sight of a shiny, sleek figure, hopping out of her hellhole. The mink scurried across the ground and out of the barn. While I wanted to focus and appreciate each and every animal as he or she found the way to freedom, I knew I couldn't do so at the expense of those who would be left behind. I had to spend every moment on the farm opening cages to allow as many as possible a fighting chance at a natural life.

I continued my work, frantically unlatching and cutting wires. While I worked, several mink ran across the top of the cages while others scurried about my feet, squeaking with joy. Before long, these feisty critters were all over the place, running this way and that, playing and fighting with each other. Now and then I would briefly stop my work to separate two of the little guys and shoo them towards the outer fences where they would find their freedom. RUN LITTLE GUYS, RUN!

A SUSPICIOUS NOISE

Suddenly I heard—or thought I heard—a slamming noise. "The mink have woken the farmers," I thought. "Here he comes." I looked to the end of the barn towards the farmer's house. Struggling to adjust my focus for such a distance in the darkness, I made out a light colored, upright figure. Were my eyes playing tricks on me or was someone standing there? I grew very uneasy and almost nauseous, as I imagined "Farmer John," angry as a wasp evicted from her nest (but much more dangerous), standing in the doorway, holding a rifle. I prepared myself for the worst and tried again in vain to focus on the end of the shed.

Better safe than sorry, I reminded myself, and quickly left the shed. I looked for my partners, and, not finding them, my anxiety increased. I moved across the adjacent field and hid in some thick, dark bushes, and watched the farm for about 20 minutes. I saw nothing out of the ordinary and no lights were turned on, so I eventually crept back and cautiously re-entered the compound. I ducked into the sheds where my friends were working, to be certain that all was well. I found them working away undeterred. I went back to my shed and continued opening the cages.

The work was exhausting and I could feel my bones ache with the monotony of the routine. But I kept going—I could never live with myself if I didn't open as many cages as was humanly possible. I lost count at 500.

TIME TO MOVE ON

I finished my shed and checked on the others to see if they needed help. Finding their sheds empty, I moved on to the next one, and we finished that one off together. Sadly, we came to our pre-designated cut-off time. Though there were many more sheds full of prisoners, we had to leave—the farmers would wake soon and the rise of the sun would provide no cover for ours and the minks' escape.

We marked some of the now empty sheds with spray paint and then retreated. As we fled, we chased many mink to the holes cut in the fence. Once on the other side, we stopped for a moment to watch the many dark figures gliding and scampering through the fields towards the creek which would lead them to their new prospective homes.

Using the moon as our guide, we found our way back to our hidden vehicle. We briefly shared our experiences as we walked—one of our team had been bitten while attempting to open a cage. All of us had found several mink dead and decaying in their cages.

We piled our soaked, sore, and muddied bodies into the car. We made frustrated faces at each other as we were excited but knew we could not talk in the car. We drove silently back down the dark roads to our campsite, where we sorted out our things, throwing all clothes and shoes into the campfire, and placing tools into bags to be discarded safely and immediately.

We talked a little more about our experiences, including what we could do better next time. We made plans to meet again, and shared warm hugs before embarking on our long journey home. During the following day's drive, we heard news reports of the raid on the radio. We smiled proudly with the satisfaction that many mink had a chance at freedom that day, that the fur trade had just become a little less profitable, and that "Farmer John" just might go out of business.

College Of Notre Dame

2000

The full story behind the unclaimed rescue of 250 mice from the labs of a small university in northern California.

The headline in the March 18, 2000 San Jose Mercury News read "*250 Research Mice Missing From College of Notre Dame: Professor Fears Lab Animals Will Not Survive In The Wild.*" Researchers at the College of Notre Dame in Belmont, California had arrived at their lab the previous morning to find damaged equipment, signs of forced entry, and every one of their mice gone.

(Editor's note: The college has since been renamed Notre Dame de Namur University.)

Animal rights activists were suspected by police and college officials, by everyone but activists themselves. When no communiqué surfaced following the animals disappearance, and with no other evidence indicating that it was an animal liberation action, it was dismissed by those few activists who took notice as a mere theft for snake food by an opportunistic college student, or frat house prank.

Unknown to all but those behind the "theft," the mice were not fending for themselves in the surrounding hills, but instead were settling into their new home, far from the reach of Notre Dame vivisectors.

Now, nine years later, this raid will finally be written into history as an animal liberation action, and the true story will be told.

Notre Dame de Namur University is a small Catholic college with a student population of less than 1,500 located on a hill in Belmont, California. In the heart of Silicon Valley, it is surrounded by what may be the highest concentration of animal research labs in the nation. Like other large biotech hubs (including La Jolla, California and North Carolina's Research Triangle Park), what happens in many of the small labs here often stays below the radar of the animal liberation movement.

Over 20 USDA-registered animal research labs lie in Silicon Valley, the belt of suburbs that stretch south of San Francisco to San Jose. Marked only by the inconspicuous signs of biotech companies, these research facilities are tucked away in well-groomed office parks, enjoying relative invisibility. Most appear no different from the internet start-ups and one-story call centers that surround them. Even tell-tale signs like deliveries from Simonsen Laboratories and Charles River could easily pass unnoticed. In these office parks lie Silicon Valley's dirty secret, the biotech nightmares where tens of thousands of animals each year are killed.

Even further below the radar are those research labs using animals the U.S. Department of Agriculture deems unworthy of protection, those falling through a loophole in the Animal Welfare Act so egregious, it leaves 90% of animals uncovered by the USDA's already feeble oversight. Any lab using only mice, rats, birds or fish in research or testing is not required under the Animal Welfare Act to register with the USDA. With no official record of these labs, we can only speculate on their numbers.

When we looked behind various biotech companies which were not on the USDA list, we found over one dozen inconspicuous buildings whose trash contained animal bedding, invoices for mice and rats or small cardboard carriers which read "Live Animals—This Side Up."

Our survey of labs in Silicon Valley had a purpose. We were planning a rescue.

To begin with we had to consider what has always been the greatest obstacle to live liberations—finding homes for the rescued animals. Finding homes is even more difficult for large animals and those who are not normally companion animals. Dogs and cats can be placed into the above-ground adoption stream with the right contact person. Rabbits are less common companions, yet homes for large numbers have been found in the past.

The animal who is liberated in largest numbers from labs often goes unnoticed: the mouse. Most who have read of the Noah's Ark-style raid at the University of Arizona in 1989 probably wondered about the level of planning needed to find enough safe houses for over 1,200 mice. Few would imagine how little space is needed for even several hundred of these animals to live comfortably.

It was decided; mice would be the subject of our rescue mission. The larger ratio of mice to other animals in research facilities ensured their accessibility, and mice can be transported with relative ease.

We were also moved by the symbolic value of reminding the public (as well as some animal rights activists) that ALL sentient life is worthy of consideration, and the message that would be sent to researchers that no matter what species they tormented, their work would be considered a target.

A mice research lab would be located, broken into, and emptied.

Arguably the riskiest component of a live liberation is the housing of animals. History tells us few are caught in the act. It is the careless post-raid talk and actions that present the greatest dangers. Potential homes must adhere to the same security code as the participants in an action. Any transgression could bring greater consequences than a few years in prison for activists—it could mean a literal death sentence for the rescued animals in their care.

After several visits to potential Underground Railroad candidates, an invitation was extended from a trusted individual: "bring all the mice you can get." Two large pens would provide space to house several hundred small mice. The mice would be housed on a porch in the day and moved into a garage at night. But this housing arrangement came with one stipulation—we must make every effort to avoid generating media coverage. No painted slogans, no communiqué.

The homeowner often had visitors and business associates in the home. The mice were at risk of being seen by visitors to the heavily trafficked house. The mice alone may not raise suspicion, but coupled with the media coverage that a raid claimed by the ALF would generate, the risk was too great. Cell members agreed to the stipulation and the plan continued on course.

With homes, and people willing to risk their freedom, one item remained: finding a lab to raid.

For two nights we took to the streets of Silicon Valley. The United States Department of Agriculture's list of labs provided us a rough course. We found that labs often cluster, and the list gave us both names and towns (more often than not the address was a PO Box or company headquarters rather than the address where the animals were held), as well as a sense of what areas harbored the highest concentration of labs. At every stop, we took a walk around the block, taking a close look at every building appearing to house a biomedical research company. Our short walks would often turn up several unlisted labs in close proximity to the registered one.

Animal use was obligatory in most of these companies, and while many outsourced their testing (to companies like HLS), most could be expected to have, at the least, mice and rats inside. Between the mega animal research complexes like Roche and SRI International, we identified numerous smaller companies which all seemed to be made from the same mold—small, one or two story buildings hidden deep in tree-lined office parks, their work only revealed by a close look for evidence through windows, in trash, or with a well-trained nose. Internet research can dig up valuable data, however it can never be a substitute for physically searching out potential targets. It is then that the most useful information is gathered and only then that the greatest opportunities present themselves.

At the conclusion of two nights of footwork we weighed the pros and cons of each target. We had not yet sought to identify access points, limiting the first phase to locating targets worthy of a closer look.

One of our first stops was Notre Dame de Namur University in Belmont. Although not on the USDA list, papers published in academic journals made public their use of mice in research. Our daytime "college student" walk-through of the campus failed to provide us with information about where the animals were housed.

Returning at night we again surveyed the campus on foot. Stepping on a cinderblock behind a nondescript building in the heart of the campus, we looked through a window. Visible at an angle, inches from being out of sight altogether, was one column of small cages stacked on shelves. It was all the information we needed. Any facility found to have animals was a potential target, and Notre Dame had unknowingly placed itself on our list.

The lab was a small, inconspicuous, one story building. The front was located directly on the edge of a heavily trafficked parking lot which, even at night, had a degree of activity. The rear backed up to a wooded hill. The confirmation of which room the animals were housed in, along with the undetectable rear access to the building, moved Notre Dame to the top of our list.

We indulged ourselves in no further delays. No waiting for a new moon, no excessive surveillance. We set ourselves instead to emptying the lab the following night. Several hours away, we purchased gloves, red-tinted headlamps, radios, a crowbar, disposable shoes and clothing, stackable storage tubs, and a large hammer to apply to both the window and any disagreeable equipment found inside.

The night of the action, we parked on the edge of campus in a dark parking lot. The action was simple by design; minimal equipment and the minimum number of people: two. We each removed two tubs from the truck, moved into the woods and up the hill. At the crest, one activist put on a headlamp and headset. Radios were checked, and that activist descended the far side of the hill to the lab's rear window.

The activist pulled out a crowbar, hoping that it would be of some use on the thick bars that were bolted to the window frames of the building. The crowbar worked brilliantly and in less than five minutes the bars had been pried from the frame and lay on the ground. The false sense of security that they produced had provided a much-appreciated surprise—the window behind them had been left unlocked.

Upon entering the activist radioed the lookout, who left their post to hand four tubs through the window. The lookout resumed their post at the peak of the hill. The work of loading the mice inside would be handled by one person.

Inside, the activist could see what the view from the outside did not reveal: two walls of cages, holding over two hundred mice. The lids were removed from each tray and the mice placed in the tubs. In twenty minutes, every animal was loaded.

The lookout received the radio call for pickup. The next several minutes would be the time of greatest risk as there would be moderate noise and no lookout as the tubs were passed out the window.

One of the activists stayed behind, while the other sprinted the mice over 300 yards to the vehicle, then resumed the post and radioed their position.

Receiving word, the activist inside began the demolition phase. Several large pieces of equipment were thrown to the floor and smashed with a large hammer. In less than five minutes, the demolition phase was complete. Receiving an "all-clear" the activist slid out the window and disappeared into the woods.

Arriving at the safe house an hour later, we took a closer look at our yield. Over 250 mice had been removed. It was unfortunate that this raid could not have a media element—the mice were in miserable shape, certain to bring objection even from members of the public who did not grant consideration to these animals commonly called "pests." Most of the mice were grossly mutated, with deformities such as crooked tails and tumors. Many of the mice were clearly arthritic, others trembled violently.

The mice were introduced to their new home—large pens with fresh bedding and many small houses and other enrichments they had spent their lives without. While not the true liberation of a return to the wild, we had offered the best life that could be hoped for.

The newspaper articles the following day brought further encouragement. The mice removed were the product of a unique lineage, and in relieving the researchers of this irreplaceable genetic strain built up over many decades, the raid had effectively wiped out a research project that began in 1928.

The last of the mice passed away in the summer of 2002, having spent the remainder of their lives in fresh air, overlooking a lush backyard garden in the hills above the San Francisco Bay Area.

The telling of this story closes the chapter on this raid, one of many which go unclaimed and escape the history books of the animal liberation movement. There are certainly many more such actions whose stories are yet to be told.

Waste no time waiting for the next story to be written—history is a thing better made than read. Take your research from the internet to the streets, and translate your rage from words to actions.

And remember what they say: the best way in is never the front door.

BAY AREA DATELINES

Police: Stolen mice won't last in wild

BELMONT Some 250 research mice stolen from the College of Notre Dame may soon die if released into the wild, said a Belmont police official.

Detective Michael Speak said the mice, which were taken Friday, have been raised in captivity and need to be kept in a controlled environment in order to survive.

Police say the mice have been missing since about 11 a.m. Friday when someone broke into a trailer behind the college on Ralston Avenue where the mice were housed.

Speak said the mice were being studied by a professor trying to determine why they were born with genetic defects. The research is being conducted to better understand what causes these defects in humans, Speak said.

He said the mice were not mistreated or used for chemical experimentation.

"If these mice are not returned in good health," Speak said, "72 years of research will cease and have to start all over."

Huntingdon Life Sciences

2001

The story behind the legendary
break-in at Huntingdon Life Sciences.

On April first, 2001, our lives changed. All of us. It was this weekend that I, along with some very dear comrades, entered Huntingdon Life Sciences, and left with 14 precious friends. In a span of three days, the entire animal liberation movement in the United States was entering a new era, with focused energy, and dramatic success. We were all changing for the better. The grassroots animal rights movement was learning to focus on specific targets, and how to use their strength to gain victories. We, the underground animal liberation movement, were becoming more focused, plugging into the campaigns of the above ground, to inspire them, to give them hope, and to promote tactics that require audacity, even if they are unconventional, while still using uncompromising vigilante rescues as the most effective way to free animals now. But of course, the most important change that weekend was in the lives of 14 beagle puppies, who we lifted from their living graves. It's hard for me to imagine now, these puppies who love sunshine and grass, and romping with each other, back in those steel cages we found them in. And they're never going back.

Huntingdon Life Sciences is a vile little lab, and they've not only tried to hide from the animal rights community, but the nation as a whole. The lab is almost entirely surrounded by woods, which was convenient for us (and the animals inside). We were able to walk around the whole perimeter of the lab unnoticed, and see the filth that passersby can't see from the roadway. The back of HLS is dirtier than a junk collector's lawn in Alabama, with chunks of asphalt breaking apart in what are supposed to be delivery driveways. Rows upon rows, and piles upon piles of empty cages become warped and oxidized from weather exposure. This brought us great joy, that HLS not only couldn't keep animals in these cages anymore, but seemed to have no use for them now, or in the future. Several large buildings in the back were filled with nothing but garbage, leftovers for a one successful scam operation, now exposed into a joke of an enterprise, struggling to give some semblance of survival.

The evening of March thirty-first, we were approaching the lab through the woods behind it. HLS resides in a town so tiny, they don't even have their own police force, and rely upon the next town over, Franklin Township, to provide them with protection. But no evil can protect themselves from the pure of heart. We put in time and effort until we learned how to outsmart them at their wicked game. There are two bodies of water behind HLS, one being a canal that divides up the police forces of the area. HLS is just within the final reaches of the Franklin Township police force. We knew that police are inherently routine in their work, seldom using any creative skills, and that they wouldn't think outside of their own jurisdiction if they knew that a "crime" was occurring. We therefore entered, and left from outside their jurisdiction. But this required crossing the canal, at times 100 feet wide, and too deep to be able to walk across. Also, we thought that nothing would mask the smell of 14 puppies like fresh flowing water.

We tied a rope to one of the trees along the shore, and sent one of our first people out in the boat to cross the canal. The oars dipping into the water silently created huge ripples that spread to both shores in a matter of seconds. We too, silent, and anonymous, hoped to create huge ripples, showing the world that the use of animals as a vehicle for human greed will no longer be tolerated-We will fight back, and We will win. At the other shore, the rope was tied to another tree. This enabled us to shuttle each other across the canal in a matter of moments. We followed the backwoods trails created by deer, passing the landmarks we had come to know like the back of our hands, the abandoned rusting septic tank, and the section of woods where the bramble grows so thick that it can only be crawled through, always approaching the growing sound of the ventilation fans, which echo through the woods for miles.

Our lookouts were all stationed, it was time to go inside. We used bolt cutters to create emergency exits every few sections of barbed wire fence, in case we needed a quick escape. This wasn't very likely though, since the security force was as threatening and effective as a 95 year-old deaf man. The fence doesn't even touch the ground in many places, leaving sometimes three and four foot gaps to slide under, and the back gate was never locked tight enough to keep us from passing in and out for previous surveillance. Perhaps to the 250 lb security guard, this was safe. We knew the precise timing of the security rounds, and that for the specific employee working that night, we had 6-7 minutes as he completed his rounds, and would return to our entry point. The security patrol was hard to miss, and always gave plenty of notice since the truck used highly visible flashing lights, and drove 5 miles per hour.

When we had initially been searching for the animal storage units, we had been erroneously looking inside the lab. Climbing up the jungle gym of pipes along the back of the main building, we were able to enter the necropsy room through a skylight that wasn't even nailed down. The first night we went, we realized that the horrors Michelle Rokke had witnessed in this same room where we stood were as true then as they were in 1997. Several operating tables were covered in evidence of painful dissections, with surgical instruments left, uncleaned, to soak in the pools of blood left on the tables overnight.

It was only by following the stench of animals living in close quarters to one another that we were able to find the only animals we saw alive at HLS. All of the sheds in the back have alarmed, deadbolted doors. But they also have ladders that lead straight up to the ventilation shafts of the buildings. We climbed up the ladder and entered the building through the unlocked door only 10 feet above the alarmed deadbolted one. The inside of the lab looked worse than any dusty old attic imaginable. Sheets of plywood created a path crossing over the cave of exposed fiberglass insulation, where tangled wires hung down casually. We tore apart the insulation, and sawed a hole through the ceiling to the floor below, where the animals were. The locked door was no match to the crowbar that popped it open in seconds.

When we entered the beagle unit, it was eerily silent. The dogs, upon seeing us, made no noise. Through the darkness, we could see the shining black of the puppies' eyes peering at us with a mixture of curiosity, and the intense fear of humans. We had waited so long for this moment. We ran from cage to cage, and flung open all the doors at once. As they saw the first puppy do it, all the others began to understand that they could get up and leave their prison with the slatted steel floor. The puppies ran all over the unit, exercising their new found freedom to run, jump, and interact with one another. Those who were small enough went into carriers, and for some of the larger dogs we affixed harnesses fashioned of rope, to guide them to liberation. We cleared the unit, and took every living animal we found out with us.

I took two dogs out with me, both the largest dog, and the smallest puppy of the lot. As we ran along a grassy trail created by powerlines, the puppy was a ball of energy, and the older dog trotted along at a pace worthy of a Sunday walk. But before we were halfway out, the puppy was getting restless, and he began to cry. The three of us stopped for a moment, and the little one kept jumping up to sniff me as I scratched behind his ears. I pulled him up into my arms, and he began to lick my face through the fabric of my mask. "I understand Little One, you're tired... You're just a baby here, fleeing for your life..." It was at this time that I appreciated the steady pace of the older dog. He seemed to know and understand that if he patiently ran, and kept moving, he would never have to return to the iron cube he had been in for what was most likely years.

The three of us crossed the canal, and knew that we were going to be safe. We were the last ones to meet up with the rest of the group, and as I loaded my new friends up for transportation, all that was visible was a sea of wagging brown and white tails, and bobbing puppies jumping all over, relishing the feeling of contact and play. Although we all moved with a stealthy silence, there was an intense feeling of celebration. The beginnings of dawn were lightening the sky to a dark blue-gray, and it was going to rain soon. Within hours, our footprints would be washed away in the mud, and the dogs would be hours away, on the long, well-deserved journey to their new lives. The coldness of winter was finally ending, and the sharp spring green glowing with new life could be seen through the darkness. It was a beautiful morning, and it was a brand new day for the animals.

14 dogs stolen from lab

THE ASSOCIATED PRESS

FRANKLIN TOWNSHIP — Authorities are investigating a burglary of 14 dogs from the Huntingdon Life Sciences laboratory in the East Millstone section of the Somerset County township.

Animal-rights activists see the early yesterday morning incident differently: They call it a "liberation."

Somerset County Prosecutor Wayne J. Forrest said the dogs were taken between 3 a.m and 5 a.m. yesterday morning.

Jeff Lapadula of the New Brunswick branch of Animal Defense League said his group received a fax from a group called the Animal Liberation Front yesterday announcing that 14 beagles had been freed.

The dogs were stolen a day before a scheduled protest at the laboratory of the England-based company.

Activists have been targeting the Huntingdon lab in Somerset County in New Jersey and two in England.

They say the firm mistreats the animals it uses in tests.

Animal Defense League organizer Darius Fullmer said in a press release that his group does not take illegal actions like the raid in which the dogs were taken — but it supports them.

"Fourteen innocent creatures have been rescued from a short life of pain and a brutal death," Fullmer said.

His group is expecting 200 protesters from around the world at a rally this afternoon.

Forrest said police would be on the scene as needed.

SCOTT NELSON FUR FARM

2001

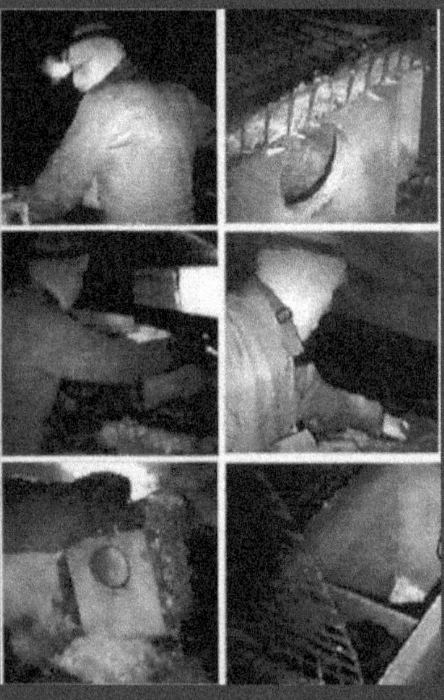

How a small group shut down an Iowa mink farm — by raiding it twice in one week.

THE ELEMENT OF SURPRISE

The element of surprise. In the A.L.F. war against the war on animals, this is our true leverage. For this war is not merely one of superior resources—a front on which they will always win—but of will, surprise, and invisibility. The fight of the clandestine guerrilla cell has been called "The War of the Flea"—an unrelenting force too small to isolate and neutralize, but whose prolonged campaign will confuse, demoralize, and sting the opponent into collapse. The A.L.F. "fights the war of the flea, and his enemy suffers the dog's disadvantages: too much to defend; too small, ubiquitous, and agile an enemy to come to grips with." One FBI agent called the hunt for the A.L.F. "like grabbing Jello." It is our under-the-cloak-of-darkness, clandestine nature in which the force of our blow lies. What they cannot predict, they cannot catch. And what they cannot catch, will return to strike again. Sometimes later that week. . .

The purpose of our reunion was unspoken. After a long separation, three activists, a closet full of equipment, and the question: Which target? The fur farms of the Midwest were a likely choice. Over one-third of the country's 350 mink farms lay in the three state area of Minnesota, Iowa, and Wisconsin. Our numerous reconnaissance missions had yet to turn up a single farm with a security system. Dozens of farms—many holding 20,000+ captives and lacking even a fence—invited demise by our hands.

This raid would be unconventional in that the decision process would not involve one established farm address resource: *The Final Nail.* Although seven years old, it still remains a useful resource for fur farm targets. But significant gaps existed between the number of farms listed, and the number known to exist through other statistics. Expanding this gap was the large number of closures since its publication. It was in this gap we would strike addresses previously unknown by the movement, farms comfortable and sleepy in their presumed invisibility, addresses we had special privilege to: Two summers previous, in one visit to a fur industry supplier, a member of our cell came away one very valuable booklet—the title itself made it good as gold: "Customer List." Cross-referenced with *The Final Nail,* several previously unknown farms were found. Scott Nelson's mink ranch in Ellsworth, Iowa was our first stop.

Whoever laid out this farm was on our side. Four sheds, barely a fence to speak of, and the mink liberator's most coveted luxury—no house on site. This target chose itself.

On a strict risk/benefit ratio, the fur farm raid is unmatched. At one time a focus of the A.L.F. in the mid-90's, mink liberation activity in the past years has slowed to the rate of nearly one a year. Newer activists are perhaps unaware of the frenzy of fur farm activity taking place at one time, with 1995 seeing 5 raids, 17 in 1996, 20 in 1997 and 10 in 1998, and many are equally unaware of this activity's ease. Security patrols of farms are almost unheard of, and the nights of reconnaissance required for many other actions is unnecessary. Three activists can free 3,000 mink in 30 minutes. A cell of five could liberate 10,000 in an hour.

Valid excuses for inactivity by activists in this area are few. Most people in this country live within a day's drive of a fur farm. Addresses can be found in *The Final Nail*. Expenses can be kept below a hundred dollars, near zero if one is resourceful. And thousands of animals can be freed by as few as two people. The three-state, five-farm spree in 1997 resulting in the liberation of over 12,000 mink—for which Seattle activist Peter Young was charged, charges he remains on the run from to this day—was said to be carried out by two people.

A.L.F. activity should not be viewed as distinct from any other "line of work." If militant vegans put the time into animal liberation that we did into our careers in the "real world," we would see animal liberation activity soar in both number and scale. For in our goal of animal emancipation, our means should really be no different than any other endeavor—legal or illegal. You size up the obstacle, teach yourself the skills, and acquire the tools. The aspiring rock climber reads books on rock climbing, takes rock climbing classes, and obtains rock climbing equipment. By the same formula, the aspiring white collar criminal isn't deterred by the arcane world of banking, finance, and credit card manufacture; s/he purchases a photo id machine, laptop computer, credit card embosser, and teaches himself the trade. It is with this mindset that the liberator must approach A.L.F. activity. One isn't deterred by a seemingly impenetrable research lab; we simply obtain alarm system manuals or attend a trade school with alarm installation classes, do the research, and deduce a method of circumvention. The locked door of a vivarium in a Biology Building basement doesn't signify defeat; a $15 lock pick set is obtained, a lock picking book purchased, and one learns to pick locks. In lab raids where alarms have prevented convenient entry via doors, the A.L.F. has continuously taken tools to concrete and made their own. The urgency of animal exploitation demands no less. The more one practices this process of overcoming obstacles, the more one realizes them to be largely psychological.

So it continues with fur farm raids. Nearby farms aren't likely to be listed in the phonebook; one simply makes a logical deduction as to whom has this information, then goes there and procures it. State/Regional fur breeders associations, fur feed manufacturers, department of agriculture offices, or fur farm equipment suppliers are located, visited, and their trash is taken and inspected for addresses. Fur farm targets with guard dogs aren't abandoned; the cell merely obtains the necessary sedatives as though s/he were a legitimate dog "owner" requiring such. The alarmed farm isn't avoided; the alarms are identified, researched, understood, and circumvented. This is a very simple matter once one clears away the cloud of mystique surrounding A.L.F. activity.

Behind every spectacular mink liberation, some making national news and others closing farms forever, there is likely little more than one visit to a thrift store, one to a hardware store, one night of reconnaissance, and one of action. Wire cutters, flashlight with red screen, headbands for flashlight, gloves, mask, disposable clothing: all the tools needed to close a farm and free its captives. But the uniqueness of the Scott Nelson Ranch begged one additional tool, never before used by the A.L.F. in a mink liberation—a video camera. This had never been done, for good reason. Few farms targeted by the A.L.F. have been fully emptied, less for reasons of cowardice than self preservation. The sound of released mink is a symphony of pleasure squeals, fighting, and excited chatter—beautiful but loud. The proximity of a farmer's house to the sheds makes prolonged presence on the site risky. For this reason, emptying a farm of all animals is rarely a certainty going in. Dedicating a cell member to video when they could be opening cages—translating to hundreds of lives lost—would be a criminal move. But this action would be unique. With no house on site, and a "stock" of barely 2000, opening every cage—and doing it in less than 30 minutes—was a certainty. A video document would achieve a two-fold purpose: 1) Giving the public its first glimpse of fur farm conditions, and 2) for activists, it would accomplish some badly needed demystification of mink liberations. It only takes one spark, they say, to start a prairie fire. Introducing uninitiated activists to the ease of a mink liberation through video might be the spark to once again bring the industry its second wave of A.L.F. raids. It was an opportunity not likely to be seen again.

We shopped around for a camera that would accommodate our needs. We bought the best, with one crucial feature: night vision. The next day, the camera would accompany us onto the farm and record what would become history.

A pre-raid walk-through of the farm was taken the night before the action to determine the presence of obstacles unseen from the road—dogs, alarms, etc.

Both deterrents used by the rare farmer, and both succeeding in absolutely nothing. With dogs, sedatives can be obtained from one or two veterinarians under the pretense of being an upcoming vacationer with a large dog requiring mild sedation for the trip. With alarms, those found commonly on fur farms (particularly the high-security farms of the Northwest) are at best smashed and ignored, and at worst the path of the alarm-beam must merely be determined and rolled under. These alarms are identified most often as black boxes on posts placed in the comer of the property. It should be noted on this topic that it was stated in the communiqué that the Arritola Mink Ranch in Mount Angel Oregon from which 10,000 mink were freed in 1997 was fortified with a "state of the art" security system.

Everything that had been noted from our drive-by was verified—security was non-existent. We familiarized ourselves with the cage latches, layout, and fence. Everything was coming together, one night with all the ingredients of a good plan: shredded cages, bankrupt exploiters, and animals running free.

24 hours later, we stood at the property line before the soft chatter of 2000 mink, calling for freedom. There is no call more urgent.

The dropping of masks marked the eruption of our advance. Wire was ripped away, posts ripped from the soil, cages opened, and in less than 30 minutes, every animal was set free.

From our communiqué:

"Fences surrounding the farm were cut away, every cage opened, and 2000 mink ran to freedom. These animals were kept 3 and 4 to a small wire mesh cage. Their rescue came at the final hour, only a month from a violent death in the pelting season. Captive-bred mink are closely related to their wild ancestors and have been shown to retain survival instincts when released - ensuring these liberated prisoners will live and thrive. The fur industry will move to condemn this action, using misleading half-truths and boldface lies. They point their fingers with blood stained hands. There is no defensible case for the taking of innocent life. Furthermore, there is no defensible argument against militant intervention to prevent this atrocity. When mink are no longer kept 4 to a small wire cage, when chickens are no longer kept packed in battery cages, when we stop calling dead animals food, when the blood stops spilling - these actions outside the law will no longer be needed. Until then, we will be tearing up fences, breaking down walls, and opening cages to free the animals. Terrorism against non-human animals will be met with liberation. In this struggle for life against greed, compassion over sadism, our only recourse is to ignore laws and risk our freedom to save lives. Were you in a cage, whose side would you be on? A.L.F"

Double Dose

48 hours later across the state in Glenwood, Iowa; Double T farms (21655 Barrus Rd.) was raided and 162 birds bred for vivisection were set free. This was the second raid at the farm, and the second within 48 hours of a mink release. The raid was taped and the video released to the media. For the second time, owner Ted Golka perhaps regrets listing his home address in *Lab Animal* magazine.

Breaking the Mold

Browsing in an electronics store, we moved across to the televisions for coverage of the release. We watched a recovery effort, with farmers from several states flocking to the scene to recapture those freed. Eighteen hours previous, mink took their first steps of freedom before our camera, and before those of the media we watched them take their last. Owner Scott Nelson appeared, smugly down-playing any permanent impact to his business, while boasting of over half the mink being recovered, and returned to cages—two things voiding the intended impact of the action. And at a meeting that night, two things we vowed to militantly correct...

2 am, six nights later. We stood at the exact spot where Scott Nelson had told reporters he was the victim of a "terrorist act," masked up and prepared to demonstrate love in its truest form.

The re-liberation took less than ten minutes.

Our communiqué released that afternoon stated:

"The first time we visited the Scott Nelson Mink Ranch, we opened every cage on the property. We intended to close the place down. Unfortunately some of the mink were recaptured. To demonstrate our complete seriousness regarding the freedom of these animals and contempt for the people responsible for these horrible places we, again, visited the fur farm and opened every cage on the property. We demand these mink are allowed to remain free. A.L.F."

That evening, Scott Nelson was back on TV—announcing his retirement from the fur industry.

Revolutionary Suicide

To all once active warriors, let each action remind you of the struggle you abandoned, of those you left behind. To every talker, full of words and nothing else, let every warriors strike against abuse be also one against your own failure. To every warrior imprisoned, accept every lab in flames as a tribute—your life is a victory. And to every animal still under the knife and behind the wire, our revolutionary suicide is for you...

Mink sprung again; farm near failure

A Canadian animal-rights group says its members returned to Scott Nelson's cages.

By STACI HUPP
REGISTER AMES BUREAU

An Ellsworth mink farm is ready to go under after vandals released its animals Tuesday for the second time in a week.

A Canadian animal-rights group that took responsibility for the first release also claimed to have made the second. Members of the North American Animal Liberation Front said they emptied the cages of nearly 1,600 mink from Scott Nelson's 15-year-old farm last week. About 600 animals were rounded up. The mink escaped again early Tuesday, along with the Nelsons' hope.

"We'll probably toss out what we have and be done," said Metta Nelson, 29, Scott Nelson's sister. "It's a little too frustrating to keep going. It's like farming. If you don't have the crop to cash in, you don't have the

See MINK, Page 4B

HAWKEYE MINK COOPERATIVE

2002

How two activists broke into an Iowa mink feed supplier to obtain addresses of previously unknown mink farms.

THE ENDGAME PROJECT

After midnight on January 13, 2002, "persons unknown" entered the pelt processing wing of the Hawkeye Mink Cooperative (1324 Main Street, Jewell, Iowa) and silently slipped away with over 50,000 pages of data on the local and national fur industry. Barely registering on the radar of both activists and the industry, this incident was marked as a suspicious yet un-notable burglary. For the first time, the true story behind this raid will be told.

THE SILENT RAID

Just before Christmas 2001, several dedicated animal liberation activists took a walk to discuss strategy for the next phase of anti-fur industry actions. The past 6 years of mink and fox liberations and arsons at key targets had served both animals and the movement well. With less than 350 farms remaining, the continuation of such tactics, along with actions aimed at taking out well-chosen infrastructure targets, could see the collapse of the fur industry by decade's end.

It was decided that the most serious impediment to continued advancement in this direction was the lack of new hard data on the industry—specifically, new names and addresses of fur farms and affiliated targets. Little new intelligence had been uncovered since the publication of the seminal fur farm listing *The Final Nail #2*, three years prior. Over 300 fur farms were believed to exist, yet barely 150 U.S. farms were listed. With over 150 addresses to be discovered, locations for many research sites and feed suppliers remaining unknown, and no new data emerging, a plan formed: to carry out an intelligence-gathering raid, erasing the information gap, and bringing the movement its final flood of addresses necessary to liberate the last of the fur farm prisoners. If properly executed at an info-rich target, this would be the last such mission the movement would ever need. The information on the remaining fur farms was out there. And what they would never turn over, we committed ourselves to take. The Endgame Project was born.

The confiscation of documents and other damning information through overnight raids by activists is not unprecedented. In 30 years of underground animal liberation activity, several break-ins have been documented, apparently (or explicitly) carried out solely as information gathering operations. This tactic has been common in the UK, where numerous raids have been carried out to confiscate data which would aid activists by incriminating animal murderers and expose their bloody work. In the US, this model was never used so effectively as the 1984 break-in at the University of Pennsylvania Head

Injury Clinic, in which dozens of videos of gruesome head injury experiments were removed and made public. This simple action ultimately shut the lab down forever. It was speculated the data contained in *The Final Nail*—which sparked nearly 50 fur farms raids in the two years after its publication—was in whole or part sourced from documents removed from fur industry research facilities during Operation Bite Back.

Possible info-rich targets included fur industry trade group offices, pelt processors, and the offices of individual farms; each with their own benefits and drawbacks. The offices of individual farms would be most easily penetrable, and have provided intel in the past, yet compared to other options they are the least likely to have data of the volume and scope sought by The Endgame Project. There was one weak link in the fur industry of which there were only a handful of locations, and inside which lay the addresses of nearly every fur farm in the country. This was certain, because their profit depended on it.

Businesses and cooperatives which delivered mink and fox feed to nearly every one of the United States' fur farms, it was deduced, had information covering the largest geographical area. The mission sought industry data of both a regional and national scope. Thus fur farm feed suppliers were chosen as the target.

After much reconnaissance, one site stood out in both its layout and size as optimal for a break-in: The Hawkeye Mink Cooperative in Jewel, Iowa. Despite its remote location, Jewel had little reason to feel immune from activists. Iowa had been the site of 6 fur farm raids in the past 4 years, and two additional raids at a pigeon farm. Two of the raided fur farms were within one mile of the co-op. (Later, Iowa would see the largest rescue of laboratory animals in 10 years from the nearby University of Iowa, in which 401 animals were removed from the psychology building.) However, despite having its address widely distributed in *The Final Nail*, and despite raids on fur farms all around it, the Hawkeye Co-op had thus far escaped being targeted by activists. When The Endgame Project was given life, this would no longer be the case.

The mission was established: enter the Hawkeye Mink Cooperative offices and leave with every piece of paper in the building.

GOING IN

We scaled down our strike team to two, the absolute minimum needed to safely execute the raid. Additional units to load and transport documents would ensure a quicker exit and less time inside the building. Yet offsetting this benefit was the drawback of exposing more active group members to the risks involved in a break-in, the payoff from which would not be immediate. There was no direct benefit to the animals in liberating data, the payoff came in what we did with the information.

The Hawkeye Mink Cooperative was one of several fur farm feed suppliers left in the country, including the Northwest Farm Food Coop (heavily damaged in an A.L.F. arson attack in 1991), Utah's Fur Breeders Agriculture Cooperative (targeted by the A.L.F. in 1997; $1 million damage), and United Feeds (burned in 1999), and there were rumors of other suppliers who existed under the radar. The strategic value of targeting feed suppliers was in their crucial role in keeping the North American fur industry afloat. On the global market, the North American fur trade is superior to the larger markets of China and Russia only in the quality of its pelts. The development of specially formulated feed is vital to this "quality," the largest source of which were local cooperatives and National Fur Foods (WI). The Hawkeye Mink Cooperative had good reason to be on guard. But there was one lesson our group had learned in our years as animal liberation activists: no building is ever as secure as one imagines, and no target anywhere is impenetrable. None.

The Hawkeye Mink Cooperative was composed of three buildings and two delivery trucks. Confiscating a delivery list from one of the trucks would be a simple way to obtain what would likely be a complete list of every fur farm in Iowa , perhaps beyond. Yet while the trucks were unlocked, the cabs were found absent of paperwork. The rest of the facility consisted of one large and elongated shed, a feed manufacturing building, and a pelt processing building. In addition to supplying feed, Hawkeye skinned and treated pelts for farms and trappers in Nebraska, Minnesota and Iowa. Reconnaissance identified the operational center of the facility to be in the northwest corner of the pelt processing building.

The facility was surveilled for one night, between 11pm and 4am. There was no activity. After discussion between the team members, it was decided that any overnight activity would be atypical in a rural setting, and the reconnaissance done to date would be sufficient.

That week, team members obtained the necessary equipment: gloves, dark clothing, a small hammer, a crowbar, radios, ski masks, and six very large military-style duffle bags. All items were paid for in cash, hundreds of miles from the target. The items were kept in sealed bags, away from the possibility of human contact, free of any trace of forensic evidence which could be left at the scene.

The day of the raid, radios were checked, time limits set, and a radio code gone over: "Yellow light" meant there was potential for danger: proceed as usual, but be on guard, don't make loud noises, and prepare for future communication. "Green light" meant all is clear. "Red light" meant severe danger: hide immediately inside the building and make no noise. And then there was the appropriately abrupt "abort." Translation: Get out.

At 12am, the two Endgame Project operatives went into position.

The break-in unit entered the property through the rear. In approaching the pelt processing building, there was no safe angle. Hawkeye Mink Cooperative was located on Main Street in downtown Jewel. The rear exposed one to view from neighboring homes. Dressed in black, the break-in unit slipped through backyards and at 12:15 arrived at an office window: the point of entry. The member confirmed radio contact with the watchperson. Everything being in place, the break-in unit removed a hammer from a backpack and punched a small hole in the glass. Reaching through, the window was unlocked and opened. Several nearby crates were stacked, and the unit slid through the window and into the first office. A quick scan was done of the window frame for alarms. Seeing none, the member moved from the first office to the second, scanning the rooms thoroughly for visible alarms. Scrutinizing all corners of the offices closely, it was determined the only alarms were on the front door, just feet from the window. The last person to leave had left the keys in the alarm control panel, next to the door. It was turned to "Off."

The operative continued on course, exiting the building and retreating across the property to await any possible police response in the event an alarm had unknowingly been triggered. After 45 minutes, there was no response, and the operation entered its second phase.

A team member re-entered the first office and removed the six large duffel bags from their backpack. The heart of the operation had begun. The member began the task of filling the bags with every document and computer disc in the building. Every desk drawer was opened, and all paperwork, publications, business cards, and anything else of intelligence value was loaded into the bags. The operative moved to the file cabinet, and emptied it of all its contents. Stacks of journals, address books, phone tree lists and sales logs were bagged without inspection.

The mission plans called for the removal of everything, with nothing left behind. The team member moved to the second office, which was given the same treatment. For expediency, individual documents were not inspected. But at casual glance it was apparent this was the largest body of fur industry intelligence entering the hands of the animal liberation movement since Operation Bite Back, with information on not just a local but national scale. When every document had been loaded, 6 duffel bags were at capacity.

The team member had been inside the building for 45 minutes, with no incoming radio transmissions, meaning no activity outside. The break-in unit radioed the watchperson: they were ready for pickup. The team of two was joined by the watchperson who left their post to aid in the transport of the six massive duffel bags to the vehicle. Each bag, nearly too heavy to lift, was pushed through the window to a team member, who ferried them across the property to the designated point on the dirt road along the property's northern border. The break-in unit returned to the office, placing in their pocket two sets of keys—one for the building, another for the alarm.

Leaving the offices in ruins, the last operative slipped through the window to meet the vehicle. In view of neighboring homes, the bags were loaded into the backseat, and the vehicle drove into the night.

THE ENDGAME PROJECT FILE

At late-morning, the team arrived at a pre-designated safe house for Phase III of the operation: taking stock of the haul and distilling down all the information into one document of hard data—The Endgame Project File. In the planning stages it was decided to extract all new, previously unknown data and reduce it to one compact file, stripped of any clues as to the info's source, then immediately dispose of the original documents. Keeping the haul for a moment longer than needed would expose the team to the unnecessary risk of being in possession of evidence which would implicate them in the break-in. The team members set themselves to the task.

For one week, the Endgame Project members poured over the nearly 50,000 pages of data, comparing it to previously known data in *The Final Nail*, and transcribing everything that was determined to be previously unknown to the movement. And of unknown information, there was much. Taking inventory for the first time made it clear, the haul was the goldmine of intelligence that was hoped for. Confiscated in the raid were rolodexes of fur industry contacts going back to the 1950s, years of Fur Rancher magazines and other rare industry publications containing addresses, stacks of American Legend auction house receipts with farm addresses and pelt counts, and every variety of document related to the inner-workings of the fur industry. As the data-mining phase progressed, it was clear nearly 100 new fur farm and other industry addresses were being brought to light for the first time. The intention of the Project members was for this data to serve as a catalyst for the next wave of action to liberate fur farm prisoners, laying the fur industry to waste forever.

Much of the paperwork would be difficult to part with, both for the significant historical value of some of the documents, as well as the difficulty translating some into streams of letters and numbers. The duffel bags were filled with priceless photos inside fur farms, fur farm research facilities, and auction houses; rare insider documents such as copies of the Fur Industry Research Council newsletter, and a booklet inviting fur farmers to an "open house" at the much speculated-about National Fur Foods Research Ranch, an experimental fur farm in Oshkosh, Wisconsin whose address had never been made public. The last page contained directions to the farm, and its location would be speculated about no more.

One week later, the last document had been scrutinized and the last note taken. Another day was taken to quickly re-scan the confiscated paperwork for missed data, and the haul—none of which would contain either a fingerprint or trace of forensic evidence—was taken to a landfill and permanently discarded.

50,000 pages had been boiled down to one document: The Endgame Project File. The 40 page document contained hundreds of addresses, names, phone numbers, directions, and info on the inner-workings and weaknesses of the North American fur industry.

Our Counterterrorism Intelligence Unit had fulfilled its intel and research phase, and the program's final stage called for a passing of the torch. The Endgame Project File was given a once-over to strip it of any remaining details which could betray its source, fact-checked against the original handwritten notes, and sorted for distribution.

Our mission fulfilled, responsibility for the next stage fell on the larger movement. The Endgame Project File was anonymously mailed to over 20 aboveground groups and contacts, none of whom were known personally to the Cointel Team. Each envelope contained a cover letter requesting the preservation and further distribution of the file movement-wide. It was our wish that the data would be distributed widely, eventually falling into the hands of those selfless liberators who knew how to apply the data best through overnight liberations of fur farm prisoners and the eradication of the industry infrastructure. We would not have to wait long.

THE AFTERMATH

On the night of August 18, 2002, six and a half months after the Endgame Project File was distributed, 2,000 mink were released from the Misty Moonlight Mink Ranch in Waverly, Iowa. Previously unlisted in *The Final Nail*, the farm's address was first unearthed in paperwork taken from Hawkeye Mink Cooperative.

In the seven years that have passed, three farms have been raided whose addresses were previously unlisted and whose locations were first revealed in The Endgame Project File. These raids have brought (temporary or permanent) freedom for over 13,000 mink. While it is impossible to know the persons behind these actions, or the source of their data, the evidence strongly indicates these actions are the result of The Endgame Project.

The cascading effect continues. Years later, in the summer of 2008, *The Final Nail #3* was released. Claiming "over 100 never-before revealed farms," it was the first publicly available update to *The Final Nail* in 10 years. In the six weeks following its release, three farms were raided in North America with nearly 10,000 mink released. Addresses of two of the farms had not been made public prior to its release. To the compilers of the Endgame Project File, the "100 never-before revealed farms" were hardly new. It appeared the yields from the Project were coming to surface.

It is not possible to know the true source of the data behind *The Final Nail #3*. And if it did have its source in the Endgame Project File, it is equally impossible for the authors of *The Final Nail #3* to know that the original source of their data was in the dusty file cabinets of the Hawkeye Mink Cooperative all those years ago.

For those who decided on the fur feed supplier as a target that night in 2002, the public disclosure of the long secret file brings final and welcome closure. Nearly seven years after its inception, The Endgame Project was officially closed.

This type of data-confiscation raid is a direct action model for the future. The casualties of the meat, dairy, egg, vivisection, and fur industries are piling up. Homes for liberated animals are scarce. The larger groups that are required for large-scale liberations can be daunting to orchestrate in a world full of individuals who are unworthy of our trust. Yet one damning vivisection video made public can save the lives of a thousand laboratory animals. One reclaimed file cabinet's contents can incite a wave of effective actions. For those without a trusted partner with whom to work, the clandestine entry model offers endless options for a one-person counterintelligence unit. The victims of human greed ask not that we act in the greatest numbers, only that we act.

By liberation, education, or confiscation—"take by night what the day never brings."

Merial Select Labs

2003

How the A.L.F. rescued over 100 birds from HLS supplier Merial Select Laboratories.

We were determined to show a little justice for the animals trapped inside Huntingdon Life Sciences by going after one of their customers.

Merial Labs was tucked away in Maryland, doing their dirty work on animals to create vaccines to keep farm animals "healthy," or rather produce more, for agribusiness. A variety of their new vaccines were then shipped off to HLS for testing.

However, behind their main facility sat a large group of smaller units, each housing chickens in different stages of life, that Merial used for their own testing. Here is where we decided to strike.

After parking our vehicle safely in the local vicinity, we made our way amongst some wooded areas, and cut our way through thick bramble. This emptied us out into the fields behind Merial. After a short recon the night before, we knew we needed a few carriers, a pair of bolt cutters, a crowbar and some warm clothes (honestly, what else does one really need?). The March winter was chilly, but as the snow began to fall harder and harder, we delighted in the fact that no lazy cop would get out of their car to check out anything, and our tracks would be quickly covered.

We were aware that the doors leading into the units were alarmed, but the geniuses inside these "lifesaving research" labs hadn't thought to also alarm the windows. Obviously, to us common "terrorists," this was our point of entry!

With our trusty tools, we cut and pried off the panels and screens and climbed on in. The baby chicks were a little startled at first—we doubt they have ever seen a couple of masked people enter that way before!

But before long we rounded them all up into our carriers and kept them stacked next to the heat lamp. We repeated the process in a couple of more units before we realized we had already liberated more than we had homes for. We were sure once our safehouse saw how adorable these little chicks were they would work overtime to find some extra homes (and thankfully, we were right!)

Our driver for the evening retraced our steps back to the vehicle, and made their way to our new pickup point. Originally we were going to transport the animals back to the vehicle the way we came in, but with the snow storm in full effect, we were determined that all of us were going to leave in style—through the front! The snow had already covered our tracks, and let's face it, it was too damn cold to walk all that way. The rest of us rounded up all the carriers, tools and 115 birds, and made our way to the van, loaded up, and turned the heat on high.

Another job well done!

We felt confident as we turned onto the open road and headed towards safety. Unfortunately, we had a full 36 hour drive until we reached our safehouse.

Upon arrival, an area was set aside to keep the chicks warm, watered and well fed. As soon as we placed them into their new surroundings, the baby chicks began scratching in the bedding, bathing themselves in the water dishes, and huddling together to settle down for a well-deserved rest.

Here, they would be starting a new life. Usually for us, this is where the story would end. In a month's time though, we would be back for a second visit.

The chicks were growing fast and had almost outgrown their area. Their original home had fallen through, and we were informed that we needed to get them to a new home, and fast. We spent a number of days driving around the countryside to talk, in person, with some of our people, and finally squared away a permanent place for the birds.

When we arrived to pick up our old friends, we were amazed at how fast they had grown! We equipped the vehicle with bedding, secure perches, beds and water bowls, and loaded up the girls for yet another long journey.

After another lengthy drive, we got straight to work getting their new living quarters squared away—allowing them to have a comfortable and dry shelter area as well as an outdoor area to scratch and play and rest in the warm sun. Now almost full grown chickens, we placed them one by one in their new home. Just about all of them were perplexed by the grass under their feet. They had never experienced it in their whole lives.

But that didn't stop them from running, stretching and enjoying themselves in their new environment. It was an honor to be able to see them go from cramped quarters in small barns out in a snowstorm, to playing in the grass in the warm spring breeze. It reminded us that animal liberation doesn't always have to be flashy stunts and expensive campaigns. It can be a couple of friends, a pair of boltcutters and the determination and creativity to see animals living free.

After resting up, we paid a final visit to our friends to say goodbye. The sun was going down and the evening stars were coming out. While some slept in the perches we made for them out of fallen branches, most cuddled together outside in a bed of soft grass, sleeping in the fresh air, for the first time. Occasionally one would rustle their feathers or shift from side to side. Every so often a head would pop up and look around at the evening sky and the green grass, almost in disbelief.

Their long journey from toxicology experiments to safe living was over, and we could all rest a little easier.

INTERVIEWS

Interviews with members of the
Animal Liberation Front

CONTENTS

INTERVIEWS

How does one interview the A.L.F.? Many activists would clamor for their knowledge. Many journalists would clamor for their story. The difficulty in accessing A.L.F. activists pre-arrest is why this is the book's shortest chapter.

Included are the seven known interviews with anonymous A.L.F. members. With the stakes so high and trust so low, only three of these were with the media, with the rest granted to activist publications (including *PETA News*, an impossible-to-process pairing in the present day).

Only six interviews with arrested members remain, and while not every A.L.F. prisoner is represented here, the scarcity of even post-arrest interviews is a roundabout testament to how good the A.L.F. are at not getting caught.

Notable entries include five interviews with participants in seminal 80s laboratory break-ins, including University of Pennsylvania and Texas Tech, none of which saw a single arrest. Darren Thurston's 1996 interview almost doubles as a "how it was done" piece, giving granular details on how he and David Barbarash rescued dozens of cats from the University of Alberta. Another notable entry, at least for its rarity, is an unpublished interview with one of defendants in the "Mass 4," a legal case involving the arrest of four people for an attempted mink release and arson at the Carmel Mink Ranch in Hindsdale, Massachusetts. Lastly, news magazine show 60 Minutes secured a lengthy interview with a purported A.L.F. cell member (who participated in a rescue at Marshall Farms, among others). This is the entire transcript, unavailable elsewhere.

Among the greatest liberties taken in this book was including the Chris DeRose interview. DeRose was never charged with A.L.F. actions himself, and as such this interview does not meet the explicit standards for this book. The decision to include was not made because he was suspected by the police (and many activists) of being the mythical "Joseph," an organizer of the west coast A.L.F. cell behind multiple large lab raids in the 1980s. (DeRose has always insisted he was merely Joseph's spokesperson and media liaison). Instead, it was included because this interview may be the closest history gets to perhaps the A.L.F.'s most prolific and mythologized figure.

While many interviews with captured members were not included for space reasons (this is a "best of"), there are only three examples of anonymous interviews that are known to exist, yet were not included. One, another *PETA News* interview with a person behind the City of Hope break-in in 1984. Two, a pamphlet titled *Interviews With California A.L.F. Activists*, which is exactly what the title describes. I once owned a copy, and can testify to its existence, but it has remained elusive for years. Three, a much smaller but worth-mentioning example: a 2000 Bay Area news feature on the A.L.F., which, similar to the 60 Minutes interview, featured a purported A.L.F. member, masked, and interviewed in a hotel room. The televised portion only included a few snippets of what presumably was a much longer interview, but it is significant as one of only a few interviews granted to the media in the North American A.L.F.'s 40+ years.

Be inspired or be incited, but extract all you can from these conversations. With the challenge and risk they require, history will enjoy very few interviews with the A.L.F.

University Of Pennsylvania: "Jack"

1984

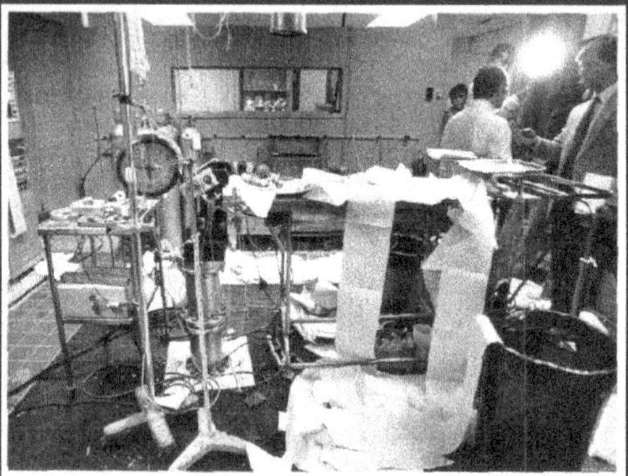

The Animal Liberation Front claims responsibility for the theft of records and the damage done at the University of Pennsylvania's animal research lab.

Interview with an anonymous A.L.F. activist behind the break-in at the Gennerelli lab at the University Of Pennsylvania

An A.L.F. member since 1982, "Jack" believes A.L.F. actions to date have succeeded because of two important factors: the time spent in careful planning and the discipline necessary to protect the anonymity of A.L.F. units.

I understand you were a member of the team that broke into Dr. Gennerelli's laboratory at the University of Pennsylvania.

Yes, and I helped a few weeks later with the second raid.

Why these two raids?

Well, two main reasons over and above my general commitment to intervene directly to help stop suffering. First, G. is absolutely notorious and his abuses, it struck me, could only be exposed through this kind of action. Everything else had been tried. As for the second raid, I had the additional incentive of knowing about two veterinarians at the school, Adrian Morrison and Peter Hand, who had traveled last year to Maryland to appear in court and defend yet another infamous experimenter, Dr. Taub.

You mean they defended the conditions in Taub's lab?

Absolutely. One of them actually went so far as to say there was nothing wrong with failing to call in a veterinarian if a monkey had a broken bone or infected wound. They pretty much said that no deaths or few deaths equaled good health! They also said there was no scientific evidence that heavy accumulation of feces caused a health problem. I remember reading that the prosecutor told the judge that if that were the case, we've wasted a lot of money on sewage systems in this country.

Why has this action received more attention than past actions?

I don't know positively, but I feel sure the tapes play a big part. Finally people can see what's actually going on in laboratories, and they can see what they're paying for. That's one reason I've been delighted with the press coverage; we've known all along how bad things are for laboratory animals, but now everyone can see for themselves.

Did you go in specifically for the tapes, or did you intend to bring out animals?

We decided to go in for the tapes, because we knew how important a step this exposure would be for all laboratory animals. But the decision wasn't easy. We had seen the baboons on the 5th floor during previous surveillance; their cages were so small, and looking into their eyes sent chills through me. It was an ugly choice because the whole place was wretched; all of us wanted to just stop the whole operation. I remember Fred Weisman's film *Primate*, where he described laboratories as having "the smell of urine and the stench of greed"; it's so disgustingly true.

You said G. is notorious. What do you mean?

I'm talking about his callousness towards the animals he uses, his consumption of large sums of taxpayer's money, and the fact that all these years he's been fine-tuning his ability to damage animals' brains, ever so precisely at this angle and this speed, so that we can make better football helmets. My brother is a dirt bike racer, and when he tells me about some of the things he and his friends do, I'm grateful he's still here at all. But he does all those wild things because he wants to; he enjoys it. PETA has a t-shirt that says: "Animals don't drink. Animals don't smoke. Animals don't wear makeup. Animals don't drop bombs. Because we do, why should they suffer?" That's how I feel.

Do you think the end of G.'s work would mean the end of head injury research?

Of course not. In fact, I really want to see money going to develop alternatives to animals. I believe we could take some real steps forward, faster and more efficiently without using animals than Gennerelli has over the last 15 years by mutilating all those monkeys. In this technological age alternatives should be sought out and developed. Right now the money is in animal experiments. Dallas Pratt's book *Alternatives to Pain* really got me thinking. Researchers claim that there aren't any alternatives—without ever trying to find them. They haven't searched their souls about what they're doing; they use animals as a matter of course. That needs to change.

Have your A.L.F. activities ever interfered with your personal life?

Actually, I look at it the opposite way. I've tried to make sure I don't take on responsibilities that will interrupt or prevent my animal work. A year ago my dog died, and I decided then not to replace her. Instead I thought I could better help other animals by making my home a foster home. I keep animals, temporarily, while people go on vacation or for any reason. I've been able to help so many animals by keeping them out of commercial kennels. Years ago I worked in a kennel for the summer. The conditions were pretty bad and this place was supposed to be one of the best. If you've ever boarded your dog, you know you aren't allowed to see the pens; the animals can sit in their urine all week and get a quick bath the day they're to be picked up. They're confused and upset enough about being left by the people they know, without having to go through substandard treatment.

What about your job?

I'm a graduate student with a full scholarship, so I'm not working now. I have a lot of studying and book work to do, but somehow, I've always managed to keep up.

How do you feel about being in the A.L.F.?

I'm proud of it. I only wish I could openly recruit classmates and other students. I have no misgivings or second thoughts about what I do, only a sound conviction that I have to do it. What I find regrettable is that I can't share my experiences with friends after a successful action. I find myself wanting to run up to someone and say, "Did you hear about the animals in such and such laboratory? After all they've been through, now they're free!" Along with being happy for the liberated ones, I feel excited about what they represent for our cause; each action we accomplish means a step forward for animal rights, because by exposing their plight, we have the opportunity to speak for them. As long as people don't know what's going on, they can't do anything about it.

Would you have changed anything about the G. break in?

I only wish we had done it sooner.

University Of Pennsylvania: "Karen"

1984

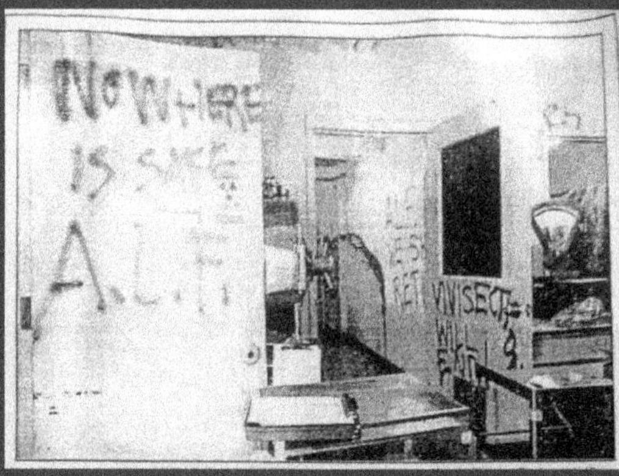

Interview with another anonymous A.L.F. activist behind the break-in at the Gennerelli lab at the University Of Pennsylvania

A member of the Animal Liberation Front tells why she broke the law for animals.

Interviewed by Len Lear for Animals Agenda

Karen, 38, a health care worker in a large eastern city, is one of the members of the Animal Liberation Front who broke into the Head Injury Clinical Research Center at the University of Pennsylvania in May 1984. In the most widely-publicized break-in of its kind, the A.L.F. stole more than 60 hours of videotapes of experiments and initiated an exhaustive campaign that led ultimately to the Center's closing.

For over 13 years, the Center had used hundreds of unanesthetized baboons to study the effects of head injuries. In the studies, which cost taxpayers nearly $1 million a year, baboons had their heads plastered to a machine which delivered blows as great as 1,000 times the force of gravity. Then, on Memorial Day, 1984, the A.L.F. team entered the laboratory and took the tapes, which had been made by the experimenters themselves as a part of their record-keeping routine.

The A.L.F. members left the tapes on the doorsteps of People for the Ethical Treatment of Animals' headquarters in the Maryland suburbs of Washington, D.C. PETA hastily edited them down to a 30-minute documentary, entitled "Unnecessary Fuss," which documented violations of the Animal Welfare Act, animal abuse and researchers' callous attitudes toward the baboons. Embarrassed University of Pennsylvania officials pulled political strings and Philadelphia District Attorney Edward Rendell launched an investigation to identify the A.L.F. members involved in the break-in; several PETA members were summoned to testify before a grand jury. Undaunted, PETA aggressively distributed copies of the documentary to other animal rights groups, to members of Congress and to the media.

Publicity about the baboon bashing at the University brought forth protest after protest, culminating with a four-day sit-in at offices of the National Institutes of Health in July 1985. On the fourth day of the sit-in, Health and Human Services Secretary Margaret M. Heckler ordered NIH to suspend its $1 million-a-year grant to the head injury lab.

Then, late in September after months of investigations and official reports, the University of Pennsylvania announced that "experiments in the lab have been suspended indefinitely." Within weeks, Secretary Heckler announced that funding to the lab would remain under suspension because the researchers had "failed materially to comply with the conditions of their grant with respect to the care use of non-human primates." In a separate action, NIH Director, Dr. James Wyngaarden, spelled out a list of major actions to be taken by the university before he would "consider any request for resumption of funding" for head injury studies involving non-human primates.

In this exclusive interview, Karen (last name withheld) was asked about her background and the reasons for her involvement with the Animal Liberation Front. Our interviewer deliberately took a "devil's advocate" approach in order to discuss the most frequently encountered questions about the A.L.F.

Were you always around animals as a child?

I grew up in a big city on the east coast, and we always had cats. My mom and dad were sensitive to animals. He didn't see the sense in hunting, for example, and I remember one time when she stopped the car to pick up a turtle and move it off the road. They ate meat, though; they never made the connection.

How did your views become more radical?

It started about ten years ago, when I became a vegetarian. I always loved cats, and somehow it occurred to me that I would never eat a cat, so why should I eat other animals? Then I began rescuing a lot of stray animals. I would find homes for them, or at least take them to a shelter that I could trust, not one that uses a decompression chamber.

Did rescuing stray animals lead you to the A.L.F.?

No. That was something different. For many years I was a waitress, a file clerk and so on, but I was going to school at night for a science degree. In the course of doing research in the library for a couple of papers, I read about things that were being done to animals in laboratories. I was really shocked. I had no idea whatsoever that these atrocities were going on. I could not believe it. Animals are used in the most cruel and horrible ways, and it's not as if it's being kept secret. It's right there in any medical library.

Could you be more specific as to what you learned that particularly disturbed you?

I learned about the experiments on "learned helplessness," for example, which have been going on since the 1950's. They would give electric shocks to dogs, and they would naturally try to jump out of the box, but the escape route would be blocked. Eventually the dogs would go crazy. They would throw themselves against the wall and wind up cowering on the floor, accepting the shock and urinating on themselves. The conclusion of the researchers is that if the animal cannot escape, s/he learns to accept the shock. This has been done over and over again—at the University of Pennsylvania, among other places.

Would you accept the notion that some of the animal research may be valid?

Very, very little has been gained from this killing that is of benefit to humans. In fact we might be farther in treating head injury victims if no animal research had been done. We've been deprived by the fact that more has not been done with human clinical studies, human autopsy studies, epidemiological studies, solid tissue cultures, computers, positive emissions tomography, and so on. Dr. Gennarelli, who was in charge of UPenn's head injury lab, even admitted that these things are not being used enough because the money is being drained off by animal research. In fact, nuclear magnetic resonance is a way to study human brain damage without using animals, but it's very expensive and the money is tied up in animal projects.

For example, the people at the UPenn head injury lab claim their research will benefit children who have suffered traumatic head injuries and brain damage. I certainly can sympathize with the parents of such children, but that still does not make this research valid. The researchers would like you to believe that if enough animals are killed, little Johnny's head will be repaired. But this is ludicrous. Considering the hundreds of millions of animals killed in research labs, we should all have eternal life by now.

Are you saying that human head injury victims have not benefited at all from the kind of research that was done at UPenn?

Absolutely. I have read every single head injury study that has been done, and not one has discussed how the human victims or the animals victims were treated after the research. The human victims and their families have been exploited and given false hope. They have been used as a shield to keep the cruelty and the money coming.

How did you come to join the A.L.F.?

After learning about the horrors of useless animal research, I began writing letters to Congress, handed out literature at tables in shopping centers and engaged in picket demonstrations. I still do those things, but I realized that other forms of action were also necessary because the killing and the torture kept right on happening.

How did you and the other A.L.F. members find out about the research at UPenn?

Very simple. Dr. Gennarelli has published all of his findings and his methods in a medical journal dealing with brain trauma. We simply read his own published reports. The details of this and other animal research can be easily found in any medical library in the country.

Did you know in advance about the videotapes, which were the key in shutting down the lab?

Yes. Gennarelli mentioned the tapes in his published studies. We were very happy when we found them, but they were far worse than we had expected. The callousness and brutality were absolutely unbelievable. The researchers made fun of the animals while they were dying, and they'd beat up one animal in front of another.

You could clearly hear them say that one baboon was "off anaesthesia" right before they started bashing in his/her head. You could see the animal trying to crawl off the table. One researcher said, "It looks like this one has a dislocated shoulder," and then he deliberately picked up the baboon by the arm, causing the animal excruciating pain, laughing all the while he was doing it. They were like Nazis. They didn't even do a proper neurological exam, and they left the animals unattended and tied to the operating table after the injuries.

How would you respond to those who say your efforts are merely condemning more animals to death since the research you disrupt is likely to be done all over again?

We are abolitionists, and if we are successful in closing down a lab, as we did at UPenn, then obviously no more animals are going to be killed there. We also had the funding cut off from the City of Hope in Los Angeles after our break-in. They were doing cancer research, but the conditions in the animal lab were horrible. Dogs were dying unattended, and one suffocated in his own fecal matter.

Don't you worry about being caught and going to jail?

I do not live in fear. I have been in on three break-ins, so I could go to jail and I'm prepared to deal with it if it happens. We are not martyrs, though, and we'd much rather stay out here, where we can do more for the animals. [Karen has no children and no husband, although she does have a boyfriend who is "supportive" of her A.L.F. activities. -Eds.]

In many of your raids, you have liberated research animals. What has happened to those animals?

We make sure they are well cared for. We feel that by liberating animals, you are also liberating people. We are on this earth to protect animals, not to exploit them. We do not have the right to use them as if they are inanimate objects. They have a right to their own lives, which should not include slavery and torture.

Don't you feel you have committed an immoral act when you have destroyed property that belonged to others?

Not when that property was used to inflict pain, suffering and death on living creatures. We have been referred to by certain critics as terrorists, but the real terrorists are those who put animals in boiling water and bash in the brains of fully conscious creatures and harm human beings by misdirecting research. If all of that is not terrorism, then what is?

University of Toronto

1986

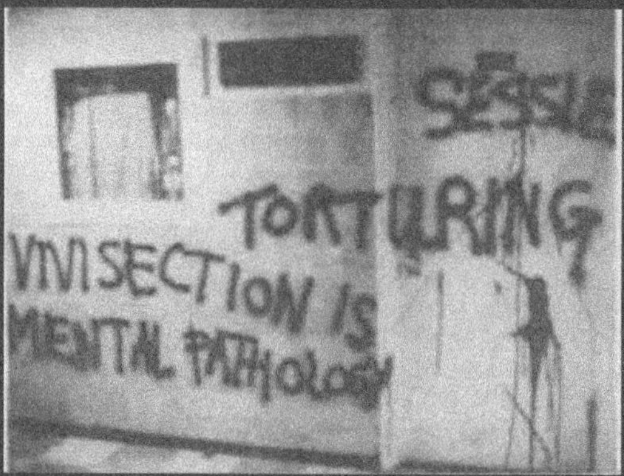

Interview with another anonymous A.L.F. activist behind the break-in at the University of Toronto College Of Dentistry.

This interview was conducted with a person who took part in an ALF raid on the College of Dentistry at the University of Toronto in Feb. 1986, where experiments take place involving the use of pain, and the measuring of facial reactions to pain. A failed attempt was made to liberate animals, but equipment was destroyed and damage exceeded $15,000.

What were your feelings when you failed to liberate any of the animals there?

I'm not sure it is possible to describe the feelings of overwhelming frustration I, and all the others involved, felt at being so close to the animals yet unable to reach them. We were separated by just a wall and even managed to get through part of that, but we just ran out of time. The feeling or frustration has not gone away, it has merely been diverted into an energetic determination to succeed next time.

Would you use violence (on people as well as researchers' machines and torture devices) if it was absolutely necessary in order to free an abused animal?

Violence is a relative term. I do not recognize the destruction of researchers' torture chambers or instruments of torture violence, merely as economic sabotage. I feel that violence against people turns off the public and it is not something I am personally comfortable with, as the ALF group to which I belong operates by complete consensus, it is therefore extremely unlikely, believing as I do, that I would find myself in a violent situation. Also, in order to reduce the chance of confrontation with a guard, etc., we investigate our targets very carefully over a long period of time.

Many "scientists" have commented that the ALF is nothing but a terrorist group akin to such organizations as the IRA and that the ALF's raids in the future are certain to lead to violence. What's your opinion on this viewpoint?

Terrorism is defined in the dictionary as "mass organized ruthlessness" or "state of terror"; terrorist is defined as "to oppress by fear." There can be no greater terrorism than the violent research going on behind the locked doors of laboratories and no greater terrorist group than vivisectors doing that which they do best—torturing animals. Accusing the ALF of "perhaps" committing violence at some unknown and unspecified time in the future is not only ridiculous but will not serve to divert our attention from reality, which is that the research community is already committing violence now, every day, against its helpless animal victims.

How do you keep infiltrators out of the ALF? Also, how can you be sure that people volunteering homes for abused or liberated animals aren't cops, etc.?

Infiltration is a serious problem but I believe we take every possible precaution against it. I prefer not to discuss the exceptional security measures taken to ensure people are not "infiltrators." Also, I prefer not to discuss the safeguards used where homes for the animals are concerned. Needless to say, they are extensive—carelessness that would result in turning an animal over to someone who would return him/her back to a laboratory is not to be tolerated. Everyone involved considers this even more important than being caught and going to jail; we know the risk we are taking, terrifying though it may be, and we made the choice. However, the animal is helpless and once liberated must remain liberated, whatever the cost.

Dr. Thomas Salamo, a member of the U of T's Faculty of Medicine and a heart surgeon at St Michael's Hospital has refused to give me an interview because "it's not a good time to discuss the research" being done at the U of T! What types of research do you know, or do you suspect are going on there? What's he trying to hide?

I don't wish to answer this question because of security and the safety of others. I cannot explain further. Suffice it to say that all kinds of research are going on at the U of T and we are aware of every detail of that research. In terms of Salamo trying to hide information—it constantly amazes me as to how secretive researchers are about their work. Are they not proud or what they are doing in the "name of mankind" as they like to put it? Could it be that they fear their research methods would not stand up in the light of public scrutiny?

Dr. William Rapley, director of animal care veterinary services at the University of Western Ontario in London, Ont. was very "nice" when I interviewed him. However, in his efforts at being so polite and "helpful," he evaded telling me what experiments the animals at UWO are being subjected to. Do you have information on what is really going on there now?

Once again, same answer as above.

I know your commitment to the Animal Liberation Front is great and that you are willing to go to jail for your actions. Are there any particular incidents that led you to these beliefs? (Why did you join the ALF?)

I am passionately committed to creating social change which will make this world a better place for all species, not just for humans. As an animal rights activist, once I had dealt with the fear of realizing that I could go to jail if caught, it seemed the logical step to become a liberator. I want to look back on my life and know I did absolutely everything I could to help stop these atrocities, even giving up my freedom, which is the greatest sacrifice one can make. It is important to realize that when liberators make this decision, they do not do so out of any sense of martyrdom, but out of a sense of necessity. Believe me, the last thing we want is to be a "sacrifice"; the animals need all of us on the "outside," rather than in prison.

Do you think that ALF raids will do anything to abolish animal research in the future? What will it take to end the torment once and for all?

I believe ALF raids are invaluable because, thus far, they have been responsible for bringing to light atrocities in research facilities—e.g., City of Hope Medical Center, the (University of Pennsylvania -ed) Head Injury Tapes, etc. It is essential that not only animals be liberated—though that has first priority—but also damning documentation against the research facility. We have to present factual evidence to the public because ultimately, they are the ones who will have to apply pressure to create changes in the system, in legislation, etc. They have to know what is going on in laboratories, indeed in every arena where animal abuse is taking place. Only by knowing the truth can the general public raise an outcry to stop this horror. And of course, in terms of the animals, the ALF is the only hope for an end to the suffering of laboratory animals. If they are not liberated, the only way a lab animal leaves the lab is when it is dead.

Canadian A.L.F. Activist

1986

Interview with a Canadian A.L.F. activist.

Under tight security, one cell of the ALF Canada agreed to be interviewed for the Front Line News. For purposes of the interview this person shall be identified only as Robin.

How did you come to join an ALF cell and why?

Getting involved was inevitable after doing a lot of investigating and finding the system allows and even encourages goons. crazies, and creeps to gain and profit from the torture and humiliation of helpless animals. I CAN'T JUST STAND BY AND NOT DO ANYTHING ABOUT IT and happily neither can a lot more of us who want to put an end to animal abuse.

How do you find laboratories to target?

There are MANY animal concentration camps of one sort or another with willing employees who don't like what they see, and so come forward anonymously with information. That, combined with our own methods of investigation, gives us a good idea of what's going on where.

Do you draw the line at physical violence? What is your reaction to the Animal Rights Militia tactics e.g. letter bombs?

After witnessing the worst kinds of violence I have ever seen in laboratories, slaughterhouses, and traplines, I understand the passionate rage the Animal Liberation Militia feels. However, for the time being my personal anger manifests itself in taking part in raids. It is obvious that support for the ALF is here in Canada and growing rapidly. Violence may set us back—it's a big risk.

Suppose you remove a laboratory animal; won't it be replaced by a new one who will have to suffer the ordeal of the experiment as it is repeated from the beginning?

They will repeat the experiments anyway, and keep repeating them ad infinitum. The only way any animal gets out of a lab under normal conditions is when it is dead. At least this way, the ALF gives some a chance to survive, and that is, after all, our main goal, as well as removing incriminating documents and evidence that will put these places out of business. I would be amazed if anyone thought I could walk out of a lab and leave all those animals behind!

How do you carry out surveillance?

With a warm coat and hot thermos.*

How do you guard against infiltrators?

That's not easy when you live in a society that pays you to fink on your neighbours. Mostly by being as careful as we can; also the format of the ALF means that individual cells are encouraged to develop independently. Therefore, one is not known to the other.

When did the first Canadian ALF action occur and what was it?

The first MAJOR action carried out by the ALF in Canada was June 15, 1981 at the Hospital For Sick Children. (Sick kids sharing the same roof as the torture lab!) 21 animals were liberated, including the earless cat that got so much media coverage.

What equipment is needed for a break in?

Jack-hammers, helicopter, and a wrecking ball.*

Any other comments you'd like to make?

Yes! Carrying an animal away from daily terror is worth the risk of possible future penalties or imprisonment. I'm not a fanatic, a terrorist, or a misguided misanthrope. I'm just enraged at a society that forces people to go outside the law to defend helpless animals. With the support of other animal rights activists and groups, we will expose the horror that so few of us see.

Finally, I urge everyone out there who has a home for a liberated animal to please let the support group know. This is our most vital need right now.

**For security reasons Robin preferred not to answer these questions!*

Texas Tech

1989

ALF TALKS!

My interview with two of the Animal Liberation Front cat liberators took nearly three weeks to set up. Finally, we met in the back parking lot of a Dallas coffee shop at 10 p.m. on a Thursday.

There, a serious young couple materialized in the darkness and introduced themselves as Dave and Jan. Both wore shaded glasses and hats that covered their hair. Jan "patted me down," checking for a hidden camera or microphone, then we all got into my car. Dave drove. After a few minutes, Jan, apologizing, slipped a scarf blindfold over my eyes.

About ten minutes later, the car stopped, and when Jan removed the blindfold, I saw that we were at a nondescript garden apartment. Over coffee in the kitchen we talked. Jan is a social worker, Dave a high school history teacher.

Jan: John Orem is what we call a career vivisector. That means he's typical of animal experimenters who make a handsome living mutilating animals with government funds. Someone on the inside said she had watched the cats suffer for years and that the ALF was her – and their – only hope. We had experts look Orem's papers over and they were sick at how stupid and cruel it was.

Me: So far he's received $900,000, hasn't he?

Dave: Yes. He's been riding the government grant gravy train, fueled with tortured cats, since 1977 and obviously plans to ride it until he retires, and the results of it all are a big fat zero.

Me: Couldn't you have contacted the authorities?

Jan: There's no point. No law's being broken. The stark truth is the Animal Welfare Act doesn't even cover animals during actual experiments. No law does. Not one! Experimenters don't even have to use anesthesia, and frequently they don't. When you complain to the funding agencies, they defend everything. To them there is no such thing as trash science, no such thing as too much pain.

Me: How did you gain entry to Orem's laboratory?

Dave: Shortly after 7 a.m. four of us went in and two of us stayed outside as lookouts. We had been in on a recky [reconnaissance] some weeks earlier. We knew exactly where to go.

Me: Were the cats afraid of you?

Dave: They were afraid of the men, not the women. They cringed and pulled back at first, as if expecting to be hurt. After we took the videos from Orem's office and gave his torture machinery what it deserved, two of us held the cat bags open while the women placed the cats gently inside them. As the others carried the cats out, I spray-painted "Don't mess with Texas Animals – ALF" on the wall.

Me: What happened to the cats?

Jan: We took them straight to a vet. Floyd was sick. The breathing tube hole in his neck was infected and he had an upper respiratory infection because his sinuses had been stripped by years of ammonium hydroxide blasts in the face. His hair was so badly matted that he had to be shaved. Cinders has peculiar stumps instead of legs. His growth has been severely stunted somehow. Black Cat had a traumatic hernia the size of a Texas grapefruit and that was removed right away.

Dave: Now they're all together many miles from here, healing inside and out with care and kindness, coming out of their shells.

Me: Why did you destroy that equipment?

Dave: Because its whole purpose is to cause pain. We didn't want Orem to pick up the phone and simply replace the cats. We want to make continuing barbaric, worthless experiments like his as expensive and as difficult as possible.

Me: Would you ever harm a person?

Dave: No. The ALF will break things, but we will never harm a living being. The vivisectors are terrorists. Every day they cut, shock, burn, poison and drive insane thousands of frightened, helpless, innocent animals. They kill without a thought. Our aim is to slow down and eventually stop their violence.

Jan: We want the public to know what's going on behind the locked laboratory doors. If they knew, they'll stop hearing the hype and help us stop the horror. That day, a lot of animals will be happy.

Interview with "Dave" and "Jan" — two activists behind the rescue of five cats from the Texas Tech lab of researcher John Orem.

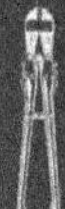

My Interview with two of the Animal Liberation Front cat liberators took nearly three weeks to set up. Finally we met in the back parking lot of a Dallas coffee shop at 10pm on a Thursday.

There, a serious young couple materialized in the darkness and introduced themselves as Dave and Jan. Both wore shaded glasses and hats that covered their hair. Jan "patted me down," checking for a hidden camera or microphone; then we all got into my car. Dave drove. After a few minutes, Jan, apologizing, slipped a scarf blindfold over my eyes.

About 10 minutes later, the car stopped, and when Jan removed the blindfold, I saw that we were at a nondescript garden apartment. Over coffee in the kitchen we talked. Jan is a social worker, Dave a high school history teacher.

John Orem is what we call a career vivisector. That means he's typical of animal experimenters who make a handsome living mutilating animals with government funds. Someone on the inside said she had watched the cats suffer for years and that the A.L.F. was her—and their—only hope. We had experts look Orem's papers over and they were sick at how stupid and cruel it was.

So far he's received $900,000, hasn't he?

Dave: Yes. He's been riding the government grant gravy train, fueled with tortured cats, since 1977 and obviously plans to ride it until he retires, and the results of it all are a big fat zero.

Couldn't you have contacted the authorities?

Jan: There's no point. No law's being broken. The stark truth is the Animal Welfare Act doesn't even cover animals during actual experiments. No law does. Not one! Experimenters don't even have to use anesthesia, and frequently they don't. When you complain to the funding agencies, they defend everything. To them there is no such thing as trash science, no such thing as too much pain.

How did you gain entry to Orem's laboratory?

Dave: Shortly after 7am four of us went in and two of us stayed outside as lookouts. We had been in on a rocky reconnaissance some weeks earlier. We knew exactly where to go.

Were the cats afraid of you?

Dave: They were afraid of the men, not the women. They cringed and pulled back at first, as if expecting to be hurt. After we took the videos from Orem's office and gave his torture machinery what it deserved, two of us held the cat bags open while the women placed the cats gently inside them. As the others carried the cats out, I spray painted: "Don't mess with Texas animals – A.L.F." on the wall.

What happened to the cats?

Jan: We took them straight to a vet. Floyd was sick. The breathing tube hole in his neck was infected and he had an upper-respiratory infection because his sinuses had been stripped by years of ammonium hydroxide blasts in the face. His hair was so badly matted that he had to be shaved. Cinders has peculiar stumps instead of legs. His growth has been severely stunted somehow. Black cat has a traumatic hernia the size of a Texas grapefruit and that was removed right away.

Dave: Now they're all together many miles from here. Healing inside and out with care and kindness, coming out of their shells.

Why did you destroy the equipment?

Dave: Because it's whole purpose is to cause pain. We didn't want Orem to pick up the phone and simply replace the cats. We want to make continuing barbaric, worthless experiments like his as expensive and as difficult as possible.

Would you ever harm a person?

Dave: No. The A.L.F. will break things, but we will never harm a living being. The vivisectors are terrorists. Every day they cut, shock, burn, poison and drive insane thousands of frightened, helpless, innocent animals. They kill without a thought. Our aim is to slow down and eventually stop their violence.

Jan: We want the public to know what's going on behind the locked laboratory doors. If they know, they'll stop hearing the hype and help us stop the horror. That day, a lot of animals will be happy.

University Of Arizona

1989

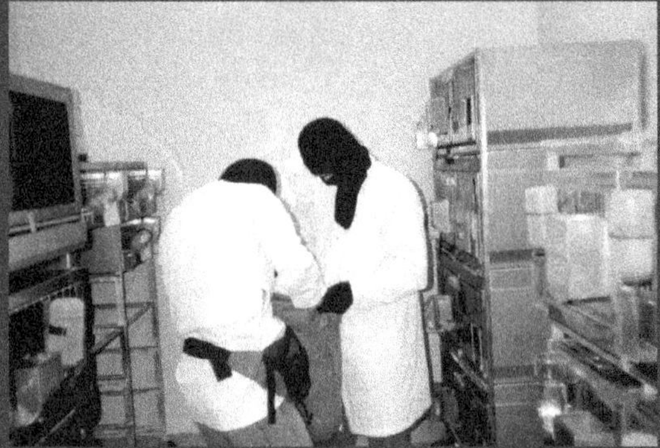

Mainstream newspaper *The Tucson Citizen* interviews a person behind the largest lab raid in US history.

The ALF: 'Fanatics' Or 'Liberators'?
by Carla McClain.

They are called terrorists, anarchists, violent fanatics and criminals by their detractors.

They are the Animal Liberation Front—the highly trained and highly secretive underground animal rights army that spans two continents and seeks to release all animals from what it believes is cruel exploitation by man.

To accomplish that, ALF members strike under cover of night and black hoods. They break down doors and windows, vandalize equipment, destroy records, set fires, set bombs, spray red paint, and steal—or "liberate"—animals.

They commit crimes for the sake of animals, especially animals in medical experimentation, and have rarely been caught or convicted.

Serious argument is going on within the animal rights movement over such tactics. Some believe the peaceful non-violent civil disobedience taught by Gandhi is the only way to stop pain and suffering. But others point out that it was not until A.L.F. broke into animal laboratories that the public got to see what was going on inside, and some of the practices were halted.

To date, the group has struck 85 times in this country and freed thousands of animals from universities and medical laboratories. Its most damaging bit was a $3.5 million fire at the University of California at Davis.

On April 3, A.L.F. members invaded the University of Arizona, setting two fires, taking more than 1,200 animals and causing some $250,000 worth of damage. They left behind a press release claiming credit for the raid, signed their initials on walls in red paint, made headlines across the country, and vanished.

For obvious reasons, the A.L.F. does not show its face to the public. However, in a rare exception in its 15 year history, members of A.L.F. — those who struck the UA — have been persuaded to talk to the mainstream press, in an interview with the Tucson Citizen.

What was your role in the raid on the University of Arizona?

My role was to get the animals out of the labs, get them into the vans, and get them away from the university. We took them first to a veterinarian. I won't be able to tell you any more details about the raid itself.

What condition were the animals in and what have you done with them?

The rabbits had shaved raw spots, and appeared to be intended for some kind of skin patch testing. Some of the mice had wounds, almost as if they had been chewed by other mice. Others were very sick with cryptosporidium. It was pitiful. They had horrible diarrhea. They were covered in liquid feces. Mice are naturally very clean animals. Rats and mice groom themselves very much the way cats do. The other animals were basically healthy, but obviously not well cared for. Those with the wounds were oozing and gaping. They lived in very tiny, bare cages.

Were you aware that the infected mice pose a hazard to the public health, that the virus they carry could prove fatal to infants or immuno-suppressed people?

"Crypto" is a very benign disease in most people; it produces mild flu-like symptoms for a short period. We did not take the mice to the homes of immuno-suppressed people. We took them straight to a veterinarian, which is where they will stay until they are healthy. We are the only ones who were exposed. We thought about that, but none of us got sick. The rest of the animals went on the underground railroad. Some are in foster homes, waiting to be placed, some are in permanent homes. They are now scattered all over the country. None of them is in Tucson.

The VA raid made a lot of people angry and frightened. You set fires, you damaged and stole public property. You didn't just "liberate" a few animals. People see this as crime, violence, even terrorism. How do you justify that?

Unfortunately, right now there is no other way to rescue animals, to prevent their (sic). I don't like to risk going to jail. This was not done on a whim. Right now, we have to rely on the U.S Department of Agriculture and the National Institutes of Health (US agencies) to protect animals in the laboratory, and this isn't happening. As just one example, James Wyngaarden (head of the NIH) called the University of Pennsylvania head injury lab "one of the best in the world" and that's frightening. The head injury lab was where they held inadequately anesthetized baboons in vises and then used a device to smash their heads. It was the ALF that broke in and got the films of these animals in agony, that showed the callousness of the researchers toward the animals. It was only after the public saw these films that the NIH had to stop funding this research, and the lab was shut down.

When you see this kind of thing, you realize that medical research is not benign, as we are told, that the animals are not always anesthetized, as we're always told. The federal Animal Welfare Act, which is the only law there is, only covers the care of the animals, not how they are used in experiments. You can do anything you want to an animal as long as the cage is cleaned, there is food and the water bowl is filled. The experimenter doesn't even have to use anesthesia if he thinks it will interfere with his results.

But why the fires and the vandalism, too?

It is valid to destroy any property that is used to harm animals, to harm any being that feels pain and fear. By vandalizing the labs, you make it more difficult for research to continue. You also make it more expensive to do it. And you make people who are considering experimenting on animals think twice about going into that. I do think that, in a way, it is much the same thing as the abolitionists who fought against slavery going in and burning down the quarters or tearing down the auction block or the whipping post—whatever is being used to subjugate the slaves. It's very much the same thing. I think it sends a message to researchers about how serious this is. Sometimes when you just take animals and do nothing else, perhaps that is not as strong a message.

Do you equate the enslavement, the "use" of humans with the enslavement and use of and use of non-human animals? Is this really the same thing?

No, of course humans and non-humans are not the same. No. But we can't make decisions based on who has the higher power of reasoning, who can talk, who is supposedly a "higher" being than another. Just because I eat spaghetti and you listen to Mozart, does that give you the right to cause me pain? To take my life? To have control over me.

The only judgment we can make, the only ethical judgment, is whether someone has the capacity to feel pain and fear—to suffer. If a being feels those things, and animals do as much as you or I, then we have no right to cause them pain or fear. Just because a dog can't read a book or drive a car doesn't give me the right to feed him a quart of Drano to find out how toxic it is. The dog feels the agony of that as much as we would; he convulses just as we would.

The philosophy that drives the ALF is research the belief that animals do not belong to us. They don't exist for our use- not to eat, not to experiment on. They are individual feeling beings with their own lives to lead. They have a right to see the sun and live with their companions in the same way that we do. They have the same right not to have pain inflicted on them that we do. And beyond that, because man does have dominion over animals, we have an obligation to do whatever we can to protect them.

But when you go in and set fires, you risk killing a human being. What if the night janitor had been caught in there that morning at the VA? What if some students you didn't know about had been studying there all night and they had died in one of those fires? It is said that it is only a matter of time until the ALF kills someone with these tactics.

I would like to say that every care was taken to make sure no one would be harmed. We felt sure that the fires were set in such a way that they would not harm people and we took every precaution. It is possible to make sure. We know what we are doing, and it is one of the rules of the ALF that no one will be injured. Property yes, people no. No one has ever been harmed in an ALF raid.

In this raid, for example, we decided that if a guard showed up, we would not knock him out or in any way manhandle him. We decided we would take no physical action, we would be caught red handed rather than harm the guard. The ALF has never hurt anyone, yet researchers are harming animals every day. And they call us terrorists; that's a little ironic.

It is important to remember that the real violence is being done to animals in the labs. If someone caught you and put you in a cage and fed you poisons and pesticides or starved you or electroshocked you, you would hope someone would break in and rescue you. If you saw someone shocking or burning a kitten in the street, you would run up to and take that kitten away from that person, even if he or she owned it. You'd do it. People bum and blowtorch and shock animals in the labs, they drive them insane, they kill them, that's the reality, but it is going on behind closed doors that no one can get past. That doesn't mean we should ignore it.

But why not try non-violent disobedience instead of violence to accomplish these goals? People who did that Gandhi and Martin Luther King,

for example- literally changed the world, and ended whole eras of pain and suffering.

I have participated in civil disobedience a number of times. It's a very valuable and effective tactic to bear public witness against the wrong done to animals, and I will continue to do it. But for civil disobedience to really change things, you need great numbers of people to do it. Although animal rights is now a national movement, it is still young and we need to inform people about what's really going on in the labs, and the break-ins are doing that.

What has been revealed by lab break-ins?

Well, the list is long, but here are some of the worst. First, the head bashing lab at the University of Pennsylvania.

A couple of years before that. One of the first exposes was the research of Edward Taub in Maryland, which was done on monkeys supposedly to help stroke victims. He cut the spinal nerves to cripple the monkey's limbs, then using electric shock, tried to force the monkeys to use the crippled limbs. Alex Pacheco (now head of People for The Ethical Treatment of Animals) went undercover in that lab for four months and documented and photographed how the monkeys lived in constant fear, how they mutilated themselves, chewed off their own fingers, the filth they lived in. After Pacheco went to the police, the lab was raided and the research finally was shut down.

A raid in 1984 at the City of Hope in California found animals used for cancer and infectious disease research were kept in conditions so bad that they were dying even before they got into the experiments. Dogs had inhaled their own feces, monkeys had died of exposure or been killed by other monkeys. It was revealed the animals were suffering terribly.

Another was the raid on the SEMA lab in Maryland, which contracts to do research for the federal government. There, baby chimpanzees were being used for AIDS and hepatitis research. Again, the documents and the videos taken showed an extremely high death rate due to miserable conditions- monkeys driven insane in isolation chambers, steamed to death when pipes broke, suffocated when the ventilation system failed. Others were starved to death when their feet caught on the slats of their cages and they couldn't get to their food and no one noticed. Chimps are animals very close to man in their social needs and physical reactions, yet this is how they lived. After hearing about this raid, Jane Goodall asked for a tour of the SEMA lab and when she got out of there, she said it was the second worst day of her life. The worst day was when her husband died. There are many more (examples).

But, at least in the case of the VA, a lot of people reacted angrily to the fires, and those who set them, and it seemed as if the raid backfired as far as your public relations go. Could you be making more enemies than friends this way?

We have discussed that possibility. It's a concern. I understand it can happen, but the point is people have been trying for the past 100 years by the usual means- letters, protests- to stop the use of animals in experiments, or even just to make it more humane. But what has happened is the use of animals has increased in savagery, if anything, because of new technology that is used now. It is time to look at other methods.

Even if we do alienate some people, the benefits outweigh that- saving the lives of individual animals, and finding out what actually is going on behind the closed doors that the public is paying for but is told nothing about.

The ALF and animal rights groups claim that no good whatsoever comes out of animal medical experiments. Even if we concede that a chunk of it is repetitive and does not produce results, there is no denying that such life-saving breakthroughs as the polio vaccine, insulin, organ transplant surgery, and cancer drugs evolved out of animal experiments. Would you forego those lifesaving treatments altogether?

Even if you put aside the ethical position that we do not have a right to do this to beings capable of suffering, in a very large sense, when we do animal experiments, we are actually harming human health. I know that sounds strange. Let me explain.

Using our tax dollars on animal experiments is taking public money away from helping humans. As just one example... at Yale University, 3 million dollars a year is being used for addictive drug experiments on cats and monkeys. That's three times the amount available in the whole state of Connecticut for drug treatment centers for sick human beings. People are ruining their lives and dying all over the country because there are such long waiting lines to get into drug treatment centers.

Another example. There is very little money available for long-term care for the disabled people, to help them live normal lives. But Edward Taub can get millions to cripple monkeys. Babies are born every day retarded and with birth defects because their moms do not get adequate prenatal care or enough food, yet we pay big sums to prove that baby monkeys go crazy when their mothers are taken away from them at birth. The infant mortality rate for black infants in the nation's capital is higher than it is in Costa Rica. How can we justify pouring millions into animal research when we know what these human babies need but aren't getting?

Beyond that, researchers take credit for breakthroughs in such things as ending epidemics of infectious diseases, when history shows that it was improved sanitation systems and techniques that get the bulk of the credit for that.

Transplant surgery is interesting. Yes, they spent years experimenting on animals to transplant organs and to test the artificial heart. Yet every human being given a transplant in the early days has died, if not on the operating table right after. It took years of human transplants before they got it right. The first humans on the artificial heart suffered debilitating brain damage due to strokes—something all that animal work never even suggested would happen.

The polio vaccine—as far back as 1949, scientists knew how to grow the polio virus in human cell cultures, and it was recommended that a vaccine should be developed that way. But that was ignored and animals were used because it was a longtime habit and much more convenient. So the rhesus monkey population in India was nearly wiped out by that research.

It has always been more cheap and convenient to use animals, when there are other, better ways, given a little scientific creativity. But we just don't bother.

The Centers for Disease Control recently did a major study of the leading U.S factors affecting the U.S death rate. The most influential factor, accounting for 51% of all deaths, was lifestyle. Environment—pollutants and toxins—was second at 20%. Heredity was third at 19%, and medical intervention was the last at 10%. Yet by far, most of the money goes into animal experiments for that last and least influential factor.

Who are you-are you a professional activist or do you have a normal everyday life? Why did you decide to take such risks for this cause?

I think I am a pretty normal person- I have a job, a house, a mortgage. My job is in social work. I got into the animal movement years ago during my first year of medical school. I dropped out in my first semester because of the dog lab. I couldn't handle cutting open live dogs and killing them for that purpose. I'm embarrassed to say now I did nothing about it at the time except to leave school. Since then, I have done a great deal of reading, and I started thinking about how we use animals, reading medical journals, and I wondered why we had the right to do these things. Over time, I became a vegan.

Before you can join the ALF, you are checked out thoroughly, for your sincerity, your commitment, your commitment, for years of action in the movement, for a willingness to go to jail if you have to. It is not easy to get into the ALF. To be honest, I'd really rather have a normal life, and devote myself to growing a garden maybe. But now that I know what goes on in the labs, on the factory farms, I can't ignore it. I feel a sense of personal responsibility about what society does to animals.

It is as if I were living in Nazi Germany an in my town there was a Buchenwald and I knew it and I did nothing. People who tried to stop those horrors got killed for it. At least I won't be killed for this.

OK, what's next for the ALF?

Well, as soon as we finish placing the UA animals, there will be another raid. We are looking forward to that. I will be in many more of them.

Darren Thurston

1996

Hallway of the Ellerslie cat & dog facility.

Convicted A.L.F. activist reveals the how-to's behind a break-in and rescue at the University Of Alberta, and his subsequent arrest.

How did you get involved in animal rights?

I started getting involved in the hard-core/ alternative/straight-edge music scene in 1985/6 and through that got involved in animal rights/ liberation. I stopped eating meat and, shortly after, stopped eating dairy and eggs. I formed an Animal Rights group called Citizens Organized for Animal Liberation because none of the local AR groups wanted to do civil disobedience actions or even demonstrations. They would do their annual anti-fur pickets and the odd anti-rodeo and anti-circus pickets and sit on the fence the rest of the time.

What led you to take a more militant approach to animal liberation and join the A.L.F.?

First off, animal rights organizing was very frustrating. I saw animals every day getting killed and tortured for human greed, vanity and food, while people wanted to write letters and talk to vivisectors about the 'problem.'

Secondly, you can't join the Animal Liberation Front. It has no central command, address, or membership list. The A.L.F. is everywhere. It's composed of dedicated people who take the first step and do something~smash a window, glue a lock, spray paint a butcher shop, free some mink, burn a meat truck, liberate some animals from a laboratory. Remember, YOU ARE THE A.L.F.! And the animals need you NOW.

How did you learn to do A.L.F. actions?

I never really learned from anywhere or anyone. But I do remember an old adage that "practice makes perfect" or something along those lines. For those that would like to learn the finer details of how to do certain things, they are available in numerous booklets.

What security precautions did you see activists take while involved in the A.L.F.?

Physical security was a major concern of everyone as it always should be. You have to assume that every word you say over a telephone is being heard, pay telephones included. Never talk inside anyone's home or vehicle, both can and are bugged very easily.

The best cover of course is to have never been involved in above-ground animal rights organizing at all. Animal Rights groups are the first place the police will start looking for suspects. Police regularly video tape demonstrations so they know who is active. More and more activists are forming small tight knit groups of close friends that they can work with. We are also seeing activists both here in North America and in England go underground so that they may continue direct action against the animal abusers and/or avoid arrest.

What was the University of Alberta doing to the animals?

I had done some research in the University library and found information about the ongoing experiments at the University of Alberta such as the testing of drugs on primates, spinal cord research on cats, smoking experiments on dogs, etc. A lot of the cats that were liberated would have ended up having their spinal cords broken and drugs tested on them.

How did you obtain that information?

A lot of it came from lab animal research journals and other University publications at the University libraries. The vivisectors love publishing papers of how they torture and mutilate animals in order to get further research grants. It doesn't take that long to figure out how to use any University's computer search functions and check out ongoing experiments and specific researchers.

What did you do to prepare for the raid?

I watched the entire facility for numerous days and nights familiarizing myself with the normal routine of the facility; the time the staff came and left work, when staff that lived on the farm/facility were at home and when they went to sleep, at what time University security did their routine checks. I also obtained both road and aerial maps of the area from local libraries.

The facility was quite large—it has approx. a dozen buildings including breeding facilities for mice, cows, pigs, sheep, dogs and cats. Two caretakers (both vivisectors) lived in separate houses on the facility.

Any other planning?

I picked a night that I knew would be quiet, a new moon when there would be very little moonlight. We also made a visit to the facility the night before the raid to make sure everything was in place and to familiarize everyone of what the facility looked like and what their roles were.

What equipment was necessary to do the raid?

Hmm...... Well, let's see; crowbar, large ball-peen hammer, portable electric drill, radios, radio frequency-scanners (so we could listen to both University Security and the Police), pick-up truck, cat carriers, paint, large bags.

How did you carry all of the equipment inside?

There wasn't all that much equipment needed, a duffel bag and back-pack worked fine.

How did you handle the security systems and enter the building?

The facility had a security system including an ADT card entry system at the front door, and an intrusion alarm system—the vast majority of the facility was totally insecure though. There were numerous windows that it would have been very easy to break and enter through, including windows directly into the large cat colony cages. There were many doors that could have been opened in a variety of different ways; pushing hinge pins out, drilling large holes right through, drilling or picking locks, or forcing the locks with a crowbar. Mysteriously though, the door we went to, which opened directly into the cat kennel room, was left unlocked?!

What did you do when you entered the building?

Immediately went to work getting the cats out. The most important part of the action was getting the animals out safely. Once that was done the other tasks could be completed; finding and taking important files and of course economic damage.

There was approx. $100,000 in damage done to the facility. Could you tell us what equipment you damaged and why?

There was only one small laboratory in the dog and cat kennel we were in. We damaged as much as we could in the entire building after all the cats were safely away from the facility. Damaging torture devices and other equipment makes them inoperable to torture and kill animals anymore otherwise they could go back to torturing animals the very next day. Destroying the actual instruments of torture is practical. It ensures that the sadism will be stopped at least temporarily. It also ensures that they will be wasting money (which would have otherwise gone to vivisection) to hire extra security and install expensive alarm systems.

How did you damage it?

Inside the laboratory itself, we forced open every locked storage cabinet, dumping the contents on the floor, smashed sterilizers and other equipment and splashed red paint everywhere. In their office, boxes of files pertaining to illegal sources of the dogs they used and research were taken, everything else was scattered on the floor and then soaked in muriatic acid. Throughout the facility, slogans were spray painted, red paint splashed on walls, electrical cords cut, toilets and sinks smashed.

There was also one delivery truck outside used to transport animals from the facility back and forth to the main University lab, it had paint stripper dumped all over and the tires slashed and was also spray painted with slogans.

How did you leave the "blood" marks on the wall?

Red paint that had been thinned a little and placed into several plastic 2 liter soda bottles, which made it very easy to splash anywhere and everywhere.

What did you wear during the raid?

Coveralls to keep clothes underneath paint free, gloves, inexpensive throwaway shoes and balaclavas (in case of video security cameras.)

How did you get the animals out and how many were there?

The cats were originally going to be placed in large cloth bags and then carried to an awaiting vehicle and placed into cardboard cat carriers. Upon putting the first cat into a bag it was promptly shredded. So much for that plan—plan two went into effect as the cardboard cat carriers were carried two at a time across a long field, two cats placed in each box and then carried all the way back to the awaiting vehicle. 29 cats were liberated all together.

How long did the University raid take?

The entire time inside the facility probably took 3 hours or so, mostly because it took so long transporting the cats across a field to the truck.

How did you re-home the animals?

I did not take part in the re-homing of the animals. The cats were supposed to go to a home that would hold them for a while and then send them off to other homes where they could live out their lives free. The homes didn't get set in advance as they were supposed to. With a lot of hard work and stress, homes were finally found.

Is there anything you would have done differently?

The film and video footage taken and sent to the media had too many traces of where they were taken and helped police to track down the motel we used after words. More thought definitely needed to be put into not leaving any trace of location as to where the photos were taken.

How did you get caught?

An informant named Jessica Sandham. She was a woman who had rented a motel room where the cats were to be taken after the raid (where video and still photographs for the media were taken). Jessica who rented the room didn't have to show any identification at all but instead showed her own and did not tell anyone else that she had done this. Investigators, who started checking every motel/hotel in the entire city looking for similarities to the media, video and still photographs tracked down the motel we used. The room was rented by Jessica who was already in the National Crime Index Computer (unknown to me or her at that time) as a suspected animal liberation radical which of course rang big warning bells. After placing her under physical surveillance for over a week, on June 19th members of the Integrated Intelligence Unit knocked on her door and asked her to answer questions. Instead of saying "NO COMMENT" or "call my lawyers" or "fuck off," she went with them to answer questions.

She was questioned for 4 1/2 hours on video-tape (unknown to her). Where the police tried all the typical police tricks and traps and she went for them all and talked freely about all she knew including rumors about the UofA raid. The police led her questions and tried to scare her by mentioning the so-called increasing "violence" in the animal liberation movement and my completely legal possession of several firearms.

What happened to Jessica Sandham?

Jessica Michelle Charlotte Sandham (DOB Jan. 31/1973) is free, has always been free and was never arrested, we know immediately after the arrests she moved to another city and has since moved back to Edmonton and lives with her parents (12033-4t St., Edmonton, AB, Canada 403-479-1898). She was immediately disowned by the animal liberation community in which she was active. She has been labeled a traitor and informant in Canada.

Can you tell us about your initial arrest experience?

I was arrested Friday June 19th at approx. 5:30 pm. I had just finished working at a small store where I was the manager. The police, who had placed me under 24 hour physical surveillance since June 3 (two days after the action), knew where I was. I was standing at a transit stop when I heard a car screech to a stop behind me. As I glanced over my shoulder I saw two large men, obviously cops, jumping out with guns drawn.

I was originally charged with 4 counts (Break and Enter, Mischief over $1000, Theft over $1000 and including a conspiracy charge that was later dropped) related to the UOfA liberation, after I was taken to the police station. I was then put in a holding tank and finally brought into an interview room with one of the cops. He proceeded to ask me a huge list of questions, to which I responded with little except that I would like to talk to a lawyer. As I was being arrested, the police were also executing search warrants on my partner's and my apartment and a friend's home. A warrant was also issued for the arrest of a friend of mine, Grant.

Can you explain your experience with the courts and jail?

I was finally processed after about 5 hours at the police station and 12 hours sitting in a holding tank at the Remand Center and moved to a really dirty and cold dormitory with 80+ other men. Next I was called out again and taken over to the police station to be charged with another 3 charges (arson and two mischief's). These charges were in regards to two actions at Billingsgate Fish Market.

One was in December 1991 when the store and 4 large fish delivery trucks were spray painted with slogans, tires slashed and incendiary devices left on their front seats. Three of the incendiaries ignited causing approx. $75,000 damage. The other action (also at Billingsgate Fish Company) was the following month when their store and three replacement rental trucks were spray painted with slogans and tires slashed.

After a few days, I finally got moved into a unit in the Remand Center, bunked up with a hyperactive 18 year old car thief, and another 56 'children' on one of two units called "the zoo" (so-called because of all the fights and craziness in general).

I finally obtained a good lawyer, one of the top lawyers in Alberta, who took the case for a very low expense. He did his best and more a lot of the time. I would have much rather had an animal activist lawyer, but there's just not that many around in Canada.

About four days after my arrest late one night just after lock-up, I got called out again and was brought over to the police station to be charged with yet more charges. This time I was charged with another 7 charges related to damage done to three billboards carrying advertisements for the Fur Council of Canada. At one of the signs a note was left for Hook Outdoor Advertising telling them to stop running the ads or it would be their most expensive advertisement campaign ever. At the end of December the A.L.F. entered Hook's yard and wrote a long message on the side of one of their vans telling about the horrors of fur production and one of the boom trucks was gutted by fire, another charge of arson. On Jan. 1, 1992 at Oullette Meat Packers, a van had it's tires slashed, side window smashed and a timed incendiary device was left on the seat. Both the building and van were painted with slogans. The incense sticks had gone out (according to court testimony) for some reason—extreme cold, wind? And so one more attempted arson charge and another mischief charge. The police were telling me they want six years in prison.

Approximately June 29, 1992 a Canada-wide arrest warrant was issued for David Barbarash and photos of David were circulated to television stations and newspapers.

David was wanted for three charges related to the UofA liberation (Break and Enter, Mischief over $1000, Theft over $1000). The Royal Canadian Mounted Police visited several activist's homes in B.C. looking for David. David disappeared underground.

My attorney had seven separate bail hearings to try and get me released on bail, even with numerous conditions, to no avail. I was refused on the grounds that I 'was a threat to society' and that 'I may not appear for trial'. Even after my family offered to put up property and $50,000 cash for my bail. At the bail hearing before mine one day, the same judge granted bail for a person convicted of murder that was facing a trial for manslaughter.

Early September 1993, I finally got my 4 day preliminary trial, after I'd been inside for over 14 months. Jessica Sandham took the stand and testified about her role in the UofA liberation - renting a motel room, buying paint and meeting with several people from 'out of town'. She also talked about the Billingsgate arson and how I had allegedly said that it looked like it would have been easy or was easy. The police testified all about the actions that I was charged with. My attorney got the police to answer questions about the surveillance they undertook and we learned that they had me and my residence under 24 hour physical surveillance in December 1992 for three weeks. June 3rd two days after the UofA liberation they had set up 24 hour physical surveillance on me and Grant, both our residence's, Jessica, and several 'targets' that they hoped might get 'hit'. They had placed legal 'bugs' on both mine and Grants phones and also a 'bug' in my residence. We also got the police to testify about involvement in the case from the FBI, BATF and Michigan University Police. Members from all three had actually traveled to Edmonton to take part in a second search of my residence, looking for more 'evidence'. Police also testified that the FBI took photocopies of all of my files, an entire filing cabinet. So four days later it was over and now it was time to wait for a two week trial.

After a few weeks I finally heard that my trial date was not going to be for another 8-12 months and I would be in jail the whole time. The situation re: the UofA and the Billingsgate arson charges wasn't looking all that good because of evidence against me. My attorney had been trying to get me a deal where I would plead guilty to the UofA and the Billingsgate arson charges and I would get out with time served, the other charges would be dropped. On Oct. 12, 1993, I plead guilty to three charges—Break and Enter to Commit Theft and Mischief (UofA liberation) and arson (Billingsgate fire). I was acquitted of all the other charges against me. Later that day I walked out a free man after 15 1/2 months inside.

Within one week after I was out, I got a visit from the chief investigator, serving me with appeal papers. The police and prosecution didn't think that my 15 1/2 months locked up was enough. They wanted me to serve several more years. On March 8th, 1994, five months after I got out, the appeal was heard at the Alberta Court of Appeals (the highest court in Alberta). The Appeals Court reserved their decision. Their decision came several weeks later; they sentenced me to another two years, less a day inside. I was taken into custody immediately and shipped back to the Edmonton Remand Center.

From Edmonton Remand I was transferred and spent 4 1/2 months in Calgary Correctional Facility (Spy Hill) and then 5 months at Fort Saskatchewan Correction Facility (The Fort). A lot of my time was spent on the phone helping out with other prisoners' support including Rod's (who had just been arrested) and working towards an early release. I spent my spare time reading, writing, playing cards, and working out. Time went by a lot quicker than in the Remand Center because there was a little more to do.

Finally out Jan., 1995, I was granted an early release under probation and partial house arrest. I accepted it and was out yet again. For 4 months I was to be home from 6pm till 6 am, parole workers would call every night to make sure I was home and also knock on the door every other day or so. I also had to see my probation officer every week. After approx. 5 months, I was finally finished with the house arrest portion of my probation and now just had to visit every two weeks. Two days before completing it, my probation office ordered me over the phone to attend a meeting at his office on one hour's notice—I refused. The next morning when I called him, he told me to turn myself in—he had pulled my probation because I was allegedly seen at the airport boarding a plane (I was not allowed to leave Edmonton without permission as part of my probation conditions). After contacting my attorney for advice on what to do, he told me that they could pull it at will and that I would likely have to serve another two weeks until my sentence expiration. Three days later I turned myself in and served another 10 days.

What happened to your co-defendant in this case?

Grant was arrested the day after me on June 20th on nothing other than complete speculation. He was charged with the same four counts related to the U of A liberation that I was. Approx. ten days later he was released on $4000 cash bail and stiff conditions including moving 3 hours away to another city to live with his parents, a curfew and report once a week until his trial. Grant did not have a criminal record and was 29 at the time. At Grant's trial several months later the prosecutor gave him a stay of charges because they had no evidence at all.

How long were you in jail?

All together, just under two years.

What was prison like?

It was the first time I had been to jail in my life so it was quite eye opening in the beginning. I didn't know what to expect really. You got used to the routine really quick—you don't have much of a choice. Overall it really wasn't that bad though.

Did you fear for your personal safety while in prison?

No. Things were a little crazy at times, I got into several fights over my beliefs.

Did prison have any effects on you?

Being imprisoned strengthened my resolve even more. It gave me the chance to improve my mind and body. I got involved in weight training and jogging which strengthened my body. It made me realize even more that we need to keep up the pressure on animal abusers around the world on every level, both above-ground and the underground. We can win this war! I certainly knew that if I was caught doing A.L.F. activity, I could end up serving time in jail. But those are the risks we take. Every A.L.F. activist must be ready to go to jail rather than incriminate other A.L.F. activists or do anything that would put the animals' freedom at risk.

Do you have any regrets?

I wish we could have taken every animal there.

What words of wisdom do you have for other activists?

Don't let anything get you down, there's a lot of bad stuff happening out there, and things are pretty tough sometimes. Actions can still be done and NEED to happen. Work with as few people as you need to, make sure you know them all VERY well and KEEP YOUR MOUTH SHUT! You don't need to spread rumors or gossip about other activists and actions or about your own. I'm in this for the animals—if you're not, get the fuck out.

David Barbarash

2001

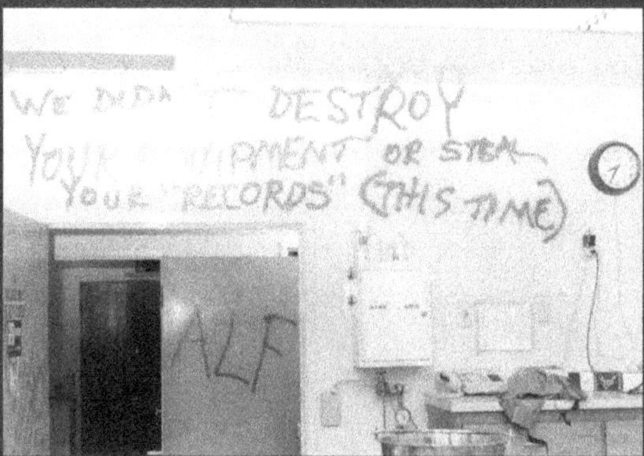

Convicted A.L.F. activist and former A.L.F. spokesperson discusses a wide range of direct action related topics in this lengthy interview.

What is the ALF?

The Animal Liberation Front isn't really an organization, but more of an international movement of animal liberation activists who believe conventional methods of protest aren't enough to obtain the goals of animal liberation, and that there is a moral justification for taking action outside the law. Activists operate anonymously, usually at night, in cell-like structures of two to eight or more people. Sometimes you could have an ALF activist going out alone to spraypaint a wall, but usually even for simple actions like that you'd want someone looking down the street.

Members of the ALF follow a strict code of non-violence. This means that there will be no harm, injury or death occurring to any animals, human or non-human, during the course of an action. We don't consider the destruction of property a violent action, because we don't believe you can do violence against something that isn't alive, that cannot feel pain.

The goals of the ALF are to liberate animals from laboratories or other places of abuse. We set them free into the wild whenever it's feasible, as in the case of mink or fox from fur farms. For obvious reasons animals liberated from laboratories aren't set free in the wild, but are placed into homes. In fact finding homes for these animals is just as much a part of the action as taking them out of the labs.

As well as liberating animals, the ALF participates in what we call economic sabotage: we destroy property used to abuse, torture, and kill animals. We draw parallels with the freedom fighters in Nazi Germany, who liberated prisoners of war and destroyed equipment used by Nazis to torture or kill their victims. There was moral justification for taking action then, and we believe there is today as well.

The ALF doesn't have a hierarchy of species: we don't place humans above animals so far as their inherent right to live, and to live without being tortured. We don't see a fundamental difference between a human killed in a gas chamber in Nazi Germany or a mink gassed on a fur farm.

What's the scope of the ALF? Is it six people doing one action per year?

It's hard to gauge the scope because we don't hear about every action, for example spraypainting walls, or going to McDonald's and breaking windows.

We do hear about the main actions—the arsons, the liberations—and the last few years have seen a sharp increase in actions against laboratories and university research facilities. Prior to that, those kinds of actions had dropped off for quite a while, as those facilities had become more aware of our tactics, and increased their security. But just last year we had four or five attacks on university research facilities or vivisection labs in North America, including animal liberation from these labs, in addition to any number of smaller raids on slaughterhouses, fur retailers, fur farms, and so on. Also we're seeing an increased use of fire through the use of incendiary devices.

Which of course necessitates getting the animals out first.

Fires aren't set at any structures where lives could be involved. I guess it's possible that if all the animals were released the facility would be burned, but normally the ALF are only able to remove a certain percentage of the animals.

How does someone choose which to remove?

It's hard, especially when you know what's going to happen to those you leave behind. I was faced with that dilemma in a raid I did in Edmonton. We took out twenty-nine cats, but had to leave the rest behind. We also had to leave the dogs, and all sorts of other animals. You have to find homes for the animals before you do the action, so if you've found homes for thirty cats and five dogs, that's all you can take, unless you want to risk trying to place them afterwards.

For basic security reasons, the people who house the animals likely aren't the same as those who release them. Instead the people who create sanctuaries for these animals are part of a loose network we call the Underground Railroad, after the slave liberation movement.

So there's a fairly large support network.

As is true for any underground or revolutionary network, the ALF wouldn't be as effective if there wasn't a support network. I don't have any direct contact with ALF members, but I'm considered part of the support network, because I'm the media liaison. Then there's a support group in Guelph, Ontario, that raises funds for imprisoned ALF activists, and publicizes actions and issues in their magazine, Underground. In addition, there's an informal network of animal rights activists in the aboveground movement who support the work of the ALF. The Underground Railroad houses rescued animals and sometimes even ALF activists. Without the support of these people, the ALF wouldn't be nearly so successful.

How is contact made between the actual liberators and the Underground Railroad without giving away the liberators' identities?

That's a risk. ALF activists have to personally approach individuals they think are sympathetic and able to care for animals. When I talk about the Underground Railroad, I don't mean there's a formal network communicating with each other. Instead, it's an informal group of people who care about animals and are willing to take them in. If there are real security concerns, the ALF activist would have a trusted intermediary make the contact. The ALF always operate on a need-to-know basis, generally only talking about actions among themselves. If the activists are smart at all, they don't boast or brag about their actions to other people, or use the phone, or anything like that.

Where did the ALF come from?

It started in the United Kingdom in 1976. Before that, in the 1960s and early 1970s, animal rights activists began the Hunt Saboteurs Association, which sabotaged fox hunts by blowing whistles, calling off dogs, and so on. That movement continues to this day: it's very large, and strong enough that the Labour government of Tony Blair is considering banning fox hunting. That was really the perfect issue to start with, since fox hunting is such an easy target. It's so cruel, and there are obvious class issues involved.

In the early 70s, some members of the Hunt Saboteurs Association formed another organization called the Band of Mercy so they could focus on more issues, and also so they could begin employing other tactics, such as property destruction. In 1973 the Band of Mercy set fire to a pharmaceutical company, and in 1974 and 1975 they liberated animals from lab animal breeders and vivisection labs.

Some of these activists eventually served jail time. When Ronnie Lee got out in 1976, he reformed the Band of Mercy into the Animal Liberation Front. By 1979 they'd made their first appearance in North America, when a group under the ALF banner raided New York University and liberated a couple of dogs. They emerged in Canada in 1980 with a raid on the Hospital for Sick Children in which they liberated some cats. That raid led to a famous picture that made the front page of the Toronto Star of a cat without any ears. For the last twenty years the actions have been accelerating.

The last few years have seen the development of the ELF, or Earth Liberation Front. An offshoot of Earth First!, they're similar to the ALF in their tactics and philosophy, except their focus has expanded to include the earth and ecology as well as animals.

Being a much newer organization, the ELF doesn't have as many actions under its belt, but there've been some huge ones. They're responsible for the most costly act of economic sabotage ever in North America, burning down five structures, including a huge restaurant, at a ski resort near Vail, Colorado.

The ski resort was expanding into a public roadless area—some of the last lynx habitat in the state—in a massive act of environmental destruction (and corporate welfare). Five days after legal remedies were exhausted and the ski expansion was given the go-ahead, ELF activists burned down the buildings, at a cost to the corporation of twelve million dollars. Since then a grand jury was convened which targeted local environmentalists, but no charges have ever been laid, or suspects identified. I think the costliest act of economic sabotage before that here in North America was in 1987, when the ALF burned down the UC Davis Diagnostic Laboratory, which was under construction. The cost for that one was about five million dollars.

I need to add that when we talk about the costs of economic sabotage, those are only the immediate costs. We hope of course that we'll convince them not to rebuild, at the risk of facing similar consequences again. But even if they do rebuild, the actions will continue to cost them because they've had to increase their security. And they know they're always a target.

There are other costs associated with sabotage, too. If you just burn down a structure like a fur feed warehouse, you've got a million and a half dollars worth of damage, and that's it. But if you destroy the computer equipment in a university laboratory, you're taking out five or ten years of research, much of which has to be redone, or may even be lost forever.

I read all the time – maybe a few times a month – about activists destroying genetically engineered crops. Is that the ELF?

Sometimes. But most of those actions have been claimed by various groups like Reclaim the Seeds, Future Farmers of America, and so on. These groups are springing up all over; there is tremendous discontent with the status quo, and it's manifesting all over in action.

Does the ALF do any hacking?

There was a faction of the ALF called something like the ALF Internet Task Force that targeted companies with a program called floodnet, generating a huge number of emails to certain accounts and overloading their systems. They only did that a couple of times, and I haven't heard from them since. I do know that those actions happen all the time, but it's very rare for them to be claimed by the ALF or any other group.

How heterogeneous is the ALF?

Since it's an underground movement, we obviously don't know precise demographics. But we have an idea based on who's been arrested and convicted. In North America we've had everyone from young punk kids, anarchist teenagers, to people in their twenties and thirties like myself and my cat rescuing partner, Darren Thurston, to grandmothers and older women like the Chatham Five, who were convicted of releasing mink from a fur farm in Chatham, Ontario.

There've been a fair number of studies done on the animal rights movement, and they used to say the average animal rights activist was a middle-aged, middle-class white woman. I'm not sure that's still true. I think the ALF is made up of those people, and people with dreadlocks, and people who believe animal rights is the only issue and don't concern themselves with any other social justice issues, and people who're aware of racism, sexism, homophobia, and who work on all those issues. I have to say, however, that at least for now there aren't a lot of people of color in the movement, with some exceptions, like Rod Coronado, who is half Yaqui Indian, half Mexican.

I've heard of him.

Like myself, Rod Coronado has been involved with non-violent direct action for many years. I remember in 1989 when I and four friends were facing charges in Toronto for spray painting a KFC and other minor ALF actions, Rod and two of his friends were facing similar charges in Vancouver. But before that he took responsibility for a Sea Shepherd action which involved scuttling Icelandic whaling vessels and destroying a processing plant. Rod has also served time in jail for leading an ALF campaign against the fur industry which involved releasing animals and burning down fur research labs.

How do you respond to the label you get so often in the corporate press, about being eco-terrorists or animal rights terrorists?

I completely reject the terrorist label. People who have a vested interest in abusing or killing animals aren't going to want to understand what the ALF is about, and will try to make sure no one else understands, either. So they paint ALF or ELF activists as terrorists. But here's my question for them: Where's the body count? Show me the people who've died or even been injured as a result of animal liberation actions. Show me even a fire-fighter injured putting out a blaze caused by the ALF. They can't, because no one has ever been injured.

I'll tell you what has happened, though. Activists have been bombed. Activists have been shot. I can show you people who've been beaten up and put into the hospital at regular fur protests, and people who've had all their teeth knocked out with baseball bats. I can tell you about ALF activists who've been shot in the back. I could show you a list of animal abusers—people who for a living do violence on animals—who've used violence as a way to combat animal liberators. I can't find one instance of a victim of violence from an animal liberator, yet we are the ones who are constantly labeled as terrorists. It's absurd.

What about the razor blades?

A group called the Justice Department, an extreme faction of the animal liberation movement, has said they're willing to harm humans to further animal liberation goals. They have carried out these booby trapped razor blade letter campaigns in England, the U.S. and in Canada, targeting individuals associated to animal cruelty and abuse. It's not unusual in human society to have people bent on doing violence and harm to others, and the animal liberation movement is no different. Same goes for the anti-abortionists, the black liberationists, native sovereignty, and others. The Justice Dept. is very clearly a small minority, and the vast majority of animal rights supporters are non-violent. But even when you analyse the JD razor blade actions and the amount of actual harm they can inflict on someone, how does that compare to what faces animals in labs or those being hunted? I'm not going to justify that kind of violence, because I don't believe in it, but I don't think causing razor cuts on fingers equates to terrorism, not compared to what's been inflicted on activists by animal abusers, certainly not compared to what, for example, the

US military does on a routine basis, and absolutely not compared to the vast torture of non-human animals on which our system is based.

Even if we include the razor cuts – and I realize the razors were not sent by the ALF—it seems the level of effort that goes into squelching the ALF is often out of scale with the damage—and I'm thinking of the liberations and sabotage—they actually do.

The level of repression is out of scale only if you use a common sense philosophy of how the world should work. The ALF may not be dangerous in terms of actual damage we cause, although we have caused millions of dollars of damage to industries like fur farming, but we're very dangerous philosophically. Part of the danger is that we don't buy into the illusion that property is worth more than life, which is one of the fundamental and generally unstated assumptions of our culture. We bring that insane priority into the light, which is something the system cannot survive.

I remember that when I was in jail for liberating cats and creating a bit of property destruction—not using fire or anything, just spraypainting—I was denied bail because, as the judge put it, I "was a danger to the public."

And you're a vegan. . . .

I don't even eat honey, because I don't like to harm any living being. But during my time of incarceration I saw people come and go through the jail's revolving door who beat their wives or girlfriends, who got in fights on the street, who knifed people. For them, bail was generally set at five hundred or a thousand dollars.

We asked the judge even to set my bail at some ridiculously high amount, like $100,000, but he said no deal. There really is something wrong with our culture. If you beat up a stranger, it's not a problem. If you beat your wife or girlfriend, it's not a problem. If you commit crimes for purely selfish motivations—you want to get rich, you want things—it's not a problem. But if you commit crimes for political reasons, it's dangerous, because it threatens the structures our society is based on. Animal exploitation industries like animal agriculture, medical research, and the pharmaceutical industry form some of the bases for our society. They go to the core of what we're about as a so-called civilization.

But there's another reason for the repression. Activists in the ALF and the

ELF organize on a very anarchic structure, and are extremely adept at taking actions without getting caught, and without leaving forensic identification. They know how to use internet security, they know how to travel anonymously, and they know how to create funding for their actions. But here's the thing: for the most part the activists are very normal people, living normal lives, many even having normal jobs. That is a real threat to the state, because I think those in power understand—perhaps not on a conscious level, but certainly in their guts—what this could lead to when enough regular people decide they've had enough of this illusion of a society, and want to do something about it, want to make a change. Not necessarily for animal or earth liberation reasons, but because they're sick and tired of getting paid six dollars an hour for a shitty job, or getting pushed around by the cops because of their skin color, or they're just fed up because they want to be living genuine lives, feeling genuine emotions, and doing something meaningful.

Perhaps even more important than the actions of liberation and sabotage themselves are the ideas and possibilities the ALF and ELF offer to normal people about how they can organize and take action in a safe, focused, and direct manner.

They also offer tangible victories, something that's extremely rare at least in the environmental movement.

We're seeing victories in the animal liberation movement, more in Europe and England than here. We're starting to see bans on fur farming in countries like Belgium, or local governments adopting measures banning animals in circuses or the importation of wild dolphins and whales.

The fur industry is decimated in England, where only a couple of fur farms remain. Through continued protests and raids, we were able to shut down the main breeder of cats for scientific research, as well as many breeders of dogs for research. England is a special case, because there's such a strong movement there, but all over we're winning these real victories, actually shutting down these places of torture.

I love the fact that even when the actions are small, the activists are still taking the offensive. Most of our environmental battles are purely defensive: trying to stop this or that piece of destruction.

The actions are about taking responsibility. That's what the ALF is based on.

It's saying, "I'm tired of waiting for the people we're petitioning to take action to stop animal abuse, because they're either not doing it or they're taking too long and animals are still dying." If I'm going to take responsibility for these animals' suffering, these animals' pain, which I know is continuing every day, every hour, I've really got to take some action to stop this moral outrage.

I've read in the corporate press that the ALF is out to rob people of their pets.

Of course not. Where do you think the animals we liberate from labs end up?

I need to be clear about how the ALF chooses targets. Each individual cell decides for themselves what they'll focus on, and what tactics they will use. One cell might decide to focus on chicken liberation and may choose to raid a factory farm and save some chickens. Another ALF group might choose fur farming and release mink. Yet another might target meat trucks with incendiary devices. Because of that absolute autonomy on the part of the individual cells, you never know who or what the ALF will target.

That said, it's been pretty standard that the ALF doesn't normally target the individual fisherman or hunter or pet abuser, although they do find issue with all of these. Tactically it's much stronger to focus on larger targets, industrial targets, ones that are going to make a difference. If you're going to spend all that time and energy and money, if you're going to risk blowing your cover, if you're going to risk felony charges and major time, you don't want to waste it on something of little significance or consequence.

I see an analogy to my own environmental work, in that although I oppose all industrial forestry, I often work with independent loggers against transnational timber companies. The loggers and I both know that in our lifetimes the opposition is more theoretical, because we're both so busy fighting this much larger enemy.

That's analogous, but not completely. Although some of our main targets in the fur retail industry include Niemann-Marcus, Macy's, and Bloomingtons, we also target mom and pop fur retailers. The same is true for butchers and slaughterhouses. The reason is that there may be only two or three fur retailers in a city, and if you want to eliminate them all, you want to eliminate them all, no matter the ownership. Sometimes the big department stores are easier to target, because they're not making a lot of profit off their furs right now, meaning if you cause them to sustain a lot of monetary damages they can be convinced their fur trim line isn't worth the trouble. Obviously if the store's only focus is on furs, it will be harder to convince them to quit the business, but we have had fur stores shut down because of repeated attacks on their windows, or from fires.

How do you respond to criticism that by interfering with animal research you're killing children: if you hadn't liberated any cats, the researchers would have cured leukaemia by now.

Animal research has provided a few stopgap measures for some of society's ills, such as environmentally-caused diseases like cancer or AIDS, and more generally science has managed to create some pharmaceuticals that enable people to live longer. But science hasn't cured these diseases, and for a number of reasons I don't believe it ever will.

To start with, they're using animal models, which is a fraudulent science. You can't give a mouse Altimeter's, create some procedure that helps the mouse, then say, "Let's apply this to humans and see what happens." If you're going to look at these diseases, you've got to look at humans, you've got to look at clinical studies and trials, and you've got to look at the environment.

Cancer is a great example. It's a disease of western industrial civilization. This is, of course, true of so many of the diseases we're inflicting on ourselves. Look at the chemicals and poisons we eat in our food, breathe in our air, and drink in our water. Look at the stress people are under in their daily lives to go to work, provide for their families, pay their bills, and live under this repressive so-called democracy that resembles nothing so much as a large prison.

Another reason it's fraudulent, and why cancer won't be cured, is because "curing" it is a multi-billion dollar industry. People making six or seven digit salaries as administrators in cancer institutes and pharmaceutical corporations are not going to turn off that cash-spigot. They'll do anything to keep their business going, including torturing millions upon millions of animals.

You keep talking about torture, but I hear in the corporate press all the time that the animals are actually quite well taken care of. There are laws on the books saying they have to anaesthetize animals before surgery, and so on.

Well, they don't use anaesthesia when they do studies on pain. The cats I rescued from the lab were destined to have their spinal cords broken to study how to repair them; I can't imagine there would be no pain involved. Baby primates will have their eyes sewn shut in deprivation experiments. Vocal cords are often severed so that the animals can't scream during their torture. Have you ever had surgery? Sure, you were anaesthetized during the surgery, but afterwards did you feel any pain? Of course you did. That's why they give you pain medications afterwards.

But it all comes back to the bigger philosophical point, which is if you consider both humans and non-humans as having an inherent right to live free from torture and abuse, then there can never be any justification for torturing a non-human in order to find a cure for a human-species related disease. It's our disease, it's our shit, and we've got to deal with it. There can be no justification for creating this kind of horror on another individual because we have a belief that humans are greater than this other species.

This may not be a fair question, but if by torturing 5700 mice, or 570,000 mice, or whatever, they could find a cure for leukaemia, would that be okay?

I don't think it's a fair question because I don't think it's going to happen. So far as the question itself, I would turn it back around and point to medical research the Nazis did on Jews and others they considered inferior. Is that research ethical? I don't think so. Simply considering another inferior doesn't convey to us the right to torture them, even if we believe we may gain useful information by doing so. It's a ridiculous question anyway, and one I get all the time. If you really want to stop kids from getting leukaemia, or any kind of cancer, don't put chemical and oil refineries above their aquifers, or spray Roundup on our food, or leak toxic waste into our rivers and oceans.

The question is also racist and classist. Here's why: we've got over six billion people on the planet, the vast minority of whom live in North America and are white. Yet whom are these cures supposed to save?

I remember reading several years ago that for the price of a single B-1 bomber, about $285 million, we could provide basic immunization treatments, such as shots for chicken pox, diphtheria, and measles, to the roughly 575 million children in the world who lack them, thus saving 2.5 million lives annually. The point is that saving the lives of children is never the point, despite the rhetoric.

Exactly. Billions upon billions of dollars are spent and millions upon millions of animals are tortured, all in the illusory hope of creating cures for a minority of individuals on this planet, a minority who abuse their bodies and the environment, and then say, "Well, I've got cancer because of all this shit I'm eating and drinking, and stress, and the society we live in, so let's kill a bunch of animals because we in North America deserve to live longer."

You mentioned that the culture resembles a prison. You've done some time.

It's funny: when I got out of prison and its extreme regimen back into so-called free society, I said, "Wow, we still have prison walls, we still have prison guards. We have a little more room to run, but it's still a prison. There's not much difference. Even in terms of the food we're offered." It was a real eye-opener.

I don't mean to demean the experience of the students I teach at a prison, but I've got to tell you it reminds me so much of school, only now the hall monitors carry mace.

Prison concentrates the most violent bullies of high school into one tiny contained area. I'm talking about both the inmates and the guards. The guards are there, obviously, because to some extent they enjoy being part of that over/under mentality.

How did you end up in jail?

On June 1, 1992, Darren Thurston and I raided the University of Alberta bioanimal kennels in Edmonton. This was a holding facility that took in cats and dogs mostly from farmers—whom they paid about forty bucks per cat they caught around their barns—or breeders and prepped them before shipping them to different research facilities within the university. They started them on special diets or gave them drugs. We took out twenty-nine cats, and created about $75,000 worth of damage to the building.

Were a lot of the cats feral?

Yes. In fact there were four or five we couldn't catch because they were too scared.

How does one find a home for a feral cat?

Some people—like farmers with barns—will take feral cats. In our case, finding homes even for twenty-nine cats wasn't a problem. After we carried the cats out in individual boxes, we went to a motel room and took some videos and pictures for the media. That was my downfall, which I'll talk about in a minute. Then we sent out press releases, and delivered the cats first to a vet to make sure they weren't diseased, and then to their homes.

Not to incriminate anybody, but are the vets usually in on it, or do you just go in and pay for someone to look at twenty-nine cats?

These are vets who are also animal rights sympathizers. They can pretty well guess what's going on. It would be too dangerous to use just any vet, especially after the press hits.

Anyway, Darren got caught because the authorities found his fingerprint on a bottle of paint we'd used inside the facility. We'd worn gloves, of course, but evidently his had a hole in it.

One little detail can trip you up. . . .

My mistake was even worse. We put up a banner that said ALF as a backdrop in the motel, then did some video work, cleaned the place up, and split. The police tracked down the motel room from the video and dusted it for prints. They found a piece of tape left on a curtain rod used to hang up the banner, and on the tape I'd left a thumbprint. That was how I got nailed. They put out a warrant for my arrest, but by that time I was already in the United States, where I stayed for two years until I was apprehended in an FBI roadblock in California, which was very exciting.

Were you underground in the States?

Yes, though not completely, because I was still associating with known animal rights activists, and my friends.

Were you going by your own name?

I had false ID. But the Feds figured out where I was, and waited for me on a road leading from a friend's house. It was all very surreal. There were probably fifteen cops, all behind their car doors with their guns drawn. Through a bullhorn they ordered me to use my left hand to open my door, then to get out and kneel on the pavement, hands on my head. After they had the cuffs on me they crouched towards my car with guns drawn to make sure my car was secure.

Tell me again how much damage you did in your action.

Seventy-five thousand dollars.

How much did they spend to get you?

I've been under investigation since 1995. I'm sure they've spent millions of dollars on me. I'm still always under investigation, and still always under surveillance. I guess you could say it's my form of personal economic sabotage against the state.

Anyway, I got arrested, and spent the next three weeks in nine different facilities in California till I was formally deported. I was sent to the Edmonton Remand Center, which is a holding facility, where I was denied bail. I spent four months altogether before I pled guilty to being an accessory after the fact to breaking and entering

After the fact?

They could only place me at the motel. Thurston got hit harder because his print was at the scene, and also because he faced a charge of arson from a previous action. He served a total of two years. After having been the subject of an international manhunt, and being called a danger to the public, I got sentenced to time served and probation.

What's the longest any ALF activists have been put away?

Rod Coronado was sentenced to fifty-seven months, but that included a non-related charge. He was convicted of theft and destruction of federal property for taking a cavalryman's journal from the museum at Little Big Horn. I'm not sure how much he would have gotten had he not been connected to that one. In any event, he served fifty-seven months and is now free.

What does it cost to do an action?

Cost depends on scope, and usually comes in the form of gas money and motel rooms, if you choose to sleep in motels when you're on the road or doing surveillance. An action happens in one night, but there might be nights or weeks of surveillance first.

An interesting letter came out of an ALF cell after an action last year. The raid was against a facility—Biodevices, in California—that vivisects on dogs for pacemakers. The ALF activists took all forty-six dogs, which was an incredible feat. . .

Where could they put forty-six dogs?

That's why it was so incredible. I can't imagine where they found homes for that many dogs. So far as carrying them out, they probably got a bunch of boxes or doggie carriers, and rented a one-ton truck.

Wouldn't it be dangerous to rent a truck?

There are ways to do it. You can have fake ID. Or a sympathetic person with an alibi can offer a credit card. Then if that person ever got subpoenaed before a grand jury, she or he would have to decide whether to talk or to go to jail for not cooperating.

Anyway, one of the activists in that cell wrote a letter taking issue with the fact that once the facility was emptied, they hadn't burned it down. Evidently, some of the other activists within the cell hadn't wanted to do that. The interesting point of the letter was that the action had cost $7000, and if the cell had just been interested in saving dogs, they should have gone to the pound, where they would have saved a lot more lives for their money.

The letter writer has a point.

I think the effect of this raid was more dramatic and long term than going to the pound, but the letter implicitly raises the very good question of the distinction between symbolic and non-symbolic action.

Saving forty-six dogs from the pound would have been a purely non-symbolic action, in that you're not making a point. Writing letters or doing protests is purely symbolic, in that no actual animals are saved. I think that the ALF tries to stay away from either of those poles. A lot of ALF/ELF members are motivated to do what they do in part because they believe much of the environmental movement has been reduced to symbolic posturing that does little more than waste time and energy. Sure, symbolic actions gain some media benefit, raise some public awareness, but they don't really get us anywhere in terms of saving habitat or saving the lives of animals. We're not seeing real movement, real progress. Every time somebody hangs another banner, we get a little slogan across, and the picture is in the paper or on TV, but what have we really accomplished? But no matter what the effect of freeing those dogs from Biodevices was on discourse, the truth is that those activists saved the lives of forty-six dogs from lives of open-heart surgery, and the torture that goes with that.

What would you hope ALF and ELF actions ultimately lead to?

I'd hope they lead to a larger number of people understanding that it doesn't take a special person to take action, that anyone can take action, and that we have a moral responsibility and obligation to take action against torture and abuse, whether that torture and abuse is of humans, non-humans, or our environment. Our planet is being killed, animal species are being killed, and we have a responsibility to stop this killing any way we can.

I would hope that after hearing about the action at Vail, some people would stop and think, "Wow, some people felt strongly enough about the lynx that they burned down five structures thousands of feet up a mountain and got away with it." I would hope a lot of people would be inspired by that, and they would take action on the issues that are close to their own hearts. I would hope that these actions would cause them to stop and think about their own lives.

How many people are disgusted by slaughterhouses? If a couple of normal, everyday people can go into a slaughterhouse and remove chickens—give these chickens lives—and in so doing make a strong statement of their opposition to those kinds of horrendous crimes against nature, then anybody can do it.

How can anybody do it and still be safe? After all, we're talking about felonies.

First, I'd say people should watch out for provocateurs. The FBI has long made a habit of infiltrating movements. That means you should work with people you know and trust.

Second, there's plenty of good information out there about security, and there are plenty of people trying to make that information as widely known and understood as possible. A website, called the Frontline Information Site, has a vast amount of information about security: how not to leave forensic identification or evidence behind, how to conduct yourself among your friends and co-activists in terms of talking and not talking, and stories about how one person started working with the ALF.

Lots of this information is available for anyone who wants to look for it, either on the web, in booklets distributed by animal rights groups, in magazines like The Earth First! Journal, or No Compromise, or Live Wild or Die, or Underground.

Probably the most important single piece of information is for people to keep their mouths shut. Very often people get busted not because of any great police detective work, but because of their own mouths, or the mouths of other people. Darren and I were a different story, and Rod Coronado was a very different story: several people spent several months a piece in jail because they wouldn't cooperate with the grand juries investigating Rod.

I want to go back to the question of what you want. On the biggest scale, because industrial civilization is killing the planet, and killing us, I want to bring it down, causing as little damage to human and non-human life as possible. Does the ALF/ELF want that?

I don't think bringing down industrial civilization is an explicitly stated goal of the ALF or ELF, but I do think it's implicit in the goals they do state. Some of the explicit goals include: ending the agrifood business; ending the pharmaceutical industries; ending the vivisection industries; ending the animal-clothing and animal-entertainment industries; ending industrial logging; ending massive development and road-building. These all add up, at least in my own mind, to that larger goal of either bringing down industrial civilization, or at least radically altering the way this society works and the way people relate to their environment and other species.

How will change come about?

I don't think the actions of the underground groups by themselves can stop vivisection, factory farming, and so on. It will have to be the combined efforts of the ALF and the above-ground animal rights groups who protest, and the elderly men and women who write letters, and the people who do outreach, education: all that stuff is going to work toward a radical change in consciousness. The question, I think, is and always has been whether that radical change will come soon enough, before "it's too late."

We're already in the midst of the apocalypse.

Yes, we are in the midst of the apocalypse. Given the current course of civilization, I'm extremely pessimistic for the survival of our species, and for the survival of many other species. None of that stops me from taking action, because I wouldn't be able to live with myself—and this is probably true for most activists—if I sat back and got a job and watched TV, when I knew something is going on. Once you know something's very wrong with our culture, you can't not do something, even if you're not sure that whatever you do is going to make a difference. You have to do something.

Often after I give talks, someone will ask, "If things are so bleak, why don't you just quit?" The truth is that it never occurs to me to quit.

I don't think it's easy for people like us to quit, because once you have the knowledge, once you have the understanding, the consciousness, you're stuck with what you know. And what I know is this: the environment is being destroyed, which means of course we're destroying ourselves. I know if we are to survive, we have to really expand our consciousness, our circle of understanding and awareness, to include the environment, and to include the suffering of others, human and non-human alike. And I also know that if we give a shit about anything else besides ourselves and our money, then we need to start doing something, whether it's joining the ALF or ELF underground, writing a letter, picketing in front of a fur store, or stopping a Wal-mart from coming into your community. Simply being born a biological human doesn't automatically make you a human being and give you membership in human society. In order to become fully human and to be a member of any sort of human society we would care to join, we have to take responsibility—take active responsibility—for the actions of our species and of ourselves. Sitting on the fence just doesn't cut it. You might as well be dead.

Rod Coronado

2003

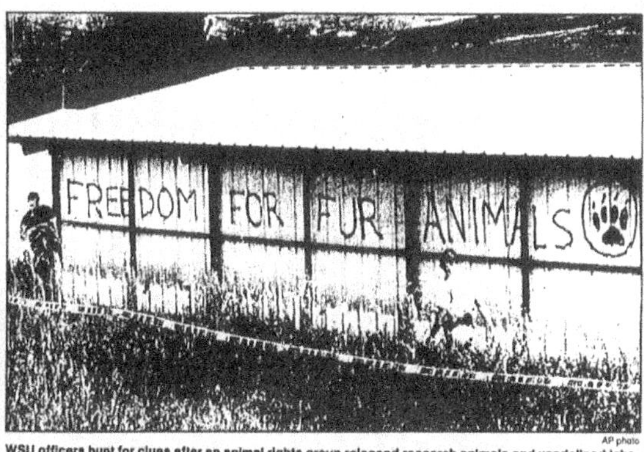

AP photo
WSU officers hunt for clues after an animal rights group released research animals and vandalized labs.

After serving 57 months in prison and completing probation for A.L.F. arsons targeting the fur industry, Rod Coronado gave this long-form interview.

How did you first get involved with the struggle for animal liberation?

When I left high school in 1984, I started working with Paul Watson and through Sea Shepherd met my first vegetarians. In I 986 I became one, even though I had already become involved with direct action against whalers and furriers. But 1987 was the year I started my own ALF cell, so I'd say that is when I really began my personal struggle for animal liberation as opposed to reforms or believing animals will ever win legal protection.

What first got you interested in taking direct action?

Seeing Paul Watson confront seal killers on the ice floes of Newfoundland in 1978. When I saw that it was possible to organize and intervene to prevent atrocities against wildlife and the earth, I knew that's what I must do. That was only months before I read about Paul ramming the pirate whaling ship, the Sierra, in I 979. When that happened, I gave up on the animal welfare groups I had joined and began to direct all my support towards direct action.

What were the charges you pleaded guilty to, and do you feel your efforts were worth the penalty you faced?

I pleaded guilty to aiding and abetting the arson at Michigan State University's Experimental Fur Farm in 1992, and theft of government property-that being a 7th Cavalryman's journal from the 1876 battle of Little Big Horn. It was a spontaneous action in response to the one-sided portrayal of the battle in the museum that did not recognize that at the time the U.S. was itself in violation of the Ft. Laramie Treaty and Custer's 7th cavalry illegal invasion. I offered to return the book when the truth was told but ended up burning the book instead.

Since then, the battlefield has installed a Native American director and is currently building a monument to the Lakota and Cheyenne warriors who died that day defending their people and homelands. Custer got what every U.S. soldier deserves, a rubbing out. Hell yeah, it was worth it. Four years in prison for eight years waging a guerilla war against animal abusers that cost them millions, saved hundreds of lives and struck fear into the cold, black hearts of the animals' enemies was a good trade-off, considering I was facing twelve years for the ALF charges alone. There were literally dozens of raids I was never charged with, so as a direct action warrior, I think it was a worthwhile sacrifice for tasting true freedom that I will never forget. Given the choice, I'd much rather go to prison for four years than not having fought the battles that I did. That was just one battle; I don't think of it as having "done my time." We all need to "do our time," not as prisoners but as warriors. Isn't that what living is, as opposed to what surviving is? I've lived a good life, I've let it be known whose side I'm on, and I have no regrets (except for wishing I'd never been caught, so I might have burned more torture chambers to the ground).

Can you tell us a bit about your years locked up in prison, what the conditions were like, and how you dealt with that time?

I spent my first three months in a minimum security prison at the foot of Mt. Graham, a sacred site to my people, which I defended while on the run. I was boosted up to medium security because the prison authorities believed me to be an escape risk because of my relationship to that place. I spent the next three and a half years outside Tucson working as a landscaper because I refused to work for UNICOR, the prison industry, because they manufactured equipment for the U.S. military (air-force helmet bags). I also refused to do any kind of work that involved the maintenance of that internment camp. So I watered plants and chased away my boss whenever he'd approach my area with herbicides.

One of the highlights for me was nursing a kangaroo rat back to health. I snuck her into my cell, and she used to crawl onto my chest while I was sleeping and stare at me. As a Native American, I was able to participate in sweat lodge ceremonies every Sunday where I could re-affirm my commitment to defend Earth. I helped organize an animal pow-wow, produced a zine for supporters on the outside and another zine for those inside. I did radio, T.V. and newspaper interviews in person and over the phone, especially after a successful ALF or ELF raid; I corresponded with hundreds of activists across the world; and I studied resistance struggles in Northern Ireland, Mexico, Chile, Peru, Spain, and France. And of course wrote for *No Compromise* and the *Earth First Journal.* I was constantly debating and discussing our movement's goals with the general prison population as well as regularly attending the Humanists Society and Nation of Islam's meetings. I wrote *Memories of Freedom,* began work on my own book, and did prisoner support for various ALF activists. At times I was more active inside than sometimes outside of prison. I worked out every day, never left my cell without a book, and read the *New York Times* and *USA Today* every day, as well as the weekly, monthly, and quarterly newsletters of about a dozen groups involved in human, animal, and earth liberation. I made a commitment to improving myself as well as demonstrating to my captors that they had not broken my spirit, and instead only galvanized my determination to be an enemy of their terrorist state. All these things I believe are obligations of ALF warriors in prison. Prison isn't a time to relax. It's a time to strengthen mind, body and spirit for the fight that lies ahead when you are released.

What kind of support did you receive as a prisoner, and what do you think can be done to improve the level of support our prisoners receive?

I received a tremendous amount of support because, fortunately, I had name recognition and over ten years of history with the animal rights and environmental movements. Out of three and a half years in medium security, I received mail everyday except about four days. The greatest thing done to offer me support, though, were the seventy raids against the same fur farm industry I had fought. That's the best form of support. Otherwise I think it's up to the individual prisoner to determine what kind of support is best.

As I mentioned, most of my time was spent on activism, but some supporters inquired about other interests, so I also would occasionally receive a country western music magazine since I've always been an in-the-closet honky tonk man—yee haw! Having money in my account was always nice, as were visits. I personally also loved group letters written at EF! and other gatherings. The slimiest non-support actions were those by armchair scum who criticized my legal defense when I was at my lowest. To them I have no words, just a pop in the mouth if they are ever brave enough to say to my face what they spewed on their chat rooms and email lists. Our warriors have every right to choose the legal defense that suits them best, as long as it does not include testifying against other warriors. It's for no one else to judge. It's their asses, not yours, that are on the line.

With prison sentences against underground activists becoming increasingly harsh, how do you feel these activists can best prepare for the possibility of imprisonment?

By acquainting themselves with federal sentencing guidelines for their crimes before they are caught, and if you can't do the time, don't do the crime. Otherwise, you weaken our entire struggle while also jeopardizing the freedom of your comrades. It's also my own opinion that one should be familiar with the sacrifices made by other P.O.W.s in other struggles. When you know what goes on in the prisons of Northern Ireland, Peru, China and Turkey, you can't help but be grateful for doing time in a first world country. I hear Holland's prisons are great!

You were very active in the fight against the fur trade prior to your arrest. Could you say a few words about the past highlights of this campaign, and what you feel would be most effective in the upcoming years?

It was my cell's job to liquidate the research and development base for the fur farm industry in America. I'd say with the four raids we carried out on researchers receiving grants from the fur trade we were maybe 60% effective? Highlights for me were the closure of OSU's Experimental Fur Farm and the total destruction of the USDA's Predator Control Research Facility at Utah State University. For the future, I don't want to say publicly what I think would be best. The path of war is a sacred and honorable tradition, and plans for war should only be discussed around the campfire in the company of other warriors, not movement theorists.

Do you view animal liberation as being part of a larger struggle? And if so, what is that struggle about at its core?

Definitely. It's part of a struggle that has been fought for hundreds of years. You should hear what Lakota warriors like Crazy Horse used to do to miners, trappers, buffalo hunters and wolf killers when they caught them. Far from Gandhian nonviolence! Those of us in the animal liberation and radical environmental movements are simply the modern counterparts to the fort and wagon burners of yesteryear. What honorable company we keep!

But even before then, there were entire nations in Brittania, Europe, Africa and Asia who defended the natural world with a lot more aggression than our movement has ever used. It's not our job to redefine the struggle, only our duty to carry the torch of uncompromised resistance. When we root ourselves in the power and ancient spirit of the earth we not only advance the cause of animal liberation, but our own as well.

It has always been the tradition of this resistance to empower oneself in the tactics and strategies of the guerrilla that refuses to recognize the authority of an occupying army and oppressive government. To me, animal rights is what one fights for within the system. You cannot achieve animal liberation without the dismantling of economic systems dependent on animal abuse. Animal liberation is not about reforming the system. It's about rebuilding a society where all life on earth matters, where the five-fingered people are simply one strand of a web that is held together by the recognition that only through living harmoniously with Earth can we ever truly be free.

Equally, animal liberation to me is about recognizing the inherent evilness of the petrochemical, agricultural, biotech and other industries that may not overtly slaughter billions of animals, but whose business practices equally result in the commodification of our animal relations. It's not enough to be vegan. We in the animal liberation movement need to strive toward a more simplistic way of life that acknowledges the anti-earth and anti-animal impacts of all consumerism. Animal liberation activists need to be less self-righteous and more open to the lessons of sustainability and low-impact living. It's not just about screaming and smashing windows; it's also about recreating the kind of society we believe is a practical alternative to the destructive lifestyles of a first world nation.

What level of importance do you put on efforts to broaden our movement and educate the public about animal concerns and veganism?

In my own activism, I invest very little time in such efforts. Not because I believe them to be ineffective; I just believe such tasks are better left to groups like PETA, who have unlimited resources to achieve such aims. I'd rather see us in the animal liberation movement focus on what we do best: direct action. I mean, each one of us does this kind of work on a daily basis every time we interact with the non-vegan public. It's also important to remember that often it is illegal direct action that results in a greater public interest in our beliefs, as well as exposure of the evils perpetuated behind the locked doors of laboratories, furriers, factory farms, and circuses.

As a long-time participant in the struggle for animal liberation, what do you view as our movement's strengths and why?

Our greatest strength is our ability to operate outside of the systems of state control. Our refusal to accept modest reforms is the true demonstration of our commitment toward total animal liberation. Call it zero tolerance or a policy of non-negotiation with terrorists and hostage takers, but our greatest strength comes when we base our tactics and strategies not on their capability for winning public support, but more importantly on the ability to inflict maximum economic damage to the corporation profiting from animal and earth abuse. Very few strategies accomplish this as effectively as economic sabotage.

With the abuse of animals running rampant, how would you recommend

activists pick what campaigns they choose to focus on?

That should be determined by where one lives. If it's near a large university, then maybe it should be vivisection on campus. If you live in Texas or other predominantly ranching states, your targets should be the livestock industry or whatever prominent animal abuse exists.

It frustrates the hell out of me when I see animal rights activists protesting Red Lobster or some other vague target, while entire industries that lie vulnerable escape attention. We need to target vivisection breeders and suppliers in our hometowns, as well as support campaigns like SHAC. These tactics work just as well against all animal abusers. It's nowhere near enough to participate in animal protests. We need to be relentless every day (and especially night) of the year.

What would you say to activists who support direct action but don't feel confident enough to undertake such actions themselves?

I'd say that's only an acceptable response for someone who has instead chosen to support direct action in other ways like renting "clean" cars, homing rescued animals, serving as a media spokesperson for raids, funding a local ALF cell, you know, all the other vital work that allows the ALF/ELF to remain effective. Otherwise, you 're not an animal liberationist, but what the abolitionists used to call an obstructionist because you claim to support animal liberation but fail to engage in and support the actions that best represent animal liberation. It's like what my old friend Paul Watson used to say: "Talk's cheap. It takes money to buy whiskey!"

In closing, I'd just like to say god bless the ALF and ELF and especially those behind the scenes, the "little old ladies" who have never wavered in their support for direct action. Without them, we'd be lost. I'd also like to say there is no greater honor than that to be found in representing the victims of injustice. The empowerment I have felt in reintroducing a mind to the world or watching an animal research lab burn to the ground is incomparable to any feeling of empowerment one receives from working within the system. Also, nothing we experience in a jail or prison can compare to the pain inflicted by governments and corporations. The state murders, tortures and destroys, and we must fight them using force if necessary. Remember that, and good luck. Now get out there and do something to make our future descendants as proud as we are of the actions of our warriors of the past. La lucha continua! (The struggle continues!)

Carmel Mink Ranch

2003

In this unpublished interview, a person arrested for an attempted raid of the Carmel Mink Ranch in Massachusetts tells their story.

What are you able to say about the night of November 26th, 1996?

Three activists and myself were arrested outside of Hinsdale, MA. We were charged with several felonies for releasing mink and attempted arson. The fur farm had been hit by the A.L.F. twice before we were arrested.

When I mentioned to a friend I was interviewing you, he wanted me to ask if you were the person from the Mass 4 case who led the cops on a lengthy foot chase through the woods.

Yes, it was me. It started when we saw flashing blue and red lights driving into the fur farm. We all jumped a fence and ran into the woods. Shortly thereafter, we split into two groups. One group headed directly to the car and was arrested. My group approached the car from the opposite direction of the fur farm. Meaning we intentionally made a large circle to approach it from an unsuspected direction. When we reached a hill that overlooked a car, we saw that the car was being watched. At this time, a person from a nearby house saw us and called the cops. The cops drove up the hill and the chase was on again. My group split when we were nearly surrounded and the cops yelled, "Stop, or we shoot!" I immediately started to run. I fell down a gulch and broke through the ice into a pond. I climbed out of the pond and headed up out of the gulch. When I reached the top of the gulch, I found myself in a trailer park. I was running through the trailer park to reach the woods on the other side with the intent of heading into New Hampshire. But, when I was halfway through the trailer park a cop sped up on me. I ran through people's yards and over bushes so he couldn't follow me. He got out of the SUV and chased me on foot. He eventually tackled me. We rolled and I was able to throw him off. I started running again. Other cops arrived, and four cops tackled me to the ground. They overpowered and arrested me. Everyone was already in custody at the police station. They overheard the whole chase on the police radio in the station.

Talk a little about the jail experience. You mentioned to me you backed off from activism after your release. Was this a direct fear-response of the jail experience? To what do you credit your political or priorital shift after jail?

The worst thing about jail was all the talk about material things from other inmates. You're locked in there and people talk about all the things they own on the outside. Some inmates have pictures of stereos, jewelry, cars, and whatever else. And the TV is blasting most of the day. The only time I got into any sort of confrontations was because I couldn't stand hearing those things non-stop. Other than that, most of the inmates thought what we were charged with was cool and wanted to know more about it. Jail didn't change a thing, besides making me more calculated. My tactical shift happened after the legal mess was wrapped up. It was catalyzed by weaknesses in the animal liberation movement. The largest flaw was that people were and are insincere. By this, I mean that they are more into being liked in the animal liberation scene than being down for the cause. The phoniness of the movement pushed me further towards an inner struggle and community building.

From personal experience, what is your assessment of support for imprisoned activists, and those in serious legal trouble? Was there a significant gap between the talk and actual support?

I believe there was a gap. At the start, we received an overwhelming amount of support. But then, many agreed with the legal strategy we took. They wanted us to martyr ourselves for nothing.

Give us a quick rundown of your history of activism.

Few years with Food Not Bombs, founded the Boston chapter of Coalition to Abolish the Fur Trade, worked as public research director for a national animal rights group, founded Mass Hardline, founded the New Eden Project and Paia / Hawaii Hardline.

How did you get involved in the animal rights movement?

In my early teens, I was introduced to vegetarianism through the Hardcore scene. Then about 12 years ago (1991), a friend encouraged me towards veganism and animal liberation. Hardcore further indoctrinated me. From there I accepted Hardline. I later moved to the Northeast with the intent of promoting Hardline and militant veganism.

You were heavily involved with the animal liberation movement of the mid-90s – working for a national AR group, organizing a CAFT chapter, and then your arrest in 1996. You were a dedicated activist. What are your reflections on the successes and failures of this era?

In the mid-90s the animal liberation movement was almost justified being called a threat. Direct action for animal liberation was happening at a rate not seen before in North America. The largest success was the move from actions like spray-painting graffiti to liberations, arson, and pipe bombings. The largest failure was that so many activists accumulated an arrest record for civil disobedience actions, when they could be doing actions that have more impact. Not that civil disobedience doesn't have its place, but it shouldn't be the priority. If you think its murder, act like it.

What are your current feelings on the A.L.F., E.L.F., and animal/earth oppression in general? Do you still see these as urgent issues?

They are urgent issues. In many ways, I do not believe the earth and the animals will be saved, but that in no way negates our duty to fight oppression and deal out justice. Winning or losing is not a factor. The fight, and how we die is what matters.

Are you still in touch with your codefendants? What are they up to now?

I am not in touch with them. It is my understanding that all three are still vegan. One is now a lawyer, and the other two.... I don't know.

Based on your stories alone, Boston in the mid-90s sounded like a very hectic time – demos erupting into brawls, legal entanglements for your friends, etc. Do you reflect on this as a period of righteous activity, or just the product of youthful naiveté?

It was righteous activism. We made serious progress for the cause and along the way built many friendships.

You mentioned a couple of your friends were involved in a legal case that was not publicized and I don't think many people heard about.

They were charged with the attempted torching of a veal slaughterhouse. They were arrested before they ignited it. They got a felony apiece and didn't bother getting support from the animal liberation movement. In hindsight, they would have, but at the time didn't feel they would benefit from it.

As someone who has been in the hot seat facing serious charges with co-defendants, tell us your opinion on snitches. Is there ever an excuse? How should someone who sells out a comrade be dealt with?

Selling others out is essentially apostasy; therefore, they need to be taken out. If someone sells someone else out, and there are reliable witnesses or records, there is no excuse or discussion to be had about it. The traitor should be executed immediately.

What advice would you offer newer activists?

What is most important is to know why you are involved. To be honest with yourself about what you believe. Most ineffective actions are the result of people seeking prestige and recognition. They do things to impress fellow activists. This often undermines the efforts of others who are truly sincere. Additionally, it is important to develop certainty that the path you are on is the true path. If you know this deep in your heart, then success in all areas of life will follow.

For the second time this year, the Hinsdale mink farm was hit by a radical animal rights crew.

Animal activists free mink again; 4 arrested

By Lisi de Bourbon
Berkshire Eagle Staff

HINSDALE — Following a foot chase through a cemetery yesterday morning, police arrested four people in connection with the release of an unknown number of mink from their cages at the Carmel Mink Ranch off Route 143.

Police Chief Mark C. Green Jr. said he suspects that the incident may be related to another that occurred in August, when over 1,000 mink were freed from their cages by a group calling itself the Animal Liberation Front.

Earl and Jeanne Carmel have raised mink at the farm since the 1950s. They own and operate the Berkshire Fur Shoppe from the front of their home on Route 143.

Reached at home last night, Jeanne Carmel declined to comment on the incident and would not say whether the animals were insured.

"I don't really care to talk about it, it's under litigation," she said.

Green declined to release the names

MINK, continued on B7

Chris DeRose

2004

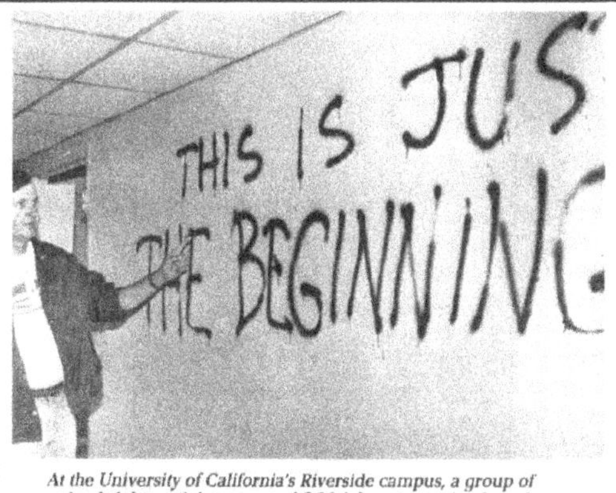

At the University of California's Riverside campus, a group of animal rights activists removed 260 laboratory animals and painted graffiti on the walls.

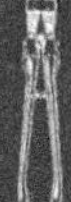

While not an A.L.F. member himself, Chris DeRose was the aboveground contact for "Joseph," an organizer behind many of the most high-profile and expertly-executed lab raids of the 1980s. Through Chris DeRose, we get what may be the closest insights we will ever receive into one of the A.L.F.'s most successful and storied liberators.

Tell us about Joseph.

I worked with him, he was with the West coast branch of the ALF and I was his intermediary between the above ground and underground groups. As such, I have been suspected of being Joseph, which is not the case. Joseph is a very dedicated person, very thorough about whatever he is going to do and he had made a commitment at that point in his life to free as many animals as possible and to expose as many facilities as possible. This is from about 1980 to 1985.

Last Chance for Animals (LCA) was founded in the heightened activism of the mid-1980s and, along with PETA, played an aboveground role in the ground-breaking liberations at the City of Hope and UC Riverside laboratories. Can you recount for us these actions and the impact they carried on, not only the particular labs, but the vivisection industry as a whole?

I think the overall effect was overwhelming simply because many of the research facilities, if not all of them, started to have a fear that they were going to be next. A lot of them started to clean up their own act, (and of course we still totally disagree with anything they were doing in there), and, if nothing else, it sent paranoia through the whole biomedical research community. This paranoia was one of the psychological things Joseph saw that needed to be done, because it [vivisection] has to be deterred from within the biomedical community, not just raids and liberating animals, so it was psychological warfare that Joseph saw being done - to let them know that none of them, not even the biggest ones, are impregnable.

LCA helped pioneer the use of direct action in US animal rights campaigning. Leading civil disobedience charges and large scale mass demonstrations, the LCA 'no-nonsense' style struck a chord. What influenced LCA in employing this approach and to what successes were they used?

There was a gap ... I look at this way—it's kind of like a pyramid, and the top of the pyramid, the pinnacle, was the Animal Liberation Front and in the bottom strata of the pyramid—you look at it with four sections, the bottom section, the biggest one, were the people that give donations, write letters, and never really come out of their homes. Just above them are demonstrations, people that come out to demonstrations, people that get physically active. Between that and the pinnacle of the ALF there was a gap. In every civil rights battle and in every movement of this sort there were always these four elements represented, and this element of civil disobedience and open direct action was missing. LCA brought it in for good reason. For example, when City of Hope had a raid and all this great material came out, it got news for 2-3 days and then it faded away. But when you take direct action and you go back to that facility a month later and two months later, you can take that same footage and same documentation and get it back out to the media and play it again. In other words, you're not just getting 1 or 2 or 3 days of media play from a raid that took months and months to plan, but really unlimited play on it. Civil disobedience and direct action are done to draw attention to an issue.

Tell us the story about the 'kick that was heard around the world.'

The kick that was heard around the world was done by Dr. Less Stewart, an activist. Basically that was a direct action we did at the UCLA Brain Research Institute around 1988. In 1988 we went and did a break-in where the brain research cat vivarium room was and we took a camera crew, a real professional TV camera crew with us. This was at 10:40AM in the morning, and unbeknownst to us at 9AM the university had a press conference to show all their fluffy cats and rabbits saying there was nothing wrong with them.

They took the media on what I call a white glove tour. At 10:40AM we broke in the doors of the cat vivarium and we showed the world what was really going on inside of there. We showed the cats with the electrodes going into their brains, their brains being exposed, the electrodes in their spines ... it was pretty horrendous. We got that news out on CNN and it went around the world. For five straight days it was the number one story in LA.

The 'kick that was heard around the world' was when Dr. Stewart kicked open the front door of the vivarium that was locked. It was a heavy, heavy duty door. He then kicked the three other following vivarium doors in. He did time because of this action, we both did. We each got 45 days in solitary confinement, in the 'hole'. I served 90 days and he got 120 for breaking and entering.

LCA is called the 'FBI of the animal rights movement because of the work of its Special Investigations Unit. The investigations are often clandestine, precarious, and illegal. Does LCA feel any contradiction in breaking the law (trespassing, etc) to 'enforce the law' with footage taken of animal cruelty?

Not at all. We feel that it is definitely justifiable. We feel it is the same thing as if there was a house on fire and a child were trapped inside. Under normal circumstances it is illegal to break into that house, and if anyone ever wanted to charge you for breaking in to save that child they technically could, but who is ever going to do that? The crime that is going on inside the laboratories far supersedes any trespassing or breaking and entering charges, and until the day l die I' II feel that it is necessary, and that it is one of the few things we have left (to combat cruelty).

Even if it ever became a major felony... if there is a crime going on behind those doors we need to expose it. It is our job as human beings, never mind as animal rights activists, to expose what is going behind those doors.

On the evening of April 16th 1987, the ALF burnt the halfway completed UC Davis animal research lab to the ground, causing over $3 million in damages. This action changed the face of ALF activism and caused an internal split within the movement about direct action. Can you help tell this story from Joseph's perspective and why he felt this divergence was wrong?

Joseph had a very strong policy of no arson and no bombings. The reason is that in this country we look at that as a terrorist act. A terrorist act does what? ... it brings in the FBI. Joseph felt that there were at least 10 more years of underground activities, liberations of laboratories, big ones like UC Harbor, UC Riverside, City of Hope. If you ever bring in the FBI that's going to put the kybosh on it because the FBI has unlimited resources to investigate you and they can pull in all the other agencies together. He knew local agencies and state agencies didn't care enough about ALF stuff or were not savvy enough to do anything about it, nor would they put the energy into it.

Joseph also found that in America, Americans always like that "taking from the rich giving to the poor," that Robin Hood-syndrome. He knew the psyche of the American public, and that they would root for the underdog, and as long these guys looked like they were doing good things helping animals, even though in the meantime they are exposing the whole biomedical research industry, that it would gain momentum, it would gain acceptance, and it would get laws changed. He felt very strong about this. Once you cross the line, now you become a terrorist organization by committing a "terrorist" act—that is the beginning of the end.

UC Davis... when that building was burnt down, they just collected the insurance. Not a thing was accomplished by it. When you go into a facility and just trash it, it just makes it look Like you are just vandals or real nut-jobs. When Joseph did it, you never saw anything trashed, machinery that was destroyed... it was so that you could not see that it was destroyed. In the back of the computer in the City of Hope action, it was one of these computers that took up a small room, the whole back of it, I think aluminum something was poured into it, and the whole machine was destroyed. Yet it didn't look like it. The image and illusion that is created by the underground is by far one of the most important things you have to bring forward. That it's not just a bunch of vandals going into a place or a bunch of "terrorists" lighting a match and burning the place down. What does that accomplish? You trash a place, and they have got a custodian to come in for six dollars an hour and clean it up. Meanwhile you've got all of this negative, negative media and media is so important. It shapes how the public is going to perceive what it is they are seeing.

Also when you destroy something on such a large scale like that, like the UC Davis building, first they said it was million dollars, then a million and a half, then three or four million—UC Davis probably made money on the deal. They probably collected the insurance. Whoever burnt it, it wasn't worth the box of matches they used. It really destroyed everything. At that point Joseph and his group were so disgusted by seeing this and the people involved in this were told never to do this. They just basically disbanded their unit on the west coast. It is a shame too, because they had it together. They had the equipment, they had the knowledge, they had the experience, and they had the record to show that they could do it. But yet—there goes somebody off to try to make a name for himself... it is very easy to light a match and run.

If one person, a homeless person, a firefighter, anyone was hurt or killed in one of these fires, or one animal—that would have been the end of the animal rights movement as we knew it at the time. Joseph and others worked so hard... PETA and other groups—it would have been the end of their work because people would have hated them because a human had died. Arson is something that is uncontrollable and you never know who is going to be in that building, or who is fighting the fire and if they are going to get hurt. Or if there is an animal in there, a guard dog, or a stray dog or cat—that is all you need to happen, one incident like that—and it's over. The opposition would play that forever. Direct action for animal rights has shifted from Bob Barker and baby Britches to the bombing of biotech buildings.

As a former actor, a reporter, and longtime Hollywood resident you know the importance of public image and the mechanisms for creating such.

What ideas and advice do you have for this element of the animal rights movement with regard to its appearance?

You can always clean up a mistake, and I don't think the image is so tarnished. The opposition is always going to try and tarnish it no matter what, but it can be changed. It [direct action) needs thought, some serious calculations on how the public is going to perceive something. The problem is, that it is much tougher to get into these research labs than it was back then, simply because of arson and the FBI is involved. When the FBI goes to these facilities to advise, they tell them to tremendously increase their security to deter these break-ins. A lot of the damage is done, and it is done forever and that is because of security. You know the same people, or person, or whatever, that had done all this stuff back then—lighting the match and running, I don't see him doing anything anymore. I don't see activities inside these facilities still taking place. Anybody interested in doing something like direct action—think about it, plan it out, it takes a long time, but one good action lasts a long time, if not forever. Small hit and run things are okay, but plan your good actions. The biomedical research community needs to be awakened. The early 1980's need to come back. It has been away too long now.

What is your take on the new breed of direct action campaigns such as SHAC that take great care to personalize their targets and employ direct tactics aimed at holding individuals (researchers, investors, biotech executives, etc.) accountable?

I think SHAC's tactics are by far the most progressive, the most thought-out, and I wish I would have even thought of these tactics years ago. I think Joseph would be very proud to see this new wave of action. This is what needs to be done much more now, especially since covert activities are becoming more difficult. The kind of tactics SHAC has taken on are revolutionary, they are great, they are effective, and they work.

No one is physically hurt and it only pinpoints and holds the bad people accountable. It is mostly the big corporations, as they are put out there publicly and I think that is what is needed. You have to think about what your opposition does not want and this is what you have got to give them. Exposing them, bringing it to their neighbors, to the media, their face, their names, their activities—that is painful. That will turn them around. I have watched what SHAC has been doing in the last four years, and I have to say I am impressed.

Do you have a favorite ALF action, or is there one that stands out to you as particularly effective?

I would say the UC Riverside raid, because of Britches. Britches kind of signifies 'ALF'. I think in this country it signifies success within the underground of animal liberation. I think it also signifies the horrors in these research laboratories, of what these people in the research labs can actually undertake. I think PETA did a good job in getting that message out there.

Another action I like, it was very brazen and one of the first, was at UC Harbor Medical where 12 dogs, we called them the doggie dozen, were taken. That was the first. There were none before that, I think there may have been a couple small ones with some rats or mice saved at NYU, but other than that there was no other with any large animals or numbers being taken.

Then, of course, the golden temple—because it really struck at the core of vivisection. The City of Hope raid, or as we called it the City of No Hope, the City of Hype, that institution was always being heralded as the golden temple of animal research for cancer, and it was exposed. What was going on at the City of Hope blew people's minds, including the people that worked there that didn't even know about some of the stuff. The conditions of the animals there were so deplorable, so bad that the actual facilities looked like Auschwitz and Treblinka.

Then also the raid on the University of Pennsylvania remains on my mind. Because of the footage they were able to get out of the facility by the researchers themselves, that to me is one of the most profound raids also. They didn't take any animals, but they got footage that shook the world and continues to do so.

Burning Rage: 60 Minutes Interviews The A.L.F.

2001

The high-profile news magazine show sits down for an interview with an anonymous A.L.F. activist.

In researching our story 'Burning Rage' about environmental and animal-rights extremists, we attempted to reach out to active members of the Earth Liberation Front (ELF) and the Animal Liberation Front (ALF).

These people aren't easy to find. Members of these groups have been involved in illegal activities like arson, breaking and entering, and sabotage. "Eco-terrorists," as they are known, have been branded by the FBI as America's top domestic terrorist threat.

On September 30th, 2005, 60 Minutes producer Graham Messick received a telephone call from a man claiming to be an active member of an ALF cell. The voice at the other end was barely audible. The reason, the caller said, was because the call was being "re-routed" to prevent it from being traced.

The caller said he had heard we had interviewed Dr. Jerry Vlasak, a spokesperson for several radical animal rights groups, who has publicly advocated the assassination of researchers to slow down what he believes is the abuse of animals. The caller wanted us to know that the Animal Liberation Front was a non-violent organization that targeted property, not people.

After some discussion, the caller said he would consider granting an on camera interview, the group's first in over 20 years according to him, if we could protect his anonymity. The man wanted to discuss this with other members of his ALF cell, and said he would call back in about a week.

We had no way to ascertain where the man was calling from or if he was who he claimed to be. In fact, throughout this process we have never learned any names, phone numbers, or any other personal information about these purported ALF members.

A week later, there was a second barely audible telephone call. The caller suggested we conduct an interview in a neutral place and mentioned Mexico. We discussed a possible interview in New York City. We told him he would need to provide details of an ALF action that only the perpetrators would know. The man said he would consider this, and would call back in another week. He didn't.

But on Tuesday, October 18th, the man called a third time. This time the voice was loud and clear. Traffic could be heard in the background, indicating to the producer that he was calling from a pay phone. The caller said "they" were in New York City and were ready to grant an interview. Right now. He also insisted that we not record his voice. Reluctantly, we agreed to film the interview, transcribe it on paper, and make no audio recording of the man's voice.

We agreed that correspondent Ed Bradley would be ready for an on-camera interview in a neutral location – a place with no security cameras on the street – between 7 p.m. and 9 p.m. that night, and that they could meet us there if they decided to go ahead. We had no way of knowing if they would show up, and no way of reaching them.

At 7:45 p.m., two masked men – whose faces we never saw – arrived. One man never talked. His job was to make absolutely sure we did not record any audio of the interview. The other man sat for the interview, which we filmed. The following interview transcript is taken from notes that were taken by producer Graham Messick and associate producer Michael Karzis:

Let's begin by asking, who do you represent? Are you ALF, ELF, or some variation or splinter group?

We're representative of an autonomous ALF cell, the animal liberation front… I can't sit here and be a voice for every ALF cell. But I can represent at least one cell.

How many people are in your cell?

It varies. I can't go into details.

Do you know people in other cells?

I can't go into that.

Do the cells communicate with each other?

Cells operate autonomously from each other and don't want to know the other people. I don't really want to know the people in other cells, and I don't want people in the other cells to know who's in my cell.

So you can't make direct contact between your cell and another cell?

There's a one-way method of communication that's from the cell to the public only…. There's no reason to communicate with any other cell.

Have you or anyone else in ALF ever given an interview before?

The last interview given like this was in the 80's… There's never been an interview given like this before.

So why do it now? Why take the risk of coming here and to talk to us on 60 Minutes.

It's a big risk. Everything we do, we look at the benefits versus the adverse consequences. We don't believe there's an accurate representation of who [we are] and what we do.

Who are you and what do you do?

The ALF is an underground movement that engages in things ranging from economic sabotage… documenting animal abuse…. Part of the reason we do what we do is to show the public what goes on behind closed doors. If people could see what goes on behind those doors, they would be outraged…

What goes on behind closed doors?

We live in a society that is founded on exploitation of life, whether it's in a lab or a factory farm. Animals feel the same pain, the same emotions as you or I… I can't endure their suffering.

Under that mask, who are you? If someone was to look at you, would you seem to be an otherwise normal law abiding citizen?

We're all normal people. We're just people who said enough is enough. I'm a normal person and I have a normal life… We just believe that to continue to turn our backs on what happens to animals is to be an accomplice to that exploitation and to be a part of it…

Most people watching would say that most normal people don't burn down research labs.

Most normal people would find it unacceptable to see animals have the skin burned off them while they're alive…to see primates that share the same DNA as humans, cut open while they are still alive day in and day out. I challenge anyone who sees this to go to a farm or a lab to see what happens. I challenge people to look at those videos. If you want to know why we do what we do it's as simple as watching those videos.

Do your friends and families know anything about what you do?

No idea. None whatsoever

Then, how can you speak for the movement if you're just one cell in this movement and the cells don't communicate directly with each other?

I'm not a spokesperson for the movement. I'm one person in the movement, one person expressing the movement. No one person can speak for the whole movement. I can speak for ALF in broad general terms. The ALF guidelines speak for themselves.

Have you been involved in "direct actions?"

I have. I won't go into specifics. I would like to go into specifics. But since we are America's number one domestic terrorist threat, it isn't worth it. I can speak generally, but I will provide proof of who I say I am.

Generally, without naming specific events, what have you done?

We've liberated animals in labs, from fur farms, breeders… destroyed property.

Destruction of property? Arson?

I can't be specific.

How did you destroy property? Arson you wouldn't admit to?

I can destroy property by throwing a brick. But telling somebody what I did, like an arson, what would I benefit from a sentence of 80 years behind bars?

I'm just trying to get at what it is that you do? I mean… if you picket in front of somebody's house, that's one thing. If you burn down a lab that's another thing.

I can say that I support arson generally. We support arson. Extreme times call for extreme measures. We don't choose our methods. If picketing worked, I'd be the first one out there. If writing letters worked then I'd be writing letters until my hand fell off. But it doesn't work… the status quo is exploitation of life.

Do you consider arson "non-violent?"

I don't look at it as being violent or non-violent. Many people think you cannot commit a violent act against a piece of property. The debate goes on and on. The question should be how violent is it to rip the skin off a mink's back, anally electrocuting a fox, that's violent. To equate destroying property with killing is something I don't understand.

But why take the risk of going to prison?

I think it's a risk worth taking. I've been to hell, and I've seen what goes on in those labs, and seen what happens to animals. After seeing that I cannot, not act.

It's hard for some people to imagine, I mean people can imagine fighting for their freedom or even fighting for someone else's freedom but a lot of people can't understand fighting for the freedom of animals. I mean forever man has domesticated, killed animals for subsistence.

We also know that some of the greatest thinkers of our time have refused to hurt animals. Some have chosen to hurt animals. Some chose to hurt, others, not. I chose not to hurt animals.

But you could make the argument that raising animals, domesticating animals for your own survival is a natural state of things? Would you accept that argument?

I don't accept that the commodification of life is natural. I don't accept that rampant heart disease is natural, the rates of asthma in the cities have gone up and that 13 year old girls are growing breasts because of the hormones that are in their food. That is not natural…

So in some places where people still live in what we would call a primitive society, you see tribesman into the water off their island homes with a spear and stand there looking for a fish and then kill that fish, and that's food for him and his family. That's not natural?

I can't speak to what I don't know. At the same time there's a difference between eating to survive and commodifying life. There is a difference between commodification and surviving to live.

And when you say commodifying what do you mean by that?

I think it becomes a lot easier to exploit when you turn something into a commodity... when you objectify something it's easy to exploit. By commodification, we live in a society that discards life for money.

Do you know Jerry Vlasak. You know who he is? Calls himself a spokesperson for the cause, for your cause. And he says it's time to start killing people who do research on animals?

Well, we appreciate that he likes to consider himself a spokesperson, but he doesn't operate with our endorsement or our support or our appreciation, the support of the ALF. We have a strict code of non-violence. Not a single human being in the 20 to 30 year history has ever been harmed in an ALF action.... That's not luck, it's a pretty good record.

I mean there are some cases, for example Daniel Andres San Diego is suspected of carrying out three bombings. One of which he set a bomb to go off an hour after the first bomb. Fortunately for the first responders, they spotted that second bomb and disarmed it. If they hadn't, they would have been hurt. I'd say that was lucky for them?

I don't have much knowledge of the specifics of the case.

Does Dr. Vlasak speak for anyone in the movement?

I don't know who put Dr. Vlasak in the position he's in. It wasn't us, the ALF.

He says that every social movement eventually resorts to violence. Would you agree with that?

I think looking at history, many social movements have resorted to violence.

And do you think that yours will resort to violence?

As I said before, we don't choose the methods. We don't choose the weapons.

We liberate life, destroy property. We have guidelines of non-violence.

If you destroy my property, that's violence against me.

Our intention is not to coerce, not to terrorize, not to threaten individuals. But I do believe that myself and the warriors I've worked with have saved countless lives… I've saved dogs and puppies that have lived their whole lives in a cage and released them to run around in a field and the dirt for the first time. If that's violent, then fine. If taking puppies out and letting them roam. And I believe every one of those lives has value. If that's violent, fine.

What about Daniel Andreas San Diego, who is suspected of carrying out three bombings in California, and threatening people's lives. What do you think of his actions?

[No answer.]

But he [San Diego] set off a nail bomb, and he threatened to car-bomb or shoot the president of a big company that does tests on animals… Isn't that pretty much what Jerry Vlasak is advocating?

I've never made [a] delineation between a bomb as being violent or a milk jug filled with kerosene as violent. I don't know what to say…. We have put the lives of a security guard above the lives of hundreds of animals. It's a judgment call, an ethical dilemma. We don't claim to have all the answers.

You do see, from your perspective that the life of one man is worth more than the life of dozens of animals?

I can't say that I cannot say one man's life has more value than hundreds of animals… because operating under ALF guidelines we never harmed life. A 30 year history of never harming a human being.

Is there a place where you draw the line? I mean, is there a line between non-violence and violence?

We don't throw bricks at people. We don't set people on fire, buildings when there are people inside. We don't assault people when we carry out actions.

You say that violence against a building, destroying a building is not

violence. So what I'm wondering is how do you get from non-violence to violence?

If a human being is injured, it cannot be an ALF or ELF action. By virtue of the guidelines, it's not an ALF action.

So you came here to say to us tonight that the ALF, the ELF are non-violent and will not escalate beyond arson. Is that right?

I think it is interesting that in today's political climate, that we are America's top domestic terrorist threat; but, we haven't killed anyone. But the neo-Nazis have maimed and have murdered and they're not considered a terrorist threat. I think it's abysmal. Animal activists can face more time than a man who rapes a woman, I think it's because it challenges the status quo.

Is there anything else that you'd like to add?

I think our general sentiments or objective are similar, to stop the destruction of life.… It's amazing to me we're having a conversation about violence in relation to the ALF and ELF when we have Monsanto and Dow Chemical, Exxon and companies who are hurting and murdering people with their by-products… I don't have hope. The fact we are having a conversation about my tactics being extreme or violent while corporations are making a killing, literally and figuratively, and while their stocks are going through the roof, is amazing to me. To focus on us, that we are America's top domestic terrorist threat, is amazing to me.

After the interview, the man sat down, still masked, and gave us details about an ALF crime. It turned out to be a break-in and theft of 33 beagles and 11 ferrets from a place called Marshall Farms in upstate New York. He said as they tried to gain entrance, they made a series of nicks and cuts into the fence surrounding the facility before realizing they had brought the wrong equipment, and scaled the fence. He called it a "rookie mistake."

60 Minutes confirmed that there was indeed a break-in and theft at Marshall Farms in North Rose, New York on December 5, 2001. Marshall Farms breeds animals for research and sale. Scott Marshall, a representative of the company, wouldn't discuss details of the crime and the New York State Police in Albany wouldn't release copies of the police report. But there were accounts of the crime in animal rights publications and the local press.

THE A.L.F. STRIKES AGAIN

When pressed, the man mentioned another incident, this one all the way across the country in Salinas, California. He claimed his ALF cell "liberated 24 rabbits" from a breeder, and "the owner was sleeping 15 yards away when we did it." 60 Minutes found an account in the San Jose Mercury News from May 2001 about a break-in at a medical research company outside Salinas in which more than two dozen rabbits were stolen. The San Diego Union Tribune reported that "activists struck while members of the family… were elsewhere on the property."

Peter Young

2007

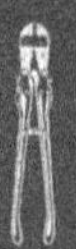

Raiding fur farms, step-by-step.

How many Midwest farms did you surveil during the fall of 1997?

Between 35 and 50. We traveled eastward across Montana, South Dakota, Iowa, Minnesota, and Wisconsin. We spent the daytime driving past farms and the nighttime on them. We walked the sheds of every manner of farm, from single sheds to farms imprisoning 80,000 mink. We walked the Fraser Fur Farm compound and stared in the eyes what may have been more lynx than existed in the wild in the entire state of Montana. We encountered masked scarecrows with signs reading "A.L.F. Stay Away." We were chased from farms on foot on more than one occasion, and by cars from several more. We looked at a lot of farms, many of which have been hit in the years since. It brings me immeasurable pleasure to read of farms I visited, whose captives I had to leave behind, being raided years later. I hope I'm alive to see the day one or both of the Zimbal mink farms (WI) has every cage opened.

We received a tremendous amount of information on the farms we surveilled via the discovery process of my legal case. Dozens of pages of confiscated notes we had taken on farms were turned over; in addition to numerous police reports listing often detailed information on, and addresses of, fur farms in areas where we were accused of actions. I believe all the fur farmers who wrote my judge asking for the harshest possible sentence were not aware photocopies of their letterhead and (unpublished) return addresses were turned over directly to my lawyer. Again, as with raids that are carried out in the wake of an arrest, we see it doesn't pay for an industry to encourage the imprisonment of animal liberators.

What was your intention with this campaign?

To get as many animals out of those cages as we could before pelting season. The fact that some of the farms shut down was an unanticipated yet welcome side effect.

Describe this period (1996 to 1998) of underground activism against the fur industry.

An anecdote to illustrate the pace at which farms were getting raided from 1996 to 1998: We had discussed surveilling farms in Idaho, including one in Preston ID. We decided against it, and did not visit any farms until Montana. We would later read that literally the night we were to have visited that farm, every one of its 5,000 mink were released by individuals unknown. Later, when we received the various police reports from that period it was revealed there were others surveying farms in the same three-state area, sometimes visiting the same farms we had only a day apart. That three groups were out simultaneously seeking farms to raid illustrates the momentum at the time. Had we sustained this pace, there would be no U.S. fur industry today.

Talk about how you located fur farms. Were all farms you visited listed in *The Final Nail*? Did you draw from other sources?

The Final Nail was a starting point. To this day it is the best resource for fur farm addresses, although it has many gaps. To locate unknown farms, and find street addresses for those where only a "rural route" address was listed, we had to call on our creativity. This pre-dated the internet as we know it, and hard-copy material was our sole resource. The sources from which we drew the most info: local phone directories, business directories at the library, and agricultural survey maps at university libraries. Above them all, fur industry trade publications like Fur Rancher provided the most leads. And then there were those farms we found by turning down "Fur Farm Road." Sometimes they hide in plain sight.

What did you look for in choosing one farm to raid over another?

We looked at many farms, and couldn't hit them all. There were features we looked for which disqualified some farms and beckoned us to others, which I will leave unmentioned to avoid giving the fur industry insight into the workings of those working to rid them from this earth. We should be reminded there have been farms raided with everything from perimeter security to guard dogs. Activists should take from this that "security" is only a deterrent if you let it be. Farmers should take from this that when animal liberators have you in their sights, cash in your chips because you're getting raided either way.

What did you do with the car while you were surveilling or raiding farms? Did you have a driver, or did you park?

Parking is an exercise in creativity. Cornfields, farm service roads, nearby non-residential buildings, and any place that will not arouse suspicion are all options.

Having a driver would be sensible in an extreme case where parking was an impossibility. There are too many variables that could necessitate quick and premature flight from the premises to chance having to wait for pickup from a circling driver. We parked every time.

Talk about removing fencing. How did you remove the fences surrounding a farm to allow the mink an escape route?

There is no correlation between the apparent fortitude of a fence and the ease with which it can be dismantled. Often the most intricately constructed fences are held together by only a few pieces of wire affixed to posts. When the wire is cut, the entire fence falls. Generally a small pair of wire cutters is sufficient, with larger bolt cutters sometimes being necessary. We took down 400 feet of fence in Medford in less than 20 minutes with fewer than 50 cuts.

What equipment did you bring to the farms?

Dark clothes, facial covering, gloves, headlamp with red screen (making it barely visible at a distance), bolt cutters, and wire cutters. That's it.

Is there anything you wish you had used which would have made the action safer or more effective?

With all actions, as in life, I believe low-tech and streamlined is best. Trust your senses and work with the absolute minimum needed to accomplish the goal.

That said, the complications that came from our policy to always be in eyeshot of each other on the farm could have been avoided with radio contact. For that reason, I would see no good argument against using radios during an action. We never procured radios for the simple reason that we were short on money and the animals were short on time.

Describe a mink shed.

One to four rows, partially walled, with a very crude saloon-style door, if any. There is not much to it. When you've made it that far, the hardest part is behind you.

Are there any security precautions you encountered at the farms (security guards, cameras, alarms, etc)?

In the 35 to 50 farms we visited during the fall of 1997, I saw one video camera and no alarms. In the farms I've visited in the Northwest, I've seen over 10 farms with perimeter security and several with video cameras. Thus there are serious regional differences in security. The perimeter alarms I've encountered are invisible beams, which, most of the time, can be rolled under. I would suspect there is close to zero chance cameras on a farm are monitored overnight, and would not consider them a deterrent.

Is the opening of the cages self-explanatory?

It's always self-explanatory but never consistent. Latch styles are numerous. In addition to simple latches, there are nesting boxes which are most often removable and provide the best option for mink to escape. Occasionally cages are wired shut individually, easily remedied with wire cutters.

Other than your over-arching conspiracy charge, you plead guilty to an explicit perpetrator role in releasing 2,500 mink from a Medford, Wisconsin farm. What can you tell us about this action? How long did it take, and what were the obstacles?

Medford WI was at one time known as "Mink Capital USA" (while still a contender, the title today would likely go to Morgan, UT). There are several farms in or around downtown, and at least a dozen in Medford and outlying areas (some may have closed in the years since). The house was a safe distance from the sheds, and altogether there were no obstacles to speak of. The entire action took one hour.

In light of the numbers you give in your university talks, that 2 people can release 1000 animals in 15 minutes, what do you feel are the reasons behind the abundance of small mink releases in which only 1 to 200 mink are freed?

I know exactly what this is because I almost fell victim to it. None of the available literature forewarned of the decibel level created by even a few dozen mink given their first taste of freedom. When you're in someone's backyard at 1am, and being detected means going to prison, if you're not prepared for the wall of noise it can be an immediate cause for flight. The fear dissipated the first time I left a farm and became aware that what is deafening inside a shed is almost inaudible just 25 yards away.

There are certainly other reasons for aborted raids, such as discovery by farmers, which has been known to happen. Relative to just 20 years ago, there are only a handful of farms left and I would hope animal liberators would invest the preparation time to ensure they release 10,000 animals over finding themselves unprepared and leaving after releasing only 10.

What lessons can we learn from the past 10+ years of fur farm liberations? What have been our mistakes?

Mistakes: Not maintaining the momentum of the mid-to-late-90s that would have brought the end of the U.S. fur industry. And squandering risk-exposure on periphery targets (such as fur stores) in areas where farms or infrastructure targets are within a day's drive. A mink release on the right farm will be a much less risky endeavor than breaking the windows of a fur store. This is less a criticism than a call to cater every action for maximum impact.

Did you issue communiqués for your actions?

We issued no communiqués. There are pros and cons to issuing communiqués, and for live liberations, I see more pros than cons. Generally I think communiqués are a necessary element to any large-scale, successful action. Whatever our reasons at the time, we did not make any claims of responsibility and were focused solely on getting to the next farm. There was a plan to issue a communiqué after leaving the Midwest, making public all the intelligence gathered during our investigation of farms - from unknown addresses to farm layout and more. These notes were confiscated by the FBI during the seizure of our vehicle, and this information was never made public.

Among fur industry actions you were not a part of, which stand out as most impressive, and what can we learn from them?

The examples of multiple raids taking place back-to-back, such as the 5 raids that took place in 10 days during August of 1998. Anyone who thinks fur farmers are on too high alert now to successfully empty their farms should take note there is no farmer on higher alert than one within 3 hours drive of a farm that had been raided the night before. Yet still liberators have still slipped in, released animals, and slipped out undetected. We should have an evidential basis for our fears, not vague assumptions rooted in a default-bias towards the path of least resistance.

Offer your analysis of the direction mink and fox releases should take in the future.

Bigger raids and more of them. There's nothing more to say.

ESSAYS

Writings from the Animal Liberation Front

CONTENTS

ESSAYS

For a law-abiding activist, penning words about their work is a low-effort, zero-risk endeavor. To an admitted felon, it requires legal risks and a laborious security protocol.

As such, we rarely see dispatches from behind felony lines unless prompted by urgent stimuli. While a communique is almost obligatory, writings untied to a specific action—like those here—are exceptional.

There is an urgency to these words, as demonstrated by the effort required to write them. If the A.L.F. had one chance to address the rest of us, what message would they send? The essays here are a product of that question.

The Eco-Terrorist's Telegraph

Imagine you operate in an A.L.F. cell in one corner of the country. You've amassed enough experience that you have information of benefit to other A.L.F. cells. Yet without the option of cross-cell communication, you have no ability to reach them.

Imagine also you operate in an A.L.F. cell, and have a message to the broader above-ground movement. You want to continue your work, yet are seeking a commitment of support should you be caught (to use one example from this collection). Your anonymity prevents direct contact, and you have no ability to reach them.

In both these scenarios and many more, your only option is to write an essay, submit it to an above ground platform, hope they publish it, and hope your intended audience reads it.

In the aforementioned "cross-cell communication" category, we find multiple examples of "open letters to the A.L.F." here—letters at once *from* the A.L.F., and *to* the A.L.F. Among them, "Bulletin To Fur Farm Raiders" (on lessons learned releasing mink), and "Making It Count" (on limiting your risks to high-impact targets). Perhaps the most exotic A.L.F.-to-A.L.F. message is "Fire Is A Good Tool" (title mine), an open letter expressing one A.L.F. cell member's regrets after their 1999 rescue of 46 dogs from a laboratory in

California, and wishing they had burned the lab down behind them. This anonymous letter was published in the *Earth First Journal*, and reveals dissent not just within the A.L.F., but within individual cells.

Aiming their message a different direction are several direct challenges to the above-ground animal liberation movement. One, a direct call-out to activists whose support for A.L.F. prisoners is highly conditional, leaving the A.L.F. with no certainty they will be supported if arrested. Another confronts activists with a naïve belief the obligations of the A.L.F. fall on anyone other than themselves. And convicted mink liberator Kevin Olliff challenges "A.L.F. supporters" with their false sense of accomplishment in lieu of real contribution.

Probation As Podium

Like most sections, this one can be classified into two categories: The anonymously-authored, and the former-prisoner-authored.

In the latter, Rod Coronado's output exceeds all other convicted A.L.F. members (beyond his book *Flaming Arrows*, another book's-worth of essays exists, with over two dozen writings published across *Earth First Journal*, *No Compromise*, *Bite Back*, *Underground*, and more). Three significant essays were chosen from his work—including a fugitive communique, circulated while on the run, outlining conditions for his surrender; and "Open The Cages"—the most in-depth and well-informed look at the facts and myths of mink releases.

On the cusp of falling outside the guidelines for this book were two essays by JP Goodwin, convicted of breaking windows at a Memphis fur store. While I've excluded most content related to small-scale property damage, these essays fit into the bigger history of higher-impact A.L.F. activity through his work cheerleading the A.L.F. in the early days of their fur farm campaign (unofficially dubbed "Operation Bite Back Part II").

Another highlight, David Barbarash giving the raw numbers (vs. emotional distortions) around how many A.L.F. members actually get caught. A poor ability to assess probability of arrest may deter more actions than any other factor, and this essay attacks baseless myths with hard facts.

Open Enrollment At The A.L.F.

The A.L.F.'s most persistent message in this chapter is one that's impossible to miss, repeated in nearly every essay—a plea for action.

The reader would best heed this call, and take note the A.L.F. doesn't ask for "supporters"—they ask for participants.

Reforming the Fur Industry, ALF-Style

1992

Anonymous essay on destroying the fur industry.

The entire fur and trapping industry can be eliminated within three years. Two years ago we stated that it could be done in five, and so far it is going according to schedule.

Although there seems to be renewed interest in trapping and fur farming, 40% of all fur farms have gone out of business and trapping license sales have fallen as much as 75% In some states. Fur stores are dosing left and tight and It seems that most department stores are dropping fur- related items. They are on the run, but they're preparing for a last-gasp comeback and the pressure must be increased.

Of course, education tactics are very important, but the Animal Liberation Front focuses on direct action. First, let's address the trapping issue. Get a copy of a magazine called The Trapper and Predator Caller. If you can't find a copy, call them at 1-800-258-0929 and ask them who sells their publication in your town. (Note: Do not ask them to send you a copy. If you do, they'll have your name and address. Never use a private phone when you use an 800 number. The caller's number may automatically be recorded by the company being called. If your state permits the phone company to sell caller-identification services, make all local telephone calls from a pay phone. And make all toll calls from a pay phone to avoid them being listed on your phone bill.) The magazine lists trapping supply companies, and the state trapper associations along with the officer's names and addresses.

Call these people and act interested in trapping. If possible, find out where they are setting their traps. Consider the possibility of having a quiet little party in the trapper's fur shed where they keep their traps, pelts, and assorted equipment.

Trapping is a business and if you destroy their means for doing business, they just may go out of their murderous business, if not their moronic minds.

Now for some heavier anti-trapping fun! There are four big trap manufacturers left in North America for steel jaw legholds, soft catch legholds, and body grip traps. They are Woodstream (the biggest which makes Victors and Conibears) in Lititz, PA; BMI in Willoughby Hills, OH; Duke Traps in West Point, MS; and Bridger in Ogden, UT. Just for the record, a turd named Harry Winter in Willits, CA is manufacturing a trap called the Dog Proof Coon Trap.

Shut these places down and we would cripple the wild fur industry severely.

Remember they doubtless have security guards. Every hit makes them tighten security so be cautious and make it count! Group security is absolutely essential so don't tell anyone.

Be warned that trappers and fur farmers are likely to be strong and armed and woods wise. Their livelihood (deadlihood) involves intimacy with blood, guts, and murder. They are not likely to be finicky when dealing with anybody they believe is mucking about with their income.

Other important targets are the publications of the fur trade. The National Trappers Association (major anti-animal rights group and publisher of American Trapper Magazine) has offices in Bloomington, IL. Fur-Fish-Game, the other of the three major trapping magazines, is in Columbus, OH.

The Trapper and Predator Caller is published by Krause Publication, Iola, WI. There are two trade journals catering to the retail fur industry: Fur Age Weekly in Glenwood Landing, NY, and Fur World in New York City. Destroy these means of communication within the industry and their traps, and the whole industry will be hurting.

In 1990 there were 660 fur farms left. Chances are there is one within a two to three hour drive of where you live. Contact the murderers listed in the back of The Trapper and Predator Caller and tell them you'd like to visit a fur farm because you may want to start your own. They might tell you where one is located. Unless the farmer lives right there, this should be an easy hit. If you visit them during the day, consider what to do about your appearance, vehicle, and license plate.

On mink farms, there are usually a number of mink 3-4 years old used as breeding stock. The rest are less than a year old. Releasing the breeding stock and other adult-sized mink into the compound not only disrupts the whole process, but severely handicaps the farmer in differentiating breeding stock from the sale animals. Such mischief can ruin the next year's breeding plans. When this happened to one mink farm two years in a row, it shut down.

Spraying the animals with non-toxic dye, the way Greenpeace and Sea Shepherd spray seal pups, ruins the commercial value of the pelts. There are various colors of sheep dye that are non-toxic. Be careful not to spray the animals' eyes and ears.

Other sites that need a heavy dose of justice are distribution centers of the processed furs: Seattle Fur Exchange, Seattle, WA; D. Cohn Fur Processors, Greenville, SC; National Superior Fur Dressing, Chicago, IL; Russ Carmen Lures, New Milford, PA; Hudson Bay Co. Fur Sales, Corstadt, NJ; Crown of MN Inc, Minneapolis, MN; Klubertanz Equipment Co., Ederton, WI. To locate them, let your fingers do the walking. Your local phone directories are good for something besides creating profits for clearcutters.

Retail fur stores, listed under "fur" in your yellow pages, are the easiest hits. Glue the locks, spray paint the merchandise, etch the windows. Be creative and go for maximum impact.

This guide is a waste if action is not taken. This is war in defense of the innocent. The risk we take is nothing compared to the suffering caused by the fur industry. Put these words into action. There's no time to waste. Good luck and total secrecy.

Fugitive Communique

1993

Statement from Rod Coronado, sent from his life underground while on the run for a series of arson attacks and liberations carried out against the fur industry.

(ALF) spokesperson, Rod Coronado, who has been hiding due to threats against his life from the Federal Bureau of Investigation (FBI) and the fur industry, is willing to surrender to federal authorities under the following conditions.

1) That all grizzly bears held hostage as experimental subjects by Washington State University (WSU) be released to a wildlife rehabilitation center approved by People for the Ethical Treatment of Animals (PETA 301-770-8969) and Earth First! (406-728-8114), with the intent of returning the bears to their native homeland from which they were removed.

2) That WSU issue a public statement promising never to capture or acquire more endangered species as research subjects or for any other purposes.

3) That all tax-payer supported research being conducted on mink, coyotes and otters by Washington State University, Oregon State University, Michigan State University, and Utah State University be suspended.

Although the Coalition Against Fur Farms (CAFF) and the ALF do not approve of the incarceration of any native wildlife, Rod Coronado believes that the hostage exchange of one species for another is a reasonable alternative. If these three conditions are agreed to, and met, and negotiated through PETA and Earth First! — I, Rod Coronado, will turn myself in to federal authorities in Montana at the tribal headquarters of the Blackfoot Nation. As part of the agreement, I, Rod Coronado, swear to cooperate fully with Grand Jury Inquisitions into ALF activity that I am suspected in, relating to the defense of native wildlife and the environment. I swear to testify and answer all questions relating to my role as a spokesperson on behalf of the ALF, and as the Coordinator of the CAFF.

I, Rod Coronado, believe that my non-violent actions in defense of the earth are innocent acts to protect the ecological integrity of this country's natural heritage. This statement of conditions of surrender is in no way an admission of guilt to charges laid by the United States Government, or any other law enforcement agency. It is my belief that with a fair trial, the citizens of this country will recognize that the real acts of terrorism committed on university campuses in the last eighteen months, are those carried out by Oregon State researcher Ron Scott, Washington State researcher John Gorham, Michigan State researcher Richard Aulerich, and Utah State researcher Frederick Knowlton.

Recent attempts by the FBI to portray me as a fugitive evading arrest are standard practices by the US Government to convince the public that I am guilty and that I am a violent criminal — the first steps in justifying the assassination of Native American activists who choose to maintain their cultural and religious beliefs.

Through the example of US history, it is my understanding that if I was to continue my defense of Native American wildlife and lands, then I would be murdered by the FBI or people within the fur industry. The FBI, while questioning David Howitt in June 1992, acknowledged a threat against my life. In May 1992, when the FBI and the Bureau of Alcohol, Tobacco and Firearms (BATF) raided my mountain home in southern Oregon, the presence of automatic weaponry in my attempted arrest is a testament of the US Government's willingness to use deadly force to squash my representation of Native American wildlife, and those who defend that wildlife.

In over ten years of non-violent resistance to the destruction of native wildlife and lands, I have never caused an injury or loss of life to any living being. Through my obligation as a citizen of the earth, I have only ever targeted the implements of life's destruction, i.e. whaling ships in Iceland. I have never, nor will I ever, carry or use firearms or explosives in my defense of my earth mother. My religious beliefs recognize the sanctity of all life and would never allow me to justify a violent act that would result in the loss of life. It is only because of the FBI's record of violence against Native Americans such as Anna Mae Aquash, Leonard Peltier, Una Trudell, Pedro Bisonette and other American Indian Movement (415-552-1992) activists that I avoid contact with the US Government by living a life in hiding.

In the Spirit of Crazy Horse,
Rod Coronado
Coordinator, Coalition Against Fur Farms
Spokesperson, Animal Liberation Front

Life Underground

1994

Anonymous essay on going underground for animal liberation.

Hey! You out there! Are you awake? Have you really taken a good look around lately? Have you noticed what's going on? We have less forests now. We have more roads and concrete. We have less species of animals and plants now. We have more polluted air, water, and food. Life is dying all around us while corporate fucks and the brainless masses concern themselves with money and things. Have you noticed? If you get your news primarily from the corporations through TV and newspaper, you probably haven't noticed. The struggle for liberation and freedom for all species and the Earth continues. It's time to notice. It's time to help the struggle. It's time to get involved, because there just isn't much time left. If you're interested, read on. If not, go back to watching America's Most Wanted. You never know, you might just see your friends there. Then will you care?

The April 94 issue of *Militant Vegan* reports that there have been "more than 20 acts of sabotage and liberation in just the first 2 months" of 1994 in North America. By including vandalism and other minor attacks, the list grows to over 40. That's not counting what we'll never hear about these figures mean that some kind of action happens almost every day.

This year we've taken some blows as well. In Edmonton, the prosecutor of an A.L.F. activist appealed the sentence handed down to Darren Thurston and put him in a cell for 61/2 months so far (of a 2 year sentence) on top of the 141/2 months he already spent inside. In Spokane, Kim Trimiew and Deb Stout were imprisoned for months for refusing to talk to the grand jury about the A.LF.; this was Kim's second time behind bars for refusing to testify. David Barbarash served 4 months after being picked up at gunpoint by the FBI/BATF. The latest news is that Rod Coronado has been arrested after 2 years of freedom from the feds—now they want to keep him in jail until he is 99 years old. Arizona has become the most recent state to create laws specifically to criminalize animal liberation activists. There are already federal laws in place.

Grand juries are continuing until at least mid-1995 in five states (OR, WA, Ml, UT, LA). Direct FBI harassment of activists continues in at least 3 states so far this year.

Does this sound pretty bad to you? We need to remember that what this all really means, what it reflects, is the growth of our movement. There are now more brave sister and brother warriors forming cells and tribes and taking action. What it also means is that we have to be much more careful and smart in our daily activities. The "political climate" is not what it was ten or even five years ago. Now, in the mid-nineties, mistakes will be hard and costly. Follow the basic rules: don't use phones for anything, use only safe addresses for mail, shut your mouth - do not say anything to anyone, etc., etc. You know it all, right? Well, I hope so.

As the evolution of the struggle continues in this way and the attempts to squash it increase, we will see more of our brothers and sisters either in jail or on the run. We need to accept this as a reality because people do fuck up, and sometimes the feds do get lucky. We need to prepare ourselves for the increased repression. The first steps to take are to thoroughly clean your home, to get new i.d., and to start stashes of needed things such as money, food, gear, etc.

It doesn't matter whether you are active or not. If you have any friends or connections at all to active resistance fighters, then you may find yourself in need of i.d. at some point. Making your home safe means having all personal letters, diaries, photos, papers and magazines advocating illegal activities, and any related items such as that timing device you have been working on for months, it means having all this stuff out of your home and into a safe place. It may seem a bit inconvenient and perhaps unnecessary, but I tell ya, 5-10 years in a cell will be a lot more inconvenient. Also remember that someone else's actions in your city or neighborhood could precipitate a raid on your home even if you had nothing to do with it.

If you are an active warrior, you should consider ending your public life and begin your private one. There are a few activists who are living this way now, and so far none have been caught [since this was written, two underground North American activists have been captured by the feds.-ed]. One thing to consider is that all the people the feds are physically harassing right now, and all the activists who are or have gone to jail, have all been public people with all connections leading to their homes, jobs, friends, etc. An activist is much more secure and safe away from prying eyes, if s/he is a private person. A private life as an activist means not going to any public political rallies and demos, meetings or similar events. It means dropping out of a public existence as much as possible.

In this private life many new issues will come up that are sometimes not so easily dealt with. This includes loneliness and isolation, especially if you make a complete break from traditional friends and family. This is why the idea of a tribe is so important. We need each other for our psychic and emotional well-being, to enable us to cope and survive. This break from those friends and family does become necessary when you realize that those who lead public lives often do not fully understand your security needs. Many mistakes will happen such as mentioning your name over the phone or in the presence of others who will repeat the information to someone else. Your friends will do this, no matter how many times you've tried to explain the situation to them. Until your friends and relatives really and truly understand the level of security you need, it is wisest to have as little contact as possible with them. For those who do begin to understand, encourage them to get a safe address, and if you have one yourself (which you should) you can now safely communicate with each other through the mail.

Other issues that will come up tend to revolve around home and money. About the former, it is best not to live with people who can testify as to whether you were home on a certain day, or what firearms you have, or where you might have travelled. Will your housemates be brave enough and have the integrity to refuse to answer questions to an agent or a grand jury? Will they too choose jail over talking? Do you really know their breaking point? Think about it.

Perhaps your current home situation needs to be changed. Living on your own or with your comrades is the best: Living on the road is also an alternative. Whatever you decide to do; do it safely. No phones, no mail, do not arouse the suspicions of your neighbors. We are now in the era of safe actions and safe living.

The central issue that will keep coming up is the one of money. If you've been thinking ahead and have been part of the slave force, maybe you've put away a few thousand. Or maybe you've got some left over from grandma's inheritance. Eventually though, your personal supply will run out. A job is out of the question when you're leading a private activist life. Besides, there's so much real work to be done. So how will you survive? Surviving costs money, whether it's for food (you will need to cut down on shoplifting as it poses a huge risk to your survival) or for research work or for those tools, or for gas or for the occasional car rental or motel room. It all adds up.

Unfortunately, money is the one thing I haven't completely figured out yet. You can try your folks or your working friends to donate to your needs, or maybe you or they know of richer sympathetic folks. For those of you reading this who have been approached for money, or know of activists who need it, put your thinking caps on to figure this one out. The reality is, without the cash flow, ain't nothing much gonna happen.

This may sound so dire and depressing and especially difficult. This road is certainly not for everyone. Careful consideration must be given to this decision. Hard questions must be asked of yourself: Do I really think that letter writing, petitioning, marching, shouting, civil disobedience, and banner hanging will really change anything before it's too late? Is it almost too late already? Is there something more than needs to be done? Am I one of those people who needs to be doing that "something more"? There's nothing more this planet needs right now than committed Earth warriors. Think about it.

One thing I would like to touch on briefly is one not many people give much thought or credit to. That thing is magic, specifically, magical protection. Amid your scoffing and teasing I can happily say that there is magical energy to tap into. Most of my protection, outside of all the practical precautions I take, comes from my faith in the magical realm.

This is not to say I've ignored my own advice or acted callously, but much of my safety and security is greatly enhanced by my knowledge and understanding and "tuning in" to the magic around me. I look at it as a kind of chaos of energy which engulfs and connects every being and place. Once you learn to see signs of the energy, and begin to connect with the chaos around you, you can tap into the protective energies. There is no rule of how to do this; everybody must find their own way which suits their particular way of relating. A lot of it has to do with faith and a lot has to do with your connection to other like-minded souls and well as the natural world. Anyway, I'm not writing to convert you non-believers. All I'm saying is just open yourself up to the potential and the possibilities. What have you got to lose?

We have an incredibly enormous task on our hands, which is to help bring the madness to an end. The planet and all creatures on it have suffered long enough at the hands of humans. As conscious people we have the responsibility to stop the destruction, and to do that we must stop the humans and their criminal corporate enterprises. Earth warriors need help from you as soon as possible, and we need as many new dedicated souls as possible to join in the struggle. And, we need all the help magic can provide for us as well.

I want to talk a bit more about the support role. Fact is, most of you reading this, no matter how much you agree with the idea of resistance and direct action, will not participate in it or be prepared to involve yourselves in full-scale resistance. That's unfortunate, but not a complete waste. Truth is, in order for any level of direct action campaigns to continue and flourish, we need people who are not directly involved to offer much needed support. Here are some ideas, some of which have already been mentioned but they can be stressed over and over again.

You likely know someone who is involved in illegal actions. Help to maintain their security. How? By not asking them questions such as "Where are you going?" or "Where have you been?" By not talking about these people to your friends or strangers, casually, over the phone, or otherwise. By refusing to answer questions about them posed to you by anyone, either a close friend or the FBI. By opening your door to them when they need a place to crash, no questions asked. By offering them money when they come through town, because they need it, and their sources are few and far between. Like I said before, money is the main issue as far as support for an underground life and for continued actions. If you've got a job, consider putting away a set amount each month to support the underground. You may not know anyone now who is in need but in all probability you will sometime in the future. Hit up your wealthy friends and relatives, and they don't need to know what it's for.

There are other things to start acquiring and stashing. Nonperishable food such as grains and canned goods will always be useful. Know anyone who works in a health food store or even a Safeway? With the approach of world disorder, you yourself might just benefit from a well thought out survival plan. Aside from stashing food and money, you might also want to consider acquiring a gun and lots of ammo. Personally, I have no use for such things in 1994, but who's to say what might happen in 5-10 years. Every year it's getting harder to get a weapon for personal defense, so the smart thing to do would be to get that stuff now while you still can and simply stash it in one of those army ammo boxes buried in a spot in a national forest or somewhere. I would suggest either a 9mm or 38 with as much ammo as you can afford. If you never need it, great! But if you do need to defend yourself in the future, you will be prepared. The important thing to remember here is that there are people now, our friends, our brothers and sisters, who are, in 1994, on the run, avoiding police detection, trying to continue this struggle which we all believe in, carrying out actions for the Earth and the animals, and who are barely surviving and only just surviving due to the support, minimal though it is, and goodwill of some people and friends like you. Ideally, in my fantasy world, every one of you would immediately quit your jobs and your public lives and start your private underground life of activism and resistance. I know that won't happen, so the next best thing is for ya'll to start putting into place measures to support our comrades. Remember, we're out here on the front lines, and we need you! Let's support our troops!

Using Direct Action Against The Fur Trade

1995

How to destroy the fur industry using A.L.F. tactics.

It appears as if we are seeing a dramatic increase in the number of direct actions (DA) being carried out by the Animal Liberation Front (ALF) and similar direct action groups. It is my view that we must be strategic, intelligent, and focused if we want to be successful in the long run. If we take out the weaker animal abusers now, our resources and targets will not be so stretched in the future. Specifically, if we completely defeat the fur trade now, the meat, dairy, vivisection, etc. industries will be easier to handle in the future. Divided they fall, right?

"Direct action" is a term that can apply to many forms of activism but is commonly used in reference to live animal liberations and acts of economic sabotage (property damage). Direct action has been an important part of every successful social movement's history. The Underground Railroad, the Boston Tea Party, etc. are several actions where people risked their freedom for the better treatment of an oppressed group. Some criticize direct action but it should be noted that 1) without radical action, a society will not consider discussing an issue such as animal rights that requires such a change on the individuals part, 2) life is more valuable than an inanimate object such as a furriers windows, 3) direct action causes animal abuse to be cost prohibitive by causing insurance rates to rise, and 4) live liberation's achieve the desired goal immediately. To let an animal suffer on a farm and do nothing because of some sort of "respect for the law" is repulsive.

I would like to discuss ways in which DA (direct action) can be effectively used against the fur trade. I will discuss live animal liberations first. Basically, there are three ranch-raised fur animals: mink, fox, and chinchilla. Mink and fox are genetically wild and will survive when released into the woods. Minks can travel five miles a day while fox can travel twelve. They disperse quickly so there should be no worry that a habitat will be wrecked by a massive release of fur farm animals.

Mink and fox do bite so heavy gloves are a necessity. They can be grabbed and dropped on the other side of the fence. Don't ever put them into bags together as many A.LF. cells do when dealing with other animals. These particular species are very likely to start fighting when piled on top of each other. One idea is to cut holes in the fence around the compound and then open all the cages so that the animals can find their own way out. Plenty of escape routes should be provided. None should lead the animals towards a busy road. Also, release type actions should take place between late May and late October. If before then, the animals will be too young and if after this period, there may not be enough food available.

The chinchilla is a small herbivore that is native to the Andes mountains in South America. They can't be released into the wild and if liberated, should be given good homes. There are several things that should be taken into consideration concerning post-raid chinchilla care.

An important one is that they have a hard time tolerating extremes above 80 degrees F. If you should liberate chinchillas, please make sure that the person providing their new home has been educated about their special needs. Chinchilla care books are available at the book store and library.

Fur farms can still be hit even if a live liberation is not possible at that time. In October through December, the pelting stock (those about to be killed) will be the same size as the breeding stock (those kept to produce more animals). If all of the animals are released into the compound then the fur farmer won't know which are the breeders and which are the pelters. He will have to pelt them all out and spend thousands of dollars on new breeding stock. This is so annoying that sometimes they just give up for good. If anyone uses this tactic, they should make sure every animal cage is opened as it is hard for us to know which shed contains breeders and which doesn't. If a couple sheds are left untouched, then you might miss the breeding stock completely and the purpose of the hit will not have been achieved.

Non-toxic dyes can be sprayed on the animals' backs to ruin the economic value of their pelt. This is better than nothing, but as with the last described tactic, the animals will still be killed. The processing room and the feed storage barns can be hit as well. Malecky Mink Ranch in Yamhill, OR was put out of business when the A.L.F. burned down their processing barn. Arson should only be used when it can be guaranteed that the fire will not spread to the sheds the animals are in.

Fur farmers have specialized tractors that dispense feed on top of the cages. These vehicles can be trashed in a number of ways. One easy one is to buy a bottle of muriatic acid at the hardware store. This costs about three dollars for one or two gallons. Simply pour it all over the engine and leave.

Your state department of agriculture may have a list of fur farms in your state. You can call and ask and if they ask questions say you're a potential fur farmer looking for breeding stock. It may be wiser to contact the Coalition to Abolish the Fur Trade. They have a small fur farm list, and while their list may not be complete, at least they won't tell who ordered the lists from them. For security purposes, claim you need the list for research and investigations. Their address is: PO Box 40641, Memphis, TN, 381 74, USA. Try and send $1 to cover postage and printing.

Economic sabotage can also be employed. This simply involves smashing fur shops' windows, squirting super glue into the locks, spray painting, filling bell peppers or Christmas ornaments with paint and "paint bombing" the building, etc. To be effective, a place should be hit repeatedly. Every hit causes security to increase so go for maximum destruction.

Send press releases about fur hits to the Coalition to Abolish the Fur Trade.

It's past time to end the fur trade for good. Let's take to the streets and stop the killing. Action speaks louder than words.

Using Direct Action Against The Fur Industry

1995

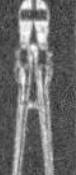

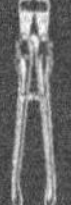

More tactical guidance from an A.L.F. member on taking down the fur industry through direct action.

The A,L.F. can defeat the fur industry. Remember all of the lab raids and animal liberations that took place in the eighties? Imagine if the same amount of energy and enthusiasm was put-into attacking fur farms in the nineties. I think that the fur industry would be crushed.

All fur animal species, except chinchilla, can be released into the wild and survive. They disperse quickly and travel many miles in a single day so there is no need to fear a huge ecological imbalance as a result of a massive mink liberation.

Malecky Mink Ranch was torched in Dec. 1992. The fur farm industry tried to decline that this was an A.L.F. action for quite some time. Eventually they could no longer hide from the truth as pieces of an incendiary device were found. Presumably they wanted to cover this up so that other mink ranchers wouldn't be scared out of the business. If scores of fur farms were raided then the industry would be devastated and many would stop raising fur animals for fear of losing their entire investment. Remember, most fur farmers do this part time and are not solely dependent on mink and fox to make a living. Therefore they are much easier to push out of business as opposed to a chicken farmer, etc.

If A.L.F. cells were to raid fur farms, one thing should be remembered. The animals aren't old enough to release until after May. Also, they must be liberated before late October because otherwise winter will have set in and they won't have time to learn how to efficiently hunt for food as most prey species will now be more difficult to catch. ·

National Fur Foods in New Holstein, WI is doing major research to make fur farming more profitable. The same is true for Wildlife Pharmaceutical in Fort Collins, CO. I'm surprised that these two companies haven't been targeted yet. The A.L.F. completely shut down the mink research center at Oregon State University and crippled several other fur animal research centers. National Fur Foods could be the strongest remaining.

On the retail level, I think all activist groups should really hammer the department stores that still sell fur. I would bet that they sell as much, if not more fur, than regular retail furriers. This is because they have more walk-in traffic, a better advertising budget, and their own charge accounts. Also, they can be forced to get rid of fur because they aren't solely dependent on the sale of such items. The thing to remember is that one or two spaced out actions aren't enough. Persistence is the key!

The Coalition to Abolish the Fur Trade, PO Box 40841, Memphis, TN 38174, has a list of fur farms which they sent out to anyone. For yours and their protection, claim you need it for research and investigations.

Then, pass the lists around to everyone. Let's not let them hide these hellholes anymore! I really believe that the A.L.F. can finish the furriers off. The body count is rising in the fur concentration camps.

Are we going to lose ground and then the whole battle, or are we going to fight harder than ever and liberate every last animal?

TOTAL LIBERATION
anonymous

Spread Your Love Through Action

1995

Open letter from Rod Coronado,
written in prison.

On March 3, 1995, I pled guilty to aiding and abetting a fire at Michigan State University (MSU) that destroyed 32 years of research intended to benefit the fur farm industry. The Animal Liberation Front (ALF) claimed responsibility for the raid, the seventh in a series of actions dubbed "Operation Bite Back" which targeted fur farms and universities engaged in tax-payer supported research jointly funded by the fur trade. I also pled guilty to one count of theft of US Government property; in particular, a journal belonging to a 7th Cavalry Officer killed at the Little Bighorn near Crow Agency, Montana in 1876. This negotiated plea agreement is the result of a seven year investigation by the FBI into my activities, and the federal government's continued targeting of indigenous activists who assert their sovereignty and continue their fight for cultural survival. It is also the culmination of nine federal grand juries that have lasted over three years, subpoenaed over sixty political activists, jailed four for six months each, and harassed and intimidated countless others in the hunt for members of the ALF.

In return for the guilty pleas, the US government promises not to seek further prosecution of me in the remaining districts investigating the ALF, nor subpoena me to testify against others suspected of ALF activity. The price I pay for not testifying against my compatriots is a three to four year prison sentence.

Prior to the plea agreement, I was the sole defendant in a seven court indictment alleging that I was responsible for a nationwide coordinated effort to cripple fur farm research and development. With a lifetime commitment to protect the earth behind me and in front of me, I must choose carefully the battles in which I fight, and the arenas in which I fight them.

Like most indigenous people, I am unable to match the limitless resources of the US government in their efforts to incarcerate me, nor am I able to adequately defend myself amidst laws that criminalize the preservation of our sacred earth mother.

This is only the latest attempt by the US Government to make an example of those who break free from the confines of legitimate protest. At a time when ecological and cultural destruction is commonplace and within the perimeter of the law, it sometimes becomes necessary to adhere to the highest laws of nature and morality rather than stand mute witness to the destruction of our land and people. I believe it to be the obligation of the earth warrior never to be ashamed of one's own actions to honor the sacred tradition of indigenous resistance. Therefore, I accept full responsibility for my actions and remain grateful to have had the honor of serving as a member of the ALF as their spokesperson and supporter.

With a record of over 300 animal liberation actions and rescues in the US without injury or loss of life, yet thousands of lives spared from the horrors of vivisection and fur farming, the women and men of the ALF remain to me some of the most respected of non-violent warriors in the struggle to save our planet. MY role in the MSU raid was a non-participant, acting as a conduit for the truth hidden behind locked laboratory doors. While in Ann Arbor, Michigan, awaiting instructions, I received a phone call from an anonymous ALF member detailing the raid for inclusion into a press release. Later, I received research materials and evidence seized during the raid. These documents would have exposed taxpayer sponsored research benefiting the fur farm industry, and experiments where mink and otters are force-fed toxins and other contaminants until they convulse and bleed to death. Accompanying these documents was a video tape of the cramped and unsanitary conditions mink and otter endure at MSU's research laboratories. My desire to release this information to the public was greater than my desire to protect myself from rabid investigations by the FBI and the ATF. Seventeen months later, I was indicted by the Michigan grand jury based on this evidence.

Earlier in the month of February, 1992, I was at the Little Bighorn River in Montana. I went to the site of the infamous battle and was shocked at this, the only monument I know of that glorifies the loser. In further disgrace to the warriors who lost their lives defending their families and homelands, the monument paints a one-sided story of the conquest of the indigenous peoples of the Great Plains by the US military. The truth remains that George Armstrong Custer and his 7th Cavalry were an illegal occupational force trespassing in clear violation of the Fort Laramie treaty of 1868 to attack peaceful encampments of non-combatants in the heart of the Lakota Nation.

The theft of the Cavalryman's journal is a reminder of indigenous discontent with the treatment of our heritage and culture by the US Government.

Over the last ten years I have placed myself between the hunter and the hunted, the vivisector and the victim, the furrier and the fur bearer, and the whaler and the whale. These are my people, my constituency. It is them that I owe my life. I have chosen to continue the time honored tradition of resistance to the invading forces that are ravaging our homes and people. Many people have been tortured, murdered and imprisoned on this warrior's path, yet we must continue to stand tall against the tyranny that has befallen this continent in the last 503 years. As warriors we must accept that prison awaits those who are unwilling to compromise the earth and her people when we choose to remain allegiant to fellow warriors whose identity remains unknown. We are all Subcommandante Marcos, Crazy Horse and the ALF. Never, ever, should we forget that in order to achieve the peace and liberation we strive for, some sacrifice is necessary. This will not be the first time an indigenous person has gone to prison while upholding the obligation to protect our culture, homelands and people, and it most definitely will not be the last. It is with total love that I say good-bye to my earth mother for a little while to enter the concrete and steel prisons of US Government reserves for its discontent citizens. Such rewards await those who must give their lives and freedom to prevent destruction of the most beautiful planet in the universe, our life-support system, our beloved mother earth.

To those who have fought beside me: you will always be my friends and families and for you I will give up that which I love the most, my freedom. I will face prison rather than speak one word against those on the frontlines of the battle to protect earth. Our relationship is a sacred one. And in your freedom I pray that you spread your love through action that continues to rescue all that remains wild. Never surrender!

Though we may never see each other again in the trenches of the struggle for animal and earth liberation through illegal direct action, in my heart I will always hold you closest. Be patient my friends. I have not forgotten those already behind bars, those in the traps and in the rifle sights of man's ignorance and greed. It is time for me to hand over my role as a "hero" to the animal and environmental movement to others whose faces are not yet known.

To you I give the responsibility to preserve and protect what is left of the splintered nations of others we call animals. In your hands lie the future of this centuries-old struggle, in yourselves you must find heroes. Now you must take the risks rather than cheer on those who have walked before you. Carry her spirit well, and shower yourselves in her beauty when in need of true power. I have been brought back home to my people, the Yaqui Nation and it is to them that I now return to satisfy the restless spirits of my great grandmothers whose cries I must answer.

Sometimes we are forced to do things we do not like when we are warriors.

On this land that I now live, where my ancestors are buried, the great warrior Geronimo sometimes found it necessary to surrender to the enemy in order to recruit young warriors for future battles. We are a patient people. Never forget the beauty, magic, love and life we fight so hard to protect and that others have given so much to defend.

Our pain and sadness is very real but so is our happiness and joy as we witness the coming Spring. I will always be beside you and you may always find shelter in my home. I love you all, and in you I place the hopes for a rebirth and a rekindling of our sacred relations to all animal people and creation.

Forever in Your Honor and in Her Service.

Rod Coronado-Wiiko Yau Ura
Pascua Yaqui Tribe

Fur Wars Heat Up: A.L.F. On The Warpath

1996

After being jailed for attacks on fur stores, JP Goodwin took a leadership role in the aboveground anti-fur movement, and cheerleading A.L.F. actions against the fur industry that surged in the mid-1990s.

It was reported in the last issue that the Animal Liberation Front had declared war on fur farmers and was going all out in an intense campaign for mink liberation. June, July, and August saw as many actions against mink farms as the whole year before that.

On June 7th the A.L.F. made their first attack against a Utah fur farm. The A.L.F. had already smashed one local retailer up so many times that they had put a sign in the window reading "No Fur Products Sold Here Anymore." This time they went into the Fur Breeders Agriculture Co-op in Sandy, and liberated 50-75 mink. Apparently this raid marked the beginning of what appears to be a long, hot summer for Utah fur farmers.

Three weeks later the A.L.F. struck again, this time in Riverton, Utah. They reported that some mink were dead in their cages while others were piled up under the cages, rotting in the other mink's feces. Some mink were cannibalized, and the whole place was filthy. The A.L.F. opened the cages and freed 1000 mink who ran into nearby fields enjoying their new found freedom.

At some point in the month of June the A.L.F. struck in Washington state. We don't have any details except that 80 mink were liberated. This cell did not report the name of the city, name of the farm, or the date that it happened.

July 4th turned out to be a true independence day for animals. In Langley, British Columbia the A.L.F. raided the Akagami mink ranch and released 400 animals. We called the mink farmer posing as reporters and spoke with his wife. She claimed that the mink would starve to death as they hadn't been trained to hunt for food. She then shot holes in that myth by claiming that the liberated mink had killed and eaten a dozen geese in the area. So much for starvation!

On the same night, another A.L.F. cell raided the Latzig mink ranch in Howard Lake, Minnesota. Another 1000 mink were liberated this time. This led to massive media coverage. Myself and Freeman Wicklund from Animal Liberation League did numerous media interviews and debates, explaining that now these mink had a chance at life, whereas before, death was certain.

The Minneapolis Star Tribune ran quotes from CAFT refuting the fur farmers' claims that the mink wouldn't survive. The public was educated to the fact that mink have escaped from fur farms in many places where there were no native mink populations. Not only did they survive, they reproduced. This proves that ranch raised mink still have the natural instincts necessary for survival in the wild. The alternative is death in a gas chamber, or by broken neck.

Another A.L.F. cell reported that they were going to carry out a third raid on Mac Ellis Fox Farm in Tennessee, but that the place was now out of business. Apparently this is a result of last fall's raid which saw the release of half the fox on that farm.

The A.L.F. didn't stop there. The next target was Holt Mink Ranch in South Jordan, Utah. Utah fur farmers are scared. They have been installing heavy duty fencing with aluminium plates along the top that make a lot of noise when someone tries to go over them. Holt had installed this sort of fencing, but the A.L.F. took it apart, cut it down, and rolled up. They also smashed the new locks on all of the cages. 3000 mink were released, but police arrived and the group had to evacuate. TV news reported that damage to breeding cards alone amounted to $35,000.

The A.L.F. struck next in Hinsdale, Massachusetts at the Carmel Mink Ranch. 1,000 mink were released. The August 10th action led to national coverage. Even CNN reported on the raid. Two nights later the A.L.F. was in Alliance, Ohio for another break in that led to the liberation of 2,500 mink. Though some mink have been recovered at each site, many are now free, and the industry is going ballistic.

These raids have been very successful. So successful that the fur industry will do almost anything to stop them from occurring. They have put out a $100,000 reward for the arrest and conviction of any A.L.F. activist involved in a fur farm raid. One fur auction house has taken out an insurance policy for any fur farmers which ship through them. They are worried that their farmers will start closing up as a result of this. They are already spending millions of dollars in extra security nationwide.

The industry has produced a booklet that they are sending out to farmers. This booklet describes security techniques that they can adopt. Security techniques which the A.L.F. dismantled in Utah, putting the industry to shame. We haven't gotten a copy of the booklet yet.

Sadly, some so-called "animal defenders" are not so supportive of these raids. Ann Davis of the Salt Lake City, Utah based Animal Rights Alliance has stated that she has already talked to the FBI, and will continue to do so. The

FBI is working for the fur industry. Anyone that works with them is working hand in hand with the fur trade and is a traitor. If you don't want to be investigated then don't associate with turncoats. With friends like these, the mink are screwed.

Let it be stated loud and clear, that myself and the Coalition to Abolish the Fur Trade support these actions 100%. We will never, ever, ever work with anyone who helps the FBI stop the A.L.F.. Put yourself in the minks place and think of how it must feel. Merritt Clifton of *Animal People* magazine has spread outright lies and misinformation about the mink liberation campaign. Would these people rather see these mink piled up in a gas chamber while the fur trade gets rich? Apparently so.

Fortunately, most animal rights activists realize that this is one of the best things to happen in a long time. The A.L.F. looks like they won't stop, and the authorities are nowhere near catching them.

Fur Wars Intensify

1996

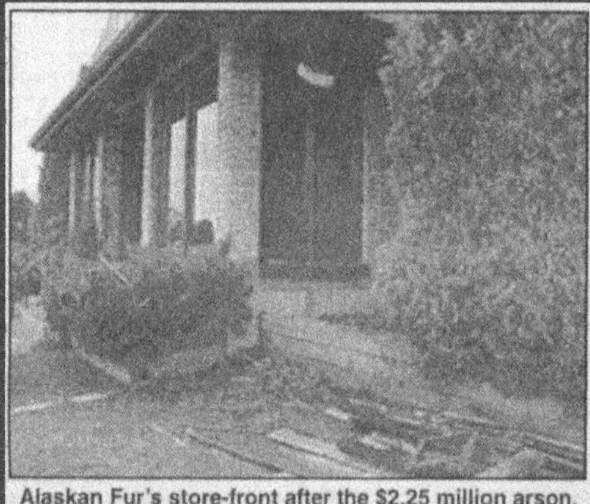
Alaskan Fur's store-front after the $2.25 million arson.

"A.L.F. Close Two Farms! $2.25 Million Blaze At Alaskan Fur!"

Second article from JP Goodwin, documenting the A.L.F.'s then-surging anti-fur campaign.

The A.L.F. has been very busy in the last few months and this increase in action couldn't have been more timely. As we move into both the fur retail season, and the killing season on fur farms, underground activists are striking out, trying to stop as much of the suffering as possible.

A.L.F. cells have been attacking fur retailers with window smashing, paint bombs, and glued locks. Active cells have been creating headaches for furriers in Minneapolis, Washington, DC, New York City and Dallas among others. A communiqué from a Dallas group claimed that they had even sprayed muriatic acid (available at hardware stores) through a furrier's mail slot, and apparently doused the room.

Fur farms still continue to be the A.L.F.'s number one target, and with good reason. Demand from Asian countries is making fur farming profitable, very profitable. It is conceivable that we could destroy the retail fur industry in North America and Western Europe, but if growth continues at its current rate, China, Russia and South Korea could consume enough fur within five years to keep fur farmers very busy.

There are some potholes in the road though. If there is a shortage of fur, and current demand cannot be met, then fur will not take off in those areas. If the fur farm industry is shut down by direct action then Asian demand will be irrelevant. There are about 450 mink farms in the US, along with a hundred or so small fox farms, and another hundred or so chinchilla farms. If the A.L.F. continues with an increased pace in 1997, then it will be interesting to see which fur farmers can remain in business.

It was reported last issue that the A.L.F. had raided the Jorney Mink Ranch in Alliance, OH. Justine Jorney is the president of the Ohio Mink Breeders Association, and the A.L.F. is gunning for her. Her farm was raided again on September 28th, and this time 8,000 mink were released. News footage claimed that this farm was struggling to survive after the second raid. Mink were seen several cities away, doing just fine. This farm is three times bigger than the average mink ranch, and its collapse would be a major victory for animal liberation.

The A.L.F. carried out 6 raids in October. On October 2nd the A.L.F. attacked the Paul Westwood Fur Farm in Salem, UT. 1,500 mink were released and breeding records were destroyed.

Moving quickly to the New England area, the A.L.F. attacked the Gauthier Fur Farm in Lindboro, NH. 35 fox and 10 mink were released, and property was damaged. A local news station did an interview with a disguised individual (voice over, etc.) who claimed to be in the A.L.F.. Killing footage from fur farms was shown on the news, along with the interview. This led to more public education than could ever be accomplished with letter writing or passing out flyers.

On October 11th the A.L.F. made a second raid on Carmel Mink ranch in Hinsdale, MA. The Carmel's had installed infra-red security beams which shot out over the tops of the cages. When a cage was opened, the current was broken, and presumably an alarm would be set off somewhere. The A.L.F. went to work anyway, opening 75 cages before the farmer came out and chased them off.

The next fur farm raid occurred on October 23rd in Lebanon, OR. Arnold Kroll lost 2,000 mink in a raid that made major headlines throughout the state. A.L.F. cells in Oregon have already forced the Oregon State University Experimental Mink Farm and Malecky Mink Ranch out of business. Hopefully, they will continue the tradition and shut the last 27 Oregon mink farms down.

Just a day later, the A.L.F. was in Utah for the fifth time. During the early morning hours of October 25th the A.L.F. raided the Reese fur farm, and released 2,000 mink and 200 foxes. It began to appear as if Utah, which has more fur farms than any other state, would set the tone for the battle over fur farms in the coming years.

Newspapers have stated that some Utah ranchers are sleeping in their trucks with shotguns cradled in their arms. Those who are in bed at night are so paranoid that the slightest noise has them jumping up and running outside. Some farms have put up heavy duty electric fencing, and installed flood lights. I guess this was to put the finishing touches on their concentration camp appearance. Others have security dogs, security guards and/or hourly patrols. Either way, the A.L.F. has proven that they will by-pass all of this and free the animals, one way or another.

The campaign continued with another repeat attack at the Bennett Fur Farm in Victor, NY. This time the A.L.F. had to cut down 3 perimeter fences to gain access to the compound. This was a huge mink ranch until the A.L.F. targeted them last April. Now the A.L.F. states that they had 40 or 50 empty sheds, and the group could only find a small number of foxes. 46 of these fox were liberated, and breeding records were destroyed, before an incoming security truck forced them to evacuate.

Perhaps one of the most devastating anti-fur actions taken by the A.L.F. this year was on November 12th at the Alaskan Fur Co., a retailer in the Minneapolis suburb of Bloomington, MN. Someone threw an incendiary device through the window, destroying the first floor of this two story furrier. $2.25 million in damage was done.

At this point, the A.L.F. has not claimed the action, but most people suspect that it was anti-fur militants. Alaskan Fur Co. had been targeted for spray painting, etc. in years past. After the news reported the fire, the Coalition to Abolish the Fur Trade sent out a press release supporting the attack. This led to a media feeding frenzy. All 4 Minneapolis TV stations ran it as the top story, and one even showed fur farm footage as well. CAFT members did several radio interviews and debates, and there was extensive news coverage in Minneapolis and St. Paul newspapers.

Marsha Kelly of Fur Commission USA refused to directly debate a CAFT representative, and then spent most of her airtime talking about meat and vivisection, etc. This falls in line with her statement to Fur Rancher magazine in the Fall of 1992. At that time she claimed that the fur industry must direct attention to other, more accepted forms of animal exploitation. "It is not in our best interest to focus on ourselves" she said. I wonder why that would be?

The fur trade claimed to be on a rebound, but we shall see what really happens. So long as the A.L.F. maintains constant pressure, it is safe to say that many will feel it is a wise business decision to leave the fur industry.

If Not You, Who?

1996

Anonymous essay challenging activists to make their actions consistent with their rhetoric, and start taking risks to save animals.

In today's society, those who rescue animals from places of abuse and cause economic damage to institutions of earth and animal exploitation while revealing the horror that is committed against them, are terrorists. In today's society those who burn, maim, electrocute, shoot, trap, poison and torture animals are sportsman, scientist, farmers, and businessmen and women. We live in a society where these convoluted perceptions of good and bad are force-fed to us as the value-system that the government claims makes us the most free society in the world today. In school, work and family we are sometimes brutally reminded that to stray from the accepted norms of society is to be ostracised from it, which all too often is followed by police repression of us social deviants and potential "domestic terrorists."

Many authoritarians in this society speak of our "war for independence" and pride themselves on their heritage of building a democratic society out of a harsh and forbidding wilderness. In North America, the dominant worldviews (both moral and legal) that we are intimidated into accepting is nothing short of the forced indoctrination of a foreign value system from an invading force occupying our homelands which has historically sought to destroy all human cultures that strengthen and maintain our connection to earth and animals.

Each of us in our own hearts knows it is wrong to force-feed poisons to rabbits, rats and mice or any animal for that matter, but how many of us are willing to violate the "laws" of our society and commit the "crime" of breaking and entering, grand theft, and destruction of property to stop it? Once we cross that line, it takes us from peaceful protesters to alleged felons in our pursuit of the bond to earth and animals. Animal Liberation Front activists face many years in prison, huge fines and restitution, long periods of probation where violations mean more years in prison, loss of certain constitutional rights such as the right to keep and bear arms, to vote and the bearing of a "scarlet letter" which prevents employment, international travel and almost always guarantees government harassment for the rest of their lives. Such is the price for taking our opposition to animal abuse and earth exploitation beyond the accepted perimeters of protest.

So why risk all in order to save a few animals and lessen the profit margin of the government sanctioned vested interests who destroy nature? Because we're tired of waiting for others to stop unquestionable evil in this world.

We're tired of being dragged from the picket line and watching truckloads of animals going to slaughter, of bulldozers rolling toward the destruction of wilderness animal homes. Where civil disobedience in our movement mostly centers around drawing attention to the abuse and exploitation of animals and earth, A.L.F. actions seek to rescue the prisoners of that abuse and hinder if not cease that abuse by destroying the machines and tools of life's destruction.

Through sharing the very same goal, the difference in tactic and regard for man's law matters greatly in the eyes of the slanted scales of justice. Legal strategies that might be proven effective in one realm may not apply in another, the only similarity being the motive behind the action. So why does the A.L.F.· continue to participate and advocate tactics that seriously threaten their personal liberty and physical freedom?

Because what we endure in a prison cell or at the wrong end of a fur farmer or law enforcement officer's gun is minuscule when compared to what our governments have allowed to happen on this continent to animals in the last 5 centuries. Though the A.L.F. may never receive the support or participation of as many who support or participate in civil disobedience and protests, these are some of the reasons A.L.F. activists have chosen to sacrifice certain unnecessary liberties to ensure fundamental liberties for animals.

Anyone who has ever seen video or photographic documentation of animal abuse (often obtained by the A.L.F.) can relate to the feelings of powerlessness and inability to stop the torture. Screaming your lungs out on a protest line and even getting arrested in acts of civil disobedience are ways that we manifest our rage and anger, but often the feelings of impotence return and we are left facing the continued torture and abuse of literally billions of animals.

For A.L.F. members a life of obedience to laws and values that sanction the destruction of all we love is no life at all. How can we as fellow members of the same species responsible for such cruelty and global destruction, as we now witness today, not do all that is humanly possible to stop it? One need only rescue one individual from the fate of the vivisection laboratory or fur or factory farm to experience the satisfaction and peace that comes with knowing that at least one prisoner has escaped. Any feelings of insignificance from such an action when compared to the thousands not liberated are erased as you witness the joy and love for life that all animals are capable of expressing when released from their misery. I will never forget the reward of watching a little female guinea pig I once knew being received with such gentle love and compassion by an elderly woman who warned me of animal dealers who kidnap pets for vivisection.

Little did she know (or need to know) of the impending fate of our little animal relation had the A.L.F. not rescued her from the vivisection supplier who had already sold her to a lab for LOSO testing. Thousands of guinea pigs are tortured in vivisection laboratories every year, but at least this one wouldn't be.

Fighting factory farming can also leave the average activist feeling overwhelmed when simply being vegan doesn't stop millions of chickens from being forced to live a cramped existence on egg farms. Yet it doesn't take more than even the smallest backyard to build a chicken coop that would be heaven to 6 or 7 laying hens. Many times I have broken into egg farms to help rescue a few chickens who were precariously clinging to life in their squalid conditions, and it has been a true blessing and beacon of hope to see these intelligent animals recover from their confinement. Within days, even chickens are capable of somehow remembering how to dust-bathe, scratch for bugs and worms, and roost at night. Social structure and individual personality returns to all animals when given the opportunity.

When one liberates any animal from a certain death with the guarantee of life incredibly better than any other in its intended fate, a victory is achieved for all who believe in the rights of animals. We remind ourselves and others of the inherent worth of all life and how the values and laws of the society we oppose deny not only animals but also ourselves true freedom. ·

So open up your home to rescued animals and assist others in finding homes for the liberated. Let it be known to fellow activists that you can support certain types of animals and maybe the A.L.F.'s Underground Railroad will come knocking on your door. And if you know of someone who would feed and care for animals if a coop or other facilities were built on their property then get out there with a hammer, nails and recycled lumber and build it.

And when it's built don't wait for the A.L.F. to find tenants, get out there and get them out yourself. For the urban guerilla or activist who wants to really impact the cycle of animal abuse, economic sabotage is the A.L.F.'s salvation. How often we all have stood in front of university torture chambers on that one day a year we dedicate to laboratory animals, only to go away at the end of the day knowing that for the 364 other days that year the animals will be used and abused as if they weren't the living, breathing, and feeling sentient beings that they are. Yet in one night animal research laboratories have been shut down, hundreds of animals liberated and research experiments ruined by A.L.F. attacks.

Though the tactics may appear extreme to the uneducated or unaware, the A.L.F. has always countered that the true extremists and terrorists are those who, in the light of day and fully within the bounds of the law, conduct painful experiments on animals. Many above-ground activists find it easier to support live animal liberations with their happy endings, but for the animals left behind there is no happy ending when the torture chambers are emptied but not destroyed.

To this day, the greatest impact caused in vivisection laboratories and other A.L.F. targets has been through arson. In June of 1991 when the A.L.F. torched Oregon State Universities Experimental Fur Farm, a handful of activists no different from yourself, accomplished every anti-vivisectionists dream. Not only was the 65 year old laboratory shut down and every research project destroyed, but information obtained from the vivisectors own records helped contribute to numerous raids on other fur farms and laboratories. Most often animal rights activists are mistakenly led to believe that animal research laboratories are secured fortresses, but such is not always the case. All it takes to find out is for every animal liberation activist to adopt a vivisection center in their area and spend late nights observing the nightly habits and routines of maintenance and security staff if any. After a few weeks you may be surprised to discover that a window of opportunity is available, enough to allow liberationists the opportunity to strike. Once you have balanced the scales of true justice by making your own rules in the fight to defend animals and the earth through illegal direct action, you will have discovered what our enemies fear most, the unleashed fury that is the A.L.F.

Federal investigators, biomedical researchers, fur industry officials and other pro-animal abuse forces rarely talk of their fears of a demonstration, protest, or civil disobedience. What really keeps them up at night are the lightning strike raids of the A.L.F. The current $100,000 reward for the capture of an A.L.F. activist speaks the truth of what animal abusers fear the most.

So why not try pursuing the shortest path to animal liberation? Think of all the risks you would take if your very own dog or cat was being tortured in a vivisection laboratory and then try to explain the difference between your own companion animal and the millions of animals in research lab, factory and fur farms today. Remember, animals are our brothers and sisters in this world. They are innocent beings who know not why they are being punished at the hands of man. Let's not forsake them and leave them to the fate of the merciless. The A.L.F. will not forget our connection to the natural world and the animal people and will continue to strive towards a harmonic relationship with ail fife. We do this because of love not hate. Governments can imprison us, but they cannot break our spirit.

Please join us in our quest for immediate and total animal liberation.

Open The Cages

1996

Prison essay from Rod Coronado on the facts vs myths of raiding fur farms.

On October 23, 1995 the Animal Liberation Front (A.L.F.) opened the cages on the Dargatz Mink Farm in British Columbia, Canada freeing 2,400 mink into the surrounding countryside. The liberation from the Dargatz Mink Farm was the first in what now has become 12 liberation raids by the A.L.F. of fur farms in North America in less than a year. The result has been the release of approximately 11,000 mink, 30 fox and one coyote from the intensive confinement that would have led to death for all prisoners.

The release of animals from fur farms is nothing new. In the former Soviet Union, Iceland, mainland Scandinavia, Western Europe, Britain and Newfoundland, Animal Liberation raids as well as accidental and intentional escapes from fur farms have resulted in mink and some fox being introduced successfully into the natural environment.

In Britain, the ecological impact of these releases has been measured, and as liberated mink conveniently fill the ecological niche left by Britain's now extinct otter population, the negative impact has been minimal. In Iceland's island ecosystem, and in parts of Scandinavia, mink has been slightly more destructive to the ecological balance. Never has the question of formerly captive mink's survivability been questioned by those in the know, only the level of impact these beautiful fierce predators have as they successfully re-adapt to a wild life.

NORTH AMERICAN MINK

In North America, it's a whole different story. Although there is a Eurasian species, mink are believed to be native to North America with the theory that the Eurasian species originated from North American ancestors who crossed the ice bridge between this continent and Asia. Previous to the "discovery" of the "New World," mink were one of the many aquatic animals that flourished in virtually every lake and waterway in North America except the desert regions.

The war against the mink nation that continues today, began when the first Europeans invaded their homeland. When the Mayflower first rounded Cape Cod, Massachusetts in 1620, already Jamestown, Virginia was the hub of an extensive fur trade. A price list from 1621 records mink among other animals fetching up to ten shillings apiece on the market to which modern day fur farmers can claim as their bloody lineage.

The fur trade can also accept responsibility for causing the extinction of the native mink's saltwater cousin, the sea-mink. Nearly twice the size of their freshwater relations, and recorded as inhabiting the whole Northeastern North American Seaboard, and all that remains of this being are two skins and a pile of bones. That and of course the memory of one furrier who before the American Revolution recalls the pelt of the sea-mink selling for five guineas. And so it is, by the end of the 19th century, fresh-water mink were severely depleted from their former range in all of North America by a fur industry thirsty for the blood of this continent's fur animals.

BEGINNINGS OF MINK CAPTIVITY

Unlike their European and Scandinavian counterparts, mink farmers in the United States and Canada began the attempted domestication and economic exploitation of mink often from live captured wild mink populations. In the 1920's this new element to the fur trade began.

In 1925 Kent Vernon's family in Northern Utah (now president of the Utah fur-breeders Co-Op) live-trapped chicken-killing mink from the wild and began breeding them in captivity. In 1927 the U.S. Government opened its Experimental Furbearer Research Station in Corvallis, Oregon (shut down by an A.L.F. raid in 1991) and began experimentation in different techniques to breed wild mink in captivity. With overexploited mink populations unable to satisfy the demands of an increasing demand for fur, trappers across North America began to captive-raise wild mink, and in the 1930's discovered fur mutations that altered the minks fur color. Now just 70 short years later, mink farmers are still battling the still dominant wild DNA of captive mink that causes these normally free-roaming solitary animals to contract diseases from close confinement, self-mutilate and even cannibalize their own kind. All for the price of a fur coat.

MINK INDUSTRY RESEARCH

Beginning in 1990, I researched mink farms by visiting over 25 in Oregon, Washington, Utah, Idaho, Montana, and Michigan. What began as a quest to document conditions and killing techniques on fur farms quickly turned into the study of the first ever attempted domestication of a North American predator. What I learned both by my research and by the rescue rehabilitation, and release of sixty mink from a Montana farm leads me to conclude that all captive mink should be released, in one way or another, from their prisons we call fur farms.

Highly intelligent, fierce and very adaptive, mink are anything but successfully domesticated. Arguments by the fur industry that mink are domesticated are ludicrous. Like all wild animals held in captivity, some mink when released from their cages will fare better than others. Many factors will contribute to successful mink reintroduction as does the impact they will have on their surrounding eco-system. These are issues that I will address in this article.

INFILTRATION

In 1990-91, I spoke with many mink farmers and researchers who, believing I was a mink farmer, instructed me in ways to avoid my mink from losing their recessive genetic structures that gave them the fur quality and color variation that separated them from their wild relations. Captive mink are genetically 95% similar to their wild counterparts. The only difference besides behavior being fur color and quality which is solely maintained by a scientifically controlled diet, which is key to maintaining their genetic differences from wild mink. Black and dark mink being the closest genetically to wild mink.

Jim Leischow, a second generation mink farmer from Kenosha, Wisconsin described to me in a discussion at the 1991 Seattle Fur Exchange auctions how without a scientifically controlled diet, mink on any fur farm would lose their recessive genes, and over-powered by their dominant wild genetic structure, return to their wild roots in just a few generations. Leischow also detailed how a mink escapee that breeds with a wild mink would produce offspring that in one more generation would have lost all traces of any altered genetic structure.

IMPRISONED MINK STILL WILD

The difference between mink and other animals raised in intensive confinement is totally incomparable. Not only are all other domesticated livestock ungulated and herbivorous but they have also been domesticated for well over a thousand years. The closest comparison, which is hardly applicable, but for the sake of argument will be used, is the domestication of the common house cat. Originating in ancient Egypt, the cat has had over two thousand years of domestication, yet still this feline predator is proven capable of surviving in the wild as feral populations in the U.S. and Britain will attest to.

Once again, survivability is not the issue but impact on their native species. Captive mink are so far away from successful domestication that they are rarely caged together unless with their own off-spring, and then only until they reach sexual maturity. Self-mutilation and cannibalism, which is not uncommon on mink farms, is yet further proof of a wild animals' behavior as it attempts to deal with the neurosis caused by intensive confinement. Anyone who has ever been on a mink farm has heard the incessant scratching mink will make as they attempt to escape or attack their captive neighbors, separated only by a plastic or metal divider. This also is common behavior of a wild predator unfamiliar with close proximity to others of its own species. The psychological as well as physical torture associated with the confinement of mink naturally accustomed to solitary wandering is beyond our comprehension.

Genetically speaking mink are predominately still wild. Separated from their wild ancestors only by a controlled diet. Physiologically they are identical. What remains as the greatest division between wild and captive mink is predatory instincts and natural behavior which dictates how they hunt, find shelter, build nests and forage. Fear of other animals is minimal as mink are renowned for their fearlessness.

MINK REHABILITATION PROJECT

These separations were the basis of personal research into the potential for rehabilitation and release of the 60 mink I had purchased in Montana in 1990. The Coalition Against Fur Farms (CAFF) began as a rehabilitation project, the objective being to determine the feasibility to reintroduce native mink from fur farms back into their natural habitat. In January of 1991 the trials began as CAFF volunteers placed mink in cages four times as large as their previous enclosures and introduced natural objects such as logs, rocks, plants, and gallon baths.

Fur farmers had assured me that escaped captive mink had at least a 50% chance of survival, and CAFF hoped to increase that figure as much as possible. The introduction of a 12"x6" bathtub allowed the mink their first opportunity to acquaint themselves with water besides that which came from a small water nozzle or dish. Their response was to fully submerge themselves and spin in a cycle that quickly splashed all water out of their baths. This would be followed by grooming sessions in which the mink dried themselves and maintained utmost cleanliness, yet another sign of a healthy wild animal.

Once the mink had built up muscular strength after their time in a fur farm's cramped conditions, we began to nurture hunting instincts. Though morally opposed to the killing of animals, CAFF felt that the survival of our captive mink could not be guaranteed without a minimal amount of live-animal feeding. We knew that our project would later be used by others to determine the potential for successful reintroduction of fur farm prisoners, and so chose to do everything possible to ensure not only their survival but also their survival without human dependency. This also meant live-feeding which would teach them how to hunt rather than scrounge near or where humans were. This would ensure greater independence and less likelihood of human/mink interactions.

The mink in our project dug into their instinctual memory to remind themselves how to first seize the prey with one bite, then without releasing it, crush down until the skull or neck was broken. Then the mink would scour the logs and rocks for others that may have gone unnoticed. Once assured of no other present prey, the mink would return to the kill and eat everything or place the remainder in its nest just like wild mink. Once the mink had learned to kill and had tasted live food, they refused to eat the scientific diet we had been supplied by National Fur Feeds.

THE RELEASE

Finally, we released the mink to natural waterways across the Northwest's many forest lands. Always far from human habitations. And never within a 5-mile radius of another captive released mink of the opposite sex. We wanted to ensure the breeding only with wild mink. We also waited until the natural breeding season had passed so as not to burden the mink with the upbringing of offspring in their first season of freedom.

Our mink releases were filled with encouraging signs that the mink would survive. On one release a mink quickly found an abandoned animal burrow, and as we left we could see its head peeking out watching our departure. Another release had a young female mink burrowing under a log, gathering twigs and grass building a nest. Still another mink found a mouse hole, and burying its nose in it began to dig frantically. On many releases near streams the mink were quick to explore the shore of the water, eventually plunging in and swimming completely submerged, playing with pebbles and rocks with their forepaws. Returning to one release site weeks later I quickly found mink droppings and tracks near the creek and the dropping contained hair from a preyed upon animal. Most of the behavior exhibited by our mink was not learned, but simply returned to them as they found themselves in their natural element.

THOUGHTS ON LIBERATIONS

It is my belief that the liberator becomes responsible for the lives of the liberated when she/he endeavors to free them. Ideally, the liberated will become truly independent of human needs and achieve complete liberation. But until then, there are a number of factors that liberators can influence to increase the possibilities of a liberated mink's survival.

The time of year the liberations take place is the highest priority. The best time being May and January, the worst being during the breeding and kit-bearing season. Releasing an impregnated mink increases the needs of the liberated mink for food and shelter, female mink naturally raise their kits alone. Releasing mink once they have given birth to a litter will also mean abandonment of kits, although some might be foster-raised by another mink mother.

Of course, it cannot be overlooked that all captive minks are destined for death, and there is room for debate as to which kind of death is more desirable, a mink being the only one to surely know. Still I have hesitated to release mink from fur farms near heavily travelled roads knowing a large number would become road kills. This is yet another moral dilemma the liberator must face when they decide to open the cages. Personally, I have seen mink watching as the gas-chambers are wheeled down the rows of cage, and seen them screech frantically and attempt all manner of last minute escape as it becomes painfully evident that they will die.

There is also the very compelling argument for liberation that even with the recapture of 100% of all released mink from a targeted farm, that the breeding has still been completely disrupted as farmers have no way of separately identifying their breeder mink from their pelter mink. A mink raised to be pelted will often be in a much smaller cage than a breeder mink. For this reason, liberators would do best by releasing mink from both large and small mink cages so as to confuse the two. As of yet mink farmers have not devised methods of tagging, branding or tattooing individual animals except for labelling on the cage. For this reason it is always advantageous to remove all record-keeping cards from cages when releasing mink.

Transportation of mink either a short distance from cage to guard fence or a larger distance is best achieved by securing the mink individually in its nestbox. A small flat piece of sheet metal is often used to divide and block the hole leading from the nestbox to cage at which point the nestbox can then be removed and the hold blocked with a gloved hand or more permanent means for long transportation. Despite the average liberators aversion to leather, nothing protects human skin better than a thick pair of leather welding gloves which usually can be found lying around a mink farm. With criminal DNA testing liberators should take every precaution not to leave a blood trail of their own. Remember, you are dealing with a wild predator unfamiliar to kind human hands.

Often given the choice, a mink will leave the immediate area once outside of the guard fence, which usually is a 5-6 foot fence lined with sheet metal to prevent escape should mink get out of their cage. If left inside the guard fence often a mink will linger simply because of the smell of food or other mink cages, and also because of the familiarity of its own nestbox which is all it has ever known.

Once a large number of mink have left the guard fence area the quickest method of natural distribution is waterways. Without interference from the irate mink farmers attempting to recapture his furry investments, mink will not overcrowd themselves in the wild. It is not uncommon for a mink to travel 5 miles in one night (they are mostly nocturnal) and a large number of mink released in one area will not stay concentrated but will travel until they establish a territory all their own, searching out other mink only to breed.

ECOLOGICAL IMPACT

This leads us to the issue of ecological impact caused by mass mink liberations on their new environment. There will be noticeable impact on local prey populations, and for this reason, liberators should research target areas to guarantee that the sensitive habitat of a vulnerable endangered species is not nearby. Mink will attack almost anything, I've seen mink chasing large dogs and heard a story of one seen flying through the air attached to the leg of a large heron, the mink unwilling to release its targeted prey.

Mink will kill beyond their need, and for this reason caution should be taken when releasing mink near large concentrations of small animals. Mink are ferocious. Long persecuted at the hands of man, native predators are continually routinely killed by ranchers and other gun-toting humans. Much like the coyote has filled the ecological niche the wolf has left behind and by doing so extended its own historical range, so also do mink have the potential to fit nicely into the niche otters and other predators have left as their numbers are continually reduced by humans. Native mink populations are still drastically reduced, and given large-scale mink liberations, individual mink are sure to redistribute themselves to their former habitat with a little help from their two-legged friends.

There should not be hesitation to reintroduce captive mink into their native habitat. The ideal environment being underdeveloped areas with a nearby water source and infrequently used roads. As A.L.F. liberators open the cages, they not only liberate an individual animal but the whole species. Mink, fox, bobcat, and lynx farm liberations are not only a blow to a fur farmers' profits, but also a boost to North America's ravaged environment. With an absence of natural predators, prey populations often explode causing undue harm to their environment. By releasing fur farm prisoners, liberators are guardians of healthy eco-systems.

Before one single animal abuser can argue the merits of a captive fur animal's impact on the natural environment, they must first address the overall impact the whole domestic livestock industry has had on the earth. It is no coincidence that the number one reason behind predator eradication is the protection of politically powerful livestock interests. Still it remains that for the mink nations of North America the shortest path on the road to animal liberation lies from the opened cage to the outlying guard fence.

Now it is time for liberators across the continent to follow the lead of the A.L.F. in British Columbia, Washington, Utah, Wisconsin, Tennessee, New York, and Minnesota and take action to liberate the four-legged prisoners from the war on nature.

Until all fur farm prisoners are free.... Open the Cages!!!

Support Our Prisoners

1997

Anonymous members of the A.L.F. issue this statement to the aboveground animal rights movement on the importance of supporting A.L.F. prisoners.

In recent years as the Animal Liberation Front escalates its campaign of direct action against the fur trade, the animal liberation movement has seen the capture of six of its members by law enforcement. Already ALF members are serving lengthy prison sentences in the US. As the prospect of other ALF members following suit increases with our actions, we as ALF warriors call on the animal liberation movement to clarify its support for our captured and imprisoned comrades.

We ask for a clarification that will hopefully mirror the conditions for support afforded to ALF members in the UK, where the organization originated. The primary condition is that *ALF members do not testify against any other member*. All other conditions pertain to the carrying out of ALF actions and do not impose conditions for support once captured.

In recent months, through inter-ALF correspondence and communication, it has been learned that ALF members composing the Mass 4 and Ohio 2 have come under blatant animal liberation movement condemnation for their legal defense decision-making process. This condemnation has come from the movement and activists who, less than two years ago in Washington DC, publicly pledged their support for the ALF and our actions, but who have since then repeatedly withdrawn that support and spread verbal condemnation of ALF members for not adhering to a legal defense strategy that non-ALF members recommend. The latest duplicity of non-support concerning the Mass 4 and Ohio 2 originates from the same source and is identical to the basis of attacks against imprisoned ALF member Rod Coronado who accepted a plea bargain on lesser charges and received support from a national mainstream animal rights organization.

The Animal Liberation Front now believes that these are not isolated incidents and that withdrawal of support from the animal liberation movement is an occurrence that will continue to repeat itself until the movement decides collectively whether it will support the ALF unequivocally as long as they do not testify against comrades, or only when they follow the advice and direction of those who are not at risk of imprisonment. We feel that the direct action struggle has witnessed monumental impact against the fur trade in recent years. And as such, as ALF members we believe that in order for this struggle to survive and grow, the ALF must know that its warriors, once captured, will have the support of the aboveground movement of which it is a part, when we need it most—when our members face years in prison as a result of the actions against industries and institutions who disregard public opposition to animal abuse.

While some may believe that unconditional support for the ALF does exist within the animal liberation movement. One need only ask captured ALF members or current ALF prisoners in the U.S. to learn of widespread condemnations that have been expressed to them personally from activists claiming to support the ALF. They have been attacked for choosing to decide for themselves the best defense of ALF members in court. As long as one ALF member, after having risked life and freedom to rescue the victims of animal abuse and when facing years in prison, must face such hostile criticism from our supposed closest allies, then there exists a serious impediment to the creation of the type of ALF support necessary to sustain our planned long-term resistance. The Mass 4 and Ohio 2 were not sentenced to prison and Rod Coronado will only serve 4 years in prison rather than 12. These are outcomes that the ALF considers beneficial to each individuals' further participation in animal liberation activities. And best of all, these positive outcomes were accomplished without testifying against fellow ALF members.

Each legal battle that arises after the capture of an ALF member is unique and dependent on a variety of factors, all of which must be considered before anyone can accurately predict the outcome. Past criminal history, whether arson was involved, whether the judicial jurisdiction is city, county, state or federal, whether the defendant is rich or poor, black, or white—all these things influence the process of criminal justice in our unjust society. Then there is the simple political influence that accompanies most ALF court cases, dependent on the targeted animal abuse target's economic significance to the community, or the political influence it has bought through campaign contributions. The days of expecting justice for the animals and the earth from the same legal system that sanctions their death and destruction are not forthcoming.

Nor can justice be expected when legally defending ALF members who have willingly engaged in criminal activity to attack economically and politically powerful institutions such as animal industries. Achieving justice in such a corrupt system cannot simply be accomplished by challenging that system on its own ground, as has been proven to revolutionary struggles whose direct action strategy has been criminalized in other countries. Nor is the animal liberation movement prepared to sustain support for the long term prisoners that such a strategy would create. That is why it has always been ALF policy to only stipulate that members do not testify against other operatives when captured in order to receive support. No one who considers themselves an ALF supporter should condition that support on whether his or her advice or direction is followed.

The ALF is not a hierarchical organization. Our survival is guaranteed in part due to our cell-like structure that decentralizes operational activities to best ensure continuation of our campaigns. There is no central authority to whom we are beholden. In following a few basic guidelines, we or anyone reserves the right to claim ALF membership and maintain the right to determine how best to carry out operations and legal defense. That independence in the decision-making process of being an ALF member does not stop after capture.

No animal benefits from the imprisonment or those who would defend them without restriction when free. And no ALF member should feel pressured by the aboveground movement that supports them to pursue a legal strategy that is not his or her own decision. The very real chance of imprisonment—and the strength required to endure such a consequence—demands that a person rest assured that such a situation is only the result of his or her own actions and not anyone else's. No ALF member should be coerced into pursuing martyrdom or a legal strategy that expects justice or success through the courts or media. The effectiveness of the ALF is to be measured by its actions outside of the legal system, not from within it. Captured ALF members should be supported in any decision that will return them to the struggle as soon as possible, without needlessly risking further imprisonment for the hope of any secondary effects that satisfy the aboveground, but not necessarily the underground, movement. Captured ALF members have sacrificed enough already, and if any aboveground activist believes they should sacrifice more, they should shut their mouths, step forward, join our ranks, and set an example with their own freedom and action rather than with that of another.

The ALF is a covert operations organization employing guerilla warfare tactics and encourages self-empowerment that leads to successful direct action. By encouraging all of our members to be their own leaders, we believe that no one but ourselves should guide us into action. Whether that action be on a fur farmer's property or in a courtroom, ALF members reserve the right to decide how to best defend themselves against legal prosecution from an establishment that views us as criminals and terrorists. We cannot expect justice from those who sanction true acts of terrorist themselves. By condemning ALF members for their decision-making process, the animal liberation movement is inadvertently saying to its present and potential direct action warriors that unconditional support by the aboveground movement is not guaranteed and, in fact, that the possibility exists that they might instead be condemned by those who claim to support them the most.

The ALF is the only army the animals have. When all other tactics fail, liberation from torture and death can only be delivered through illegal direct action tactics, as successfully practiced by the ALF for more than 20 years. It is time the animal liberation movement decides if it can meet the challenge of providing the support necessary to ensure that the ALF continues, or watch it collapse as more and more of our members are abandoned to face the legal consequences of their actions alone.

A.L.F. Bulletin To All Fur Farm Raiders

1997

How to optimize fur farm raids for maximum impact and minimum risk.

By now I'm sure you've all read *The Final Nail* and know of a bunch of fur farms in your area with animals eager to be liberated.

Due to the recent continent-wide barrage against the animal torturers, you should expect security to be tightened. If you the would-be raiders, here are some tips:

1. Guard dogs may be an option but they probably won't be near the cages. Security guards may be hired. Cameras may be placed at some of the larger fur farms. Still undeterred? Read on. Always survey the area before-hand, possibly on a different night than the raid.

2. Tools: thick gloves; common-brand shoes which will be thrown away later; flashlight with red cover over the light (red attracts less attention and does not blind you or take away your night-vision—the red cover can be made of red grocery bags and tape if need be); razor/knife to cut the nets around each shed, bolt cutters for fences and locks; small wrecking bar; walkie-talkies (perhaps, if this is a team effort). Carry no ID or key sets or change. Individual keys, like the key to your getaway van, can be carried as long as they don't rustle. Emergency money bills should be carried.

3. Fur farms that imprison mink and fox hold between a hundred and a hundred thousand animals. They are made up of long sheds side-by-side with open sides. Inside are row upon row of cages about three feet off the ground. The sheds are always aligned north to south to make for even light distribution and proper pelt development. Sometimes there will be a wall surrounding all the sheds, sometimes each shed is individually enclosed in a net or fencing.

4. After a survey of the area, decide on an escape route for your animals away from roads. Then decide on escape routes for yourself in case you wake the neighbors. You may wish to place a member of your troupe as "watch-dog."

5. Gloves at all times, no fingerprints. Do all the setup work first. Cut the bottom of the nets or fence around each shed. Open up sections of the fence around the perimeter, only a few will do.

6. Start at the shed farthest from the farmhouse. You'll figure out how to open the cages. Start opening at one end and work your way down. Don't worry about the animals, they'll find their way out. After you've finished the first row of cages, go onto the next. Some of the animals will fight or play. You

can separate them or leave them alone. The noise can be unnerving, though. You'll notice sounds from the mink that they didn't make in their cages. The animals will "coo" as they run along when before all you've heard were hisses and shrieks in the cages.

7. After you have finished the last row of cages in the shed closest to the farmhouse go back and check on the other cages. If breeding cards are on top of the cages, you can take them. It will be an amusing scene of mayhem. Animals will be jumping out of cages and running about everywhere. They will be frolicking and darting through the exits you created beforehand. You can leave when all the cages are open - the animals will find their own way out.

8. But your party may be disrupted early. If the farmer is awakened by you he will probably come running with a flashlight. Immediately leave quietly. He may know what is going on and call his neighbors and police before coming out to try and surprise you. CAREFUL!

9. At the very least, the priceless breeding info will be lost forever. And chances are the "lost" animals will not be insurable either. Each animal saved is about a $35 kick in the ass to the fur farmer. Multiply this by 1000 or 10,000 and we're talking major eco-tage.

10. Be careful if fur farm raids have occurred in your area. Be extra careful if you hit the same farm twice.

Letters From The Underground

1997

The story of one anonymous A.L.F. activist and how she embarked on a campaign of direct action for animals.

To begin, let me say that while associating with animal rights activists (something I try to avoid), I often hear people speaking thrillingly about articles they've read in the press or seen on the news about animals being liberated, laboratories being trashed, lorries being torched, fast food restaurants being burned to the ground, etc. Along with these conversations it is practically guaranteed that one or more persons will exclaim the greatness and empowerment of the action followed by a "Gee, how do I hook up with these people?" Also heard is, "Why don't these lads contact me?" or "How do I get involved with that group?" There are many others, but all basically asking the same thing: "How do I get involved?" This is how I found the answer to that question.

After reading stories about lab break-ins and fur stores being torched, I, too, desperately wanted to join this group. But how? There was really no place to start. All of my friends in the animal rights movement had less interest in illegal direct action than I did, and even those who showed some interest were completely clueless as to how to meet these people.

At one point, I wrote to an animal rights group letting them know that I would be willing to help them raid a lab. Needless to say, that letter went unanswered. Finally I realized what I was doing. I was waiting for someone with a plan to drop in out of the blue and ask me to join in a lab raid. Now stop and think about this. Would anyone who put hundreds of hours in planning a covert, illegal direct action that could land them in prison for years risk asking a basic stranger for help simply because he or she is a vegetarian or belonged to the local animal rights chapter?! NO! (At least not if they want to stay active and out of jail.)

So how did I, or a better question is, how do you, end up "joining" the Animal Liberation Front? That's easy. Come up with your own plan! Really. It's not as hard as you think. Let me repeat this important point which everyone must realize: Come up with your own plan. This is very important.

One of the reasons there is not a lot more illegal direct action happening is because there are only a few people willing to invest the time and energy necessary to choose a viable target, research the facts, recon the place, and conduct any other work necessary to execute a successful direct action. There are always plenty of people who want to help in the actual execution of the plan, though not many people are willing to dedicate and invest the time, money, energy, and stress that go along with the planning. People are always willing to share in the "excitement," but not in the actual work. Simply put, no one wants to help bake the bread, but everyone wants to eat it.

OVERCOME THE EXCUSES

Many people will easily shrug off planning a direct action for many reasons. (Nearly all are mere excuses which could easily be overcome.) One of the most overused reasons is people tell themselves they don't know anyone who could help in the final execution of the plan. For example, they don't know who could find homes for X number of animals; they don't know who they could trust as a lookout; they don't know who could loan or rent them a vehicle to use, etc. I want to emphasize here that if you are faced with a problem like this, continue on!

There are many bridges that one can foresee that look uncrossable during the planning of an action. These problems seem unresolvable and often discourage people from continuing on with their plan. Again I must emphasize: continue. These problems either solve themselves or are more easily solved when you actually reach that point of the plan. (The other option usually being the plan is aborted for some other reason long before the problem ever had to be confronted.)

Something else that should be thrown in here is that you should expect about four out of five plans into which you've invested time and money to fall through. Again, this shouldn't deter you. If you approach direct action with the knowledge that most of your plans may not work, then you should not be discouraged from battling on if some of your plans do fall through.

Though it is not necessary, before taking any direct action, one should read as much literature as possible on the topic. This is much easier to do now thanks to a "revival" in the grassroots animal rights/liberation movement. If possible, any literature pertaining to illegal activities should be mailed to a fake name at a post office box or private mailbox center. If this is not possible, perhaps a well-trusted friend (who could handle police/federal harassment and is not involved in illegal activities themselves) would be willing to have it sent to his or her place. Another possibility would be to get this information off of a web site (from a library, campus, or cyber-coffee shop computer).

Though some of these security precautions may seem ridiculous, paranoid, and unnecessary, you will be thankful you followed them if you continue to increase the frequency, severity, and effectiveness of your actions, thus producing more intense local and federal investigations.

AN ARMY OF ONE

But, wait a minute! You still don't know if there is anyone you can trust. This does not mean that you shouldn't consider doing an action. When I realized that no one was going to drop in and ask me to help them with their plan—when I finally realized that I was the A.L.F.—I decided to target a fast food restaurant that I had noticed as appearing vulnerable.

My first step was realizing that I was the A.L.F. and that it was up to me to find a viable target, in this case the fast food restaurant. Though I still didn't know who could help me with this plan, I proceeded to scope it out the next few nights, still thinking I would find someone to help me.

Though I had no experience at "casing a joint," it came very easily and naturally. Between 2:00 and 3:00 a.m. (the time I decided would be safest to strike the place) I carefully scoped it out. Some nights dressed head to toe in my jogging gear (now is not the time to be caught there in your balaclava), I jogged up and down the street past the restaurant. I was careful to look for possible activity inside the building, check on any employees' cars in the parking lot, judge the amount of traffic, the amount of police presence, determine how well the parking lot and building were lit, scan for any drive thru or security cameras (to look out for and to sabotage!), etc.

Other nights I walked my boyfriend's dog up and down the street looking for the same things. In no time at all I was very familiar with the activity of the area (and had walked two emergency escape routes I would take should I be interrupted). I was soon confident with this target. Unfortunately, I still didn't know anyone I would trust enough to divulge my plans to. I knew what I wanted to do.

The day before I was going to execute my plan, I drove to a neighboring town, bought superglue, spraypaint, and some garden gloves from three different stores, making sure to pay in cash at each store. That evening I went for a walk wearing my gloves and ended up picking up two large rocks and half of a brick that I determined was small enough to carry around and handle, yet big enough to smash through the thick plate glass windows of a fast food restaurant.

THE FIRST ACTION

Though I would have felt a bit more comfortable with a partner to lookout for me, I was tired of waiting around for apathetic and unmotivated people.

That night, dressed in black from head to toe, I went jogging. As I got near the restaurant I slowed to a walk. Seeing that there was no traffic around and facing a dark and empty-looking building, I approached the restaurant. Walking briskly across the lot, I pulled my mask down over my face. At the rear of the building I quickly took off my black backpack and got out my supplies. I quickly filled the two back door locks with superglue and small pieces of paper clips that I had snipped especially for this occasion. I then proceeded to spraypaint slogans over the entire back of the building and on the side with the drive-thru.

This done, I peeked around the building. Headlights were approaching from up the street so I just remained calm and motionless. My stomach dropped when I saw it was a police car. The cop then drove by without slowing down or looking my way.

Delighted, I walked around to the front of the building and quickly tossed all three projectiles through three separate windows! I saved this part of the action for last because of the loud sound it would make. And with the three explosions of glass, I quickly sprinted through one of my pre-arranged exits and into a residential area where I quickly vanished. I then removed my black turtleneck and balaclava, ditched them in an apartment complex dumpster, and went home.

My point here is that with enough planning, determination, and self-confidence, one person can pull off a successful action! Of course, the "bigger" or "more severe" the action, the better it may be to have a lookout with clear communications to you. Nevertheless, one person shouldn't feel helpless and inactive because he or she doesn't know others who are willing to take illegal direct action. Besides, taking action is your first step in feeling out potential comrades who share the same philosophy as you and are ready and willing to take action.

LOOKING FOR PARTNERS

It is really very difficult to explain to someone how they can find close, trustworthy partners who are willing to take the same risks and are knowledgeable and strong enough to withstand heavy bouts of police interrogation, intimidation, and harassment. Though you never plan to be faced with this situation, it is a realistic risk and you and anyone you work with should understand with a firm knowledge that if this situation arises, you and anyone you work with will not cooperate at all with any law enforcement agencies!

There is no cut and dry pattern or formula for choosing or finding partners. THIS IS GOOD. If there was a pattern or formula, it would open the door for infiltration of law enforcement and corporate agents. However, by executing the fast food action by myself, it led me to a second person whom I later hooked up with.

FRIENDS AND COMRADES

Another member of our current cell really was not "chosen." We had merely known and trusted each other since high school when we used to forge passes out of study hall so we could skip school and go swimming in the river.

We had both been vegetarians (and outcasts) in high school and I taught him about animal rights as he shared with me his views of deep ecology. It wasn't long before we started working together. My point here is that there was no formula with which to evaluate my friend. Merely, I had spent years with him as a best friend and we pretty much knew each other inside and out.

These are the best kind of partners to have since you already have an established relationship and friendship that no law enforcement agent would be able to make up. So I'd like to emphasize that this is the best way of "finding" a partner: working with someone you have a history with. And, always trust your intuition. If someone doesn't feel right or you get "weird vibes" from him or her, DON'T work with that person! The opposite is true here also, but I don't need to explain that since, when you find that true connection, the feeling is pretty much unmistakable.

The other partner I connected with after the fast food restaurant action had a long history in the environmental movement. I only shared my interest in illegal direct action with her after she had complained to me consistently about a billboard advertising animal products and how someone should correct the billboard so consumers would know exactly what suffering that product really hid.

After hearing repeated complaints from my friend (was she checking me out, too?), we went for a walk. Here I told her that the billboard she hated so much appeared to be easily accessible (I had already re-conned it) and that if she wanted to help redecorate it, that would be jolly.

Needless to say, she thought this was a grand idea and, within a matter of days, the billboard had been corrected. Red paint bombs made from Christmas ornaments also gave the appearance of blood running down the advertisement.

CRITIQUING THE ACTION

The day after the billboard action, my friend and I went on another walk (we NEVER talked in a house or car!) to discuss and critique our action. This may seem silly to some, but it is the best way to learn from your mistakes and make improvements for further actions.

Meetings like this—restricted to only those involved with the action—are great to learn from. Other than that they should never be discussed again. In this case, we realized that the warning system we had set up to warn of cops (a loud whistle) didn't work. I had been warned twice of police in the area by her whistle, but I was never sure when to resume work on the billboard. Also, the whistling merely attracted attention to my partner rather than to me.

Because of this, we ended up putting together our savings and buying a police scanner, frequency book, and a cheap pair of two-way radio headsets. Because of the headset's low price ($49.95 for the pair), I knew they would not be reliable for an action where the lookout is a long distance away. Nevertheless, they would suit our needs for more billboard, fast food restaurant, and fur shop actions.

BUILDING TRUST AND SOLIDARITY

These are the actions that should be done most often to build up confidence, unity, and comradeship. The more of these types of actions done, the more competent, confident, and experienced you and your cell will become, and you can soon "move up" to bigger and better actions. (Bigger and better being defined here as larger actions with more severe amounts of damage being done to the target. This, of course, includes arson attacks.)

These actions will come in time if you and your partners stay active and build up a unity and confidence that becomes almost intuitive. Myself and the two individuals I currently work with have almost a psychic connection in which we usually always know what the other two people are thinking. This will not happen overnight and, if you expect it to, you will be let down. That is why I must emphasize motivation and persistence.

It took me about two years of actions like this and now I currently work regularly with two separate cells and a handful of other people who occasionally seek my assistance. Through persistence and perseverance you will build up a network of resources including tools, money, people, and experience.

If you tell yourself that there are no suitable targets to strike, you should stop and ask yourself if this is what you really want to be doing. If it is, just go to the nearest phone book and let your fingers do the walking. The yellow pages will give you the names, phone numbers, and addresses (and a map of the local area) of countless animal exploiters. This is an invaluable and easily accessible resource, available 24-hours a day in any city or town you may find yourself in.

In one instance, our cell drove two states away to "remodel" an establishment profiting off of animals' deaths. Once there however, we realized this would not be possible. Instead of going home disappointed, we simply went to the nearest pay phone and let our fingers do the walking. Before we left that state, one animal abuse establishment had been completely destroyed!

FUNDING YOUR ACTIONS

Your actions will, to a slight extent, be limited by your funding. Therefore, it is very important that absolutely NO money is spent frivolously. However, once you decide that you will be taking direct action, the first thing you should do is set up a fund.

Don't use your own personal bank account or ANY bank account. All financial transactions must be off the books and receipts for expenses (tools, gas, etc.) should always be destroyed. There are a few different ways of increasing your fund. If you or any of your cell mates (no pun intended) have a job, you may want to immediately put 10 percent (or more) of each paycheck directly into the fund. With three employed people, this can quickly increase the size of your fund in a short time.

Another possibility would be for someone to adopt your cell. Though this may sound far fetched, it's not. However, adopters, I feel, cannot be actively sought. In my experience, adopters have had a long history with cell members and share the same philosophy. The only thing keeping them out of the trenches themselves is something like a physical disability, a family with children, a prominent job or political position, etc.

Again, for security reasons, donors should not be "looked for" or "asked" as much as simply "found" or "known." Remember, having a long and trusted history with the person is probably the safest way to prevent leaks or infiltration. Also, donors should never make contact with the cell (only the known individual in the cell). And, of course, the donor should never know of any plans or potential targets. If the donor wants to know what their money has been up to, they can have newspaper clippings anonymously mailed to them or to a pre-arranged post office box.

Donors should be made aware of the RICO laws as well as the most current "anti-terrorism" legislation that has been passed. It's also good to know their feelings on arson, explosives and other controversial tactics before they receive clippings of such events. Remember, security precautions with donors are important and necessary to insure the safety of both the cell and the donor(s).

If you have donors asking too many questions, wanting to meet other cell members, etc., you will want to remind them of the necessity for security. If they persist, or you feel uncomfortable, it may be time to find different donors. Remember to use common sense and to always trust your intuition. Finally, and most importantly, don't rip off your donor! Donors need to be thought of and respected as fellow members of your cell, despite their physical absence. Remember, they are helping to make your actions possible. Don't misuse funds. This is the quickest and easiest way to lose a donor and the cohesive trust of your cell.

Another quick and easy way to save money for your fund is to eliminate or greatly reduce your cost of living. This can happen in a variety of ways and forms, but a few brief examples include getting clothes and supplies from free boxes, dumpster-diving, Salvation Armys (and their drop boxes), garage sales, flea markets, etc.

Also, when traveling, (and at home) eat your own food! Good road trip food includes sandwiches, bagels, trail mix, fruit, bread, etc. Tupperware makes it easy to take cooked rice, pasta, baked potatoes, etc. along for those longer road trips. Also, this food can be acquired from food boxes, dumpster-diving, free lunch groups, etc. Taco Bell bean burritos without cheese are NOT an acceptable road food as money is too scarce to be going to the PepsiCo corporation (which exploits animals) or even to a private restaurant that serves animal parts as part of their menu.

In other words, turn away from the consumer-trained frame of mind and become more autonomous and self-sufficient as a cell. This seems to be a harder transition for people living in a big city or suburban area, but it is just a matter of self-discipline. Try to wean yourself (and your cell) off of all that Babylon tries to addict you to. You shouldn't be seen in a Taco Bell in a strange town the same night that the McDonald's next door is going to burn down anyway!

Another big savings is to camp while you're on the road. Besides saving you $20 to $50 a night, you don't have to worry about being recognized by an employee, signing your name, presenting ID, being on a "security" camera, having your vehicle recognized, etc. Besides, camping will give you a little time to communicate with nature and let you reflect on why you're doing what you're doing. The electricity from motel room lights, televisions, phones, etc. help to scatter and disrupt thinking anyway. Having a clear mind makes for clearer thinking and better decision-making - every cell should have.

In bigger actions where two or three cells might need to meet to discuss plans, media work, etc., a motel may be needed. In this case extra security precautions need to be taken on renting the room, parking in the area, entering and exiting the building, etc. Common sense and experience will help with these precautions. DON'T take security risks.

Despite your low cost of living (my only expense is gas money), there will always be expenses to pull off an action. From gas money to tools to clothes, you will need a source of funds. Of course, more time and energy may be needed to fundraise if you want more sophisticated tools (which you will want for more sophisticated actions), such as police-quality walkie talkies, night vision goggles, a 200 channel scanner with headset, vehicle(s) and whatever else your cell needs to insure a safe and successful action.

Another way to increase your action fund is by fundraising, you know, the good old fashioned way like having a garage sale, bake sale, tabling, car wash, etc. We've done this many times. Whether you're just passing out literature, selling books, selling vegan goodies, etc., always have a donation jar available. Of course, you can't tell people you are raising money for illegal activities and since I don't like to lie to people, I always raise funds to "help animals."

For more specific inquiries, I explain how this money will end up "informing" and educating the public about animal abuse. Of course your fundraiser doesn't have to have anything at all to do with animals (which is much more secure) but that will have to be something for the fundraisers themselves to decide. Also, take advantage of any school fairs, Earth Day events, street fairs, concerts, etc. to raise money. Remember, the heavier the traffic, the heavier the donations.

If you are fund-raising for a legitimate organization, funds need to be diverted before they are turned in or recorded. There really are countless ways to make and save money for your cell's action fund: garage sales, campus organizations, concerts, short-term jobs, funders, etc. Your imagination is your only limit. Don't let lack of funds prevent you or your cell from taking action.

If this is happening, then you need to concentrate on fundraising until you have enough money to execute your plan(s). Just remember, money is the root of all evil (it fuels animal exploitation). Be careful with it, use it wisely, and don't let it disrupt the cohesiveness of your cell. And, in the end, make the animal abusers the ones to really pay.

Making It Count

1998

On the strategic value of striking high-impact targets.

Greetings Comrades,

In the interest of speeding the process of animal liberation, I want to throw out some strategic comments to help people better direct their energies.

These comments are related to the United States· and Canada solely. The current political climate as it relates to animals, and economic considerations, are entirely different in other countries. Some of this may be relative to England, Sweden, or whereever else, but this is primarily meant for North American readers.

To get right to the point, our cell believes that actions against fast food restaurants and small butcher shops are, at this time, a waste of time. Notice that I said "at this time." We are concerned about activists risking arrest at a place where the impact from the action is going to be rather insignificant.

Actions against the meat industry can be highly beneficial. But smashing a window at McDonalds isn't even a drop in the bucket. Live liberations of farm animals, on the other hand, is always great for the individual animal and can be a great propaganda tool. The lab liberations of the 80's were highly successful in publicizing vivisection, especially when videos were given to the press after the raids. Similar actions today against factory farming would be priceless.

Acts of economic sabotage would have much more impact against an actual factory farm, than against a multi-billion dollar corporation. KFC and Burger King won't even feel the loss of a couple of windows - but a factory farm can be shut down if all the equipment is damaged. This is especially true if their particular product is suffering from a low market value at the time of the hit.

Putting a fast food restaurant or small butcher shop out of business doesn't save any animals. People will still buy meat, just somewhere else. These places deserve to get smashed up, but is this what we want to risk long jail sentences with? Meat trucks, however, are good targets. This way the distribution of the product itself is affected. If done on a large scale, it can have an impact directly on meat consumption. We are simply asking activists to think their actions out and to go for larger objectives, instead of acting with little forethought.

With the fur industry, it is conceivable the whole thing can be brought down by ALF attacks. Any fur target is strategic since we can put the whole industry under.

Fur farms are suffering big time and the continuation of the current campaign will shut the remaining farms down, no matter how high Russian demand pushes the pelt prices.

For vivisection any property owned by a vivisection university is fair game, but cells need to finish campaigns that they have begun. Don't stop with one action, follow through.

Just think your actions out and go for real change. Our cell does not sympathize with McDonalds at all—we just think that we need to avoid arrests when the action that led to the bust doesn't have a chance of producing any tangible results.

An A.L.F. Cell

Smashing The Fur Trade Quickly & Effectively

1998

Mike and Eva Del Conte sort through debris after Thanksgiving morning fire at her store

Finishing off the fur industry through direct action.

The North American fur farming industry is on the verge of collapse. In 1998, Russia experienced an economic crisis that brought their fur trade to a halt. This is significant because in 1997 Russia consumed half of the world's fur skins.

To make matters worse for mink farmers in America, the usual disease problem became more widespread. Distemper killed many caged fur animals, damaging the fur farming industry's profit margin even more.

The third major factor that has devastated the fur farming industry is the Animal Liberation Front (ALF). Since late 1995, the ALF has raided approximately 50 North American fur farms, releasing close to 100,000 animals.

This has cost the industry millions of dollars and provided a shot at life for countless mink and fox.

If these raids continue, the industry will collapse completely. The question is, will the liberations continue?

In 1997, 21 North American fur farms were raided by ALF freedom fighters, people just like you and me. In 1998, less than 10 fur farms were raided in North America.

Internationally, the fur farm raids increased dramatically with Poland and Ireland seeing their first raids ever.

North America saw a decline in direct action against the fur trade. Despite the decline, fur farmers are as paranoid as ever. Leo Weisdorfer, the owner of the largest fur farm in Oregon, admitted to having spent $38,000 on security in 1996 alone. This demonstrates the long term value of ALF mink liberations. By attacking a handful of farms, the ALF has forced the entire industry to spend millions of dollars on security. Fur farmers are very concerned about being raided and the pressure is pushing some out of the business.

The Animal Liberation Front is not a structured organization with a membership list. The ALF is nothing more than people who get together with their most trusted comrades and fight back for the animals. Anyone who carries out a non-violent direct action for the animals can consider themselves a part of the ALF.

Will the fur farming industry collapse? That depends on the commitment of those who don't want mink gassed and foxes anally electrocuted. We have an opportunity to completely finish off an industry built on the systematic torture of forbearing animals.

Economic and social factors have given us an advantage. The majority of fur farmers are at retirement age and want to protect the money they have left. Times are tough for mink farmers.

A major liberation campaign carried out now would be the final nail in the fur industry's coffin. Many mink farmers are making decisions about whether or not to stay in business.

Now is the time to strike. There are less than 400 mink farms left in the United States. At the end of the year there should be none.

If you believe that fur is murder, then act like it!

Ten Rules For Direct Action

1999

Ten commandments for effective A.L.F. actions.

1. Make sure the operation will be effective. Never waste time (much less risk a jail sentence) with an operation which you feel will be ineffective.

2. Hit the enemy where they least expect it and where it will hurt them the most.

3. Almost all sabotage should be carried out at night.

4. Timing must be perfect as the longer an operation takes, the greater the chances of something going wrong.

5. Work only with people you trust. Undercover cops who infiltrate activist groups are extremely dangerous. Work in small groups or cells, consisting of no more than four to six people.

6. All operations should be simple and fast and several means of escape should be planned .

7. All equipment should be concealed. Volatile substances should be handled with extreme caution.

8. The safest tactic should always be used. Except when absolutely necessary, elaborate commando operations should be avoided. Pick your targets carefully, as mindless, erratic vandalism will lead to a loss of popular sympathy.

9. The need for secrecy is obvious. Security and secrecy must be maintained without reservation. If it is not, you deserve to be caught.

10. Any member who breaks the code of the group should be cast out immediately and permanently.

Fire Is A Good Tool

1999

One of the A.L.F. activists behind the rescue of 46 dogs from a California laboratory reflects on the action, and their regrets.

Greetings from the ALF! The last weekend of August 1999, 46 dogs were liberated from behind the horrifying walls of a lab supply provider called Biodevices. Every animal at the facility was taken and placed in loving arms, leaving the prison empty of all life. If it had been up to those carrying out the action, Biodevices would have been burned to the ground, never to reopen. Unfortunately, and I mean that with all the rage and passion conceivable, part of the underground railroad that was accepting the dogs was unwilling to follow through with their part if fire was involved. So, those inside did as much damage as possible by means of spray painting, smashing, destroying records and flooding by leaving all faucets turned on. The jars with formaldehyde holding hearts, brains and other organs were left alone.

This action took years of recon and preparation. I arrived knowing very little about the logistics but expected to be challenged mentally, emotionally and physically. I am familiar with cities and how they operate, but my first time encountering the area in which Biodevices was located provoked a fear in me that took a while to accept. There were video cameras on nearly every streetlight, a police communication center a few doors down, a police training center across the wash and a handful of 24-hour businesses with security on surrounding streets. My heart and spirit believed the liberation was possible, but my mind was overcome by the amount of work, organization and planning that still needed to be perfected in such a short amount of time. There were many details to be covered and new ones constantly forming. Each moment of each day needed to be carefully utilized. Each person's ideas, strengths and input were crucial. There were arguments and misunderstandings. These things helped us to know ourselves and each other better and to trust that we were each 100-percent ready. Thank you all for working so hard, for believing, for putting aside your differences and fears.

I encourage all you warriors, new and experienced, to go underground and follow what is strong in your hearts. Often an idea or action seems impossible to carry out, but there are cracks in the cement and others out there who feel the same as you. Maximum destruction often takes no more time or energy than minimum damage.

As I reflect back I smile to know that 46 dogs are free and have a bright dog future. But there is also a deep aching to know that Biodevices will reopen and acquire more dogs to enslave, torture and kill.

Fire is a good tool. Use it wisely. I wish we had.

How Many A.L.F. Activists Get Caught?

2002

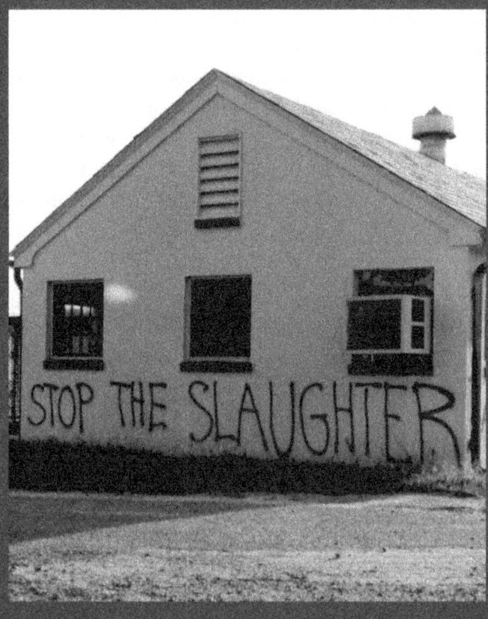

Former A.L.F. prisoner David Barbarash examines the relative rarity of A.L.F. arrests.

How many ALF activists really get caught? The short answer: not very many.

The Animal Liberation Front has been active in North America for more than twenty-three years. Over the past two-plus decades, dedicated activists have carried out literally thousands of actions. Working under the cover of darkness, they have engaged in everything from minor property damage – such as spray painting buildings and gluing the locks of animal abusers – to live animal liberations, and even major economic sabotage in the form of setting fires that have destroyed or caused major damage to the properties of animal abusing companies.

With so many people – probably several hundred – having been involved with illegal activities over such a long period of time, one might think there would be a long list of criminal convictions and prisoners serving jail time for their actions. The reality is, thankfully but not surprisingly, the exact opposite.

Every year we hear about a small handful of people who have been caught for ALF (or ELF) activities, and although much attention is placed on them, they are anomalies. Because there are no big news stories every time an activist or ALF cell does not get caught, all we remember are the stories that talk about those who do get caught. All this might give you the wrong impression that great strides are being made by law enforcement to "crack down" on illegal actions.

Indeed, it seems that almost every time I read comments from an FBI spokesperson, on the one hand they're saying, "we've got some good leads," or, "we will infiltrate and catch the ALF," or some other nonsense.

Out of the other side of their mouths, however, they frequently remark on the "shadowy" nature of the ALF and just how difficult it is to catch these people.

The reasons activists get caught are:

- They are working with a person who is weak and who testifies before a grand jury or gives a statement to police.
- They are already under surveillance and are caught in the act.
- They leave a piece of forensic evidence behind at the scene of the action.

By far, the majority of ALF activists are caught because of someone else snitching on them, not because of any great investigative techniques of law enforcement. The simple reality is that the FBI and police need snitches to solve the vast majority of their cases.

Practicing good security measures is a basic premise for underground activities, and, aside from leaving no evidence behind at the scene, this includes keeping your mouth shut. Most importantly, though, it involves making intelligent decisions about whom you choose to work with. In fact, I would say your decision about your fellow activists is probably the most important decision you can make, as it will likely make the difference between staying free or going to jail.

There is a plethora of information, both printed and online, detailing the intensive security measures activists need to follow in order to avoid capture. It seems, given the reality of few arrests, that the great majority of activists are successfully following these directions.

Abolition. Liberation. Freedom.

2004

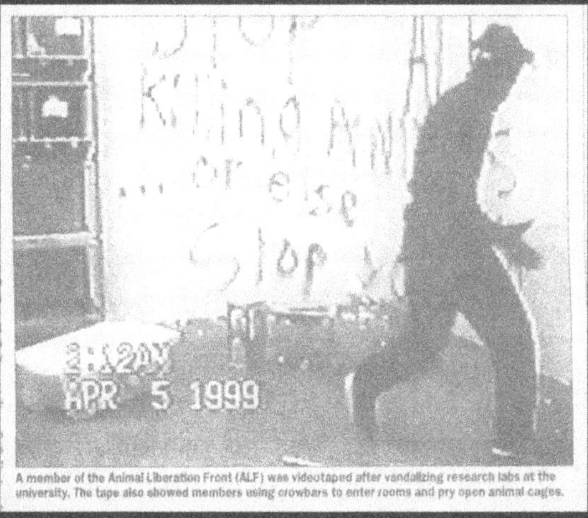

A member of the Animal Liberation Front (ALF) was videotaped after vandalizing research labs at the university. The tape also showed members using crowbars to enter rooms and pry open animal cages.

Former A.L.F. prisoner Gary Yourofsky writes on the necessity of the A.L.F., facts and myths of direct action, and who the real "terrorists" are.

For weeks after the events of 9-11, I was transfixed by the news media. CNN, MSNBC, FOX-News, The Today Show, Peter Jennings, Dan Rather, Brian Williams. Report after report. Image after image. The collision. The fireball. The smoke. The collapse. The rubble. The debris. Ground zero. The panic. The response.

As a national lecturer on animal rights, and one of the country's most outspoken animal liberationists, I believe I speak for the entire movement when I tell you that we have the utmost empathy for every innocent victim of the World Trade Center and Pentagon attacks. We mourn human tragedy as much as animal tragedy. The notion that animal rights activists are anti human is an outrageous lie.

We choose to be activists for other species because billions of innocent animals are murdered without so much as a disquieting tinge of guilt from the masses. We are vegans because we realize that violence and hatred must be destroyed at its root, in our everyday habits of consumption.

Missed Opportunities

Shortly after the 9-11 attacks, my faith in humanity was restored temporarily because I witnessed such an outpouring of love, empathy, compassion, and community. The world was condemning evil and the taking of innocent lives. In our unity to find the perpetrators, I wondered if we would understand that murdering any living being was wrong. I hoped that, by a collective awakening to compassion, the terror that humans inflict upon innocent animals for food, clothing, sport, entertainment, and research would end or at least abate.

In a moment of optimistic speculation, I pondered whether the camouflaged-hunters lurking on American soil, skulking in the distance with guns and bows, waiting to terrorize and kill more than 200 million innocent animals annually—might throw their weapons to the ground?

Would the animal researchers who terrorize 50 million dogs, cats, primates and mice annually in vivisection procedures have a revelation? The March of Dimes experimenters who sew shut the eyes of kittens and ferrets to see if blindness affects their brains would surely stop their barbaric acts of terrorism.

After the 9-11 bombardment, the researchers at the Oregon Regional Primate Research Center—who electro-ejaculate primates in order to obtain sperm for their breeding colonies—would make the connection now. Surely, the animal research community was going to be arrested and charged with acts of terrorism.

Would terrorist fur-farmers and trappers be sent to prison for breaking the necks of mink, anally electrocuting foxes, genitally electrocuting chinchillas and catching wild animals in steel jaw leghold traps?

Would humankind realize that animals do not want to be our food, clothing, entertainment and research specimens? Would we finally understand the words of British Bishop William Inge when he said that if animals ever formulated an organized religion, the devil would be depicted in human form? And would we finally seek to change that image?

Would Gandhi's immortal words of peace -"The life of a lamb is no less precious than that of human" - be recited at every school across America?
But not a damn thing changed in human attitudes toward fellow animal species. The routine violence of human customs was swept even further under the rug. The repetitive talk of people revolting against evil sickened me because it was clearly hypocritical and deceitful.

Shamefully, it seems that the hatred that humans have towards non-humans is so vicious, bitter and entrenched, that a thousand peaceful Gods and Goddesses couldn't eradicate it. For that brief moment, though, I saw a glimmer of hope. Reporters, civilians and government officials kept saying "we will destroy the evil." Unfortunately, they were only referring to the evil people who disrupt the rest of society from performing its own evil deeds.

Each meat, dairy and egg-eater is responsible for the death and dismemberment of more than 3,000 land animals and thousands of marine animals throughout their lifetime. Annually, in the US alone, around 10 billion cows, pigs, chickens, turkeys and other animals live in concentration camps. Within the first year of their pathetic lives, they're sent to killing-houses where knife-wielding terrorists slit their throats, drain their blood and dismember their bodies, all-too-often while the animals are still conscious and aware. Sadly, I realized that any lesson learned in the wake of 9-11 was not going to change that.

Path To Liberation

If people truly want to end terrorism, then they should discard animal flesh from refrigerators, toss bows and bullets into the trash, insist that universities close down their vivisection laboratories, demand that department stores close their fur salons, make circuses shift to only human performers, abolish the rodeo once and for all, and support the courageous ALF humanitarians who liberate animals from places of terror. People who yearn for a compassionate world should have nothing but praise for these amazing altruists. Otherwise, any talk of peace, civilization and justice will remain the most hypocritical rhetoric that has ever existed.

Remember, just because an act might be classified as illegal does not make it morally wrong. And just because an act is legal does not make it the best avenue for facilitating substantive change. Laws have always been broken by free-thinking, radical individuals who realize that it is impossible to make progressive changes within a corrupt, discriminatory system.

Nelson Mandela, Rosa Parks, Martin Luther King, Jr., Mohandas Gandhi, Henry David Thoreau and Jesus, to name a few, were routine, radical law-breakers who went to jail many times for disobeying unjust laws. We see them as heroes today, but in their time they were considered by many to be law-breakers, villains and radicals. "Radical" has a negative connotation in society today. However it is simply the Latin word meaning "root," and what radicals do is to bypass pseudo-solutions and get to the root of a problem. Everyone should realize that all social justice activists were considered radical in their time. It is only after social justice activists die and society begins to evolve and comprehend their actions that the "radical" is placed on a pedestal and embraced. Without question, ALF liberations are akin to Harriet Tubman and The Underground Railroad which assisted in the liberation of blacks from white slave-owners. In fact, a wise ALF adage—from an unknown individual—states: "If we are trespassing, then so were the American soldiers who broke down the gates of Hitler's death camps. If we are thieves, then so were the members of The Underground Railroad who freed the slaves from the South. And if we are vandals, then so were those who destroyed forever the gas chambers of Buchanwald and Auschwitz."

One must understand that ALF raids have two goals; giving enslaved animals a chance at freedom and causing major economic damage. As a movement, we must stop living in fantasyland by believing that those directly involved in torturing and murdering animals, and profiting handsomely from it, will listen to reason, common sense and moral truth. The vast majority will not. If they did, there wouldn't be an animal liberation movement because they would have understood the cruelty of their ways by now and adopted a vegan lifestyle.

I am aware that some activists like Howard Lyman and Don Barnes were former abusers of animals who had epiphanies and changed. That's why I said most will not listen to reason. I didn't say never try to educate and enlighten. But in the vast majority of cases, it is just a fantasy to believe that direct abusers collectively will change. What those involved in animal exploitation will listen to, however, is damage to their profits and livelihood. Only if we make their blood businesses unprofitable, will they cease the violence against the animal kingdom.

Remember, since the inception of the animal liberation movement, no human has ever been injured or killed during a liberation or an act of economic sabotage. We need to stop accepting the lies propagated by the media and the corporations who murder animals for a living. ALF activists are not terrorists; those who abuse animals for a living are! ALF activists are not criminals; those who enslave, torture, mutilate, dismember and murder animals for a living are! Activists who liberate animals should not go to prison; animal exploiters should! It should never be viewed as a crime to try and forcibly stop hatred and discrimination and terrorism; it is an act of compassion and courage.

All animals are simply disenfranchised nations in search of the one thing that every sentient being demands: FREEDOM! They are not property. They are not objects. And they are not commodities. The earth and its inhabitants do not belong to humans, under any circumstance. So when inanimate objects—like buildings and machines—are destroyed during an animal liberation, the property-destruction issue is justified because an animal's inherent right to be free trumps economic damage, and buildings that exist to torture living beings deserve to be eradicated forever!

Let Them Read Lies

I believe one main reason why the ALF does not yet have broad public support is because of the lies spewed by animal exploiters and the distortions reported and perpetuated by the mass media. Sadly, animal-killers and their supporters will go to any length to deceive and mislead the public into believing that they are the victims and not the animals. Having inside knowledge of what animal liberation entails, let me give an example of how the propaganda machines work.

On March 30, 1997, I was part of a mink liberation effort at the Eberts Fur Farm in Blenheim, Ontario. We released 1,542 mink from their cages, but were apprehended shortly thereafter. The media reported four lies that are typically issued by the fur industry after liberations: (1) the mink froze to death after freedom; (2) the mink starved to death overnight after freedom; (3) the mink caught pneumonia and became stressed out after freedom; (4) the mink were run over by cars on rural roads at three in the morning after freedom.

Let's look at the facts.

(1) Mink are clothed in natural fur coats which make it impossible to freeze to death, especially during the pleasant month of March/April, which is when my Ontario raid took place.

(2) It takes several weeks for mink to starve to death. It cannot happen overnight. In fact, authorities involved in the Ontario mink liberation stated that the liberated mink raided a nearby chicken farm for food, incontrovertibly exposing the starvation lie. As for the chickens, my heart goes out to them. But my enmity is still inflamed by the 250 million Americans who kill and eat 9 billion chickens to satisfy their meat-addictions. If humans didn't enslave chickens, mink wouldn't raid chicken farms. If humans didn't enslave mink, the ALF wouldn't raid mink farms.

On rare occasions, some people claim that mink attack companion dogs or cats. I have yet to see any proof of this happening. Not one photo of a dead body or a pile of canine or feline bones. So, I believe this is another ploy to divert attention from the real victims; the mink. Even if the mink did attack a dog or a cat, many times dogs attack cats, cats attack birds, and so on. This just proves two other points. In the last 100 years of mink farming, not one wild gene has been bred out of these animals. And after thousands of years of dog and cat domestication, they, too, still possess their wild genes. Being raised in captivity in no way impedes an animals' chance of surviving in the wild.

It should be noted that in the late 90s after the Frye Fur Farm in Illinois was raided—and thousands of mink were given a chance to escape—the fur industry issued a press release claiming how much the Fryes loved and cared for their mink. The release stated the Fryes routinely picked up and played with the mink. Yet, across the waters in England that same year, a liberation of 10,000 mink took place. That release stated that everyone should hide their dogs and cats and children because the mink were vicious animals who would attack and eat everything in sight. Isn't it remarkable that Illinois mink are sweet and cuddly, yet English mink are rapacious and vicious?

The fur industry's public relations people are masters of doublespeak and thereby hide their atrocities from public view. It is obvious that the fur industry can't even get their lies straight. And that's because one lie leads to another.

(3) Mink do not spontaneously contract pneumonia or stress when they are not in cages. Being kept in a cage for your entire life causes stress and neurosis. Freedom is the cure for caged-induced stress and neurosis.

(4) There are no cars on rural roads at three in the morning except for those of fur farmers and police who are trying to recapture the liberated mink. If they backed off and let the mink go, rarely would there be a mink-car casualty.

The fur industry knows that if people were aware of the five methods of death used on mink, foxes and chinchillas, virtually no one would buy a fur coat. The anal electrocutions, genital electrocutions, gassings, neck-breakings and toxic chemical injections are purely evil. So, the fur industry's spin doctors have devised some glittering propaganda in order to divert attention from the heinous methods of death, and the prejudiced media are all-too happy to report them uncritically. The industry and media conspire in an attempt to make animal liberations appear foolish and describe the actions as creating more harm than good.

Any wildlife biologist or veterinarian who is not associated with the fur industry or does not own a fur coat will admit that mink and foxes are wild animals who will undoubtedly survive after being set free. They also will admit that no amount of genetic breeding can take away animals' innate, instinctive survival mechanisms. And let me be perfectly clear: Freedom does not cause death! Hunters, meat, dairy and egg-eaters, fur-wearers, leather-lovers and animal-experimenters cause death!

According to the fur industry, 400 mink instantly died after my Easter Sunday raid. Yet on my request, the lawyers asked them to provide proof of the purported 400 dead mink. They were asked to do so by either bringing in photos, dead bodies or testifying under oath. They declined all offers.
Not surprisingly, the death toll quickly descended from 400 to 300 to 200 to 100 to 12. Subsequently, during my three-day trial when I was convicted and sentenced to six months in prison, the furriers brought in photographs of two dead mink who allegedly died the night of the raid.

Now, I did not believe the authenticity of the photos, but for argument's sake, let's say that two mink were run over by the cars of the fur farmers who were trying to recapture the freed mink. Those two deaths are unfortunate. But every mink in the concentration camp was going to die. Opening the cages was the only chance any of them had. The act was justified.

The job of an ALF activist is not to guarantee safety and freedom, but to give incarcerated animals an opportunity to live in freedom. Unfortunately, 1,000 mink were recaptured because they never found the holes in the fence in order to make it across the street to the luscious miles of fields. (According to some authorities who spoke on the condition of anonymity, the official numbers of the Ontario raid were 1,542 released, 1,000 recaptured, 540 escaped and two dead.) However, of the 1,000 recaptured mink who never made it off the grounds through the cut fence-holes, the best news was 70-80 percent of the pregnant ones miscarried their fetuses. The animal rights community does not want animals bred into enslavement. A miscarriage is infinitely more humane than a lifetime of imprisonment, horror and eventual murder.

It's truly disheartening when the media and a majority of society get so upset when enslaved, tortured and soon-to-be-murdered animals are liberated. Yet, these same individuals don't get upset when enslaved, tortured and soon-to-be-murdered animals—who spend their pathetic lives inhaling the fumes of their own excrement—are gassed, anally electrocuted, genitally electrocuted, injected with toxins or have their necks broken manually.

Taking statements without questioning the source is contemptible. Why would responsible journalists heed the words of the police, who are experts at manipulation, and abject furriers, who collectively murder 40 million animals a year for money? If journalists would think rationally instead of trying to fit into the sleazy world of media hype, they could actually produce a brilliant story on ALF humanitarians and the current paradoxes in our society.

People who put their lives on the line for a cause should be commended not condemned. Dr. Martin Luther King, Jr., once stated, "There are some things so dear—some things so precious—some things so eternally true—that they are worth dying for. And if a person has not discovered something that he or she is willing to die for—then that person isn't fit to live." I wholeheartedly concur!

The Aftermath

For my random act of kindness and compassion on behalf of the tortured and doomed mink, I spent 77 days in prison. (Hilma Ruby, my lone, upstanding compatriot out of the five, spent 60 days in prison.) Canadian Judge A. Cusinato sentenced me to six-months in the Elgin Middlesex Detention Center in London, Ontario. A deportation parole was issued, though, and I returned to Michigan after serving 77 days at the maximum security lock-up.

Before being carted off to prison, I was able to address the judge:

"I stand before this court without trepidation and without timidity because the truth cannot be suppressed today and the truth will not be compromised.

Mohandas Gandhi, one of the most benevolent people to ever grace this earth, once said, 'Even if you are only one person the truth is still the truth.'

The dilemma we face today is whether this court chooses to acknowledge the truth. The following statement is for everyone's edification.

One day every enslaved animal will obtain their freedom and the animal rights movement will succeed because Gandhi also proclaimed, 'All throughout history the way of truth and love has always won. There have been murderers and tyrants and at times they have seemed invincible, but in the end they always fall. Always!'

The true devoted humanitarians who are working towards the magnanimous goal of achieving freedom for animals cannot be stopped by unjust laws.

As long as humans are placed on a pedestal above non-humans, injustice to animals will fester because without universal equality one type of equality will always create another type of inequality. There will be no compromise here today because the truth cannot be compromised.

My presence in this courtroom today is paradoxical. I ask this court: If it is NOT a crime to torture, enslave and murder animals, then how can it be a crime to free tortured, enslaved and soon-to-be-murdered animals?

Humankind must climb out of its abyss of callousness, its abyss of apathy and its abyss of greed. Enslaving and killing animals for human satisfaction can never be justified. And the fur industry must understand that the millions of manual neck-breakings, anal and genital electrocutions, mass gassings, drownings, and toxic chemical injections can never be justified. And, the snaring of millions of free-roaming animals in steel jaw leghold traps, who die slow, horrific deaths, is unjustifiable as well.

There will be no compromise, for the truth cannot be compromised. The schism that this court has created among the five co-accused has been sealed.

Now that I have been convicted, through my volition and in a symbolic protest of the unjust conditions that animals endure, a hunger strike will begin tomorrow at 7:30 a.m.

For every mink that ever languished in a tiny cage and was savagely murdered at the Eberts Fur Farm, I will go hungry. And for the 40 million other animals worldwide who have the skin ripped off their backs in a disgusting display of barbarity, in the name of vanity, I will go hungry.

And if this court expects me to experience an apostasy, meaning an abandoning of my beliefs, it is sadly mistaken. In April of '97, when I was incarcerated for 10 days in a Chatham jail, I briefly experienced, vicariously, what a caged animal goes through. And, thanks to that 10-day bail hearing, my empathy for every mistreated animal intensified.

No matter what I go through during my incarceration and hunger strike, will be nothing compared to the everlasting torture that innocent animals endure on a daily basis.

And if this court is alarmed by my honesty, let me close with a quote from slave abolitionist William Lloyd Garrison:

'I will be as harsh as the truth and as uncompromising as justice. On this subject, I do not wish to think or speak or write with moderation. I am in earnest. I will not equivocate. I will not excuse. I will not retreat a single inch. And I will be heard. The apathy of the people is enough to make every statue leap from its pedestal and hasten the resurrection of the dead. My influence shall be felt in coming years, not perniciously but beneficially, not as a curse but as a blessing, and posterity will bear testimony that I was right.'

There will be no compromise here today because the truth cannot be compromised."

The Struggle Continues...

During my 77-day incarceration, I felt lifeless, moribund, and enervated. Not from any sort of punishment or correction the system thought it doled out, but from the lack of public compassion and activism for animals. Apathy is a bittersweet plague which leads to nihilism. And nihilism is the father of inertia which results in the death of one's emotions.

The majority of people submersed in the aversion of revolution have destroyed their humanity. If one cannot feel, see, nor understand the preciousness of this earth and all of its inhabitants, then why should he or she be blessed with the gift of existence? This planet should be a replica of the most beautiful place imaginable, a place where humans view animals with awe and respect. What a pathetic life I must have led before I heard the cries of the enslaved and the tumult of the animal kingdom. Activism engulfs me. My life is this struggle. From liberator to educator, I continue to fight for interspecies justice.

Do Not Support The A.L.F.

2012

An "anonymous liberator" behind one or more actions in the 2010's challenges activists to stop "supporting" the A.L.F., and start *becoming* the A.L.F.

The Animal Liberation Front is in desperate need of fewer supporters. It has far, far too many, and the madness has to stop somewhere.

The supporters are legion in their black t-shirts – tapping away at laptops, surfing crowds at shows, bussing tables at the local vegan eatery, distributing zines. Thousands of them share their support every day on Facebook and Tumblr. They post and re-post, like and comment. They are ever proliferating.

But, sadly, while all of this reaches new heights in the frenzy of the internet, the underground is largely at a standstill in the real world. ALF support, at one point a recruiting mechanism subservient to the action that it helped empower, has now become the main event. So, since it no longer serves its purpose, it is kindly but firmly requested that you abandon your support. Take off your t-shirts – here is the wake up call. If you are able-bodied and you have built an entire social identity around 'supporting' sabotage and liberation, you are now required to go out and do those things. Your support will not be missed. You will no longer be able to hold on to the comfortable fiction that it ever mattered in the first place. And you will not be able to speak about your nighttime activities, so you will miss out on scene points.

But you will be able to relish accomplishments far more meaningful than anything you could ever do on Instagram or at a show. When you are old and your tattoos have faded, these memories will still be clear. You will be able to make a true and direct impact in the midst of a cold and vast system. And you will be able to look a creature in the eyes and save her life. For those who truly believe, it will be no sacrifice to change roles and take risks in order to keep alive this thing they hold so dear. It takes no specialized skill, only common sense and courage.

Perhaps, as a community, it is time for us to start changing our lifestyles through a new collective paradigm. If you are a self-identified 'radical' who spends their life going to work and watching movies with friends, the only thing currently separating you from the average American is ideas. This must no longer be acceptable.

We cannot explicitly speak about, and thus cannot socially reinforce, a culture of underground activity. However, we certainly can build a "culture of crime," whereby we encourage not only disrespect (easy and functionally irrelevant) but disregard for the law. Jaywalk, shoplift, trespass, whatever – get acquainted with ignoring the rules as a way of life. Start in an area where you feel comfortable, get your friends doing it, and then put what you learn to use in the dead of night.

Accompany this with a culture of institutional privacy – encryption for casual conversation, proxy web surfing, releasing ourselves from the need to share every move we make on social media. While it is most important that individuals take action, these collective steps might be useful.

As for those who do not change, who continue to post their blogs or write their songs, they should not be given the respect or recognition that they seek. It is not respectable to align oneself in words with a phenomenon based on action. And when one gains social clout from doing so, it is parasitic, or at the very least cowardly. It contributes to an activist culture where such inaction is somehow a reasonable, even honorable, manner of behavior.

While others offer liberation and risk prison time, these individuals offer 'support' and risk too many high-fives. But those whose support is only as good as their own comfort can keep both.

Press officers, convicted operatives, and the disabled can continue to speak up for the ALF. If actions surge to an all-time high, but no one is sharing the news on Facebook, the animals won't mind. They do not care about our theories, ideas, beliefs, or our drama. They are in desperate need of fewer supporters and more actors.

If your support for the Animal Liberation Front is genuine, it will end tonight.

I Used To Break Into Labs To Free Animals

2014

An A.L.F. member reflects on their history rescuing animals, and the lives they saved.

One day while walking on a New York sidewalk, a couple stopped in front of me and embraced. I noticed that as the woman held her partner, she peered over his shoulder, with her eyes affixed to the reflection that they cast in a large plate glass window adjacent to where they stood.

I changed my path and made an effort not to walk between the couple and their reflection in the window. It seemed as if the woman wanted nothing more than to capture this reflection and emotional embrace in her memory. Who was I to stand—metaphorically (and literally)—in the way of that?

Their Moment Triggered Something in Me

Walking past that couple on the sidewalk triggered me to reflect on my own cherished memories. Some memories were obvious in their bliss—like the day I got married, or the day my son was born—but others were more nuanced and I spent the rest of the evening considering those. Until that moment I had never considered that some of my most profound memories have been bottled up, never to leave my lips for fear of state actors holding me accountable.

Accountable?

I began to feel like a bloated water balloon, still affixed to a running tap: bursting was inevitable, and I was already leaking…

One day shortly thereafter I was taking my son and our dog Morgan for a walk to the park. Morgan's eyes are starting to glaze over with age, and it's only in a vast open field at the rear of the park that I let her off her leash. In the field she does not have any risk of running into anything and every time I unhook her leash, she dashes off, running as fast as she can, usually in a giant figure eight pattern. On this day she did the same but unexpected to me, in that very moment, seeing her run free and unhinged my balloon popped. I found myself crying and adrift in a whirlwind of emotions.

I thought to myself of just how many days I spent talking about negative things (state repression, court cases) or reciting bewildering and often disheartening statistics about human consumption of animals, and just how few days I spent talking about freedom, about liberation, and about this beautiful and deeply spiritual idea of animals as individuals.

I wanted to take this opportunity to reflect on some of these individuals.

Renee

Renee was a rhesus macaque monkey. Renee had spent 11 years in confinement, her health was ailing, and her future uncertain. She was never experimented upon, but rather was listlessly awaiting experiments at another facility. I sat for two hours in a thunderstorm before jumping the gates to the compound where she was held and bringing her to sanctuary.

Every year I think about Renee. I'll never forget how Renee, despite being in an animal carrier, still managed to tear up the back seat of my mother's car. I'll never forget about how her prolonged poor health rendered her barren, and I'll never forget about how her inherent desire to be a mother made her the perfect guardian for an infant monkey who ended up at her sanctuary a year later. I'll never forget this selflessness in Renee. Renee gave something priceless to that little monkey and moreover, years later she would give me something priceless.

Alice

Alice was born at a breeder for vivisection and lived for six months in a holding pen for reserve research animals, en route to testing facilities. I opened Alice's pen and carried her to safety. I had to run over a mile and a half with Alice before reaching our exit vehicle and while I was running, Alice threw up on me. Before getting in the car with Alice I put her down. I saw her sway and then land on her side. She was motionless for nearly a minute. In this moment of desperately trying to understand what was happening to Alice my comrades and I began to yell at each other. We fumbled to find her pulse; we thought the worst and my friend to my right began to cry. Then, almost as fast as she fell down, she sprang back up, wagged her tail and licked me in the face. We would later learn that Alice had an ailment that impacted her equilibrium, but would ultimately live a long, happy and healthy life.

This was the first time in Alice's life she felt anything other than concrete under her feet. It was overwhelming for both her and us, because in that moment we both received something very special.

Oscar

"It only made sense to intercede"

Oscar was also born into a facility that bred waterfowl for vivisection. Oscar would have but six months before he would end up on a necropsy table, unless someone interceded. It only made sense to intercede.

In our months of advance reconnaissance, we took notice of Oscar. He had a limp, one leg was shorter than the other, and he was only partially covered with his plumage. He was at a disadvantage from the peers with which he shared his installation, yet we'd watch as every night he and a dozen others would pile together to keep warm. On the night when we freed Oscar from his confines, he rode on a truck with hundreds of those peers.

Our trip was nerve-racking. We hoped to reach the sanctuary by sunrise. The temperature outside was in the 50s but the back of the truck was 80 degrees and climbing. Every stop we made to open the back of the truck to allow cool air in was another risk of being caught and every moment above 80 degrees was another risk to the safety of the birds inside. When we arrived, the walls of the truck were wet with condensed sweat.

We met the sanctuary owner. The man was a saint, and I felt guilty that he actually thought my name was Holden Caulfield. He led us to where we could unload our friends, an adapted Quonset Hut reminiscent of a miniature airplane hanger with a greenhouse top and an exit to an adjacent field and pond.

Oscar's friends, in a brilliant chorus of noise and motion, ran en masse toward the pond and dove in. It was so brilliant, it almost felt choreographed. But I quickly became concerned and asked the sanctuary owner if the transition from a hot truck to the cold waters of a Pacific Northwest pond were dangerous. He acknowledged these concerns and suggested we wade out into the pond and begin clapping our hands to wrangle our friends back in. Slowly, they made their way from the pond back to the warmth of the hanger, shaking the water off in what looked like celebratory dancing, but then we saw Oscar…

Oscar was stumbling on himself and his breathing was erratic. He was not shaking the water off.

We dried Oscar with towels and moved him to an adjacent warm space by himself. We wanted him to feel safe; we wanted him to feel loved; we wanted him to recover from whatever shock he was experiencing, but he did not. Oscar died that afternoon.

I have never been able to forgive my recklessness of that day. But I also know

I will never be able to capture in words the awe of seeing Oscar and his friends celebrate their first day of freedom. Oscar and each of his friends gave me lasting inspiration and insight into the very act of being alive and free.

This is a Thank You Letter

This is a letter to Renee, to Alice, to Oscar and to the 281 other beings I removed from abuse. In freeing you I learned things not only about you, but also about myself. I learned that fear of repression for what many consider my criminal acts, although tangible and real, is only as strong as you allow it to be. I learned that giving an individual a new option for a new future—one free of abuse—is not only liberating for those freed, but also for those doing the freeing, and this feeling stays with you, forever.

Years later I, too, would find myself in a cage, incarcerated for my tenure as a radical activist. And while prison is an overwhelming and at times terrorizing experience, I found myself when there calling upon my memories of the efforts I made to free others. I found something comforting there, something that made me realize that those days when I restored someone else's freedoms were the freest days of my life. No matter how large or how small, each of these individual situations mattered…

All That Counts Are The Animals You Save

2014

In a letter from prison, convicted A.L.F. activist Kevin Olliff issues a challenge to activists to confront "trifles of human privilege," keep their focus away from intra-movement debate, and on saving animals.

In prison, you want to know that others are taking up where you left off. So when people ask me what they should do to support prisoners, I tell them to send movement news. Even in the grayest correctional bubble, word of critters scurrying from concentration camps is enough to bring a sense of freedom flooding back into any activist's veins.

But these days, when I hear the latest, it often has the opposite effect. So much of the news seems to be drama, divisiveness, and internet declarations. I will avoid specifics, but suffice it to say that none of it contributes to achieving our objectives – and none matters to animals on the verge of death in their cages.

I am lucky that I will never know a fraction of those animals' hardships, but I do know that one of the hardest aspects of life in a human prison is the constant feeling of others looking over my shoulder. Guards look over my shoulder for adherence to prison regulations, inmates look over my shoulder for conformity to their culture, feds look over my shoulder to catch me slipping on recorded phone calls and visits. There is no escape.

And yet, regrettably, this problem will not end with my incarceration. That is because the talkers and dividers in my own movement love looking over the shoulders of others. I prefer my animal rights with only four guidelines, but these people have more rules than a parole officer. They insert themselves into activist's private lives without a warrant or probable cause. And they insist on ideological rigors unrivalled by the FBI. When it comes to taking the focus off the animals, they are better cops than the cops.

Perhaps my ego isn't big enough, but I have never been under the impression that my own ideas somehow represent the absolute key to right and wrong in the universe. So when I became involved in a modern international social movement, I suspected that I might meet an individual or two who didn't act or believe exactly the same as me. Troubling as that may be for some, involving yourself in activism means involving yourself with a diverse bunch of people. Some of us are lawyers, some of us are felons. Some of us go running, some of us eat dessert. Some of us have photo projects of vegan runners or vegan desserts. Some of us are promiscuous, some married, some neither – and some both. I'm not defending or deriding any of these choices. To be honest, I don't really care. Neither should you.

If you dislike someone or their opinion, feel free to simply not talk to them. It does not help to gossip, quibble, or drag the whole movement into it. The same goes for who-said-what on the internet about which ideological (read: irrelevant) position, or the inclusiveness of the editorial decision-making process for your local group's last Facebook post. Time to spare on these trifles is a human privilege.

To me, that such things are even noticed is puzzling. But that they impact our activism is tragic. It breaks my heart that this nonsense becomes a top concern for the minuscule segment of humanity on whom the animals have to rely. And as much as it may weigh upon me, for them it is a death sentence.

When your passion burns, you often light those around you with the same fire. This is what makes dramatic people so dangerous – their bitterness tends to catch on. But this is also a source of strength for the sane: Every truly dedicated activist – who holds this struggle in their heart, who refuses to be sidetracked by negativity and cliquishness – is in turn shining a light for others. Young people getting involved deserve to find out now that what really matters isn't your politics, your popularity, or how many times you can use the word "organizer" in reference to yourself. All that counts in the end are your tangible achievement for animals.

COMMUNIQUES

Statements of responsibility for A.L.F. actions

COMMUNIQUES

When compassionate raiders break down the doors to a university lab and spirit animals to freedom, they have only one opportunity to deliver their message: the communique.

Issued anonymously (and untraceably) in the hours or days following an A.L.F. action, these dispatches from the animal liberation underground offer activists their sole chance at managing public perception, educating the public, admonishing animal abusers, and inspiring others to take up crowbars and make animal liberation a reality... *tonight.*

Pre-internet, news outlets and above-ground groups would tell of receiving packets of info via the mail (or doorstep) in the wake of high profile A.L.F. raids—packets containing various combinations of typed communique, copies of confiscated documents, photos, and video.

Today, they tell of communiques arriving via inbox, via disposable accounts and public computers surely never to be touched by the raider's hands again.

Once disseminated, these snapshots of history often fade from view and memory, evading the history books through the hyper-info-transience of the digital age. Yet history was meant to be told, and ALF communiques are the history of a movement—history as told by those who made it.

Unavailable to explain themselves publicly by the very nature of their work, the communique is the press release of those without a call back number, the stage for those in hiding, the microphone for those without a voice.

Of all names claimed by those who work above the law for animals, the Animal Liberation Front holds the title of most used, and most recognizable. When the guidelines of the A.L.F. are found to be too confining—or the pressures of its history too great—there are those who do their work under different banners. Included are dispatches from the Animal Liberation Brigade, Vegan Straight Edge, and others. Common to them all, the understanding that in some battles, working within the law will win you favor from the police, and little else.

The communique is the most consistent, unfiltered glimpse we have into the minds and motives of "the animals' last hope."

Communiques serve the under-appreciated purpose of forcing visibility. When animal abusers thrive on staying under the public's radar, their response to a large-scale action is often to pretend it didn't happen. And when impossible—deny it was animal liberators (see E-L Labs, 3- 89, University of Iowa, 11-04). The communique puts exploiters in a rare defensive stance, an uncomfortable place for those guilty of the indefensible.

With the communique, the necessary conditions of their composition bring all the mystique of the prison-scribed memoir or message in a bottle from a lost ship at sea. They bring up images of road-worn liberators, the morning after in an obscure rural town, fighting sleep over a note pad, debating the finer points of style and message before disseminating the final product and living to fight another day... and night.

The general communique adheres to the who/what/when/where/why formula, but the tastes of the anonymous authors varies slightly more on the issue of tone. Most consistent is the utter seriousness and sense of urgency that is requisite to any A.L.F. action. But some offer undertones of humor, while others do not stray in the slightest from a staunch revolutionary battle-cry. On either end of this spectrum, no matter the taste of the audience, their words cannot be reduced to mere rhetoric. Inherent in the communique is the integrity of the authors—integrity in their willingness to put action before their words.

The communique is the story of the A.L.F., in one of the only ways available to them to tell it.

What is included

Included are all known communiques for North American A.L.F. (and A.L.F.-adjacent) actions deemed "significant" by the editors. This includes all large-scale sabotage actions and live liberations (exceptions below).

What is not included

Not included are communiques for small-scale property destruction, and in limited cases, some opportunistic animal liberations (e.g. a mouse freed from a glue trap).

Notes:

Altering communiques for publication was done sparingly and not without careful consideration. Only very limited edits were made, in cases of spelling or small formatting changes. With the authors unavailable for comment, we accept some of these "mistakes" may have been intended for reasons unknown.

For many communiqué's we relied on a single source, which may or may not have included the entirety of the original statement. Multiple instances exist where a communiqué appears to be incomplete, yet there exists no source material to confirm. We always drew from the best and most complete source available.

CONTENTS

CONTENTS

KEWALO RESEARCH LAB | 1977

May 29th, 1977
Honolulu, HI
Two dolphins removed from lab, transported to the ocean, and released

Early this morning two slaves were freed in Honolulu. They had been kept in a circular enclosure five ft. high for the last six years, during which time they were kept in total isolation while undergoing remorseless experiments.

These innocent prisoners were Bottlenose dolphins, the same species as the famed 'Flipper'. These dolphins possess a highly developed language and intelligence compared to that of a human.

The dolphins were safely transported to a carefully chosen location where they will start a new life of freedom. They will never again know the nets of a captor or the relentless probing of scientific research.

A statement of our feelings was left at the Kewalo Basin Marine Animal Research Lab.

TORONTO HOSPITAL | 1983

June 26th, 1983
Toronto, Ontario
Five cats liberated

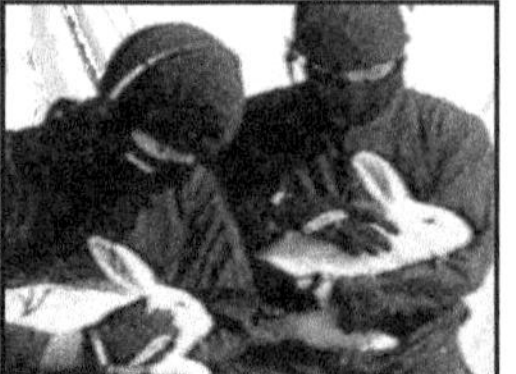

On Sunday, June the 26th, the Animal Liberation Front liberated 5 cats from the Toronto Western Hospital and experiment equipment was destroyed. The animals have been placed in homes.

Chronic experiments which involve prolonged suffering are being carried out at the hospital on baboons, squirrel monkeys, rabbits, dogs, cats and rats.

Repetitive heart surgery is being done on dogs yet at McMasters University a computer duplicates heart attacks in man. It duplicates the whole circulatory system and a patient's reaction to whatever treatment and drugs that are given. It even speaks English. Unfortunately, the animal research lobby is powerful and represents businesses which include drugs, household products, cosmetics and the military.

The dogs and cats were given to the hospital by municipal pounds Also, some were given to the hospital by the University of Toronto's Department of Lab Animal Sciences, which also receives animals from municipal pounds, and from dog nappers and other illegal dealers in Quebec.

In our society, living creatures are not respected and valued for their existence, but are treated as commodities. Farm animals are beef, wildlife is game, fur animals are pelts, dogs and cats are pets to be traded, and unwanted pets are vivisection material. Laws which condone and encourage tormenting, mutilating, and murdering millions of sentient beings in Canada alone each year are wrong. Therefore, the Animal Liberation Front will not hesitate to use illegal direct action to rescue and liberate animals, and to continue our campaign against abusers...

UNIVERSITY OF TORONTO | 1986

February 16, 1986
Toronto, Ontario
Break-in & attempted liberation

Early this morning, members of the Animal Liberation Front made entry into the animal concentration camp of the U of T's dentistry building. Messages were left for the chief animal torturer, commandant Sessle, and his Nazi cohorts.

Sessle is a specialist in administering chronic pain by implanting electrodes in the tooth pulp of primates and subjecting cats and rodents to massive facial mutilations and other mindless cruelties.

Lab areas sustained extensive damage as part of the ALF's economic sabotage campaign against the scum who torture animals.

February 16, 1986
ALF

SYDELL'S EGG FARM | 1986

June 4, 1986
Hartley, DE
25 hens liberated
First documented factory farm rescue in North America

Animal Liberation at Mid-Atlantic Factory Farm!

On Wednesday, June 4, 1986, the Farm Freedom Fighters liberated 25 laying hens from a Mid-Atlantic battery egg operation. According to Farm Sanctuary, the spokesgroup for the liberators, this is the first direct farm animal liberation ever conducted in the United States.

Farm Sanctuary was alerted to the liberation when an anonymous caller contacted the group early Wednesday morning and identified himself/herself as a member of the Farm Freedom Fighters. A videotape of the actual liberation, photographs and a detailed description of the liberation was left for Farm Sanctuary. The videotape contains footage of the liberators, the battery egg operation, and the hens. The tape also shows the liberators spray-painting slogans such as "Animal Auschwitz" and "Battery cages are torture chambers" on the walls of the hen warehouse. A note was left for the egg producers urging them to stop using battery cages. **(Copies of the videotape and photographs are available upon request - contact: Farm Sanctuary, P.O. Box 37, Rockland, DE 19732, U.S.A.).**

The Farm Freedom Fighters targeted the egg industry because it is one of the largest abusers of farm animals. Over 95% of the eggs sold today are produced in the battery cage system where four to five laying hens are crammed into a bare wire cage commonly measuring 12" x 18". The extreme overcrowding results in extensive feather loss, skin damage, and feet malformations. The raising of laying hens in these stressful conditions poses serious health hazards for humans as well. The birds are fed enormous quantities of antibiotics to reduce the high disease and mortality rates resulting from intensive confinement systems. Many medical experts fear the rampant use of antibiotics is creating antibiotic-resistant bacteria in humans, a condition which renders life-saving drugs useless.

According to a statement made by the Farm Freedom Fighters, "This action is the first of many farm animal liberations. Our war against farm animal oppression will continue until all farm animals are free from the brutality of factory farms."

CHESTER'S CHICKENS

1986

June 6, 1986
Newmarket, Ontario
106 chickens rescued

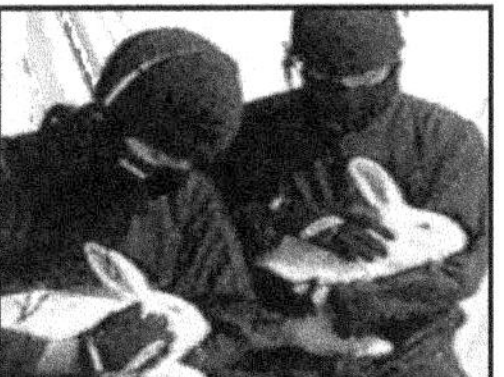

June 6, 1986 - Newmarket

One cell from the Northern ALF raided the premises of Chester's Chickens in Newmarket.

In order to get into the main chicken concentration camp, we had to cross a huge field which was overlooked by the Highway. In order to escape being 'picked-up' by headlights we had to crawl on our faces for most of the way. The farm itself was well-lit by floodlights and surrounded by two fences. We quickly cut our way through these and made our way into the main building.

Inside we stopped, mesmerized by the sight of thousands of chicks - so many that they covered the entire floor of the building. It was like looking at a living yellow carpet with bright lights beating down from the ceiling!

We immediately began to liberate chicks - 106 in all, and before leaving sprayed slogans everywhere - mainly 'Chicken Lib' and 'Scum'. In two's and three's we left the building, separated, and came together later at the designated meeting place.

The chicks have all been placed in good homes where they now get to go to sleep in the dark at night!!!

UNIVERSITY OF OREGON

1986

October 26, 1986
Eugene, OR
264 animals liberated, $120,000 damage to labs. Original typed statement.

A.L.F. STATEMENT

An open letter to:

Mr. Paul Olum
Mr. John Mosely
Mr. Greg Stickrod
Mr. Richard Marrocco
Mrs. Barbara Gordon-Lickey
Other concerned officials, administrators, staff and faculty at the University of Oregon.

The Animal Liberation Front would like to carify the issues and respond to some of the accusations made in connection with our raid and rescue action at the University of Oregon on October 26, 1986:

I. This act was, first and foremost, a mission of mercy; a nonviolent direct action carried out solely on behalf of the animals which were rescued, in order to free them from lives of forced confinement in steel cages inside sterile laboratories, and to allow them to live their lives under conditions more in line with their biological, psychological, and behavioral, as well as physical, needs.

Secondarily, but no less important, it was an act of outright retribution aganist Drs. Gordon-Lickey and Marrocco; an expression of total rage and anger over the sadistic and brutal acts she has committed against hundreds of innocent baby kittens during her 17-year career as a vivisector, and our frustration over the failure of efforts to stop her.

With this liberation, it was also our intention to demonstrate our unwillingness to accept the status quo of animal use and exploitation in principle, even when carried out in accordance with established requirements of the law. We openly concedethat we found few instances of non-compliance with guidelines of the Federal Animal Welfare Act governing humane care and treatment of laboratory animals, in comparison with violations we have uncovered at other institutions , most notably the University of Pennsylvania, the University of California at Riverside, and the City of Hope medical center. This, however, is not enough. The fact that these animals were foced to live in a state of permanent confinement in unnatural and artificial environments, i.e., caging systems, is ample justification for our action. In further support of our cause, though, are the cruel and brutal acts of physical and surgical mutilation these animals are forced to undergo; acts which constitute crimes against morality, as well as blatant violations of the dignity and sanctity of life itself. This is totally unacceptable.

Furthermore, though we do not accept the concept of ownership applying to living beings, most A.L.F. members are hard-working, tax-paying citizens, and our tax money was used to "purchase" these animals, including the cats and kittens in the breeding colony. We have not only as much right as Gordon-Lickey to determine how they will be allowed to live their lives, but even more right, since she has excercised such poor judgement in this regard by depriving them of thir most basic and fundamental rights, including their freedom, their eyesight, and life itself. Therefore, all we have done is "relocate" those whom we are rightfully entitled to relocate.

2

II. Regarding the physical damage we did to facilities, equipment, and property: the Animal Liberation Front acts based on principles of nonviolence. We have never, nor will we ever, knowingly harm any living being(s), human or nonhuman. This does not extend to non-living, non-sentient objects. To act in a manner consistent with our policy of peaceful and non-violent resistance, we must destroy the instuments of death and destruction. Also, we realize that every penny'sworth of the dollar-value damage we cause represents money unavailable for the purchase, mutilation, and slaughter of living animals. This includes the cost of expensive and sophisticated security systems now neccessary to keep us out of research facilities, and the animals in.

Additionally, it was the cutting of the eyeballs, as much as anything else, that compelled us to include the vandalism and destruction as an expression of pure, outright rage, in addition to the liberation of the animals, as a part of our action. It was the cutting of the eyeballs and the sewing shut of the eyelids of innocent newborn kittens, particularly during the intortion/extortion experiments (1978-80) and the "artificial squint" experiments (1972-74). The destruction of the X-ray machine in particular, was in direct retaliation for the surviving kittens from the eye rotation experiments being chemically paralyzed, restrained in a stereotaxic device, and having their skulls cut open in order to probe their brains with needles and tungsten microelectrodes during visual testing while still alive, prior to being killed. Likewise, it was neccessary to totally demolish the primate stereotaxic device which we found in the back hallway of bldg. 114, in order to insure that it would never agin be used to restrain and immoblize live non-human primates while electric shocks are conducted directly into their brains through concentric bipolar electrodes wired to an electic generator, as Mr. Marrocco has done many times in the past, and plans to continue doing to live crab-eating macaque monkeys. Not cruel, Mr. Marrocco? No pain whatsoever? Then you should have no objections to impartial observers not connected with the University, the press, and members of the humane/animal rights community being present to observe, record, and photograph this procedure in the future. Expect to be contacted soon so that arrangements can be made. Incidentally, Mr. Marrocco, consider yourself extremely fortunate that we allowd you to maintain possession of those monkeys. The one and only reason we did not take them along with the other animals is that adequate homes and caretakers could not be found for them in advance. Leaving them behind was one of the most difficult things many of us had ever done. We will never, ever forget the look in their eyes.

By the way, the "$10,000" microscope was destroyed in about 12 seconds with a 36-inch steel wrecking bar that we purchased at a Fred Meyer store for less than five dollars. We consider that a pretty good return on our investment.

III. In addressing the public response of University officials and vivsectors to the entire incident, we find it ironic to see such a sympathetic display of compassion and concern for the resued animals by those who obviously consider them as nothing more than "research tools"; replaceable commodities to be used up and discarded at will. This is evidenced by the fact that these individuals, as a matter of routine, commonly mutilate and kill such animals, (including over 8,000 at this institution during 1985), and would have done so to many of these particular animals had we not rescued them.

We despise Mr. Stickrod, in particular, for the slick and clever P.R. job he has done in misleading and decieving the public and the news media concerning the facts of this issue in order to elicit public sentiment for his case. We think he would make an excellent politician. His outright lies to the press, however, are disgusting, and are an insult to what little credibility he has. His claims that none of the animals which we rescued were

3

used in clinical experimentation, for instance, are false. The purpose of the cat breeding colony in Science I is to insure a constant, year-round supply of baby kittens for Gordon-Lickey to use in her visual deprivation experiments. All 10 of the kittens we rescued, as well as the 6 since born to Bootsy, were destined to suffer that fate.

The number of animals officially claimed by the University to have been rescued (150), is also incorrect. We counted nearly 140 of the white rats alone, including newborns and juviniles, which we took from the main rat room of bldg. 114. This is not even counting the 16 brown and white adults kept seperate in the back room. In addition, we took all 12 of the adult cats in the breeding colony, along with the 10 kittens, including Bootsy and her then-unborn litter, for a total of 28 cats, not 18. The total count of animals rescued was well over 200.

Contrary to Mr. Stickrod's statement that "in all instances the equipment that has been damaged has been the machinery for animal care and not for the research work," the primate stereotaxic device mentioned earlier, which we also filmed in our videotape, was in no way used for the care or treatment of any animals, but was in fact one of the most sinister instruments of torture ever devised by the human mind. We took particular delight in destroying it.

As for Mr. Stickrod's and Mr. Weston's impassioned cries about how the rescued animals "are not being cared for," and would have been better off left in the University's "care", these slick but vain appeals to public sympathy are ridiculous, and will not be taken seriously by anyone with even the vaguest notion of how these animals are forced to live - and die. The photographs we have released to the press are ample evidence that they have been placed in private "safe" homes where they will be cared for in a manner befitting their dignity as individual, sentient, living beings. All of the rescued kittens, for example, will be allowed to retain the normal eyesight they were born with throughout their natural lives. They will be allowed to grow and live unconfined by steel bars; to run, jump and play, climb a tree, hunt, chase a ball, or just sit and think cat thoughts, as cats were meant to do. The rabbits, with the exception of those unfortunate few who were recovered under uncertain circumstances,* are now able to feel the goodness of the earth beneath their feet and the warmth of the sun above them. They love the fresh cabbage, lettuce, and carrots they receive daily, and have proven to be quite affectionate. The rats, for the first time in their lives, are able to stand up ontheir rear legs and stretch to their full height, a new experience for them after living in the low-top containers in which we found them.

Also ironic is Mr. Stickrod's concern for the interests of hard working taxpayers, as if they would be billed directly and seperately for the over $50,000 cost of the damage we caused. In actuality, most of this amount, covering repair and replacement of equipment, will be deducted from grant funds already awarded, and will, as stated earlier, displace funds otherwise available for the purchase, abuse, and slaughter of live animals, which

* To the best of our knowlege, all animals were placed in good, safe homes; we rely on an intricate underground railroad network, much like the one used to transport fugitive slaves to the free states of the North in the last century, to bring all of the animals to sancturary. However, much like the railroad of the 1800's, not all of the oppressed always find their way to freedom, due to unfortunate circumstances beyond our control; thousands of blacks were returned to the torment of slavery, and now 10 rabbits have been returned to their tormentors at the University of Oregon. At any rate, this represents but a small percentage of our total effort. Over 200 former victims are now free from the torture and death of vivisection.

4

the taxpayers would have had to pay for anyway. Furthermore , $50,000 pales in comparison to the approximately $1.2 million which Gordon-Lickey has already spent over her 17-year career as a cat butcher. Mr. Stickrod fails to mention that she is even now billing the taxpayers nearly $350,000 for her current project, which is expected to consume another 300 baby kittens. We challenge Stickrod, Gordon-Lickey, or anyone else to present any tangible results from these vast sums of money and animal lives, even a single documented case where the eyesight of a human was saved or improved.

Lastly, the statement implying that only animals, and nothing else, were taken in our raid is an outright lie. You know full well that we have the color slides - over 400 of them - which we found in the office of room 304 of Science I. These may prove more damaging than any other part of our effort, for they provide undeniable proof of the accusations made by us and others, including some of the most gruesome, repulsive, and incriminating examples of the systematic torture of living animals that takes place behind the locked doors of your institution. The revelation you have been dreading is imminent, as we plan to release many of these to the public and the press shortly.

IV. In closing, we would like to state that, aside from having to leave the monkeys behind, our only regret in connection with our action was that it was neccessary to go to such extremes in the first place, when it would have been so simple, and much less costly on your part to avoid. We are aware that you (University officials, faculty, and administrators) were given ample oppurtunity to address and respond to the specific concerns of the animal rights community over a reasonable length of time. Yet, through selfishness, greed, and an incredible display of arrogance, primarily on the part of Mr. Moseley, Mr. Stickrod, and Mr. Marrocco, you refused. You have now paid a high price for that arrogance. We sincerely hope that, among other things, this will serve as an example for other individuals and institutions to think long and hard, and consider carefully before making the same mistake.

Your repeated vain attempts to pacify and placate the animal rights community by pointing to the creation of the Institutional Animal Care and Use Committee (IACUC) are an excercise in futility. This committee would provide little more than comic relief if the implications of its existance weren't so tragic. Considering that this body is composed almost entirely of individuals with strong vested interests in the continuation of animal abuse and exploitation by maintaining the status quo of current research and experimentation at the University of Oregon, it is a classic example of the proverbial "foxes guarding the chicken coop." The IACUC is clearly in violation of even it's own inadequate guidelines, particularly those relating to the sociological, biological, ecological, psychological, and behavioral requirements of animals. Anyone with even an intuitive understanding of animal ethology would agree that no animal care committee which allows the kind of offenses against animals that this one does is a committee that cares even remotely for the interests of the animals it oversees.

Be realistic. You really didn't expect to continue jacking the animal rights people around the way you have without eventually running up against active resistance, did you? As you probably realize by now, as others have in the past,this particular political movement is no longer willing to accept such arrogance, and has grown strong enough to back up that unwillingness. And, as you have seen firsthand, though the A.L.F. is but a small and militant faction of the animal rights movement, we are fully capable of making our point in an extreme and dramatic way when we desire to do so. We see our actions as small victories in the larger war being waged by humanity against the planet earth and all it's occupant life forms. We, of course, have aligned ourselves with the latter side in this conflict, which is no longer a passive struggle

Oregon State University

1991

June 10, 1991
Corvallis, OR
OSU experimental fur farm burned down, closed forever. Original typed statement.

A CALL OF THE WILD

Written on the eve of the raid on Oregon State University's Experimental Fur Farm.

Let it be recognized that the Earth, and all life upon it, is under massive attack by human forces that would destroy all of nature for the sake of economic, and personal gain. We are at the most critical stage of ecological destruction in human history, with every form of indigenous non-human, and human life threatened with continued exploitation, and biological extinction.

If the animal nations, and the land they live in to survive, then we must act now.

Hundreds are murdered every minute, thousands every hour, and millions of animals are slaughtered everyday. All for the meat we eat, the leather and fur we wear, and the countless other by-products fed to our society by the earth-destroying industries involved in animal abuse. The reasons behind predator control, and over-grazing, are to protect the interest of the livestock industry. We know the facts, and even who is doing it, now is the time when direct action speaks louder than words.

Over the last fifteen years, the Animal Liberation Front has maintained an active role in covertly challenging the institutions of animal abuse, and also environmental destruction. The Animal Liberation Front has rescued thousands of animals from vivisection laboratories and suppliers, factory-farms, fur-farms, and other places where they were being imprisoned, and tortured. The Animal Liberation Front has also caused tens of millions of dollars of damage to property being used to destroy life, by continuing an effective campaign of "economic sabotage". But this is not enough!

In order to topple the infrastructure of animal exploitation it is necessary to launch a full-scale guerilla war against animal, and earth abuse industries. Unlike any other war, the war fought by the Animal Liberation Front in the last fifteen years, has been one where life is the highest value, not real estate, or political power. It is a struggle where we retain a moral high ground above our enemies because we attack only the machines and property of destruction, and not those that operate them. To justify the destruction of life, is to forfeit our call for respect of all life. The defense of nature and animals can be attained without more killing. The full benefits of economic sabotage have yet to be tapped by the animal, and environmental movements.

It is time to continue the re-evolutionary process that will spare natural diversity, and non-human beings from the remorseless path of modern society. It is time to be acknowledged as a part of the solution, not a part of the problem. There is no more middle of the road, or fence to sit on any longer. It is time to abandon our biological prejudice, and speciesism that prevents us from risking our own freedom to obtain that of an imprisoned sister or brother.

If we truly believe in an affinity with all life on Earth, then let us now defend it by all means necessary.

There can be no true freedom as long as one of our non-human family members is imprisoned by the power of human-kind. The destiny of the Earth is in our own hands. We can choose to spend our precious time and energy on mild reforms, and temporary victories, or we can strive for total liberation of the animal nations by refusing to accept the ineffective avenues of change that governments offer us. We must never expect the power-structure to release its strangle-hold on nature and animal-kind voluntarily. Nor can we expect to liberate the animal nations through the sanctioned methods of the very institutions that oppress them.

It has been one-hundred and twenty years since human tribes aggressively challenged the United States Government to defend animal life. Unfortunately for Western North America, and all that lived upon her, that battle was lost. But the struggle has just begun again. In the spirit of the buffalo, prairie wolf, and laboratory rat, we must organize an effective underground movement that can maintain a relentless campaign of economic sabotage against the anti-life corporations that mutilate animals, and ravage their homelands. we must continue our attacks, and strike repeatedly until the anti-nature forces are beaten down from their dominating platform of oppression.

For too long we have tried to reach the hearts of the heartless, while our sisters, and brothers have continued to fall. We have appealed for peace on every level governments have offered us. Always with the same disappointing results. We can no longer compromise the lives of those we have no right to represent at the bargaining table of anthropocentric society. There is no more time to wrestle with philosophies that place animal life below that of property. To disregard the sanctity of life is a moral crime, as well as a breaking from the laws of nature. There is no longer a use for passive resistance, such tactics are only effective against an opposition that respects life. There is only time for aggressive self-defense of the innocent victims of human greed, and patriarchy.

The genocidal war being waged against the Earth, and all that live upon her, is unjustifiable, and unacceptable to human beings that still embrace compassion, and freedom as higher values than material wealth, and power. It is very important to recognize in our struggle, that the forces that exploit the Earth, and animals, have amassed too much power, and authority, in order to fight them overtly. We must not offer our own lives as fodder for the police. They have all the guns, and money, but we have the spirit of nature on our side and sabotage must be the Earth's revenge.

This is only one human voice from the front-lines of the war to protect animals, and defend the Earth. There are few of us, and many of them. We are tired, and grow weary. We desperately need others to fight the struggle, or the Animal Liberation Front will exist only as a memory, like the native riders of the Great Plains.

As is the case with many other members of the Animal Liberation Front, I am ready to die for the defense of our Mother Earth. We will not escape the clutches of the government forever. For this reason, we must recruit new members if we are to turn the tide of animal exploitation. This is a call to those who can no more turn away from the cries for freedom emitting from every research laboratory, factory-farm, fur-farm, circus, and wilderness. A call to individuals who can no longer tolerate the screams of pain from our non-human sisters, and brothers. You are the Animal Liberation Front and the animal nations need you.
Do not send money to ease your conscience, do not attend more police monitored demonstrations, and do not write letters to political waste-paper baskets.

Instead organize, stratagize, and act now. Locate friends that you trust that feel the same way you do, then keep your mouth shut. Remember, one individual can make a difference, and a group of people can change the world. Do not look for romantic adventure, or self-gratification in this struggle. In autonomy is the birth of true personal liberation. There will be rewards, and they will be beyond your wildest imaginations. They will come as you fight for freedom with others in the night. They will come everytime a fur shop you strike goes out of business, everytime an animal you liberate runs free, and everytime an animal concentration camp you torch burns to the ground.

There will come a time when we ourselves begin to fall, when we are the imprisoned animal behind bars. It will not be the first time someone is imprisoned because of their adherence to the laws of nature. Then is when we must remember that whatever happens to us in a jail cell, is little compared to the torture inflicted upon animals by industry, and government. With good security, and common sense, we can deny the opposition a victory over us, and the Earth. We can remain free. It has been seven years since my first Animal Liberation Front action. Governments cannot imprison ideas, and spirit, neither can they squash the voice for freedom, and struggle for justice for all. To government, nothing is more dangerous than a people that rise above their control, and empower themselves with the self-confidence to act against state-sponsored terrorism.

We must also discover that liberation is a process that begins with ourselves. It must be your first Animal Liberation action. It will come as you question, and reject the guidelines and laws of our society forced on us since birth. Values and beliefs that have only served to breed apathy, and insensitivity to the crimes being committed daily around us. Rules of society that have allowed so much death and destruction to continue against the Earth, animals, and ultimately, ourselves. We must instead strive to live with one another in a non-oppressive, life-respecting way that allows for us to rediscover all that the Earth offers us if we only choose to listen. Listen to the language that others have forgotten, and what others have attempted to destroy.

I do not speak for myself only, but try to also speak on behalf of those without a voice. Through the years I have seen their eyes behind the wire, and have witnessed their agony in death. It is a very real tragedy, what we do to our fellow beings on Earth. Rather than hate ourselves because of what our species has done, we must show the animal nations that all of human-kind is not evil. We must make our own lives an example of how peaceful coexistence can become a reality. It all starts with you. The strength of a small group of people is limitless when we start to break free.

As we raid Oregon State University's Experimental Fur Farm tonight we will see hundreds of animals in cramped cages that will be killed this November. We will try to save some of them. For the rest, I will beg of you to throw down your petitions, and pick-up your pry-bars. Membership in the Animal Liberation Front begins with your first "illegal" direct action on behalf of animals.

Animal liberation is literally only a stone's throw away, it must spread to your local butcher shop, fur salon, and chicken farm. May the flames of animal liberation engulf every structure representing animal and Earth abuse. The Animal Liberation Front must never die, for if it does, the hopes of freedom for billions of animals will be forever drowned in the business as usual attitude of the animal abuse industries.

For the women, and men of the Animal Liberation Front, I call on you to join us as warriors of a new society, one that will include all species in our global community. A place where the cry of the coyote, and song of the whale mean as much as the voice of any human. May we rescue natural diversity and all animals that belong in it, from ecological genocide at the hands of patriarchal domination. Be driven not by anger, or frustration, but by love and desire to be free in a world where all are equal.

Western Wildlife Cell Member
ANIMAL LIBERATION FRONT

MALECKY MINK RANCH | 1991

December 21, 1991
Yamhill, OR
Processing shed burned down, farm closed

December 21 1991 – Western Wildlife Cell members of the Animal Liberation Front (A.L.F.) raided Malecky Mink Ranch in Yamhill, Oregon, and set an incendiary device that destroyed the processing plant of this farm near Salem.

Intelligence sources revealed that the fur farm was to be sold, with intentions to continue exploitation of fur animals. Malecky Mink Ranch was a recipient of information from Oregon State University's Experimental Fur Farm and had developed innovative methods of commercial exploitation of mink for the fur trade.

No mink or humans were injured in the A.L.F.'s fourth action against the United States Fur Farm industry. Fleshing machines, drying drums, skinning racks, feed mixers, freezers, and a workshop were all effectively destroyed in this economic attack against the tools of death and destruction.
This action was taken to avenge the lives of mink murdered on the ranch in the past and to prevent the further imprisonment of native wildlife in the future. 750,000 mink are slaughtered every winter in the Northwest for trade and four million nationwide on over (illegible –ed.) fur farms.

The Animal Liberation Front also announces a new campaign against the fur trade, one that directly targets the insensitive humans who wear fur garments. We will fight the fur-wearers in the streets. No longer shall the ecological arrogance of the public supporters of the fur trade go unchallenged. A.L.F. members shall arm themselves with battery acid and dye, and will inflict damage on the furs worn by humans. Fur is for four-leggeds, not two. The lives of fur animals will be avenged.

The fur industry is responsible for the demise of not only native north american wildlife, but the destruction of Native peoples' cultures as well. Over the last four hundred years this barbaric industry has waged a genocidal war against animals and humans. Through the introduction of social and physical disease, the fur trade has forced native people to participate in their bloody practice, or perish like so many animals in traps and cages.

It is time to eliminate this anthropocentric profit-centered beast before the last howl is heard. A.L.F. calls on all peoples to join in the battle against this ecologically destructive regime, and to defend the defenseless from the oppression of our own species. We must destroy that which destroys the animals, earth, and ourselves.

On behalf of the mink, fox, bobcat, lynx, and coyote nations. A.L.F. shall wage non-violent war against the fur trade. Until the last fur farm is burned to the ground.

Animal Liberation Front, Western Wildlife Cell

Blaze razes Yamhill mink plant

An activist group takes credit for the fire, but officials say it may have been accidental.

By Dave Berns
The Statesman Journal

A man claiming to belong to a radical animal rights group said his organization set a fire Saturday that destroyed a Yamhill mink processing plant.

But authorities said the single-alarm blaze at Malecky Mink Ranch in rural Yamhill County may have been the result of an accidental fire.

The anonymous telephone caller told KGW-TV that the Animal Liberation Front set the 5:45 a.m. fire that destroyed a single-story building at 7931 NE Keller Lane.

Chief Vic Knutz of the Yamhill Fire Protection District said the blaze was being investigated as possible arson, but he questioned the legitimacy of the 9 a.m. phone call.

"I'm not sure there's any proof of that at this time," Knutz said of the caller's claim.

No one was hurt in the fire, which was quickly brought under control. But mink ranch owner Hynek Malecky said that his 10-year-old business was destroyed.

"This was my lifelong dream," he said. "We are hard-working people. We were never on welfare or nothing. I put all my money in the business, and now it's all gone."

Malecky said that he raised between 3,000 and 4,000 mink annually and processed their skins to sell to a New York company. No animals were lost in the fire.

Officials from the Oregon State Police arson team and the U.S. Treasury Department's Bureau of Alcohol, Tobacco and Firearms coordinated the investigation.

Sgt. Ethan Wilson of the Oregon State Police said: "There's no evidence at this time to indicate it was anything other than an accidental fire, but the investigation is continuing."

Two Yamhill County Sheriff reserves were scheduled to remain at the site overnight. Sheriff Lee Vasquez said the security was requested by Malecky's insurance company, which wanted to make sure the area would not be tampered with before insurance investigators arrived.

The Animal Liberation Front is a secretive organization that claimed responsibility for June arson attacks on an Oregon State University mink research farm near Corvallis and the Northwest Farm Food Cooperative in Edmonds, Wash.

In October 1986, group members broke into a University of Oregon psychology lab and freed 125 monkeys, rabbits, hamsters and rats.

UNIVERSITY OF ALBERTA

1992

June 1, 1992
Edmonton, Alberta
29 cats liberated, extensive damage to labs

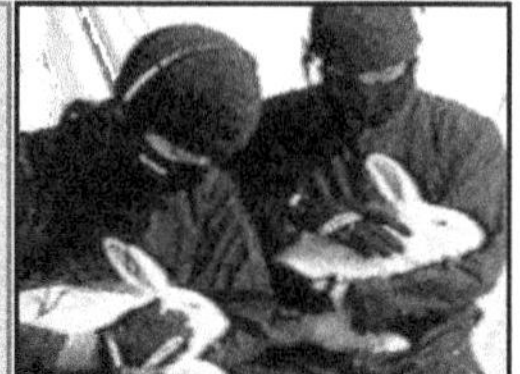

The Animal Liberation Front takes credit for a raid early this morning at the University of Alberta's Ellerslie Research Station 127 St and 9 Ave SW. We have liberated a total of 29 cats from this prison farm, removed research documents, and destroyed research equipment and records.

The cats were to be used in useless and painful experiments in research labs across the U of A.

The A.L.F. believes that humans do not have any rights to inflict pain and suffering on any species.

The cats, most of whom were former pets, have been given veterinary examinations and will be placed in homes of caring people. We are saddened to have left behind hundreds of animals including more cats, many dogs, goats, sheep, mice, rats, deer, pigs, and elk.

Documents show that approximately 80,000 animals are vivisected each year by the U of A. Experiments university researchers inflict on animals include sensory deprivation, exposure to disease, toxic substances and radiation, among the endless horrors.

The black and white film we've sent to the Edmonton Sun and Edmonton Journal show the actual liberation in progress. It also shows along with the video we sent to the CBC and (illegible – ed.) affiliate, the cats in the arms of the liberators.

All animals have an inherent right to live their lives free from human interference. Today liberation and economic damage are part of an ongoing campaign against all animal torturers which will end only when the last animal is free and the last lab is burnt to the ground.

The Animal Liberation Front urges everyone to join us in celebrating Environment Week by liberating our four-legged brothers and sisters from their wretched prisons.

Animal Liberation Front

MICHIGAN STATE UNIVERSITY

1992

February 28, 1992
Lansing, MI
Two mink liberated, office torched

Early on the morning of February 28. 1992, the Great Lakes Unit of the Animal Liberation Front (ALF) struck Michigan State University's experimental fur farm in East Lansing. Minks were in cramped cages, and foxes and otters were seen on the premises, held in equally poor condition. Gas chambers used to kill minks at the poultry research [lab] were damaged.

The office of head researcher Richard Aulerich at Anthony Hall was also raided, and records detailing abuse against experimental subjects were confiscated. Key chains made from the minks' severed paws were found in the office of the mink research department.

This action is in retaliation against the torture and slaughter of native Michigan wildlife by Aulerich and his associates. Minks are born to be wild, not to be research tools in ten-inch cages. Over the past seven years, the minks of Michigan have been held captive and subjected to attempted domestication to provide fur. [See photo below.]

As a pioneer in the field of mink research, Aulerich has helped fur farmers in America exploit and execute millions of animals with regard to neither their ecological importance or their psychological well-being. He has served as the fur farm industry's problem-solver when it comes to tragedies resulting from the intensive confinement of tree-roaming predators.

It is obvious that MSU is being used by this special interest group as a research center that satisfies the monetary greed for people who exploit wildlife for fur. As a recipient of tens of thousands of dollars from the Mink Farmers Research Foundation and the USDA. Aulerich uses the facilities of MSU to further his own career status and the financial well-being of a socially unacceptable industry. (Now as the American fur farm industry declines— 600 farms, USDA figures, 1991 —Aulerich must search for new industries to support his dirty work. His very career depends on it.) But the animals aren't the only victims.

The taxpayers and students are pawns in the game of industry supported institutions and institution-supported industry.

In research papers taken. Aulerich states that wild minks, as predators high on the food-chain, are highly susceptible to environmental toxins. He therefore contends that they are ideal and promising candidates for experimentation. Vet the effects of fungicides and herbicides, such as PCBs, have already been well documented. Aulerich is simply exploiting the public's concern over environmental pollution. In his own words minks suffered from "wasting syndrome," bloody stools, 40 percent loss of body weight, stomach ulcerations, high kit mortality, anorexia, and "hyperexcitability. If these farcical attempts at solving environmental degradation continue, so will ALFs attacks against mink research at MSU.

In regard to the research of human-induced deafness in minks, Aulerich need not create more victims of this unfortunate handicap. Deaf minks produce no data that can be accurately extrapolated to humans. Rather than spend precious research dollars on non-human models, Aulerich should work with deaf humans who can communicate their trauma, and with it, create concrete findings to benefit other deaf individuals. Such clinical work is the only acceptable alternative to animal research.

ALF envisions a human-animal relationship that respects the ecological integrity of fur animals in their native environment. ALF seeks not to place animals on a higher ethical platform than humans but simply to ask fur animal researchers such as Aulerich to return all hostages to their homelands. If ALF is considered terrorist due to our prioritizing of life over profit and property, then we accept that label with pride. But ALF sees terrorism as the forced ingestion of toxic substances into innocent victims, gas chambers operated for vanity, and the continued environmental destruction by chemical companies ready to poison the earth and its inhabitants for money.

If the war on the mink nations continues, so shall ALF's campaign—until the last mink cage is empty, and its prisoners running free. WE HAVE JUST BEGUN TO FIGHT!

For the foxes, otters and minks at MSU's fur animal concentration camp,

[signed] Animal Liberation Front, Great Lakes Unit

USDA ANIMAL DAMAGE CONTROL

1992

October 24, 1992
Millville UT
29 coyotes released, two buildings torched, $600,000 damages

On October 24, 1992 earth warriors broke into the USDA Animal Damage Control's (ADC) research facilities in Northern Utah. Twenty-nine coyotes were released from outdoor pens, and over $150,000 of damage was inflicted on ADC buildings and research equipment. Raiders first cut holes in pens of captive coyotes at the Predator Research Facility in Millville, Utah, a quarter mile from forest lands. The coyotes we released were being subjected to experiments to test traps and poisons to be used against native wildlife by ADC. Students from nearby Utah State University told of seeing coyotes vomiting, bleeding, convulsing and dead in the pens of the US government research station.

ADC Project leader Fredrick F. Knowlton (801-750-2508) has spent the last twenty years killing tens of thousands of coyotes in research to develop more effective control methods of native predators, in particular coyotes and wolves. In turn, his research developments are manufactured by the USDA's ADC program to be used by sheep and cattle ranchers as the arsenal for the war on indigenous wildlife.

For the coyotes that we helped escape, we only hope that we gave them a chance to be who they are, and not what the livestock industry wants them to be. Under the protective shield of the new moon, coyotes warriors moved swiftly in an attempt to defend imprisoned wildlife. Like shooting stars, a dozen coyotes were seen running towards the forest once freed. Other coyotes attempted digging to escape while others lay sick and dying, too weak from ADC poison trials to save themselves.

With a shrill war cry, a band of warriors next descended on the actual Predator Research Facility (PRF). Once inside, we discovered research offices filled with coyote and wolf skulls, piles of traps and snares, and signs for experimental pens that read, "DO NOT FEED." With war clubs swinging, we smashed computer and research equipment used against our animal sisters and brothers. In a cooperative deal with the Utah State University, the PRF operates as the US government's only coyote "Ecological and Behavioral Applications Project." It was then decided that we would start a fire at the lab which destroyed a third of the facility, and caused serious structural damage to the rest of the vivisection laboratory. Our objective was to rescue as many imprisoned coyotes as possible and cause maximum damage to predator research data that threatens the continued existence of the last wild predators of North America.

As the morning sky rose above the flames of the PRF, coyote warriors rode to the Utah State University campus in Logan, where Knowlton's office is located. Just 50 yards from the police station, raiders entered his office and began confiscating valuable predator research files and computer discs. Warriors discovered records detailing the illegal dumping of over two tons of radioactive coyote bodies, losses of radioactive collared goats in field experiments, and tests where coyotes were left in leg-hold traps and snares for more than 18 hours. Documents detailing protocols for force-feeding of toxic poisons, and records of aerial shot-gunning of research coyotes are enough to justify the rescue mission. Acts by ADC researchers such as intentional starvation of coyotes are crimes against nature, and will be dealt with by an animals' tribunal. Coyote warriors hope this attack hinders the ADC program, and if it does not, expect more.

At coyote-killer Knowlton's office we lit another fire. This one in broad daylight to demonstrate our love for the wild nature of the Coyote Nation. Much of Knowlton's ongoing predator research was destroyed in the ensuing blaze in the National Resource Building.

For the last 100 years, the US government has waged war against native American predators on behalf of livestock interests who graze cattle and sheep on wildlands. Wolves, coyotes, cougars, bears, bobcats, foxes, badgers and other wildlife by the hundreds of thousands have fallen victim to the ADC's poisons, traps, snares and aerial gunning campaigns. Much like other agencies of the US government, the ADC has never spared, or shown mercy to the members of Native American tribes of animal people. Millions have been slaughtered, and millions more will be... Unless some bodies do something.

As the US government attempts to criminalize acts of defense of the American wilderness and wildlife, fewer people will hear the truth behind the real terrorist acts of the FBI and ADC. We must escalate our efforts to preserve all that is still wild.

The US government says we used sophisticated radio-controlled explosives. Earth warriors use the power of fire, the purifying cleanser, to return man's evil to the earth. Researchers say animals we release will starve, be hit by cars, or pose threats to humans. Our sisters and brothers have always been a threat, because they are free, that is why ADC kills them in experiments that smashes their bones with traps and guns, not cars. ADC researchers starve coyotes, the earth mother does not. The FBI says we are from a radical, secretive loosely organized Animal Liberation Front. We are not radical, we choose to conserve life, not destroy it. We are not secretive, our voice has been heard since the harmonic balance of nature was first broken by human domination. Yes, we are the animal liberation front, we are also the earth, air and water liberation front. In the US government's eyes we are the spirit of everything wild, yet to be tamed or controlled.

No longer must we let government-controlled media labels divide us. We are one people. We are bound together by a 500 years resistance to ecological and cultural genocide As the Animal Liberation Front, we have existed as one warrior society in the midst of the greater earth struggle. Our beliefs are not the product of twentieth century European philosophers. Our fight is the same fight as the Mohawk, Dine, Blackfoot, Lakota and Apache. We believe in animal rites, not rights. We stand with those fighting for the Black Hills, Mt. Graham, Kalmiopsis, Badger-Two-Medicine, and every other struggle for self-determination. If there is one undeniable common ground, it is the enemy. In Earth First! we see ourselves. In the American Indian Movement we see ourselves. Red, brown, white, fur feathers and fins, we are all sisters and brothers. For a rebirth of the harmonious relationship with all life, let us no longer stand apart, but TOGETHER.

We are only as strong as our weakest link. No more genocide against the peoples of earth. No more divide and conquer. There are only two kinds of people, those who say there are two kinds of people and those who do not. For Peg Millet, Mark Davis, Keith Kioller and Jonathan Paul. For the Grizzly, wolf, coyote and mink. They are all family. They are all imprisoned because they believe in a way of life separate from the US government empire.

DARGATZ MINK RANCH | 1995

October 26, 1995
Chilliwack, BC
2400 mink liberated

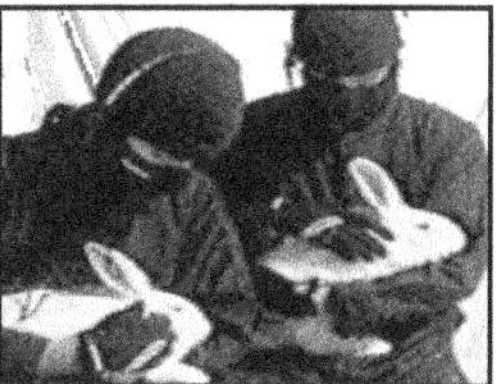

"Man's inhumanity to man is only surpassed by his cruelty to animals."

On the evening of October 26, a cell of the Animal Liberation Front visited Dargatz Mink Ranch (10282 Reeves Rd, Chilliwack, B. C.) and on November 13 we visited Rippin Fur Farm (27413 8th Avenue, Aldergrove, B.C.). To verify the authenticity of this notice, allow us to describe the occasions. Mr. Dargatz has nine and one half mink barns (8 in use) and Mr. Rippin has nine mink barns (all in use). Each barn generally has four rows of cages - two inner and two outer. At Mr. Dargatz's farm, a full barn contains about 64 cages in each outer row and 81 cages per inner row, while at Mr. Rippin's farm a full barn contains 288 cages per outer row and about that many for each inner row. About one cage in ten was already empty. Mr. Dargatz also has goats inside his mink compound.

We were disappointed but not surprised with the one-sided media coverage. As purveyors of the status quo, they say our actions are careless and futile. They broadcast the words of Mr. Rippin and Mr. Engh (Canadian Mink Breeders Association - Chris Engh, 30030 Burgess Mt. Rd. Langley, 8. C.) as though it were plain fact. They say our friends are domesticated. We in the A. L. F. say they are wild animals placed in cages. They say those who don't get hit by cars will just starve or drown. We say that some have and undoubtedly will be hit by cars but in rural Aldergrove or Chilliwack, the odds are that most won't. Similarly, some may starve before adjusting back to the natural world. As for drowning, well that's just a crock - even domesticated terrestrial animals such as dogs and cats can swim. They say we are terrorists and criminals with no respect for property. We aren't out to terrorize anybody, we simply want to save lives and end this terrible trade. While trespassing and minor barn damage my violate B. C. law, their notion of sentient creatures as "property" violates Natural Law. Mrs. Engh, token female of the fur business, says "Next to hunting humans, this is the worst." Regarding what her husband does [fur farmer], we say "Next to bunting humans, this is EQUAL."

It would have been nice if either BCTV or UTV at least showed the tiny cages and their effects on our friends, to say nothing of the other things that Mr. Rippin and Mr. Dargatz do to them there. Instead, they say our friends are cold and hungry, practically trying to find their way back to their cages. What bull! These farmers don't care about the welfare of these animals - they would have been slaughtered and skinned in a matter of weeks. Their sole concern is the damage we have done to their profits. All we did was give our friends a fighting chance to escape from that scheduled slaughter. Mr. Engh even goes so far as to present one of the mink as his pet and say in a soft and gentle voice, "I don't know how these people can be so cruel." These animals are not their pets! The farmers aren't trying to save them from death - the want to deliver that horrifying death personally and receive the blood money. We can think of few things crueler in this world than the confinement of a living, feeling, intelligent and wild animal to one or two cubic feet of life so that they can be murdered and mutilated to further the hedonistic pleasures of some thoughtless man wishing to decorate his woman. There is no logical justification for the slaughter of these animals. Nobody needs a mink coat except those mink.

Releasing our 2,000 friends at Mr. Dargatz's farm and 4,000 friends at Mr. Rippin's farm were two of the most satisfying things that we have ever done. Some of them were rather friendly; others were curious with their new found freedom; some were terrified by our presence, while many just showed signs of dementia caused by their living (loosely defined) conditions - pacing back and forth, tailbiting, cannibalizing, etc. After their jailbreak, many of our friends took off and never looked back, many wandered around exploring the new world, while many simply played a little too loud at Mr. Rippin's ranch as this seems to have woken our kind farmer and his neighbours. We would have freed all 10,000 of our friends had not farmer Fred's arrival necessitated our departure. We regret that many of our friends have been enslaved once again, especially now that they have had a taste of freedom. Why we recognize that our actions will financially damaged Mr. Rippin and Mr. Dargatz, their employees and their families, we have come to realize that this concern is secondary compared to the amount of pain and suffering that they would cause if left alone. They reap profits from that which simply should not be. We hope that someday they will see how truly wrong the things are that they do.

CLARENCE JORDAN FUR FARM | 1995

November 16, 1995
Olympia, WA
300 to 400 mink liberated, aborted attempt to burn down building

Friends, comrades and armchair liberationists,

In the early hours of Thursday, November 16th, 1995 The A.L.F. carried out a raid against Clarence Jordan's mink farm. Three to four hundred minks were released and an attempt at burning down his storerooms, refrigeration unit and killing shed was aborted because he came out.

This action was an attempt to shut down his operation down permanently and we regret that we failed at this mission though many minks got to taste freedom. Clarence has recently secured his cages with extra wire I suspect as a response to earlier attacks in British Columbia.

In continuing struggle we fight for the animals,

A.L.F.

200 minks released from cages at farm

Vandals freed about 200 minks at a farm near Olympia and damaged cages and other equipment, the Thurston County sheriff's office said Thursday.

Damage was estimated at $75,000. The farmer was working Thursday to round up the animals set loose overnight.

The owner asked that his name and the location of his farm not be disclosed.

This was the third episode of vandalism at mink farms in the region in recent weeks. Tuesday, vandals released 5,000 minks at a farm in Langley, B.C. A mink farm in Chilliwack, B.C., was hit last month.

- The Associated Press

ZIMBAL MINKERY | 1996

January 15, 1996
Oostburg, WI
200 mink liberated

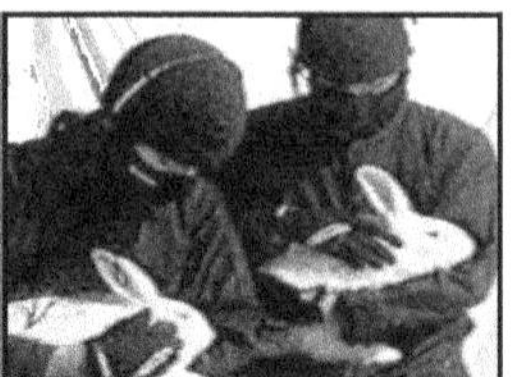

Greetings from the Animal Liberation Front. Late on the night of Monday, Jan. 15, we raided a mink farm in Sheboygan WI. The mink farm was owned by Bob Zimbal, and was located on Washington Rd. 200 mink were liberated. The A.L.F. opened cages and released these wild creatures into their natural habitat. These mink were part of a 20,000 strong breeding herd. They spend their entire lives in tiny cages, breeding offspring for the fur trade. Their offspring are taken from them, raised in intensive confinement, and then gassed. Their lives are destroyed for a mere luxury Item. Now, these mink have a chance at life. Beforehand, death was certain.

More is coming.
For Liberation, A.L.F.

Fur protesters claim 'credit'

All but 2 animals set free in raid on mink farm in county back in their cages

PRESS STAFF, AP

A group of animal rights activists has claimed responsibility for releasing 200 animals at a Sheboygan County mink farm a few days after a demonstration at a fur farmers' convention in Oconomowoc earlier this month.

A group calling itself the Animal Liberation Front took responsibility for the incident when it notified the media Monday via a fax sent by the Coalition to Abolish the Fur Trade.

The coalition stages demonstrations throughout the country and organized a protest Jan. 13 at the convention of the International Mink Association in Oconomowoc.

All but two of the mink were returned to their cages at the Zimbal Mink Ranch in the town of Sheboygan, said Robert Zimbal, who operates the business. About half of the mink refused to come out of their cages. The others were found milling around the fenced-in property.

Zimbal said he assumed the two missing mink were dead because they were domesticated animals and did not know how to survive in the wild.

The Sheboygan County Sheriff's Department investigated the break-in, which was reported Jan. 16. The incident is believed to have happened late on Jan. 15 or early in the morning of Jan. 16.

Deputy Inspector James Hoffmann said his office had turned up no solid leads in the break-in.

"We will review the fax received by the media to determine if there is anything of value in it as part of our continuing investigation," Hoffmann added.

Zimbal did not know why his farm, which has about 16,000 mink, was targeted by the group.

"If you think of any type of farming, you raise the animal for a purpose," Zimbal said Monday. "Like other kinds of farming, like cows or chickens, we give them the best care. The better care we give them, the bigger and better the animal."

Last week's incident was the second time in the past several years that animal activists took responsibility for releasing mink at the Zimbal farm.

In September 1989, about 100 mink were released and signs at the entrance at the ranch had been tampered with to create a

Turn to MINK / A2

BENNETT FUR FARM | 1996

April 4, 1996
Bloomfield, NY
1700 mink liberated

This communique is being sent to various media and animal liberation groups.

In the early hours of Thursday, April 4th, A.LF. activists released 1,700 minks from the Bennett fur farm In Bloomfield, New York. The mink farm is located about 20 minutes southeast of Rochester, off of route 64. ·

A.LF. activists broke into the compound, cut several holes around the fence, and released the minks from their cages. The cages were tiny and coated in excrement and filth.

Mink are genetically wild animals. THEY ARE NOT DOMESTICATED! Moat will adapt and survive after being released into the wild. Spring is arriving, so there won't be a shortage of food. The A.L.F. recognizes that a small percentage may starve before adapting, but most will not. Now they at least have a fighting chance to live, whereas before this raid, they would have certainly been murdered for the bloody fur trade.

Mink also disperse quickly (travelling up to 12 miles a day), so no habitat will suffer as a result of the mink being released.

The Animal Liberation Front Is an illegal International movement dedicated to ending the exploitation of non-human animals. They carry out direct action, usually through economic sabotage, property damage, and live liberations. The A.L.F. operates under the policy that life is more important than "property."

UTAH FUR FARM | 1996

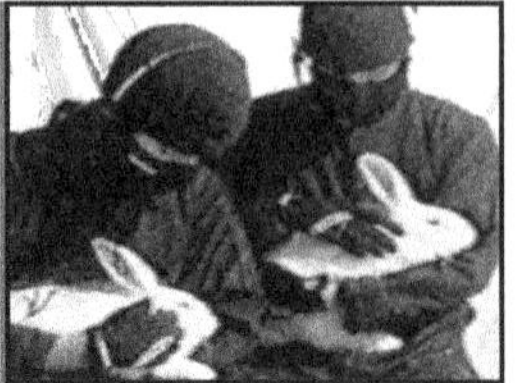

June 21, 1996
Riverton, UT
Hundreds of mink liberated

Early morning hours of 6/21/96 hundreds of mink were released from 12190 South Redwood Rd. in Riverton, UT. Upon earlier entrance to the farm we discovered dead mink in cages (who were there at the time of the raid some days later). Some were swept under the cages lying in the other mink's feces. Some were half eaten by others. Upon this we decided to move fast, before more mink meet the same fate.

More such actions are coming.

Murderers beware.
-A.L.F.

ANOTHER MINK FARM RAID

An underground animal-rights group that broke into a Riverton mink farm Friday and opened 1,000 cages now has a $100,000 bounty on its head. Most of the minks were found inside the farm near 12000 S. Redwood Road, although 12 or 13 still were missing, said Dale Christensen, a Fur Breeders Agricultural Cooperative executive. Christensen said six or seven minks were killed when they were run over by cars or drowned. The Fur Commission U.S.A., a national mink farmers group, has offered a standing $100,000 reward for information that leads to the arrest and conviction of Animal Liberation Front members who conduct raids. ALF has hit mink farms around the country. Alex Slack, member of Coalition to Abolish the Fur Trade in Salt Lake City, said the farm was raided because of what the group sees as poor living conditions at mink farms and cruelty of killing the animals. He said he did not participate in the raid, but he sympathizes with the group. On June 7, ALF members also tried to free 45 minks from the Fur Breeders Agricultural Cooperative in Salt Lake County. Only four minks escaped.

LATZIG MINK RANCH | 1996

July 4, 1996
Howard Lake, MN
Several hundred mink liberated

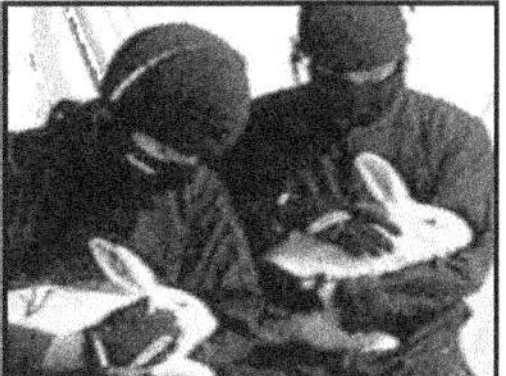

HAPPY INDEPENDENCE DAY!

In the early hours of July 4th, the Animal Liberation Front released several hundred mink from the Latzig Mink Ranch 809 Cty. Rd. 7 SW in Howard Lake, MN.

After being released from their cages, many of the mink escaped through a large gate in the fence which we opened; many others were lifted over the fence to freedom.

The farm is located a short distance from water, in an area resembling the animal's natural habitat.

We recognize that some of the released mink may not survive but for these genetically wild animals they have at the very least been given a fighting chance at life, as opposed to certain death within five months if they had remained In their cages.

We will not allow the suffering and the slaughter of animals in fur farms to continue without resistance, and will continue in direct action against all forms of animal abuse.

-A.L.F.

HOLT MINK RANCH | 1996

July 17, 1996
South Jordan, UT
1000+ mink liberated

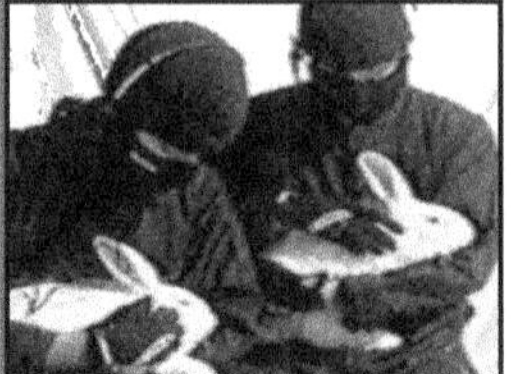

In the early morning of July 17 well over 1000 mink were released from their prisons into the wild where they belong. Holt Mink Ranch at 10291 South 1230 West, South Jordan, UT 84065.

The fur farmers are scared, they are all stepping up security. Mr. Holt had just installed a new fence and used wire to lock each and every cage; but as you can see this proved to be useless.

This new fence was simply cut down and rolled up leaving the animals plenty of room to escape. The locks were cut or ripped open, causing plenty of damage to the cages. What Mr. Holt did not or does not understand la that nothing will stop us.

Original plans were to open every cage, but a cop arriving on the scene forced us to leave. Breeder cards were also destroyed.

Once again, more actions are coming. The time is now for animal liberation.

A.L.F. till next time!

JORNEY MINK RANCH | 1996

August 12, 1996
Alliance, OH
2500 mink liberated

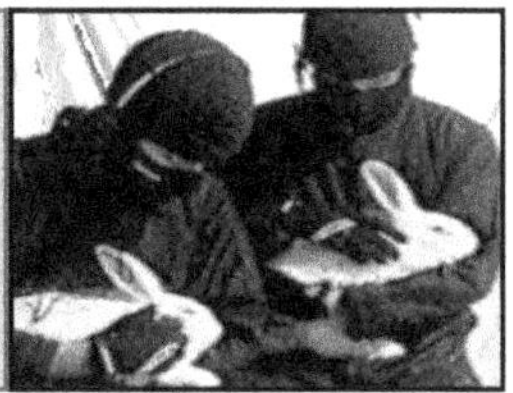

Early morning hours on August 12, 1996 the A.L.F. liberated 2500 mink from Justice Jorney's mink ranch In Alliance Ohio.

As the cages were ripped open we were amazed at how quietly and patiently each mink waited for its tum to be liberated. They felt mud beneath their feet for the first time and splashed playfully through the rain puddles.

As we skulked our way through the corn and saw the ranch for the first time, one work jumped into all of our minds… Auschweitz. The mink were crammed five to a cage with no apparent source of food or water.

We refuse to allow the barbaric imprisonment and murder of innocent creatures for the vanity of selfish humans. As long as there are animals suffering at the hands of humans, there will be the A.LF.

-A.L.F.

HEGER COMPANY | 1996

September 9, 1996
South Saint Paul, MN
Attempted arson

The Animal Liberation Front claims responsibility for the attempted firebombing of Heger Co., a fur farm feed supplier in South St. Paul MN in the early hours of Sept. 9th.

In a city of so much misery (the South St Paul "Livestock Market" tortures and kills hundreds of thousand of cows, pigs, and sheep each year) the action was done not only to protest the atrocities against life, but to directly bring about change, and speed the decline of a dying industry.

We intend to learn from our mistakes and return!

BENNETT FUR FARM | 1996

October 29, 1996
Victor, NY
46 foxes liberated

A.L.F. COMMUNIQUE

"The Animal Liberation Front is claiming responsibility for the following action that occurred in the early morning hours of Oct. 29, 1996 in Victor, NY.

The ALF entered the Bennett Fur Farm by cutting through a series of *3 different fences.* We saw remnants of older fences that had possibly been cut down on previous raids. The fence nearest to the sheds had metal sheets on the top of it so as to make noise if they were being tampered with, but this proved a frivolous security precaution as they were easily by-passed. Once inside the actual fur farm, we came across countless empty sheds, possibly 40 or 50, which each shed could have housed several hundred animals each, but all were empty. This could have been because of previous successful raids on the farm, or we may have been too late as the killing season may have already claimed the lives of our animal friends.

We continued onward hoping to find at least a few sheds with animals still in them. Nearing the front of the farm, we heard animal noises and followed them to a shed. Inside were dozens and dozens of silver foxes. They were making a tremendous amount of noise as we searched the shed. We opened a total of at least 46 cages and destroyed the breeding cards on all of the cages inside that particular shed. Liberation for all of the foxes would have been possible if we had not been interrupted by a security truck that forced us to evacuate.

The foxes seemed reluctant to leave their cages once they were opened, so at times activists would climb inside of the cages and usher them to freedom.

This is the second known raid on this particular fur farm. All in all, forty six foxes were liberated, fencing was cut through and torn down, and ALF slogans were spray painted on various sheds throughout the farm.

We will be back - as long as there are animals trapped inside that concentration camp- we will fight for their release...
Much more to come from ALF!!

JACK BROWER FUR FARM | 1996

December 25, 1996
Bath, MI
150 mink liberated

Our.intent was to throw a special Christmas party for the mink held captive there. Upon arriving, we discovered that we were unexpected guests. To our surprise and delight, there were no surveillance cameras and no guard dogs to greet us or announce our arrival.

We set to work immediately with our handy-dandy tin snips. We cut several openings through both the inner and outer fences surrounding the 6 sheds housing the mink. When we entered the shed area, we found that three of the sheds were empty pelting stock housings. The other three were filled with anxious white mink restless to be free. After the rear door of each shed was removed {so that the mink could run out without having to run past their rescuers), each cage was opened.

Those that didn't climb out immediately (most practically threw themselves out of those tiny wire cages!) were lifted out and released. One ferocious little guy would not let go of the glove of one human helper and had to be carried outside the perimeter hanging from a glove. Once laid on the ground (glove still gripped in his teeth), the mink took a look around and realizing that he was at last free, finally released the mitt and bounded across the snow to a nearby woods and away. We wish him and the others (some 150 mink we estimate) very happy lives.

There was no better Christmas present that we could have received than the sight of all those beautiful creatures playing about, chasing each other, and finally running away. But no party would be complete without "decorations," so we liberally decorated the structures with festive green paint wishing all a Merry Christmas from the ELF! And just think, less than $30 worth of gas, tools, and paint was all we needed to throw our mink party!

NUMEROUS ACTIONS

1996

1995-1996
Southern California
Numerous sabotage & liberation actions claimed in 1995 to 1996

ANIMAL LIBERATION FRONT COMMUNIQUE

Dear SG, - It's been a while since we've corresponded, but we've been busy. We extend our gratitude to all activists fighting for our precious animals. We wholeheartedly support your effort to pay special attention to our fellow warriors who have the misfortune to be incarcerated• we must let them know that they are in our hearts and our thoughts at all times!

Here is a report on actions that occurred between 1995 and 1996 to date.

POPEYE'S (fest-food operation selling chicken) was targeted three times. They were spray painted with slogans expressing our feelings about their meat-peddling business. They were also treated to glued locks.

KENTUCKY FRIED CHICKEN (more scum like the above) was twice the recipient of our redecorating talents; slogans were painted all over their walls and block fencing, and their locks were rendered inoperable in the usual manner.

BURGER KING was beautified with slogans such as MEAT IS MURDER; they were hit twice. Their carnivorous customers were unable to enter the next morning because of non-functioning locks, courtesy of superglue.

Another object of our outrage and artistic endeavors was an Italian restaurant featuring SIX different veal dishes on the menu. Their back walls, side walls, fences, parking lot, and porch were refurbished with slogans such as VEAL IS CHILD ABUSE and SCUM. Front and back locks were also glued. Hit #2.

RED LOBSTER was sloganized and glued - they had to replace several locks as well as clean up their walls, (hopefully having to repaint). Hit #3.

LEATHER STORES (2) were hit, painted with slogans (WEAR YOUR OWN SKIN) and superglued.

McDONALD'S had their doors, walls, parking lot, and menu spray painted with MEAT IS MURDER as well as comments on their practice of supporting deforestation. Locks were glued.

WINNICK'S FURS was painted with FUR IS DEAD and had their front locks glued; the back lock was already glued - someone was there before we were! Hit 13.

WOODLAND HILLS FURRIER, a particularly resistant bunch, were treated to glued locks once again. Hit #10

A BABY PIGLET was liberated from an institution Intending on turning her into sausages. She was placed in a loving home and is doing fine.

A HEN AND A DOG were liberated separately from abusive owners. The hen was half-starved and had a wound on her neck. She was placed in a loving home and Is now the beautiful, happy bird she deserves to be. Her new human companion reports that she loves to be held and petted. Likewise for our canine friend!

TWO RABBITS were rescued from owners who were planning on killing them. They were placed in loving homes where they are now doing fine.

The above took place In Southern California. We are doing what we can when opportunity presents itself. We hope we are making a difference, however small. Whether you write letters, contribute money, or participate in an active A.LF. cell, all of your efforts are needed and appreciated in our battle to liberate our animal friends.

Animal Liberation Front

RANCHO VEAL | 1997

February 19, 1997
Sonoma, CA
Truck at veal slaughterhouse torched

We placed 4 incendiary devices in a double, semi-trailer truck used for live animal transportation: We used a total of 5 liters of flammable liquid, which we placed in the engine, the top of the cab and the connecting wheelbase. We had a direct link to the fuel tank. We confirmed that there was the fire ignited through visual confirmation...

This is just the beginning of a war… our war for your end has begun.

THE OUTDOORSMAN | 1997

February 28, 1997
Indianapolis, IN
Hunting supply store set on fire

In the early morning Friday, February 28, the ALF hit a hunting and trapping store on the far south side of Indianapolis. The Outdoorsman promotes the murder of innocent life through the sale of hunting and trapping equipment and by selling magazines and other literature advocating the torture of animals. Windows were broken, slogans were painted, and the back of the wooden building was burned.

JACK IN THE BOX | 1997

March 6, 1997
Perris, CA
Under-construction Jack In The Box restaurant burned down

Thur. Mar. 6. 1997
Perris. CA. USA

Though Jack in The Box Burgers fast food chain is responsible for the deaths of millions of animals every year, they didn 't gain that much publicity until they killed several humans in recent years and made thousands more severely ill by serving them animal carcasses.

However, on March 6, 1997 Jack was about to have some of his karma come back to him (or at least to his CEO puppet-masters.) Members of the Animal Liberation Front (A.L.F.) entered the construction site and quickly searched it for any living creatures. When the building was found clear, two incendiary devices were placed and set.

In a matter of a couple hours, Jack no longer had a box. The entire building was destroyed! The following day, a contact reported driving by the area and seeing nothing but a black, charred, collapsing frame of what once was going to be a fast food restaurant.

This tactic is so effective we encourage everyone out there to do their homework, be careful, and help rid our planet of this cancer called fast food.

-A.L.F.

DOUGLAS BURGERS | 1997

March 6, 1997
Lake Elsinore, CA
Attempted arson at restaurant

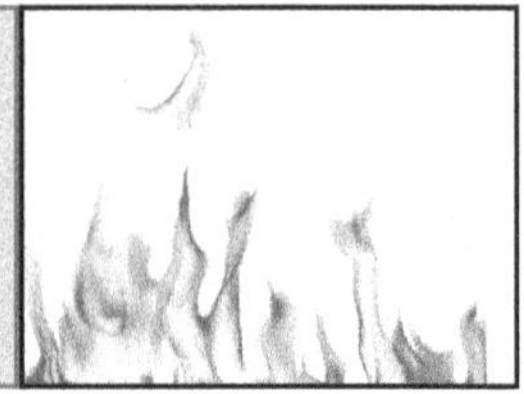

In the wee hour morning of Thursday, March 6, 1997, members of the Animal Liberation Front closed in on their target. Douglas Burgers located in Lake Elsinore, California was nearly finished with construction of their 23rd restaurant.

Despite an extremely heavy police presence in the area with regular patrols around the construction site, the freedom fighters were able to gain access to the grounds. After snipping through the construction company's security fence, operatives gained access to the building and quickly searched both levels for any human and non-human animals who may have been sleeping inside the building. When the building was found completely vacant, operatives quickly set to work assembling two incendiary devices and splashing the building with kerosene.

Then, after hiding inside the building for about another twenty minutes until patrol cars left the area, the incendiary devices were lit and the ALF'ers made their quick but stealthy exit. Unfortunately, the devices never ignited. (Operatives who placed them believe that the base of the incense sticks used were too moist from the kerosene to ignite - only the sponges should be covered in fuel!) Though this building still stands, this action demonstrated to all animal killers that no amount of security will make them immune to the A.L.F.

MORE TO COME!

FUR BREEDERS CO-OP

1997

March 11, 1997
Sandy, UT
Country's largest mink feed supplier bombed

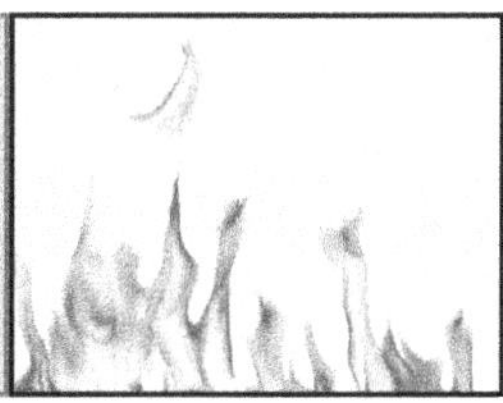

In the early morning hours of March 11, we attacked the Agricultural Fur Breeders Co-Op in Sandy, Utah... firebombs were set in four trucks and the main offices. More attacks will be forthcoming unless the demands of political prisoner Jeff Watkins are met.

Six bombs did an estimated $750,000 damage to this Salt Lake County mink-feed plant. No one was hurt.

Pipe Bombs Chew Up Mink-Feed Plant

BY VINCE HORIUCHI
THE SALT LAKE TRIBUNE

Six pipe bombs exploded at a Salt Lake County mink-feed plant Tuesday, causing $750,000 damage to a building and five trucks. Violent animal-rights activists claim they are behind the bombings.

"They're claiming responsibility, but we have no idea at this point," said Salt Lake County Fire Capt. Frank Dalton.

A bomb ripped through the second story of the main building at Fur Breeders Agricultural Cooperative at 8400 S. 700 West and ignited a fire that spread through most of the floor, Dalton said. The powerful blast shot metal shrapnel onto a parking lot.

No one was inside the building at the time of the blast.

Ben Flitton, a truck driver for Fur Breeders, was asleep with his wife and 2-year-old son in a building on the site when the first explosion knocked him awake about 1:45 a.m.

"If it was enough to shake a building, buddy, it's big," he said.

Flaviano Garcia, a plant mechanic who lives in a trailer at the site, said he heard five blasts in about a 10-minute span.

"They were good-sized explosions," he said.

Five of the bombs were planted underneath trucks used by the company to transport mink feed to Utah and southern Idaho farms.

The explosions ruptured the metal fuel tanks on the trucks that did not catch on fire. About 150 gallons of diesel fuel, battery acid and other fluids spewed from the trucks onto the plant parking lot but did not start a fire outside.

"It caused a major pollution problem," Dalton said.

About 60 firefighters from Salt Lake County, Sandy, Midvale, West Jordan and Murray fought the fire and had it contained in 20 minutes.

Authorities spent much of Tuesday searching for other explosive devices in the building with two bomb-sniffing dogs from the Salt Lake City International Airport. No other bombs were found.

By Tuesday night officials had reopened 700 West, which was cordoned off for most of the day.

The blaze in the plant destroyed the administration offices containing computers and financial records, said Dale Christensen, chief financial officer for Fur Breeders, the second largest U.S. provider of mink feed.

"The FBI has labeled them terrorists, and that's exactly what they are," Christensen said of the radical animal-rights activists.

J.P. Goodwin, the national director of the Dallas-based Coalition to Abolish the Fur Trade, claimed Tuesday that he got a phone call from someone taking responsibility for the bombings. While Goodwin and his organization do not claim to know who did the bombings, he agrees with the act.

"If it hurts them [fur breeders] in the pocketbook, it's OK by me," he said.

One violent animal-rights group, the Animal Liberation Front (ALF), has claimed responsibility for a number of firebombings and incidents of vandalism in Utah in the past several years.

By 1995, there were more than 40 incidents in Salt Lake County at meat plants, mink farms, and even ice-cream parlors.

ALF also claimed it released mink from more than 1,000 cages at mink farms in Salt Lake County, including one at Fur Breeders last June.

EBERT'S FUR FARM | 1997

March 15, 1997
Blenheim, Ontario
1542 mink liberated

Greetings from the Great Lakes Earth Liberation Front. Furriers beware the ides of March! Like the evil Roman empire before you, your kingdom of cash and cruelty will fall by the weight of its own iniquity (or with a little help from our friends). On March 15, our band of eco-anarchists paid a visit to the Eberts fur farm in Blenheim, Ontario on Mink Lane Rd. We were amazed at the openness of the operation. The sheds were practically next to the main road, with no attempts being made to hide the farm from the public. This made our work somewhat more difficult, as traffic constantly passed us while we were on site. There were some 12 sheds, though at least a few were empty. We cut several holes in the perimeter fence, but also opened the driveway gate leaving plenty of exit routes for our friends to choose from. We entered the first shed and had some trouble opening the cages. Once we figured out the latches, we started opening the cages and collecting the breeding cards. When possible, we damaged the cages. The mink were ready to party, rushing past us to the nearby safety of wooded farmland. We also knew that Rondeau Provincial Park was not far away, offering plenty of suitable habitat for our sleek brown buddies.

One of our group left a spray paint autograph on the feed shed, just to let them know that we care. When we had released about 240 of our captive comrades, a truck pulled up to the front gate that we had already pried open.

Saddened to leave without finishing our intended business, we managed to escape detection by hopping the back fence and meeting our driver up the road. Though it is maddening to have been so close to freeing so many, we are somewhat comforted by Mother Jones' words: 'Mourn the dead and work like hell for the living!"

UC DAVIS | 1997

March 18, 1997
Davis, CA
Attempted arson at under-construction animal research lab

We took this opportunity to end primate research and to cause as much financial loss as possible to the biggest enemy to animals on the West Coast. We will not allow UC Davis to imprison, torture and murder millions of animals, year after year.

Let this fire light the way for others to follow. Let them know that this evil towards the earth and animals will not be tolerated and that fighting for their liberation is more important than a respect for laws that protect slavery and exploitation.

We did this on the 10th anniversary of the fire set by the ALF in April, 1987, which destroyed the Veterinary Diagnostic Laboratory at UC Davis - the first successful act of fire sabotage by the ALF in the U.S., causing $4.5 million in damages.

We also dedicate this action to all animal liberation and earth liberation activists currently in jail, and on hunger strike for the millions of animals killed every year in the U.S. using the leghold trap.

Be patient. Our war for “their” end has only just begun.

ACME POULTRY | 1997

March 23, 1997
Seattle, WA
Chicken slaughterhouse broken into, offices trashed, three chickens rescued

The Animal Liberation Front (A.L.F.) takes responsibility for the early morning raid of the Acme chicken slaughterhouse (1024 S King St. in Seattle WA) in the early hours of 3/23/97.

Every year in this country 6 billion chickens are tortured and slaughtered for our own selfish consumption. These innocent beings never bask in the sun or spend one moment free from pain. This selfishness will no longer be tolerated.

We entered the massive killing rooms, sabotaging forklifts and other machinery. We also entered two offices in which we destroyed all paperwork by pouring acid and paint over them. We also found 3 chickens left for dead on the killing room floor. We loaded them up and liberated them from a life of certain death.

The video shows 2 of the 3 chickens resting peacefully in our arms. They have been placed in loving homes where they will be able to live out their lives free from torture.

Something all animals (human and non-human) deserve.

Until all are free ...

A.L.F. - Puget Sound Unit

LIBERATION NOW!!!!!!

ARRITOLA MINK RANCH | 1997

May 30, 1997
Mount Angel, OR
10,000 mink liberated. Excerpts from original handwritten communique.

We are simply humans who have followed a call to action with more love than fear. The animals enslaved in exploitative industries today are waiting for you...

The intense joy of seeing a living creature taste freedom for the first time is truly indescribable. Animals locked in cages don't have a voice so you may not hear their cries every day. They still feel pain...

This action took place not as an act of 'eco terrorism' but an act of love...

Not one of the mink imprisoned would ever have been allowed to walk more than one foot in any direction, living their short lives with an unpardonable death sentence...

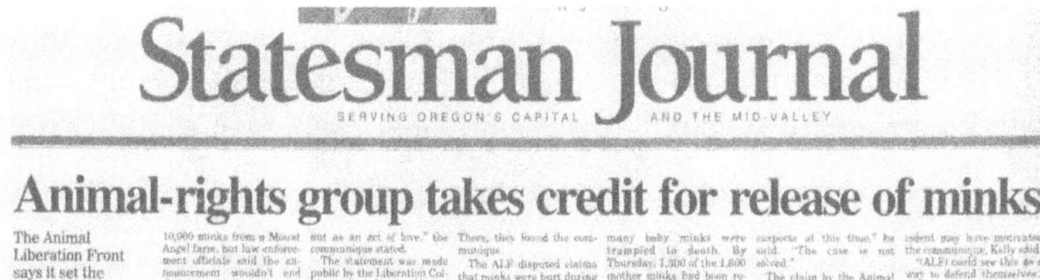

Statesman Journal

SERVING OREGON'S CAPITAL AND THE MID-VALLEY

Animal-rights group takes credit for release of minks

The Animal Liberation Front says it set the animals free as an act of love.

BY SUZANNE MARTA
The Statesman Journal

PORTLAND — An animal-rights group claimed responsibility Thursday for the recent release of about 10,000 minks from a Mount Angel farm, but law enforcement officials said the announcement wouldn't end their investigation.

The Animal Liberation Front, a group that promotes freeing animals used for commerce, released a communique that both claimed responsibility for and defended the act.

"This action took place not as an act of 'eco-terrorism' but as an act of love," the communique stated.

The statement was made public by the Liberation Collective, a Portland-based human- and animal-rights organization.

Liberation Collective member Craig Rosebraugh said his roommate received a telephone call from a person using a disguised voice Thursday morning telling him to look on the porch. There, they found the communique.

The ALF disputed claims that minks were hurt during the incident.

"Contrary to the lies of the popular media, no animals are harmed in any act of liberation," the communique said.

Law enforcement officials who were at Rick Arritola's fur farm Saturday said many baby minks were trampled to death. By Thursday, 1,300 of the 1,600 mother minks had been recovered.

Claiming responsibility for acts like the one in Mount Angel is not uncommon for groups seeking media or political attention, Marion County Sgt. Doug Garrett said.

"We don't have any solid suspects at this time," he said. "The case is not solved."

The claim by the Animal Liberation Front came as no surprise to Fur Commission USA spokeswoman Marsha Kelly.

"There was never any doubt in my mind," she said. "The incident has their signature."

Public outcry about the incident may have motivated the communique, Kelly said.

"(ALF) could see this as a way to defend themselves," she said.

Those responsible for the attack on Arritola's farm could be prosecuted under the federal law for terrorist acts against animal enterprise. The crime is punishable by a fee based on the damage, and/or one year in prison.

CAVEL WEST | 1997

July 21, 1997
Redmond, OR
Horse slaughterhouse torched, closed forever

Greetings,

On Monday, July 21, 1997, under nearly a full moon, the Animal Liberation Front paid a visit to the Cavel West Horse Murdering Plant at 1607 SE Railroad Avenue in Redmond, Oregon. About 35 gallons of vegan jello was brought in with the team. Next, a number of large holes were drilled into the rear wall of the slaughterhouse office to bypass potential alarms on the doors or windows. Next, the area that housed the refrigeration units was located and again large holes were drilled through the wall at that part of the slaughterhouse. Two teams then poured the jello into the numerous holes and quickly began to assemble the three electrically-timed incendiary devices that would bring to a screeching halt what countless protests and letter writing campaigns could never stop. While these devices were being assembled some members of the team entered a storage shed/office/ construction site (all part of Cavel West's operations) and left the remaining 10 gallons or so of jello for dessert. Then two gallons of muriatic acid was poured into the air conditioning vents to taint and destroy any horse flesh that may have survived the fire. Finally, the incendiary devices were set to ignite at exactly the same time. Unfortunately, as the battery was being connected to the device at the refrigeration unit, a spark started that entire area on fire! Fortunately, we had very thorough back-up plans in case anything went wrong and this insured that our departure went quick and smooth. At least $1,000,000 of damage has been done and the entire plant is currently closed and out of operation! The media blackout of this action is intense and thorough but you know what?... The horses don't mind.

ANIMAL LIBERATION FRONT
Equine & Zebra Liberation Network

WILDLIFE PHARMACEUTICALS | 1997

August 19, 1997
Fort Collins, CO
Attempted arson at fur farm supplier

The premises of Wildlife Pharmaceuticals Suite 600, 1401 Duff Dr., Fort Collins, CO 80524 (970) 484-6267 was raided. After holes were drilled an incendiary attack was made. Unfortunately only minimum damage was sustained.

Wildlife Pharmaceuticals is the solitary manufacturer of Prime-X melatonin implants for the fur farm Industry in North America. The implants are used by mink and fox farmers to unnaturally speed up the fur growth process allowing the animals to be killed 4-6 weeks earlier.

Pounding the final nails into the fur industry,

Animal Liberation Front.

IDE FUR FARM | 1997

September 1, 1997
Downer's Grove, IL
3500 mink liberated

We opened cages and freed at least 3,500 mink. Hundreds of breeding cards were tom up or smashed. Theses innocent creatures now have a chance at freedom, where otherwise they would have faced a life of confinement and death in this fur farm concentration camp.

BEWARE to all animal murderers! THE ALF IS WATCHING YOU!!!

During the Labor Day weekend, vandals released 4,000 minks from the Charlie Ide Fur Farm near Downers Grove. All

ADAM'S FOX FARM | 1997

September 20, 1997
Anderson, IN
200+ foxes liberated

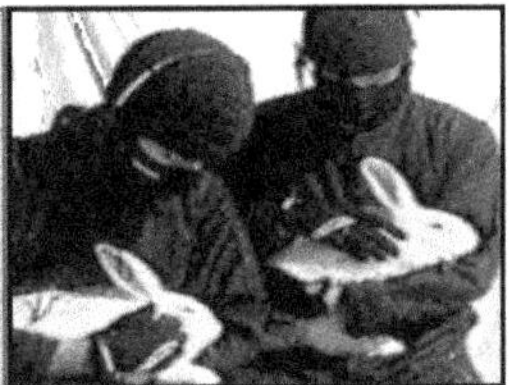

On the early morning of Saturday, September 20, the Animal Liberation Front raided Adam's Fox Farm in Anderson, Indiana.

Upon reaching the house of the fur farmer, the liberators snuck around the property hiking through a field. While the liberators were still some distance from the cages, the fox could be heard barking. Upon this occurrence, the AL F. knew they had come to the right place. Next it was necessary to cut one of three fences in between the clearing and the actual cages.

After cutting the first barbed wire fence, and trekking through the thick woods for some time, another barbed wire fence faced the liberators. Luckily, the barbed wire fences created little difficulty to the operation as they were easily cut in various places with large wire cutters and peeled back.

Soon after hiking another distance through the woods another sort of chicken wire fence was discovered and cut in two large swaths, so as to let the fox escape. Upon reaching the cages, another fence, about two to three feet tall was encountered which was stomped to the ground almost in its entirety to allow the fox to easily transcend it to freedom.

The first cages we came upon were empty, but they were the only ones. After coming to the edge of that row, about eight more full rows of twenty cages each were found. Each cage had one or two fox imprisoned within. The cages were about fix feet long mesh wire with wooden boxes on the end with metal tops on them that merely had to be pulled off or pushed up to allow the fox to jump out. The fox never made a sound once we began opening cages. They were all quite timid and most would look at the liberator for a second before turning its back until we were safely out of their sight. As we opened the cages very few were jumping out immediately, but as they are quite timid creatures, they began to jump out as we were leaving.

Each of the eight rows had about twenty fox, and some cages had two fox in them. Every cage was opened except for one row in which the cages appeared to be bolted shut; therefore, about 200 foxes were liberated that night.

Also, as the cages were being opened, another escape route was found from the area where the cages were kept. A large gate that led to a field and freedom was opened, and some of the fox were seen to have found it before the liberators left.

Animal Liberation Front

FRYE MINK FARM | 1997

October 5, 1997
Crystal Lake, IL
5000 mink liberated

The farm has approximately 40 sheds. Surrounding the concentration camp was a chicken wire fence 4 feet high. Attached to the top of the fence were strips of sheet metal suspected to deter mink from climbing over or to make noise if any unwanted guests attempted to climb over. Above the fence was one electrical wire. For unknown reasons there was no electrical current running through it.

We were prevented from rolling the fence up because it was buried in the ground at the bottom. Instead we cut holes 2 feet high and 15 feet or more across in 3 sections. The chicken wire was folded down along the ground so as to allow the mink to run away.

We cleared 8 regular stock breeding sheds each containing 400 cages with measurements 18" x 12," x 6" (l x h x w). The wooden nesting boxes were lifted from each cage. The mink would climb out if not already in the boxes when lifted out. 5 sheds with breeding stock mink were cleared along with the breeding stock of 3 sheds filled half with regular stock and half with breeding stock. Each full shed contained 200 cages each measuring 18" x 12" x 12" (l x h x w). Some cages contained two mink in each. The nesting boxes were unattached from the front leaving an exposed opening for the animals to jump out of.

The breeding cards in each cleared shed were torn from the beams above the cages and thrown mixed together in the excrement below the cages.

Cables to a tractor were cut, the electrical system's wires slashed, and the water pumping system sabotaged.

An estimated 5,000 mink were liberated.

Stores will be attacked and farms raided until the whole industry is destroyed and all animals are free. Millions of animals are slaughtered each year at the hands of the fur industry and by their support from callous and selfish humans. This is the season of blood.

Fur farmers and animal murderers beware! THE ANIMAL LIBERATION FRONT VISITS YOU NEXT!

The Frye Fur Farm near Crystal Lake lost about 400 minks Oct. 5 after vandals cut exterior fences and released about 5,000 prized animals from their cages.

The saboteurs also took the animals' pedigree and breeding records, devaluing by thousands of dollars the worth of the animals that were eventually found, said Steve Frye, who runs the farm with his father, Larry Frye.

PALMER MINK FARM | 1997

October 6, 1997
Preston, ID
5000 mink & unknown number of foxes liberated

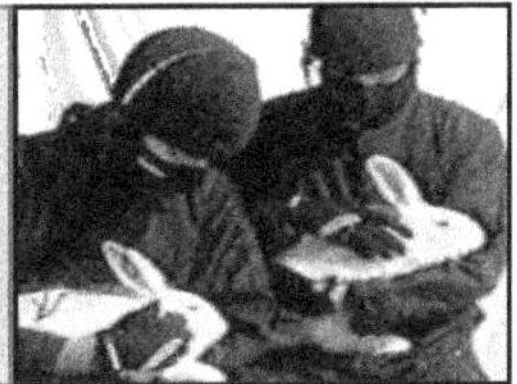

The mink quickly climbed out of their prison cells, jumped to the earth, and excitedly ran through the fields, enjoying their first taste of freedom, ever. The foxes, being much more shy and cautious (and a bit neurotic after spending their entire existence in small, filthy cages) did not exit their cages as anxiously as the mink. Nevertheless, we did witness a handful of foxes leave their cages and one sprint away from the farm, never slowing down or looking back! A water pipe in one of the sheds was also broken.

-A.L.F.

LAIR FOX FARM | 1997

November 5, 1997
Fort Wayne, IN
125 foxes liberated

In the early morning hours of Wednesday, November 5th, the Animal Liberation Front raided the Lair Fox Farm on Shoaff Rd. (owner Blaine Leffers).

As we approached the farm we noticed a bright flashing light and heard loud music blasting from a radio. This was an obviously weak attempt to deter liberators from breaking in and setting the prisoners free.

The cover of the loud noise from the radio allowed us to cut two 8 foot long and 3 foot high holes in the surrounding fence. Once inside, we opened the cages. A total of 125 foxes were liberated. "Free the Enslaved-ALF" was painted on a wall. All of this was accomplished in full view of a security camera on a nearby barn. As we left, we saw many of these bluish-silver foxes run to freedom.

BLM HORSE CORRAL | 1997

November 29, 1997
Burns, OR
600 wild horses liberated, corral set on fire

The Bureau of Land Management (BLM) claims they are removing non-native species from public lands (aren't white Europeans also non-native) but then they turn around and subsidize the cattle industry and place thousands of non-native domestic cattle on these same lands.

[This action was taken] to help halt the BLM's illegal and immoral business of rounding up wild horses from public lands and funneling them to slaughter.

This hypocrisy and genocide against the horse nation will not go unchallenged! The practice of rounding up and auctioning wild horses must be stopped. The practice of grazing cattle on public lands must be stopped. The time to take action is now. From an investigation like the Associated Press' to writing the BLM to an action like ours, you can help stop the slaughter and save our Mother Earth.

Animal Liberation Front
Earth Liberation Front

FLORIDA VEAL SLAUGHTERHOUSES | 1998

October 1997 & May 4, 1998
Wimauma, FL & Lauderhill, FL
Two veal slaughterhouses torched

The A.L.F. claims responsibility for the May 4 arson attack at Florida Veal Processors Inc (6712 State Rd. 674), a slaughterhouse in Wimauma, FL.

The action was done on behalf of the hundreds of thousands of calves every year in the American veal industry who are kept in isolation, denied freedom of movement and fed a deliberately unhealthy diet for the entirety of their short lives until they are slaughtered at a hell like Florida Veal Processors.

The ALF. also claims responsibility for the October 97 arson at Palm Coast Veal Corp. (3698 NW 16th St) in Lauderhill, FL.

USDA WILDLIFE SERVICES

1998

June 1998
Olympia, WA
Building torched, $1.5 million in lost research & $400,000 in damages

This year for summer solstice the A.L.F. and E.L.F. decided to honor the wildlife of the great Pacific Northwest and the forests they call home by having a bonfire (or two) at facilities which make it a daily routine to kill and destroy wildlife.

The arrogant humans who make money by killing and destroying nature would have the public believe that beaver, deer, and other wildlife are responsible for the decimation of our public forests - not clearcutting!

That cougars just trying to survive their genocide-not human expansion and habitat decimation-are the problems!

So one tax-payer-supported government facility researches more efficient and economical ways to destroy our wildlife while a second tax-payer-supported agency puts that research into practice. In addition, a third tax-payer-funded organization-the state Department of Natural Resources-conducts insect control experiments and genetic research.

This action was done in solidarity with Josh Ellerman and in recognition of his courage and commitment to the animals.

-The Real Wildlife Services

UNITED VACCINES | 1998

July 3, 1998
Middleton, WI
310 mink released from research farm at fur industry supplier

Approximately 7 PM, in the evening of July 3 1998 the Animal Liberation Front and the Earth Liberation Front carried out a daylight raid on the United Vaccines experimental research fur farm in Middleton, Wisconsin, near Madison.

Two large holes were cut in the perimeter fence of the compound and one large section of fence was completely torn down. Inside were 3 sheds, one was empty, one containing caged mink and one containing animals resembling possibly the Black-footed ferret of [sic] a variety of pole-cat. Neat the sheds were two double rows of cages covered by liftable roof segments. All cages containing animals were opened, some requiring cage doors to be bent to allow for escape. All prisoners were seen climbing out of their cages. 310 animals liberated. Each cage in the fenced in area was numbered and each mink had small black tags on both ears. Light bulbs smashed out in all sheds and a weighing scale smashed.

"INDEPENDENCE DAY FOR FUR FARM PRISONERS" spray-painted on a storage barn. 3 windows smashed alarm to go off and force liberators to evacuate before causing more damage.

This facility also contained a fenced in area with empty fox cages. This room we suspect is where laboratory tests are conducted on the animals.

The experiments conducted at the United Vaccines laboratories and research farms are solely to decrease "profit-losses" incurred by premature deaths on fur farms. The cause of these deaths can be attributed to the widespread [sic] on the farms due to close confinement, malnourishment, poor sanitation and the psychological stress of captivity. The blatant disregard for the mink and fox nations' well-being is apparent in this industry, which cares only about fur quality and maximum "production" and death.

The Fur farming industry plays a crucial role in the devastation of delicate ecosystems. Fur farm waste run-offs contaminate local bodies of water, poisoning fish supplies and suffocating aquatic plants. Disruption of this balance adversely affects all plant and animal nations and their interdependent relationships with the ecosystem.

This action commemorates the worldwide struggle for independence from occupation and is dedicated to Josh Ellerman for his dedication to defend Mother Earth and her animal nations.

Returning the prisoners back home, the Fur War continues.

-ALF and ELF

ALF activist cuts perimeter fence at United Vaccines

MARMOTECH | 1998

July 4, 1998
Dryden, NY
150 woodchucks liberated, labs damaged

For the past 20 years, Cornell researcher Bud Tennant has been subjecting woodchucks to procedures we would not allow to be performed on our worst enemies during times of war. Tennant owns a facility called Marmotech, Inc. (181 Midline Rd.), where he breeds woodchucks and infects them with various diseases. He then tests the effects of various chemicals on the infected animals, which usually results in a gruesome outcome. Tennant's experiments range from the horrendously cruel to the outright bizarre. A recent project involved developing an "electroejaculation device' to force woodchucks to release semen for breeding purposes.

During the early hours of Independence Day, 1998, activists from the Animal Liberation Front entered the Marmotech facility and opened approximately 50 cages containing an average of three woodchucks each, and left the door ajar to permit the animals' escape. When the A.L.F. departed, most of the woodchucks were moving toward the door.

Three who happened to be in carriers were brought outside directly and released. According to data cards on the cages, these animals were all disease free. Unfortunately, the ALF. had to leave behind several hundred more who had been infected with woodchuck hepatitis virus and other diseases. The A.L.F. took and destroyed the data cards on these cages as an act of sabotage against this callous treatment of fellow creatures. All log books and other information were also confiscated and disposed of and vials of infectious serum were removed from a refrigerator to spoil.

The liberation was timed to coincide with the time of year in which young woodchucks leave their family unit and begin fending for themselves.

Since some of the woodchucks at this facility were wild caught, it is assumed that they will readily return to life in the wild. Those who have always lived in cages may have a harder time of it. but surely it will be better than being killed by "intravenous injection of excess pentobarbital," as would be their fate otherwise. Since the facility was in an area surrounded by fields and woodlands, the now free woodchucks should be able to find plenty of vegetation to feed on.

How someone can make a living off the intense suffering of others is something we will never understand. The sickest part of the situation is that our government actually pays Tennant and his mad scientist friends to conduct these atrocities. However, Tennant is merely confirming information which has already been gathered from human population studies and clinical evidence. Furthermore, safe and effective vaccines are already available for hepatitis. Tennant is merely satisfying his own curiosity about every minute detail of a specific type of hepatitis found only in woodchucks. Until this tyrannical and obscene use of our tax dollars stops, the Animal Liberation Front will be there to correct such injustices.

We will never forget looking into the eyes of creatures doomed to a horrible death and not being able to save them. More actions will be forthcoming.

Animal Liberation Front

Activists release 150 of lab's woodchucks

By FRANKLIN CRAWFORD
Journal Staff

DRYDEN — Members of an animal rights group called the North American Animal Liberation Front claimed responsibility for breaking in Marmotech Inc. on Midline Road in Dryden early Saturday morning and releasing 150 woodchucks and destroying research data.

"Activists from ALF opened approximately 50 cages contain-

'This is not civil disobedience. This is criminal behavior.'

— **Bud Tennant, a Cornell University researcher who owns Marmotech Inc.**

WESTERN OREGON RABBIT GROUP | 1998

July 21, 1998
Philomath, OR
3 rabbits liberated

The ALF takes responsibility for the freeing of three female breeding rabbits from the Western Oregon Rabbit Group. The rabbits are now safe in a good home. This is in no way a victory for those still imprisoned- We will keep fighting. ALF

HIDDEN VALLEY FUR FARM | 1998

August 20, 1998
Guttenburg, IA
330 foxes liberated

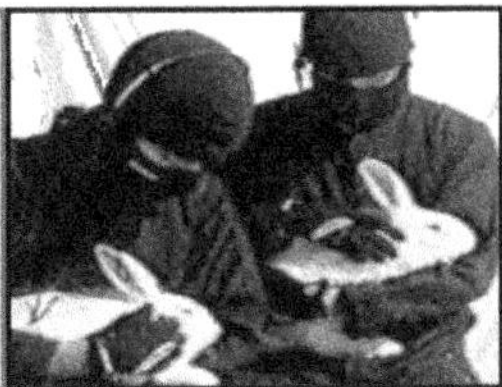

In the early morning hours of Thursday, August 20, 1998, ecoanimal warriors raided Steve Hansel's Hidden Valley Fur Farm in Guttenburg, Iowa.

After following a sign indicating the location of the fur farm, liberators traveled miles of gravel road to reach this fox concentration camp. The fox could be heard screaming and barking from hundreds of yards away, which made the task of finding the prisoners less difficult.

Upon entry to the compound, operatives were surprised to find no fences enclosing the area. On the grounds, two large sheds stood. Each of these were capable of containing six rows of fox cages.

Further inspection revealed one empty shed and one shed with two rows of cages. This second shed imprisoned about thirty fox. The area behind these sheds appeared to have once been used for more sheds. Old wooden frames littered the ground in this area. Reportedly this farm also contained members of the mink and ferret nations; however, none of these were found. We suspect Hansel's stock has decreased in recent years.

Near the sheds six long rows of individual breeders cages stood. Most of these cages contained two fox each. The cages measured about six feet long by two and a half feet wide. The rear of each cage was separated into a nesting box. The nesting box doors were concealed under a layer of sheet metal that could simply be lifted up. Each of the nesting box doors underneath were secured with unlocked clips.

Although these could be opened, another exit was necessary for the prisoners' escape because in most cages the nesting areas were closed off to the animals inside. Therefore, operatives opened cage doors located on the top. The doors on the top required liberators to pull back a metal latch and lift up the hinged wire mesh door.

All thirty cages containing fox in the shed were opened and some of the imprisoned fox were lifted out to freedom. Approximately 150 breeder's cages, all that were found, were opened. Some of the fox were seen running around the compound. An estimated 330 members of the fox nation were liberated in all. This concentration camp imprisoned many kinds of fox. Coat colors varied from white to red to dark brown and black.

In addition to the release of prisoners, two feed machines, one in the shed and one in a nearby barn, were sabotaged and had wires cut. In a large building near the barn, operatives peered through windows to discover large amounts of tools and processing equipment.

This was all done in view of the farmer's house.

Gaia's blood has been spilled for far too long. We took it upon ourselves to reclaim justice for our Earth Mother and all of her children. The time has come for the two-footed animals to reestablish their link with the four-footed animal nations and the earth of which we are all a part.

This action was done in solidarity with the warriors of the Chatham 3. We will not forget our comrades. Our brothers' and sisters' forced inactivity will not abate the ALF's resistance against the capitalist death machine.

Smashing the fur industry piece by piece,

Animal Liberation Front

Fur farms ransacked, foxes freed

ISEBRANDS MINK RANCH | 1998

August 21, 1998
Jewell, IA
1500 to 3000 mink liberated

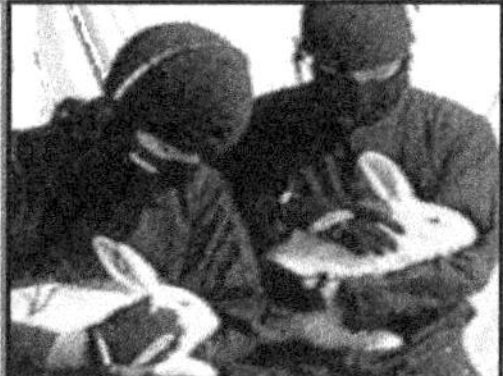

On the morning or Aug. 21, 1998, the Animal Liberation Front struck the lsebrands Mink Ranch at 3221 Queens Ave. in Jewell, Iowa. 1500 to 3,000 mink were set free.

Let this raid be a call to action. It is time for all those who oppose needless suffering to start the attack.

This is the third fur farm raid in the Midwest this week, let's make this only the beginning.

By brick, boltcutters, or fire, this is the dawn of liberation.

On Midwestern fur farms, security is almost always non-existent. A fur farm raid is a simple, low risk operation. The only things separating life from death of the mink in these dens of suffering are a latch on a cage and your own fear.

Now is the time for activists who are unwilling to risk their freedom for the animals to question their own dedication and conviction. Many will wear an A.L.F. t-shirt, but will not jeopardize their middle class lifestyle to end the suffering of others.

Compassion and reverence for life needs to be extended beyond the human, beyond the puppy, to include the confined poultry chicken, the victimized dairy cow and the fur-bearing slaves.

ANIMAL ABUSERS PREPARE FOR JUSTICE

A.L.F. - We strike again

ZUMBRO RIVER MINK | 1998

August 28, 1998
Rochester, MN
3000 mink liberated

In the early morning hours of August 28, 1998 the Midwestern Wildlife Unit of the Animal Liberation Front raided the Zumbro River Mink Concentration Camp.

Breeding Information for over ten thousand mink was torn from above cages and trashed on the ground. An estimated 3,000 mink nation prisoners were released from cages.

A portion of fence was rolled over away from the road to decrease the risk of released animals crossing the road. Surrounding the compound on both sides were houses. The sheds were clearly visible from the road. This prevented liberators from freeing more prisoners. The total number of captives in the camp ls an estimated 15,000 in seven sheds.

The placement of this concentration camp is highly beneficial to the release of wildlife such as the mink. Nearby the camp Is large forest area and across the street Is the Zumbro River which runs far north of town. These mink will now have a chance to establish themselves in the local ecosystem and regain the natural instincts which the confinement of fur farm imprisonment had all but destroyed.

Operation Bite Back will be continued through the efforts of the Animal Liberation Front, Earth Liberation Front and the Wild Minks. Nothing will deter us Guardians of Mother Earth. The animal nations will be set free to live again as one with the forest.

Animal Liberation Front,
Midwestern Wildlife Unit

BROADVIEW EGG FARM | 1998

September 19, 1998
Burlington, WA
11 chickens liberated

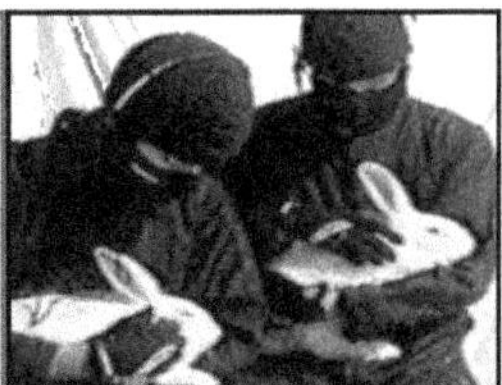

In the early morning hours of Sept 19th, 1998 the Animal Liberation Front liberated 11 chickens from the Broadview Egg Farms in Burlington, WA.

We entered the premises by cutting away a perimeter fence. We then made our way to one of the four massive barns. We used a crowbar and mallet to dismantle the locks and entered the barn.

There we found 11" x 17" cages holding untold 1000's of chickens, 4 to 5 to a cage. We immediately filled 11 birds into our carriers, where they sat anxiously awaiting their departure. We quickly documented a hellish concentration camp for egg laying chickens. These living, feeling creatures are kept in horrifying, intense confinement in small wire cages. Video footage was taken of the nightmarish condition the imprisoned chickens are forced to endure for their entire lives. We left various messages; "freed by ALF," "torture will end," "murder," & "ALF."

As we left our hearts sank knowing the countless numbers we left behind. We then placed the 11 birds into loving and safe homes to enjoy the freedom they have never known.

The meat, dairy, & egg industries are responsible for suffering and murder on an epic scale. Veganism is the answer to end this holocaust. Unfortunately, education of the public is a slow process, and the animals confined for our greed do not have time.

The Animal Liberation Front rises to their call to end their suffering and save their lives. Animal abuse industries wish to keep the public ignorant to the suffering involved in their products...

THERE IS NOWHERE TO HIDE. ANIMAL MURDERERS BEWARE. THERE IS JUSTICE COMING...

BLM WILD HORSE CORRAL | 1998

September, 1998
Rock Springs, WY
100 wild horses liberated

In mid-September, 1998, the Animal Liberation Front and Earth Liberation Front raided the BLM's wild-horse corrals in Rock Springs, WY.

Although an arson attempt on their office and vehicles had to be aborted, we did manage to free up to 100 wild horses.

The fact that the BLM hasn't informed the public about this event (they are publicly "owned") only shows that the BLM wants to continue their business of slaughtering horses for foreign dinner plates without public scrutiny and keep their genocide against America's Wild Horse Nation out of the American public's consciousness. Until the BLM ceases this campaign of "equine-cleansing" our campaign against the BLM will only intensify.

End the wild horse round-ups NOW.

Animal Liberation Front

PIPKORN MINK RANCH

1986

October 26, 1998
Hermanville, MI
5000 mink liberated

5000 Mink Freed

10/26/98; Hermansville, MI -

On the early morning hours of Monday, October 26, the Earth Liberation Front entered the Pipkorn Inc. Mink Ranch in Hermansville in the Upper Peninsula of Michigan. Seven holes were cut in the perimeter fence, and a large gate was opened allowing the prisoners to escape. Approximately five thousand cages were opened.

The farm held captive many different breeds of mink; however, most of those released had white fur. Many were seen leaving the compound and entering the surrounding woods as the liberators left. This action was done in defiance of the recent government repression waged by the grand jury's indictment of two falsely accused activists from Washington state. The Earth Liberation Front will not be intimidated by this government's actions or fur farmers' recent threats of violence against liberators.

As corporate destroyers burn in the west, wildlife nations will be liberated in the north.

Earth Liberation Front

DAVIDSON'S FUR FARM | 1999

February 13, 1999
Annandale, MN
6 foxes liberated

On the night of Feb. 13th 1999, the A.L.F. visited Davidsons Fur Farm in Annandale MN to release victims of vanity that are kept in horrible conditions within this concentration camp with the release of 6 fox (all we could find).

The mink sheds were found to be abandoned and the visible existence of coyotes and wolf that were unfortunately not able to have been released at this time.

Over the past few months the following farms have been found abandoned:

Keith Fortunes - Atwater, MN
Johns Ranch - Hamil, MN
Cannon Falls Ranch - Cannon Falls, MN

More will be found, more will be closed. Continue comrades in the fight for true freedom, with resistance in mind for those that are currently being hunted by our government.

By bricks, by boltcutters, by fire.
ACT

UNIVERSITY OF MINNESOTA

1999

April 5, 1999
Minneapolis, MN
Break-in at two buildings, extensive damage to multiple labs, 116 animals liberated

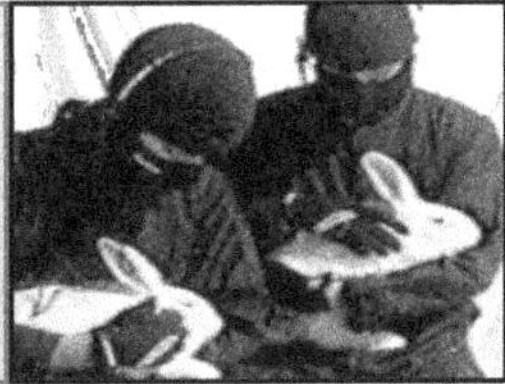

The Animal Liberation Front decided to start lab week early this year by raiding laboratories at the University of Minnesota in Minneapolis.

The following animals will never be harmed again at the hands of vivisectors:

27 Pigeons
48 mice
36 rats
5 salamanders

Elliot Hall, the Psychology Research building, where the animals were rescued from, had the walls painted with slogans, cages and equipment damaged, doors broken and research documents were also taken and are currently being reviewed.

Lions research building was also visited and had virtually all equipment on the 4th and 2nd floors severely damaged. Vivisectors own video footage of experiments were taken along with computer files and research notebooks.

This shows that lab raids can still be successfully completed. A video along with still pictures will be arriving to selected groups which should be immediately released to the public.

Our hearts go out to our friends that could not be taken. Their futures depend on you...

Act now
Animal Liberation Front

CHILDER'S MEAT COMPANY | 1999

May 9, 1999
Eugene, OR
Building torched

In honor of Mother Earth and all the cows who have their babies stolen from them to help furnish the meat and dairy industries, the Animal Liberation Front chose Mother's Day 1999 to pay a visit to Childer's Meat Company on Airport Rd. in Eugene, OR.

Using 20 gallons of a diesel fuel/unleaded mixture, four 5-gallon buckets were strategically placed near the two-story office building containing the companies business records and along the main building near a natural gas line. Using two kitchen timer delays, with another two-timers as back up, there was plenty of time to leave town before the Mothers Day celebration really ignited.

As long as companies continue to operate and profit off of Mother Earth and Her sentient animal beings, the Animal Liberation Front will continue to target these operations and their insurance companies until they are all out of business.

Happy Mothers Day

Arson suspected in Eugene blaze

About 40 firefighters respond to the early-morning fire at a meat-packing firm.

The Associated Press

EUGENE — A fire tore through a meat-packing business near the Eugene Airport early Sunday, destroying a two-story office building, a shipping dock and a refrigeration unit.

Police believe the fire, which caused an estimated $150,000 damage to Childers Meat Co., may be arson-related.

The fire was reported by a passerby who noticed the flames and called 911 at 3:13 a.m. About 40 firefighters were called to the blaze, which took about three hours to control.

Fire Marshal Mike Thrapp said the fire originated in two places outside: the office building at the front entrance and on the building's west side near a natural gas line. The fire quickly spread to the second floor, where it was burning through windows when firefighters arrived., Thrapp said.

The fire didn't damage the business' meat-processing facilities, but co-owner Tim Childers said operations can't continue until the water and electricity services are restored. He estimated the business might be running within a week.

The business, which employs 40 people, ships meat to Oregon hotels and restaurants. Childers didn't want to speculate on who might have started the fire.

WORLDWIDE PRIMATES

1999

June 25, 1999
Miami, FL
Truck set on fire

The Animal Liberation Front takes responsibility for the firebombing of a truck at Worldwide Primates, Inc. (7780 NW 53 St., Miami, Florida), the business of modern-day slave trader/ primate dealer Matthew Block and his family.

The action is in support of the 1999 Primate Freedom Tour.

Animal Liberation Front

KRIEGER FUR FARM | 1999

August 3, 1999
Bristol, WI
3000 mink liberated

In the early hours of the morning on August 3, 1999. We, the Animal Liberation Front, infiltrated a modern day death camp. This camp is located in Bristol, WI, and it holds an estimated 30,000+ captive mink.

Once on the grounds of the farm, ALF activists proceeded to destroy breeding records. These breeding records were found hanging over the cages on ridged pieces of wood or metal. It appears that Krieger tried to hide his records by stapling regular blank breeding cards closer to the cages. Activists destroyed the breeding records of four complete sheds.

A.L.F. activists then began to liberate mink. Krieger had incarcerated a large number of mink in groups of 4-6 in single cages. And while this over-crowding is inhumane and unsanitary, it made our jobs extremely easy. As the cages were opened, mink began to escape immediately. They knew that the time of liberation had arrived.

The conditions on Krieger's death camp were the worst we have ever seen. There was filth everywhere. The sheds were decrepit and unmaintained. Throughout the farm there were open ditches full of feces and urine. In several cages, we saw the decomposing corpses of dead mink whom were just left there to lie. These dead mink were surrounded by their fellow inmates.

This farm was targeted not only because of Krieger's exploitation of the mink nation (although that would be reason enough), but because Krieger's farm is a direct supplier of Neiman-Marcus Department Stores. Through their support of such a farm, Neiman-Marcus shows absolutely no regard for Life or the eco-system.

It appears that Neiman-Marcus is allied with Krieger and his fellow murderous farmers in their love of profits and greed over Life and Freedom. The

Animal Liberation Front declares an open invitation to anyone who would dare to stop these groups' sick reign of terror.

Now is the time for direct action. The only terrorism is the one we allow to exist. Until all these death camps are closed, we will continue to liberate.

In defense of the animal nations and Mother Earth,

Animal Liberation Front

GENE MEYER FARM + UNITED FEEDS | 1999

August 8, 1999
Plymouth, WI
2500 mink liberated, fur farm feed supplier burned down

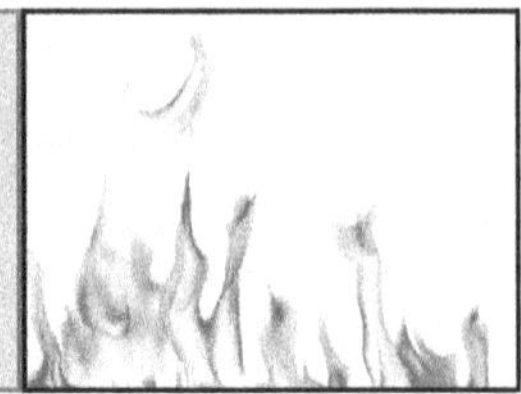

In the early morning of August 8, 1999, We, the ALF entered Gene Myers Fur Farm in Plymouth, Wisconsin and opened every single cage on the property. Tears came to our eyes as we watched thousands of mink run to their freedom in nearby fields.

Once we had finished sweeping the farm, we headed off to United Feeds, which is the major feed supplier of this concentrated fur farming area. We entered the building and checked from top to bottom to ensure that no living thing was inside. After walking throughout the building and seeing the sick huge bins of animal innards and organs, we knew that we had to end this operation. Four incendiaries were strategically placed throughout the building, ensuring that it would burn to the ground.

We will not stop or be stopped until every cage is opened and every oppressed creature is free.

1999 will be a crippling year for this blood-soaked industry. This action is dedicated to our comrades on the run. You are not forgotten.

More to come...

ALF

Associated Press

Firefighters battle a blaze at United Feeds Inc. in the town of Greenbush early Monday.

BIO-DEVICES

1999

August 29, 1999
Orange, CA
46 dogs liberated from vivisection supplier

Because vivisection is nothing more than economically-induced scientific fraud the Animal Liberation Front targeted a supplier of dogs to research laboratories, many of whom were stolen or falsely acquired from homes like your own from USDA licensed B-dealers.

In the early morning hours of August 29, 46 dogs (many injured from surgeries) were liberated. Not one was left behind!

They have now been examined by a doctor of veterinary medicine and placed in good loving homes where they can live out the rest of their lives free from torture.

The building, located at Collins and Eckhoff in Orange County, California was damaged and many messages were left, such as "Animal Liberation" and "Vivisection is Fraud."

This rescue mission proves that animal liberations can still occur if people are willing and determined to empower themselves and take the steps necessary to free the animals.

This liberation is dedicated to Alex Slack, a true animal liberationist victimized by the federal government, who chose to take his own life rather than betray his friends and the animals. As long as animals are exploited, tortured, and killed for profit there will be an ALF.

Making animal liberation a reality,
A.L.F.

GUNNINK FOX FARM | 1999

September 12, 1999
Chandler, MN
100 foxes liberated

On September 12 the A.L.F. visited Calvin Gunnink at 446-80 Ave, Chandler, MN and released 100 fox before having to leave.

Unfortunately hundreds more fox and lynx were unable to be released. Our hearts go out to our captured warrior Justin Samuel and to others still on the run.

The A.L.F. cannot be stopped.

WESTERN WASHINGTON UNIVERSITY | 1999

October 24, 1999
Bellingham, WA
Basement labs broken into, 31 animals liberated, offices trashed

On the morning of October 24th, the Animal Liberation Front raided the Western Washington University department of psychology animal labs in Miller Hall, liberating 3 rabbits and 28 rats and destroying 2 offices, including the office of notorious and sadistic primate "researcher" Merle Prim.

The entire contents of Prim's office - including all research papers and books on surgical technique were piled on the floor and soaked in 2 gallons of muriatic acid. The office of the animal "caretaker" was devastated and all documents related to animal torture destroyed.

We entered the building after midnight, first destroying Prim's lifetime of research derived from torturing primates, and seizing crucial documents related to animal research. We then made our way to the animal labs in the basement, locating a set of keys in an unlocked office. We made our way through the animal rooms, entering 7 rooms and rescuing 3 rabbits and 28 rats from the hands of deranged vivisectors. Sadly we were unable to liberate 8 rabbits due to electrode implants, but documented their horrendous condition on video. We also came across large lizards that were not able to be liberated.

All seized documents and video shot will be made public.

A warning to all vivisectors: 3 LAB RAIDS, 6 MONTHS, YOU'RE NEXT. This war - the revolution on behalf of animals continues.

The hammer of vegan justice falls.

-Animal Liberation Front

We strike again.

WASHINGTON STATE UNIVERSITY | 1999

November 20, 1999
Puyallup, WA
Building broken into, multiple labs trashed

In the early morning hours of Saturday the 20th of November, the Animal Liberation Front took a stand against the commodification of life by raiding the Washington State Univ. Dept. of Animal Sciences Poultry Research lab in Puyallup, WA.

We smashed out a window and entered the lab, making our way to the animal rooms which were found to be empty. We proceeded to smash every computer and piece of lab equipment in the facility.

The instruments of torture once used to experiment on live birds have now been reduced to a mere pile of rubble.

This raid marks the second ALF action against vivisection in the last month, and signals an ALF renaissance. Our sister and brother warriors are hearing our call - TAKE ACTION!! The coming year will perhaps be the most active ever.

And to the vivisectors: We know what you're doing to the animals. We never forget, and we never sleep.

This action is dedicated to the accused ALF prisoner, Justin Samuel - you are not forgotten. And to the 9+ billion murdered in America each year for food and science, we're doing all we can.

Animal Liberation Front

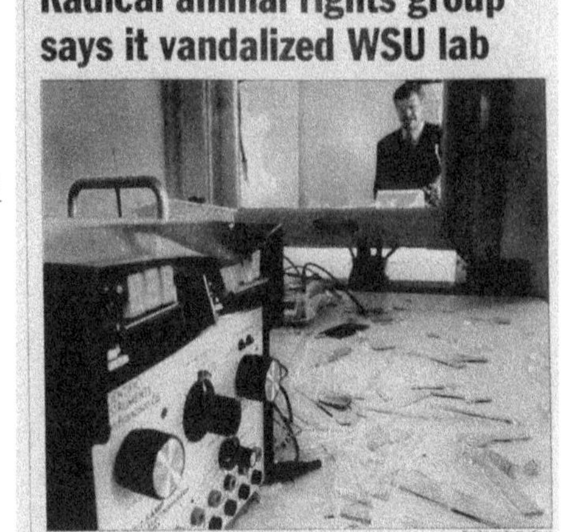

Radical animal rights group says it vandalized WSU lab

R&R RABBITRY | 2000

January 5, 2000
Stanwood, WA
23 rabbits liberated

The Animal Liberation Front is claiming responsibility for the January 5th liberation of 23 rabbits from R & R Research and Rabbitry, a research facility and laboratory animal breeder in Stanwood, WA.

We entered the compound in the early morning hours and emptied a shed containing their entire next day's shipment of rabbits.

These beautiful creatures were slated for delivery to pharmaceutical R&D labs and gory trauma research at Seattle-area hospitals.

We were unable to gain access to the labs and damage was minimal, but 23 rabbits have been placed in loving homes where they will live out their lives free from torture at the hands of sadistic biomedical researchers.

This is the 4th liberation of animals destined to die under the knife in the past year. Lab raids are back, slaughterhouses are being firebombed, mink are running free... A vegan insurrection is underway. This is a revolution for the animals, we will not stop until they are all free.

We're breaking down doors to get them out, and this is only the beginning...

Risking our freedom for theirs - Animal Liberation Front

MULTIPLE BAY AREA TARGETS | 2000

December 1999 to February 2000
Bay Area, CA
Multiple arson and sabotage actions across numerous targets

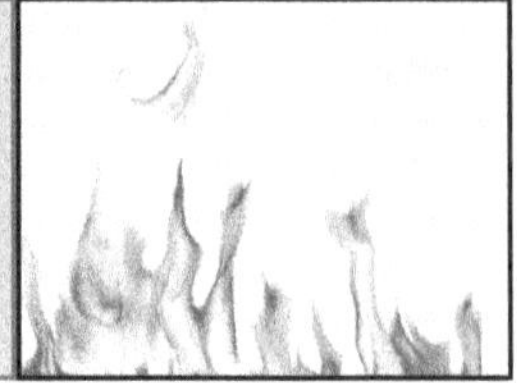

We, members of the Animal Liberation Front, claim full responsibility for the following actions of animal defense:

- Fulton Poultry Processors, Fulton - 4 incendiary devices - Dec. 20, 1999
- Rancho Veal Corp., Petaluma - 5 incendiary devices (office, storage, trucks) - Jan. 03, 2000
- Petaluma Farms, Petaluma - 5 incendiary devices (office and trucks) - Jan. 15, 2000
- Primate Products, Redwood City - flammable material placed through mail slot - Jan., 2000
- B & K Universal, Fremont - 4 incendiary devices (trucks) - Feb. 25, 2000
- Neiman Marcus, San Francisco - 29 windows smashed - Feb. 27, 2000

There will be no stopping us. Our war for the end of animal abuse has begun. No amount of blood money will save them from us. We will not stop until their industries of rape, enslavement, torture, and murder are destroyed.

ALF

The communique pertains to actions at the following locations:

Fulton Processors 1200 River Rd., Fulton, CA 707-546-8482
Rancho Veal Corp. 1522 Petaluma Blvd. N., Petaluma, CA 707-762-6651
Petaluma Farms 700 Cavanaugh Lane, Petaluma, CA 707-763-0921
Primate Products 1755 E. Bayshore Rd., Redwood City, CA 650-368-0663
B & K Universal 3403 Yale Way, Fremont, CA 510-490-3036
Neiman Marcus 150 Stockton St., San Francisco, CA 415-362-3900

DAI ZEN EGG FARM | 2000

May 7, 2000
Stanwood, WA
212 chickens liberated

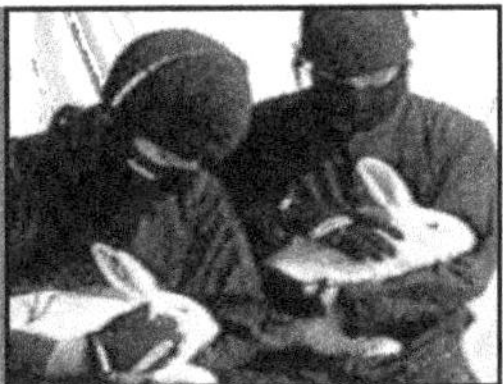

The Animal Liberation Front is claiming responsibility for the liberation of 212 egg-laying chickens from an egg farm located on Hwy 20, just west of I-5 in Burlington WA on Sunday, May 7th. The horrific conditions inside were documented on video (video to be released shortly) showing the life of these birds that is worse than death. All animals freed were placed into loving homes.

The birds inside this factory farm, as shown in the video, were crammed into filthy wire cages no larger than an 11" x 17" cage, roughly the size of a half sheet of newspaper. It is there that these animals live for years, standing on wire, surrounded by feces and rats (both dead and alive), deprived of food, and often packed in with their dead cellmates. The odor of waste and death inside was overwhelming. These modern day egg farms are animal torture chambers.

Recently, the Northwest was shocked to learn what egg farms are like on the inside, when above ground animal rights groups exposed the conditions inside nearby Amberson Egg Farms in Lake Stevens. The unfortunate reality is that Amberson's was just one common example of how billions of chickens are forced to live inside nightmarish egg farms. Farm Fresh Eggs is just one more example. Our video plainly shows it was not. If these farms had glass walls, they would not exist.

The ALF carried out this raid to rescue 212 chickens from their hellish prison, and to expose the conditions in which these innocent, sentient animals are kept in to produce eggs for consumers who are unaware of the suffering behind their food.

We ask the public to consider veganism - the elimination of all animal products from one's diet - to put an end to this suffering.

This raid was carried out by a small cell of compassionate individuals whose decision to cross the line was motivated by a reverence for life - what have these sentient creatures done to deserve such torture?

Until all are free...
the animal liberation front

Animal-rights group liberates 240 hens to 'loving homes'

BURLINGTON, Wash. – Member of the Animal Liberation Front staged a nighttime raid to free chickens from a farm west of here and placed them in "loving homes," the animal rights organization said.

A worker at Dai-Zen Farms, west of Burlington on State Route 20, confirmed Monday that about 240 hens had been taken from the farm, which has more than 30,000 laying hens.

Jose Luis Soto said wire cutters were used to snip cages and free the chickens. He said 57 cages were damaged.

– *The Associated Press*

SUNNY-CAL EGGS | 2000

June 24, 2000
Beaumont, CA
613 chicks liberated

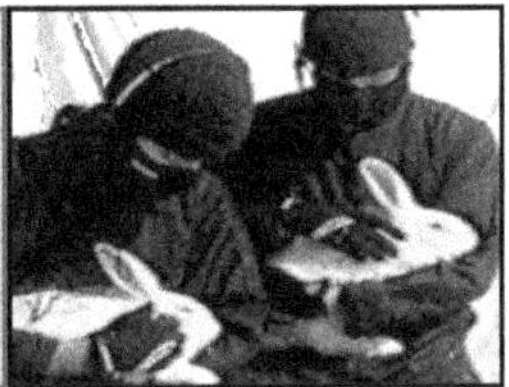

With the June 24th premier of Hollywood's new film "Chicken Run," the Animal Liberation Front (A.L.F.) exposed the truth behind egg farms. The A.L.F. is claiming responsibility for the liberation of 613 chickens from Sunny-Cal Eggs in Beaumont, CA (east of L.A.).

As audiences watched "Chicken Run" for the first time, the A.L.F. took action by breaking into sheds at this modern day concentration camp. We obtained video documentation of the horrendous and inhumane conditions inside this factory farm.

Billions of real live chickens suffer immensely on real battery egg farms every day. Just like those in the movie, each and every one of these chickens has her own personality, the capacity to suffer and a desire to live. And just like the characters in the movie, the owners of such animal concentration camps care about nothing more than profits. To maximize production and profits, 4-6 birds are crammed into cages barely larger than half a sheet of newspaper.

All 613 chickens were placed in homes and will never spend another day in a cage. These birds will never have to live and endure the endless torture and misery placed upon them by this cruel industry. They will never have their beaks cut from their bodies with a hot blade. They will never be killed simply because they can no longer produce eggs for human consumption.

With vegan dog treats and manipulation of gates, we fenced off guard dogs, cut through 5 perimeter fences and entered massive compound where we carefully loaded the chickens into carriers and delivered them to safety. Until human beings learn to take responsibility for this earth and all her creatures, it will remain necessary for compassionate individuals to act outside the law on behalf of the innocent.

GO VEGAN
- A.L.F.

GENESIS LABORATORIES | 2000

August 28, 2000
Wellington, CO
Hole drilled in wall, 179 birds liberated from labs

The Animal Liberation Front is claiming responsibility for the liberation of approximately 179 animals from Genesis Laboratories (10122 NE Frontage Rd., Wellington CO) in the early morning hours of August 28th, 2000.

Genesis Laboratories performs wasteful, redundant and cruel toxicology experiments on hundreds of wild animals annually.

Under the guise of "science," vivisectors at Genesis live trap animals in the Colorado wilderness, confine them to inhumanely small cages such as those we found inside the lab, and poison or otherwise torture these innocent creatures to death. 179 animals are now out of this torture chamber.

An outdoor aviary holding wild Bobwhite birds held for future use inside the lab was located, the pen walls cut away with wire cutters, and approximately 100 birds allowed to escape.

We then cut into an adjacent aviary where 11 ducks were loaded into carriers and taken to a getaway vehicle.

The main laboratory was our next target. Using a high speed drill and 3/8" drill bit, several holes were drilled into the wall of the building. Bolt cutters were then used to cut away a 3' X 3' hole in the corrugated metal siding. Fiberglass insulation was stripped away, and an additional hole was cut into the drywall, giving us direct access into a room holding an additional 68 Bobwhite birds. These birds were held in tiny wire cages allowing no room to fly or walk. The cages were cut into and all 68 birds loaded into carriers for delivery to a getaway vehicle.

Moving further into the building with the intent of liberating every last animal, we stepped into the path of a motion sensor in the laboratory hallway, sounding alarms and demanding a premature retreat. This unfortunate technical error forced us to leave behind hundreds of animals held throughout the building including additional birds, prairie dogs, squirrels, ferrets, and wild mice and rats.

All rescued animals were confirmed to be wild and native to the region, taken to a wilderness area, and released to live out their lives free from the bloodthirsty grasp of conventional "science."

When darkness falls, their laws enforcing savagery are voided and we will do what is necessary to liberate the animals.

For the end of the meat, dairy, vivisection, fur, and all animal exploitation industries.

- A.L.F.

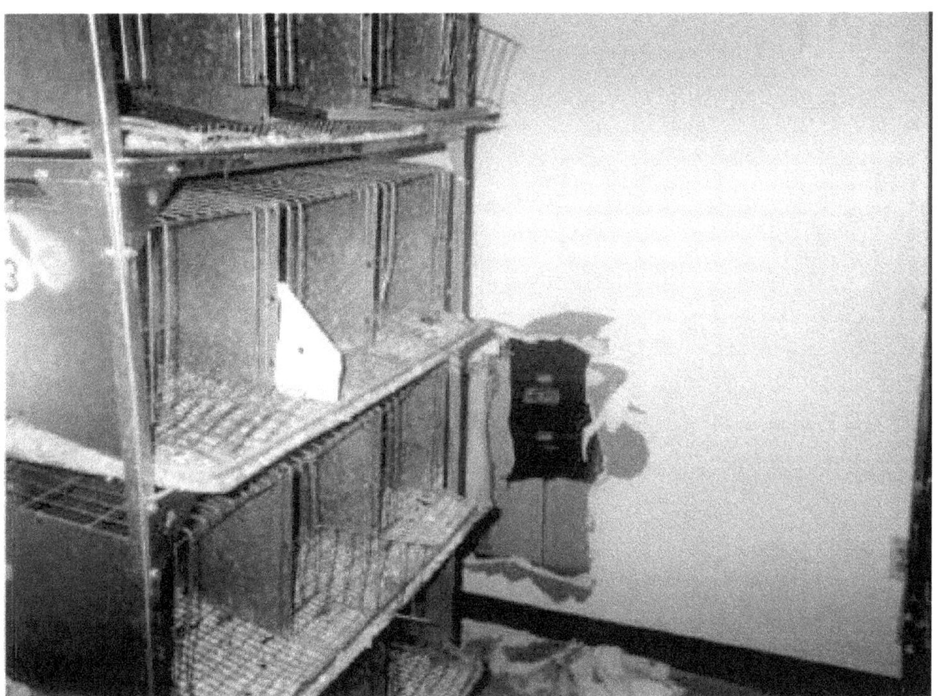

WHISTLING WINGS | 2000

September 3, 2000
Hanover, IL
750 ducks liberated

In the early morning hours of September 3rd, 750 ducks and a countless number of ducklings were liberated from Whistling Wings (www.whistling-wings.com) in Hanover, Illinois, the largest "producer" of live Mallard Ducks. They are a supplier for hunters and researchers whose methods of shipping baby ducks include UPS and the United States Postal Service.

We cut holes in the fences, opened all of the cages and barn doors for the ducks to escape to freedom. It is our hope that they will find a new satisfying life on the nearby Mississippi River.

A.L.F.

DREWELOW & SONS MINK FARM | 2000

September 7, 2000
New Hampton, IA
14000 mink liberated in largest mink release in US history to date

The Animal Liberation Front is claiming responsibility for the largest liberation of animals in history – the release of 14,000 mink from the Earl Drewelow & Son's Mink Farm, 2477 239th St, New Hampton IA; during the early morning hours of September 7th, 2000.

Handheld cutting tools were used to strip away two entire sides of the farm's fencing, giving the mink an escape route. Inside the sheds we found a horrific scene – thousands of mink crammed 2-3 to a tiny wire cage, waiting to die in a mess of waste and cobwebs.

Any attempt by the fur industry to dismiss the Drewelow & Son's Fur Farm as an isolated example should be considered a lie. The A.L.F. know from experience these conditions to be the industry standard.

Every cage was opened and 14,000 mink released to freedom.

The fur industry will be quick to respond to this beautiful act of compassion with baseless cookie-cutter form responses, in an attempt to discredit our actions and divert attention away from their sadistic industry. These standard lies from the mouths of murderers will be preemptively rebutted here:

Lie #1: "The mink will be hit by cars" – The absurdity of this statement is that before liberation, death was 100% certain. Every animal on the farm was bred to die. While it is true a small number may be hit by cars, most will not, and if nothing else they have been given a chance at freedom.

Lie #2: Mink are domestic and cannot survive in the wild" – Mink are in fact only one or two generation removed from their wild cousins and have not yet had their wild instincts bred out. The "Mink Rehabilitation Project" led by convicted A.L.F. liberator Rod Coronado proved this a decade ago. Mink legally purchased from a fur farm were released into the wild and shown through observation to retain natural survival instincts and thrive in the wild after a lifetime in a cage.

Lie #3: "Most of the mink were recaptured" – Mink travel several miles a day. Most mink had dispersed into the surrounding fields before the liberation was complete. A few may be recaptured, but only a handful.

Our hearts go out to those few recaptured who were given a shot at life and now have only suffering ahead.

Lie #4: "The A.L.F. are terrorists" – Every action carried out by the Animal Liberation Front is an act of compassion, with the only intent to save the lives of sentient creatures. These actions are carried out with no benefit to ourselves, except peace of mind knowing we have done all we can to rescue animals from the torture chambers and concentration camps of the meat, dairy, egg, fur and animal research industries. Their freedom is our victory.

We break the law in adherence to a higher law – one which state animals are not commodities, not objects, but sentient creatures with a right to live. We will fight for the lives of these animals as if they were our own.

Animal murderers beware – the A.L.F. is watching and there is
no place to hide…

Metro / NE Iowa WATERLOO-CEDAR FALLS COURIER SUNDAY, SEPTEMBER 17, 2000 PAGE B9

Minks still straggle in after ALF raid on New Hampton business

- Drewelow now taking extra precautions in guarding farm.

By REBECCA KLINE
Courier Staff Writer

only around 35 percent of the 14,000 minks have been found and returned.

"We are seeing minks that haven't eaten anything, and they are about half the size that they were (before the release) and they are pretty ornery," Drewelow said.

increased security tenfold, and we are on high alert for something like this to be happening again."

Guards are on the farm day and night. Drewelow said that is the only way he can stay in business.

As far as the Animal Liberation

and when you have to factor in people attacking you, that is a lot to deal with," he said.

He predicts this sort of ecoterrorism will occur again, possibly at his farm, in the near future.

DOUBLE T FARMS | 2000

September 9, 2000
Glenwood, IA
Every bird liberated from vivisection supplier

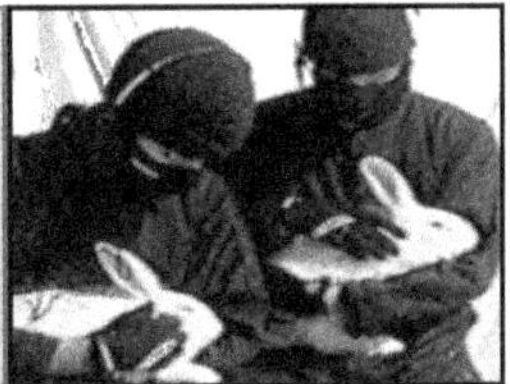

The Animal Liberation Front is taking credit for the liberation of 215 pigeons from Double T Farms (21655 Barrus Rd., Glenwood IA; Owner: Ted Golka), a breeder of animals for vivisection.

Double T Farms breeds thousands of birds annually for the purpose of being tortured to death in biomedical research laboratories. Access was gained to the pigeon shed through an unlocked door.

63 pigeons were placed in containers and loaded into a vehicle for transport to a wilderness area out of state. We were unfortunately logistically unable to transport by vehicle any more than these 63 pigeons. The remaining 152 birds were loaded into tubs and manually transported through nearby fields to wooded areas a half mile in every direction and released to freedom. Every pigeon was taken.

Any attempt by the vivisection industry to claim these birds were unable to fly or survive in the wild will be denounced here as false. All pigeons took flight immediately upon release. The "domestic" pigeon is a myth. We have full confidence in the survivability of these birds. While a percentage of the animals may become victim to wildlife as part of a natural predator/prey relationship in the wild, we accept this as the birds' role in the natural order, certainly preferable to confinement to a cage and torture until death inside the lab of one of the mad scientists who abound at our nation's universities and pharmaceutical companies.

Atrocities committed on pigeons in labs exposed by the A.L.F. in the past include the electrocution of live pigeons inside psychology labs at UC-Riverside in 1985 where nearly a thousand animals were liberated, and starvation experiments inside the University of Minnesota which was raided by the A.L.F. in 1999.

We are the only hope for these animals.

Millions of animals are shocked, cut open, blinded, and subject to more of the most barbaric and sadistic forms of torture ever devised by the human mind. This idiocy is carried out by sick, bloodthirsty madmen who slither through the halls of research institutions, leaving a trail of broken bones and blood.

Data from animal studies is not applicable to humans. Every dollar spent on biomedical research is a waste and the entire premise of this multi-billion dollar industry a fraud.

The A.L.F. has risen up from this society's dry well of compassion. Our compassion is for all life. Anywhere animals are killed or imprisoned for meat, fur, eggs, dairy or any other purpose will be considered a target. These are acts of compassionate vigilance in defense of all living creatures, and we will only stop when they do.

The animals' only hope
- A.L.F.

WEBER MEAT PACKING

2001

March 2, 2000
Queens, NY
Two trucks torched

In the early morning hours of March 2nd, we planted two incendiary devices underneath two trucks belonging to The Schaller and Weber Meat Packing Plant in Astoria, Queens. The incendiary devices did an unknown amount of damage to the trucks, although it was evident that the trucks caught fire.

Until the institutional abuse of animals is put to an end we will continue to destroy the property used to exploit innocent life.

This action was carried out in support of Andrew Stepanian, and Frank Ambrose, both dedicated members of our strong above-ground support groups. The unjust treatment of these activists will never intimidate us into stopping our activities.

We will not stop until they do,

- The Animal Liberation Front

SUNNY-CAL EGGS | 2001

March 17, 2001
Beaumont, CA
In second raid at the farm, 468 chicks liberated

In the early morning hours of March 17, 2001, members of the ALF liberated 468 young chickens from Sunny-Cal Eggs in Beaumont, CA. These animals will be placed in good homes where they will never be crammed into a cage, and forced to stay awake all hours to produce more eggs (more profits). This is the second time this farm was raided—last June, 613 baby chicks were liberated, and video footage of the horrendous conditions on this farm was released.

ALF

CORNELL UNIVERSITY

2001

April 28, 2001
Westhampton, NY
232 ducks liberated

Communique for 4/28 Lab Raid
Cornell Duck Research Facility

On the evening of Saturday, April 28th Animal Liberation Front activists liberated 232 3-month old ducklings from the Cornell Duck research Laboratory located on Old Country Road in Westhampton, Long Island. The action served to both liberate these beautiful creatures from exploitation, abuse and terror, and to provide a damaging blow to factory duck farming industries.

The Cornell University Duck Laboratory works to provide vaccines, hormones, and supplement technology to factory farmers in order to maximize their profits. This research will allow farmers to have a quicker growth rate of their ducks and allow their ducks to survive even further torture under smaller confines of battery farming. This research is not "pro-animal" it rather maximizes profits for an industry of animal murder, animal exploitation, environmental degradation, and greed.

To rebut the ludicrous claims made by the lab, all ducks were brought cross-country to a sanctuary where they will live their lives on many acres in peace and serenity, with the care of veterinarians, ample food, and most of all, free of fear of violence and murder.

The ALF

ICRC COMPANY | 2001

April 28, 2001
Castroville, CA
28 rabbits liberated

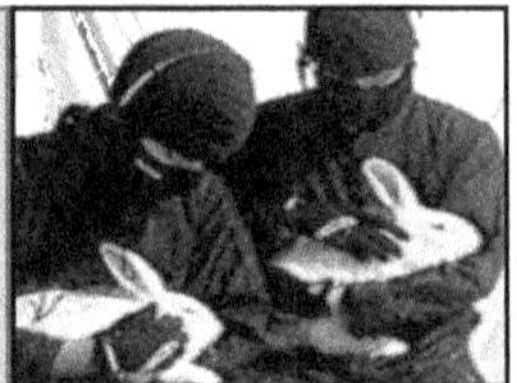

To celebrate World Week For Animals in Laboratories, The Animal Liberation Front is claiming responsibility for the liberation of 28 rabbits from ICRC Company (950 Dolan Rd., Castroville, CA) in the early morning hours of Saturday, April 28th, 2001.

Cutting through one fence and dodging motion-detecting lights we made our way to the outbuildings, where we witnessed rabbits confined in cramped cages barely able to move. Noticing that the undertakers of this abhorrent operation were still awake in their bedroom watching television, we quietly loaded as many rabbits as we could.

These gentle animals will be placed in loving homes and will never have to live their lives in agony and then murdered under the guise of "science." While these modern-day torture chambers continue to exist, our actions will only become more bold. We will not rest until these innocent creatures are no longer the victims of human viciousness, and while the vivisection industry continues to mutilate and torture millions of animals annually, when night falls, the laws supporting these death-camps mean nothing.

-ALF

MCDONALDS | 2001

September 7, 2001
Tucson, AZ
McDonalds burned down

On Friday night, 9/7/01, activists working in the interest of both the Animal Liberation Frontline and the Earth Liberation Frontline torched a Tucson, AZ, McDonald's, causing more than $500,000 in damage. The fire raged from 3 am until roughly 5:30 am, and left the building completely unusable. This action is meant to serve as a warning to corporations worldwide: You will never be safe from the people you oppress. Globalization is nothing more than the government sanctioned rape and murder of the earth's resources, and we, the people, will never stand for it. As long as this country continues to cater to the greed of corporations and ignore its responsibilities concerning human rights, animal rights and the environment, we will work in opposition. As long as the president supports free trade and pushes for "fast track" trade authority, we will act in opposition. As long as corporations enslave workers in other countries, waste our natural resources and torture animals, we will unite and stand in opposition. We are NOT a select few; we are the majority. The workers and the poor are strong, and we will no longer accept your inexcusable transgresses. We call upon you to pay it all back.

In support of all of those fighting for freedom on the frontlines – we will never compromise.

McDonald's fire may be linked to activist groups

By LA MONICA EVERETT-HAYNES
Citizen Staff Writer

The initials of animal and environmental rights groups were sprayed on a fast-food restaurant that burned this weekend, but authorities are not saying whether the groups were responsible for the fire.

The McDonald's at [illegible] N. Campbell Ave. was set ablaze around 3 a.m. Saturday, said Capt. Joe Gulotta, a Tucson Fire Department spokesman.

Police are investigating the total loss of the restaurant as an arson, Gulotta said.

The initials "ALF" and "ELF" were spray-painted on the side of the building and flashed across local television news screens yesterday.

The initials could stand for Animal Liberation Front and Earth Liberation Front. Law enforcement agencies across the country have blamed both groups for vandalism at scientific laboratories, luxury homes, business offices

INITIALS, cont./Page 5A

■ WENDY'S bowing to pressure from an animal-rights group, Wendy's Restaurants nationwide will alter the way it obtains eggs and chicken. Story, Page 5A

COULSTON FOUNDATION

2001

September 20, 2001
Alamogordo, NM
Building torched at primate lab, $1 million in damages, lab closed one year later

A.L.F. claims responsibility for the million dollar fire set in the maintenance building at The Coulston Foundation (TCF).

TCF has the largest colony of captive chimpanzees in the world and has been in violation of even the minimal standards of the animal welfare act for years. the USDA has brought more charges against TCF than any other research lab, yet it refuses to enforce the law and shut this horrific institution down. TCF is in such a deplorable state that the national institutes of health has pulled its funding and TCF also lost their accreditation as a research lab. TCF is under attack by legal groups and individuals across the country and is teetering on the edge of bankruptcy.

chimpanzees share more than 98% of the same DNA as humans and live in complex social family groups in the wild. at TCF, they live isolated in prisons of concrete floors and metal walls, with no other "enrichment" items besides an occasional ball, tire, or TV set. during nights of observation, we heard the chimps and macaque monkeys periodically scream and crazily pound on the walls, sounds we will never forget.

A separate, anonymous video crew with no knowledge of our action plans filmed the disgusting conditions of this place. The audio track on this raw video footage was removed because the crew talked to the chimps to try and calm them down. The footage shows a crew member feeding them raisins. some of the chimps were eager for this friendly contact, but others only rocked themselves, nearly catatonic, in the corners of their cages.

We wanted to liberate all these animals but because of difficulty in moving and sheltering them, especially since they're infected with HIV, hepatitis and herpes, we decided the best way to help them was to cause as much economic damage to TCF as possible. Every precaution was taken to avoid injury to the animals, personnel, security and firefighters.

We intend for this act of nonviolent economic sabotage to bring an end to this truly evil institution. if any investors consider bailing out TCF, they'll have to factor in large financial losses from direct action.

For the animals, A.L.F.

BLM HORSE CORRAL | 2001

October 17, 2001
Corvallis (Susanville), CA
200 wild horses liberated, hay barn torched

In opposition to the Bureau of Land Management's (BLM) continued war against the Earth - the Earth Liberation Front targeted the Wild Horse Holding Facility in Corvallis, California on October 17th, 2001. For years, the BLM has rounded up thousands of wild horses and burros to clear public land for grazing cattle. Many of these wild animals are sent to slaughter.

We cut through and removed four 60 foot sections of wooden fence to corrals holding more than 200 wild horses in order to free them from captivity.

After moving domestic horses to a safe distance we set four timed incendiary devices aimed at destroying two barns, two vehicles and one office building.

In the name of all that is wild we will continue to target industries and organizations that seek to profit by destroying the Earth.

Earth Liberation Front

SCOTT NELSON MINK FARM | 2001

October 16, 2001
Ellsworth, IA
2000 mink liberated

The Animal Liberation Front is claiming responsibility for the liberation of 2000 mink from a fur farm in Jewell, IA (Tollman Rd.) in the late hours of October 16th, 2001. Every animal was released.

Fences surrounding the farm were cut away, every cage opened, and 2000 mink ran to freedom. These animals were kept 3 and 4 to a small wire mesh cage. Their rescue came at the final hour, only a month from a violent death in the pelting season.

Captive bred mink are closely related to their wild ancestors, and have been shown to retain survival instincts when released - ensuring these liberated prisoners will live and thrive. The fur industry will move to condemn this action, using misleading half-truths and boldface lies. They point their fingers with blood stained hands. There is no defensible case for the taking of innocent life. Furthermore, there is no defensible argument against militant intervention to prevent this atrocity. When mink are no longer kept 4 to a small wire cage, when chickens are no longer kept packed in battery cages, when we stop calling dead animals food, when the blood stops spilling - these actions outside the law will no longer be needed. Until then, we will be tearing up fences, breaking down walls, and opening cages to free the animals. Terrorism against non-human animals will be met with liberation.

In this struggle for life against greed, compassion over sadism, our only recourse is to ignore laws and risk our freedom to save lives. Were you in a cage, whose side would you be on?

A.L.F.

DOUBLE T FARMS | 2001

October 18, 2001
Glenwood, IA
In second raid at the vivisection breeder, approximately 162 birds liberated

In the early morning hours of October 18, 2001, the Animal Liberation Front visited Double T Farms (21655 Barrus Rd., Glenwood, Iowa.), a breeder of birds for vivisection.

We located the pigeon shed, and cut through the wire mesh perimeter. 62 pigeons were found and released. These pigeons were destined for a cruel and senseless death at the hands of vivisectors.

All possible nesting boxes were emptied, and breeder tags were removed from each bird. The shed was also damaged. A second aviary containing ducks and geese was located, and 50 yards of netting cut away, allowing approximately 50 birds held captive within to escape.

A third aviary holding approximately 50 geese was similarly ripped apart, and those geese who did not immediately take flight were picked up and taken outside.

Approximately 162 birds were released.

This is the A.L.F.'s second visit to Double T Farms , and there will be further visits until Ted Golka's operation is shut down.

Risking our freedom for theirs.
A.L.F.

SCOTT NELSON MINK FARM | 2001

October 23, 2000
Ellsworth, IA
In second raid at the farm in a week, every recaptured mink re-liberated, farm closes

10/16/2001 A.L.F. liberated 2000 mink at Scott Nelson Mink Ranch in Ellsworth, Iowa
10/23/2001 A.L.F. liberates all recaptured mink at Scott Nelson Mink Ranch in Ellsworth, Iowa

The first time we visited Scott Nelson Mink Ranch in Ellsworth, Iowa we opened every cage on the property. We intended to close the place down; unfortunately, some of the mink were recaptured.

To demonstrate our complete seriousness regarding the freedom of these animals and contempt for the people responsible for these horrible places we again visited the fur farm and opened every cage on the property.

We demand these mink are allowed to remain free.
A.L.F.

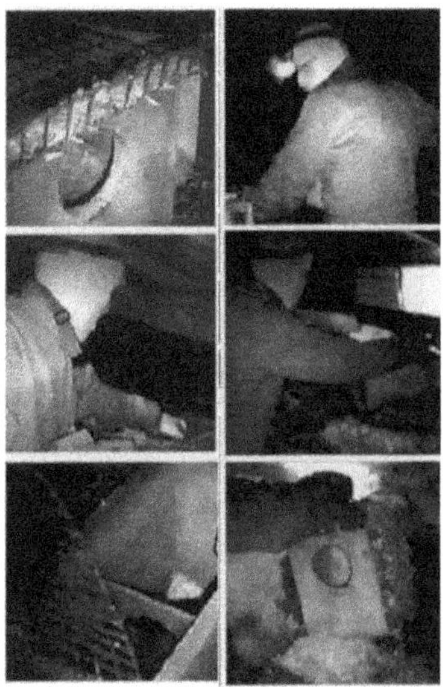

MARSHALL FARMS | 2001

December 5, 2001
North Rose, NY
30 beagles and 10 ferrets liberated from vivisection breeder

On the evening of December 5th, we visited Marshall Farms in upstate NY, liberating 30 beagle puppies and 10 ferrets. After outsmarting constant security patrols, we scaled the electrified fence, breaking through the door of one of the approximately 50 sheds of animals. Inside, we found hundreds of beagle puppies waiting to be shipped to vivisection labs, transferred from one small cage to another, destined to be killed. Before the next security patrol, we packed up 30 puppies and 10 ferrets and stole away into the night with them, taking them away from their hellish life, and giving them a life filled with freedom and joy.

As a breeder for Huntingdon Life Sciences, Marshall Farms would have ensured that these animals had a tortured, painful life suffering in labs. Beagles are routinely poisoned to death and abused at the hands of callous workers at HLS. Workers have been caught punching beagle puppies in the face, shaking them and throwing them against walls, and dissecting living animals for "research data" that even technicians admit is faulty. These 40 animals will never have to endure such brutal conditions.

This action is dedicated to Barry Horne, whose life's work brought attention to the suffering of animals in laboratories everywhere, and whose actions inspired people who care about animals to act on their behalf, even if it means risking your freedom for theirs.

Let this action serve as a warning to all who aid Huntingdon Life Sciences in killing 500 innocent victims every day that you cannot hide from justice.

ALF

SIMS POULTRY | 2002

May 3, 2002
Bloomington, IN
Delivery truck torched

The Animal Liberation Front is claiming responsibility for the early morning May 03 attack on Sims Poultry Processors in Bloomington, Indiana. While it may not be an actual slaughterhouse, Sims Poultry was targeted because of its role in the industries of animal exploitation and murder. The ALF will not rest until all businesses profiting from the misery and death of the innocent are destroyed.

Record numbers of chickens are being raised and killed for meat in the U.S. every year. Nearly ten billion chickens are being hatched in the U.S. every year. These birds are typically crowded by the thousand into huge factory-like warehouses where they can barely move. Chickens are given less than half a square foot of space per bird while turkeys are each given less than three square feet. Both chickens and turkeys have the end of their beaks cut off, and turkeys also have their toes clipped. All of these mutilations are performed without anesthesia, and they are done in order to reduce injuries which result when stressed birds are driven to fighting.

Today's meat chickens have been genetically altered to grow twice as fast, and twice as large as their ancestors. Pushed beyond their biological limits, hundreds of millions of chickens die every year before reaching slaughter weight at 6 weeks of age. These institutionalized practices begin with the premise that living beings are mere commodities to be 'processed' and consumed.

Despite the state's ongoing campaign to discredit and dismiss the movement for animal liberation, we will not shy away from acting to save the lives of innocent beings. As long as there is animal suffering, we will wage a non-violent war against their oppressors.

As long as there is animal suffering, there will be the Animal Liberation Front.

ALF

MISTY MOONLIGHT MINK RANCH | 2002

August 18, 2002
Waverly, IA
2000 to 3000 mink liberated

The Animal Liberation Front is claiming responsibility for the liberation of 2000-3000 mink from the Misty Moonlight Mink Ranch (1842 140th St., Waverly, IA, Owner: Nick Demuth, phone: 319-276-3350) in the early morning hours of August 18, 2002. Two sides of the perimeter fence were cut away and five sheds emptied. No cage was left unopened.

This raid is the ALF's latest effort to liberate all non-human captives from torture, confinement, and murder. This marks the 6th raided fur farm in Iowa; of these, 3 have closed forever. This campaign to rescue Iowa's victims of science and agriculture will continue until every animal confinement operation is empty and every slaughterhouse is burned to the ground. In the fight for the freedom of these animals, all is justified. To echoing screams of the living and images of the dead, we raise our boltcutters for their freedom - by any means.

For their lives, we lay down our own,
ALF

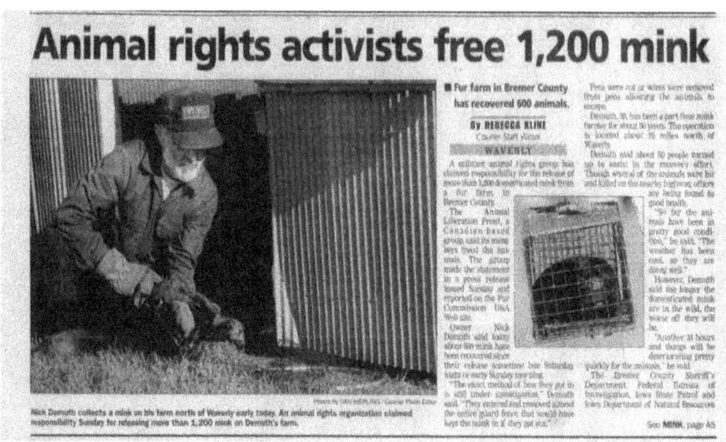

Animal rights activists free 1,200 mink

■ Fur farm in Bremer County has recovered 600 animals.

By REBECCA KLINE
Courier Staff Writer

WAVERLY

A militant animal rights group has claimed responsibility for the release of more than 1,200 domesticated mink from a fur farm in Bremer County.

The Animal Liberation Front, a Canadian-based group, said its members freed the animals. The group made the statement in a press release issued Sunday and reported on the Fur Commission USA Web site.

Owner Nick Demuth said today about 600 mink have been recovered since their release sometime late Saturday night or early Sunday morning.

"The exact method of how they got in is still under investigation," Demuth said. "They entered and removed almost the entire guard fence that would have kept the mink in if they got out."

Pens were cut or wires were removed from pens allowing the animals to escape.

Demuth, [illegible], has been a part-time mink farmer for about [illegible] years. The operation is located about [illegible] miles north of Waverly.

Demuth said about [illegible] people turned up to assist in the recovery effort. Though several of the animals were hit and killed on the nearby highway, others are being found in good health.

"So far the animals have been in pretty good condition," he said. "The weather has been cool, so they are doing well."

However, Demuth said the longer the domesticated mink are in the wild, the worse off they will be.

"Another 24 hours and things will be deteriorating pretty quickly for the animals," he said.

The Bremer County Sheriff's Department, Federal Bureau of Investigation, Iowa State Patrol and Iowa Department of Natural Resources

See MINK, page A5

Nick Demuth collects a mink on his farm north of Waverly early today. An animal rights organization claimed responsibility Sunday for releasing more than 1,200 mink on Demuth's farm.

MINDEK BROTHERS FUR FARM | 2002

May, September, & November 2002
Harborcreek, PA
In three separate actions, a feed barn is torched, and 250+ mink liberated

At 2:00 AM on November 26, 2002, anonymous cells of the A.L.F. and the E.L.F. visited the Mindek Brothers Fur Farm (4200 Shannon Road) in Harborcreek, Pennsylvania. Before disappearing into the night, a large fire was set which completely destroyed the farms feed barn and its contents, causing extensive financial loss.

The A.L.F. is also claiming responsibility for releasing 200 breeding mink in May and 50+ in September from the same farm.

Working together, cells from A.L.F. & E.L.F. demolished this feed facility due to its role in the systematic torture and killing of thousands of innocent creatures yearly - animals which possess the same complex emotional/physiological traits as loved household pets, yet are denied all reasonable consideration and confined to a miserable "existence" in tiny wire cages hardly large enough to turn around in.

Imprisoned in fur factories, these solitary creatures are forced to endure intensive confinement for the entirety of their lives, next to, or not uncommonly, packed into the same excrement and disease laden cages as their doomed relatives. In their natural state, these animals maintain a vast territory encompassing several miles. However, on fur farms such as this one, most of these semi-aquatic animals "enjoy" less than 24 inches of space, living on chicken wire, exposed to incredible levels of disease, cannibalism, and weather extremes. With what is essentially still a wild animal, these squalid conditions produce a perpetual state of chronic distress, unimaginable to human beings. This stress leads to severe psychosomatic illness, causing disturbing behaviors like self-mutilation, cannibalism, and incessant pacing and scratching in attempts to escape from their prison.

After experiencing the blistering heat, filth, intensive confinement, and other amenities of the mink shed for half of a year, they are either gassed, electrocuted, or have their necks snapped. If they are genetically superior, they often stay on the ranch indefinitely in such conditions, only to be killed in the same manner when they lose their usefulness.

These cells have witnessed all of these things and more just as disturbing, first hand at this farm, and feel that they must pose this question to the public.

Would this deplorable situation be allowed to continue if the animals happened to be cats, or puppies perhaps, rather than their canine relative the North American Mink? Clearly, it would not. Brutality is brutality - these animals are no less deserving of basic "rights" than the animals we call our friends, and the law protects as such. Thus it is, in the face of this glaring hypocrisy, with their very real suffering in mind, that we take the justice and mercy that the law fails to provide into our own hands, and provide it for those who cannot act in their own defense.

The economic value of a dead body or a frivolous luxury item cannot be compared to the inherent value of a life - thus unnecessary killing is absolutely unjust. This has been recognized by much of the rest of the world, and in multiple cases, fur farming has been completely banned by other "first-world" governments. It is time for the world's most accomplished and proven terrorist, the United States, to respond and follow suit. If it does not, this inexorable struggle on behalf of innocent life will continue.

The E.L.F. took part in this action on behalf of the Earth, due to the target's extreme pollution of surrounding streams and groundwater with excrement and offal runoff. The fur trade's codependent relationship with the ecological nightmare of factory farming and other such nefarious forms of animal agriculture alone, completely necessitate our action in defense of life on Earth. If the owners of the destroyed facility wish to be left alone, they should permanently close their operation, providing clear proof that they have done so. If this is done immediately, and this communique is released to the public UNALTERED, individual members from each of the cells responsible for this action will turn themselves in. If this is not done, the rest of the mink ranch WILL be demolished. Other components of the mink ranch operation may also be targeted.

In defense of life,
A.L.F. / E.L.F.

MERIAL SELECT | 2003

February 27, 2003
Berlin, MD
115 chickens liberated from chicken industry pharmaceutical supplier

In the early morning hours of February 27, 2003, the ALF liberated 115 chickens from Merial Select Laboratory (10026 Main Street, Berlin, MD, 21811, Phone 410 641-2060, Fax 410 641-0768).

In the midst of a snowstorm, we made our way to the animal housing units. Using crowbars and boltcutters, we bypassed the alarmed doors by prying and cutting our way through the window panes and wire mesh. After crawling into several barns, we loaded 115 baby chicks into carriers and brought them to safety.

They have been taken to temporary housing to live in a period of isolation to ensure that the possible diseases they have been infected with do not spread to others. Afterwards, they will be moved to permanent homes to live freely. Merial Labs will tell you their research into new vaccines is "helping" animals. The truth is, they are creating vaccines to maximize an animal's life inside a factory farm in order to increase profits from the commodification of life.

Countless animal research facilities commit their atrocities in Maryland, but Merial was targeted specifically because they are a client of Huntingdon Life Sciences. Any friend of HLS is an enemy of the ALF. We know who their clients are. We are out there, and you're next.

Until all are free...

The Animal Liberation Front

ROESLER BROTHERS FUR FARM | 2003

August 26, 2003
Sultan, WA
10000 mink liberated

The Animal Liberation Front is claiming responsibility for the liberation of 10,000 mink from a Sultan fur farm (339th Ave SE - dirt road east of landing strip). Fencing was removed and nearly every cage opened. It has been shown through such efforts as the Mink Rehabilitation Project that farm raised mink can survive and flourish in the wild. All industry responses stating the contrary are lies. All institutions of animal exploitation – regardless of any attempts to conceal their bloody operations - will be located and the animals liberated.

-A.L.F.

We would also like to express our utter contempt for those who cooperate with the authorities in their hunt for animal liberators - especially snitch Justin Samuel of San Diego currently attempting to reassimilate into the animal liberation movement. May you forever live in guilt, shame, and scorn.

CHIRON

2003

August 28, 2003
Emeryville, CA
Two ammonium nitrate pipe bombs detonated at Chiron headquarters

In the early hours of August 28th volunteers from the Revolutionary Cells descended on the animal killing scum Chiron. We left them with a small surprise of 2 pipe bombs filled with an ammonium nitrate slurry with redundant timers. This action came about because Chiron has continued their murderous connection with Huntingdon Life Sciences even though they have been exposed numerous times as some of the most egregious animal killers in the industry.

Chiron, you were asked to sever your ties with HLS, you were told, and yet you continued your relations with them. Now it is time for you face the consequences of your actions. If you choose to continue your relations with HLS you will no longer be subject only to the actions of the above ground animal rights movement, you will face us. This is the endgame for the animal killers and if you choose to stand with them, you will be dealt with accordingly.

There will be no quarter given, no more half measures taken. You might be able to protect your buildings, but can you protect the homes of every employee?

From Palestine to Euskal hernia, from the jungles of Colombia to northern Ireland, the struggle will continue until all of the oppressive institutions are destroyed!

For animal liberation through armed struggle, the Revolutionary Cells

-Animal Liberation Brigade

LOUISIANA STATE UNIVERSITY | 2003

September 24, 2003
New Orleans, LA
Labs broken into & trashed at inhalation toxicology lab, $200,000+ damages

(Editor's note: Only excerpts of this communique have been preserved)

These gas chambers subject suffering animals to daily doses of cigarette smoke and industrial pollutants causing pain, suffering, and death...

It should be clear that animals do not deserve to be tortured and die in this pointless research.

The Animal Liberation Front will continue to target animal killers until the day of empathy and compassion replaces cruelty and exploitation.

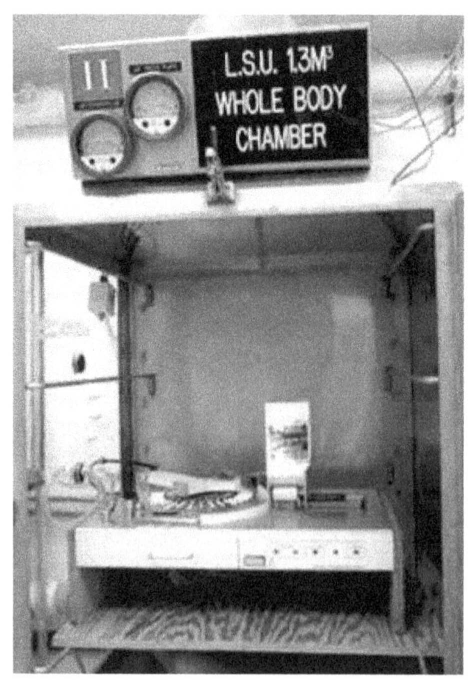

SHAKLEE | 2003

September 25, 2003
Pleasanton, CA
10 lb ammonium nitrate explosive detonated at Shaklee headquarters

On the night of September 25th volunteers from the Revolutionary Cells attacked a subsidiary of a notorious HLS client, Yamanouchi.

We left an approximately 10lb ammonium nitrate bomb strapped with nails outside of Shaklee Inc, whose CEO is both the CEO for Shaklee and Yamanouchi Consumer Inc. We gave all of the customers the chance, the choice, to withdraw their business from HLS. Now you all will have to reap what you have sown.

All customers and their families are considered legitimate targets. Hey Sean Lance, and the rest of the Chiron team, how are you sleeping? You never know when your house, your car even, might go boom. Who knows, that new car in the parking lot may be packed with explosives. Or maybe it will be a shot in the dark.

We have given all of the collaborators a chance to withdraw from their relations from HLS. We will now be doubling the size of every device we make. Today it is 10lbs, tomorrow 20....until your buildings are nothing more than rubble. It is time for this war to truly have two sides. No more will all of the killing be done by the oppressors, now the oppressed will strike back. We will be non-violent when these people are non-violent to the animal nations.

In memory of all of those fallen before us in the war for liberation: Jill Phipps (animal activist), Barry Horne (ALF), Olaia Kastresana (ETA), Arkaitz Otazua (ETA), Angayarkanni (LTTE), Babu (LTTE), Bobby Sands (IRA), Patsy O'Hara (INLA), Carlos Guiliani (anti-globilization martyr), Lee Kyung-hae (farmer and anti-globablization victim), and many more on numerous other fronts. We won't forget you, we won't let your deaths be in vain.

Gora Euskadi Ta Askatasuna!
Up the Real IRA!

Long live the Popular Front for the Liberation of Palestine!
Viva La Fuerzas Armadas Revolucionarias de Colombia!
Long live the Frontu Di Liberazione Naziunalista Corsu!
For the creation of Revolutionary Cells!
For Humyn, Earth & Animal Liberation!

Bringing the bomb and the bullet back into amerikan politics,

Revolutionary Cells—animal liberation brigade

The revolutionary cells exists as a front group for militants across the liberationary movement spectrum. We are anarchists, communists, anti-racists, animal liberationists, earth liberationists, luddites, feminists, queer liberationists, and many more things across various other fronts. Where ever there is oppression there are those unwilling to idly stand by and let it occur, and those people make up the nucleus of the revolutionary cells.

Who are the revolutionary cells? It is an anti-gmo activist destroying a GMO crop, it is a basque youth driving a car packed with explosives destined for a Spanish politician, it is a queer bashing back, a rape victim putting a bullet in the rapist, a Corsican nationalist planting a bomb at a French bank, it is a Cincinnati riot in response to police brutality, an animal liberationist shooting a vivisector dead on his doorstep. In short it is the spirit of resistance realized. It is moving from politics to praxis.

Anyone who takes part in the war against the oppressive hierarchies in this world can consider themselves a member of the Revolutionary Cells.

Revolutionary Cells Guidelines:

1. To take strategic direct action (be it non-violent or not) against the oppressive institutions that permeate the world.
2. Make every effort to minimize non-target casualties, be they human or non-human.
3. Respect a diversity of tactics, whether they be non-violent or not.
4. Any underground activist fighting for the liberation of the humyn, earth or animal nations may consider themselves a Revolutionary Cells volunteer.

UNIVERSITY OF IOWA | 2004

November 14, 2004
Iowa City, IA
Multiple labs and offices in two buildings broken into & trashed, 401 animals liberated

The Animal Liberation Front is claiming responsibility for the liberation of 401 animals from the University of Iowa in the early hours of November 14th, 2004. All animals on the third floor of the UI psychology department —88 mice and 313 rats—were removed, examined and treated by a sympathetic veterinarian, and placed in loving homes.

Additionally, two animal labs and three vivisector's offices were entered and all contents relating to animal research were destroyed.

These are:

4th Floor - Spence Labs:
Vivisector Ed Wasserman's lab entered. Dozens of computers and devices used in experiments on live pigeons were destroyed.

Basement - Spence Labs:
Lab of vivisector Mark Blumburg and others entered. Surgical equipment and small animal stereotaxic devices, as well as "shock boxes" and other instruments of torture destroyed.

4th Floor - Seashore Hall:
Primate researcher Joshua Rodefer's office entered. Computer discs, hard drives, paperwork and photos showing Rodefer's work confining drug addicted primates in small glass boxes removed. The remaining paperwork detailing his monstrous work addicting primates and rats to narcotics was soaked in acid and the computer destroyed.

1st Floor - Seashore Hall
Primate researcher Amy Poremba's office entered. Computers destroyed, documents removed, and the remainder soaked in acid.

This raid was carried out to halt the barbaric research of the UI Psychology Department's 7 primary animal researchers: Professors Poremba, Freeman, Blumburg, Johnson, Robinson, Rodefer and Wasserman.

This was not thoughtless vandalism but a methodical effort to cripple the UI psychology department's animal research. Only equipment in rooms where animals were confined and tortured were targeted. Only computers belonging to or used in the work of vivisectors were destroyed. Only documents of animal researchers were doused in acid. The acid a deliberately chosen paper dissolving agent.

Our goal is total abolition of all animal exploitation. Achieved in the short term by delivering the 401 animals from UI's chamber of hell. And in the extended term by shutting down the labs through the erasing of research and equipment used in the barbaric practice of vivisection. The entire raid was a careful and deliberate 5-pronged assault on UI's animal research.

Behind the laboratory doors we found drug addicted rats, rats subjected to stress experiments involving loud noise, rats undergoing thirst experiments, unanesthetized rats with protruding surgical staples and oozing wounds, and mice and rats affixed with grotesque head implants.

Inside the labs of UI's Psych Department, we found a bloody torture chamber showcasing the cruelest whims of our earth's sickest minds. Professors Freeman, Poremba, Rodefer, Johnson, Robinson, Blumburg, and Wasserman are monsters. Tonight 401 animals are spared their reach.

Our deepest sadness is reserved for the animals on the 4th Floor kept from our arms, those we were unable to save, including hundreds of mice and rats, pigeons, guinea pigs, and 8 primates.

No animals were released into the wild. All 401 were placed in comfortable, loving homes.

We acted as operatives not only of compassion, but good science. Animal research is not only cruel but hazardous—as data derived from the animal models is not applicable to humans and therefore dangerous.

Our bypassing of UI's sophisticated, key card-access, 4-walled security system (perimeter, elevator, corridor, animal room) should be interpreted as a two-fold message:

1) Our utter seriousness in achieving animal liberation.
2) If you torture animals and we not be stopped from liberating them.

On the ears of these monsters who know only profit and blood, who hide behind unjust laws, our breath has been wasted. Justice for the victims of vivisection will be achieved not by the blows of boycott nor protest—but of our sledgehammers to laboratory doors.

Let this message be clear to all who victimize the innocent: We're watching. And by axe, drill, or crowbar—we're coming through your door.

Stop or be stopped.
A.L.F.

Communique Addendum 1.0

The continuation of vivisection is maintained only insofar as it remains outside public sight and scrutiny. The ongoing research uncovered at UI's Psych Dept. is of such a sadistic nature as to be inexcusable by all but the sickest minds. UI code requires all animals be kept behind locked doors of windowless rooms, and most often on floors locked to the public. UI has also tagged this raid as mere vandalism and denied an animal liberation motive despite numerous slogans left painted at the site, all to divert attention from its animal research. We confiscated paperwork from UI's 7 primary researchers to give the public a glimpse into the sickness
kept from their eyes:

Prof. Freeman:

Drills holes into the skulls of rats and affixes head implants in neurology experiments involving "electrical brain stimulation." Rats removed from his lab were grossly disfigured by surgically implanted devices on the skull.

All animals in his lab were rescued.

Johnson:

Exposes rats to a series of "chronic stressors" including loud noise and strobe lights for the aim of "experimentally induced depression." Also performs experiments involving the withholding of water from rats.

All animals in his lab were rescued.

Blumburg:

Currently subjects infant rats to prolonged cold exposure. Famously deranged mind on record as stating the cries of animals in labs are an automatic response and convey no more emotion than a sneeze.

All animals in his lab were rescued.

Poremba:

Currently confines 8 rhesus monkeys in the NE corner of the Psych building's 4th floor, subjecting them to numerous stressors including reward/punishment experiments. Places primates in a "behavioral conditioning box," also known as a "shock box," where primates are subjected to shock experiments. Inside her office we found pieces of primate brain encased in glass and blueprints to the building.

Rodefer:

Addicts primates and rats to cocaine, methamphetamine, and PCP in redundant drug experiments. His drug possession license filed with the DEA stipulates the drugs be kept in a locked safe in the building's basement. However 2 stashes of narcotics were found in his 4th floor office, including the inside pocket of a jacket, suggesting he is himself addicted to the drugs he has for years forced on animals.

Addendum 2.0

Because of the established link between violence towards animals and that towards humans, we offer as a public safety measure the home addresses of UI Psych Dept. vivisectors:

Mark S Blumburg
536 S Summit St
Iowa City IA

Spouse: Jo McCarty
354-7339
Office: E232 SSH
Lab: 315 Spence Labs

John H Freeman
1054 Red Oak Park Rd.
Tipton IA
886-1289
Spouse: Elizabeth Freeman
Office: E224 SSH
Lab: 307 Spence Labs

Kim A Johnson
1401 Bristol Dr
Iowa City IA
338-5617
Spouse: Marlene
Office: E20 SSH
Lab: 318 + Basement B13 Spence Labs

Amy Poremba
1330 Highland Ave
Iowa City IA
354-2618 (home)
319-594-1084 (cell)
Spouse: Mark
Office: E124 SSH
Lab: 4th Floor, Spence Labs

Scott Robinson
1110 10th St.
Coralville IA
351-9455
Spouse: Karen
Office: E234 SSH
Lab: 317 Biology Building

Joshua Rodefer
861 Normandy Dr
Iowa City IA
339-9842 (home)
331-3419 (cell)
Spouse: Pamela Keel
joshrodefer@myrealbox.com

Edward Wasserman
1252 Oakes Dr.
Iowa City IA
354-9785
Spouse: Mary Losch
Office: E222 SSH
Lab: 4th Floor, Spence Labs

Tuyet Nguyen
(assistant to Rodefer)
923 12th Ave
Corallville IA
319-339-7827 (home)
621-3668 (cell)

Lab Assistants to Rodefer:

Lindsey Guynn 350-2082
Josh Fillinger 319-430-9792
Gina Huss 563-299-3434
McCabe Kenny 319-431-3615
Violet Lucca 319-431-3615
Lab Assistants to Poremba:
Imelda 621-3079
Bethany 337-8220
Christina 708-334-9556
Damon 358-2946

SEABOARD SECURITIES

2004

December 30, 2004
Tequesta, FL
Office of HLS supplier broken into and trashed

Last night we broke into the offices of Seaboard Securities (HLS market maker) in Tequesta, Florida (17713 SE Federal Highway, Ste 100). We emptied a file cabinet of its files, and smashed several computer monitors and a television. Here's a message to Kevin, Dennis, Cristian, Adam, Guy and the rest of the Seaboard Securities staff: we now know where you live; we will not hesitate to take this fight to your doorstep if you continue to do business with Huntingdon Life Sciences.

GNK DEER FARM | 2005

January 18, 2005
San Miguel, CA
Entire herd of deer released from venison farm in US's first recorded deer liberation

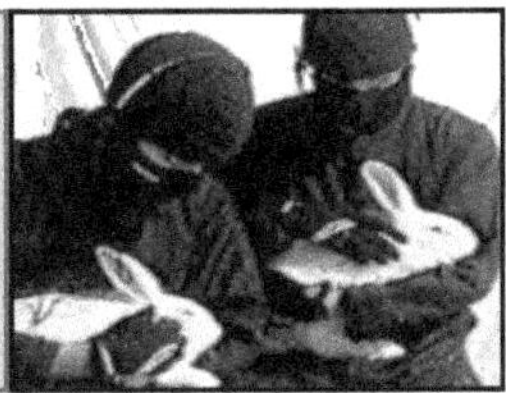

The ALF is claiming responsibility for the release of the entire deer herd from GNK Deer Farm (65801 Big Sandy Road., San Miguel, CA. (805)467-3705) in southern Monterey County in the early morning hours of January 18, 2005.

The pen was located in the rear of the property and over 1/4 of the fence was cut away, releasing the deer into the mountainous countryside.

GNK Ranch - owned by former LAPD Sergeant Gerd Konieczny - is one of the 3 largest deer farms in California and hosts an on-site deer slaughterhouse.

We believe this to be the first ever deer liberation in the US. Freedom for these creatures - for whom death is a certainty- was a simple and unskilled operation. Hundreds of deer farms operate in this country. We encourage compassionate people everywhere to locate farms in their area and tear down their walls.

The venison industry remains small. Our hearts go out to victims of the larger problem, the billions of lives we are unable to save - cows, chickens, pigs, mice, rats, and others - casualties of the meat, dairy, vivisection and other industries of suffering and blood. Their pain is our own.

For the liberation of the helpless we will strike,

A.L.F.

Animal rights group admits freeing fenced deer

More than 30 deer were allowed to escape from a venison farm in southern Monterey County early Tuesday and an animal rights group is claiming responsibility, Monterey County sheriff's Cmdr. Tracy Brown said.

GNK Ranch workers discovered that nearly 500 feet of fence had been cut away from the 8-foot-high posts, allowing 34 European fallow deer to escape into the hills.

CRIME

Brown said more deer escaped but returned to the farm on Big Sandy Road near San Miguel.

The fence surrounded a two-acre enclosure that housed up to 400 deer raised for slaughter, with their meat being sold mainly at San Luis Obispo County markets.

Although an investigation is ongoing, a fax sent to local media outlets claimed the Animal Liberation Front carried out the act.

The ALF credo calls for "direct action against animal abuse in the form of rescuing animals and causing financial loss to animal exploiters, usually through the damage and destruction of property," according to the ALF Web site.

Because many actions of the ALF are illegal, activists tend to work individually or in small groups, with no centralized organization. Brown said authorities have not heard any other reports of similar incidents in Monterey County, or any involving the ALF.

The FBI has been contacted by local law enforcement, which is seeking the suspects in the case on charges of trespassing and vandalism, Brown said.

WOODLAND FARMS | 2005

February 27, 2005
Tranquility, CA
12 ducklings liberated

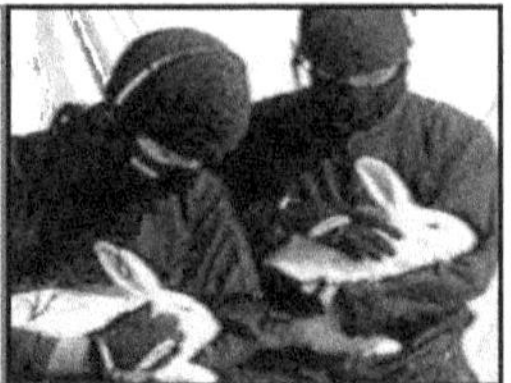

Each year, approximately 24 million ducks are killed for food. Most are warehoused in large sheds with nothing but sawdust reeking of ammonia, a bit of food, and 'nipple drinkers' as their only source of water. They live in these conditions until 7 weeks of age when they are slaughtered.

In the early morning hours of February 27, 2005, we liberated 12 ducklings from 29755 W. Jefferson Avenue, Tranquillity, CA 93668, a farm owned by Woodland Farms, a subsidiary of Maple Leaf Farms. Maple Leaf Farms, the largest producer of duck meat in North America, murders over 14 million ducks each year.

Ducks are waterfowl. In the wild, they spend a great deal of their day in water, immersing themselves in it and preening. The ducklings that we rescued from the Woodland Farm in Tranquillity would never have seen a body of water during their short lives in the factory farm. Now at least these 12 ducklings are in a loving home where they can swim every day and live out their natural lives free of oppression.

Until all animals are free,
a.l.f.

LITTIG FOX FARM | 2005

April 1, 2005
Bluffs, IL
Dozens of foxes liberated

To all those who refuse to give in,

In the early morning hours of April 1st, our small band of dogooders made our way through muddy fields and grassy mounds to descend upon a fox factory farm owned by Kerry Littig (1774 Eagle Run Rd, Bluffs, IL 62621). She is the top breeder of silver foxes in the U.S.

Until now she probably thought that she was pretty safe since her address has never been made public. We found you Kerry, and more importantly, we found the foxes you imprison, force to suffer, and finally mutilate all for your own profit and the vanity of others.

Only the breeding animals were on the farm, so we knew this wouldn't take very long. After removing the majority of the surrounding fence, we entered the shed, removed all of the breeding information and finally opened every single cage, releasing dozens of foxes into the surrounding countryside. We hope with all our hearts that some make it!

Kerry better believe that we will come back, time and time again, until this hellhole is closed once and for all.

This action was done in absolute solidarity with all of those forced to flee in order to escape the state's repression, and most of all FOR PETER, who made it seven years. You inspire us immensely and are with us in every passing moment.

Strong Hearts Forward!
the Animal Liberation Front

LOUISIANA STATE UNIVERSITY | 2005

April 22, 2005
Baton Rouge, LA
Labs entered through a vent, trashed, and 21 mice liberated

In celebration of World Week for Animals in Laboratories the Animal Liberation Front is claiming responsibility for the liberation of 21 mice from Louisiana State University in the early hours of April 22nd, 2005.

Breaking through a vent in a side door, animals on the seventh floor of the LSU Biology Department building—21 mice—were removed, examined and treated by a sympathetic veterinarian, and placed in loving homes.

No animals were released into the wild. All 21 were placed in comfortable, loving homes.

LSU's Animal Cruelty Facility lab was also vandalized in addition to giving 21 mice new lives free from torture, solitude and suffering. Aquariums were smashed, windows broken and paint stripper poured on outer walls. Spray-paint was used for slogans and further vandalism of the labs, and the locks were glued on doors to any rooms that housed no animals.

Our deepest sadness is reserved for the animals on the 7th Floor kept from our arms, those we were unable to save, including hundreds of mice, dozens of rats, birds, rabbits, and turtles.

The cold solitude of the cage and the deafening silence of sterile, windowless laboratory rooms on the top floor of a building, with no chance to interact in the outside world or with one another is torture enough. Add to that the despicable cruelty of those human beings who've shown no compassion for the screams from animals in their never-ending, painful experiments and you can see where our sadness, and our anger, comes from.

We acted as operatives not only of compassion, but good science. Animal research is not only cruel but hazardous—as data derived from the animal models is not applicable to humans and therefore dangerous.

Our aim in inflicting as much economic damage as possible is to drive up the cost of animal experimentation until this sadistic psuedo-science is no longer economically feasible.

Our aim in liberating animals should be obvious. Giving them a new life free of the hell that is the LSU ACF. For 21 mice, we've done that.

To vivisectors everywhere, you know your profession is one of cruelty and unnecessary suffering.

Stop now or be stopped.

Always for the animals,
A.L.F.

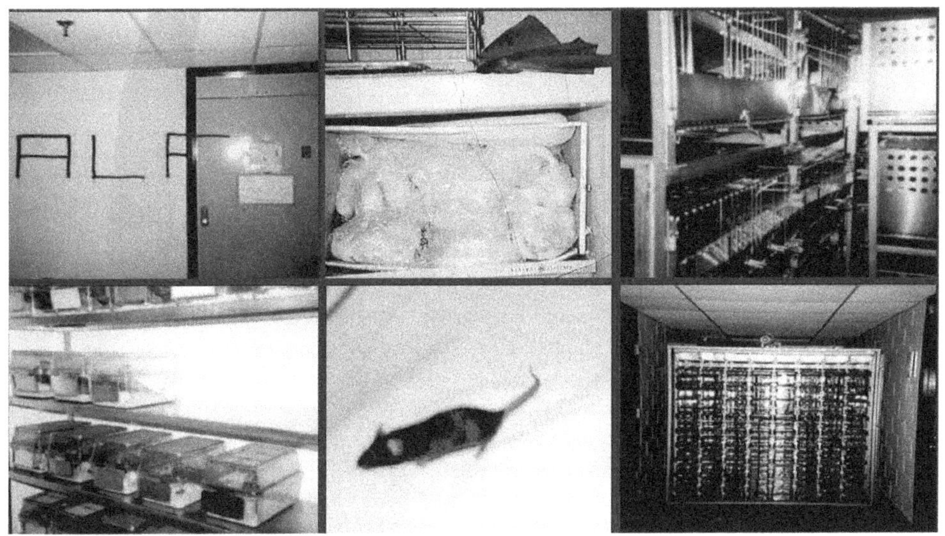

CONNECTICUT EGG FARM | 2006

March 25, 2006
Litchfield, CT
120 chickens liberated

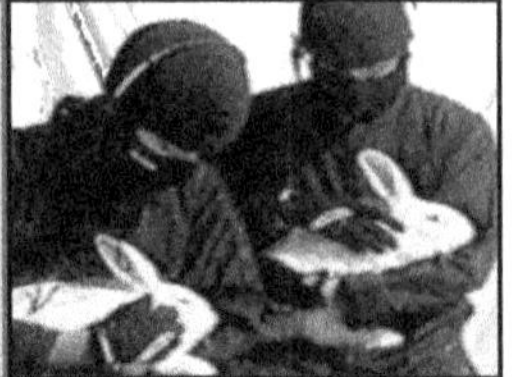

On the night of March 25th we entered an egg laying chicken farm in Litchfield CT and rescued 120 chickens from a lifetime of suffering. The chickens are now living in peace and comfort in a sanctuary where they will never again have to endure the terrible conditions of factory farms.

Chickens are highly intelligent, social creatures who experience pain and think, suffer, and feel happiness as humans do. Inspired by others, and guided by our hearts, we took action to liberate them from their horrendous suffering and can only hope to inspire others to take similar actions.

While we would like to see our above ground comrades strongly united in common cause, we feel obligated to express our disapproval of the Animal Liberation Press Office. We do not recognize their authority to speak for us, nor do we consider their views on violence representative of the underground animal liberation movement.

Until every cage and human prison is empty, for the Earth and the Animals.

LATZIG MINK RANCH | 2006

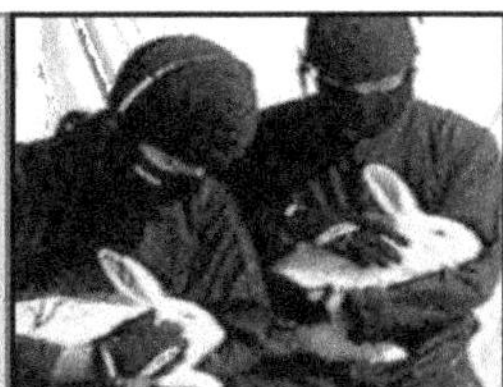

April 29, 2006
Howard Lake, MN
Entire breeding stock liberated

To all those who refuse to give in,

In the early morning hours of April 29th, our small band of dogooders made our way through muddy fields and wet forests to descend upon Latzig Mink Ranch in Howard Lake, MN. It has been ten years since the A.L.F. last visited this farm, and it has been too long since there has been a liberation.

Only the breeding animals were on the farm. After cutting several holes and opening [a] gate in the surrounding fence, we entered the main breeding shed. All of the breeding information was removed and destroyed. Every cage was opened, releasing hundreds of mink into the surrounding countryside.

Imprisoned in fur factories, these solitary creatures are forced to endure the intensive confinement of only a few square feet of cage, compared to the miles of territory these animals would enjoy in the wild - their natural state. Even if these animals die after being released into the wild, it is better there than at the hands of those who would otherwise imprison them and cause them to suffer.

It is better to die after a life of running free in the wild under starred skies while chasing their prey, as these animals are supposed to do, than to die a death brought about by gassing, anal electrocution, or snapping of the neck. How do you think these animals would prefer to die: after a lifetime running free in the wild under starry skies, or after a lifetime of confinement ended by a brutal murder of gassing, anal electrocution, or a snapped neck - a murder all for the profit and vanity of others.

Many of the mink scratched and paced in their cages, searching for ways to escape. We aided them by removing the nesting boxes and opening the cages. Initially, many of the mink had trouble walking because of the deplorable and cramped conditions of the cages. All cages contained at least two mink, but many contained several more. By the time we had finished, many had darted to the freedom that sat on the other side of a broken fence. We hope with all of our hearts that some of these beautiful creatures make it!

This is the second A.L.F. liberation in the midwest done in absolute solidarity with Peter Young, whose unparalleled bravery and determination serves as an inspiration to us all.

To all of those who smirk at the fate of Peter and other captured activists, remember this: we have broken, closed, and burnt down more of your farms, more or your labs, and more of your businesses than you have been able to capture activists. As in the case of Peter, for each year that one of us faces in prison, there will be an equal, if not greater, number of liberations in response. Your attempts at scaring us and making an example of our comrades will not work.

Finally, to all fur farmers, furriers, and profiteers of death, this is the last warning: close down your businesses, or with boltcutters, fire, and storm, we'll do it for you. You can try to scare us, you can try to imprison us, and you can even try to kill us, but the day we stop will be the day that the last animal has been freed from its cage.

Let the third and final part of Operation Bite Back commence!

For Absolute Liberation,
the A.L.F.

P.S. Peter, I hope this helps raise your liberation to letter ratio.

DELAWARE EGG FARM

2006

June 5, 2006
Unnamed location in DE
35 chickens liberated

This past weekend 35 hens were liberated from a large battery cage egg facility in Delaware. In the middle of the night we simply entered the unlocked facility (after scouting several locations), removed one to two hens from many different cages so as to give those who remained a tiny bit of extra space, and once all of the hens were set to go we were off into the night. As we moved across the grass outside they were eerily quiet, taking in the fresh night air for the first time in their lives. Each of these is a sentient being who up to this point has lived a life of pain and suffering, and now each has freedom and peace for the rest of its days.

To all of the old activists whose bandanas are dusty, and to all of the young ones who don't yet know how much is possible - get off of MySpace and get out on the farms, labs, and everywhere else where beings live in constant pain. You are their only chance.

Animal Liberation: don't call it a comeback, we've been here for years.

GRIGGSTOWN QUAIL FARM | 2006

December 20, 2006
Princeton, NJ
250 quail liberated

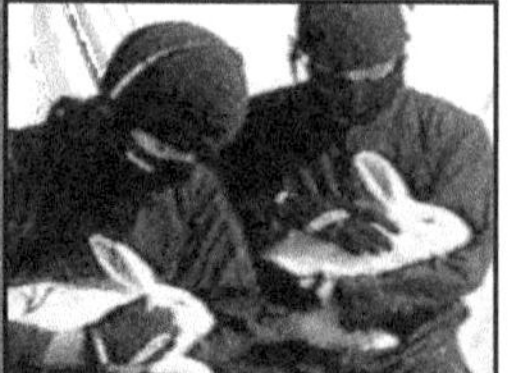

Last night we gave an early Christmas present to around two hundred and fifty of our friends at the Griggstown Quail Farm in Princeton, NJ. After clipping through the fencing we cut out large sections of the canopy covering three pens, then flushed several hundred quail, pheasants, and partridges out into the starry sky and freedom. The farm is located by a waterway and open fields, and we wish our friends the best of luck in establishing new lives.

To the animal abuse industry, welcome to post-Animal Enterprise Terrorism Act America: not one damn bit different.

Sincerely, the ALF

FBI seeks vandals who hit quail farm

Animal rights group claims responsibility

THE ASSOCIATED PRESS

NEWARK — The FBI is looking for animal rights activists who vandalized holding pens at a Somerset County quail farm, leading to the deaths of several dozen birds they released in the name of stopping animal cruelty.

CARPALOGICS | 2006

September 20, 2006
Gilbertville, MA
23 rabbits liberated

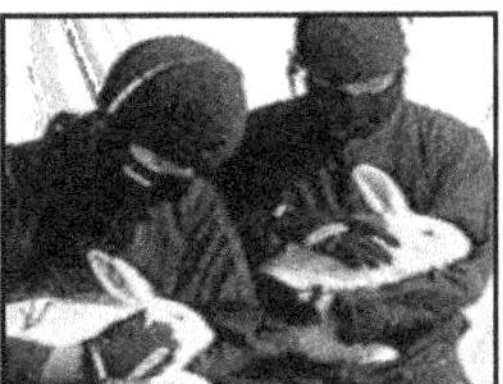

In honor of the SHAC-7, 23 rabbits have been liberated from Capralogics, a vivisection lab in rural Massachusetts. Jake, Lauren, Kevin, Andy, Josh, and Darius, as well as their 17 other lop-eared friends who have yet to be named, are all safe from the hands of those who had imprisoned and tortured them in the name of profit.

Capralogics is a small company that does contract testing on rabbits and goats in both the U.S. and the U.K. Some of the photos submitted with this communique, taken by a Capralogics employee in the U.S., show the way rabbits are treated by this terrible company - their bodies restrained in head-locks, their skin shaved off so they could be injected with various compounds. When the experiment concludes they are terminally bled, meaning they are cut and left to bleed until their life has drained away. Then, as the pictures show, they are thrown into the surrounding fields for coyotes to eat.

Of course, once we found out about this we could not let it continue without trying to rescue some of the animals. So in the middle of a warm, foggy night, we hopped the cheap fencing around Capralogics' property and entered one of their four rabbit housing sheds. There were no locks to pick, no windows to pry open, no doors to bust down - the sheds are open structures and we simply had to step over a gate to enter them. One by one we went down the rows of small cages, each containing a rabbit which had most likely never felt the sun on its fur or the grass beneath its paws. Every cage in the shed was opened and we took as many rabbits as we could, 23 total. Several other rabbits were let loose into the surrounding field. With luck they will live their last days in freedom, but even if they get caught or killed as least they have had one decent night in their otherwise tortured lives.

SHEPHERD'S EGG FARM | 2007

November 1, 2006
Spanish Fork, UT
102 chickens liberated

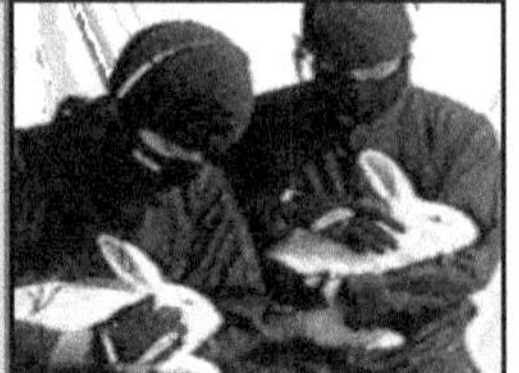

On the night of Thursday November 1st, the Animal Liberation Front entered a shed at Shepherd's Egg Farm near Spanish Fork, Utah to liberate as many hens as possible from this living hell.

In this single shed out of several, we saw literally tens of thousands of hens suffering in conditions even worse than we imagined.

Words cannot sufficiently capture this nightmare. They were so crowded in battery cages they could hardly move at all, let alone spread their wings. They all had significant feather loss from struggling to get through the wire cages to escape for their lives. Many birds had their heads or wings stuck in the wires of their cages, and were left to die because they could not reach any food or water.

Their beaks had been mutilated by factory workers. Everyday they must breathe in the overwhelming and disgusting stench from the mountains of manure below their cages. It should be no surprise that none of these birds receive one bit of veterinary care for their numerous injuries and diseases. There was a hole in the floor of the farm for workers to throw dead birds into a garbage can below (see footage). While the view inside Shepherd's Eggs was gruesome, it is in no way unique. These cruelties can be found in all modern egg farms, including so-called 'free range' facilities.

We moved quickly to remove as many birds as we could. We knew that Shepherd's Eggs cared so little about their birds that they would likely not even notice that they were gone. We took one or two from each cage, so the remaining chickens would have a little more room. The exploiters will try to scare consumers out of supporting this liberation by saying we increased a risk of some sort of biological contamination. This is a lie. We took every possible precaution to ensure we wouldn't harm the hens or ourselves, including being covered head to toe with all of the necessary bio-safety gear.

Altogether we rescued 102 hens. All hens received veterinary care and were placed in loving homes. They ran around their new homes with joy, appreciative of their first experience of freedom.

None were released into the wild. In their new homes they all have access to the outdoors. They can all breathe in fresh air. They are able to dust bathe and scratch the soil, instead of metal wires. They will all live out their full lifespan here instead of being killed when no longer profitable. In other words, these chickens can finally live like chickens.

All sentient animals, like these chickens, will always suffer as long as they are seen as nothing more than objects whose exploitation leads to increased profits and cheaper food. The only solution is to simply stop buying eggs and other animal products. Less than 1% of the hens at Shepherd's Eggs could be rescued today. It's up to consumers to save the other 99%.

Until consumers become responsible and stop paying the exploiters, you can count on the ALF to continue hurting their profits directly through property destruction and other forms of economic sabotage. Around the world the ALF is making progress and saving lives. This action is dedicated to all animal liberation prisoners including Barry Horne. Barry died six years ago today on a hunger strike. He would still be alive today if it wasn't for the stubborn cruelty of humanity. We will never forget Barry and we will never forgive the exploiters.

A.L.F.

MARR'S MINK RANCH

2007

November 6, 2007
Deming, WA
150 to 200 mink liberated

better late than never:

this delayed communique was inspired by the recent ALF action in Oregon.

in the early morning of November 6th, an estimated 150-200 mink were released from a fur farm on Cornell Creek Road off of highway 542 in northern Washington. this action was planned and carried out by a single activist working alone.

no excuses. do something.

SCRIPPS MERCY HOSPITAL

2008

February 10, 2008
San Diego, CA
Vivarium entered via unlocked door, 47 rats liberated

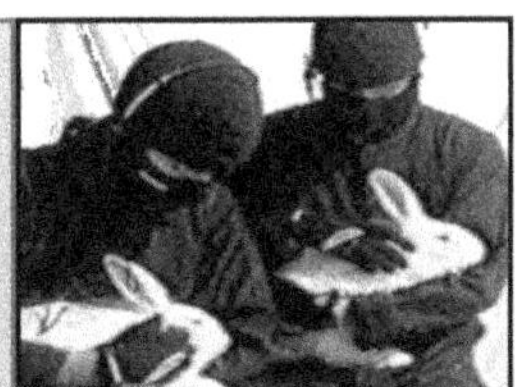

Recently, concerned citizens rescued 47 rats who were apparently part of a breeding program at Scripps "Mercy" Hospital in the Hillcrest area of San Diego. We entered through an unlocked door and found these beautiful innocent creatures living in squalor. Eight were crammed into each tiny barren cage. Their white fur was matted in urine and feces. Their babies were to be stolen from them and tortured in useless experiments, but now they are in loving homes where they will spend the rest of their lives as individuals, rather than research tools to be discarded when no longer necessary.

Who are the terrorists in this situation: those who peacefully rescue neglected beings from abuse and cruelty, or those who terrify, torture and destroy innocent life?

This recuse is dedicated to the brave people who speak out and more importantly act in support of direct action and rescue.

JEFFERSON FUR FARM | 2008

April 21, 2008
Jefferson, OR
40 mink liberated

We, the masked avengers of the Animal Liberation Front released around 40 Blue Iris mink from the breeding stock at Jefferson Fur Farm, 1477 SE Talbot Road, Jefferson, OR. Breeding records containing genetic history were also permanently destroyed. It will be a hard road ahead for these mink and their offspring, but with our help they now have a chance at survival.

These animals are not capitalist commodities to be bought and sold for fashion or vanity, but unique individuals deserving of liberation from human exploitation. Even if some of the mink do not make it we feel it is better to die free, then at the hands of their speciesist captors.

To the Posches, owners of Jefferson Fur Farm: Consider this your first warning. Tear down this death camp and let the mink live free. If you don't we will be back to finish the job.

To others concerned with the well-being of fellow living beings. First and foremost, go vegan. If you've been vegan for a while, it's time to start looking up animal abusers in your area and doing the research for how to effectively cripple them. Work in small affinity groups, be cautious always—macho never, and never give information if captured. It's time for animal rights to move beyond consumer sub-culture, towards an active liberation movement, which threatens the capitalist commoditization of life and the speciesist ideology itself.

We want to make it very clear that we will not be intimidated by the states continued witch hunt against the earth and animal liberation movements. Draconian prison sentences and repressive legislation will not deter us from our goal of total earth, animal, and human liberation. For every liberator you throw in prison, there will [be] two more to take her place. For every activist's house you raid, there will [be] ten times that many cages emptied. You can take our freedom, but you will never extinguish the flame that burns in our heart. Let your passion mirror the animal's oppression and our persecution.

A.L.F.-Cascadia

Feds investigate mink release at Jefferson farm

ALF claims credit and issues a threat; all animals caught

BY DENNIS THOMPSON JR. AND RUTH LIAO
Statesman Journal

Federal authorities were investigating the attempted release of about 50 mink by members of the Animal Liberation Front from a Jefferson farm, officials said.

FBI agents spent Wednesday morning gathering evidence at the Jefferson Fur Farm, agency spokeswoman Beth Ann Steele said.

The released mink were discovered about 6 a.m. Monday, Steele said. Farmworkers caught them all before they could get away.

"Guard dogs started barking right away, and the owners woke up and were able to recover the mink," Steele said.

A press release placed online Tuesday by the Animal Liberation Front contained an apparent threat against the farm's owners. It was signed by ALF-Cascadia.

"Consider this your first warning," it read. "Tear down this death camp and let the mink live free. If you don't, we will be back to finish the job."

The ALF is considered a domestic terrorist group by the U.S. Department of Justice, and its threats are taken seriously, Steele said.

The group's press release referred to them as "masked avengers" and acknowledged that some of the freed animals likely would not survive their release.

"It will be a hard road ahead for these mink and their offspring, but with our help, they now have a chance at survival," the release read. "Even if some of the mink do not make it, we feel is it better to die free than at the hands of their speciesist captors."

The Marion County Sheriff's Office is assisting in the investigation.

The perpetrators destroyed breeding records, said Teresa Platt, the executive director of Fur Commission USA.

Platt's Coronado, Calif.-based association represents mink farmers in 28 states and keeps track of ecoterrorist incidents. Platt estimated the loss of the records was $5,000.

"Everybody in Oregon and agriculture has probably gone on alert because of this," Platt said.

rliao@StatesmanJournal.com or (503) 589-6941

Online

See this story at **Statesman Journal.com** to read articles about 9,000 mink released from a Mount Angel farm in 1997.

MCMULLEN MINK FARM | 2008

August 19, 2008
South Jordan, UT
Over 600 mink liberated

This is a local soldier out of Utah just letting you guys know of a raid that just happened last night at the South Jordan, Utah McMullen Mink Farm, 300 plus mink were released with all their breeding records destroyed. Good news, haven't seen this done in a while so it had to be done.

RIPPIN MINK FARM | 2008

August 23, 2008
Aldergrove, BC
4000 mink liberated

On Saturday Aug 23, activists entered a mink farm in Aldergrove BC CANADA and released approx 4000 mink. The farm is next to Aldergrove Lake Park which provides over 200 acres of water habitat for them to survive. Operation Biteback is in full force, let these arrows be our tears......

Here are the addresses to other mink farms in the area. The ones which have stars are confirmed to have animals on them at this time and are in full operation.

6811 Bradner Rd Abbotsford BC
28945 McTavish Abbotsford BC
28340 Townshipline Rd Abbotsford BC
4764 Lefeuvre Rd Abbotsford BC
711 256th Aldergrove BC
25498 Fraser Hwy Abbotsford BC

Shut them down.

MULTIPLE TARGETS | 2008

2008
Numerous locations across Canada
33 birds liberated in five separate actions

We've been busy, sorry for not sending a report earlier!!

British Columbia, Canada: These actions were done over the past year:

Activists rescued 25 battery hens from 3 different farms on 3 different occasions. One farm where 17 hens were rescued, eggs were smashed and doors were ripped off the hinges, this farm is now closed down for undisclosed reasons.

Eight turkeys were also rescued from 2 different farms, on two separate locations.

None of these farms were locked and we encourage others to walk through their unlocked doors as well...

The Fraser Valley of British Columbia is a factory farm HELLHOLE and we will be back to save more lives from these animal terrorists!!

You'll here from us again, ALF

WORLDWIDE PRIMATES | 2008

September 10, 2008
Miami, FL
Outdoor pens cut open, 20 to 24 monkeys liberated

Late on September 10 we entered the compound of Worldwide Primates (16450 SW 180th Street, Miami, Florida) and cut large holes in 4 outdoor cages. Each cage held 5 or 6 monkeys.

There is no doubt that monkeys can survive in Florida. There are hundreds of wild monkeys in colonies across the state. Worldwide Primates is surrounded by fruit farms.

Worldwide Primates is the business of convicted baby orangutan smuggler Matthew Block. He spent one year in prison and then went back to work importing and selling primates to vivisection labs.

Mr. Block, we haven't forgotten you. Your work is still criminal in our eyes.

Animal Liberation Front

ASTORIA MINK FARM

2008

October 17, 2008
Astoria, OR
1500 mink liberated

In the early morning hours of October 17th, a lone activist infiltrated the fur farm at 92659 Simonsen Road in Astoria Oregon.

About 1,500 mink were released from their cages with at least 200 of these being breeding stock. The fact that there is no fence around this farm should help ease their escape.

This action is being claimed for the vegan straight edge community. not as a self-congratulatory ego boost, but in the vain hope that it might spur others into action. It has become apparent that the combined tactics of record collecting, sing-alongs, and militant posturing have failed to stop those who abuse innocent life. once we accept this then we can stop squandering our potential and choose a more effective plan of action.

I would like to close by offering a piece of advice to the owners of this farm, to the owners of the other farms in the Astoria, OR area (it was simply by luck of the draw that your farms weren't chosen), and to ALL fur farmers: find a new profession. fur farmers are a dying breed. get out before you are forced out.

"your laws will have no meaning past the setting of the sun."

-VSE

CANADIAN EGG FARM | 2008

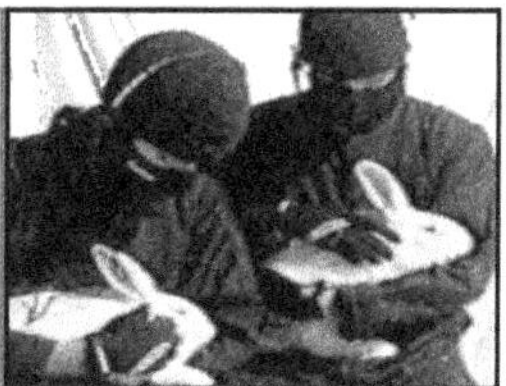

November 27, 2008
British Columbia
20 chickens liberated

On the night of Nov 27, 20 'free range' hens were liberated from a British Columbia egg farm. Activists entered the barn through an unlocked door and found the hens, many of them too weak to move while lying on the metal grated floor surrounded by other dead and dying birds. The hens are almost completely featherless, all of them have been debeaked right back to their nostrils, and their bottoms are swollen, infected and red.

Free range is not good enough, organic is not good enough, go vegan and leave the animals in peace.

This action was done in solidarity with the turkeys who were mutilated and dismembered on the Aviagen turkey farm in West Virginia which was exposed recently by undercover investigators. We will not stand for these constant attacks on our animal brothers and sisters, you will not get rid of us as we are only getting stronger.

ALF Canada

CSL GAME FARM | 2009

April 18, 2009
Corneltus, OR
Pheasants liberated

In the early hours of April, 18 2009, after making our way through muddy fields we descended upon CSL Game Farm (7401 NW Kerkman Rd, Cornelius, Oregon) a breeder of 'game birds' for the meat industry. Outdoor pens housing pheasants and quail were opened giving the birds a chance to escape into the night sky. The exact number that got away is unknown, but we hope it is many.

We reject the anthropocentric world view, which regards non-humyn animals as commodities — resources to be bought, sold and exploited for humyn interests.

We are not interested in 'welfarist' reforms for bigger cages and longer chains or menial legislation that only reinforces the status of non-humyn animals as 'property'. This is why we take direct action: to save the lives of animals here and now — not standing on the sidelines waiting for others to act, but realizing that the only thing standing between an animal and its freedom is a latch on the cage door.

This action was inspired by and carried out in solidarity with Utah grand jury resister Jordan Halliday and all those who refuse to compromise in defense of all life on this planet.

SCIENTIFIC RESOURCES INT'L | 2009

May 18, 2009
Reno, NV
Building torched, estimated $300,000 in damage

In the early morning hours of May 18th, four incendiary devices were planted at Scientific Resources International, a supplier of non-humyn primates for use in vivisection labs all over northern Nevada. The concept of animals existing as "resources" is utterly despicable, and we vow to do all in our power to run businesses like these into the ground. "For only a fool would cling to this world as it is" –ALF

Animal group claims credit for Reno blaze

BY SCOTT SONNER
ASSOCIATED PRESS

Animal rights activists have claimed responsibility for a fire that gutted the Reno business office of a company that ships monkeys from China for scientific research in the United States and elsewhere.

plier of non-humyn (sic) primates for use in vivisection labs all over northern Nevada," the message read. "The concept of animals existing as 'resources' is utterly despicable, and we vow to do all in our power to run businesses like these into the ground."

Vivisection labs are used

YLIPELTO'S FUR FARM | 2010

July 27, 2010
Astoria, OR
Eight incendiary devices planted: boat, car, forklifts, and a barn torched

We delivered eight incendiary devices to the lovely folks at Ylipelto's Fur Farm, at 92659 Simonsen Loop Road in Astoria on the morning of July 27th. It is nice to see that the enslavement, torture, and death of thousands of innocent creatures affords certain people luxuries like boats, nice cars, and various (expensive, no doubt) farm machinery, and we were more than happy to alleviate them of these. A careful attack sent structures up in flame both in the front and rear of the property, simultaneously. We hope that this can leave an impression on our friends, Veikko & Eeva, that making such a living off of the subjugation of sentient creatures (for something as selfish and disgusting as the fashion industry, no less) will not be tolerated. We hope that others like them will also consider where their priorities lie (the nearby Wilkinson & Stunkard farms, to name a couple), and decide whether or not they'd like to be next.

–Don't think that you'll be given a choice; your actions serve as your voice.

HARVEY BECK MINK RANCH

2010

September 9, 2010
Granite Falls, WA
400 mink liberated

In the early hours September 9th 2010 the ALF paid a visit to the Beck's fur farm in Granite Falls, WA. Thanks to the news reports we know that we released aprox. 400 of the mink there and all we can say is that it wasn't enough. We wish that there had been time that night to free all the prisoners that hell hole contains. We are heartbroken for everyone left behind but take solace in the fact that we will do better the next time.

This action is dedicated to one who will only be known as x/one blue/one brown/all heart/x

ALF

OREGON DEER FARM | 2010

October 9, 2010
Molalla, OR
Deer liberated from farm

On the morning of October 9th, we raided a deer farm located at 32155 S Grimm Road in Molalla, OR. A large section of fencing was stripped away allowing the captive deer herd a chance to escape into the surrounding forest. The venison meat industry remains small in this country, but as long as they exploit sentient animals, they will remain a target of the ALF. For the animals enslaved, mutilated, and murdered by this society: we will be tearing down the fences to set them free.

–Animal Liberation Front

VERMONT FARM | 2010

November 14, 2010
Unknown location in VT
20 turkeys liberated

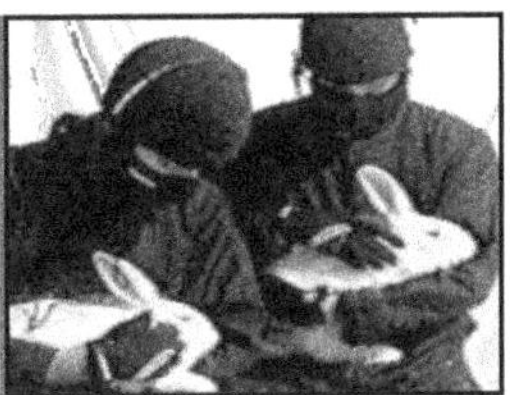

During the early morning hours of November 14th, members of VT ARM liberated 20 turkeys that had been cruelly forced into a small pen without shelter. The pen had been set up alongside a road as a marketing ploy. The decision to liberate the turkeys was made after it was learned that they were to be murdered that morning. It took the extraction team less than 5 minutes to breach the fence and liberate the turkeys. As a parting gift members of ARM slashed the tires of the mobile slaughterhouse, which had been parked less than 20 meters away, while the driver sat in the front seat smoking. Uncle Sam spent thousands training us to be the best and now those who think they can profit off the suffering of animals will learn that we are. We will use whatever means necessary to liberate animals, prevent cruelty and punish those who commit acts of cruelty. To the Bushway criminals, Happy Thanksgiving.

DAMASCUS ELK FARM | 2011

August 29, 2011
Clackamas, OR
Dozens of elk liberated

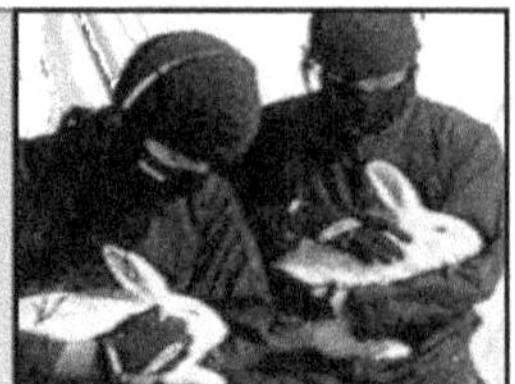

On the night of August 29th, a small band of animal liberationists crept quietly onto the property of Damascus Elk Farm located at 23255 SE Highway 212 in Clackamas, OR. This farm raises dozens of Roosevelt Elk for commercial slaughter. Once we made it to the elk pens, wire cutters were used to successfully remove a large section of fencing from one of the pens. Unfortunately due to a disturbance, we had to cut our action short and we were unable to open the remaining pens. The total number of animals (if any) that got away is unknown, but the intent of our action should be made perfectly clear: to prevent directly the violence that is inherent to animal agriculture and to liberate sentient animals back into their native habitat.
Across the country there are thousands of elk and deer being held captive on farms, waiting to be liberated back into the wild. These acts of liberation are generally low risk and can directly save the lives of animals. Elk and deer farms have little to no security and the small size of the industry makes these farms particularly vulnerable to sabotage.

With this act we attempted to remove the last barrier between these wild creatures and their new, free lives. Link by link, these barriers will be dismantled in our society, to create a new ethic of freedom and accountability. Assist us in the struggle for liberation, or stand on the wrong side of history.

For all those imprisoned.
-Animal Liberation Front

CARL SALO FUR FARM | 2011

September 24, 2011
Astoria, OR
Approximately 300 mink liberated

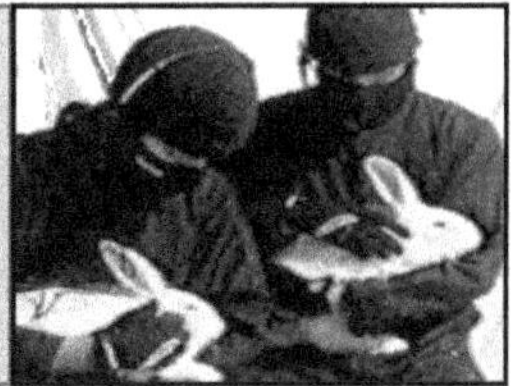

On the evening of September 24, we visited the mink farm on Savola Road in the outskirts of Astoria, Oregon, cutting holes in their fences before making our way through their sheds and opening cages.

Capitalism is cancerous and deadly to every life it comes into contact with. We're not interested in reforms and stall tactics, nor in the continuance of a culture that views lives as an economic resource.

On these cooling autumn nights we warm our fingers on the breeding records we took from your sheds and throw into our fire, and take comfort in seeing that some of us still have it in them to run into the wilderness beyond the fences.

For those whose sympathies lie with laws and commerce over lives, look around: retailers and restaurants are catching fire, windows are broken, tires slashed, and security costs are rising. Now might be a good time to consider another line of work.

This action was dedicated to the radical teachers, gardeners and foragers, to those embezzling from corporations, sharing indigenous skills, setting fires, molotoving cops, and all those working to challenge capitalism's deathgrip in their own communities. Your work inspires us.

Fewer calls to action, more action.
The Gordon Shumway Brigade

ROCKY MOUNTAIN FUR | 2011

September 26, 2011
Caldwell, ID
Building torched

In the early morning hours of September 26th, a visit was paid to the Rocky Mountain Firework & Fur Company, a shop that (quite foolishly) sells both highly flammable and explosive toys, and the chemically-treated skins of thousands of tortured animals (among some other nasty things, like trapping supplies). A hole was drilled into their storage space, and several gallons of fuel were pumped through, as well as multiple other charges being set beneath an adjoining structure. Ignition devices were set to finish up our work, once we were safely on our way.

By oppressing innocent life, you've lost your rights. We've come to take you down a notch. Stay in business, and we'll be back.

Yours truly,
The Arson Unit

Activists Say They Set Fire at Idaho Fur Seller

BY JOHN MILLER
Associated Press

BOISE • Animal rights activists said they pumped fuel into an Idaho fur and fireworks retailer before imal Liberation Front, Vlasak said. They warned that the store must close its doors permanently.

"Stay in business, and we'll be back," their message said.

MILLER'S MINK RANCH | 2011

October 12, 2011
Gifford, WA
1000 mink liberated

In the early morning hours of October 12th, we entered Miller's Mink Ranch on Addy-Gifford Road in Washington, and took down every breeder card in one of the two large, main sheds. We opened approximately 3/4 of the cages, many of which had more than one animal, freeing more than a thousand animals. We also took 3 individuals and released them at different locations.

We chose to do this not because we believe that humans wearing fur is inherently wrong. Rather we think that the callous disrespect with which the fur industry treats the animals is despicable. The fact that it has become an 'industry' for the vanity and fashion of the rich is what we hate. In the Pacific NW the fur industry represents more than just animal abuse and species-ism. Trapping, killing, and skinning fur bearing mammals for profit was one of the first steps of westward expansion and manifest destiny in this area. It was one of the first parts of the colonial process that decimated many Native people and cultures. The fact that the fashion and fur industries point to Native people wearing fur as their justification of the factories of death is inexcusable. These people responsible have no personal or cultural ties to the native people who were here first, in fact, they are a part of the system that destroyed their way of life. The current way of 'farming' mink, fox, bobcat, and lynx does not bear any similarity or have any hint of the same respect for life and nature that the native tribes and cultures around here have.

We are not asking for better conditions for farmed mink, for a more humane way of caging wild beings. Mink are fiercely territorial animals in the wild, with territories that can be miles long, usually along waterfronts where they can swim and hunt fish and small mammals. This freedom is their birthright as wild creatures. The approximately 2 square feet in which Miller's Mink Ranch cages two and sometimes three mink for the whole of their lives is unspeakable. It is unfortunately the standard for mink farms the world over. The agony and frustration at never feeling more than wire under paws that were meant for swimming and pursuing prey can only be wondered at. Some mink's fervor for freedom is so great they bite the wires of their cages until they break their teeth.

We would like to dedicate this act to every rebel warrior who died nameless and whose rage and bravery went unseen and unknown, to all who struggle against oppression, even with no light at the end of the tunnel in sight.

VERMONT FARM | 2011

November 16, 2011
Unknown location in VT
Second rescue at this "road side holding pen," 18 birds liberated

During the early morning hours of November 16, VTARM members liberated 16 turkeys and 2 geese from a road side holding pen. The same location had been visited the previous year. Power to the lights surrounding the outside holding pen was cut by the security team and two cameras installed after last year's visit were removed. The extraction team utilizing NVGs cut the fence and liberated 16 turkeys. In addition the security team disabled 2 ATVs and liberated 2 geese located during the visit. In all the operation took less than 10 minutes. We enjoyed our visit "farmer Bob" now consider yourself out of business, you don't want us coming back for a third time. We will use whatever means necessary to liberate animals, prevent cruelty and punish those who commit acts of cruelty. This liberation is dedicated to Walter Bond and all of the other political prisoners: you are in our thoughts and actions every day, thank you and happy thanksgiving!

HARRIS RANCH | 2012

January 8, 2012
Coalinga, CA
Largest feedlot & slaughterhouse in California targeted, 14 trucks torched

At about 3:40 am on sunday, january 8th, 14 cattle trucks caught fire at the harris feeding company in coalinga, ca. containers of accelerant were placed beneath a row of 14 trucks with 4 digital timers used to light 4 of the containers and kerosene-soaked rope carrying the fire to the other 10 (a tactic adapted from Home Alone 2 [if you're going to try this make sure to use kerosene, gasoline dries too quickly]). we weren't sure how well this was going to work, so we waited until there was news reports before writing this. we were extremely pleased to see that all 14 trucks "were a total loss" with some being "completely melted to the ground."

we're not going to use this space to expound upon the horrors and injustices of factory farming. there is more than enough armchair-activists and those of passive politics who are more than willing to do that (anything to keep from getting their hands dirty). we, the unsilent minority (the 1%, if you will), choose a more direct form of action.

we're not delusional enough to believe that this action will shut down the harris feeding company, let alone have any effect on factory farming as a whole. but we maintain that this type of action still has worth, if not solely for the participant's peace of mind, then to show that despite guards, a constant worker presence, and razorwire fence, the enemy is still vulnerable.

finally, to all those who fantasize and romanticize about direct action yet remain on the fence: there is a lot of stuff that needs to be destroyed and we can't count on spontaneous combustion and careless welders to do all the work.

until next time…

MULTIPLE TARGETS | 2012

January & February, 2012
Oregon & Washington
Nine chickens liberated from two farms in Oregon & Washington

Some small actions:

January 2012: 6 hens were removed from an intensive egg farm located in the Willamette Valley of Oregon.

February 2012: 3 chickens were rescued and re-homed from a broiler farm in Washington state.

Escaping the horrors of the factory farm, these individuals will live out the remainder of their lives in freedom in open fields.

Solidarity with non-cooperating green scare prisoners and those on the run.

Every life counts,
ALF

QUEENER RIDGE PHEASANT CO. | 2012

March 14, 2012
Scio, OR
75 to 150 pheasants liberated from canned hunt breeder

Last night, the night of March 14th, we infiltrated the property Queener Ridge Pheasant Company (40485 Queener Drive, Scio, OR) which breeds ringneck pheasants primarily to be murdered in commercial canned hunts. After jumping a barbed wire fence, we made our way to the main breeding facility where we dismantled a huge section of an aviary that held between 75-150 pheasants; liberating them into the night sky. Although the number of animals freed represented only a tiny fraction of the thousands more still held captive on this farm, we feel that every life saved–no matter how few–is a victory.

Ringneck pheasants are a naturalized species to this region and are specifically bred to retain their wild characteristics and instincts, so we have no doubt that these animals can survive in the wild upon release. Otherwise doomed to a life of confinement and brutality these sentient animals now have a fighting chance at survival.

For an industry whose only purpose is the infliction of violence against sentient animals for entertainment and pleasure, the only ethical choice we can make is to set your animals free.

Against all domination,
–Animal Liberation Front

OREGON EGG FARM | 2012

Mid-May, 2012
Willamette Valley, OR
Four chickens liberated

During the second week of May 2012, two activists entered an egg farm located in the Willamette Valley of Oregon. 4 hens were removed from the premises and placed in good homes where they will live out the rest of their natural lives. This is the same farm where 6 hens were liberated last January.

This action was done to save these individual animals from the torture and misery intrinsic to industrialized egg production, as well as to demonstrate that although we may not be able to free every animal, we can free some. This was done in full solidarity with the anarchists and animal liberationists facing state repression here on the west coast and abroad.

Freeing the prisoners.

ALF

**We are intentionally omitting the name, address, and specifics of the farm targeted. The relatively small number of animals taken will most likely, once again, go unnoticed by the farmer and will hopefully allow us to take advantage of the non-existent security on this farm for future raids and investigations.

D&S FOX FARM | 2012

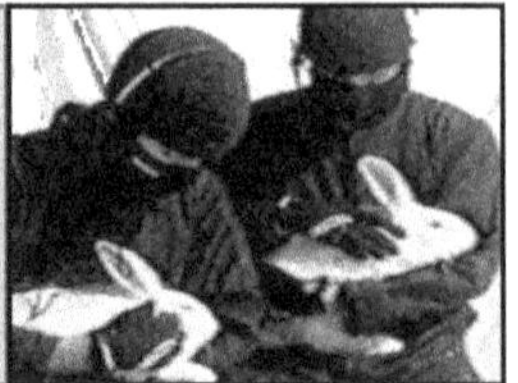

August 5, 2012
Elkton, VA
13 foxes liberated

On the night of August 5, the Animal Liberation Front visited the only known fur farm in the state of Virginia, Scott Dean's D&S Fox Farm in Elkton. We opened every one of the few cages at D&S, giving thirteen beautiful foxes a chance at new lives in the nearby Shenandoah National Park.

As we watched a few of them immediately scurry off to freedom, we damaged the machinery that allows Dean to continue his day-to-day operation confining and torturing these sensitive creatures.

Dean, it appears that this is a hobby providing you only supplementary income – it is our commitment to free your prisoners and cost you more than you make until you shut down.

To those nationwide who also seek justice for the innocent, your nearest fur farm is at most a state away.

Take action for animals.
-ALF

PRIMROSE PHEASANT FARM

2012

September 21, 2012
Canby, OR
Dozens of pheasants liberated

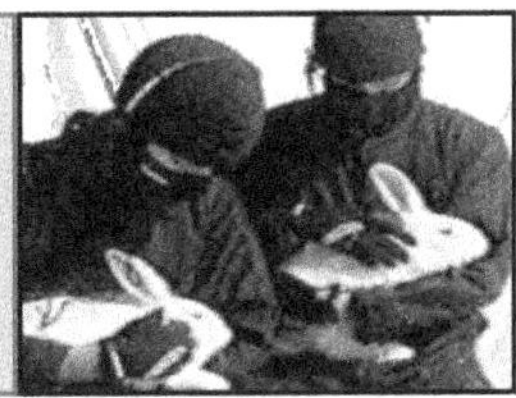

On the night of September 21, 2012, saboteurs tore open a lone flight pen located at the newly incorporated Primrose Pheasant Farm (27368 S. Primrose Path Canby, Oregon), releasing dozens of slaughter-bound ring-necked pheasants into the countryside.

Naturalized populations of ring-necked pheasants have resided in the Willamette Valley for hundreds of years and the surrounding farmland serves as ideal habitat that these captive bred non-domesticated birds can undoubtedly survive in. Destined otherwise to be killed by butchers and sport hunters, these sentient beings will now get the chance to live out the rest of their natural lives in the wild.

For the silent ones..
A.L.F.

ASH GROVE PHEASANT FARM | 2013

July 22, 2013
Riverside, CA
Unknown number of pheasants liberated

On the night of July 22, the masked rescuers of the Animal Liberation Front entered the Ash Grove Pheasant Farm at 10540 Victoria Avenue in Riverside, California. As the farmer slept just feet away, the fencing was torn open with wire cutters. Four of the six pens on the property were breached, giving these beautiful beings a chance at freedom.

Wildlife farms are everywhere. Their victims can be immediately released, with no rehoming necessary. This life saving action took no specialized skill, less than twenty-four hours of planning, and fifty dollars. With basic tools and determination, anyone is capable of destroying the barrier that stands between an animal and their freedoms.

Stop fraternizing about it. Stop fantasizing about it. Stop frightening yourself out of it. You know you want to – just do it. Wild non-humyns await their release from prisons in your neighborhoods.

'For only a fool would cling to this world as it is,'
A.L.F.

SHELLI FRAZIER FUR FARM | 2013

July 27, 2013
Plains, MT
One bobcat liberated

In the early morning hours of July 27, the Animal Liberation Front visited the property of Shelli Frazier at 6934 Highway 200 in the town of Plains, Montana, completely surrounded by the beautiful Lolo National Forest. Frazier applied in 2006 for a permit to imprison bobcats on her property in a fur farm that she hoped would eventually grow to sixty cats. Despite already making a living breeding horses, she perhaps felt that this could be a lucrative side business. We arrived at her unpublished address determined to correct her mistake, and watch her investments run free into the wilderness.

Exploration of the site revealed that the force of economics had already precluded any need for the force of boltcutters – strewn about this disgusting and decrepit property were large empty cages, the rusted remains of Shelli Frazier's dreams.

It was not until we checked every single run in an empty cat hutch tucked at the back of the northern lot that we found the tragic consequences of her business ineptitude. In one of the runs, huddling against the back wall, surrounded by rotting food, mildewed wood, and his own feces, was a lone bobcat.

The sight of a creature so majestic in a state so pathetic cannot be done justice with words. We have yet been unable to determine why Frazier kept him and him alone, but if it was a sense of sentimentality, it certainly was not evident from his treatment. Emaciated and filthy, his beauty was evident even through the matted fur and traumatized stare, with his bushy jowls and black ear tufts. To be in such proximity to this creature, staring into his haunting yellow eyes, changed every member of our cell. We could only speculate as to how he had suffered and what he had seen, but we could know with certainty that he deserved a shot at freedom. We opened his cage and left.

Shelli Frazier is not the only cruel human ever to keep such noble cats in tiny cages in Lolo National Forest. More than two decades ago, Rodney Coronado visited Cole MacPherson's bobcat prison in the town of Lolo just an hour's drive south of Plains. MacPherson's farm was Frazier's fantasy – a shed of sixty pacing, neurotic, traumatized large cats. Though he was forced to close shop around 2005, the ALF still keeps tabs on MacPherson – today, he continues his dental practice in Missoula. This should be a lesson to Frazier. If you ever again hold wild creatures captive on your land, we will breach it to free them.

Animal Liberation Front

Additionally, though we generally avoid airing internal issues in communications such as this, we felt that this small action, unlikely to attract media attention, would be appropriate to do so: As an ALF cell, we adhere strictly to the guidelines, including a policy of total nonviolence. Because of our desire not to be misrepresented to the media in this regard, we have in the past very clearly requested that NAALPO not publicize or speak to the press about certain actions of ours. NAALPO has flagrantly disregarded our wishes in this regard. When a press office claiming to represent the ALF directly scoffs at the requests of the ALF, this should be a scandal within the animal rights movement. Those of us underground risk our freedom and sometimes lives rescuing animals; the least we can expect is a press office that is responsive to us. We regret having to hash this out here, but due to our anonymity we have no other recourse. We hope that NAALPO will respect our wishes in the future – it seems to us that its very legitimacy would hinge on this.

CINDY MOYLE FUR FARM | 2013

July 28, 2013
Burley, ID
2400 mink liberated

On the evening of July 28, 2013, friends of wildlife entered the Burley, Idaho, mink farm of Fur Commission USA Board Member Cindy Moyle, compromised the perimeter fencing, and set up roving surveillance of the on-site night watchman. We then liberated the entirety of her breeding stock into the wild, emptying over twenty-five percent of this wildlife prison.

Illuminated in the moonlight, 2400 of these wild creatures climbed out of the cages where they had passed their entire lives in isolated darkness, to feel the grass under their feet for the first time. Their initial timidity quickly became a cacophony of gleeful squealing, playing, cavorting, and swimming in the creek that runs directly behind the Moyle property. They will live out their new lives along the Snake River watershed.

Cindy Moyle is a current Board Member, and former Treasurer, of the Fur Commission USA. After the recent leadership shuffling in FCUSA, we felt that the Moyle Mink Ranch would be perfect to test out the efficacy of FCUSA's new emphasis on farm security.The Moyles are a mink dynasty in Idaho, operating up to eight farms, their own in-house feed operation, and a tannery. Those doubtful of our resourcefulness and guile have in the past called the Moyle farms impenetrable. Indeed, this is the first time that anyone has attempted action against one of them.

Having now had the pleasure of testing them ourselves, we wholeheartedly approve of the new FCUSA security guidelines. We are happy to see FCUSA members increasing their overhead on security – it means they are only that much closer to bankruptcy when we raid their farms. In the case of the Moyles, the breeding records we destroyed represent over thirty years of painstaking genetic selection. There will be no recovering these genetic lines.

Aside from their operations harming helpless animals, the Moyles have also been federally investigated for exploiting undocumented workers and trafficking endangered species. Mike Moyle, ex-mink farmer and the current Idaho House Majority Leader, has used his political position to block Idaho neighborhoods from being able to declare his family's foul and fly- infested prisons to be public nuisances.

The fur industry will no doubt propagate falsehoods regarding this act of kindness.

They will claim that we are terrorists. We say that if peacefully opening cages is an act of terrorism, then the word has no meaning. It is appropriately applied to the mass imprisonment and killing of wild animals.

They will claim that these mink are domesticated animals and will starve. Documentation on the success of farm-bred mink in the wild is extensive, so we will add only our experience watching these naturally aquatic animals, who had spent their entire lives in cages, head instinctively for water and begin to swim and hunt.

They will claim that conditions on mink farms are humane. We ask why, then, they try only to hide those farms from the public, pushing for legislation to criminalize the taking of photographs. The mink that we freed from the Moyles lived in intensive confinement in their own waste. Their suffering was plain to the eye, and their yearning for freedom plain to the soul.
They will say that our raid may inspire copycat actions. We say that it undoubtedly will. It is a glorious thing that we live in a world where individuals regularly demonstrate the ultimate act of compassion – risking their freedom for the freedom of others.

They will say that we will not stop short of the complete and total end of the killing of animals for their fur. On this point we are in total agreement.

We act with love in our hearts.

EE WILSON WILDLIFE AREA

August 15, 2013
Corvallis, OR
5 pheasants liberated

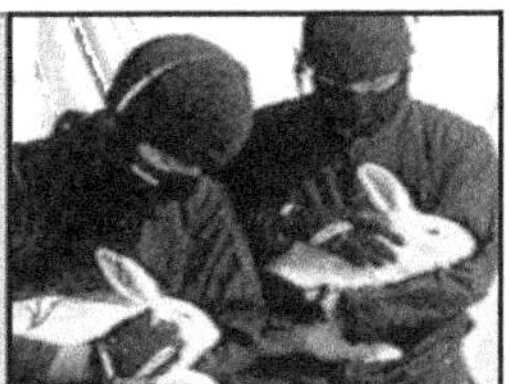

On the night of August 15th the masked liberators of the Animal Liberation Front carried out the rescue of wild pheasants and quail from the Oregon Department of Fish and Wildlife game bird exhibition pens at the EE Wilson wildlife area (north of Corvallis). Wire cutting tools were used to completely cut open 2 of the game bird pens and partially cut open 2 others giving 3 ringnecked pheasants, 1 white pheasant, and 1 mountain quail a chance to escape into the surrounding wildlife area. If it wasn't for a car pulling into a lot next the pens, forcing us to make a premature departure, the rest of the dozen or so birds would have been given a chance at freedom as well. This action is no victory for those left behind.

The EE Wilson wildlife area was once home to an ODFW breeding program that bred pheasants mainly to be released to repopulate state hunting grounds. The ODFW discontinued this program in the late 1990's, however they still keep a small number of birds on this site as a tourist attraction. It is sad and pathetic that these wild birds would have to spend their entire lives in a cage for any reason, let alone for something as trivial and frivolous as being put on display for the public.

There are over 100 registered captive wildlife facilities in the state of Oregon that imprison pheasants, quail, mink, elk and other wild animals. These facilities generally contain little to no security, require little to no specialized skill set to raid, and hold animals which in many cases can be directly liberated into the wild. All it takes is a little determination and a $15 pair of bolt cutters to make animal liberation a reality.

In solidarity with anarchist prisoners Marie Mason and Eric Mcdavid. For the silent ones and all those on the run.

For freedom and dignity,
Animal Liberation Front

ROYAL OAK FUR FARM | 2013

August 26, 2013
Simcoe, Ontario
750 mink and 50 foxes liberated

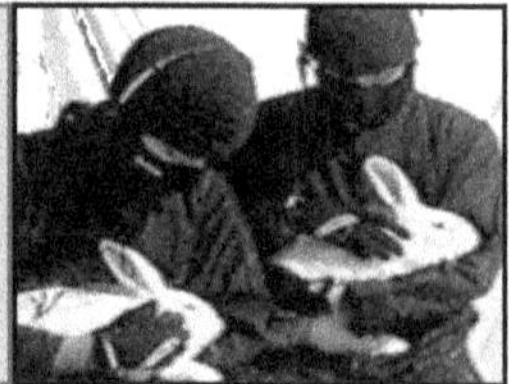

In the early morning of August 26, 2013, the ALF raided Royal Oak Fur Farm in Simcoe, Ontario. We approached the fur farm and laid down in the tall grass so we could watch the guard's building for any sign of movement. Once we were satisfied it was empty, we cut the bands that attach the chainlink fence to the poles and then tore a large area of fence down at the back of the farm and opened the front gate. We estimate we released about 750 mink and 50 fox. The fox almost seemed to understand what was happening because once they realized they were free, they wasted no time leaving their cages and escaping through the holes we made in the fence. After the fur farmers house lights flicked on, we quickly started pulling off breeding cards and tossing them around the empty cages, and then made our retreat through the corn fields with a noisy group of mink experiencing their first taste of freedom. We won't stop until this, and all fur farms are empty. - ALF

RYKOLA MINK FARM | 2013

September, 2013
Ebensburg, PA
Unknown number of mink liberated, breeding records destroyed

Last night, the Animal Liberation Front opened hundreds of cages at the Rykola mink farm located at 557 Colver Road in Ebensburg, Pennsylvania. We lost count of the number of wild animals freed into their natural environment, due to the animals being housed in atrocious conditions, four to tiny cob-webbed cages. Words cannot describe the filth and blinding stench of this farm.

As expected, the animals wasted no time escaping from their barren prisons into the natural world.

In addition to opening cages, we destroyed hundreds of breeding cards, many with notations of price, which ran from $1,000 up to $10,000 per animal.

We want to reiterate, as several recent ALF communiques have, the ease of animal liberation. We possess no specialized skill set or expensive tools. A sense of determination and a desire for justice go a long way.

Pelting season is just weeks away. Look up *The Final Nail* and find a farm near you. Let the final stage of Operation Bite Back commence. We can destroy this industry that has destroyed so many.

OVARD MINK FARM | 2013

September 13, 2013
Wanship, UT
20 mink liberated

THIS FRIDAY THE 13TH WAS AN UNLUCKY ONE FOR HAROLD OVARD AS HE AWOKE TO HIS BLOODY BUSINESS HAVING BEEN RAIDED BY A MINK LIBERATION BRIGADE WARRIOR.

BREEDING RECORDS DESTROYED, 20 MINK LIBERATED FROM A HELL OF HUMANITY'S MAKING.

FOR T, K, AND ALL PRISONERS OF THIS WAR.

LIBERATE!

– ANONYMOUS

ABBOTSFORD MINK FARM | 2013

October 2, 2013
Abbotsford, British Columbia
800 cages opened at mink farm

During the early hours of Wednesday, October 2, the Animal Liberation Front raided a mink farm near Lefeuvre and Downes Road in Abbotsford, about an hour from Vancouver. The entire perimeter fence at the back of the farm was cut before over 800 cages were opened to allow the mink a chance to escape to freedom.

The surrounding ecosystem was ideal mink habitat, marshlands and dense forest where the animals made a swift escape.

Contrary to popular belief, the Canadian mink industry is anything but humane. The cages the mink were locked in were full of feces and mostly rusted shut. Mink living in cages together had fought and plenty of the animals were covered in severe wounds. Some cages had dead animals, clearly left for weeks.

A myth put out by the mink industry claims that they cannot survive in the wild, once released but that was proved as just myth when a BC Wildlife Biologist stated that no one could tell him that they would not survive in the wild. This was a direct quote from a Vancouver Sun Article, published just after the release.

We stand in solidarity with the brave few who have taken direct action to free mink across the United States and Canada this year. Let this continue. Pelting season is still weeks away and the time to empty cages is now. The farmhouse we raided was only 50 feet from the barns. Do not let the closeness of the farmhouse deter you from liberating animals. They need it now more than ever.

To those who say the animal liberation movement is dead, think again. How can animal liberation be dead if the Animal Liberation Front is forever?

You cannot kill an idea, and we will not be ruled by fear.

Until every cage is empty,
The Animal Liberation Front

MYHRE MINK FARM | 2013

October 7, 2013
Grand Meadow, MN
250+ mink liberated

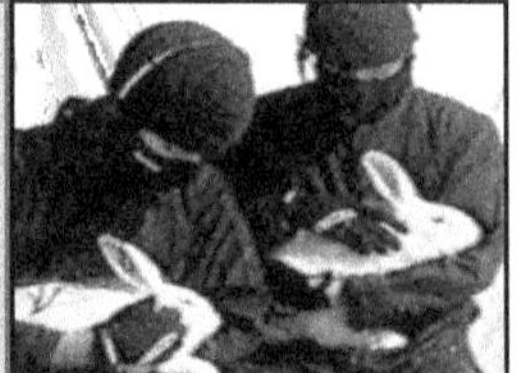

On October 7th, an individual working alone emptied a mink shed at the Myhre Mink Farm on Highway 16 in Grand Meadow, Minnesota. At least 250 fur-bearers ran to the lake directly behind the property. These animals needed very little help to freedom. As the cages were being unlatched, many of the individuals pawed it open themselves to make a dash. They are not domesticated and their spirits are not broken. Many of these mink screeched loudly at the sight of human hands, having only known the murderous hands of Einar Myhre. The only thing keeping these animals imprisoned is our own fear and a simple latch on a cage. A wild existence for them is only feet away. Make animal liberation a reality.

This is the ninth U.S. fur farm raid of the year. This level of activity has not been seen for nearly twenty years.

To the fur farmers of the world, we have nothing to say to you. We offer only this prayer: The rest is secrets. Silence now. If night has fallen, sleep well.

HOME OF NAFA EXECUTIVE | 2013

August 26, 2013
Sun Prairie, WI
House flooded

Around 7:00am on August 26, a cell of the Animal Liberation Front entered the backyard of Brian L. MacMillan, 1245 Mockingbird Lane in Sun Prairie, Wisconsin. Brian is the Vice President of Wild Fur Operations at North American Fur Auctions, the largest fur auction house in North America. Brian is a terrorist who deals in the skins of wild animals tortured and killed in steel-jaw leghold traps. The counter-terrorists of the Animal Liberation Front broke his double paned window, and inserted his own garden hose; completely flooding his home.

Most people would be amazed at the sight of a bobcat, a creature so majestic and free. Brian's empty heart sees only profit.

There is no doubt Brian and NAFA will attempt to portray themselves as victims. They have the audacity to call us terrorists, when every penny they have made is at the torture and subjugation of what is wild and free. All who contribute to industries of earth and animal destruction shall take note. There is a higher law.

Animal Liberation Front

DOYLE CHECKETTS MINK FARM | 2013

November 14, 2013
Craig, CO
200 mink liberated, farm subsequently shut down

On the night of November 14th, the Earth Liberation Front visited the previously unknown Colorado mink farm of Monte Ages, located at 622 Valley View Drive in Moffat County. This is one of the smallest mink farms in operation, so opening nearly every cage took very little time. The mink understood our mission and quite literally flew to the ground to make a dash for freedom. To cause the deranged Mr. Ages more financial trouble, breeding cards were removed and strewn about, and thrown in the piles of mink waste.

Michael Whelan will offer the same tired lies in response to this action. He advises farmers to 'sympathize with the poor, lost animals.' The lost wild animals who are now able to move freely, who will no longer be subject to Michael and his friends preferred methods of execution in the pelting season just two weeks away.

The truth is that mink are not domesticated. They are captive bred, and only for the quality of their pelts. Mink are aquatic animals who are solitary in the wild and travel several miles per day. The surrounding area of Moffat County is pristine wildlife habitat. The ones who escaped this wildlife prison will now live out their lives along the Little Snake and Yampa Rivers.

Mr. Ages has plans to move and expand his operation to 35591 North Hwy 13 in the town of Craig. This will not be tolerated. Your dreams of despoiling Northwest Colorado, contaminating our drinking water, and exploiting native american wildlife will turn into a nightmare. There will be consequences when darkness falls.

We send a salute to those courageous few who continue to fight alongside the earth and animals, even as your work is overshadowed by the bloggers, video editors, and all manner of self-aggrandizing activists.

FRASER FUR FARM | 2014

March 7, 2014
Ronan, MT
Breeding records destroyed at largest known wildcat farm in the US.

In the early morning hours of March the 7th, anonymous individuals breached the property lines of Fraser Fur Farm, a target of anti-fur activists and compassionate individuals for nearly a quarter century. Our motives were borne of a fierce love for wildlife, and a torn heart forced to watch as bobcats and other wild creatures have been made to endure intense confinement and the inevitable fate of a horrendous death at the hands of those who seek to profit from their skins. Fur-farming is a truly despicable industry, and the neck-breaking, rib-cage stomping, anal-electrocutions, and gas chambers must be put to an end by all those with love and courage in their hearts.

After entering the compound, we quickly discovered various methods of security deterrence, including motion-sensor floodlights, fortified fencing, active guard dogs and two houses on-site, one of which say less than 100 feet from the bobcat pens which were our target. Nonetheless, our task was to disrupt as best we could the fate which awaits these fur-bearing animals. Upon entering the bobcat enclosures, we viewed these majestic creatures reduced to market commodities and felt shame that such humans would bestow an existence like this. Some cowered toward the backs of their cages; others slowly inched toward us, curious as to the motives of these last-night visitors; and still others quickly began thrashing about, violently throwing their bodies as a clear expression of the torment inherent in their captivity. Now is our time to lend a hand toward their freedom, and return to the wild.

We quickly began the process of destroying all breeding records. This non-violent act is to ensure the loss of irreplaceable genetic lines, rendering the breeding stock of a given fur-producing business lost. It is with tremendous sadness in our hearts that despite our best efforts, cages were unable to be opened before being run off-site by awoken residents.

This act was meant not to inflict violence against those who profit from this business, or to instill fear and terror in a world already rife with such things. But simply as a gesture of solidarity and love toward those trapped in cages. We, and all others born with enduring compassion in their hearts, will continue to risk freedom in service to others, so long as captivity and violence is the status-quo. We hope and pray for the day when those who reap profits at the expense of all that is sacred will be made to stop the violence, until the last fur farm meets its end.

For all those, human and non-human, continuing to struggle for dignity and peace on occupied land.

ROBERT ROMAN FOX FARM | 2014

September 25, 2014
Anamosa, IA
30 foxes liberated

The Animal Liberation Front is taking responsibility for the release of 30 foxes from a fur farm in Anamosa, Iowa in the late-evening of Thursday, September 25th 2014. 10 years after the 2004 raid of the University of Iowa, the ALF has returned to east-central Iowa.

The farm targeted was:

Robert Roman
23778 Fairview Road
Anamosa, IA 52205

The majority of fencing on the farm's east and west sides were stripped away. The fencing on the north was enveloped in heavy brush and unlikely to be a point of passage, while the south abutted a shed retrofitted with living quarters, with lights on and a car outside, indicating we were not alone.

An advantage of releasing foxes over mink is that foxes are silent. As a result, the proximity of fox pens to a farmer's house is irrelevant, as we have shown.

Future visitors to fox farms should be aware that foxes are extremely timid. Unlike mink they should be encouraged to exit their cages as a vital ingredient of any fox rescue.

A point worth repeating: This entire action required $40 in gas, $20 in tools, and only a few hours to execute.

The past two years has seen a tenfold increase in the number of known fox farm addresses. The animal liberation movement is now in an unprecedented position to wipe out fox farming in the United States. Fox farms represent the softest of targets for these reasons:

• Fox farms are small, with animal numbers usually in the dozens.
• Foxes are silent (mentioned above).
• Foxes are rarely a primary income source for farmers, who can be more easily persuaded to discontinue fox farming.
• There are under 150 fox farms known to exist.

Foxes are genetically wild. There is a large and thriving wild fox population in Iowa. We encourage the media to maintain their professional integrity by seeking comment from actual wildlife biologists about the survivability of farm-raised fox, not fur farmers or their trade groups.

To be clear, our mission extends far beyond fur. We aim to eradicate all animal-exploitation industries – meat, dairy, egg, animal research, and beyond. We encourage the public to adopt a vegan diet first; raid farms second.

A final message to activists: The ALF doesn't need your passive support. We need your active participation.

Animal Liberation Front

Dedicated to accused mink rescuers currently under federal indictment in the United States, and activists making history in Eastern Europe.

EE WILSON WILDLIFE AREA | 2014

December 28, 2014
Corvallis, OR
3 pheasants liberated

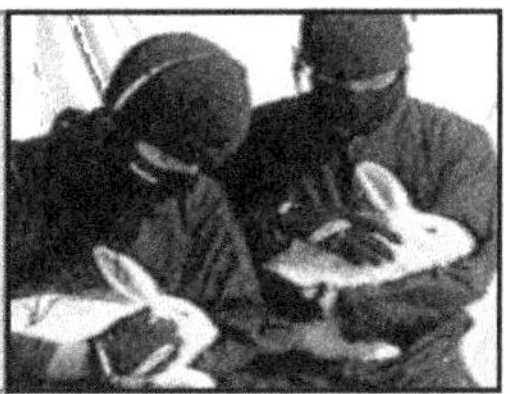

On Sunday night a pen was cut open at the Oregon Fish and Wildlife game bird exhibit located in the EE Wilson Wildlife Area giving 3 ringneck pheasants a chance to escape into the wild. This action was done to both spare these wild animals from life of captivity and to challenge the societal norm that regards non-human (as well as human) animals as commodities.

Holiday greetings to earth liberation prisoner Marius Mason and to the accused mink liberators brought up on federal 'terrorism' charges for allegedly freeing mink from a midwest fur farm.

-A.L.F.

HARLAN LABORATORIES

2015

June 7, 2015
Mississauga, Ontario
Trucks torched at laboratory animal breeder

Mississauga, Ontario, Canada - Early in the morning of June 7, 2015, the Animal Liberation Front planted incendiary devices under trucks belonging to Harlan Laboratories. Harlan is a company owned by Huntingdon Life Sciences. They are responsible for supplying research animals and animal feed to vivisectionists. This action was undertaken in order to eliminate this evil company's means of transportation, to disrupt the systematic torture and murder of innocent animals, and to cause as much monetary damage as possible. Fortunately, news reports have said that the devices ignited successfully, damaging one truck and completely destroying the other. Our only regret is that the flames were extinguished before they had a chance to spread to Harlan's offices. In solidarity with those fighting the oppression of mink on fur farms in St. Mary's - A.L.F.

WISCONSIN FOX FARM

2015

October 23, 2015
Burlington, WI
One rabbit, two foxes liberated

In the early hours of October 23rd, 2015, I took a pair of bolt cutters to the back fence of the fox farm on Hospital Road in Burlington, Wisconsin.

The first imprisoned animal found was a twenty pound rabbit in a small wire bottom cage. She was either a neglected pet or a source of food. I did not have the resources to bring her with me, and released her into the field behind the property. It was a difficult decision, but at least she spent some of her life hopping free and feeling the earth beneath her feet before meeting her fate.

There were only two foxes found on the property. They were tall, beautiful and black with glowing eyes. I crawled into one of their cages in an attempt to pull one out, but she only growled and retreated. They would only come out if I backed away and watched from afar. As soon as they were out of their cages, they joyously galloped around in circles. It was the most beautiful thing to see. I did not wait to see if they made it through the holes in the three layers of fencing that kept them imprisoned.

Raiding a fur farm can easily be done by a single person with enough courage and love to do so. I'm sorry this raid was not more fruitful. This action is in solidarity with Walter Bond. Fool though he may be, Walter is a hero for animals and a comrade who is not to be forgotten.

'Life shrinks or expands in proportion to one's courage' — Anais Nin

ESTACADA GAME FARM

2016

February 28, 2016
Beavercreek, OR
50 pheasants liberated

On the night of February 28th, in an act of love, 50 ringnecked pheasants were liberated from the Estacada Game Farm in Beavercreek, Oregon.

These birds would have otherwise been sold to sport hunting outfitters and killed for entertainment. The pheasants thrashed through the air in all directions as they made their way to freedom in the surrounding fields and meadows.

This action is dedicated to the memory of Clément Méric, an anti-fascist vegan who was murdered by neo-nazi skinheads in Paris, France in 2013. We will never forget, we will never forgive.

-ALF

Note: We request that the North American Animal Liberation Press Office not speak to the media on behalf of this action or associate themselves with this action publicly in any way.

NORTH AMERICAN FUR AUCTION | 2016

May, 2016
Toronto, Ontario
Arson attack on North America's largest fur auction house

Last week I gained access to the rooftop of the North American Fur Auction and sabotaged air conditioning units.

I also lit several petrol bombs to send a clear message to those who make their living killing and torturing animals that the times are changing. This action was done in solidarity with all the lovely persons giving freedom to animals trapped in fur farm hell.

Toronto ALF

LICHTY FUR FARM | 2016

August 24, 2016
Linwood, Ontario
Hundreds of mink liberated

A LETTER TO THE PUBLIC

LAST EVENING WE TOOK A ROADTRIP TO LICHTY MINK FUR FARM 5531 SCHUMMER LINE LINWOOD ONTARIO WHERE THOUSANDS OF ANIMALS ARE NEEDLESSLY KILLED EVERY YEAR FOR THE STUPIDITY OF FASHION.

WE CUT HOLES IN THE FENCE AND OPENED THE CAGES TO HUNDREDS OF MINK SETTING THEM FREE TO THE NIGHT

WE ARE PROUD THAT WE CAN MAKE A DIFFERENCE IN THE LIVES OF THESE ANIMALS

CONFINING AND KILLING LIVING BREATHING BEINGS FOR CLOTHING IS AN ABOMINATION AND ATROCITY WHEN WE CAN EASILY MAKE CLOTHES FROM SYNTHETIC MATERIALS WITHOUT BLOODSHED

LICHTY FUR FARM IS INDISTINGUISHABLE FROM A PUPPY MILL

THE SPACE EACH MINK HAS IS BARELY ENOUGH TO TURN AROUND AND THESE ANIMALS ARE TREATED NO BETTER THAN DISPOSABLE TRASH

THESE DEATH FACTORIES THAT PASS THEMSELVES OFF AS FARMS FLY IN THE FACE OF WHAT IS DECENT AND JUST

ANY LAW THAT ALLOWS FOR ANIMALS TO BE TORTURED AND ABUSED HAS NO PLACE AND NO RIGHT TO BE RESPECTED BY RESPONSIBLE PEOPLE

THIS LIBERATION IS DEDICATED TO ANITA KRAJNC FROM TORONTO PIG SAVE WHO STANDS ON TRIAL TODAY FOR SIMPLY GIVING WATER TO THIRSTY PIGS ON SLAUGHTER TRUCKS.

THIS IS A MOCKERY OF JUSTICE AND AN ABSURDITY OF REASON THAT A LAW WOULD CRIMINALIZE AN ACT OF KINDNESS

MOTHERS AGAINST FUR FARM CRUELTY

SLAUGHTERHOUSE TRANSPORT TRUCK | 2018

November 30, 2018
Montreal, Quebec
Single pig liberated from a transport truck

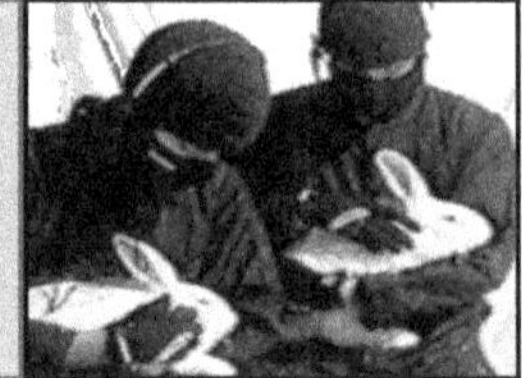

Today a lone wolf animal liberation front member liberated a piglet off a truck filled with hundreds of piglets. Sadly he was only able to get one off as the truck was at a busy truck stop and he had to work fast. This took place in the outskirts of the Montreal Quebec Canada region. This picture is with him and the piglet after they reached a safe distance. The piglet has been sent to a undisclosed location where it will live out its natural life free from ever being harmed instead will see nothing but the purest form of love.

TURKEY FARM | 2020

June 20, 2020
Unknown location, Canada
Turkey liberated from factory farm

Over 20 million turkeys are brutally murdered every year in Canada to satisfy the human's fetish for flesh. They are kept in horrific conditions but even if the conditions were idyllic, their lives are not ours to take.

This facility is 'free range & organic.' Or that's what they like to claim. There is evidence this farm feeds turkeys antibiotic laden food to promote rapid growth. They are fed antibiotics from the time they are dumped inside the shed until they're loaded onto a hauler.

Unfortunately, sometimes even with the best care and endless love, they don't make it when rescued at this stage in their life. She was almost 3 months old when she was taken out of that shit hole. She felt love, kindness, sunshine, fresh air, dirt and made friends with ducks, hens &
roosters. She is no longer with us because her body was so damaged that it simply gave out on her. She was surrounded by people who loved her and left this world peacefully.

Animals cannot wait for people to change their lifestyles.

Exploiters should live in fear, anxiety and torment for the heinous crimes they inflict on our animal comrades. It's about fuckin time they feel exactly what non-humans feel.

We are not playing nice anymore.

IDAHO AND UTAH FUR FARMS | 2020

Late summer, 2020
ID & UT
2000 mink liberated in two separate actions in two states

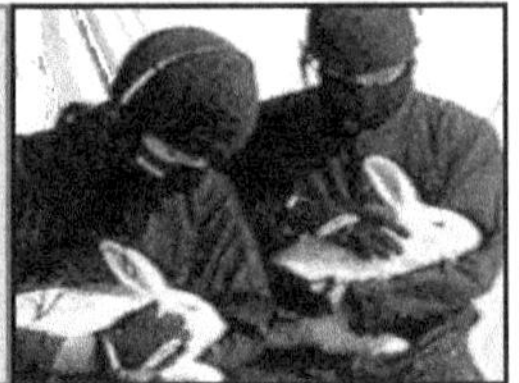

Late this summer animal liberation activists carried out two raids on fur farms in Idaho and Utah. Fencing was ripped down and nearly 2,000 mink were released allowing them to clamor toward freedom. Both farms sat near the edges of mostly undeveloped public lands, allowing plenty of habitat for the newly freed native predators.

Walking through a large field, quietly climbing a barbed wire cattle fence, and crossing the road in clear view of the house associated with the first farm proved easy. It became clear there was no visible electronic security, and the activists bet heavily that the faint barking was from a neighbor's property, or at least from a dog contained within the fur farmer's house.

Cage after cage, row after row, shed after shed, latches were opened and nesting boxes removed allowing the mink to escape to their rightful home. They spaced out the releases in order to disperse the noise from disturbed mink away from a singular location. The surreal and beautiful moment where the mink explored in the moonlight will be carried in the hearts of those that gazed upon them for a lifetime. The approving chorus from coyotes in the nearby hills still echo in their ears.

Days later, these activists found themselves before another sprawling fur farm complex. Watching for nearly an hour to be sure there was no movement from within the compound, they sat patiently, preparing to penetrate the property and rip down another fence. As they sat they could hear the scratching and faint chirping of imprisoned mink.

Beneath a bright moon, nearly full and neon pink behind the haze from the massive nearby wildfires, they proceeded to the perimeter. Cutting vertically though the chain link from top to bottom in two places 20' apart, they prepared the fence to be felled by just a few quick snips along the top when the time came. This helped disguise the preparations should a security vehicle pass. The small wire cutters they thought to pack this time also quickened their work on the chicken wire at the base.

Several sheds were completely emptied. Its previous inhabitants were much more lively than the last farm too – screaming, running, and climbing the eight foot tall perimeter fence. More than 1100 were released and then the fence was toppled for all to make their escape.

Caging the wild is a heinous offense against life – against freedom. Every cage is worth emptying, and to begin this work is not difficult. Pressure from animal liberation activists, a declining demand for the products and economic downswings have come together to push the archaic fur industry further than ever towards full collapse. Wiping fur farms off the landscape is a worthy and attainable goal. What's needed now is for the reader to reflect on what is stopping them from picking up where others left off.

As the fur industry teeters on the brink of collapse these efforts intend to push it over the edge. At this point, actually, finding operational farms seems to be one of the hardest parts. The rest is straight forward.

These activists lamented at one point that this activity wasn't better training for assailing human prisons, too, but know any action can sharpen skills useful for confronting every industry.

HOW-TO GUIDES

How the Animal Liberation Front carries out their actions.

CONTENTS

HOW-TO GUIDES

Transporting animals, picking locks, reporting actions, and not getting caught—all questions that face the aspiring liberator.

In both skill and volume, North America's A.L.F. occupies a place deep in Europe's shadow. A shorter history, fewer elaborate actions, and less of them in total. Every A.L.F. tactic was carried out first, and bigger, in Europe before arriving in North America. While the UK A.L.F. was setting fires in the 1970's, we didn't light our first match until 1987. If the A.L.F. was drilling holes through lab walls in the 1980s, we didn't import the tactic until 2000.

And our "novice apprentice" position is inevitably reflected in North American A.L.F. how-to guides. If those behind some of North America's most elaborate and well-executed raids—University of Minnesota, University of Iowa, University of Arizona—are still among us, they aren't sharing their secrets. A truly advanced how-to guide from North America has yet to be written.

"Never tell everything – you might educate the enemy."

The most circulated guide, titled *An Animal Liberation Primer*, is at best entry-level. Spray painting and clogging drains are a righteous annoyance, yet sets one's sights low in light of the A.L.F.'s demonstrated potential.

As Darkness Falls places only slightly higher demands on the reader, expanding its tactical coverage to a degree, yet still leaves anyone aiming for maximum impact to invent their own playbook.

The skill and impact level increases with *How To Sink Whalers*, clearly written from a place of experience with marine mechanics. While there is only one known application of this tactic (see: "Reykjavik Harbor") this guide leaves little question it is an all-inclusive manual for a niche form of high-impact sabotage.

The Final Nail deserves its own commemoration essay for directly inspiring the release of over 100,000 mink and foxes from the cages of fur farms, and shutting down a significant percentage in the process. Whereas other how-to guides leave out the question of "But where?" and any list of target addresses leaves out the question of "But how?," *The Final Nail* brought both together in a spark that set off a total siege.

The animal liberation model *The Final Nail* introduced alleviated the biggest obstacle to live liberations (homing animals), with the best attributes of any A.L.F. action (the ability to save a large number of animals with low risk). *The Final Nail* then sealed the deal with a state-by-state directory of fur farm addresses. The result was explosive, and it remains unquestionably the highest-impact piece of A.L.F. writing to date.

(It was revealed in a 2006 court case that former A.L.F. prisoner Darren Thurston compiled the first two editions. Numbers 3 and 4 appear to have different authors.)

Next, a collection of how-to material published in *No Compromise* across several years. In including these, I took a small leap of faith that the authors possess their implied A.L.F. pedigree. With such a small pool of activists able to credibly instruct on tactics such as arson and lab raids, the reader must trust the authors either participated in such actions, sourced their knowledge first-hand-from those who have, or did such an academic deep-dive as to not lead anyone legally or tactically astray. By publishing this material, I expect the authors have a legitimate A.L.F. resume, yet accept the possibility of something less.

Improvisational Illegality: All That Matters Is If It Works

There can be more than one truth, more than one playbook, and more than one way to commit a felony. With such a limited written output, there is little opportunity for dissenting views between cells to reveal themselves, and without this diversity, the content here takes on the weight of Tactical Doctrine and not the opinions of some people, some of the time, in some contexts.

Which is a long way to say: There is room for improvisation and deviation from the material here, and very little should be taken as immutable truth.

Among the debatable points:

- "You can never be too paranoid." (In my experience, the need to hyper-manage all potential risks kills more actions than anything else, with most success coming from a sober assessment of risk, balanced with the reward—not the analysis-paralysis of mitigating every risk to zero.)
- "Never liberate an animal you don't have a home for." (Also from experience, the quickest way to find a good home for an animal is to put yourself in a situation where you have no choice but to find a home. You'll figure it out.)

- "Never do actions close to home." (An ideal but impractical precaution that sounds good on paper, but in practice, diminishes the number of actions massively by demanding every activist cross state lines to carry out A.L.F. actions.)

The measure of a good tactic is not if it conforms to the guidance presented here. The measure of a good tactic is if it saves animals.

The Victory Is In The Blindspots

A manual can set the framework, but it can't hold your hand. Ultimately, the most important elements of successful A.L.F. actions are the ones that can't be taught.

Among them:

- "Where to home animals?" (This will come down to the strength of your extended network and nothing else.)
- "Where to find people to work with?" (Same.)
- "How to get in?" (Read this book cover-to-cover and you are unlikely to find the same method of entry twice. Physical access is highly situational. Best way to get in is to show up.)
- "How to conquer fear?" (You can't use the same mind that created the fear to conquer the fear. Using fear as fuel and taking action in spite of it is the only remedy.)

If you need a paint-by-numbers template that requires nothing of you but to show up, then work for a non-profit. The A.L.F. is not for you.

The Burden Of Knowledge

Remember that those who have achieved the greatest victories had little-to-none of this material to work with. The level of knowledge imparted here brings with it an elevated obligation.

And to those who accept that obligation yet still have questions, remember:

"When you have a strong enough 'why', the 'how' takes care of itself."

Area Mink Farmers on Alert

BY MYCHEL MATTHEWS

mmatthews@magicvalley.com

BURLEY • Local mink farmers are keeping a low profile since a recent "call to action" posted online by the radical Animal Liberation Front.

The ALF on June 1 released the fourth edition of its 58-page instruction manual, "The Final Nail: Complete Guide to Destroying the Fur Industry."

"The Final Nail is a blueprint for committing a felony," said Michael Whelan, executive director of Fur Commission USA based in Oregon.

"It's terrorism — that's exactly what it is," Whelan said. Some mink farmers sleep with "guns by their bedsides. This is their livelihood being threatened."

An Animal Liberation Primer

1993

Perhaps the most widely circulated A.L.F. how-to guide, *An Animal Liberation Primer* presents a beginner's look at carrying A.L.F. actions both small and large.

An Animal
LIBERATION
Primer
THIRD EDITION

Compiled and edited by:
@nu

The content herein in no way is intended to encourage or discourage anyone from participating, or not participating in the activities described. The information is for your general interest only.

DEDICATED TO
THE K.F.C. FIVE
AND
"S", Who died in the prime of life after liberating many animals from the chambers of hell. We are so few, and now we are one fewer. We shall carry on...

IT'S NOT THE CAT WHO NEEDS HIS HEAD EXAMINED

Foreword

This booklet has been produced to be a tool, a tool to empower the average person to make a difference in this world. It has been compiled from numerous sources, into a condensed volume of animal liberation tactics. Read this booklet once and then twice and then again. Make sure you know it inside out, before setting out to do anything.

Who are the ALF?

Members of the Animal Liberation Front are activists who directly intervene to stop animal suffering. At the risk of losing their own freedom, while following ALF guidelines:

ANIMAL LIBERATION FRONT GUIDELINES

- To liberate animals from places of abuse, i.e. fur farms, laboratories, factory farms, etc. and place them in good homes where they may live out their natural lives free from suffering.

- To inflict economic damage to those who profit from the misery and exploitation of animals; and

- To reveal the horror and atrocities committed against animals behind locked doors by performing non-violent direct actions and liberations.

The ALF and Direct Action.

As part of their personal campaign against animal abuse, ALF activists do not eat animal flesh, and many of them use no animal products at all. They come from all social classes, age groups, professions, races, religious and political persuasions, and all are prepared to go to jail , if that is what it takes to end animal suffering. They are committed to doing all that it takes to end animal abuse, short of harming any living being.

Direct action for animals began in England in the early 1960s when a group called the Hunt Saboteurs Association was formed. Hunt "Sabs" physically disrupt hunts by laying false scents, blowing hunting horns to send hounds off in the wrong direction, and chasing animals away to safety. The Hunt Saboteurs have effectively ended many traditional hunting events all over England.

In 1972 a group of Hunt Saboteurs decided that more militant action on behalf of animals was necessary and thus the Band of Mercy began. the Band of Mercy, named after a group of animal rights campaigners in the nineteenth century, smashed guns used on bird hunts and sabotaged hunters' vehicles by slashing tires and breaking windows. The group also began fighting other forms of animal abuse, setting fire to pharmaceutical laboratories and burning boats used for hunting seals.

In 1975 two members of the Band of Mercy, Ronnie Lee and Cliff Goodman, were caught trying to break into a laboratory and were sent to prison. After the arrest, support for direct action grew, and in 1976, the Animal Liberation Front was set up. Since that time, tens of thousands of animals have been rescued and millions of dollars worth of damage has been caused. It has been reported that ALF actions occur at the rate of 75 per week in Britain, ranging from raids on research laboratories to smashing the windows of fur shops. Today there are animal liberation groups in Britain, the USA, Australia, Italy, France, Germany, Canada, New Zealand, Austria, Denmark, Ireland, Japan, Netherlands, Spain and Sweden. While there are no formal communications between the groups, they all share the same goal: to save animals from suffering HERE and NOW.

One ALF member put it this way:

I see participating in ALF's raids not as a momentary forfeiture of the highest human values - goodness, generosity and the like - but rather as an embodiment of them... We feel a sense of urgency for the animals whose pain and imminent death is absolutely real to them today.

ALF - The way we were.

This article discusses ideas that could be adopted by a local animal liberation group, it is based on personal experience of several ALF groups operating in the south of England between 1982 and 1984. We did for a while perfect a system where we could move from seeing to raiding an animal abuse centre in a matter of 48 hours; the number of animals we rescued ran into several thousands - with a record of 250 on one night from a vivisection dealer. We raided everything from schools which bred animals for dissection, up to major laboratories where there was 24-hour security and intricate alarm systems, although the majority of our actions were against factory farms and vivisection breeders.

We started out as a group of four people with one car. At our height there were as many as 50 active members split into several sub-groups, some of these sub-groups are still active, although the majority of our members have now ceased to be active--the pressure of living under the continuous threat of possible arrest taking its toll on many of the more active members.

Finding people to work with is the hardest of all your tasks. At the moment we see a spate of people who have become involved in groups, who, when arrested make statements incriminating themselves (let me mention here that *no one has ever got off by making a statement*); worse than this is the disturbing development of people making statements naming other activists and giving details of raids they have been involved with (in the criminal world this is known as "grassing" or "snitching").

In the prison cells some people make a belated and somewhat pathetic attempt to save their own skin by telling the police what they want to hear. But despite the police promises, snitching has never saved anyone's skin and when it comes to avoiding a beating in the cells, the police in general only use violence in interviews when they think it will get results. When people have been hit, and they begin to talk, the police are encouraged, while if they stay quiet "Mr. Nasty", is shepherded out of the interview room and "Mr. Nice" apologizes and appeals to you personally. People who believe in what they are doing and recognize the personal risks they are taking in advance of their of their arrest will not snitch. Those *people who snitch cannot really believe in what they are doing*, otherwise they would have the confidence and the peace of mind to recognize that in a direct action campaign some arrests are inevitable, and although they are unlucky to be arrested at that particular time, the struggle will go on. Their role once arrested is to say or do nothing to impair the struggle.

It is very important that the calibre of people is high and that you never work on a job you are not happy about. In a group you need some solid un-shakeable characters, young people without much insight are not a good idea. Look for commonsense, people not prone to showing off, no big egos and no one who boasts about what they've done or are about to do. The *longer you know people the better* and try never to ask someone to get involved unless you are confident that they are interested.

Finding a target: Your local animal rights group probably has a very good idea where the local labs, breeders, fur farms and battery units are, although unless you are already involved it is probably best to keep well clear of the local animal rights group; it is after all the *first place the police will come looking for information* on likely activists. Always study the location on the map and learn to recognize where you are in relation to roads, streams, footpaths, etc.

The first visit to a target should be during the day. Park well out of the way and approach the target on foot. Try to get as close as possible, look for ways in and ways out (not necessarily the same). Begin to develop your plan–where will you park? Which buildings will you enter? Which route will you take in? Where will your look-out be? Where will your break in point be? (seldom the front door). Where is anybody likely to disturb you? Once you are back in the car, try and sketch a map immediately so that you remember everything.

After seeing the place close up it is a good idea to retire to a distance and study your road map. Look for some ideal parking spots: in rural areas these will have to be off little-used country lanes, in the town it may well be in a housing estate. You may also decide that there are some convenient footpaths running around the back of the site, walk the length of these, but don't stay around the immediate area of the site for long enough to arouse suspicion.

Once you have seen all that you can during daylight, clear off and make a draft plan. Next, return at night, try out your route and find its weaknesses. Get as close to your target building as possible, ideally right up to the break-in point. Check the locks, doors and window fittings, look for signs of alarms, and general security.

Having surveyed the target area, make sure that your route in and out is *as simple as possible,* stick to hedges, count field boundaries, note the number of gates etc., anything that will make the route nice and easy. Try not to use wide open spaces as part of your route, hedges make you invisible in the dark. It is vital that you walk the route once at night before the job, as darkness is disorienting and places can look very different.

A good time to do a job is at new moon; if you live in the city you'd be surprised how much light is given out by the moon. Winter is ideal with its early dusks, late dawns, and cold, rainy, windy nights–no farmer is going to want to get out of bed at two in the morning just because he has heard a noise that could so easily have been the wind.

Once you are sure of the route, go there at the time and day of the week that you are planning to do the job, and do a complete walk-through. Park where you will be parking, walk the exact route and stay at the break-in point for as long as you need to there on the night. If everything works out then you are onto the next stage.

It cannot be stated enough that unless there are clear and obvious advantages *you should not take ALF actions during the day.* Darkness, and knowledge of the area around the target will ensure your escape, on foot, however many police units arrive. In 1981, an ALF group was stranded in the fields surrounding a beagle breeders' at Ross-on-Wye, the police had swooped on their transport and arrested their back-up driver. The group, with beagles, were at one time just the other side of a hedge from parked police vehicles; the group escaped and got the beagles away by traveling as fast as possible, on foot, across country, eventually contacting a supporter who arranged transport for them to be picked up.

However wrong things go on the night, don't give up–a clear head, good planning and determination should give you an edge on the police.

Once your group has got off the ground you should develop a core of people responsible for tools, planning raids, the initial break-in, the look-outs, and the organization of people and vehicles on the night. This group should enter the target area first, set up look-outs, check the area over, and when they are satisfied, break in and locate the animals. Only then should "the carriers" be brought in; their job is to bag or box the animals quickly and quietly and then leave. If the target has no alarms and no one on site the advance group could conceivably go in hours in advance and prepare everything so that the carriers and their vehicles are there for as short a time as possible.

One person should be responsible for collating all information on homes, so that when you find homes for fifty hens you do a battery unit, when it's thirty rabbits or ten dogs you do a breeder. In many ways the homing network needs to be bigger than the ALF group, ideally with 4 or 5 people who can take and disperse animals, re-homing them *outside of the animal rights movement*. It is this ability to disperse animals so that your homes are never used up that will permit you to become an efficient animal liberation group. In general those people involved in the homing network *should not be in the ALF group* as it would be a very damaging blow should those people be arrested. Only members of the core group of activists should have contact with the homing network.

Tools are a vital consideration. You will need two pairs of bolt-cutters and two crowbars (large and small) a pair of diamond-tipped glass cutters, walkie-talkies and a rope. Have a proper tool-bag to carry them in, never touch them without wearing gloves, even when buying them, and always clean them between jobs. The blades on your bolt-cutters should be changed regularly--always after a lab job, and run a file over the end of your crowbars as they leave distinctive imprints on whatever they have jimmied open. The tools should *always be kept at a safe house* in between jobs. A safe house belongs to someone who *is not in your group* and not going to come to the attention of the police.

When you plan a job, it is advisable to have a plan "B" if things go wrong. Work out what you are going to do if you come across a guard or if the police arrive, which could be when you are going in, in the middle of the job, or on the way out with animals. Whatever happens don't panic, it only wastes time. You should have worked out which way to run, and who should be with you. You should know what could go wrong with your plan and have an easy solution to it when it arises. When it comes to running away it is probably best to all leave the site together heading in the same direction to a pre-arranged rendezvous point 3 or 4 fields away; from then on it may be better if you split up and travel in groups of three or four in different directions.

When doing a job you must have confidence in those who you are working with. When you appoint one or more lookouts you must be sure that they know what they are doing, that they are not frightened, and that should anything go wrong they will be able to notify you of what is happening. Once you are inside a place, you should just get on with your job, looking over your shoulder only wastes time. Do not panic if the animals begin to make a lot of noise, this is not unusual. Chickens and rabbits make a lot of noise but beagles are notorious and can be heard for miles; always remember that you have a lookout so get on with your job and the sooner you get out of the sheds the sooner the animals will quieten down.

If disturbed you should collect people and leave quickly, most people who discover you will be quite happy to frighten you off their property and then call the police. Unless you are confronted by a farmer who is literally shooting at you with his shotgun, you should not abandon anyone. Security guards are easier to deal with as the property is not theirs. Their job is not to be a hero but to phone the police, although any sign of weakness on your part may encourage them to grab hold of a tailender, so the rule is–don't panic, leave together, and leave quickly.

Parking a lot of vehicles for a raid can look suspicious, one way around this is to go out several hours earlier and park the carriers' cars in different streets in a nearby town or village. The whole of the carrying group can then be brought in by the vehicle which will leave with the animals, alternatively the carriers can come in, from different directions to a rendezvous point near the animal abuse centre and the animal transport only arriving when the group has got its hands on the animals–either arriving at a specific time, or being called up with a radio when the job is complete.

Whatever the plan always make sure that the animal van is the first away and has the safest route out of the area. It is important that if you decide to rescue animals *you are prepared to fuce a prison sentence*–the animals must be protected and if that means a choice between you going to prison or the animals being taken back, then you will be released, for the animals there is only one way out.

Although it is good to do jobs on home territory, you should consider travelling out of your area on occasions, the further you travel, the less chance of the police guessing that it was your group. It is important *not to get into a routine* of doing jobs on the same night of the week in the same police district. It is only when the police recognize a pattern of jobs that they will have the opportunity to start fishing for you.

Clothing is a very important consideration as police forensic science is now very advanced and can identify clothing, hairs, foot-prints, tools, paint, etc. In one criminal case forensic scientists proved that a discarded shoe was responsible for a foot print at the scene of the crime, they then managed to identify fibres inside the shoe as consistent with the fibre of thirteen different pairs of the defendant's socks. The police have access to highly sophisticated techniques, in practice these will only be used once they are convinced that you are the culprit, and they then can justify the enormous expenditure which is not acceptable for routine testing.

Wearing boiler suits can be a good idea as they cover your clothes, you can wear your party clothes underneath; when you reach your transport on your way home you can strip off the boiler suits, straighten your hair and look very presentable should you be stopped by the police. This works even better if you have a mixture of girls and boys in the car, then if you are randomly stopped by the police you can have a story to bluff them with, you could have been to a party, a wedding, etc. It is a good idea to have rehearsed false names, although this is complicated for your drivers if the vehicle is registered in their own name. It is a good idea to wear socks over your shoes, this prevents tell-tale footprints being left in the soft soil, and ensures that when you get back to your car your shoes won't be covered in mud. Always wear gloves, and never believe that a quick wipe with a damp cloth will remove your fingerprints.

Within a direct action campaign arrests are ultimately inevitable, either through bad luck, bad planning, good police work, a frame-up or an act of "god". The fact that you have been arrested does not necessarily mean that they have enough evidence to charge you, and if you are charged you will have the opportunity in court to give your defence. In the police station there is only one rule, "Never Make A Statement". In the war soldiers were instructed that should they be taken prisoner they should tell their captors their name, rank and serial number; in the animal rights movement it is name, address and date of birth, beyond that you should reply "no comment". Other interrogation techniques involve asking you what you had for breakfast, how long you have been a vegetarian, who do you live with, where did you meet and who planned the raid. Refuse to answer all questions, and NEVER MAKE A STATEMENT.

Other more interesting police tactics are when the police bring an item of evidence into the cell and tell you to pick it up with the obvious result that your fingerprint will be left on it, (it is particularly important to be wary of handling match boxes if you are being interviewed for arson). It has happened in the past that the police have walked into a cell with a quantity of cannabis and explained how easy it would be to plant it on the accused - so demonstrating their ability to frame you.

Sooner or later the police will inevitably try to frighten you, with their forecast of a long prison sentence if you don't help them, and eventually there will be the threat of physical attack. The physical assault rarely amounts to more than a bit of pushing around. It is designed to show you that they are loosing their patience and demonstrate that they can do what they like to you. It is very unwise to attempt to retaliate against your attacker. If you are more seriously beaten in a police cell you should roll into a ball with your back to a corner and your head tucked well down into your chest. NEVER MAKE A STATEMENT.

When and if you use the press it is worth considering your policy towards claiming actions. It is *not a good idea* to claim all your actions under a distinctive name, or to organize your press releases in a way which identifies the actions with one group of activists, this merely helps the police to put those actions together and start drawing a pattern about the way the group works. In general the national press are overwhelmingly hostile to animal liberation groups and so it is often a waste of time dealing with them.

If you phone through a press release to a paper they may well record it, if you send a letter they may well give the letter to the police so always be brief. You should explain why the target of the raid was chosen, how many animals they use, what they use them for and if possible provide a photo of the conditions inside. If you do supply a photo then remember it will be sent to the police as soon as the papers have finished with it. Unless you have a member of the group who is prepared to train themselves in the use of a video camera there is little point in attempting to use them on a raid. They are cumbersome and unless you know what you are doing the results will be unusable.

It is probably unwise to build up a trusting relationship with the local press, or with a particular reporter, second-rate reporters would claim to support anyone to get a story. You should always consider the implications should this "trusted" reporter tell the police all they knew.

What you have read in this article is a summary of the ideas used by our group, they illustrate the way in which we worked. If nothing else we proved that with hard work, commonsense, a passion for animal rights and the initial advantage of being unknown to the police, it is possible for a relatively small group of people to launch a campaign as we did which not only saves hundreds - and if you are lucky thousands - of lives, but can cause serious disruption to sections of the animal abuse industries.

Interviews with Animal Liberation Front Activists.

How did you become members of the ALF?
We are not members of the ALF, in fact the ALF has not one single member. We are ALF activists by virtue of the fact that we carry out actions, whether on an occasional or frequent basis. Immediately after superglue has been squirted into a fur shop lock the person/s involved becomes an activist. This is exactly how we became involved in direct action four years ago.

How do you go about carrying out actions?
There are a number of aspects that one has to take into consideration.

First and foremost it's important to have a look around the region at all the targets, laboratories, as many of the factory farms as one can find, hunt kennels, fur shops, slaughterhouses, etc. If actions have taken place already in your home area then it may be a good idea to go for the most straightforward, squirting paintstripper from a lemon juice squeezy, or a washing-up liquid squeezy bottle over the van(s) of an animal exploiter, gluing up fur shop locks to start with, then progress to factory farms which generally are not alarmed (there is the odd one that is, particularly the very large food chain store ones). If no actions, or only one or two small actions have taken place, it may be beneficial to go for a laboratory, the reasoning being that once things start happening in your area the labs, if any, will invest in more security measures. *There are still labs with only minimal security.* The animals are not necessarily in the labs at all times and there is usually an animal house in a separate building where animals are held until needed or in some cases are bred there. We can usually gain access to the grounds (we're not put off by the usual security fence with strands of barbed wire at the top, these can be climbed with practice–we use the concrete posts as a support and wear 2-3 pairs of gloves when learning), we usually find the building with animals have fans operating, pumping out the stale air in the unit and fresh air in. We can smell which one has animals within.

With factory farm units we can tell what kind of animals, if any, are in the units by simply placing our ear against an air duct on the side of the unit or at the door, listening and smelling. Or we try shining a pencil torch, with colored plastic held over the end by an elastic band, through any openings. In fact we double or triple the layers of plastic so that only the minimum of light gets through, not only reducing the chance of anyone else seeing but shine a bright light onto battery hens and they may well make a lot of noise. We always try the door handle etc. and have been pleasantly surprised a couple of times to find it is not locked. With experience one can often tell what animals are held in a particular unit by its shape, size and building materials used.
When looking at potential targets we don't take balaclavas etc. We also make a point of emptying our pockets of everything including door keys, discarding matching jewellery etc. before setting out, in case we drop anything. If we need to cover our faces a scarf is fine and we

wear gloves of course. We also carry bird watching books and binoculars.

The syringe-type applic
handy, but expensive. I
tubes can have a small h
drilled in the cap (b) to
narrow stream of glue
lock.

How do you carry out actions against shops involved in animal exploitation?

There are a number of ways in which we cause them financial loss. First is the length of time they are open, remembering the slogan "time is money" we place small pieces of wire, a half-inch long, or match sticks in Yale locks, screws/washers into mortice locks and then squirt in superglue, both to the locks in the front door and any side or back door. When completed any shutters on the windows have the locks similarly treated. A few days before the action we walk around the shops in the early evening to check what types of locks are installed so that we have an idea of how many pieces of wire/match, tubes of glue etc. we require. Returning on the night between 7-8 P.M. (we don't wander around the shops after the bars have closed when the police are expecting trouble, and shirt and tie doesn't go amiss), we walk up and down to check no police are standing in a doorway as they sometimes do in shopping centres. All clear and a bunch of us stand close to the door eating a bag of chips and talking, shielding the person gluing the lock, it only takes a few seconds. This is usually done by a female activist who has the materials in a small plastic bag under her clothing, if we were to be spotted acting suspiciously there is far less chance of a female being searched. We would of course be able to say which bar we have all just been to. Some stores have the type of handles on the doors that can be locked together with a bicycle lock. Any messages are written either with paint (not on widows which are easy to clean–we go for the brick/woodwork) or with a felt-tip pen. Where circus posters on walls are concerned we write the work "CANCELLED" twice on 8.5" by 14" paper in felt-tip pen, photocopy it, cut the copies in half so we have two "CANCELLED" strips and paste them over the posters. We also type up a "cancelled" note informing the shops that display posters in their windows of a mix-up of dates and asking them to take down the poster in their shop, also informing them that the complementary tickets they received for putting up the posters in their

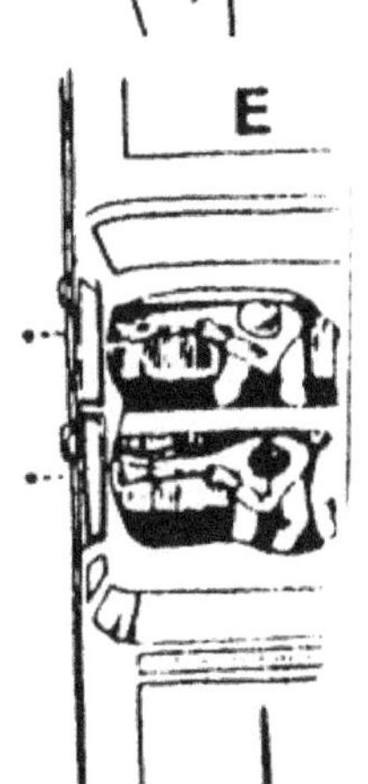

shop will be honored when it takes place. To push up their insurance premiums we damage the windows. Up until recently this involved using a ball-bearing and Black Widow slingshot.

SLINGSHOTS

This versatile tool can be used to knock out any windows even put holes in so-called "shatter-proof" windows. In the illustration you see the compact and easily concealed type slingshot (a). Missiles must be small, dense, and relatively round (b). Avoid irregularly shaped objects (c) as they don't fly straight. Small rocks, steel ball bearings and large nuts (d) are suitable. In illustration (e) you can see how one or two catapulters can hit a target from a passing car. Be careful you slingshots do no extend out of the car window.

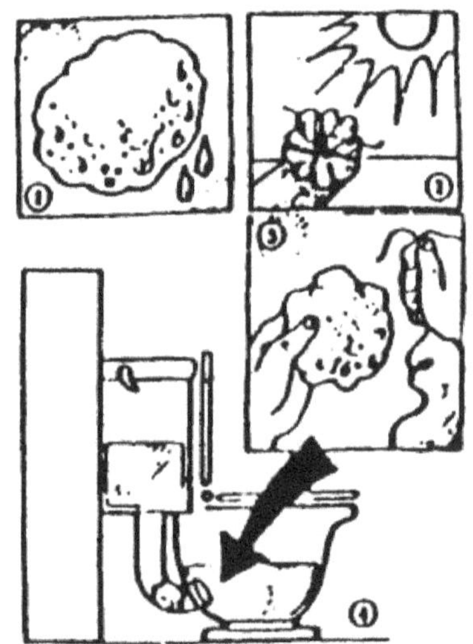

1. Wet a sponge.

2. Wrap the sponge tightly with a string and let it dry. When dry, it should be half it's normal size.

3. Remove the string.

4. Introduce the sponge into toilets or water drains to plug them up as the sponge swells.

Why and how do activists destroy vehicles and buildings?

We would first like to point out that damage to property does save animals. All the units at a factory farm can be destroyed in one night, a number of factory farmers have gone over to free-range egg production after a devastating action, some have been closed down. Laboratories have to spend more on security in order to retain their insurance, this money often comes out of their research budget, money that would have been spent on experimentation. Broiler sheds are a favorite target for destruction. Through modern growth promoting anti-biotics and various drugs the broiler hen reaches its maximum weight in an incredible seven weeks. The units are then cleared of the hens, many with broken limbs, which are slaughtered, processed for supermarkets and eventually the dinner table. The dirt and dead hens are cleared, the units disinfected and made ready for the new chicks. Shortly after the disinfecting is the time to burn them down as this disinfecting process scares away rodents. Some of the biggest destruction jobs have been successfully carried out by two people. A number of the buildings were worth half a million dollars plus also many vehicles have been trashed by just two people. The method used for factory farm units/laboratories etc. is for one person to carry two carrier bags full of torn-up clothes, the other person carrying a gallon container of gasoline in one carrier bag and boxes of firelighters in the other. Alternatively, rucksacks can be used (and disposed of afterwards). A newspaper and a box of matches are the only additions required. The container of gas and the boxes of firelighters are wrapped in cling wrap to eliminate any smell from them if we are using public transport, in which case newspapers cover everything in the bags. Everything, absolutely everything, has been carefully wiped(of fingerprints) including any crowbars used to gain access.

At the target area one acts as a look-out while the other gets into the building. If it's a wooden broiler unit (the doors are often left open when being cleaned) both carrier bags containing the old clothes are placed in a corner, the inflammable liquid is poured onto the old clothes drenching them, some can be poured on the wall for good measure. The boxes of firelighters are half opened and placed on top against the wooden walls. Using a piece of rolled up newspaper that is lit with a match, the firelighters are then lit while standing a few feet away. This is in case we have any inflammable materials on our gloves. The box of matches is tossed on top. If it's in a lab, slaughterhouse, etc. furniture is placed around one bag, the second one is placed in another room, again surrounded by furniture, and lit in the same way as above. Where there are a number of units/buildings either the largest building is destroyed or we go for the lot, transporting the materials by car. We will have already confirmed that there are no people or animals in a target building, our first job on the raid is to check the building(s) thoroughly.

Black plastic bin bags or sacks full of old clothes (one for each unit/building, more if possible depending on circumstances), half to one gallon of inflammable liquid to each bag/sack is required (the liquid being bought a gallon at a time from different sources). On top of each is placed a box of firelighters half opened (2 or 3 packets, even better, though not necessary). The sack is tilted so it leans against the corner of a wooden unit so that it can't fall away from the side panels while burning. The materials are driven to the units separately. If only one car is used, the sacks full of jumble can be stashed with a person left to keep an eye on them, then the gas, and finally the boxes of firelighters, newspaper and box of matches.

Trashing vehicles, all that is required is gasoline or paraffin. If the doors will open (as they often will with trucks) the gas is poured over the dash-board and seats, if need be a window is forced. If it's a car that is alarmed an old sheet is laid on top, inflammable liquid poured over and firelighters placed under each tire (a refinement that can be carried out against anything with tires, eg. tractor of a factory farmer). The firelighters are lit and the lighted paper tossed on top of the gas drenched sheet. If the fuel tank eventually goes up on a truck it may travel 20-30 yards. If the truck is not this distance away from a house or unit with animals in it we release the handbrake and push it beyond this distance.

If for some reason a truck cannot be destroyed outright and excellent tactic is to buy a tin of grinding paste, per truck, and mix the contents with oil. The resulting paste is poured down the oil pipe into the engine, this process ruins the engine. Once, sometime after one of these actions had been successfully carried out a particularly well made enclosure was built by the firm around the trucks with several dogs on the loose. Consequently a further raid would have proved difficult so a successful hoax was executed. Empty grinding paste tins were thrown over the fences, the firm informed of another raid. Finding the empty tins they had the engines stripped before finding it was a hoax. Also sugar, sand or water is added to fuel tanks.

ETCHING FLUID

ALF activists have discovered a new "weapon" which has successfully been used in some areas and will soon doubtless catch on in others. Sheffield ALF initiated the idea when they squirted "etching fluid" over more than fifty windows in the city in a continuation of their campaign against House of Fraser stores which have Edelson Fur departments. The stores attacked were Rackhams and Cole Bros. The fluid eats into the glass. Following the stir that this caused, the ALF in Merseyside used etching fluid on travel agencies where tickets were on sale for circuses using animals and the windows had to be replaced. There was also success with is in Stirling, Scotland, when the windows of two bloodsports shops and a fur shop had to be renewed after slogans were written on them with etching fluid. Then a dairy van had its windscreen doused with the fluid in London. The windscreens are particularly good targets, since they have to be replaced before the vehicles can be driven.

Glass etching fluid is available from craft and fine art shops. A small bottle costs about $20 but the expense is well worth it when one considers the reduction of risk to an activist using it–there is none of the noise.

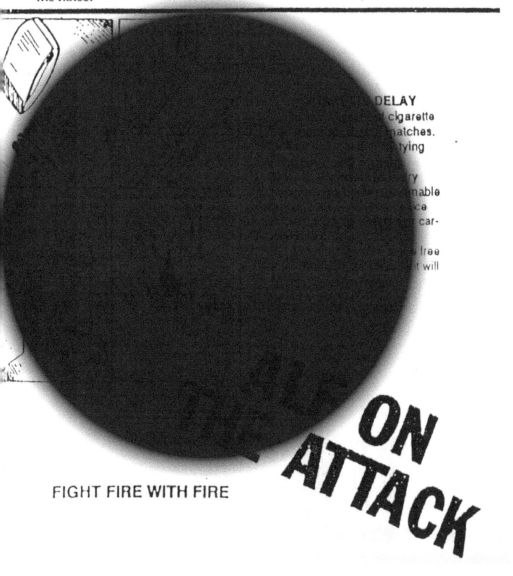

DELAY
cigarette
atches.
tying
ry
able
ce
car-
free
will

ON ATTACK

FIGHT FIRE WITH FIRE

How do you force locks open, to gain access to laboratories, etc.?
There are a few different methods the first is to try prying it off with a crowbar. Second method is to cut it off with a pair of bolt-cutters (keep them very sharp). The third is to use a battery-powered electric drill with a new 1/8 inch high speed drill bit. Depending on the hardness of the lock you may need more than one drill bit. Make sure you don't buy cheap bits--they will only let you down. Most keyed locks are pin-tumbler types whose basic operating principle can be seen in (A). When a key is inserted, it pushes up on spring-loaded pins of various lengths. when the tops of these pins are in perfect alignment with the "shear-line" the entire "plug" in which the key is inserted can be turned and the lock opened. In most locks, all of these parts are made of brass to prevent corrosion and it's relative softness makes drilling easy. As you can see in (B), the drill is used to destroy the pins along the shear line. You should be careful not to drill too deeply into the lock since this can damage the locking bar deep inside making it impossible to open. Drill in only to the depth of the keyway (3/4-inch in most padlocks and 1-inch in most doorlocks). A "drill stop" found with the power tools in a hardware store can be used to pre-set this depth and prevent drilling too deep. Now inserting a pin like a nail, will keep the damaged remains of the top pins above the shear line (C). Otherwise they will drop down and prevent the lock from opening. You may need to put the drill bit in a couple of times to chew up any pin fragments that might interfere with opening. You may need to put the drill bit in a couple of times to chew up any pin fragments that may interfere with opening. Finally, insert a narrow-bladed screwdriver (D) into the keyway and turn it to open the lock. Remember practice makes perfect, buy a cheap lock or two and practice at home.

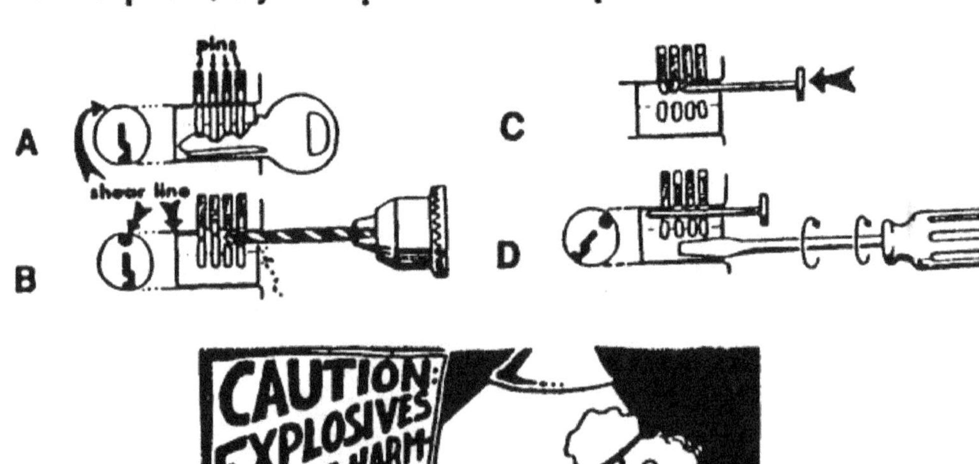

ALF
END THE
SLAUGHTE

KEEP YOUR MOUTH SHUT

If you are arrested or taken in for questioning by the police--DO NOT SAY ANYTHING. Keep your mouth shut. The only information they are entitled to is your name, address and date of birth. If they ask any other questions reply "NO COMMENT" or "I DO NOT WISH TO SAY ANYTHING" and STICK TO THAT ANSWER.

The police may appear concerned,
"That was a silly thing to do wasn't it?"
"NO COMMENT"
They may be angry,
"Tell us what we want to know or we'll break every bone in your body."
"NO COMMENT"
They may appear friendly,
"Now if you just tell us what you did and why you did it, we'll forget about the charges."
"NO COMMENT"
They may try to glean other information from you,
"Do you know anything about so and so?"
"NO COMMENT"
They'll often tell lies,
"All your friends have confessed and have now been released. You're on your own now, and they've told us all about your involvement in it, so you might as well tell us yourself."
"NO COMMENT"
Remember--These bastards have been training for years in the art of extracting information from people. Any mood or feeling they put over is totally contrived, and aimed towards getting you to make a statement.

If they threaten to keep you in for longer if you refuse to make a statement, don't listen to them--they are lying. You will undoubtedly be kept in longer if you do make a statement, as once they have found they can crack you, they will push for more and more information.

Helping the animals extends far beyond damaging and liberating--it includes keeping your mouth shut in the police station. An imprisoned activist is a useless activist. Every time you open your mouth another animal dies because there is one less activist to save it. You are therefore doing the movement more harm than good. Remember this when you are taken in.

It is policy that any activist when arrested and questioned, gives names to the police of other animal rights activists will be given no aid from any of the Support Groups.

DOES IT MATTER?

Does it matter who is responsible for any of the ALF actions?
What matters is that these things have been done--by whom is not important.

It is no fun being questioned by the police about something, especially if you know who is responsible. So, you don't want to know. The more people that know about an action, the greater chance the police have of finding the activists. It only takes one person to be interviewed and to crack, and many more are dragged into the shit. Also, people have the habit of telling "just one more person", who also tells "just one more person......"

Any activist who boasts about what he/she has done has only themself to blame if someone snitches on them, but if they bring other names into it....... A closely-knit, water-tight group is the most effective and the hardest to crack.

We have enough to think about in steering clear of the police. Do we really have to have our job made harder by friends asking questions which they shouldn't want to know the answers to?
If you are one of these people--think once...think twice...SHUT UP!
Let's get on with the task at hand.

WHAT THE ALF SHOULD NEVER BECOME-- THE EUTHANIZATION FRONT

This is an all too real future possibility... with the shortage of homes for liberated animals, risk in homing and some being too sick to live out a reasonably healthy life, sad to say some might turn to ... uh-oh... euthanization.

Some might even turn to relying on euthanization, "liberating animals they plan to euthanize and claiming to the media, "they're now in safe homes". This would defeat the entire purpose of the animal liberation front.

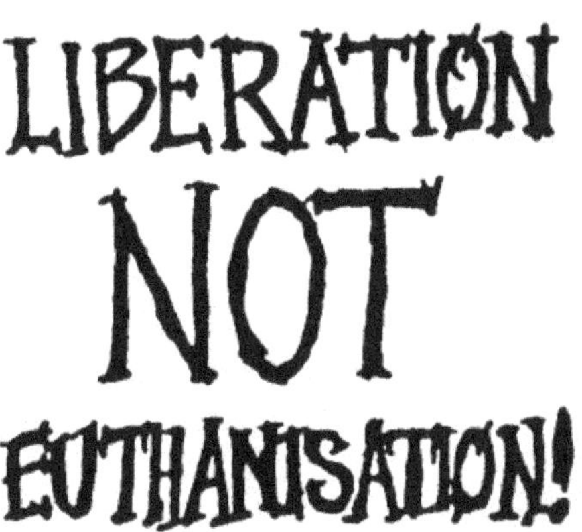
LIBERATION
NOT
EUTHANISATION!

EUTHANIZATION IS NOT LIBERATION!
DO NOT LET THIS HAPPEN!

When Drastic Measures are Required

Are you mad enough to do something rash? Relax...consider the situation carefully. Know the background of the target--go for big business, greed establishments. Remember, the enemy is bigger than us one million fold! Don't waste efforts on the little guy who may be barely feeding the family--hit the major conglomeration! Expose their atrocities!

When the situation calls for drastic measures, arson, a traditional ALF tactic, is an easy, quick way to cause major financial damage.

Arson is extremely dangerous. It is the duty of the activist to be sure nobody, animals or humans, are inside the building before the blaze. If this action is to be seen as an act for ethics then it must be committed carefully!

Remember, arson is a serious crime, a felony punishable by a massive fine and heavy prison sentence. Arson, like other acts of terrorism, carries no statute of limitations, so investigations can continue indefinitely (US law). Also realize, arson has a bad name. Conservative and even liberal/semi-radical activists cringe at the so called "violent" act of blazing.

Commit all crimes in silence! Even your best friends can be squeezed by the heat! Careful! Careful! No evidence! No evidence!

-Cinderella

An Argument for Economic Sabotage vs. Live Animal Liberations.

Yes, full scale animal/human liberation is our goal and the image of the black clad agent of mercy with beagles and bolt cutters is heartwarming. Still, given the enormity of the enemy and the staggering numbers of animals abused, we must consider if putting forth huge efforts to free a handful of creatures is really worth it.

The hardest part is finding homes for the liberated animals and every one is a live piece of evidence. Can we realistically screen every home and know nobody will squeal about a beakless chicken or a barkless dog? A dozen rabbits, rats or guinea pigs quickly become 12 dozen!

Live liberations require larger teams and much more time, plus you leave with more evidence than you go in with. An act of sabotage is quicker, requires less follow-up, less people, less evidence and gets 'em where it hurts the most--their funding!

-Cinderella

Sitting high amidst rocks and wood in my treetop nest looking down over the glittering lights of the city, I ponder and I fret.

The black highway snakes down into cement megopolis. A distant siren wails and, like the commuters creeping home through the haze, an icy drop of dread slithers up my spine and I quiver.

One drop of blood, thinks I, one tiny drop of hope. In all the shit piling up one crimson drop of hope is a terrible thing to waste. So few who really care... And to you, the few, the fistful of rocks breaking windows, making noise, sounding alarms--A word to you--Caution.

The arena's on fire and the temperature's rising. The recent past has seen a furious increase in action--The ALF now ranks among the top 3 on the FBI's list of terrorist groups.

1987 hit an unprecedented high damage tally reaching, by my estimates, somewhere over the ten million dollar mark, including the first US arson attack, the multi-million dollar blaze getting the newly constructed state of the art research lab at U.C. Davis. (Actual figures may be higher. Still it's just a speck of shit splattered on the lab toilet!)

Then, in 1988, the first attempted bombing against a vivisector resulted in the arrest of one woman whose goal may, or may not have been to blast the living shit out of the head researcher of a private Connecticut medical lab. (Police allegedly received a tip that there might be violence there that night... However, she was set up by an agent provocateur from Perceptions Security hired by the medical lab)

Be careful! We can't stress this enough! Do what needs doing and cover your trail. Don't tell your activities to anyone before or after you do it.

-Be smart--always pretend the enemy could be smarter than you. Always have an alternate way out. Know who the real enemies (the big ones) are. Don't be predictable.

-Work alone or in small groups (3-4) comrades you know and can trust 100%. Your life and freedom my depend on that trust.

-Vow to yourself and your team an oath of secrecy. Talk to no one outside. Don't talk about plans on the phone. Never, ever talk to cops. If you brag or squeal you bring the whole movement down with you.

-Go big time! Remember that with each action the odds of getting caught stack up against you. Don't piddle around. Make it count!

Maximum Destruction--Not Minimum Damage!

-Cinderella

TAKE BACK THE INITIATIVE!

Fed up of crawling on your hands and knees, asking for concessions here, concessions there...laying yourself down as cannon fodder at demonstrations...giving the state a chance to photograph and keep a file on you...wasting money on pointless bus-fares to non-starter events...AND STILL GETTING NOWHERE?

That's not to say that all demonstrations are pointless, of course. Some can be, and are, very effective in making animal abusers aware of the extent of opposition to what they are doing. They also serve as a vehicle through which we can communicate with people, and make them look up and take notice of what we are saying. The sort of demonstrations which are pointless, are the sort where everyone trudges around, has a good time, listens to a few speakers and then goes back home to the armchair again.

And meanwhile the murdering and exploiting bastards throughout the world sit back sipping champagne...

"That wasn't too bad was it? Who was it this week?"

"Greenpeace, I think, or it could have been those animal rights people."

"Oh well, it was fairly quiet, no trouble, a nice demonstration--just what we like to see. I hear that there were also lots of arrests, so that's a few more people too occupied with the courts to be able to do anything really threatening."

"Yes--people should be able to vent their feelings in a peaceful way, as long as they go through the right channels. After all, what would we do for a living if these people got too out of hand? And they don't honestly think that the government is going to listen to them do they?!"

All that energy, time and money wasted--and STILL animals are suffering and dying, no nearer to freedom.

Imagine two laboratory dogs talking,
"Did you see those thousands of people today speaking out for us? Good wasn't it!"
"Yes! But just imagine what could have been if they'd all split up into small groups, and come for us and smashed up property instead!"
So--where do we go from here?
The answer lies in taking back the initiative. You do the calling, don't sit back and wait for the police to come for you, or for the next demonstration to be called. Take up the offensive and force the oppressors on to the defensive. If you think that these people will give up what they have got by us asking nicely, I pity your naivety. For god's sake--WISE UP!
Where money is involved, people won't give up until they are forced to give up, until they can see that their dirty business is not going to profit them, and that people are going to pick up their shit and throw it back...harder.
This is war--and I make no apologies for the terminology. It is a war with a difference, a war built out of compassion and respect for our fellow living beings. They cannot wait hundreds of years for the next reform. They are dying in their condemnation. Furthermore, we are not going to get animal liberation through legislation--GOVERNMENT IS PART OF THE WHOLE PROBLEM.
The whole political system is interwoven with, and propped up by big business. Political parties are funded by big companies and multinationals, and in return, you can bet that politicians look after the interests of these companies. In fact, many politicians have shares in these companies or the prospect of a good job after leaving the political arena...
Every time we acknowledge such people by asking them to do something for us in the mode of reform (through letters, petitions, Mobilization For Laboratory Animals, etc.), we increase their power over us by giving them the belief that they have some power over us and can act on our behalf. And every action which reinforces a politician's power, reinforces the laws of this land and lets them stay there just a little bit longer--the same laws which condemn people and animals in their thousands.
We cannot rid ourselves of the effect by ignoring the cause.
Reforms have the effect of pacifying people, deflecting them from the real issues at stake, and giving the impression that politicians really do care. But of course they care...care for what?...

AS A PROTEST

So often, in reports of ALF activities, we read that the activists carried out the rescue of animals, caused damage etc. as a protest against the persecution or cruel treatment of animals.

Sometimes the media automatically inserts the word "protest" but more often it comes from the activists themselves in their claim of responsibility. So what is protest? According to my dictionary, the relevant meaning would be "statement of dissent or disapproval" or a "remonstrance". Is this really what the ALF is, or should be, all about? To me, the answer is quite definitely, "NO". Should ALF attacks which cause hundreds of thousands of dollars damage annually to property connected with animal abuse be regarded merely as a "statement of disapproval"? Is the rescue of thousands of animals every year from vivisection, factory farming and other cruelties only a "remonstrance"?

A protest is an action which calls upon somebody else to do something. To protest against vivisection, for instance, is to call upon the vivisectors to give up, or upon the government to outlaw the cruel practice. And in the end, protest is powerless because, if ignored, it can take the situation no further–

To be truly effective, ALF action must go beyond , and be seen to go beyond (especially by those who carry it out) mere acts of protest. The ALF must exist, and see itself to exist, not just as another protest group but as an organization whose actions are intended to directly bring about change.

Animals should always be rescued whenever possible, but the main aim of ALF actions must not be protest, but economic sabotage.

Actions carried out, not for the sake of their own effect, but as some kind of adjunct to political campaigning are doomed eventually to failure. This is because the "needs" of the political campaign will decree that the action falls short of what is truly effective. Thus we have the spectacle of activists entering laboratories and other animal abuse centres to cause only "limited damage" and just to take documents and photographs when the whole place could have been torn to pieces. Fools, are you proud of your restraint? Pleased that you did not "go too far", so that political ambitionists can once again ride upon your backs? Are you happy to have wasted a golden opportunity?

RECENT ALF ATTACKS IN NORTH AMERICA - 91/92 (Probably more happened, as this is all from 2nd hand sources:media reports and movement & opposition newsletters.)

CANADA-1991

Feb.-Edmonton AB-The ALF paid a visit to the house of a vivisector from the University of Alberta who has been killing dogs for over 11 years. They painted his house and two cars, slashed all the tires, and smashed two front windows of this house.

March-Edmonton AB-J. Rose, a store that sells furs, has their mural and wall painted, locks glued, and windows smashed. Darek's Furs had their windows smashed.

June-Edmonton AB- Derose Bros. Meats had their shop painted with slogans and two trucks were spray painted, daubed with paint stripper, and had their windsheilds sprayed with etching fluid. $2000 damage.

August 20-Edmonton AB-Two trucks belonging to Derose Bros. Meats were spray painted and one was set on fire. $17,000 damage.

September-Edmonton AB-Paris Furs had "SCUM" daubed on their front window with etching fluid. They have since installed a video camera monitering their front window.

November- Edmonton AB-Two meat sellers and two furriers got the usual treatment.

December-Edmonton AB- Three Fur Council of Canada billboards were paint bombed.

-Dec. 14 Three delivery trucks of Billingsgate Fish Company were spraypainted, had their tires slashed, and were set on fire. The building was also painted with slogans and a sign damaged with paint bombs. A fourth device failed to ignite in another truck. $100,000 damage.

-Dec. 30 Activists set ablaze a truck belonging to Hook Advertising and spray painted others with slogans, $10,000 damage. Hook signs carried ads from the Fur Council of Canada earlier in the month.

CANADA 1992

January 1-Edmonton AB-Ouellette Packing Plant was spraypainted and had paint bombs thrown at it. Their van was spraypainted, tires were slashed, and it was set on fire.

January 3-Alberta-The Animal Rights Militia claims to have poisoned 87 Cnadian Cold Buster chocolate bars in Calgary and Edonton because of University of Alberta vivisector Larry Wang's 16 years of animal experiments which led to the invention of the bar.

January 4-7-Calgary AB-2 fur stores had their windows smashed, 2 more got etched windows, 4 meat sellers were spray painted and a fish shop had its windows etched.

January 8-Edmonton AB-A delivery truck of Ouelette's Packers had its tires slashed.

January 9-Edmonton AB-Billingsgate Fish had all three of their replacement trucks spraypainted, and 18 tires were slashed.

February 7-Calgary AB-Fur stores were damaged.

June 1 Edmonton AB-29 cats were liberated from the University of Alberta. Documents were taken and equipment was destroyed.

December 25-Victoria AB- A new ALF cell smashed windows at McDonald's and painted slogans.

UNITED STATES-1991

Minneapolis, MN- During 1991, at least four meat shops were attacked with painted slogans, smashed windows, and/or locks glued.

Memphis, TN- During 1991, large numbers of animal abusing businesses are attacked in the usual manner.

January 1- Chicago, IL-Cook County Hospital's Hektoen Laboratory was raided, and 11 rabbits and 10 guinea pigs were liberated. Dried fruit and bananas were given to imprisoned baboons.

June 10- Corvallis, OR-Oregon State University's Experimental Fur Farm was broken into, and activists destroyed equipment and a data base, and set fire to a storage shed. $62,000 damage.

June 15-Edmonds, WA-The ALF planted incendiary devices at the Northwest Fur Foods Cooperative, a major supp;ier of fur farms and the OSU program. $800,000 damage.

July-Memphis, TN-McDonald's regional office had a dozen windows and two doors smashed.

August 13-Pullman, WA-At Washington State University, 7 coyotes, 6 mink, and 10 mice were liberated and $50,000 damage was done to two laboratories.

December 21-Yamhill, OR-An incendiary device destroys the processing plant at the Malecky Mink Ranch.

UNITED STATES-1992

Memphis, TN-Numbers of attacks on animal abuse businesses in the usual fashion.

January 13-Walnut Creek, CA-"Corrosive chemical" thrown on the windows of a fur store.

February 28-Lansing,MI-$100,000 damage done to Michigan State's mink research program,as documents are taken and offices burned.

June-Memphis,TN-fur stores attacked with painted slogans and smashed windows.

Summer-Indiana-Hoosier Trapping Supplies was spray painted and a fur delivery van in Indianapolis was damaged.

?-South Carolina-The Vegan Front trashed a fur store.

July 5-Park Rapids, MN-3000 people were evacuated from the Park Rapids Rodeo after a bomb threat by the Animal Rights Coalition Force.

July 7-Chicago,IL-An attempt was made to burn a fur billboard.

August-San Francisco, CA-Anti-fur protestors noticed that fur and leather shops in the Union Square area had their windows chemically damaged.

August-Memphis, TN-Fur store spraypainted.

August 9-Memphis, TN-Police arrested 3 Hardliners while they were painting a fur store. 2 others were arrested the following day.

October-Minneapolis, MN-Swanson's Meats had windows of its delivery trucks smashed and slogans painted.

October 24-Milville and Logan, UT-Two Animal Damage Control labs at Utah State were burned abd 25 coyotes liberated. $100,000 damage.

November 8-Minneapolis, MN-5 trucks at Swanson's Meats were burned and locks to the building were glued. $100,000 damage.

SUPPORT GROUPS

The purpose of the SG is to support the work of the ALF by all lawful means possible. This includes: support and defence of the ALF, unifying supporters of the ALF, educating the public as to the need/rationale of direct action, encouraging implementation, providing a communication forum through the Combat newsletter, providing defense funds for ALF activists and raising funds for all of the above activities.

The Animal Liberation Front consists of small autonomous groups of people all over the world who carry out direct action according to the ALF guidelines. You cannot become a member of - or an ALF activists - by joining or writing to any ALF Support Group, which are completely separate organizations.

Any group of people who are vegetarians or vegans and who carry our actions according to ALF guidelines have the right to regard themselves as part of the ALF.

The Support Groups (SG's) have been formed for those who wish to support the ALF without breaking the law. We encourage the participation of all activists, in addition to those who are either unable to or do not wish to perform direct action.

Feel free to contact the Support Groups for any information, please enclose a couple of dollars if possible to cover postage and printing costs.

MAIL SECURITY

If you are a member of an active cell, send any clippings, or your own report, with date, time, place and a few details about the action. Send your reports on plain paper, using block capital letters or a public typewriter that many people have access to. Wear gloves at all times so your fingerprints are not on the paper, envelope or stamp. Do not give your address and don't lick the stamp or envelope - wet it with a sponge. Remember, you should expect that all of the support group's mail is opened and read by the authorities

ANIMAL LIBERATION FRONT SUPPORT GROUPS

ALFSG-CANADA
Box 75029, Ritchie Stn.
Edmonton, Alberta
T6E 6K1 CANADA

ALFSG (U.K.)
B.C.M 1160
London, WC1M 3XX
England

Action for Animals
P.O. Box 152
Lutwyche
Queensland 4030
Australia

ALFSG (FRANCE)
B.C.M. 1160
London, WC1M 3XX
England

ALF PRESS OFFICE
BM 4400
London/WC1N 3XX
ENGLAND
(NOT a support group!)

Friends of the ALF
"Vrien den van het DBF"
Oude Gracht 36
3511 Ap Utrecht
The Netherlands

DBF (SWEDEN)
Box 2051
S-265 02
ASTORP 2
Sweden

APATHY NEVER!

How To Sink Whalers

Driftnetters, And Other Environmentally Destructive Ships

1993

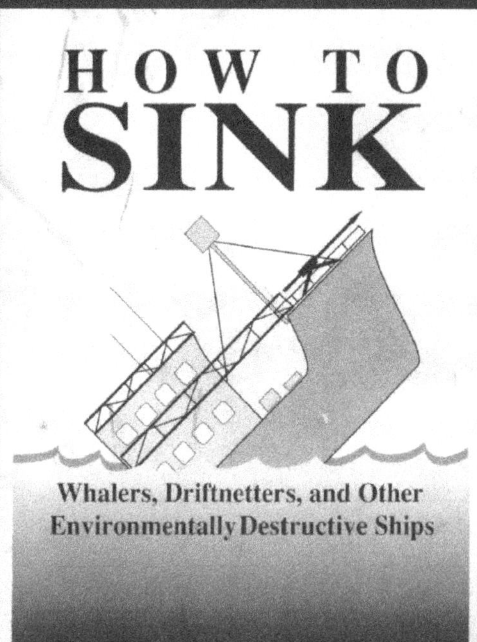

A guide to sinking ships that are used to kill animals.

HOW TO SINK

Whalers, Driftnetters, and Other Environmentally Destructive Ships

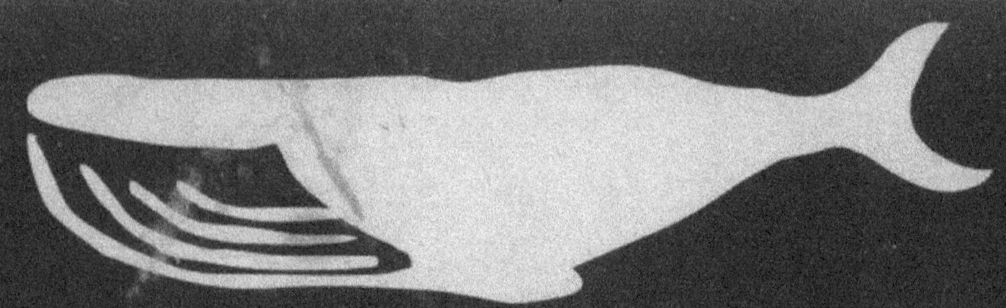

How To Sink Whalers, Driftnetters, and Other Environmentally Destructive Ships

Before we begin, I have a few rules that I must first interject. Rule number one, no guns or explosives. I will *never* advocate them. We want to protect all life. You can sink whalers, driftnetters, and toxic-dumping ships by scuttling them. Using explosives can obviously risk life and will definitely be very counterproductive with the media. If you get caught with them, you can expect to do *long time*. If you are still interested in explosives, then stop right here and go get a U.S. Navy Seals manual and a U.S. Army Improvised Munitions book. But read no further. And rule number two, no actions against the navies that might be guarding these ships. We only want to get the culprits.

When a ship goes underwater, salt water does terrible damage to all mechanical, electrical, refrigeration, and naviontic systems. Sea water is amongst the most corrosive liquids known. Even if they refloat the ship (and often they must if only because the sunken ship is now blocking the harbor), the ship will be out of commission for many months. The financial damage done to the ship is often over one-half the value of ship. We have cases where we have scuttled ships (the two Icelandic whalers for example) where the ships were refloated only to be scrapped. Those ships never killed another whale.

One other thing that I must mention: Scuttling ships is *not* a college prank. It can be *deadly serious*. Get caught in Norway and you'll do time. Get caught in Kaohsiung harbor in Taiwan and, after a forced interogation, they might deposit your body at the bottom of the harbor. This is not kids' stuff. Never forget that 'SINK' is a four-letter word. You have been warned.

But with the scuttling of ecologically destructive ships comes the possibility of doing literally tens of millions of dollars of direct and economic damage. We are talking *mega-tage* here. The joy of bringing down a whaler, of sticking a harpoon up their collective asses, can be one of the great pleasures in an eco-warrior's life. It can be the most-treasured of feathers in one's spiritual war bonnet.

Tool List

It is our experience that you can quickly and easily get almost all the tools you will need in the country where you will be doing the scuttling. In fact, you must. We would not recommend going through customs with a one-meter long set of bolt cutters. We ourselves have never had difficulty in getting all the tools we need in the country where we are to do the scuttling. Often there are pawn shops around seaport towns and you can buy what you need there. We would advise buying your tools in some town other than where the ship is. It may not be a good idea to stay in the town where the ship is docked. Yes, the best traveler leaves no footprints, and the best ecoteur leaves no monkey-prints.

There are two items on our list that you will have difficulty getting locally. Those are the lock-picking set and the CS tear gas. Both are important. You could disassemble and smuggle a small lock-picking kit into the country where you are going, but if you get caught with it, that will be the end of your action.

Do *not* fly with tear gas. If you can safely obtain it or something else equally nauseating in the country where the action is to take place, then definitely do it.

Necessary Tool List:

- large bolt cutters, at least two-feet (60 centimeters) long
- large pipe wrench
- large crescent wrench
- large pry (crow) bar
- phillips and flat-blade screwdrivers
- vice grips
- flashlights and headlamps
- lock-picking kit (and knowledge of how to use it! there are books that explain how to do this)
- gloves, waterproof clothing, tarpolin
- a dark set of disposable clothes (black is always the most fashionable color for scuttlers)
- flexible rubber gloves
- a complete change of clothes.
- two long, heavy-duty high quality pad locks per ship
- a half-full bottle of hard liquor
- soap and water to clean up with

Optional—But Very Helpful—Tools:

- two-way communications system
- small, portable, acetylene cutting torch
- CS tear-gas canisters—slow release type. If not obtainable, substitute some other nauseating, but non-poisonous agent.
- collapsible sea kayak (depending upon the site)

The critical factor in sinking a ship is being able to sneak aboard it *undetected*. If you can do that, you can bring the ship down. *The actual mechanics of sinking the ship is not nearly as difficult as locating the ship and boarding it undetected.*

All ships come to dock for repairs and preparation for the next season. It is at this point that it is possible to sneak aboard the ship for scuttling. There will be times when no one is on board the ship. We do not think that you can scuttle a ship when someone else is aboard it. They will detect you. Nor would it be desirable to try. Typically, nights and holidays are the best times to board any ship undetected. The ships may be moored next to the dock, or anchored out at harbor. You may need a collapsible kayak to get to it. Or you may have to 'borrow' a rowboat. You must be able to determine when no one is aboard. This can require much observation. But in some cases when we have found the boat, we have determined immediately that no one was aboard (for example, no tracks in the snow on or around the ship). We have then gone in and sunk that ship on the spot.

Each situation is different. With increased observation, you run the risk of being observed yourself and blowing your cover. If they become suspicious of you, you will *not* be able to sink the ship. Surprise is everything. At a certain point, you must decide whether the action is 'do-able' or not. If you think it is, then at a certain point you must decide when it is time to *go in for the kill* and do it.

Be sure to get the right ship. Make sure that it is an active whaler or driftnetter or whatever. Only sink the ships that are guilty of environmental devastation.

Now, Our Thirteen *Proven* Steps On How To Sink A Ship

STEP 1 BOARD THE SHIP UNDETECTED

I advise that you first board the ship and then hide yourself and your tools. Wear rubber gloves at all times and *do not take them off*. You can hide in the stairwells, in the middle of gear stacked on the deck, or wherever. You could carry a tarpolin and hide under it. Then wait: For ten or fifteen minutes, *do not move*. If someone has seen you board the ship, this will give them time to come searching for you, and you will find out if you have been seen or not. If they are going to catch you, it is much better that they catch you while you are just trespassing, rather than sabotaging. The penalties are not nearly as severe. You should have a half-full bottle of hard liquor with you. Take a swig or two so that you have booze on your breath. If they catch you, you should try to pass yourself off as just another drunk sailor in port. In many port towns, this is not very unusual. Also, if you think you are going to be caught at this point, try to dump your toolbag into the water. If they find both you and the bag, your toolbag will be very incriminating.

STEP 2 GET INTO THE ENGINE ROOM.

You may have to cut or pick locks, use pry bars, or even cutting torches to get in. But quite possibly, *the doors will be wide open*. Typically, the entrance to the engine room is near the stern of the ship. Once you get into the ship, *keep going down*. The engine room is at the bottom of the ship. Eventually, you will find it. Its door may be locked. If so, you will now be able to open its lock in privacy. The engine room is an oily, toxic-waste filled area. Typically, you will get dirty with the rust and oil in this room.

STEP 3 FIND THE SEA WATER INTAKE VALVE.

All large ocean-going ships have salt water intake valves and piping. These ships need salt water for deck-cleaning, fire-fighting, and for cooling their massive diesel engines. There are no air-cooled diesel engines out at sea. Usually, the coolant radiator from the diesel engine is bathed in a steady stream of cool sea water. The best way to find the sea water intake valve is to *follow the piping*. Ocean-going ships typically will have four or five different types of plumbing. Fresh water, salt water, fuel oil, engine oil, and hydraulic fluid. The salt water pipes are generally the widest. The sea water intake valve is almost always located in the engine room. The trick is to keep following the pipes to the thickest one that appears to be attached to the side or the bottom of the ship. It is at this point that the sea water enters the ship.

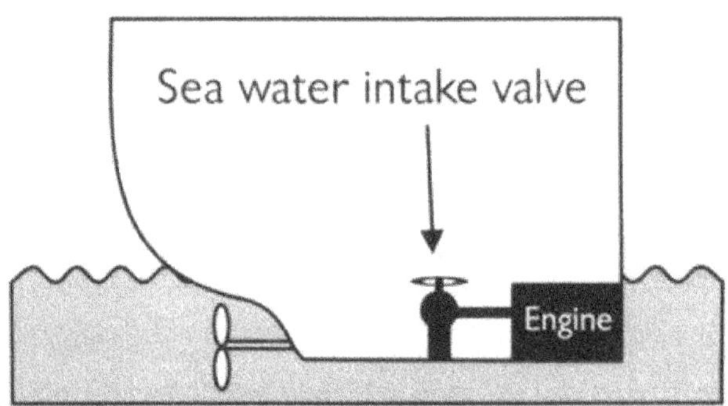

The sea water intake typically is at the bottom of the ship, but it can be on the side.

There is one exception that I should mention now, that of ships with keel-cooling systems. Keel-cooling ships are ships that pump their engine coolant directly into cooling pipes attached to the keel (outside) of the ship. They do not use internal heat exchange with salt water. Keel-cooling ships typically just stay in colder waters. Norwegian whalers use keel-cooling systems. But ships with keel-cooling systems still have salt-water intake systems. They still need sea water for deck-cleaning and firefighting. Their sea water intakes are not as large as those on non-keel-cooling ships, but they are still plenty adequate for scuttling. When we sank the Norwegian pirate whaling ship the *Nybrena* on December 27th, 1992, it had a keel-cooling system.

STEP 3 CLOSE THE SEA WATER INTAKE VALVE.

This is the master valve that controls the entrance of all the sea water coming into

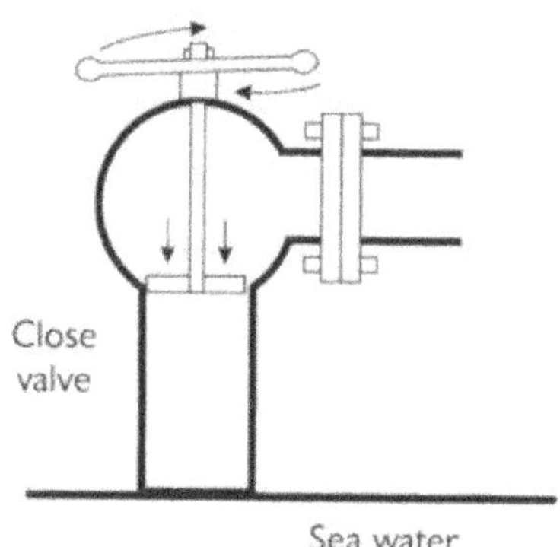

the ship. You need to close this so that you can you can cut off the pressure to the piping. If the ship is in dock for any amount of time, they should have closed the valve already. But we have boarded ships and found the valve left open. We have had to shut the valve, do our work, and then reopen the valve to sink the ship.

STEP 4 REMOVE THE HANDLE FROM THE VALVE.

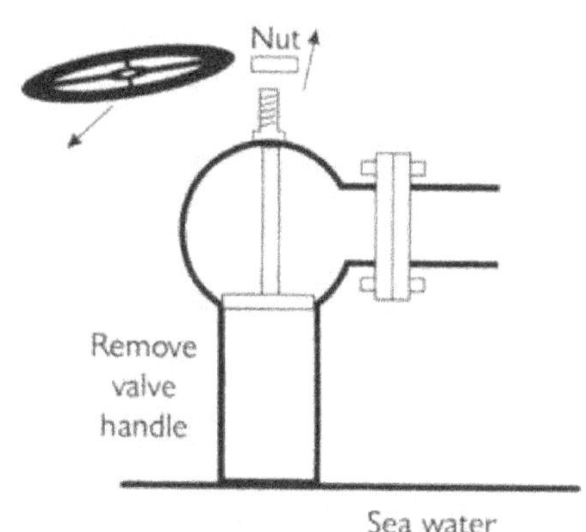

The valve handle may look either like a steering wheel or a lever type handle. Take it off. You will probably have to remove a retaining bolt that is holding the handle on. Do it and then pull the handle off. Hide the handle somewhere away from the valve stem. When you are done, we should just have a valve stem protruding outward from the valve.

We take the handle off so that if they find the ship in the process of sinking, they cannot easily shut off the valve.

STEP 5 NOW DISCONNECT THE PIPING COMING OUT OF THE VALVE.

Now that you have closed the valve, you have removed the water pressure from the system and you can work more easily. You must now use your pipe wrench, crescent wrench, and perhaps vice grips to remove the pipe or plating that is near to the intake valve. The larger the pipe you remove, the better. You will have to improvise here. Study the pipes and find one that you can take off. As you are taking the bolts off, do not be surprised

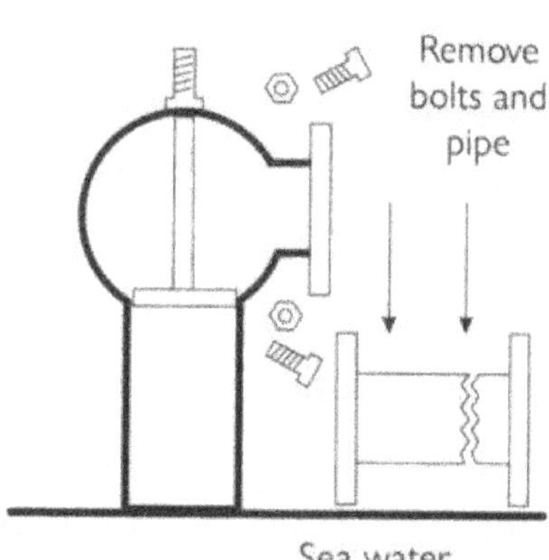

if water starts spraying out. This is water that is already in the system and you are now bleeding it out. It will stop draining shortly.

Please note: *Remove the pipe*. Do not just loosen it. Take your time and take all the bolts off and *remove it*. Carry the pipe away from where you disconnected it. You are getting close.

STEP 6 GATHER UP ALL YOUR TOOLS AND PUT THEM BACK IN YOUR BAG.

Gather up *everything that you brought aboard*. Everything. You want to be ready to make a quick exit.

STEP 7 NOW OPEN THE SALT-WATER INTAKE VALVE WITH YOUR PIPE WRENCH

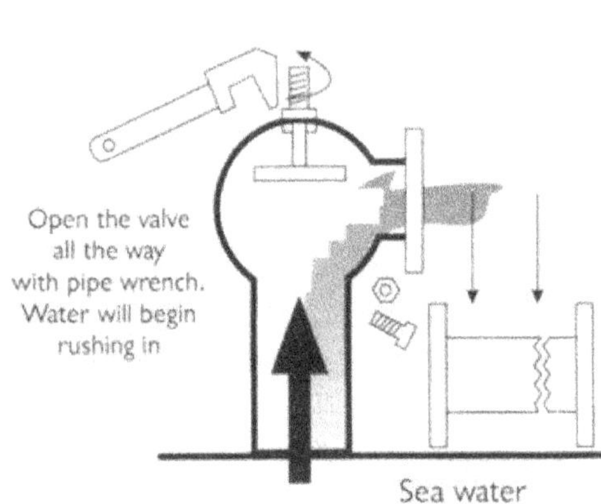
Open the valve
all the way
with pipe wrench.
Water will begin
rushing in
Sea water

This is the moment you have been waiting for. Put your pipe wrench on the valve stem and open the valve.

Salt water should begin spraying all over the place. Keep turning the valve stem until the valve is fully wide open. The ship has now hit the fan. Then lean on the pipe wrench and push it as hard as you can. Try to break the valve while it is locked wide open. We give bonus points for this. We want to jam that valve so tight that no one will be able to close it before the boat sinks.

Please note: This is the 'high pucker factor' part of the action. Don't be surprised at this point if your arse, in and of its own volition, bites five kilos of metal right out of the scaffolding that you are sitting on. If so, we excuse you.

STEP 8 BASH THE VALVE STEM WITH THE PIPE WRENCH.

Hit it *hard* with the pipe wrench to try to bend it out of 'true' and further lock the valve wide open. Do whatever you can to further jam the valve in a wide-open position. While you are doing this, water will be flying all over the place and the engine room will be flooding right in front of you. Stay calm if you can—it *is* possible—and *just do it*.

The ship is now sinking. We advise you to spend a few extra minutes to cut and break things. You should now take your boltcutters and cut all the injection nozzles to the diesel engines. We want salt water in the engine heads and cylinders. They tend not to run very well when they are filled with sea water. The metal also oxidizes quickly. Then take a mallet and smash all the gauges that you see. Go ahead and cut any pipes and hydraulic lines that you can. You may find

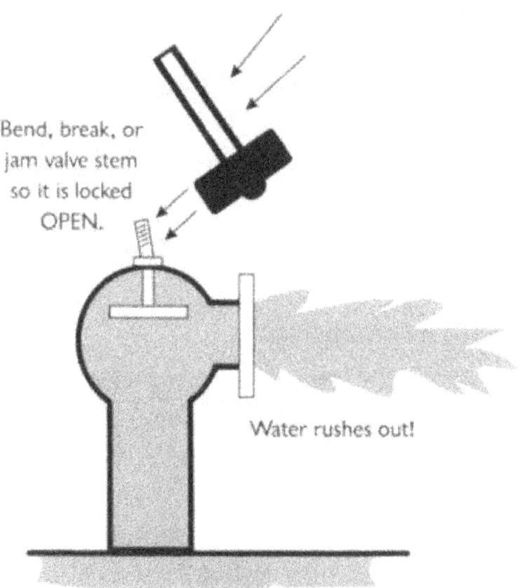
Bend, break, or
jam valve stem
so it is locked
OPEN.
Water rushes out!

yourself with extraordinary adrenalized energy and strength at this moment. If so, cutting, smashing, and breaking things can be the *perfect* way to work it off. We have found this 'bashing' period to be a time of great, albeit somewhat frantic, fun. Please enjoy this 'sinking feeling.'

STEP 9 TAKE EVERYTHING YOU BROUGHT WITH YOU OUT OF THE ENGINE ROOM.

Leave no material evidence.

STEP 10 IF YOU HAVE A TEAR-GAS CANISTER, JUST BEFORE YOU STEP OUT OF THE ENGINE ROOM DOOR, OPEN THE CANISTER AND SET IT UP HIGH SOMEPLACE.

Do *not* throw the tear gas canister into the incoming salt water. The salt water will considerably reduce the effects of the teargas. Just trigger the canister and set it near the door. Needless to say, you should shut your eyes and hold your breath while you do this. Or put on a gas mask. Then quickly shut the engine room door.

If you cannot obtain teargas, try using some other nauseating, but non-poisonous substance. There are numerous recipes for such mixtures in other books.

STEP 11 PUT A HEAVY-DUTY, LONG-HANDLED LOCK ON BOTH THE ENGINE ROOM AND THE MAIN ENTRANCE DOOR.

We may have broken their locks while entering their ship, so we feel it is only proper that we should replace their damaged property. We're not scoundrels. We also feel it to be rather improbable that *their* keys would fit *our* locks.

If they discover their ship in the midst of sinking, they will try to board it and try to pump it out. We use the locks and tear gas to buy as much time as possible.

There is a certain point when a ship gets so full of water that it hits a critical mass and cannot be rescued. The tear gas and locks help us to buy time to get the ship to that point.

Please note again: It is a serious crime to travel on air flights with tear gas. Do *not* do it. Also, the locks must have a long locking loop on them. These doors are made of thick metal and the locking arm will have to travel through thick metal before it can catch.

STEP 12 DITCH THE TOOLS OVERBOARD.

Ease them into the water with a rope on the bag. Do *not* throw them in because someone could hear the splash of a thirty-kilo bag hitting the water.

STEP 13 G.T.F.O. GET THE FUCK OUT!!!!!!!

You have two basic choices in exfiltration here. Either go underground immediately at a safe house, or leave the country as quickly as possible.

It has been our experience that it is best to leave as quickly as possible. It may take twelve hours for them to figure out that someone has sabotaged them. In the meantime, you can be long gone.

As soon as you are safely away from the ship, we advise you to take off and completely dispose of everything that you have worn onto the ship. This includes your shoes. Then wash yourself off. Remove all of the diesel fuel and salt water that you may have gotten on yourself. Then put on a clean change of clothes. We think that you should now 'dress for success'. We would not want anyone to get the wrong impression about us ecoteurs as we are leaving their country.

"Bye bye, and have a *NICE* day!"

GENERAL NOTE:

If you have not used explosives or violence against people (both of which I am totally opposed to) then generally, it will be difficult for the site country to extradite you. But they may try. Each case is different. In the past, countries have not even tried because of the potential embarrassment of a media trial. They want to keep their eco-crimes quiet. It is your personal choice whether you want to further embarrass the country where you did your scuttling by participating in such a trial. Some scuttlers have turned themselves in after the fact. Others have not. I personally want you to live on to become the '*serial sinker*'. I well understand that it is the healthy reaction of any wild animal not to knowingly enter a cage. And who wants to bother with a international legal system when their laws don't protect ecosystems anyhow? But of course, it is your choice.

HAPPY HUNTING!!!

Agent #013

As Darkness Falls

1995

AS DARKNESS FALLS...

ANIMAL LIBERATION FRONT PRIMER

A cursory guide to sabotage & live liberations.

AS DARKNESS FALLS...

ANIMAL LIBERATION FRONT PRIMER

Forward

Before you even consider undertaking any action read this entire guide, then read it again. Know every detail inside and out, particularly those parts regarding preparation and security. We highly recommend you read Ecodefense, by Edward Abbey, as well. Although oriented more towards environmental action, it is incredibly detailed and informative. If what is presented here is the kindergarten class on direct action, Ecodefense is the college course.

Dedication

This guide is dedicated to the brave men and women of the Animal Liberation Front. In this age of insanity you may be branded a terrorist, but you will one day be remembered as a selfless warrior who dared to fight for what is right.

Copyright

This guide is anti-copyrighted. Any reproduction, in part or in full, without the expressed, written consent of the authors would be greatly appreciated.

Legal Disclaimer

This guide is for your entertainment, information, and general interest only. It is not meant to encourage the activities described within. Were just writing this for the heck of it. We would never dream of encouraging someone to use the proven-effective methods presented within to free innocent beings from the depths of hell, or to destroy the tools used to torture, mutilate, and murder them. Wed much prefer you sit at home watching TV and remain apathetic.

The History of the ALF

The Animal Liberation Front has its roots in 1960s England. At this time a small group of people began sabotaging hunts there. This group, the Hunt Saboteurs Association, would lay false scents, blow hunting horns to send hounds off in the wrong direction, and chase animals to safety. In 1972, after effectively ending a number of traditional hunting events across England, members of the Hunt Saboteurs decided more militant action was needed, and thus began the Band of Mercy. They moved on to destroying guns and sabotaging hunters vehicles by breaking windows and slashing tires. They also began fighting other forms of animal abuse, burning seal hunting boats as well as pharmaceutical laboratories. After the jailing of two Band of Mercy members in 1975, word spread, support grew, and the Animal Liberation Front was begun in 1976.

Who are the ALF?

Members of the Animal Liberation Front act directly to stop animal suffering, at the risk of losing their own freedom. Direct action refers to illegal actions performed to bring about animal liberation. These are usually one of two things: rescuing animals from laboratories or other places of abuse, or inflicting economic damage on animal abusers. Due to the illegal nature of ALF activities, activists work anonymously, and there is no formal organization to the ALF. There is no office, no leaders, no newsletter, and no official membership. Anyone who carries out direct action according to ALF guidelines is a member of the ALF.

Animal Liberation Front Guidelines

- To liberate animals from places of abuse, i.e. fur farms, laboratories, factory farms, etc. and place them in good homes where they may live out their natural lives free from suffering.
- To inflict economic damage to those who profit from the misery and exploitation of animals.
- To reveal the horror and atrocities committed against animals behind locked doors by performing nonviolent direct actions and liberations.
- To take all necessary precautions against hurting any animal, human and non-human.

The third section contains a very important word - nonviolent. The ALF does not, in any way, condone violence against any animal, human or non-human. Any action involving violence is by its definition not an ALF action, any person involved not an ALF member. The fourth section must be strictly adhered to. In over 20 years, and thousands of actions, nobody has ever been injured or killed in an ALF action.

One View of the ALF

One ALF member put it this way, "I see participating in the ALF's raids not as a momentary forfeiture of the highest human values - goodness, generosity and the like - but rather as an embodiment of them... We feel a sense of urgency for the animals whose pain and imminent death is absolutely real to them today."

Does Direct Action Work?

Susan Paris, president of vivisection front group Americans For Medical Progress (AMP), admits the Animal Liberation Front has had a large impact on vivisectionists. She writes, "Because of terrorist acts by animal activists like Coronado, crucial research projects have been delayed or scrapped. More and more of the scarce dollars available to research are spent on heightened security and higher insurance rates. Promising young scientists are rejecting careers in research. Top-notch researchers are getting out of the field." The August 1993 Report to Congress on Animal Enterprise Terrorism describes the ALF's effectiveness as, "Where the direct, collateral, and indirect effects of incidents such as this are factored together, ALF's professed tactic of economic sabotage can be considered successful, and its objectives, at least towards the victimized facility, fulfilled." If we look past the "terrorist" rhetoric, we can see that its a fact - direct action works. If you don't take their word for it, ask any animal rescued by the ALF and I'm sure they would agree that direct action works.

Are You Ready for the ALF?

Direct action is nothing to take lightly. The moment you carry out your first action you are at risk of being arrested. Direct action is very demanding, physically and mentally. Are you in top physical shape? If you were being chased by a police officer, could you outrun him? Could you scale a barbed wire fence? Living under the constant stress of possible arrest can take its toll mentally as well. ALF activists should also remain drug and alcohol free, as these things decay physical and mental ability, give the police another reason to investigate you, and waste money better spent on supplies Veganism is obviously encouraged, as it is both morally responsible, and will better your physical condition. Some ALF members will also limit their association with mainstream animal rights groups, as to remain less visible to police investigations.

Finding People to Work With

One of the most important steps towards getting involved in direct action is finding people to work with. In any ALF action you are putting your freedom on the line, so you must be positive you can completely trust the people you are working with. It is essential to find people who will not sell out you or the movement should an arrest occur. You should always work with people who you know well and have for a long period of time, people who you know you can rely on. Security is an important issue in direct action, so people with a tendency to brag or who wont be able to keep their mouth shut are a bad idea. Starting your own cell is better than joining an existing one, since if you know of an existing one, their security obviously isn't too good. Asking someone if they want to get involved is never an easy thing to do. Bring up the subject in a general way and see how the person feels about direct action first, and move on from there. Cells usually consist of 2 to 5 members. Use the minimum number of people needed for each action, but don't forget the importance of look outs. Having extra people unnecessarily puts them at-risk. One person should be chosen as the leader of the group. This doesn't mean that person has any special power or privileges, and it often wont come into play at all. But if during an actions things go wrong, someone will need to make split second decisions, and in this case there is no time for democracy. Progress as a group, starting with minor actions to get used to each other, discussing after each action what went well and what didn't, and discussing how to improve and hit harder.

Getting Started

Before you even think about undertaking any action, read. Know this guide inside and out. Before you do anything you'd better know how to do it right, or you may wind up in a lot of trouble. As with anything, the first time is the hardest. So start small. If your first action is a liberation of a large laboratory with high security you are going to have problems. Start by gluing locks or some spray paint. You can go about finding a target a few ways. First, you may want to decide what kind of establishment you want to target - a fur shop, a butcher shop, a factory farm or slaughterhouse, or maybe a fast food restaurant? If you are planning on getting involved in direct action you are hopefully already aware of various animal rights issues and probably know where and how to find whichever kind of abuser you want to target. Your local animal rights group is probably aware of abusers in the area, but keep in mind that local animal rights groups are the first people the police will question. The easiest way to find a target is to let your fingers do the walking. A phone book can direct you to all your local fur shops, butcher shops, etc. If fast food restaurants are your goal, you cant go down the street without seeing one. Locations of fur farms can be found in The Final Nail. Once you've begun and know what you are doing, go big. The more actions you take part in the more likely it gets that you will get caught, so be sure that when you hit you hit hard.

Planning

After selecting your target become familiar with it. You may want to study a road map and become familiar with the surrounding area. You should first visit the sight in daylight. Park well away in a non-suspicious place, like the parking lot of a large store or a side road with many cars. Approach on foot and get as close as possible. Take a good look around (without looking suspicious) and think about how you are going to do whatever it is you are going to do. Once back to your car, draw a map including everything you can remember. Now it is time to draw up your exact plan. Leave nothing to chance. Figure out every detail and be certain that everyone is completely familiar with every detail. You don't want to find yourself at the site trying to get your act together. Next, return to the site once more before your action, this time at night. Follow your route to the site just as it will be during your action. You can think of this as a dress rehearsal. Get as close to the target as you can. This should also be as close to the time of day your action will take place (actions are obviously almost always carried out at night), so that you can see what security and other factors are in effect at that time. Always plan for things to go wrong. Know what you will do if you come in contact with a security officer or police. Know which way you will run, if you will go as a group or alone, and where you will rendezvous. These recommendations are general. For something as simple as gluing locks, less intense planning is needed. For something as complex as a raid, more planning may be necessary.

Preparation

Consider leaving your immediate area for actions; repeatedly working close to home can be a tip off to police. Also be sure to not keep a regular schedule of days and times your actions take place - if the police establish your pattern its one more thing they can use to catch you. As tempting as it is, avoid hitting the same place repeatedly. This is how a good number of people get caught. If you choose to report your actions, don't name your specific group. If so, the police will know just what actions are carried out by your group, making finding you easier. Always have a story set if stopped by the police. Know where it is you will say you are coming from and going to. If you are going to be using your car for actions, remove all bumper stickers. Also be sure all lights, license plates, etc. are OK. Drive carefully and legally. Don't give them reason to stop you. Be sure to have enough gas before leaving for an action, so you don't have to stop on the way, or especially while transporting animals. Clothing is important as well. Wear nothing with identifiable markings. Consider many targets are equipped with security cameras, and always assume the one you are hitting is. Any tattoos should be covered, any piercing covered or removed. You want to wear dark colors, but all black can look suspicious, so just keep it dark but not unusual. Ski masks are commonly employed during direct action, but be ready to ditch them if need be - they can be quite incriminating, especially on a summer night. A hooded sweatshirt, a baseball cap, and a scarf are a better idea in some locations. On high risk operations you may want to get some oversized shoes from a thrift shop to avoid leaving tell tale footprints. Stuffing the toes will make them wearable. Another option is to keep a pair of shoes used just for direct action with your tools at a safe house. If this is the case, only put them on while on the way to an action and take them off on the way back, as not leave corresponding footprints around your house or on your carpet. Wearing socks over your shoes or covering the soles in duct tape also works well against footprints. For actions where the police are going to be investigating more heavily, even hairs and fibers on clothing may be a problem. In this case you can buy clothes from a thrift store just for that night, and throw them away afterwards. Another possibility on high risk operations is to wear boiler suits, which cover all your clothes, and can be removed quickly after back to the car. Always wear gloves and be mindful of fingerprints. Be careful of using thin latex gloves, since fingerprints can be left through them. Put one pair over another if you choose to use them. Fingerprints will also be left on the inside of the glove, so if you use them , dispose of them separately from any other evidence. Be careful whenever purchasing equipment for an action. Buying a gallon of bright red paint a block from home and dumping it on the McDonald's two blocks away the same day is not a good idea. Purchase everything far away from home and always with cash, as well as long before an action is to take place when possible. Be careful of using materials that will give away where you are from. For instance, if using newspapers in an arson attack far from home, using your local paper will be dead give-away. Wipe everything you are taking with you completely to remove fingerprints, in case anything is dropped or has to be left behind. You have to scrub hard to remove prints, and some soap or rubbing alcohol may help. Clean everything as if it is going to be left behind, since sooner or later something you didn't plan to leave will drop.

For this same reason you should take as little as possible with you, and connect whatever you must take to your body. A rubber band through your belt loop with each end attached to your key chain will keep it secure, even if you are being chased and have to go headfirst over a fence, etc. Even if you don't touch something while purchasing it by wearing gloves for instance, wipe it anyway so it cant be traced Obviously, do not have drugs, weapons, or anything else illegal on you or in you car during an action. If you are using tools such as crowbars or bolt cutters (this is mostly for liberations), sharpen or file them after every action, since slight markings on the tool can leave traceable markings on what is opened. Also, never keep tools at your house. If you are keeping tools used in actions, store them at a safe house. A safe house is the house of a person not involved in the actions at all, someone who the police would never investigate. Tools and clothing should never be disposed of in your own garbage. A large dumpster at a store or restaurant is an ideal place to dispose of evidence. Never buy cheap tools, especially if you are using walkie talkies. Your freedom and the animals lives are on the line, so go for the quality equipment. Before setting out for an action, spend about 30 minutes outside in the dark. This will improve your night vision. When using flashlights, regular light will ruin your night vision. Red or blue lenses will not, and are also preferable because they are less visible from a distance. Military flashlights, available at Army/Navy stores come with red or blue lenses. Another piece of equipment that can greatly increase security is walkie talkies. Having lookouts set up and connected to the team via radio can increase warning times from seconds to minutes. The Walkman/headset style are ideal, and are commonly available at Radio Shack for a reasonable price. Night vision scopes are another useful tool. They take existing light and magnify it tens of thousands of times, allowing one to virtually see in the dark. Top of the line night vision equipment is out of the financial range of most activists, but earlier models are available for a few hundred dollars at Army/Navy and survival stores. For very thorough information on radios, night vision scopes, and many other useful bits of technology, consult Ecodefense.

Security

The government is actively monitoring animal liberationists, particularly suspected members of the ALF, so watch your back. They are opening mail and tapping phone lines, so never ever ever say anything incriminating over the phone, mail, or e-mail. Always assume that you are being watched and your house may be searched at any time (they have gone so far as dismantling heating ducts while searching the houses of suspected ALF members, so never assume anything is hidden well enough). Discussing direct action works on a need-to-know basis. Never tell anyone anything that they do not absolutely need to know. Never discuss actions with people not involved, for your safety and theirs. If someone asks you about the ALF, say that you aren't involved, but you have heard or read about it. That way you can discuss the ALF without incriminating yourself. If someone says something incriminating over the phone, quickly excuse yourself and hang up before they can get another word in, then explain to them what they did wrong next time you see them in person. Keep in mind that homes, cars, and anywhere else can be bugged. Try to discuss actions in areas that are secure (where nobody can overhear), but that they would be unable to bug. Take a walk through the woods, for instance. Except for the purpose of improving your group and its effectiveness, once an action has taken place, never discuss it again. The damage was done, animals lives were saved, and that's the important thing. Bringing up old "war stories" is an unnecessary risk. All this may seem like paranoia, but the government will go to any length stop us. Besides, its better to be a little paranoid than in jail. Effectiveness Start small, then move on to bigger things. Even the simplest actions take practice to get right, so try one thing at a time until you've gotten it down. Once you've mastered the small things, use them in combination to really ruin an abusers day. Think about possibilities of combining breaking windows and paint bombs for instance. Be sure to start with the quietest parts when doing a number of things. What is outlined here are general methods used by the ALF. Every location and building is different, so after checking over your target, you should both modify these methods based on the specific area and target itself, and feel free to be creative and come up with new ways to do damage. Creativity will make you more effective, harder to catch since you are less predictable, and make whatever security they come up with less effective.

Windows

Windows are probably the easiest target available in most situations, yet large windows can cost hundreds, making them an ideal target. Glass etching fluid (hydrofluoric acid) is available in some larger arts and crafts stores. Be sure to buy out of town on specialized items like this. Its a liquid or cream that eats through the surface of glass. If you can get a hold of some, put it in some kind of squeeze bottle, one of those plastic lemon ones for instance, and off you go. If you get the cream it can also be applied with a paintbrush, allowing slogans to be written on the window. Its potent stuff, so be careful not to get it on your skin. Working quickly at the target you'll probably make somewhat of a mess with the bottle, so bring a plastic bag to throw it in after you are done. Its a quick and relatively safe way to cause some financial damage. A less expensive but much noisier method is simply smashing windows. It is loud, so get ready to run. Aside from throwing a brick or rock, a popular way to do this is with a sling shot. They are available in many sporting stores. You may have to patronize a store that sells hunting equipment to find one, but you can always offset this by returning at a later date and smashing their windows in turn. The advantage of a sling shot is that you don't have to be right next to the window to break it. Sling shots can even be effective from moving cars. Try to fire symmetrical objects such as ball bearings or nuts. Rocks or bolts will be hard to control due to their lack of aerodynamics. Whatever you shoot, be sure to wipe them for fingerprints first. It is always your responsibility to be certain there is nobody in or near the store that you could injure while firing. Shooting from totally inside the car (as in, don't hang out the side) will make detection a whole lot harder. Air guns (a.k.a. BB guns) are another option. They don't do as much damage to the window as a brick might, but they are very quick, can be used easily from inside a car, and are very quiet. You can easily roll up to a store, stop in front for a second, roll down the window, take a shot, and leave. Unless someone is standing right there, nobody will notice a thing. Most of the time they will leave a small hole with a spider web crack, about the size of a silver dollar. Occasionally they will completely shatter a window though, so be ready for it. There are generally two types of BB guns. The first look like rifles, and are powered by being manually pumped. The second look like handguns, and are powered by CO_2 cartridges. The cartridges only cost around $2 each and will give you around 150 shots. The advantage of the CO_2 style is that they are generally semi-automatic (meaning it fires one shot every time you pull the trigger). Using such a device you could take out over a dozen windows in a couple of seconds. They do look like real guns though, so if the police roll up, drop them immediately or risk getting shot. The other option for breaking windows is a hammer. Tiler's hammers are best because of their pointed design; they can be found in most hardware stores. Windows, especially shatter proof, are tougher than they seem, so use a hammer of some weight. The best time for this is a stormy night, the lack of visibility and noise of the storm providing excellent cover. You'll naturally think to hit windows in the center, but this is actually the strongest part. Always go for the corners, as these are the weak spots. Another option with windows is glass glue, which permanently sticks glass to glass. Attaching a piece of glass with a slogan painted on the inside will require them to replace the whole window.

Shutters

People in more urban areas are probably familiar with stores lowering metal shutters over their windows while closed. After having windows smashed, a target store in a less urban area may do the same. If you are dealing with the kind of shutters that are a grid, or bars, etching fluid, sling shots, or BB guns will still work fine. Its also possible to simply lock any kind of object to the shutter, making it impossible to open.

Sometimes they wont use all the holes for locks that are available on the shutter. If this is the case, put your own lock on there. Make sure its fingerprint free first. More difficult are the full shutters that don't have any holes. Hitting the shutter with a sledgehammer may work in both damaging the shutter, and possibly breaking the window if they are close enough together. A more subtle method of dealing with full shutters is gluing the shutter locks, which you can see under the gluing locks section. If they have been dumb enough to only put a shutter over the main window and left a smaller one, like on a door, uncovered - break that one, then reach in and break the main one.

Vehicles

Vehicles are another easy target. There's a great number of ways to do damage to them. When doing a set of things to a vehicle, start with the quieter parts. There are basically two different approaches that can be taken with vehicles, destruction and sabotage - the difference being with destruction vehicles are visibly damaged, and with sabotage the action is not evident until the vehicle is run and experiences mechanical problems. There are many options with the destruction method. Tires can be slashed. An ice pick, sharp knife, or anything of that sort will work. Tires, especially on trucks, are tougher than they seem, so use something thick and strong that wont break or bend. Putting a hole in the side wall will make it impossible to repair. A pair of pillars can also be used to yank out the stem (the thing you put air in through), which will also flatten the tire. A large screwdriver can damage a radiator by punching holes in it through the grill. If you cant get to the engine, you can cut wires and break various components. If you cant get to the engine, you can also cut what you can from underneath. Bring something heavy-duty like small bolt cutters, as regular wire cutters wont be able to handle metal cables and such. Either paint or paint stripper can do some damage to the paint job. Windshield wipers can be broke off, headlights and windshields smashed or painted with etching fluid, and locks glued. Windshields are made to deflect rocks kicked up on the road, so only more direct methods of breaking them, such as a hammer, will work.

With the more subtle sabotage method, it is important to leave no signs you were there, so the vehicle is run and the damage is done. If dealing with trucks, look for levers on the side of the hood to release it and open it forward. The stereotypical sabotage technique is sugar in the gas tank. This will merely block the filter, and do little damage. More effective fuel tank additives are sand or 10 to 15 mothballs. Be sure not to use sand from near home, as it can be traced. The best sabotage target is the lubricating system. If incapacitated, it will cause the engine to overheat, bind, and generally destroy itself. Karo syrup in the oil filler hole is another classic that, in reality, only effects the filter. One option for major damage is to carefully remove the oil, either by punching a hole in the oil pan, or removing the drain plug. Adding water to the oil is more effective, since it will not lubricate, but will keep the oil pressure up, keeping a warning light from coming on. Better than water is diesel or gasoline, as it will also break down existing oil. For maximum effect, look to adding abrasives to the lubricating system. The oil filler hole is not the only option here. All moving parts need lubrication, such as transmissions, differentials, and wheel hubs. Many lubrication points will have screw on caps that can be removed with an adjustable wrench. Sand can be used for this as well. However, the top of the line abrasive is the kind used to polish stones in tumblers, available in hobby and lapidary supply shops. A very fine powder grit mixed with a slightly more coarse fine sand grit will have the best chance of getting throughout the whole engine and wrecking everything. A 400 and 600 grit size mix works well. A mere half pint of this will completely destroy an engine. Pouring sand or grit can be difficult, especially at night, so here are a few ways to make it easier. Attach a couple feet of flexible plastic tubing to a funnel for increased and easier reach. Or get a grease gun, available at auto parts stores, remove half the grease, mix in grit, and apply with the gun. Another option is to put the grit in a condom, tie it off, and simply drop it in the oil filler hole. After running for 30-50 minutes the condom will dissolve and release the grit. Other options for sabotage include dropping plaster of paris or a handful of BB's into the carburetor. A box of quick rice in the radiator will expand as the vehicle runs and clog the works. A pound of salt or some Drano will eat away the copper tubing of a radiator.

Gluing Locks

Gluing locks is one of the quickest, easiest, and safest forms of direct action, and one of the most commonly used. The idea of gluing locks is that time is money, and if you can keep an abusers business closed, even for a short time, that's money lost and animals saved. Properly glued locks will require a locksmith to fix, and they aren't cheap either. In order to glue a lock, get a tube of glue, ideally the kind with the long, sharp tip, or the kind in the syringe. Approach your target, be it store or vehicle, and put a small piece of wire or similar object, less than a fingernails length, into the lock. Insert the glue tube into the lock, and fill the lock with glue.

Once the glue dries it will be practically impossible to open. Some glues are effective, some aren't. Get some cheap locks and test some out for yourself until you find what works. In order for a glue to work well it must be thick enough as to not run out of the lock, and dry solid, not rubbery. Also consider drying time. Hardware stores have a wide selection of various glues, so try to find something with both these properties. An easier way to effectively glue locks may be to take a glue tube with a wide enough opening, squeeze some glue out, fill the tube with BB's and mix them in with the glue. This way your solid material will simply squeeze out with the glue.

Paint

Paint is often a good way to get your message across and do some damage. Vehicles, billboards, and buildings are all paintable. Spray paint is one option. Splashing paint out of a container of some sort is another. Plastic soda bottles will work well there. To get more range you can put a hole in the top and screw it back on, then spray through it. Paint-bombs can be constructed by simply filling Christmas ornaments or light-bulbs with paint. Light-bulbs take some work, but are easier to come by. Cut off the bottom part of the metal, below the glass. Very carefully break out the bottom part of the glass, by the filament, inside the remaining metal ring. Fill and carefully seal. You can use a screwdriver for that. The advantage of such paint bombs is that they are surprisingly quiet. Be positive they are print-free first though. Always transport them in sealed plastic bags, in case one ruptures. Balloons can be used too, but they tend to not work as well. Paint can be inserted into soda bottles, ornaments, or bulbs using, ironically, a turkey baster. Always mix paint about 50/50 with water or paint thinner so it splatters better. Paint on glass is easy to get off, getting it on wood, metal, or stone exteriors is a lot more effective. Large markers can also work. Super-soaker type water guns filled with a paint/water mixture are effective as well. They sometimes leak and drip, so keep them in a plastic bag before and after a hit. Its impossible to wash all the paint out afterwards, making it good evidence if found, and possibly clogged after a couple uses. Bearing this in mind it may be a good idea to buy one, use it one night on a number of establishments, and dispose of it. Just remember that paint is a messy business and has a tendency to get everywhere, including all over you.

Paint stripper is another option, especially effective on vehicles. 3M Safest Strip, or Extra Strength, has the advantage of clinging to vertical surfaces. Dupli-Color makes ST-1000 Paint Stripper, available in auto parts stores. It comes in spray cans, and can eat down to bare metal in 30 minutes. Brake fluid is an effective paint stripper as well.

Sponges and Toilets

This is one of the few actions undertaken actually inside the abusive establishment, and while they are open none the less. This can be risky for heavily involved ALF members, but its a great action for those looking for simple and more low level things to do. If you are able to get access to an abusers toilet, such as stopping in a fast food restaurant to use the bathroom, here's a quick and easy way to do some damage. Get a sponge, the bigger the better. Big fluffy ones are better than hard square ones. Get it wet, and then wrap it tightly in string and let it dry. Remove the string and it will stay in its compact shape. Once in the water the sponge will expand to its previous size. So simply drop it in, flush, and hopefully clog up the toilet. If it gets deep into the pipes first, this can turn into a very expensive problem. Lacking a sponge, lots of their toilet paper can log a toilet as well. It is easier to unclog, but still a minor nuisance. A mixture of plaster and sawdust in a nylon stocking is another method.

Telephone Lines

Telephones lines are the most neglected way to easily cause a business to lose money. Once you find an abusers building, locate the phone lines coming out. Attach a weight of some kind to a strong rope, toss it over the line, grab both ends and pull. Another option is to climb the pole it is going to and to cut it. Either way, business rely a lot on their phones and this is an easy way to take them out of commission. If you see any wires, phone lines or other, at ground level, just yank them out or cut them. Careful if its electrical though!

Security Cameras

Places that get hit a number of times may install security measures, such as cameras. Don't let this deter you. As long as you are well covered, the best they can do is give them a general height of the people involved, which doesn't mean much. What they actually do for establishment is the opposite of what they are intended. Instead of protecting them, it gives you something else to break. Security cameras are expensive, and not all that hard to destroy. Aside from open cameras, look for boxes or spheres, which sometimes house cameras. They are generally up high, around ten feet up. Flood light systems are another thing you might see pop up. If you want to hit the place again but you're not to fond of all the light, try a slingshot to take them out of commission. Just remember that if they do install a security system, that means money out of their pocket, which is what you wanted anyway. It also means you're being effective, so keep it up. Just be careful not to hit the same place too often or they'll be waiting for you.

Stink Bombs

Various foul smelling agents can serve a variety of purposes and direct action. Some ideas are dropping some through mail slots, windows after being broken, trucks (especially if windows or doors are left open.), large fur sales, and hunting conventions. Numerous very weak acids have powerful and strong smells. Most well known is butyric acid, of which two drops will clear a room and one once is enough for a building. Other options include caprylic acid, caproanic acid, isovaleric acid, proprionic acid, ethyl amine, skatole, hydrogen sulfide, carbon disulfide, and n-butyraldehyde. any of these can be diluted five or ten to one with water without losing much strength. A more commonly available option are the various lures used by hunters, such as deer piss. Any of these can be delivered using a medicine dropper or hypodermic needle.

Construction Sites

If you come across an abusive institution under construction, there are many effective actions that can be carried out at this point. Firstly, however, be positive it is in fact going to be what you think it is. During construction survey stakes (wooden stakes with colored ribbons tied to the top) are used to mark such things as corners, water and sewer lines, and elevation. Simply removing these stakes, and disguising the holes will cost a few days work. When removing stakes, also look for "hub and tacks", which are 2X2" stakes pounded flush through the ground, with a nail driven in top, or sometimes marked by flags on wires. Also, reference points, which include various stakes or hubs and tacks as much as 50' away must be removed or the survey sticks can simply be replaced. More effective than removing stakes may be to move them just slightly. Although it may seem minor, removing survey stakes is considered a relatively major crime, so use the usual security precautions.

Salt greatly weakens concrete. If a large amount can be introduced into cement bags or sand piles for making concrete, foundations and the like would be weakened.

After the foundation is poured, connections for plumbing, especially sewage, are exposed. There are often covered in duct tape to avoid objects being dropped inside. If the duct tape were to be carefully removed and clogging elements such as concrete, epoxy, or plaster were dropped down the pipes and the tape was carefully put back in place it could cause major problems if not realized until the building is completed.

After drywall is put up electrical wiring is put in. Once sheet-rock or other wallboard is hung this wiring is very hard to get to. After drywall is erected, wiring can be cut in inconspicuous places like behind studs, and then taped or glued into position. Hopefully this will keep the cuts from being noticed until after sheet-rock is hung.

Arson

Arson is a big, and dangerous step up in direct action. It can be very dangerous in a number of ways. Arson is a very serious crime, so before considering it you'd better be aware of the possible consequences if caught. Fire is also terribly dangerous, so the utmost care is needed when starting one. Its necessary to be positive that no human or non-human animals will be hurt in the blaze. It is also dangerous media wise. Arson carries the heavy tag of "terrorism", and must be used wisely as not to discredit the entire movement. As dangerous as arson is, it is also by far the most potent weapon of direct action. One of the first arson attacks in the US was against a new research lab at U.C. Davis doing over 4 million dollars in damage. When constructing your incendiary device, be careful! Consider the source of the information you are using. Never, ever, ever use The Anarchists Cookbook. This was put together by a right wing individual purposely using faulty recipes in order to kill or injure people following the book. Never use information off the internet either, as much of it is from The Anarchists Cookbook or other unreliable sources. Just use common sense.

Arson can have two different purposes. The first and more obvious is to start a fire and burn down the target, be it a building or a vehicle. But devices can also be created that will only have a small fire, meant to give off heat, thus setting off a buildings sprinkler system, doing water damage to merchandise. If using this method, you should be using timed devices, set to go off at night when nobody is around. It is best to try to get the device into the store while open, rather than breaking in during the night. These devices are placed out of sight under flammable furniture, displays, etc. Putting them inside of furniture or other products may be dangerous considering the device may fail to go off on time and go off at a later time after someone has purchased it. Placing the device on the top floor is best, since the water from the sprinklers will then ideally run down to the other floors, doing damage on each. We will first discuss devices intended to start a fire, then move on to more complicated timed devices meant to set off sprinkler systems. Before using any device be absolutely sure to wipe it clear of all fingerprints. Do not assume the device burning will get rid of fingerprints. The authorities have at least 32 methods of pulling prints of burned articles. In some cases, the fire actually fuses the oil of the print to object, making it easier to read. Whenever using a flammable liquid try to use kerosene, or diesel fuel. Their fumes aren't flammable, unlike gasoline, and are therefore safer to use. Kerosene can be bought at outdoor or camping stores as well as some gas stations. Here it is especially important to buy far away from home. Purchase it in regulation red fuel containers, then transfer it to whatever bottle you are using (usually plastic drink bottles or jugs). Also, if using bottles don't fill them all the way, or as the liquid turns into a gas and expands it will cause the bottle to leak. Flammable liquid is made to have a noticeable smell, so be sure to keep it totally sealed in a plastic bag when

24 hours. The device should be placed inside the truck, on the upholstery. If you cant open a door, you'll have to break a window or use it below the truck. Before using such a device it is absolutely necessary to check the truck to make sure the driver is not sleeping inside, as is often the case with larger commercial vehicles. Any product that repels dogs and cats can also be placed around the truck for safety, especially with longer timers. Again, make sure all fingerprints are completely gone before setting off for an action and only touch it with gloves after that.

Getting Through Locks

In some actions, particularly liberations, breaking in is an essential part of the action. Locks can be dealt with in a number of ways. If you are going to be attempting to get by a lock you should take a close look at it, possibly when you check out the site your first time during the day, or more likely your second time at night. Then try to get the exact same kind of lock and see what works. You can try to pry them open with a crowbar, or cut them with bolt cutters. The other way through a lock is to use an electric powered drill and a new 1/8 inch high speed drill bit. Depending on the hardness of the lock it may take more than one bit. Never buy cheap drill bits - they'll let you down. Most keyed locks are pin-tumbler types. In this kind of lock, a number of spring loaded pins are pushed up when the key is inserted. When the tops of these pins are in perfect alignment with the "shear line", the "plug" into which the key is inserted can turn and the lock opened. In many locks, parts are made of brass to prevent corrosion.

Fortunately, brass is relatively soft and easily drilled. A drill can be used to destroy the pins along the shear line. Be careful not to drill too deeply, since this can damage the locking bar making it impossible to open. Drill only the depth of the key-way, which is 3/4 inch in most padlocks, and 1 inch in most door locks. A "drill stop", available in most hardware stores, can be used to pre-set the depth required. Once the lock has been drilled out, insert a pin, such as a nail, into the lock to press the remains of the pins above the shear line. You may have to insert the drill a few times to chew up bits of pins that are interfering with opening. Finally, using a flat-head screwdriver, turn and open the lock. This operation takes practice, so get a few cheap locks and work on it first. Books and tools for picking locks are not too difficult to come by. The other way to get past doors is to just go through them. Prying them open with a crowbar, knocking them open with a sledgehammer, are two ways. Another way is to cut a hole through the middle of the door just big enough to fit through. A row of holes drilled with a thick drill bit is one way to do this, portable power saws are another. The advantage of this method is that if the door is alarmed going through the middle may not trigger the alarm.

Liberations

Liberations are the quintessential direct action. Education and economic sabotage save animals lives in the long run, but liberating animals from laboratories, factory farms, or other places of abuse is the only way to save animals lives here and now. Liberations are probably the most complex actions, and some of the most risky. For both these reasons, an incredible amount of planning and preparation are needed. The first step in a liberation is research. You have to know all you can about the target. You have to know how many animals they have, what kind of animals, what they are doing to them, and where they are located. Once these are determined comes the most important part of a liberation - finding homes for the animals. Aside from the actual break in group, a whole other group of people may be needed for this aspect. NEVER liberate an animal that you have not found a good and loving home for. Liberated animals should be placed in homes of people not associated with your group, and hopefully not associated with the movement at all. Once animals are taken police will be looking for them, so they have to placed somewhere police will not look. Before being liberated, an animal should be completely checked over by a trusted veterinarian. Again, before planning on how to get animals out of bad situations, be certain you have a good situation to put them in once they have been liberated. Special homes may be needed for some animals considering you may be liberating animals not normally kept as pets, or with special conditions inflicted upon them by the abusers.

While caring for a dog taken from a laboratory breeder may not require special skill, the average person does not know how to care for a monkey with a hole cut in its skull and an electrode attached to its brain. As was said, liberations are often highly complex, requiring a number of people and a huge amount of planning. The people involved should each have an area of responsibility, a specialty. You will need people responsible for finding homes, researching and planning the raid, look outs, breaking in, carriers - people to get the animals out, and drivers, as well as someone to coordinate the whole thing. If possible the look outs and break in crew should arrive early so that the carriers and drivers are there for as short a time as possible. Of course have a way for lookouts to notify everyone else if things go wrong, be it an audible signal or by walkie talkies. Many animals naturally make noise when disturbed or moved, and there's nothing you can do about it. All you can do is get in, get the animals, and get out as quickly as possible. You have to have lookouts you can rely on, so that you can concentrate on getting the job done and not have to worry about watching your back. If things go wrong get everyone together and leave quickly. Most people will be happy just scaring you off, so unless literally being shot at, don't leave anyone behind.

Parking vehicles near the site may be suspicious. It may be best to have the vehicles arrive early and park in nearby large parking lots or on side streets amongst other cars. Then, they can simply pull up, either at pre-appointed times or when notified, possibly by walkie talkie, get the animals, and go. Always have the vehicle with the animals leave first. If the animals get caught they face death, if you are caught you will only lose your freedom for a short time.

Fur Farm Liberations

Almost all animals raised on fur farms can be released safely into the wild. Police and fur farmers may disagree, saying they will starve or die in the wild, but wildlife officials agree that this is a self serving lie. Of course some will not survive the wild; some animals raised in the wild don't survive it either. Do they stand any better chances on the fur farm? This makes liberating animals on fur farms much easier than those from laboratories. Fox, mink, wolf, bobcat, lynx, raccoon, and coyote can all be safely released into the wild. The only common fur animal that can not survive the wild is the chinchilla. Fur farms are also an easier target since they are more open and generally have less security, although with increasing fur farm liberations, security is quickly increasing. No huge ecological imbalance results from releasing these animals, even in massive quantities, into the wild. They all disperse quickly, with mink traveling five to ten miles a day, and fox traveling twelve. Fur farms are easily spotted, most use long sheds or rows of cages. Fur animals are kept as cold as possible, since this will thicken their coats. For this purpose fur cages are always open to the outside air, making liberation that much easier.

There are some points of safety for the animals that must be followed in a fur animal liberation. Animals are not old enough to be released until after they have been weaned. Also, they should never be released after late October, since by then winter has set in and they wont have time to learn to hunt since prey species will be more difficult to catch at this time. The best method for releasing large amounts of animals is to cut holes in fences surrounding the compound, and then just open the cages and let the animals find their own way out. Of course some will not get out, but when releasing thousands of animals it may be the only way. The more escape routes you can cut the better chances they will have. With any release into the wild some animals will be recaptured, but getting most even some of the animals to freedom is still much better than all dying. Chinchillas are a small herbivore native to South America. They are generally not killed until spring. As was said earlier, chinchillas are the only fur animal not able to be released to the wild, so they should be found good homes with people who know how to care for them. An important thing to know is that they can not tolerate temperatures over 80 degrees Fahrenheit. Books about their care are available at book stores and libraries. Even if a liberation is not possible, fur farms can still be disrupted. From October to December the "pelting stock", the animals about to be killed, and the "breeding stock", those animals left to produce more animals, are the same size. By opening all the cages and releasing them into the compound they will be unable to tell which is which. The breeding stock may be kept in just a few cages, so be sure to open them all, or else you might miss the breeding stock and have accomplished nothing. You can also destroy the breeding cards, index card sized slips which contain the genetic history (thus the value) of the stock, usually kept on the front of the cages. This action will not save the animals in the fur farm at that time, they will still be killed. In fact, they will probably kill all the animals and purchase new ones for breeding. But, such actions can cause a farm to shut down, thus saving countless animals. Its a question each individual must decide for themselves.

Another method is to take a non-toxic dye and spray it on each animal, rendering the pelt worthless. Again, they will still be killed, but possibly it will shut down the farm and save future generations.

Dealing With The Police

The following holds true for both being arrested, or just taken in for questioning. When performing direct action, arrests at some point are inevitable, so you had better be prepared for dealing with the police. Although it is true that the more actions you do the higher your chances of arrest get, and some forms of direct action are more risky than others, there is still a chance you will be arrested during your first action, no matter how minor, so be prepared. The general rule in dealing with police is to say nothing. Keep in mind that these people go to school to learn how to trick you into incriminating yourself and others. They are also avid liars, and will say anything to try to trick you. Realize that every word out of their mouth, no matter how friendly, innocent, or unrelated it may seem, is said with the goal of getting evidence against you. Just keep your mouth shut. They may try to threaten a statement out of you. They may say they will keep you in longer if you do not talk. A lie. If they see they are not going to get what they want out of you they eventually will give up. If they see you may talk they will keep pushing until they get what they want. They may threaten you with physical violence. They may even use physical violence against you. Do not fight back. Face it, your are in a police station, surrounded by cops. You aren't going to win. If you do try and fight back you will get yourself a charge of assault on a police officer against you, and some hefty jail time. It's not worth it. If attacked, try to role into a ball and protect your head with your arms. If you can get into a corner, do so. Police will only turn to violence if they think it will get you talking, so keep your mouth shut and you will keep safe. If given a phone call, do not say anything incriminating over the phone.

Call your lawyer if you have one, if not call a good animal rights group and they will help you out with one. By the way, no one has ever gotten off by giving police the information they wanted or by turning in others. Its important for ALF members to know their rights, since they are often in possession of incriminating evidence, and allowing a search to happen when you don't have to could be disastrous. When dealing with a police officer it can fall under one of three categories. The first is consensual contact. This means that you are not being held, are free to go if you choose, and you do not have to talk to the officer. This is the state you are in if they have no solid reason to suspect you of any crime and just want to talk to you. In this situation you should politely excuse yourself and leave, since talking to the officer will give him the chance to look for spray-paint on your fingers, etc. The next stage is detention. This means that they have reason to suspect you, but not enough to arrest you on. In this situation you can not leave, but of course should answer "no comment" to any questions. In order to hold you in detention they must have SAF, or Specific and Articulable Facts. Then of course there is arrest, which requires a "high level of suspicion" that you have committed a crime. Only once under arrest can you be searched, otherwise they must present a search warrant. In any situation, if they begin a search, you should clearly and repeatedly state that you object to it. Of course, most cops do not follow the rules, but knowing them can both scare a cop (once you say Specific and Articulable Facts they'll know not to mess with you) and legally protect yourself.

Federal Agents and Grand Juries

The same holds true for speaking to federal agents and when called to testify at a grand jury. A grand jury is an idea out of English government, originally used for one government group to investigate the actions of another. They were banned in the UK in 1933. In the US it is used to target and get information on citizens, particularly those involved in social justice movements such as the animal rights movement. A federal agent will call a grand jury, and people will be supeoned. If called you will be either the target, meaning the person they are trying to indicted, a suspect, meaning not the target, but still suspected of illegal activity, or a witness, meaning you aren't suspected, but they want information out of you.

Grand juries are meant to lead to indictments, but only one, Rod Coranado, has ever come about. They are more often used to get information on groups like the ALF and the people involved. In a grand jury setting you basically have no rights. You have no right to remain silent, no right to have a lawyer present. You may only have a lawyer outside the room, contactable by phone. If you refuse to answer their questions you can be placed in jail for up to 18 months. There is a way to beat them though. Resist, resist, resist. When the grand jury is called, refuse to show up. As soon as the agent is out the door after delivering the supeona, call every activist you know and tell them what is happening. If they aren't familiar with grand juries, explain it to them. Call every animal rights group you know of. Be sure to contact less deeply involved people as well and inform them of what to do, as these are the people they will target first, since they are more likely to speak. Call a press conference and speak about what is happening. Have a protest outside their federal building. Grand juries are clearly unconstitutional. The last thing they want is publicity. Speak out about this injustice and never, ever say a word to them. This is exactly what was done when a grand jury was called in Syracuse recently, and the grand jury quickly disappeared. Resist, resist, resist.

Reporting Actions

If you choose to report your actions to a support group, send news clippings or your own report, including the date, place, and what was done. Write the reports on plain paper using block capital letters, or a publicly accessible typewriter or computer, like the ones available at a library. Photocopy the report a couple times at a public copier to obscure details making it harder to trace. If handwriting it, you may want to have more than one person write each letter. For an A, have the first person write the /, the second write the \, the third write the -, making a complete letter A. This will be much harder for them to trace. Be certain not the leave fingerprints on the envelope, paper, or stamp. Obviously don't sign the report or include your address in the report or put a return address. Spell everything correctly, since certain spelling errors are often common to certain individuals. Wet the envelope glue and stamp with a sponge, don't lick them as saliva is traceable. Always drop in a public mailbox, and avoid using the same one frequently. After it is sealed and you are sure it is evidence-free, seal it in a larger envelope so that it can be safely handled. When you are dropping it off, rip an end off the larger envelope and drop the smaller one into the mailbox without touching it. When mailing in a communiqué, be careful where the post mark is from. Don't mail in a report close to your home for an action a state away. Assume whatever you send is first opened and read by the government. Dropping it of anonymously at a supportive groups office, or the house of a supportive above ground activist is safer than mailing it.

"You attack unexpectedly; causing your opponents to become exhausted just running their lives. You burn their supplies and raze their fields, cutting off their supply routes. You appear at critical places and strike when they least expect it." -Li Quan, The Art of War

The Final Nail

1995 - 2013

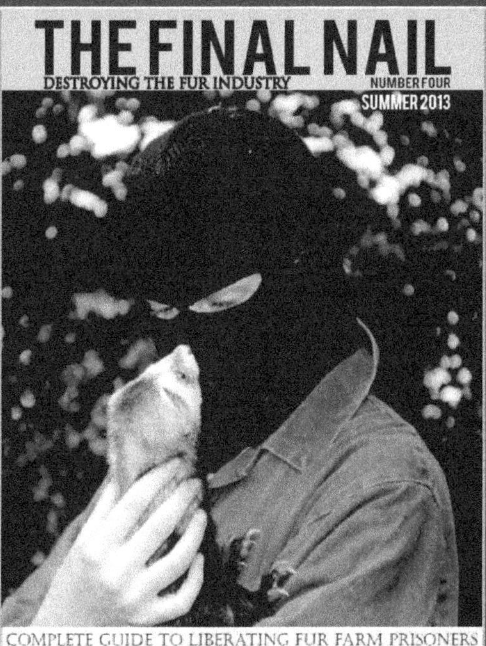
THE FINAL NAIL
DESTROYING THE FUR INDUSTRY
NUMBER FOUR
SUMMER 2013
COMPLETE GUIDE TO LIBERATING FUR FARM PRISONERS

Originally a photcopied document, the four editions of *The Final Nail* were the blueprint behind the release of over 100,000 animals from fur farms.

(Because of the large number of fur farm openings and closures since their original publication, fur farm addresses have been removed. More recent lists can be found in a document titled The Blueprint, a state-by-state diretory of known fur farms.)

THE FINAL NAIL

- Supplement #1 Fall 1996 -

For detailed information on liberating fur farm animals and destroying the fur industry read the original Final Nail (available all over). This is the firs supplement to the original Final Nail released early this summer. It is meant to go hand in hand with The Final Nail. If at all possible people should just add thes 8 pages after the last page.

In this and each and every supplement we will bring you news of: Fur Farm raids, How To updates, Security updates, New Farms, Farm closures, an corrections from the original Final Nail. The new and revised Final Nail #2 with tons of new farms, phone numbers, corrections should be out by Yule.

Operation Bite Back - Part II

Over the last year the Animal Liberation Front has made 21 fu farm raids in North America and shows no sign of slowing down

• **October 26/95 - Chilliwack, BC;** 2400 mink released at ***Dargatz Mink Ranch***, breeding information also destroyed, $383,000 losses.

• **November 13/95 - Aldergrove, BC;** 5000 mink released at ***Rippin Fur Farm***. In the early morning shortly after security guards had made their regular rounds, someone using bolt cutters cut through fences, opened every cage and destroyed 70 years of breeding information. The mink were due to be killed in a couple weeks by carbon monoxide gassing, $ 765,000 losses.

• **November 16/95 - Pleasant View, TN; *Mac Ellis Fox Farm*** raided for the second year in a row. Thirty cages were opened before a disturbance forced the A.L.F. to evacuate.

• **November 16/95 - Olympia, WA; *Clarence Jordan's*** mink farm had 300-400 mink released and slogans spray painted *"Mink Liberation"* and *"Release Mink Now"*. *"...an attempt at burning down his storerooms, refrigeration unit and killing shed was aborted because he came out. ... Clarence has recently secured his cages with extra wire as a response to earlier attacks in British Columbia." communique.* **Now Closed - VICTORY!**

The Mac Ellis Fox Farm shortly before it closed. Good Riddance!

• **January 15/96 - Sheboygan, WI; *Zimbal Mink Ranch*** has 400 mink released. These were part of a 20,000 strong breeding herd. Breeding records also destroyed.

• **April 4/96 - Victor, NY;** A.L.F. activists struck ***L.W. Bennett & Sons' Fur Farm*** cutting through double guard fences and releasing over 3000 mink. Damage estimates ran as high as one million dollars. Two years ago someone clipped a section of fence on the farm, but no animals escaped.

• **June ?/96 - WA;** 80 mink liberated from an unknown fur farm. We received word of this with little detail as to the location of the farm.

• **June 7/96 - Sandy, UT; *Utah Fur Breeders Agriculture Coop*** raided and 75 mink used in nutritional research liberated. Two sheds were half full with mink, and one of them was completely emptied out.

• **June 21/96 - Riverton, UT;** 1,000 mink liberated from ***Beckstead Mink Farm***. The A.L.F. found dead mink lying in cages, under the cages in piles of feces, with many half eaten by other mink. *"More actions are coming. Murderers beware."*

• **July 4/96 - Howard Lake, MN;** A.L.F. raiders liberated 1000 mink at ***Latzig Mink Ranch***, as part of an Independence Day action.

• **July 4/96 - Pleasant View, TN;** The A.L.F. visited ***Mac Ellis Fo Farm*** in hopes of raiding it for the 3rd time in as many years. Th group discovered that the second raid (Nov. 1995) had put the fu farmer out of business. **Closed - VICTORY!**

• **July 5/96 - Langley BC;** 400 mink were released from ***Akagam Mink Ranch***, $62,000 losses.

• **July 17/96 - South Jordon, UT;** 3000 mink liberated from ***Ho Mink Ranch***. $35,000 in damages just from breeding cards bein destroyed.

• **August 9/96 - Hinsdale, MA;** Over 1000 mink were liberated fror ***Carmel Mink Ranch***. *"Most cages were opened.... and (we) painte A.L.F. on the shed,"* said the communique. More than $10,00 damage to breeding stocks.

• **August 12/96 - Alliance, OH** 2500 mink liberated from ***Justic Jorney's*** (President of the Ohi Mink Breeders Assoc.) fur farm Slogans were also spray paintec

• **September 28/96 - Provo, UT** 8000 mink released from ***Pau Westwood's*** mink farm, breedin cards destroyed. Huge holes cu in two surrounding fences. *"Man animals were left behind and fo that we are sorry, but this war i far from over..."* from th communique. Over $20,000 i damages.

• **October 5/96 - Alliance, OH *Justice Jorney's*** fur farm raidec for the second time in less tha two months, 8000 of 15,000 min liberated.

• **October 5/96 - Lyndeborough, NH; *Richard Gauthier's*** fur farr raided, 35 fox and 10 mink liberated. Slogans spraypainted an extensive damage down.

• **October 11/96 - Hinsdale, MA; *Carmel Mink Ranch*** raided fo the second time in two months. Activists bypassed an infrared bear alarm system triggered if cages opened, 75 mink liberated.

• **October 23/96 - Lebanon, OR; *Arnold Kroll's*** mink farm raidec and 2000 mink liberated. *"As long as there are animal concentratio camps there will be an Animal Liberation Front! We'll be back."*

• **October 24/96 - Coalville, UT;** 2000 mink and 200 fox releasec from ***Devar Vernon's*** fur farm. *"This is not the end, this is a war, an we will continue to fight it."* said the communique.

The Fur Farm Industry gasps for air...

The Fur Industry has been in a frantic cramble after they realized the new wave of ttacks against the fur industry were not going way. Over 38,000 mink and 265 fox have been eleased in the last year.

Shortly after the two big raids in Canada nd another one in Washington, in November 95 the *Canadian Mink Breeders Assoc.* along ith *Fur Commission USA* offered reward of 50,000 for information leading to he conviction of .L.F. activists esponsible for fur arm raids in North America. Other ponsors of the eward fund were *North American Fur Auctions, American Mink Council, Seattle Fur Exchange and American Legend Cooperative.*

Video clip from Crime Stoppers TV segment

In late January '96 they decided that 0 g just wasn't enough and offered a $70,000 eward. And obviously feeling very frustrated gain in May the *Fur Commission USA* adds nother 30 g to the pot, upping the reward to 100,000.

Finally the fur auction houses started o think they might lose some of their best ustomers and big $$$ due to A.L.F. raids before pelting season even came around. In June he *North American Fur Auction* offers blanket nsurance to every fur farm that sells their pelts o them. The policy offers a maximum of 250,000 coverage per ranch for damages due o an A.L.F. raid. With deductible being $25,000 r 25% whichever is lower per occurrence.

In July *Seattle Fur Exchange* followed suit by offering blanket insurance to all farms that sell to it. Covering losses of up to $350,000 with the same deductible.

Fur Age Weekly while reporting that the Final Nail was distributed at the *World Congress For Animals* has down played it to fur retailers.

In September *Crime Stopper's* in British Columbia featured a segment with a recreation of the Rippin mink farm raid, and offering a $2000 reward along with the $100,000 offered by the fur industry. It was playing 4-6 times a day at different times last we heard.

The *Fur Commission USA, Canadian Mink Breeders Assoc.* and *Fur Farm Animal Welfare Coalition* have been working overtime trying to try and slow down the wave of anti-fur actions. *Fur Commission USA* has been sending out info packets with information on previous raids, militant animal liberation activists in their area, the Animal Liberation Front and even a copy of the Final Nail. Word has it they've sent them out to law enforcement agencies in at least 21 separate states and Canada.

The FBI and RCMP are investigating all fur farms raids. They also regularly help each other out with investigations and share information on radical animals activists active in both countries.

USDA Releases 1995 Satistics

446 mink farms operated in 1995, this is a decline of 3% from the provious year. These farms killed 2,691,700 mink which is an increase of 7% from 1994. The skins were valued at $143 million which is an increase in value of 72%. This is because of increased demand for furs in the Far East.

The number of mink killed will be about the same in 1996 and 1997. The new found profits the fur farmers are receiving will be used to pay off debts incurred during the last 7 years, and cover the costs of maintenance that has been neglected for years because of a depressed fur market. Unless we turn things around, the body count will definately grow in 1998.

USA Mink Farms	1994	1995
Utah	130	130
Wisconsin	78	77
Minnesota	53	52
Oregon	27	27
Idaho	23	22
Washington	23	20
Iowa	19	21
Pennsylvania	17	13
Ohio	12	12
Michigan	12	12
New York	12	11
Illinois	10	10
South Dakota	4	4
Other states	37	29

49 mink farms also raised fox. This is an increase of 2 from 1994. Probably another 50-75 people raise fox, but have no mink, so they were missed in the count.

Re-introducing fur animals to the wild

On October 23, 1995 the Animal Liberation Front (A.L.F.) opened he cages on the Dargatz Mink Farm in British Columbia, Canada freeng 2,400 mink into the surrounding countryside. The liberation from Dargatz Mink Farm was the first in what now has become 12 liberaion raids by the ALF of fur farms in North America in less than a year. *ed: 21 raids as of Oct. '96)* The result has been the release of approxinately 11,000 mink, 30 fox, and one coyote from the intensive onfinement that would have lead to death for all prisoners. The reease of animals from fur farms is nothing new. In the former Soviet Jnion, Iceland, mainland Scandinavia, Western Europe, Britain and Newfoundland. Animal liberation raids as well as accidental and inentional escapes from fur farms have resulted in mink and some fox eing introduced successfully into the natural environment. In Britin, the ecological impact of these releases has been measured, and as iberated mink conveniently fill the ecological niche left by Britain's ow extinct native otter population, the negative impact has been ninimal. In Iceland's island ecosystem, and in parts of Scandinavia, mink have been slightly more destructive to the ecological balance. Never has the question of formerly captive minks survivability been questioned by those in the know, only the level of impact these beautifully fierce predators have as they successfully readapt to a wild life.

In North America, its a whole different story. Although there is a Eurasian species, mink are believed to be native to North America with the theory that the Eurasian species originated from North American ancestors who crossed the ice bridge between this continent and Asia. Previous to the "discovery" of the "New World", mink were one of many aquatic animals that flourished in virtually every lake and waterway in North America except the desert regions. The war against the mink nation that continues today, began when the first Europeans invaded their homeland. When the Mayflower first rounded Cape Cod, Massachusetts in 1620, already Jamestown, Virginia was the hub of an extensive fur trade. A price list from 1621 records mink among other animals fetching up to ten shillings apiece on the market to which modern day fur farmers can claim as their **Continued on page F**

SKIP LEA
Chairman - FUR COMMISSION USA

PROFILE

Name: Skip Lea
Address: Alma Center, WI 54611-9707
Country: USA
Phone: (715) 964-6121
Fur Commission USA; Phone (612) 222-1080
Fax: (612) 293-0532

Skip Lea another fat slime-ball. Skip Lea is chairman of Fur Commission USA. He is known for accusing A.L.F. activists of stomping mink to death, and other asinine claims. Him and his brothers own a large mink farm in Alma Center, WI. Media reports claim that his farm has security guards 24 hours a day. Either way, he must be dealt with.

CHRIS ENGH
President - CANADIAN MINK BREEDERS ASSOC.

PROFILE

Name: Engh Chris
Address: 30030 Burgess, Abbotsford, BC V4X 2G6
Country: Canada
Phone: (604) 856-2123
Fax: (604) 857-9667

Chris Engh operates his own large mink farm at his home in British Columbia and is President of the CMBA. Chris helped set up the original $50,000 reward fund.

MARSHA KELLY
Executive Director - FurFarm Animal Welfare Coalition

PROFILE

Name: Marsha Kelly
Address: St. Paul, MN
Country: USA

Marsha Kelly: Marsha Kelly is the head PR person/spin doctor for the fur farm industry. She works for Fur Commission USA, and is known for dodging the fur issue in debate, and trying to divert attention to other animal issues. She lives in or near St. Paul, MN. Her name pops up in media reports covering anti fur actions, and she is always spreading lies about the minks ability to survive when liberated. We'll find you soon Marsha.

GRAND JURY'S

The Fur Industry is starting to feel the heat and oooooh they'r getting annoyed. They are still a huge industry that has millions o dollars available to them. They are continuing to put pressure or politicians and law enforcement agencies to treat animal rights activists as terrorists.

We should all be ready for the Grand Jury's, if they haven' already started they will. In states where there has been the mos militant animal liberation activity (we could take our guess as coulc you). If subpoenaed to a grand jury, you should call a movemen lawyer immediately or contact the National Lawyers Guild. Tel movement groups and your friends about the subpoena. **Don't try and deal with it alone.**

For basic information read *'If an Agent Knocks - Federa Investigators and Your Rights'*, for more detailed reading try *'Agents o Repression'* by Ward Churchill.

AFTER PELTING

We have found a fairly big variance in pelting time periods. So as always scouting out the farm your looking at, as much as possible wi help you in determining the best time to hit it. Watch for extra security measures around pelting season.

All pelting will be done by December and then usually all the farms will have is their breeding stock. If the weather and othe conditions are correct then breeding stock can be released.

Also after pelting season is the time when they usually let up there guard. Also if at all possible pelting/skinning/feed sheds can be burned to the ground or have extensive damage done to them using other methods: paint/acid/etc. pelting machines, equipment and feeding tractors can also be damaged.

MEDIA WORK

Media work in something that some cells don't focus on much and fo good reasons; they do it for the animals, and media work can be dangerous if you are not very careful.

The FBI and RCMP watch fairly closely the mailing addresses of radical animal rights groups that regularly receive communiques. It should be expected that all communiques sent to animal rights groups/media/etc. will be opened, possibly seized and o course checked for any forensic evidence; fingerprints saliva/hair/fibre traces, etc.

If you are going to send a communique it would be a good idea to send it to as many places as possible so that way at least one wil get there.

For those of you that are interested in doing some post raic media work - Remember to be extra careful. If you screw up you coulc get caught. Video footage and/or photos of fur farm raids are quite likely to get extensive media coverage.

FUR FARM SECURITY UPDATE

Fur Commission USA is planning seminars on farm security with security experts for fur farmers across the country. Fur farm security seminars were held this July in Utah at the annual summer school meeting of fur farmers.

A lot of fur farmers across North America are stepping up their security after all the recent attacks. Security recommendations have included; Caller ID on telephones (A great reason to use a pay phone) and having camera's on hand to take photo's of strange visitors.

Other ranchers are recommending such measures as electrified fences that not only prevent wild animal entries but also signal fence tampering. Electric fences are pretty expensive and it's not very likely that you will run into them. Watch for any attached wires or insulators on fences.

A lot of farms are using some simple precautions such as putting up extra guard fences and wiring cages shut with heavy wire. Both of these can be bypassed around with some hard work and a few good quality tools. Fences can have holes from 8 inches tall to a couple feet wide cut out of them, or can and have been taken down completely and rolled up.

Some farms are hiring security guards to do checks several times a night, especially for the months leading up to pelting season. We have heard that some of the largest farms have 24 hour security guards during the pelting season. There's not all that much that can be done for 24hr security guards (usually).

The bigger the farm the more likely (although there is always exceptions to the rule) to have some type of security system and or security guard. Proper scouting of farms should tell you exactly what you have to expect.

Activists should always be extra careful about footprints, extra large socks over top of shoes will make tell tale tracks unnoticable or better yet, buy a pair of cheap canvas shoes and dispose of them away after the raid.

Fur Rancher Summer 1996

Video surveillance system may thwart vandals

Animal rights terrorists are becoming increasingly active in their raids on fur farms in the United States and Canada, and fur farm security is an ever more important concern.

Wireless Technology Inc. of Las Vegas, NV, is a leader in the field of surveillance and security systems and has the type of technology useful to all types of farming operations.

The company manufactures video systems for security at all kinds of operations such as farms, electric substations, parking lots, etc. The King Valley Ranch in Idaho uses a Wireless Technology system to monitor its maternity ward.

The ranch wanted a system to eliminate the 2,000-foot hourly trek required from the farmhouse to a distant barn. They had installed a video system teamed with a JVC color camera and monitor.

Now the ranch personnel can monitor the maternity stalls around the clock via real-time wireless video from the rafter-mounted color camera.

Wireless Technology offers many choices in surveillance systems. One system, called the Pole Cam, consists of a video camera mounted inside a housing and attached to a tall pole such as a yard light. The camera is controlled by a handheld controller that can pan, tilt, and zoom the camera at the touch of a button.

The company says it can customize a surveillance system to meet any specific needs.

For more information, contact Wireless Technology Incorporated, 7340 Smoke Ranch Road, Suite A, Las Vegas, NV 89128-0261,Phone (702) 363-2235, Fax (702) 363-5539.

VIDEO SECURITY SYSTEMS

There are thousands of companies that sell security systems across North America. At least one has been mentioned in Fur Industry publications over the last year (see article to left).

Video security is expensive. The more bells & whistles a system has the more money it is going to cost. Usually only the biggest farms are going to have a video security system.

Video security systems can be bypassed with some work and will power. These days some type of good mask (balaclava etc.) is always needed. A little less suspicious looking is a hooded jacket and mask/bandana/etc. underneath. You never know when you're going to turn a corner and run into a video camera (fur farm or other). Non-recognizable clothing should always be worn on raids. Army fatigue jackets or nondescript pullovers and pants are a good idea. Anything recognizable should be taken off or covered, this includes jewellery, tattoo's, watch's, glasses, etc.

Reconnaissance of possible targets plays an important part in making sure everything goes smooth and that you don't have any surprise's. When scouting out farms watch for video camera's mounted on the corners of buildings and inside. Look for the tell tale attenna of a wireless system (attenna's can be as small as 18" x 18"), they may also look more like a box. If you spot camera's and no attenna's, it could be a wired video system with buried cables instead.

Do as thorough scouting job as possible so you know what to expect when you come back to do the job.

If there isn't someone watching a monitor 24 hours a day (not that likely). The camera lense's can be covered up with paint/ tape etc., so all their going to record is blackness. Taking them out by damaging or smashing the camera's or attenna's can be done, but be careful.

Some security systems can have alarms (silent or audible) that trigger when a camera is damaged or wires cut. If you know the farmer is away or have already released every animal in the place and are ready to leave the area, you should then damage any expensive video camera's, recorders, attenna's, etc. These systems are not cheap and will cost them tens of thousands of dollars.

All in all if they can't tell who you are on any video footage they might have - then great. Be Careful - If you do get caught on film, they will analyse the hell out of it, and may get little things like your height and mannerism's from studying it.

This a what the typical attenna's for video security system look like.

the fur trade can also accept responsibility for causing the extinction of the native mink salt water cousin, the sea-mink. Nearly twice the size of their freshwater relations, and recorded as inhabiting the whole Northeastern North American Seaboard, all that remains of this being are two skins and a number of bones. That and of course the memory of one furrier who before the American Revolution recalls the pelt of the sea-mink selling for five guineas. And so it is, by the end of the 19th century, freshwater mink were severely depleted from their former range in all of North America by a fur industry thirsty for the blood of this continents fur animals.

Unlike their European and Scandinavian counterparts, mink farmers in the United States and Canada began the attempted domestication and economic exploitation of mink often from live captured wild mink populations. In the 1920's this new element to the fur trade began. In 1925 Kent Vernon's family in Northern Utah (now president of the Utah Fur Breeders Co-Op) live-trapped chicken-killing mink from the wild and began breeding them in captivity. In 1927 the

U.S. Government opened its Experimental Furbearer Research Station in Corvallis, Oregon (shutdown by an A.L.F. raid in 1991) and began experimentation in different techniques to breed wild mink in captivity. With overexploited wild mink populations unable to satisfy the demands of an increasing demand for fur, trappers across North America began to captive-raise wild mink, and in the 1930' B discovered fur mutations that altered the minks fur color. Now just 70 short years later, mink farmers are still battling the still dominant wild DNA of captive mink that causes these normally free-roaming solitary animals to contract diseases from close confinement, self-mutilate and even cannibalize their own kind. All for the price of a fur coat.

Beginning in 1990, I researched mink farms by visiting over 25 in Oregon, Washington, Utah, Idaho, Montana, and Michigan. What began as a quest to document conditions and killing techniques on fur farms quickly turned into the study of the first ever attempted domestication of a North American predator. What I learned both by my research and by the rescue rehabilitation, and release of sixty mink from a Montana mink farm leads me to conclude that all captive mink should be released one way or another from their prisons we call fur farms. Highly intelligent, fierce and very adaptive, mink are anything but successfully domesticated. Arguments by the fur industry that mink are domesticated are ludicrous. Like all wild animals held in captivity, some mink when released from their cages will fare better than others. Many factors contribute to successful mink reintroduction as does the impact they will have on their surrounding eco-system. These are issues I will address in this article.

In 1990-91, I spoke with many mink farmers and researchers who believing I was a mink farmer instructed me in ways to avoid my mink from losing their recessive genetic structure that gave them the fur quality and color variations that separated them from their wild relations. Captive mink are genetically 958 similar to their wild counterparts. The only difference besides behavior being fur color and quality which is solely maintained by a scientifically controlled diet. This is the key to maintaining their genetic difference from wild mink, black and dark mink being the closest genetically to wild mink. Jim Leischow, a second generation mink farmer from Kenosha, Wisconsin in a discussion at the 1991 Seattle Fur Exchange auctions described to me how without a scientifically controlled diet mink on any fur farm would lose their recessive genes, and over powered by their dominant wild genetic structure, return to their wild roots in a few generations. Leischow also detailed how a mink escapee that breeds with a wild mink would produce offspring that in one more generation would have lost all traces of any altered genetic structure. The difference between mink and other animals raised in intensive confinement is totally incomparable as not only are all other domesticated livestock ungulates and hervevorous but also having been domesticated for well over a thousand years The closest comparison which is hardly applicable but for the sake of argument will be used is the domestication of the common house cat. Originating in ancient Egypt, the cat has had over two thousand years of domestication, yet still this feline predator is proven capable of surviving in the wild as feral populations in the U.S. and Britain will attest to. Once again, survivability is not the issue but impact on their native species. Captive mink are so far away from successful domestication that they rarely are caged together unless with their own off-spring, and then only before they reach sexual maturity. Self-mutilation and cannibalism which is not uncommon on mink farms is yet further proof of a wild animals behavior as it attempts to deal with the neurosis caused by intensive confinement. Anyone who has ever been on a mink farm has heard the incessant scratching mink will make as they attempt to escape or attack their captive neighbours, separated only by a plastic or metal divider. This also is common behavior of a wild predator unfamiliar with close proximity to others of its own species. The psychological as well as physical torture associated with the confinement of mink naturally accustomed to solitary wanderin is beyond our comprehension. Geneticall speaking mink are predominantly still wilc Separated only by a controlled diet from the wild ancestors. Physiologically they are ider tical. What remains as the greatest divisio between wild and captive mink is predator instincts and natural behavior that dictate how they hunt, find shelter, build nests, an forage. Fear of other animals is minimal a mink are renowned for their fearlessness These separations were the basis of persona research into the potential for rehabilitatio and release of the 60 mink I had purchase in Montana in 1990. The Coalition Against Fu Farms (CAFF) began as a rehabilitatio project, the objective being to determine th feasibility to reintroduce native mink from fu farms back into their natural habitat.

In January of 1991 the trials began a CAFF volunteers placed mink in cages fou times as large as their previous enclosures an introduced natural objects such as logs, rock plants and gallon baths. Fur farmers had assured me that escaped captive mink alread had at least a 50% chance of survival, an CAFF hoped to increase that figure as muc as possible. The introduction of 12" x 6" bath tubs allowed the mink their first opportunit to acquaint themselves with water beside that came from a small water nozzle or dish Their response was to fully submerge themselves and spin in a cycle that quickl splashed all water out of their baths. Thi would be followed by grooming sessions i which the mink dried themselves and maintained utmost cleanliness, yet another sign o a healthy wild animal. Once the mink ha built up muscular strength after their time i a fur farms cramped conditions, we began t nurture hunting instincts. Though morall opposed to the killing of animals CAFF fe the survival of our captive mink could not b guaranteed without a minimal amount c live-animal feeding. We knew that our proje would later be used by others to determin the potential for successful reintroduction c fur farm prisoners, and so chose to do everything possible to ensure not only their su vival but also their survival without huma dependency. This also meant live-feedin which would teach them how to hunt rath than scrounge near or where humans were This would ensure greater independence an less likelihood of human/mink encounters Then mink in our rehabilitation project du into their instinctual memory to remind themselves how to first seize the prey with one bite then without releasing it, crush down unt the skull or neck was broken. Then the min would release its prey and scour the logs an rocks for others that might have gone unnc ticed. Once assured of no other present prey the mink would return to the kill and eat everything or place the remainder in its nest jus like wild mink. Once the mink had learne to kill and had tasted live food, they refuse to eat the scientific diet we had been supplie by National Fur Feeds. Finally, we released the mink to natural waterways across the Northwest's many forest lands. Always far from human habitations. And never within a 5 - mile radius of another captive released mink of the opposite sex. We wanted to ensure the breeding only with wild mink. We also waited until the natural breeding season had passed so as not to burden the mink with the upbringing of offspring in their first season of freedom. Our mink releases were filled with encouraging signs that the mink would survive. On one release a mink quickly found an abandoned animals burrow, and as we left we could see its head peeking out watching our departure. Another release had a young female mink burrowing under a log, gathering twigs and grass building a nest. Still another mink quickly found a mouse hole, and burying its nose in it began to dig frantically. On many releases near streams the mink were quick to explore the shore of the water, eventually plunging in and swimming completely submerged playing with pebbles and rocks with their forepaws. Returning to one release site weeks later I quickly found mink droppings and tracks near the creek and the dropping contained hair from a preyed upon animal. Most of the behavior exhibited by our mink was not learned, but simply returned to them as they found themselves in their natural element.

It is my belief that the liberator becomes responsible for the lives of the liberated when she/he endeavors to free them. Ideally the liberated will become truly independent of human needs and achieve complete liberation. But until then there are a number of factors that liberators can influence and by doing so increase the possibilities of a liberated mink's survival. The priority being the time of year liberations take place. The best time being between May and January, the worst being during the breeding and kit-bearing season. Releasing an impregnated mink increases the needs of the liberated mink for food and shelter, female mink naturally raise their kits alone. Releasing mink once they have given birth to a litter will also mean abandonment of kits which sometimes can be foster-raised by another mink mother. Of course it cannot be over looked that all captive mink are destined for death, and there is room for debate as to what kind of death is most desirable, a mink being the only one to surly know. Still I have hesitated to release mink from fur farms near heavily traveled roads knowing a large number would become roadkills. This is yet another moral dilemma the liberator must face when they decide to open the cages.

Personally, I have seen mink watching as the gas-chambers are wheeled down the rows of cages and seen them screech frantically and attempt all manner of last minute escape as it becomes painfully evident that they will die. There is also the very compelling argument that even with the recapture of 100% of all released mink from a targeted farm, that still the breeding has been completely disrupted as farmers have no way of separately identifying their breeder mink from their pelter mink. A mink raised to be pelted will often be in a much smaller cage than a breeder mink. For this reason liberators would do best by releasing mink from both large and small mink cages so as to confuse the two. As of yet mink farmers have not devised methods of tagging, branding or tattooing individual animals except for labeling

These specialized tractors for feeding can be found on many larger fur farms, they should be destroyed if possible.

on the cage. For this reason it is always advantageous to remove all record-keeping cards from cages when releasing mink. Transportation of mink either a short distance from cage to guard fence or a larger distance is best achieved by securing the mink individually in its nestbox. A small flat piece of sheet metal is often used to divide and block the hole leading from the nestbox to cage at which point the nestbox can then be removed and the hole blocked with a gloved hand or more permanent means for long transportation. Despite the average liberators aversion to leather, nothing protects human skin better than a thick pair of leather welding gloves which usually can be found lying around a mink farm. With criminal DNA testing liberators should take every precaution not to leave a blood trail of their own. Remember, you are dealing with a wild predator unfamiliar to kind human hands.

Often given the choice, a mink will leave the immediate area once outside of the guard fence, which usually is a 5-6 foot fence lined with sheet metal to prevent escape should a mink get out of its cage. If left inside the guard fence often a mink will linger simply because of the smell of food or other mink cages, and also because of the familiarity of its own nestbox which is all it has ever known. Once a large number of mink have left the guard fence area the quickest method of natural distribution is waterways. Without interference from the irate mink farmers attempting to recapture his furry investments, mink will not overcrowd themselves in the wild. It is not uncommon for a mink to travel 5 miles in one night (they are mostly nocturnal) and a large number of mink released in one area will not stay concentrated but will travel until they establish a territory all their own, searching out other mink only to breed.

This leads us to the issue of ecological impact caused by mass mink liberations on their new environment. There will be a noticeable impact on local prey populations and for this reason liberators should research target areas to guarantee that the sensitive habitat of a vulnerable endangered species is not nearby. Mink will attack almost anything. I've seen mink chasing large dogs and heard a story of one seen flying through the air attached to the leg of a large heron, the mink unwilling to release its targeted prey.

Mink will kill beyond their need, and for this reason caution should be taken when releasing mink near large concentrations of small animals. Mink are ferocious. Long persecuted at the hands of man native predators are continually routinely killed by ranchers and other gun-toting humans. Much like the coyote has filled the ecological niche the wolf has left behind and by doing so extended its own historic range, so also do mink have the potential to fit nicely into the niche otters and other predators have left as their numbers are continually reduced by humans. Native mink populations are still drastically reduced, and given large-scale mink liberations, individual mink are sure to redistribute themselves to their former habitat with a little help from their two-legged friends.

There should be not hesitation to reintroduce captive mink into their native habitat. The ideal environment being undeveloped areas with a nearby water source and infrequently used roads. As A.L.F. liberators open the cages, they not only liberate an individual animal but the whole species. Mink, fox, bobcat, and lynx farm liberations are not only a blow to a fur farmers profit margin but also a boost to North America's ravaged environment. With an absence of natural predators, prey populations often explode causing undue harm to their environment and are also known to spread disease. By releasing fur farm prisoners, liberators are guardians of healthy eco-systems. Before one single animal abuser can argue the merits of a captive fur animals impact on the natural environment, they must first address the overall impact the whole domestic livestock industry has had on the earth. It is no coincidence that the number one reason behind predator eradication is the protection of politically powerful livestock interests. Still it remains that for the mink nations of North America the shortest path on the road to animal liberation lies from the opened cage to the outlying guard fence.

Now it is time for liberators across the continent to follow the lead of the A.L.F. in British Columbia, Washington, Utah, Wisconsin, Tennessee, New York, and Minnesota and take action to liberate the four-legged prisoners from the war on nature.

Until all fur farm prisoners are free...

Open the cages!!!

- Rod Coronado

THE FINAL NAIL

Destroying The FUR Industry

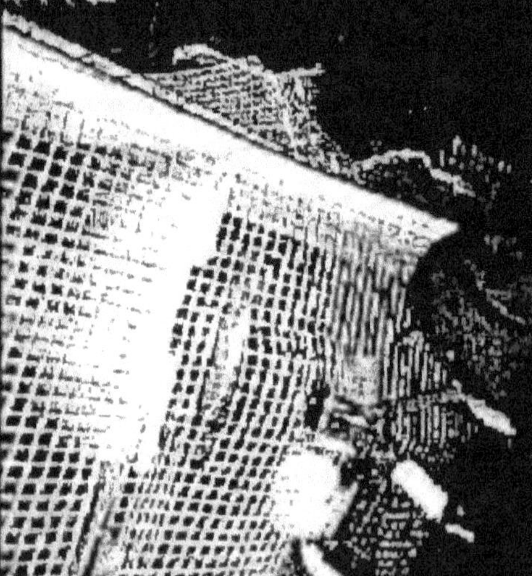

- A Guided Tour -

#2

POUNDING

After the great response to the original Final Nail and the Supplement, it is with much pleasure that we bring you The Final Nail #2. Things over the last year have picked up and taken off. It's been great to see fur farms across the US and even Canada getting raided, fur stores getting smashed up every week - fur stores have even been burned to the ground. We've reprinted the best of both publications and taken the time to update the details in them. We've added listings for dozens of new fur farms and other assorted [abusers] and also updated over 50% of their addresses and phone numbers. We've even added more new tactics and technical information. Cover photo: Animal Liberation Front activist opens a fox cage "the easy way" at Richard Gauthier's mink and fox farm in Lyndeborough, NH (10/5/96).

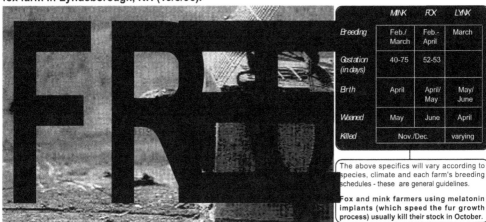

	MINK	FOX	LYNX
Breeding	Feb./ March	Feb.- April	March
Gestation (in days)	40-75	52-53	
Birth	April	April/ May	May/ June
Weaned	May	June	April
Killed	Nov./Dec.		varying

The above specifics will vary according to species, climate and each farm's breeding schedules - these are general guidelines.

Fox and mink farmers using melatonin implants (which speed the fur growth process) usually kill their stock in October.

Fur Farm Liberation as easy as 1, 2, 3...

The Animal Liberation Front can defeat the fur industry. Remember all of the lab raids and animal liberations that took place in the eighties? The same amount of energy and enthusiasm is now being put into attacking the fur industry and fur farms in the nineties. Like England, with a lot of hard work, the fur industry can be crushed. Operation Bite Back actions in the US '91 through '94 started to push the decline of the fur industry. Since late '95 as part II of Operation Bite Back there have been 43+ fur farm liberations releasing thousands of animals back to their native habitat in the US alone, not to mention countless raids overseas from Austria to Finland and more.

All farmed fur animal species: fox, mink, wolf, bobcat, lynx, racoon & coyote (except chinchilla) can be released into the wild and survive. Mink can travel five to ten miles a day while fox can travel twelve. They disperse quickly so there is no need to fear a huge ecological imbalance as a result of a massive release of fur farm animals.

All fur animal species are not old enough to release until after they've been weaned. Also, they should be liberated ***before winter sets in*** because otherwise they won't have time to learn how to efficiently hunt for food as most prey species will now be more difficult to catch.

SHEDS

Most, but not all, fur farms can be easily spotted from country roads. Mink farms consist of long sheds and can be several different configurations the most common being a single row (2 rows of cages) or double row (4 rows of cages) shed. Mink farms will vary from 2 or 3 long sheds all the way to some of the most disgusting 90+ sheds in Utah and Wisconsin. They are almost always orientated North-South for proper lighting. Some fox and lynx farms use long sheds or just rows of outdoor cages. They will vary in size from one dozen sheds to several hundred.

CAGES

Mink cages will vary in sizes but be approx.. 14" wide, 18" tall and 36" deep. They will vary in construction from area to area

THE NAILS IN

a little but farmers generally use the same designs within the area. Farms usually have one mink to a cage, although you will quite often find farms that have 2 or 3 or more to a cage. All cages will be open to the outside air.

Cages are usually latched with a simple wire catch. Some farmers have been known to actually wire their cages closed with a thick piece of wire (usually their breeders) so the cages can't be opened without a good pair of pliers or wire cutters.

Some cages will also have nest boxes at the back or on the side. A lot of cage designs have nest boxes that are removable making it very easy to just pull the nest box up and out of the cage. Removing it and placing it on the ground is all it takes to let a mink out of his or her cage.

Ideally, mink and fox can be picked up out of their cages, carried to and dropped on the other side of the guard fence. Mink will try to bite, so extra-heavy gloves are a necessity, mink will have to be picked up firmly by the scruff of the neck or by the tail.

They can also be placed in carry cages or heavy canvas type bags (only one per bag as mink are very likely to start fighting if piled on top of each other), and then released as far away as possible.

Lynx cages are usually made of your typical chain link security fence and may look more like small pens than cages.

GUARD FENCES

Another quicker, although not as reliable method for all species, is to cut several (as many as possible) holes in any

DOUBLE ROW MINK SHEDS

FOUR ROW MINK SHEDS

retaining fences around the compound and then open all the cages so that the animals can find their own way out. Plenty of escape routes should be provided. None should lead the animals toward a busy road. Farms with solid guard fences usually have gates that can be opened allowing huge 'holes' for mink to escape through.

ALTERNATIVE METHODS

Fur farms can still be hit even if a live liberation is not possible at that time. From October through December, the pelting stock (those about to be killed) will be close to the same size as the breeding stock (those kept to produce more animals).

If all of the animals are released into the compound then the fur farmer won't know which are the breeders and which are the pelters (If possible destroy the breeding information cards which are usually on the front of each cage.) The farmer will have to pelt them all out and spend tens of thousands of dollars on new breeding stock. This is so annoying and costly that sometimes they just give up for good.

You must make sure as many cages are opened as possible, as it may be hard for you to determine which cages contain breeders and which don't. If a couple sheds are left untouched, then you might miss the breeding stock completely and the purpose of the action will not be achieved.

AFTER PELTING

We have found a fairly big variance in pelting time periods. So, as always, scout out the farm you're looking at as much as possible to determine the best time to hit it. Watch for extra security measures around pelting season. All pelting will be done by late December. Then, all the farms will have is their breeding stock left. If the weather and other conditions are correct, then breeding stock can be released to the wild.

Also, after pelting season is the time when they usually let up their guard. If at all possible pelting/skinning/feed sheds can be burned to the ground or have extensive damage done to them using other methods: paint/acid/etc. Pelting machines, equipment and feeding tractors can also be damaged.

DYES

Activists in Finland and Sweden have recently begun using Henna based dyes in squeeze bottles at several fur farms. The non-toxic dyes can be sprayed on the animals' backs to ruin the economic value of their pelt. All types of fur animals (fox, mink, rabbit, chinchilla, lynx, etc.) can be dyed as long they do not have dark fur. This has put farms out of business in the past. But, as with the last described tactic, the animals will still be killed... the farmer just won't be making any money from them.

continued on next page...

Fur Rancher Summer 1996

Video surveillance system may thwart vandals

Animal rights terrorists are becoming increasingly active in their raids on fur farms in the United States and Canada, and fur farm security is an ever more important concern.

Wireless Technology Inc. of Las Vegas, NV. is a leader in the field of surveillance and security systems and has the type of technology useful to all types of farming operations.

The company manufactures video systems for security at all kinds of operations such as farms, electric substations, parking lots, etc. The King Valley Ranch in Idaho uses a Wireless Technology system to monitor its maternity ward.

The ranch wanted a system to eliminate the 2,000-foot hourly trek required from the farmhouse to a distant barn. They had installed a video system teamed with a JVC color camera and monitor.

Now the ranch personnel can monitor the maternity stalls around the clock via real-time wireless video from the rafter-mounted color camera.

Wireless Technology offers many choices in surveillance systems. One system, called the Pole Cam, consists of a video camera mounted inside a housing and attached to a tall pole such as a yard light. The camera is controlled by a handheld controller that can pan, tilt, and zoom the camera at the touch of a button.

The company says it can customize a surveillance system to meet any specific needs.

For more information, contact Wireless Technology Incorporated, 7340 Smoke Ranch Road, Suite A, Las Vegas, NV 89128-0261,Phone (702) 363-2235, Fax (702) 363-5539.

VIDEO SECURITY SYSTEMS

There are thousands of companies across North America that sell security systems. At least one has had the displeasure of being mentioned in Fur Industry publications over the last year (see article to left).

Video security is expensive. The more bells & whistles a system has, the more money it is going to cost. Usually, only the biggest farms are going to have a video security system.

Video security systems can be bypassed with some work and will power. These days some type of good mask (balaclava etc.) is always needed. A little less suspicious looking is a hooded jacket and mask/bandana/ etc. underneath. You never know when you're going to turn a corner and run into a video camera (fur farm or other).

Non-recognizable clothing should always be worn on raids. Army fatigue jackets or nondescript pullovers and pants are a good idea. Anything recognizable should be taken off or covered, this includes jewellery, tattoos, watches, glasses, etc.

Reconnaissance of possible targets plays an important part in making sure everything goes smooth and that you don't have any surprises. When scouting out farms, watch for video cameras mounted on the corners of buildings and inside. Look for the tell-tale attenna of a wireless system (attennas can be as small as 18" x 18"), they may also look more like a box. If you spot cameras and no attennas, it could be a wired video system with buried cables instead.

Do as thorough a scouting job as possible so you know what to expect when you come back to do the job. If there isn't someone watching a monitor 24 hours a day (not that likely), the camera lenses can be covered up with paint/tape etc., so all they're going to record is blackness. Taking them out by damaging or smashing the cameras or attennas can be done, but be careful. Some security systems can have alarms (silent or audible) that trigger when a camera is damaged or wires cut. If you know the farmer is away or have already released every animal in the place and are ready to leave the area, you coulds then damage any expensive video cameras, recorders, attennas, etc. These systems are not cheap and can cost them tens of thousands of dollars.

All in all, if they can't tell who you are on any video footage they might have - then great. Be Careful - If you do get caught on film, they will analyze the hell out of it and may get little things like your height and mannerisms from studying it.

Typical attennas for wirelessvideo security systems.

MEDIA WORK

Media work is something that some cells don't focus much time on and for some good reasons: they do it for the animals, and media work can be dangerous if you are not very careful. The FBI and RCMP watch fairly closely the mailing addresses of radical animal rights groups that regularly receive communiques. It should be expected that all communiques sent to grassroots animal rights groups/media/etc. will be opened, copied and checked for any forensic evidence; fingerprints, saliva/hair/fiber traces, etc. They may also end up being 'lost' and never make it to their destination.

If you are going to send a communique it would be a good idea to send it to as many groups as possible so at least one will get there.

For those of you that are interested in doing some post-raid media work, remember to be extra careful. If you screw up you could get caught. Follow all basic security precautions when mailing anything. Video footage and/or photos of fur farm raids are more likely to get media coverage.

ontinued from pg. 3

:HINCHILLAS

he chinchilla is a small herbivore that is native to the ndes mountains in South America. Chinchillas are sually pelted out in the spring. ***They can't be released to the wild*** and, if liberated, need to be given good omes. There are several things that should be taken to consideration concerning post-raid chinchilla care. n important one is that they have a hard time lerating extreme temperatures above 80 degrees F. If ou should liberate chinchillas, please make sure that e person providing their new home has been educated bout their special needs. Books are available at book ore or any library.

FUR FARM SECURITY UPDATE

Fur Commission USA has been holding farm security seminars with security experts for fur farmers across the country. Fur farm security seminars have been held at every major fur farm-related function in the last year.

A lot of fur farmers across North America are stepping up their security after all the recent attacks. Security recommendations have included; Caller ID on telephones (a great reason to use a pay phone) and having cameras on hand to take photos of strange visitors.

Other ranchers are recommending such measures as electrified fences that not only prevent wild animal entries but also signal fence tampering. Electric fences are fairly expensive and it's not very likely that you will run into them. Watch for any attached wires or insulators on fences.

It has been reported that farmers in some areas where there have been numerous raids (Utah especially) have been sleeping, armed, in their vehicles at night awaiting a possible A.L.F. raid. Especially near pelting season. In Austria and Finland activists have been shot by fur farmers, all survived, thankfully. It's a war out there - be careful.

A lot of farms are taking some simple precautions such as putting up extra guard fences and wiring cages shut with heavy wire. Both of these can be bypassed with some hard work and a few good quality tools.

Fences can have holes from 8 inches tall to a couple feet wide cut out of them, or can and have been taken down completely. A lot of farmers are putting up fences with tin guards for the top 1'-2', more to keep mink from climbing over fences than for keeping out raiders. Although they can make a lot of noise. Also most farms that have solid fences of some kind have at least one gate (some several) in them that can be opened wide for mink to escape through.

Some farms are hiring security guards to do patrols several times a night, especially for the months leading up to pelting season. We have heard that some of the largest farms have 24 hour security guards during the pelting season. There's not all that much that c be done for 24 hr. security guar (usually, but where there's a will ther a way!).

The bigger the farm, the mo likely it is to have some type of secur system and or security guard (althou there is always exceptions to the rul Proper scouting of farms should tell y exactly what you have to expect.

It is also imperative that, duri scouting missions, you leave absolut no trace that you were there. Anythi from a clipped fence, unlocked ga opened cage, missing breeding ca footprints, etc. could alert the farme thereby jeopardizing the entire resc operation and putting all members th much closer to being caught.

Activists should always be ex careful about traceable footprints. Ex large socks over the tops of shoes w make tell-tale tracks unnoticeable better and safer yet, buy a pair of che canvas shoes and dispose of them af every raid.

Any vehicles used should cleaned and vacuumed as soon possible after an action. Do a thorou cleaning job and if necessary (i.e. mud conditions, dirt access roads, etc.) y may even want to get new tires. Use go judgement and common sense. T expense of getting new clothes, tires, e is cheaper than legal fees that m otherwise occur from preventable erro It's better to be safe than sorry.

Grand Jury Update

Well we can't say we didn't warn you. In the last six months two grand juries have been convened and are being, held in Oregon and Pennsylvania.

The Oregon grand jury, to our knowledge, has so far subpoenaed only one person, Craig Rosebraugh of the Liberation Collective in Portland. On Dec. 12, Craig was issued two subpoenas to testify before the grand jury regarding the recent actions of the A.L.F. and the E.L.F. in the Northwest. One of the subpoenas was for personal materials/objects/documents as well as for Craig to testify. The other subpoena was for materials/objects/documents of Liberation Collective relating to three specific incidents. 1) The release of 10,000 mink from a Mt. Angel, OR mink farm 2) The burning of the Cavel West Horse slaughterhouse in Redmond, OR and 3) The burning of a BLM Horse Corral and horse release in Oregon.

The date he was to appear was Dec. 17th. On this date a demonstration was held at the new Federal Courthouse in Portland. Some 20 activists turned out and were welcomed by close to 50 local and federal officers. Outside, Craig was asked by an ATF Agent if he would testify and answered 'No', he was then placed in handcuffs and taken inside into the grand jury room. After Craig presented the judge with reasons why he should not have to testify, the judge refused and he was ordered to testify. The grand jury members were brought in. The questions themselves focused largely on Liberation Collective as an organization and whether or not he knew various individuals from around the country. Craig refused to answer all questions citing his fifth amendment rights. The assistant U.S. Attorney had copies of personal e-mail, newsletters, stories, etc.

After a pre-Thanksgiving communique from the Justice Department threatening to contaminate thousands of turkeys in supermarkets along the east coast, the Philadelphia based Vegan Resistance for Liberation issued a media release alerting the media to warn consumers. FBI special agent John Chesson harassed Brett Wyker of VRL trying to get him to answer questions regarding the original communique. Fortunately, as any group should see to, the original communique was already in the tra and long gone. Brett was issued a subpoe to appear before a federal grand jury Jan in Philadelphia. After filing a motion Brett w granted a three week extension, befo having to reappear before the grand jury. B will be refusing to appear before the gra jury or answer any questions they have.

Be careful and expect that we will s many more if attacks against the fur indus continue. They are still a huge industry th has millions of dollars available to them. Th will continue to put pressure on politicians a law enforcement agencies to treat anim rights activists as terrorists.

If subpoenaed to a grand jury, y should call a movement lawyer immediat or contact the National Lawyers Guild. T movement groups and your friends about subpoena. **Don't try and deal with it alo**

For basic information read *'If an Ag Knocks - Federal Investigators and Yo Rights'* and *'Grand Jury Comix'*, for mo detailed reading, try *'Agents of Repressi* by Ward Churchill.

DEVASTATE to LIBERATE

The fur farm industry has to be hit from all angles in order to ·ing it down. It's going to need both the above ground and the nderground actions. On the illegal side we need to hit all parts of the idustry, from fur farms and retail fur stores all the way to the feed nd supply industries. They all need to be hit hard in order to be evastated.

Trucks belonging to any fur related usiness are very easy targets for all type of amage and are usually worth tens of thousands dollars. The bigger and more the trucks the erier. Probably the most thorough and devasting tactic for use on trucks is the use of fire.

The processing room and the feed orage barns can be hit as well. Malecky Mink anch in Yamhill, OR was put out of business hen the A.L.F. burned down their processing barn 2/21/91) during Part I of Operation Bite Back. rson should only be used when it can be uaranteed that the fire will not spread to the sheds e animals are in.

Fur farmers have specialized tractors that spense feed on top of the cages. These ehicles can be damaged in a number of ways. If e can not be used, then there are numerous her options. One easy one is to buy a bottle of uriatic acid at the hardware store. This costs about three dollars for ne or two gallons. Simply pour it all over the engine and leave. It will at through all soft plastic wires etc. causing a fair amount of amage. Wires can be cut or pulled out, sugar or metal filings can be dded to the gas tank and oil, tires can be slashed, etc. Other items und on most fur farms that can be damaged include; feed grinders nd freezers, pelters and skinning machines.

rine Collection

has been brought to our attention that a fair amount of fox farms ossibly also some mink farms) collect the urine with buckets nderneath cages. They then sell the urine to hunters and mpanies that manufacture bottled scents for hunters to use in the eld. Simply dumping the contents of buckets under cages and any rger storage containers will cost them a pretty penny.

Acid

Acids are beginning to be used more widely in different types of actions. Unfortunately most must be bought from a chemical supply house. Some places will ask for ID, so be prepared.

Burytic Butyric acid - A yellowish acid that can be diluted 50/50 with water. It stinks to high hell and has been used for numerous applications. Dumping it on the carpet of a fur salon will usually result in the carpet needing to be replaced in order to get rid of the smell. It can also be put in a large syringe and injected through mail slots, keyways, into airducts, etc. A very damaging method is to poke a hole in a restroom wall with an awl and then empty a large syringe of acid into the wall. In order to fix this and get rid of the smell, walls may have to be ripped out.

Muriatic acid - A low powered acid that can be bought at any hardware store. It will slowly eat through soft materials like papers, etc.

Hydro-flouric acid - Also known as etching fluid. It can be diluted somewhat with water also. Will etch letters etc. into almost any glass surface after being left on for more than a couple hours. It can be bought at craft shops but is fairly expensive, it is cheaper to purchase larger quantities from a chemical supply house.

Sulphuric acid - A strong acid that will eat through paper, plastic, wires, etc. Battery acid is diluted sulphuric acid and stronger strength acid can be bought from a chemical supply house.

Marsha on the telivision news following the 11/11/96, Animal Liberation Front arson attack at Alaskan Fur Company in Bloomington, MN. Which caused $2.25 million in damages.

MARSHA KELLY

Executive Director - Fur Farm Animal 'Welfare' Coalition

Address: **1237 Birch Pond Trail, White Bear Lake, MN 55110**
Phone: **612-293-1049**

Marsha Kelly is the head PR person/spin doctor for the fur farm industry. She works for Fur Commission USA, and is known for dodging the fur issue in debate, and trying to divert attention to other animal issues. Her name pops up in media reports covering anti fur actions, and she is always spreading lies about the minks' ability to survive when liberated.

She has recently been generating more and more frequent flier points as she flies around the country doing media for the ever increasing amount of fur related A.L.F. attacks. Marsha, take our advice while you still have some time: quit your job and cash in your frequent flier points for a permanent vacation.

Fur Farm Liberations Fact & Myth...

Myth: Liberated mink will destroy native wildlife, causing irreparable harm.

Fact: It is interesting that this argument is usually preceded by the claim that the mink will starve to death because they haven't been taught to kill. If they don't know how to hunt, then they certainly won't kill any wildlife. The truth is, however, that mink kill out of instinct, much as the domestic cat does. No training or rehabilitation is necessary.

So do liberated mink destroy wildlife? Of course they destroy some wildlife. They are predators, and they help maintain the balance of nature by killing and eating prey animals. But, at the same time, they do not pose a threat to any particular species as a whole.

Mink are not specialized predators. Certain predators, like lynx, will have a principal prey that they rely on. Lynx will usually only eat snowshoe hare, otter normally eat fish, etc. On the other hand, the mink will eat anything.

Examination of mink scat shows that this animal will eat mammals, fish, birds, reptiles and amphibians. They do not specialize, but rather eat whatever is most readily available. If liberated mink ate too many field mice, then it would be easier for them to then hunt nesting birds, fish, or even snakes. When the population of one food source gets too low, mink will instinctively hunt something that is more abundant, and therefore easier to find.

Furthermore, the mink is a very solitary animal. The only time one will see mink together is when they are mating, or in the weeks immediately following their birth, when the mother is still caring for her kits.

When released, mink go in search of their own habitat and will not tolerate the presence of other mink. Mink normally have a range of just under 3 square kilometers. Being so spaced apart, it is unrealistic to assume that the mink could have enough of an impact on any particular species to make any noticeable difference at all.

Myth: Because ranch raised mink are often bred for mutant color genes, mink liberations can damage the environment by polluting the wild gene pool.

Fact: The standard mink genes found in wild populations are dominant over most mutant color genes that have been exploited by fur farmers. Studies indicate that these mutant color genes are bred out of existence in just a few short generations.

In England the entire mink population is the offspring of animals that escaped from fur farms. Despite the fact that there were no wild mink to breed with, the recessive mutant color genes have been virtually diminished by the more dominant standard genes that most ranch mink carry.

A 1986 study in Devon, England found that only 3% of the mink population was showing any sign of these mutant genes. A similar study in Scotland showed nearly the same results.

Myth: Mink in England have decimated the otter and the water vole.

Fact: Sadly, the mink became the scapegoat for the decline of the otter. Otter populations were decimated by pesticides and hunting. In recent years the otter has made a comeback, and examination of their scats has shown that contrary to claims made by mink hunters and the fur trade, otter actually kill and eat mink. Mink do not kill otters.

The water vole is another species whose numbers have been decimated by man, yet we continue to blame the mink for their problems. Studies show that in areas with the water vole, this animal still only accounts for about 2% of the mink's diet. It is doubtf that feral mink could have any noticeabl impact on the number of water voles whe they are not in any way a principal source c food for mink.

Those are the most common anti-liberatio arguments used by those that would rathe see predators confined to cages, instead c out in the wild, serving the purpose natur intended.

There have been [34] fur farm raids in Nort America, in a time span of 2 years Approximately 50,000 fur farm prisoners hav been released into the wild. If any of thes arguments had any merit, then why aren't w seeing some evidence in areas were min have been released. This doesn't have to b a hypothetical argument based o interpretations of scientifi literature. Mink have bee released in large numbers, s where is the damage? The fa is, there isn't any.

We know that they have survive One chicken farmer wrote a lett to a Utah newspaper complainin that a mink released from a farr months before had eaten some his chickens. But yet we aren seeing this ecological damage th fur trade has predicted.

In fact, the A.L.F. has done th earth a favor by raiding thes farms. In addition to stopping th mass accumulation of anima wastes by shutting these place down, they have re-introduce mink to areas where they ha been nearly wiped out. For example, th A.L.F. freed 400 mink from a fur farm i Sheboygan, WI. At roughly the same tim there was concern about the lack of min along the Sheboygan River. The A.L.F. wa the only relief that river has gotten, in regar to that particular problem.

It is estimated that as few as 150 lynx ma still exist in Montana, yet the state still allow a trapping season. Montana is the home c several lynx fur farms, and there could ve well be more lynx in captivity than in the wil

The lynx is only a few short generations o of the wild and even the Forest Service ha considered using ranch lynx fc reintroduction (see Lynx, Wolverine an Fisher in the Western United State Research Assessment and Agenda by Joh Weaver, 1993). Imagine what direct actio groups could do without all of the red tap and bureaucracy.

Until the last cage is empty......

MAXIMUM DESTRUCTION NOT MINIMUM DAMAGE

Money is what the fur industry thrives on and when you take away from their profits, it hurts them where it counts. Economic sabotage is what they listen to. This can be various types of actions including the very simple; smashing fur shops' windows, squirting super glue into the locks, spray painting, filling bell peppers or Christmas ornaments with paint and "paint bombing" the building, etc. To be effective, a place should be hit repeatedly. Just be careful & vary your schedule so that the police aren't waiting for you when you go back. Every hit causes security to increase so go for maximum destruction. Malecky Mink Ranch was torched in Dec. 1992. The fur farm industry tried to deny that this was an A.L.F. action for quite some time. Eventually they could no longer hide from the truth as pieces of an incendiary device were found. Presumably, they wanted to cover this up so that other mink ranchers wouldn't be scared out of the business. If scores of fur farms were raided, then the industry would be devastated and many would stop raising fur animals for fear of] losing their entire investment. Remember, most fur farmers do this part time and are not solely dependent on fur animals to make a living. Therefore they are much easier to push out of business as opposed to a chicken farmer, etc.

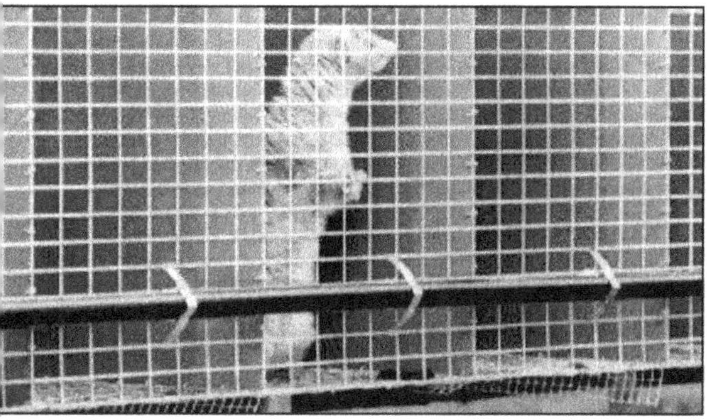

SMASHING THE FURRIERS

ire is a tool. It can be you
ower or your foe if you
ig does the amount
at fire can (try do
on dollars dama
ith only hand
lso, nothing
otential for
nd loss of
t and b
orks. B
ake d
al (h
e ina
re t
es
efo
rso
is
ou
ea
en
w
usly
olute

Vith
ere's
endia
sed fo
gs and

ition:

endiary devices are
ted in three sepa-
es: the jugs, the
nd the timed ig-
allon milk jugs
ecause they
arried using
they also
Place an
e loca-
m and
gh the
jug.
with
the
e to
the
the
safe
fuel
then
mers
oles
ponge
of the

e burns
h heads,
m and they

MINK & FOX FARM STATISTICS

	U.S. Mink Farms ('94/'95/'96)	Total pelt ('96)	Canada	Mink farms (1993/4)	Fox farms (1993/4)
WI	78/77/74	718,000	ONT	88/84	60/47
UT	130/130/130	585,000	NS	55/57	70/69
MN	53/52/40	293,500	PQ	30/22	83/59
OR	27/27/23	208,000	BC	20/20	10/8
ID	23/22/22	170,500	MB	12/11	8/5
WA	23/20/19	117,000	NFLD	6/4	68/60
IA	19/21/20	94,100	AB	6/5	19/13
OH	12/12/12	73,800	NB	4/5	71/69
PA	17/13/13	65,700	PEI	4/4	45/49
MI	12/12/9	57,000	SK	0/0	18/13
IL	10/10/9	56,700			
NY	12/11/11	20,100	Total farms	225/212	452/392
SD	4/4/?	71,300('96)			
Other states	37/29/29	93,300			

CODING FOR THE ADDRESS LIST

FR Fur Research-University and/or Private
FFES Fur Farm Equipment Supplier
FF Fur Farm
FF-M Mink Fur Farm
FF-F Fox Fur Farm
FF-L Lynx Fur Farm
FP/W Fur Processor and/or Wholesaler
FAH Fur Auction House
FFFS Fur Farm Feed Supplier
TS Trapping Supplier
FFO Fur Farm Organization
FTO Fur Trapping Organization

HEADQUARTER - BRANCH

Code	Hdq.-Branch
(1)	Ultimate Parent
(2)	Branch
(3)	Subsidiary Headquarter

EMPLOYEE SIZE

Code	Employee Size
(A)	1 - 4
(B)	5 - 9
(C)	10 - 19
(D)	20 - 49
(E)	50 - 99
(F)	100 - 249

SALES VOLUME

Code	Sales Volume
(A)	Less than $500,000
(B)	$500,000 - $1 million
(C)	$1 - $2.5 million
(D)	$2.5 - $5 million
(E)	$5 - $10 million
(F)	$10 - $20 million
(G)	$20 - $50 million
(H)	$50 - $100 million
(I)	$100 - $500 million
(J)	$500 million - $1billion

FUR IS DEAD

UNIVERSITY & PRIVATE RESEARCH
The fur industry relies on research done in labs to increase their profits through further genetic manipulation of furbearers and their feed.

FUR AUCTION HOUSES
This is where trappers and fur farmers sell the skins to retailers. This is a particularly weak point in the industry, as only a few auction houses remain open.

FUR FARM FEED SUPPLIERS
The unnatural state of the pelts of murdered fur farm prisoners is partly due to the types of special feeds developed by feed suppliers. A lot of these also have experimental fur farms.

FUR FARMS

FOX - 398 farms in Canada (as of 1994). In the U.S. 40 mink farms also imprison fox, approx.. another 50-100 farms raise fox, but have no mink and so were missed in the count.

LYNX - Approximately 40 farms still imprison lynx in North America.

MINK - Canada had 212 farms (as of 1994). In the U.S. there were 415 mink farms (as of 1996). Wisconsin 'produces' the most mink pelts but Utah has the most mink farms.

TRAPPING SUPPLIERS
These people sell leg-hold and other traps for killing wild fur animals.

FUR FARM EQUIPMENT SUPPLIERS
These are the companies that sell the cages, execution devices, automatic pelters, feed grinders, etc.

FURRIER EQUIPMENT SUPPLIER
These are the companies that sell all the tools to make the coats and other garments.

FUR PROCESSORS / WHOLESALERS
These are the people who clean up the pelts for their future use as vanity items and sell them in bulk. Not all wholesalers are processors, although a lot are.

FUR FARM ORGANIZATIONS
These are small groups of fur farmers who lobby state legislators, produce propaganda and manage sales of skins

FUR TRAPPING ORGANIZATIONS
These are small groups of fur trappers who lobby state legislators, produce propaganda and manage sales of skins

The A B C's of DEATH

Data Compilation

'ter compiling the information on fur rms for the original Final Nail and upplement from several different urces (some of them quite old), we've und there are numerous corrections.

in our sleepless quest to bring you e most up to date intelligence - we are blishing the Final Nail #2. Over 50% them have some type of addition or ange. New addresses, new phone mbers, new owners, etc.

your research and outing of any fur farms from e Final Nail listings, you ould take into consideration e following:

Some names, phone mbers and addresses may ve typos because we typed em in from our badly oto-copied original lists.
'elephone area codes have anged in a lot of areas.
Some town and city names ve changed with urbaniza- n. Check local maps.
Some of the owners have died or passed on their farms to their younger relatives. You can find the farm sometimes by just checking out everyone with same last name in town, if there is not too many.
• Rural Roads (R.R.) in some places have changed to an actual named street, check out local phone directories.
• Some named streets have changed names. Check old maps at the library.
• In a lot of states/provinces the majority of fur farms will be located in approx. the same areas or even on the same road.
• Neighbouring farms are quite often owned by members of the same family.
• And lately, a lot of them are just damn CLOSED!

Further Research

Places to look for new (and current) fur farms and other fur industry scumbags include the phone book, state or provincial agricultural dept. lists (you may need a good sounding excuse), Fur Age Weekly, Fur World and other industry publications. Active fur farming states' college and university agricultural libraries usually will have a fair amount of information. Local newspaper archives at the public library may have old articles on a local fur farm (a lot of them are family businesses and they may have been there for 10-40+ years). A lot of university, college and public libraries also have CD ROM phone directories that are free to use. Also try the internet, tons of information is available from phone, name & address searches, to maps of anywhere in the USA and more.

IO CHINCHILLAS OR RABBITS?

Yes, that's right, we've decided not to include chinchilla or rabbit farms in the Final Nail basically for the reason that they can not be reintroduced to the wild in North America. Don't fret though - we do plan on publishing a separate list for them. But, in the meantime, don't forget about your local rabbit and chinchilla farms: extensive damage can be done to farm equipment. Don't forget about the farmer's home and vehicles, all of which most likely come from blood money. Dye can also be used on rabbits and most of the lighter colored chinchilla breeds.

RR and Rt/Route are the same.
Cr = Country Road

*** denotes a farm that produced a top quality mink pelt lot, sold at fur auctions.

ALABAMA

Alabama Trappers & Predator Control **(FTO)**
P.O.Box 1385,Cullman, AL 35056
205-287-1972

Dudley Smith **(FF-F)**
RR2 Box 29713, Falkville, AL 35622

ALASKA

Alaska Trappers Assoc. **(FTO)**
HC 60 Box 288, Copper Center, AR 99706
907-479-4369

Howling Wolf Furs
121.9 Sterling Hwy., Clam Gulch, AK 99568-0000
907-567-3566
Employees: 2 Sales: C
Roger Ager, Owner

Whitestone Farms **(FF)**
Richardson Hwy. Outpost 275 (or Box 1229),
Delta Junction, AK 99737-0000
907-479-5938
Credit Rating: B Good
Employees: 25 Sales: D
Bill Greir, Owner

Yukon Flats Fur Cooperative **(FFFS)**
Po Box 283, Fort Yukon, AK 99740-0283
907-662-2667
Employees: 1 Sales: B
Michael Peter, Manager

ALBERTA

Buckskin Fur & Leather Co. **(FP/W) (TS)**
5320-1A St., Calgary, AB T2H 1J2
403-253-3459
403-252-4270 fax

Little Mountain Fur Farm **(FF)**
Carrot Creek, AB
Rick & Naoni Croteau
14 wolves, bobcats, lynx, coyotes & racoons

THE FINAL NAIL

NUMBER III | ANIMAL LIBERATION PRIMER | SUMMER 2008

COMPLETE GUIDE TO LIBERATING FUR FARM PRISONERS

AND NOW, LET'S FINISH THEM OFF

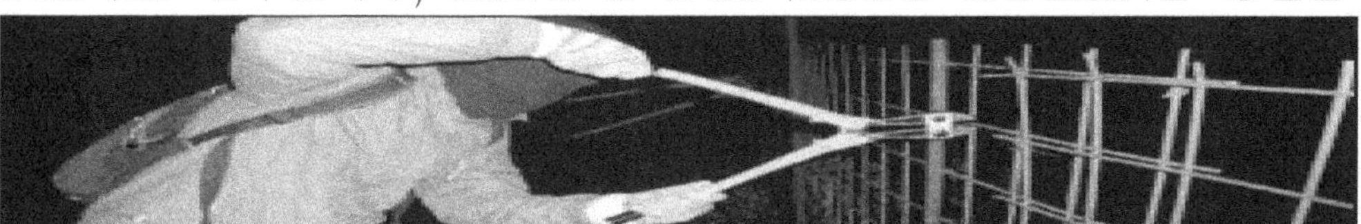

THIS REPRESENTS THE MOST COMPREHENSIVE COLLECTION OF NORTH AMERICAN FUR INDUSTRY ADDRESSES TO DATE. INCLUDED ARE OVER 100 NEVER BEFORE REVEALED FARMS, AND HUNDREDS OF UPDATED ENTRIES. THE INFORMATION HEREIN WAS POOLED FROM OVER A DOZEN SOURCES AND NUMEROUS INDIVIDUALS, NONE OF WHOM WILL BE REVEALED TO PROTECT THOSE GUILTY OF TRANSGRESSING UNJUST LAWS IN SERVICE TO THOSE HIGHER.

MANY OF THESE NEW ENTRIES ARE FOR THOSE WHO THOUGHT THEY COULD CONTINUE THEIR CRIMES IN SECRECY, ADDRESSES THE INDUSTRY HOPED WOULD NEVER BE MADE PUBLIC. THIS IS OUR ATTEMPT TO BRING ACCOUNTABILITY TO THOSE WHO SHED THE BLOOD OF THE INNOCENT EVERY DAY. MOST IMPORTANTLY, THIS IS FOR THEIR VICTIMS.

ENDGAME: TOWARDS A NEW DAWN

In 1996, a publication itled ***The Final Nail: Destroying the Fur Industry*** circulated rapidly hrough the grassroots nimal liberation movement. It offered the most comprehenisve list of nink, fox, and lynx farms o date; revealing for the irst time the physical location of fur farms across North America. Prior to 's release, there had been ive releases of fur farmed nimals. In the 2 ½ years hat followed, there were early 50 fur farm raids cross the US and Canada.

The following year, ***The Final Nail #2*** was eleased with updated nformation and many ew farms.

The Final Nail #3 offers the largest update o date, with over 100 ew farms, hundreds of pdated entries, and over 0 years of accumulated lata on liberating fur farm risoners.

With all the successes and nomentum brought by riginal ***Final Nail***, its egacy has been blemished with the revelation it's once anonymous editor had become a federal informant. As part of a plea deal in which he implicated several fugitives (as of 2008) in serious arsons, this person admitted compiling ***The Final Nail*** in 1996. There is no erasing the value of ***The Final Nail*** or any actions in a person's past, however we see with this individual that onetime assetts to our movement become liabilities, and onetime valuable foot soldiers become worthless turncoats. With revelations of this individual turning on others, becoming a drug dealer, regressing from veganism, and the various rumors of his degeneracy since 2001; he will rightfully live forever in disgrace.

In retaining the title ***The Final Nail,*** we offer no implicit endorsement of it's corrupt orgins. Rather, it is a forced reclamation, shedding the shadow of the past as we move forward towards total animal liberation.

Ten years dormant, ***The Final Nail*** is reborn.

OVER 100 NEWLY EXPOSED FARMS THE FIRST MASSIVE UPDATE OF FUR FARM ADDRESSES IN TEN YEARS

ONWARD, UNTIL VICTORY...

Fur farm liberations and sabotage in the 2000's

Since the height of activity in the 1990s, when over 60 raids were carried out in 5 years, the 2000s and beyond have seen a drop in actions, but it has not been a period without it's highlights and victories.

The first action of the new millennium took place at a location not unfamiliar to the hands of liberators: Brainerd's Fur Farm in Snohomish, WA. This farm has been raided at least 5 times, and less than two months into the new decade saw the release of 60 mink.

An attempted arson at a feed supplier in Wisconsin reportedly failed to do significant damage to the building, but the region was revisited later than year for the largest animal release in North American history: 14,000 mink released from Drewelow and Son's Fur Farm in New Hampton, IA. Iowa was the site of another spectacular release the following year. Activists released 2,000 mink from the Scott Nelson Fur Farm in Ellsworth IA, and when all but 400 of the mink were recaptured, they returned to re-liberate the captives. The farm announced its closure, and the A.L.F. had another victory.

Pennsylvania was the site of the most actions, with 4 actions since 2000. In one action a feed barn was torched. In another, Teresa Platt stepped up her PR offensive to new heights of absurdity when she claimed animal liberation activists had killed a dog during their raid of a mink farm.

The most publicized raid took place outside Seattle in 2003, when 10,000 mink were released from the Roesler Brothers Fur Farm in Sultan, WA. A media frenzy followed, which included CNN coverage and a lengthy piece in the LA Times.

In addition there have been numerous actions on the retail level, such as the fur store in Santa Clara, CA; which was closed after a single A.L.F. action.

All but a few of the farms visited in the 2000s were unlisted in publicly available fur farm lists, an encouraging trend showing both that individuals are finding farms through their own means, and showing those who make a living off the suffering of others that there is nowhere to hide.

The fur industry is a weak link in the animal abuse chain. The determined focus of a caring few can finish it off forever.

Until victory.

FUR FARM RAIDS
1995 - 2008

1. 8/13/95 Annendale, MN; Davidson Fur Farm, 1 coyote liberated.
2. 11/16/95 Olympia, WA; Jordan Mink Ranch, 400 minks liberated. **CLOSED**.
3. 11/16/95 Pleasant View, TN; Ma Ellis Fox Farm, 30 foxes liberated. **CLOSED**.
4. 1/15/96 Sheboygan, WI; Zimbal Minkery, 400 minks liberated.
5. 4/4/96 Victor, NY; L.W. Bennet Fur Farm, 1700 minks liberated.
6. 6/96 Snohomish, WA; Brainard Fur Farm, 80 minks liberated.
7. 6/7/96 Sandy, UT; Fur Breeders Agricultural Co-op, 75 minks liberated.
8. 6/21/96 Riverton, UT; Riverton fur farm, 1000 minks liberated.
9. 7/4/96 Howard Lake, MN; Latzig Mink Ranch, 1000 minks liberated.
10. 7/17/96 South Jordan, UT; Holt Mink Ranch, 3000 minks liberated.
11. 8/9/96 Hinsdale, MA; Carmel Mink Ranch, 1000 minks liberated.
12. 8/12/96 Alliance, OH; Jorney Mink Ranch, 2500 minks liberated.
13. 9/28/96 Alliance, OH; Jorney Mink Ranch; 8000 minks liberated.
14. 10/2/96 Salem, UT; Paul Westwood Fur Farm; 1500 minks liberated.
15. 10/5/96 Lindboro, NH; Gauthier Fur Farm; 35 foxes and 10 minks liberated.
16. 10/11/96 Hinsdale, MA; Carmel Mink Ranch; 75 minks liberated.
17. 10/23/96 Lebanon, OR; Arnold Krohl Fur Farm, 2000 minks liberated.
18. 10/25/96 Coalville, UT; Reese Fur Farm, 2000 minks and 200 foxes liberated.
19. 10/29/96 Victor, NY; Bennett Fur Farm, 46 foxes liberated.
20. 12/14/96 Snohomish, WA; Brainard Fur Farm, 50 minks liberated.
21. 12/25/96 Bath, MI; Jack Brower Fur Farm, 150 minks liberated.
22. 4/9/97 DeBerry, TX; Kelly Fur Farm, 10 chinchillas liberated and rehomed.
23. 3/11/97 Sandy, UT; Fur Breeder's Agricultural Co-op burned down.
24. 5/11/97 Salisbury, MD; Parsons Mink Ranch, 500 minks liberated.
25. 5/28/97 Lebanon, OR; Lou Masog Mink Farm, 80 minks liberated.
26. 5/30/97 Mt. Angel, OR; Arritola Mink Ranch, 10,000 minks liberated.
27. 7/4/97 Cle Elum, WA; David Smith Mink Farm, 4,000 minks liberated. **CLOSED**.
28. 7/8/97 Medina, OH; Tom Mohoric Mink Farm, 41 minks liberated. **CLOSED**.
29. 7/97 Alliance, OH; Jorney Mink Ranch, 500 minks liberated.
30. 9/1/97 Downers Grove, IL; Ides Mink Farm, 3500 minks liberated. **CLOSED**.
31. 9/2/97 Anderson, IN; Adams Fox Farm, 200 foxes liberated.
32. 10/5/97 Crystal Lake, IL; Frye Mink Farm, 5,000 minks liberated. **CLOSED**.
33. 10/6/97 Preston, ID; Palmer Mink Farm, 5,000 minks liberated.
34 10/17/97 Watertown SD; Turbak Mink Ranch, 3,000 mink liberated. **CLOSED**
35. 10/19/97 Sioux City, IA; Circle K Farm, 5,000 minks and 100 fox liberated.
36 10/21/97 Webster City, IA; Fassett Fur Farm, 1 mink liberated, breeding records destroyed.
37. 10/24/97 Independence, WI; Smeija Fur Farm, 800 minks liberated.
38. 10/24/97 Tomohawk, WI; Ott Mink Ranch, 300 minks liberated.

35. 10/19/97 Sioux City, IA; Circle K Farm, 5,000 minks and 100 fox liberated.
36 10/21/97 Webster City, IA; Fassett Fur Farm, 1 mink liberated, breeding records destroyed.
37. 10/24/97 Independence, WI; Smeija Fur Farm, 800 minks liberated.
38. 10/24/97 Tomohawk, WI; Ott Mink Ranch, 300 minks liberated.

39. 10/25/97 Medford, WI; Jack Dittrich Minkery, 3000 minks liberated.
40. 10/29/97 Hebo, OR; Glen Kellows fur farm, 6 rabbits liberated and rehomed.
41. 11/5/97 Ft. Wayne, IN; Blaine Leffers Fox Farm, 125 foxes liberated. **CLOSED**.
42. 11/28/97 Hinsdale, MA; Carmel Mink Rarm, 6 minks liberated.
43. 7/3/98 Middleton, WI; United Vaccines Research Ranch, 310 minks liberated.
44. 7/29/98 Sandy, UT; Fur Breeders Co-op, 6 minks liberated.
45. 7/30/98 Sandy, UT; Fur Breeders Co-op, 2 minks liberated.
46. 8/18/98 Kimball, MN; Mueller fur farm, 4,000 minks liberated. **CLOSED**.
47. 8/20/98 Guttenburg, IA; Hidden Valley fur farm, 330 foxes liberated. (The farmer mentions two actions have occurred, only one is known). **CLOSED**.
48. 8/21/98 Jewell, IA; Isebrand Fur Farm, 3,000 minks liberated.
49. 8/27/98 Beloit, IW; Brown Mink Farm, 3,000 minks liberated. **CLOSED**.
50. 8/28/98 Rochester, MN; Zumbro River Fur Farm, 3,000 minks liberated.
51. 10/26/98 Powers, MI; Pipkorn Inc, 5,000 minks liberated.
52. 11/26/98 Volo, IL; Empty fur farm sabotaged.
53. 12/2/98 Anderson, IN; Adams Fox Farm, 150 foxes liberated.
54. 2/12/99 Snohomish WA; Brainerds Fur Farm, 150 mink liberated in daylight raid
55. 2/13/99 Annandale, MN; Davidson Fur Farm, 6 foxes liberated.
56. 2/17/99 Richmond, UT; Nivison Mink Ranch, 9 minks liberated.
57. 2/23/99 Snohomish, WA; Brainard Fur Farm, 150 minks liberated.
58. 8/3/99 Bristol, WI; Krieger Fur Farm, 3,000 minks liberated.
59. 8/7/99 Escanaba, MI; Two fishing boats of a mink farmer set on fire.
60. 8/8/99 Plymouth, WI; United Feeds burned down.
61. 8/8/99 Plymouth, WI; Gene Meyer Mink Farm, 2,500 minks liberated. **CLOSED**.
62. 8/14/99 Salisbury, MD; Frank Parsons Mink Ranch, 20 mink liberated.
63. 9/12/99 Chandler, MN; Calvin Gunnink Fur Farm, 100 foxes liberated.
64. 10/1/99 Montpelier, IN; Owl Creek Fox Farm, 30 foxes painted with henna.
65. 10/25/99 Chandler, MN; Calvin Gunnink Fur Farm, 5 lynx liberated
66. 11/13/99 South Jordan, UT; Beckstead Mink Ranch, hundreds of minks liberated.
67. 1/29/00 Snohomish, WA; Brainard Fur Farm, 60 minks liberated.
68. 3/13/00 Viraquo, WI; Kikapoo Fur Foods, attempted arson.
69. 6/14/00 New Hamsphire; Richard Gauthier Fur Farm, 500 minks liberated.
70. 9/7/00 New Hampton, IA; Drewelow and Sons Fur Farm,14,000 minks liberated.
71. 10/1/00 Inidana; 30 foxes painted with henna.
72. 4/19/01 Snohomish, WA; Brainerd's Fur Farm, 200 minks liberated.
73. 10/16/01 Ellsworth, IA; Scott Nelson Mink Ranch, 2,000 minks liberated.
74. 10/20/01 Ellsworth, IA; Scott Nelson Mink Ranch, 1,600 minks liberated. **CLOSED**
75. 1/13/02 Hawkeye Mink Co-Op, Jewell, IA; break-in and documents taken.
76. 5/02 Harborcreek, PA; Minkdek Brothers, 200 minks liberated.
77. 6/02 Erie, PA; Lawrence Dana Fox Farm, all foxes liberated, breeding cards taken.
78. 8/18/02 Waverly IA; Misty Moonlight Mink Ranch, 3,000 minks liberated.
79. 9/02 Harborcreek, PA; Minkdek Brothers, 50 minks liberated.
80. 9/02 Gerry, NY; Main Mink Ranch, minks liberated and breeding cards taken.
81. 11/26/2002 Harborcreek, PA; Minkdek Brothers, feed shed burned down.
82. 8/25/03 Sultan, WA Roessler Brothers Mink Farm, 10,000 minks liberated.
83. 4/1/05 Bluffs, IL; Dozens of foxes liberated.
84. 1/29/05 Howard Lake, MN; Latzig Mink Ranch, 200 mink liberated.
85. 8/14/07 Hinsdale, MA; Berkshire Furs, 500 minks liberated.
86. 11/6/08 Deming, WA; Marr's Ranch, 150-200 mink liberated.
87. 4/21/08 Jefferson, OR; Jefferson Fur Farm, 40 mink liberated.
88. 8/19/08 South Jordan, UT; McMullin Mink Farm, 600 mink liberated

Top 10 mink producing states as of 2006, with number of farms:

1. Wisconsin (68)
2. Utah (66)
3. Oregon (18)
4. Minnesota (23)
5. Idaho (27)
6. Iowa (14)
7. Washington (9)
8. South Dakota (3)
9. Ohio (7)
10. Illinois (7)

16 mink farms in the U.S. also raise fox. There are no available USDA statistics for fox farms.

The following are other states home to "farmers who are members of Fur Commission USA":

1. Colorado
2. Connecticut
3. Indiana
4. Maine
5. Maryland
6. Massachesetts
7. Michigan
8. Missouri
9. New Hampshire
10. New Jersey
11. New York
12. North Carolina
13. North Dakota
14. Oklahoma
15. Vermont
16. Virginia
17. West Virginia

INDUSTRY TRENDS

The trend in the fur industry is towards consilidation. The year of the first mink release, 1995, there were 478 mink farms in the United States. At last count in 2006, there were 271. Yet the number of animals killed has increased. Smaller farms are declining while larger farms grow. The average mink farm in 1995 imprisoned 5,864 mink, while the average mink farm today has almost doubled to 10,547.

We are still a long way from dreams of empyting the average mink farm being out of reach to a small group of determined liberators. The largest North American animal release to date was 14,000 mink from the Drewelow and Sons Fur Farm in Iowa, and as many as 30,000 mink have been released from farms overseas

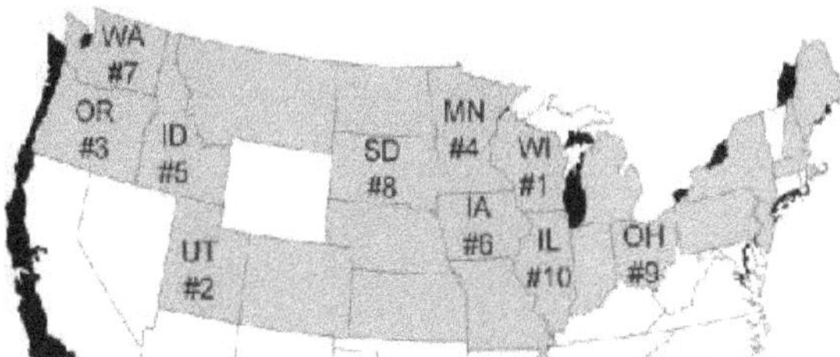

GOING FOR THE THROAT

Highlights From The Frontlines

Drewelow and Sons Farm Raid
New Hampton, IA
9-7-00
14,000 mink released

Largest animal release in North America to date. Days after the raid, the farmer reported 7,000 mink were still free.

Simultaneous Actions in Wisconsin
United Feeds fire
and
Release of 3,000 mink
Plymouth, WI
8-8-99

As fire destroyed the cooperatively owned United Feeds mink feed operation, 3,000 mink were released from the nearby Gene Meyer Fur Farm. The simultaneous action saw the total destruction of the feed operation, jointly owned by over 20 fur farmers in a region with one of the highest concentration of fur farms in the country. Additionally, Gene Meyer announced in the wake of the action he could not survive the loss of profits and would be closing.

United Feeds meeting it's just demise

Scott Nelson Fur Farm Double Raid
Ellsworth IA
10-16-01
10-20-01
Release of 2,000 mink
Subsequent release of 1,600 mink

The A.L.F. took credit for the overnight release of every animal at the Scott Nelson Fur Farm in Ellsworth, IA. In the media the following day, he announced most of the animals had been recaptured. The A.L.F. returned 4 days later and re-liberated every animal. The following day, Scott Nelson announced the farm's closure.

Operation Bite Back
Nationwide
6-91 to 10-92
*Oregon State University Experimental Fur Farm
*Northwest Fur Farm Foods Cooperative
*Washington State University
*USDA Wildlife Biology Furbearer Research Facility
*Malecky Mink Ranch
*Michigan State University Experimental Fur Farm
*USDA Predator Research Station

Operation Bite Back was a campaign to destroy the fur industry, brought to four states over 16 months. Using arson, liberations, and theft and destruction of documents; 7 key points in the fur industry were targeted in an attempt to completely eradicate the fur industry's research apparatus. Rodney Coronado was indicted for his role in this campaign and sentenced to 57 months in federal prison.

ANIMAL LIBERATION

All actions against animal abuse industries are motivated by one goal: to save lives. Whether in the short term – such as a mink release – or long term – such as the elimination of a feed supplier which will weaken the industry and bring it to its eventual collapse. Because many farms close after an animal release, the quickest way to save lives in both the short term and the long is the liberation of a fur farm's captives.

The following animals are raised on fur farms in North America, are native to North America, and can be expected to both survive and thrive in the wild:

Mink

The most commonly farmed fur-bearing species. As of 2006, there were 271 mink farms in the U.S. Mink are most often housed in long sheds. The sheds are generally only partially walled on the sides, and their contents are usually visible through the remaining two or three feet that can be comprised of chicken wire or other mesh wire. Occasionally mink are found in outdoor row pens or other non-shed structures.

Lynx

Classified as a threatened species in the U.S., it has been speculated there may be more lynx held captive than exist in the wild (Maine excluded). To date the only lynx liberation on record occurred in Minnesota in 1999, where 5 lynx were released from the Gunnick Fur Farm.

Fox

As with lynx, there are no USDA statistics for fox farms in the U.S. It is important to note that, unlike mink, fox are extremely timid and may not quickly leave their cages when released. When possible, fox should be manually removed from the property. When this is not an option, all effort should be taken to allow the maximum number of escape options, and allow the greatest amount of time to pass before the farmer discovers the release. For this reason, it is suggested fox releases happen as early in the night as possible. Fox are often held in large cages or runs that may have to be cut open individually.

Misc. Species

Other species are known to be held at fur farms, including raccoons, coyotes, and wildcats and there are reports of fur farms holding deer and skunks, among other species. One farm in Washington State is reported as raising 12 species of fur bearing animals.

MOST WANTED

National Fur Foods

Essential fur industry feed supplier. Speciall blended feed is crucial to maintaining pelt quality and keeping the U.S. fur industry competitive in the globa market. The company runs a feed production mill in New Holstein, and a research farm in Oshkosh.

Fraser Farms

Rumored to be the largest cat farm in the country. There may be more Lynx held captive on this farm than live wild in the entire state of Montana

American Legend Auction House
(formerly Seattle Fur Exchange)

Over 70% of all animal skins farmed in the U.S. pass through one warehouse south of Seattle. Twice a year – in February and May - fur dealers and brokers from around the world converge to bid on the 3 million pelts sold there each year. The industry' most crucial bottleneck point.

University research farms

At least five state universities (WSU, MSU, Idaho State, Utah State, and University of Wisconsin are known to conduct research to benefit the fur industry. Some of this research is being revealed here fo the first time. Currently the U.S. fur industry is only competitive on the global market through superior pelt quality made possible by the industry's research apparatus' of which the universities are the largest part.

A NOTE ON BREEDING SCHEDULES

TTENTION MUST BE GIVEN TO BREEDING CYCLES IN THE LIBERA-ION OF FUR FARM PRISONERS. MINK AND FOX ARE KILLED IN NOVEMBER OR DECEMBER, AND ARE NOT WEANED UNTIL MAY OR UNE. IT IS IMPORTANT TO BE MINDFUL THAT ANIMALS ARE NOT IT TO BE RELEASED UNTIL THEY HAVE BEEN WEANED. THE MINK MUST BE AT A POINT WHERE THEY CAN BE SELF-SUFFICIENT IN THE WILD. THE WINDOW OF TIME ADVISABLE FOR FUR FARM LIBERA-IONS IS JUNE TO OCTOBER. EARLIER AND THE ANIMALS MAY NOT E IN A POSITION TO FEND FOR THEMSELVES, LATER AND IT MAY BE OO LATE TO SAVE THEM.

	MINK	FOX	LYNX
Breeding	Feb./ March	Feb.- April	March
Gestation (in days)	40-75	52-53	
Birth	April	April/ May	May/ June
Weaned	May	June	April
Killed	Nov./Dec.		varying

MEDIA WORK

Media coordination adds impact to an action. eleasing 5,000 mink brings immediate relief to ose animals, while national media attention rings the animal liberation message to millions, nd deterred animal skin or flesh consumption as the potential to save thousands or millions ore. The following can be incorporated into n action to ensure maximum impact:

Photos: Documenting the conditions on a fur rm with photographs, and documenting the id itself, can inspire activists when the documentation is mailed to supportive above-ground oups and disseminated. Photos and video leased to the media after A.L.F. raids have also posed the public to many atrocities inside the ouser's torture chambers.

Video: When clandestine raiders released 000 mink from the Scott Nelson Mink Farm Ellsworth IA, they took video of the raid, leased it to the media, and gave millions of eople their first glimpse inside a fur farm. ideo is only reasonable at farms so small that ne person working a camera will not directly anslate to fewer cages that will be opened those farms guaranteed to be emptied even ith one fewer hand.

Communiqués: Issuing a communiqué detailg the action and the intentions behind it serve veral functions. One, it gives those behind nonymous actions a voice. The media can and oes pick up on content from communiqués nd incorporates them into their coverage, making your motivations clear, and countering the fur industry's inaccurate assertions of motives being anything other than compassion. Two, they serve as inspiration for others. Three, working information into communiqués can be effective to disseminate valuable info to the activist community – info such as farm addresses and farm closures. Anyone with new information for updates to this list is encouraged to distribute the info widely (preferably incorporated into a communiqué claiming an action).

THE FACE OF DEATH

Teresa Platt is the public face of the fur industry. As Executive Director of the Fur Commission USA – a trade group of fur farmers – she is the most visible full time spokesperson for the fur industry. Her tasks include media liason work in the wake of A.L.F. actions, appearing before congress to give fear-instilling testimony and encouraging tougher laws against animal liberators, and acting in numerous capacities in defense of the indefensible.

Outside her on-camera and in-print temper tantrums, she is known for the amateurish doublespeak which mark her poor PR skills. Even corporate media has yet to regurgitate the terminology she finds so clever, including "conflict gyspsies" (out of state protesters) and "abandoned animals" (released mink and fox).

With a face like the joker and a smile of pure evil, Teresa Platt hides behind the fence of the gated community where she lives on Coronado Island, CA; functioning as spokesperson for an industry that claims over two million victims annually.

Not By Word But By Deed

Raiding a Fur Farm

Equipment

Disposable dark clothing
Facial covering
Wire cutters (be prepared w/large & small pair)
Gloves
Maglight w/red screen and hands-free head strap, or headlamp w/ red screen

Optional:
Digital Camera
Video Camera
Radios (strongly recommended)

Locate The Farm

Use this directory, phone directories, trade publications, online satellite images, business databases, or more guerilla techniques to locate farms in the target area.

Dismantle the Fence

There is much variety among fences, and there are even those farms that have no fence at all. Every fence will be different, and often what at first appears to be an impenetrable fence will have flaws which become apparent upon scrutiny. Very heavy fences are often kept in place only through attachment to fence posts. An entire fence can often be felled through a small number of calculated cuts at those points where the fence connects to the posts. If the entire fence cannot be brought down, many large holes should be cut giving the animals as many escape routes as possible. The gate to the compound should also be opened. Every bit of fence cut away will likely directly translate into more lives saved. Effectively dismantling the fence should be among the highest priorities.

Move to the Sheds

Most but not all sheds will be visible from the road. They are low lying and in rows. Sheds are generally open on sides for the bottom two or three feet below the cages, making it easy to determine the animals inside. Some sheds may have crude doors, but generally expect a doorway and no door. Make a quick scan of the inside space around the door for possible alarms once inside.

Open the Cages

There are a large variety of cages and latches, and this will often vary even within the same farm. In addition to simple latches, many cages will only be opened, or opened most effectively, through the removal of nesting boxes. These are large boxes hooked to the front of the cages that can generally be lifted and set to the ground, allowing the animals to escape. Cages individually wired shut might be found, particularly for the breeders. Most often these are kept shut with a small o-ring that can be removed with one cut.

Fox cages can be found inside sheds or in outdoor rows, and vary greatly in latching mechanism and structure.

OTHER OPTIONS

Releasing within the compound

In the rare cases where a fence proves impenetrable, or weather conditions do not permit a release into the wild, the breeders and non-breeders can be released from their cages within the compound. The breeders and non-breeders will mix and the farmer will be unable to tell which is which. The farmer will be forced to pelt out his entire stock and start from scratch. This can be enough to force a farm out of business forever.

Dropping over the fence

An inefficient, but in some cases necessary, method of fur farm animal liberation is the physical transport of animals away from the farm, or manual placement of animals outside the fence. This can be useful in cases where dismantling the fence proves problematic, or the cages are too close to a house to risk the noise that follows a large mink release. There are no known cases of this tactic being employed in the U.S., yet a likely method would be to place animals individually in sacks and deliver them off site. Mink are very aggressive and heavy gloves are necessary when handling this species.

Dyes

Destroying the value of an animal's pelt can be accomplished with henna-based dyes in squeeze bottles, and has been use at several farms. The non-toxic dyes can be sprayed on the animals' backs, ruining the animal's value. All types of fur anima (fox, mink, rabbit, chinchilla, lynx, etc.) can be dyed, as long as they do not have dark fur. This has put farms out of business. However, the animals will still be killed. This is an appropriate tactic when the cages are too close to the house to release animals.

Beyond opening cages, there are other potential sabotag targets at fur farms:

Feed machines: Carts that are driven up the rows to feed animals. For information on sabotaging gas powered vehicles, read *Ecodefense*.
Vehicles: The farmer's personal or work vehicle can b sabotaged. See the book *Ecodefense*.
Processing sheds: Where the animals are cleaned an processed.
Offices: A vital organ of any business, and the potential source of valuable information on the local (or national) fur industry.

Breeding Records

If animals cannot be released, a tremendous economic blow can be made to a farm through the destruction of breeding records. Generally these are index car or above cages in the breeder shed(s). Maintaining a high quality pelt through a calculated breeding program is essential to the operation of a fur farm. Time permitting, once the perimeter has been breached, this should be the first stop in any fur farm action. Cards can be destroyed on site, or taken off site and discarded.

Recommended Reading

Books:
Free The Animals – Newkirk (History of the U.S. Animal Liberation Front)
From Dusk Till Dawn - Mann
How to Get Anything on Anybody – Book III: Guide to researching individuals and their whereabouts.

Publications:
Memories of Freedom – Wester Wildlife Unit of the A.L.F. (Account of Operation Bite Back, a direct action campaign to cripple the fur industry in the 1990s)
Interviews With Animal Liberation Front Activists

FUR FARM LIBERATIONS: FACT & MYTH

Myth: Liberated mink will cause irreparable harm to the ecosystem.
Fact: This argument is usually preceded by the claim that the mink will starve to death because they haven't been taught to kill. If they don't know how to hunt, then they cannot kill wildlife. The truth is that mink kill out of instinct, much as does the domestic cat. No training or rehabilitation is necessary.

So do liberated mink kill wildlife? Of course they hunt wildlife. They are predators, and they help maintain the balance of nature by killing and eating prey animals. Yet they do not pose a threat to any particular species as a whole. Mink are not specialized predators. Certain predators, like lynx, will have a principal prey that they rely on. Lynx will usually only eat snowshoe hare, otter normally eat fish, etc. On the other hand, the mink will eat anything. Examination of mink scat shows they will eat mammals, fish, birds, reptiles and amphibians. They do not specialize, but rather eat whatever is most readily available. If liberated mink ate too many field mice, then it would be easier for them to then hunt nesting birds, fish, or even snakes. When the population of one food source grows low, mink will instinctively hunt what is more abundant, and therefore easier to find.

Furthermore, the mink is a solitary animal. The only time one will see mink together is when they are mating, or in the weeks immediately following their birth, when the mother is still caring for her kits. When released, mink go in search of their own habitat and will not tolerate the presence of other mink. Mink normally have a range of just under 3 square kilometers. Being so spaced apart, it is unrealistic to assume that the mink could have enough of an impact on any particular species to make a noticeable difference.

This doesn't have to be a hypothetical argument based on interpretations of scientific literature. Mink have been released in large numbers, so where is the damage? The fact is, there isn't any. We know they have survived. But yet we aren't seeing this ecological damage the fur trade has predicted. In fact, the A.L.F. has done the earth a favor by raiding these farms. In addition to stopping the mass accumulation of animal wastes by shutting these places down, they have re-introduced mink to areas where they had been nearly wiped out. For example, the A.L.F. freed 400 mink from a fur farm in Sheboygan, WI. At roughly the same time there was concern about the lack of mink along the Sheboygan River. The A.L.F. was the only relief that river has gotten, in regards to that particular problem. It is estimated that as few as 150 lynx may still exist in Montana, yet the state still allows a trapping season. Montana is the home of several lynx fur farms, and there is likely more lynx in captivity than in the wild. The lynx is only a few short generations out of the wild and even the Forest Service has considered using ranch lynx for reintroduction. Imagine what direct action groups could do without all of the red tape and bureaucracy.

Until the last cage is empty......

A Brief History Of Fur War P.O.W.'s:

Chatham Three

Action: ALF liberation of 1,542 mink from the Eberts Fur Farm in Blenheim , Ontario .
Arrested: Pat Dodson, 48; Hilma Ruby, 59; Gary Yourofsky, 26; Robyn Weiner, 25; Alan Hoffman, 47. All residents of Michigan.
Charges: Each charged with Breaking and Entering and Criminal Mischief. Dodson also was charged with Possession of Break-in Tools; Weiner and Hoffman were charged with Possession of Stolen Property Over $5,000. All were freed on $10,000 cash bail.
Outcome: Allan Hoffman and Robyn Weiner inform against the others, also implicating one person in release of 1,500 mink at the farm the week previous. Sentence: 6 months in jail.

Mass Four

Action: Release of 25 mink from Carmel Mink Ranch, Hinsdale MA on 11-28-96. Can of gasoline found near scene. Third mink release at the farm in three months.
Arrested: Alex Smolak, Warren Upson, Jamie Roth, Grant Upson
Charges: Breaking and entering in the night time with intent to commit a felony, trespass, larceny of property over $250 and malicious destruction of property over $250.
Outcome: $3,100 fine, three days jail, one year probation.

Seattle Five

Action: Daylight raid of 150 mink from Brainerd's Fur Farm, Snohomish WA; 2-12-99.
Arrested: Lindsey Parme, Kyle Salisbury, Geoff Kerns, Kim Berardi and Nicole Dawn Briggs.
Charges: Second-degree burglary and first-degree theft.
Outcome: Charges against all defendants were dropped when the prosecution was unwilling to reveal their informant in the case.

Utah Arrestees

Action: Release of 3,000 mink at Holt's mink ranch, South Jordan UT
Arrested: Clinton Colby Ellerman, Sean Gautschy, Brandon Mitchener, Trev Poulson, Alex Slack. Colby turned informant.
Outcome: Two years in prison.

Ohio Three

Action: Release of 100 mink from Jorney Mink Ranch, Alliance OH; 7-97
Arrested: Jesse V. Parsh, 19, Stephanie A. MacDougall, 18, and unknown third person.
Charges: Two counts of Vandalism, two counts of Breaking and Entering and one count of Possession of Criminal Tools. All felonies.
Outcome: Each plead guilty to five felonies.

Peter Young and Justin Samuel

Actions: Release of 3,000 mink from Turbak Mink Ranch, Watertown, SD; 10-17-97; release of 5,000 minks and 100 fox from Circle K Farm, Sioux City, IA; 10-19-97; release of one mink and destruction of breeding records from Fassett Fur Farm, Webster City, IA; 10-21-97; release of 800 mink from Smeija Fur Farm, Independence, WI; 10-24-97; release of 300 mink from Ott's Mink Ranch, Tomohawk, WI; 10-24-97; release of 2,500 mink from Dittrich Minkery, Medford, WI; 10-25-97.
Charges: Four counts of Disruption of Interstate Commerce Through Threats of Violence or Extortion, two counts of Animal Enterprise Terrorism.
Outcome: Justin Samuel turned states evidence and testified against Young. Both sentenced to two years.

Fur Commission USA

225 East Sixth Street
St. Paul, Minnesota 55101
(612) 222-1080
(612) 293-0537 fax

URGENT—SECURITY ALERT

November 5, 1997

TO: U.S. FUR FARMERS
FROM: FUR COMMISSION USA
RE: ALF INCIDENT - INDIANA

Lair Fox Ranch, owned by Blaine Leffers in Ft. Wayne, Indiana, was attacked last night (Tuesday) by animal rights criminals. The guard fence was cut in two places with holes approximately 2' x 3'. All pens in the fox shed were opened, and 35 fox were removed out of a total of 99 housed on the farm. With the help of neighbors, Mr. Leffers has recovered most of the fox, but at least one was killed by an automobile, and another must be euthanized because of injuries it sustained in the animal rights attack. Local law enforcement authorities and the FBI have been notified and an investigation has begun.

This incident continues a pattern of animal rights violence in the Midwest during the last two months. Recently, there have been numerous reports by farmers of suspicious activity, including sightings of strange vehicles, and light aircraft circling fur farms. Fur Commission USA has passed along all of these reports to federal investigators, who are following up on them.

Please treat seriously any and all suspicious activity near your farm, and report it immediately to law enforcement authorities, your local FBI office and Fur Commission USA. Note descriptions of any strange vehicles, with license numbers, and any aircraft flying over your farm. In the case of aircraft, look for identifying numbers on the tail or wings.

... Wisconsin. Writer had agreed and met with Sheriff Breneman, Chief Deputy Bruce Daniels, District Attorney Shawn Mutter and individuals estimated at approximately 25 in number representing 14 different ranches of fur farms. Attached hereto is a list of the individuals and telephone numbers owning the various fur ranches.

The purpose of this meeting was believed to have been a successful exchange of information both ways between law enforcement and concerns of the ranchers. It was readily detected of the animosity and frustration exemplified by many of the ranchers and efforts were made to explain as much as possible law enforcement efforts conducted thus far in attempting to gain evidence and conduct investigations in order to determine who the responsible individuals are.

Questions were raised by the ranchers regarding the carrying of firearms if they encounter individuals on their property. It was explained as best as possible the ramifications of why carrying of firearms or any other weapons should not be accomplished. It was explained that to the best of law enforcement's knowledge thus far, that the individuals were not believed to be armed and/or dangerous and therefore having or carrying a weapon if a confrontation were to occur would likely result in heightened action for which if conducted any individual would have to account for his or her actions as any other any other law enforcement officer would.

In addition to discussing other concerns, it was recommended that certain things could be accomplished in order to improve security and awareness during this time of year when it appears that the illegal release of animals are occurring just prior to the harvest of the same.

LEAKED DOCUMENTS

AN EXCLUSIVE

It was also discussed that certain measures could be considered to help improve security and/or obtain evidence should anyone else become victims of such illegal releases of animals. One area that was discussed concerned the temporary hiring of security personnel which was felt to be beneficial in that live patrols during the nighttime hours should readily detect if entrance was made into the mink sheds and thereby hopefully minimizing the loss to the rancher. In addition individuals could contact various alarm-type security companies as it was suggested modifications could be made to perimeter guard fences to detect when and if the fence were to be cut affording an egress for the released mink. Additionally, SA BRUNER advised checking into hidden cameras activated with infrared devices utilizing infrared film in order to obtain photographs of unknown subject(s) engaged in the process of releasing the mink illegally. It was further advised that the Federal Bureau of Investigation (FBI) in no way is sponsoring or making the recommendation for any particular brand or type of equipment but merely that these types of items exist and are readily available in supporting catalogs such as CABELO's which are utilized by hunters to take nighttime photographs of wild game.

Ranchers also expressed concerns as to ultimate prosecution and types of charges which were partly answered by District Attorney Mutter and explained that potential State charges could also be duplicated by Federal charges of potentially higher significant penalties but no specific Federal violations of law were cited.

On October 29, 1997, writer received by United Parcel Service (UPS) a package of numerous documents and material from ROBERT BUCKLER, FUR COMMISSION USA, 225 East Sixth Street, Minneapolis, Minnesota 55101, telephone number (612) 222-1080. The information received also includes lists of militant animal rights activists by name and general criminal advice and techniques for followers of ALF (Animal Liberation Front) in targeting fur ranchers across the United States.

Writer was advised by BUCKLER during a telephone conversation of other individuals across the country that could be helpful in identification of ALF members from various law enforcement communities conducting extensive research on this subject. BUCKLER advised one of these individuals is Sergeant Bill Galvin, Syracuse Police Department, Syracuse, New York, telephone number (315) 425-1034, as well as, Officer Mike Larson, Portland, Washington, Police Department, telephone number (503) 823-0983. BUCKLER further advised that he has

BROMM, stated she and her husband were doing business at one time as the TWILIGHT MINK FARM. Mrs. BROMM stated, however, that she and her husband went out of business in 1990, basically because of the animal rights movement when a lot of customers stopped buying fur coats. BROMM reported that RONALD JACOBSON, formerly doing business as the L AND R MINK RANCH of rural Story City, Iowa, is also out of business, as is also CHRIS HILLPIPRE.

JIM LANGER, Norman Road, Norman, Wisconsin, was contacted and he advised that he and his brother own a mink farm at that location. LANGER stated that his farm has approximately 20,000 animals and a total loss could be as much a $1,000,000.

GARY YAUGER, 2902 Highway 310, Two Rivers, Wisconsin advised that he is the owner of a mink farm at that location. YAUGER has approximately 13,000 aninimals which he values at between $250,000 to $300,000.

With the few fur industry targets remaining, aim for the actions of greatest impact. Spray painting a feed supplier will be of little effect, and leave those who may one day attempt a significant action to deal with increased security.

Think big.
Act big.

The editor(s) of The Final Nail III would like to credit the failures of the following:

*Those liberators who turned their back on every non-human prisoner through the hedonism of meat eating.
*Jacob Ferguson, Justin Samuel and every government informant for giving the devil yet a few more human faces.
* And the FBI for keeping it interesting.

The editor(s) of The Final Nail III would like to credit the triumphs of the following:

* Those who have given us the most important moments of our lives through their comradeship and selflessness; standing by our side in the dead of night as we risked it all for total liberation.

FR: Fur Research-University and/or Private
FFES: Fur Farm Equipment Supplier
FF: Fur Farm - Species Unknown
FF-M: Mink Fur Farm
FF-F: Fox Fur Farm
FF-L: Lynx Fur Farm
FP/W: Fur Processor and/or Wholesaler
FAH: Fur Auction House
FFFS: Fur Farm Feed Supplier
TS: Trapping Supplier
FFO: Fur Farm Organization
FTO: Fur Trapping Organization
+++: Unconfirmed / Incomplete Data

UNIVERSITY & PRIVATE RESEARCH
The fur industry relies on research done in labs to increase their profits through further manipulation of housing conditions, breeding, and feed.

FUR AUCTION HOUSES
Where trappers and fur farmers sell the skins to retailers, wholesalers, and brokers. A weak point in the industry, as only a few auction houses remain open.

FUR FARM FEED SUPPLIERS
The values of the pelts are largely due to their quality, and quality is closely related to specially blended feed developed by feed suppliers. These are a crucial component of the industry and there are only a handful left. Many also have experimental fur farms.

FUR FARMS
FOX – 16 mink farms also raise fox in the U.S. as of 2006. There are no USDA statistics for fox farms and the exact number is not known.
LYNX - Approximately 40 farms still imprison lynx in North America.
MINK – The U.S. has 271 mink farms as of 2006.

TRAPPING SUPPLIERS
Businesses selling leg-hold and other traps for killing wild fur animals.

FUR FARM EQUIPMENT SUPPLIERS
Companies that sell cages, killing devices, automatic pelters, feed grinders, and more.

FURRIER EQUIPMENT SUPPLIER
Companies that sell tools to make the coats and other garments.

FUR PROCESSORS / WHOLESALERS
These are the people who clean pelts and sell them in bulk. Not all wholesalers are processors, although many are.

FUR FARM ORGANIZATIONS
Groups of fur farmers who lobby state legislators, produce propaganda and manage sales of skins.

FUR TRAPPING ORGANIZATIONS
Groups of fur trappers who lobby state legislators, produce propaganda and manage sales of skins.

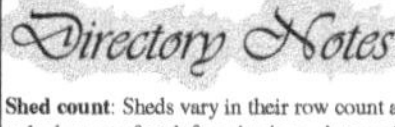

Shed count: Sheds vary in their row count and length. When possible, a shed count of each farm is given. Among farms, there can be a large variation of animals-per-cage, row count, and other variables. Shed count will loosely correlate to herd size relative to other factors, and the number of sheds will assist in approximating animal count and physical scale.

+++: Farms with this tag are requiring further investigation due to one of the following: 1) the farms are reported as not being at the address listed, 2) the current operational status of the business is in question, 3) there is a portion of the information in question (missing street address, etc) or 4) the information is unconfirmed. With creative research, these intelligence gaps can be filled and the locations of the guilty exposed in full.

Bridging The Gaps

D.I.Y. Research

Some farms and infrastructure targets are yet to be discovered. Additional intelligence gaps exist herein, such as rural route postal addresses in place of street addresses for some entries. The following reference material and tools should be used to determine the location of unlisted sites and supplement the information contained in the listings:

Business to Business (B2B) Directories
Directories for businesses that do not advertise to the public, and only sell to other businesses. It is not necessary for a fur processor to be listed in the yellow pages, but they will be found in a B2B directory. Numerous directories are available in online and print formats.

Business Databases
Business databases such as Reference USA, listing over 14 million businesses, can often be found in the reference section at libraries. Businesses can be looked up by type or name, offering site locations and other useful data.

Trade Publications
As with activists, it is by their own mouths the fur industry creates its largest problems. Trade publications such as ***Sandy Parker Reports*** and ***Fur Rancher*** are full of information such as names of key players in the industry; locations of farms; inside commentary on our movement and its impact; and specific information on the industry, what drives it, and what its weaknesses are. ***Ulrich's Periodical Directory***, available at any good reference library, lists all known trade publications by subject

Newspaper Archives
Old hard copies of local newspapers can be mined for leads on farms and other targets, uncovering leads not found online.

University Libraries
University libraries in states with a large fur industry can have a large volume of information in the form of agricultural survey maps and more.

Online Satellite Images
Scrutinize online sattelite images for insight into unknown back entrances, farm layout, escape routes on foot, and more.

Ingenuity
Ask yourself who has the information you seek, and how you can get it. The best intelligence often comes out of the greatest ingenuity.

Leave no Trace

SECURITY - AN OVERVIEW

Fingerprints
Wear gloves at all times. Never handle equipment that will be taken to the site – radio, flashlights, etc – without wearing gloves prior to the action. Be mindful of details such as prints on batteries inside flashlights.

Video Surveillance
Cameras at farms are not unheard of. Wear facial coverings at all times.

Cell Phone Tracking
Technology allows anyone to be tracked via their cell phone. Turning off the phone does not prevent against this, and time will tell if even removing the battery is 100% effective. Safest practice is to leave cell phones at home. Police agencies now have the ability to turn cell phones into microphones remotely, and monitor all conversations within earshot of a phone – even when it is turned off. Cell phones are a major liability to any clandestine activity and should be kept far away from the planning and execution of an action.

Tool Marks
Tool mark analysis linking wire cutters to cut fences at farms was the main evidence used against Peter Young and Justin Samuel. Tools should never be used for more than one action, and should be discarded a safe distance from the scene after use.

Clothing
Clothes will retain forensic evidence such as mink hair and organic matter after an action, and should be discarded. Shoes will leave unique prints, and should also be discarded. Studying shoe tread wear patterns unique to each person is another investigative tactic, and new shoes should be used for each action. Covering shoes with socks is a second option. Keep nothing after an action – no tools, clothing, maps, or notes.

Other Forensics
Humans leave a trail of hair everywhere they go. Masks must be worn to prevent against leaving hair containing DNA that can link someone to a crime scene. In Finland, saliva found at the scene of a fur farm raid was used to implicate an activist. Leave no DNA traces.

Clean car thoroughly after an action.

Other Traces
*Empty pockets of all debris before carrying out an action.
*Clean car thoroughly prior to action to ensure no misc. debris falls out when exitin[g] the car.
*Purchase nothing with a credit card. Purchase nothing used for the action anywhere nearby, even wit[h] cash.
*If in a small town, stop nowhere unless absolutely necessary – small town residen[ts] are often very aware of outsiders.
*Be mindful of soft ground at the parkin[g] location that will leave tire tracks.
*Do not bring a GPS device or use a vehicle with On Star or other tracking service.
*Do not park your vehicle in view of a surveillance camera if parking in an area wh[ere] cameras are a possibility.

Communiqués
Great care should be given to post-raid media work. Use anonymous remailers from public computers to email communiqués. Remailers are not to be absolutely trusted, an[d] attention must be given to the presence of video cameras that will capture the image of the person sending the communiqué. If the USPS is used for a communiqué or photograph/video distribution, assemble the package in a clean room with adequ[ate] gloves (single-layer latex gloves are not sufficient), and sealed w[ith] a sponge (not saliva). Tape is a magnet for traces of skin and ha[ir] – use cautiously. No handwriting. Burn all communiqué drafts including the several layers of paper under the draft that will c[on]tain an imprint. Scrutinize any photo or video to be released f[or] visibility of revealing features such as tattoos or eyes. The FBI [has] measured the distance between eyes and pupils to match suspe[cts] to photos.

No One Talks, Everyone Walks
We see through history the greatest threat to evading capture is the threat of talk. Ensure everyone in the cell is schooled in security culture. Never work with a braggart, drug addict, perso[n] untested under pressure, or one who exhibits unstable behavio[r] or heavily emotion-driven decision making. Never discuss an action after the fact – on the phone, over the computer, or in person. The Green Scare case has shown that allies can becom[e] enemies, and talking even in private can have disastrous consequences. Enact a strict code of silence.

RISKING OUR FREEDOM FOR THEIRS

THE ART OF CIRCUMVENTION

FUR FARM SECURITY IN THE 2000s

Photoelectric motion sensors. Advertising literature reads: "Create a fence you can't even see."

Since the fire storm of mink releases in the 1990s, which saw dozens of farms raided and farms shut down forever, fur farmers have taken steps to increase security. As has been proven consistently, security precautions have not prevented animal releases year after year, and farms with sophisticated security systems have been successfully emptied. Rick Aritolla of Aritolla Mink Ranch reported his farm had a sophisticated security system in place before raiders released 10,000 mink in 1997.

Fences

Fences charged with electricity are not uncommon. Generally only one or a small number of wires are charged and can be avoided. Another potential threat is tamper-sensitive fences which alert the farmer if a fence is being cut or disturbed, however there have been no known reports of any such fences being installed. As with all concerns over an invisible-yet-potential threat, one can carry out the action that would trigger the alarm, then retreat to await a response. If there is no response, it can be presumed there is no alarm.

Photoelectric Sensors

Common in the Northwest, and less so in the Midwest; these alarms often take the form of boxes affixed to posts placed in the corner of farms. The boxes transmit an invisible field which, when crossed, triggers the alarm (either silent or audible). Fields can be fan or beam shaped. With the latter, dropping to the ground and rolling under the beam has proven successful.

Dogs

The occasional farm will have a dog loose among the sheds. Effective approaches for managing loud or threatening animals will vary by situation. Optimally, dogs can be corralled into a sectioned-off area during an action.

Cameras

Occasionally farms have video cameras. Farmers have also been advised by police to install still or video cameras triggered by motion.

Security Guards

Larger farms have been known to hire overnight security guards, particularly during pelting season. This is cost-prohibitive for the average farm, yet sufficient reconnaissance should be employed before advancing on a larger farm to ensure no one is on site. Remember there is nothing that can't be circumvented with enough craft.

False Claims of Closure

One attempted deterrent seen in recent years is the false claim of closure. At least two farms claiming to have been closed in the media have since been revealed to be open. Trust no unsubstantiated media or fur farmer reports that a farm is out of business.

ACTION SPEAKS LOUDER THAN WORDS

TAKING BY NIGHT

A.L.F. Communique
401 animals liberated from the University of Iowa
November 14th, 2004

The Animal Liberation Front is claiming responsibility for the liberation of 401 animals from the University of Iowa in the early hours of November 14th, 2004. All animals on the third floor of the UI psychology department -- 88 mice and 313 rats -- were removed, examined and treated by a sympathetic veterinarian, and placed in loving homes.

Additionally, two animal labs and three vivisector's offices were entered and all contents relating to animal research were destroyed.

These are:

4th Floor - Spence Labs:
Vivisector Ed Wasserman's lab entered. Dozens of computers and devices used in experiments on live pigeons were destroyed.

Basement - Spence Labs:
Lab of vivisector Mark Blumburg and others entered. Surgical equipment and small animal stereotaxic devices, as well as "shock boxes" and other instruments of torture destroyed.

4th Floor - Seashore Hall
Primate researcher Joshua Rodefer's office entered. Computer discs, hard drives, paperwork and photos showing Rodefer's work confining drug addicted primates in small glass boxes removed. The remaining paperwork detailing his monstrous work addicting primates and rats to narcotics was soaked in acid and the computer destroyed.

1st Floor - Seashore Hall
Primate researcher Amy Poremba's office entered. Computers destroyed, documents removed, and the remainder soaked in acid.

This raid was carried out to halt the barbaric research of the UI Psychology Department's 7 primary animal researchers: Professors Poremba, Freeman, Blumburg, Johnson, Robinson, Rodefer and Wasserman.

This was not thoughtless vandalism but a methodical effort to cripple the UI psychology department's animal research. Only equipment in rooms where animals were confined and tortured were targeted. Only computers belonging to or used in the work of vivisectors were destroyed. Only documents of animal researchers waere doused in acid. The acid a deliberately chosen paper dissolving agent. Our goal is total abolition of all animal exploitation. Achieved in the short term by delivering the 401 animals from UI's chamber of hell. And in the extended term by shutting down the labs through the erasing of research and equipment used in the barbaric practice of vivisection. The entire raid was a careful and deliberate 5-pronged assault on UI's animal research.

Behind the laboratory doors we found drug addicted rats, rats subjected to stress experiments involving loud noise, rats undergoing thirst experiments, unanesthetized rats with protruding surgical staples and oozing wounds, and mice and rats affixed with grotesque head implants. Inside the labs of UI's Psych Department, we found a bloody torture chamber showcasing the cruelest whims of our earth's sickest minds. Professors Freeman, Poremba, Rodefer, Johnson, Robinson, Blumburg, and Wasserman are monsters. Tonight 401 animals are spared their reach.

Our deepest sadness is reserved for the animals on the 4th Floor kept from our arms, those we were unable to save, including hundreds of mice and rats, pigeons, guinea pigs, and 8 primates.

No animals were released into the wild. All 401 were placed in comfortable, loving homes.

We acted as operatives not only of compassion, but good science. Animal research is not only cruel but hazardous -- as data derived from the animal models is not applicable to humans and therefore dangerous.

Our bypassing of UI's sophisticated, key card-access, 4-walled security system (perimeter, elevator, corridor, animal room) should be interpreted as a two-fold message:

1) Our utter seriousness in achieving animal liberation.
2) If you torture animals we will not be stopped from liberating them.

On the ears of these monsters who know only profit and blood, who hide behind unjust laws, our breath has been wasted. Justice for the victims of vivisection will be achieved not by the blows of boycott nor protest -- but of our sledgehammers to laboratory doors.

Let this message be clear to all who victimize the innocent: We're watching. And by axe, drill, or crowbar -- we're coming through your door.

Stop or be stopped.

A.L.F.

A.L.F. Communique
21 mice liberated from Louisiana State University
April 22nd, 2005

In celebration of World Week for Animals in Laboratories the Animal Liberation Front is claiming responsibility for the liberation of 21 mice from Louisiana State University in the early hours of April 22nd, 2005.
Breaking through a vent in a side door, animals on the seventh floor of the LSU Biology Department building-- 21 mice -- were removed, examined and treated by a sympathetic veterinarian, and placed in loving homes.
No animals were released into the wild. All 21 were placed in comfortable, loving homes.
LSU's Animal Cruelty Facility lab was also vandalized in addition to giving 21 mice new lives free from torture, solitude and suffering. Aquariums were smashed, windows broken and paint stripper poured on outer walls. Spraypaint was used for slogans and further vandalism of the labs, and the locks were glued on doors to any rooms that housed no animals.
Our deepest sadness is reserved for the animals on the 7th Floor kept from our arms, those we were unable to save, including hundreds of mice, dozens of rats, birds, rabbits, and turtles. The cold solitude of the cage and the deafening silence of sterile, windowless laboratory rooms on the top floor of a building, with no chance to interact in the outside world or with one another is torture enough. Add to that the despicable cruelty of those human beings who've shown no compassion for the screams from animals in their never-ending, painful experiments and you can see where our sadness, and our anger, comes from.
We acted as operatives not only of compassion, but good science. Animal research is not only cruel but hazardous -- as data derived from the animal models is not applicable to humans and therefore dangerous.
Our aim in inflicting as much economic damage as possible is to drive up the cost of animal experimentation until this sadistic psuedo-science is no longer economically feasible.
Our aim in liberating animals should be obvious. Giving them a new life free of the hell that is the LSU ACF. For 21 mice, we've done that.
To vivisectors everywhere, you know your profession is one of cruelty and unnecessary suffering.
Stop now or be stopped.
Always for the animals,
A.L.F.

Revolutionary Cells - Animal Liberation Brigade Communique
Explosion at Chiron, Emeryville CA
August 28th, 2003

In the early hours of August 28th volunteers from the Revolutionary Cells descended on the animal killing scum Chiron. We left them with a small surprise of 2 pipe bombs filled with an ammonium nitrate slurry with redundant timers. This action came about because Chiron has continued their murderous connection with Huntingdon Life Sciences even though they have been exposed numerous times as some of the most egregious animal killers in the industry.
Chiron, you were asked to sever your ties with HLS, you were told, and yet you continued your relations with them. Now it is time for you face the consequences of your actions. If you choose to continue your relations with HLS you will no longer be subject only to the actions of the above ground animal rights movement, you will face us. This is the endgame for the animal killers and if you choose to stand with them you will be dealt with accordingly. There will be no quarter given, no more half measures taken.
You might be able to protect your buildings, but can you protect the homes of every employee?
From palestine to euskal herria, from the jungles of colombia to northern ireland, the struggle will continue until all of the oppressive institutions are destroyed!
For animal liberation through armed struggle, the Revolutionary Cells--Animal Liberation Brigade

A.L.F. Communiq
115 chickens liberated from Merial Labs, Berlin M
February 27th, 20

In the early morning hours of February 27, 2003, the ALF liberated 115 chickens from Merial Select Laboratory (10026 Main Street, Berlin, MD, 21811, Phone 410 641-2060, Fax 410 641-0768)
In the midst of a snowstorm, we made our way to the animal housing units. Using crowbars and boltcutters, we bypassed the alarmed doors by prying and cutting our way through the window panes and wire mesh. After crawl into several barns, we loaded 115 baby chicks into carriers and brought the to safety. They have been taken to temporary housing to live in a period of isolation to ensure that the possible diseases they have been infected with d not spread to others. Afterwards, they will be moved to permanent homes to live freely.
Merial Labs will tell you their research into new vaccines is "helping" anima The truth is, they are creating vaccines to maximize an animal's life inside a factory farm in order to increase profits from the commodification of life. Countless animal research facilities commit their atrocities in Maryland, but Merial was targeted specifically because they are a client of Huntingdo Life Sciences. Any friend of HLS is an enemy of the ALF. We know who the clients are. We are out there, and you're next.
Until all are free...
The Animal Liberation Front

Anonymous Communiq
Office break-in at Seaboard Securities, HLS clic
December 30th, 20

Last night we broke into the offices of Seaboard Securities (HLS market maker) in Tequesta, Florida (17713 SE Federal Highway, Ste 100). We emptied a file cabinet of its files, and smashed several computer monito and a television.

Here's a message to Kevin, Dennis, Cristian, Adam, Guy and the rest of the Seaboard Securities staff: we now know where you live; we will not hesitate to take this fight to your doorstep if you continue to do busines with Huntingdon Life Sciences.

FBI believes suspect in East Bay bombings has gone underground

By Dana Hull
Mercury News

Animal rights activist Rod Coronado had been on the run for nearly three years when he was arrested in 1994 on an Indian reservation. Agents had tracked his movements across the country based on phone records, some from an ex-girlfriend upset about her cell phone bill.

It's the kind of break the FBI is hoping they'll get in the case of Daniel Andreas San Diego, the 25-year-old suspect in the bombing of two East Bay companies with ties to a firm that tests products on animals.

Nearly a month after the FBI issued a warrant for his arrest, authorities believe San Diego may have slipped into a loosely-knit radical underground similar to the one that allowed Coronado to hide. But as cases like Coronado's show, if fellow activists provide food,

WHAT THE DAY NEVER BRINGS

JUSTICE SERVED...

Roesler Bros. Fur Farm
Sultan WA
10,000 mink released 2003

Arritola Mink Ranch
Mount Angel OR
10,000 mink released 1997

Utah Fur Breeders Co Op
Sandy UT
Destroyed by fire 1997

JUSTICE COMING...

River Jordan Mink Ranch
Lehi UT
Largest mink farm in the U.S.

Klinger Farms
Chippewa Falls WI

Fraser Farms
Ronan MT
Largest lynx farm in the U.S.

LET THIS RAID BE A CALL TO ACTION. IT IS TIME FOR ALL THOSE WHO OPPOSE NEEDLESS SUFFERING TO START THE ATTACK. THIS IS THE THIRD FUR FARM RAID IN THE MIDWEST THIS WEEK, LET'S MAKE THIS ONLY THE BEGINNING. BY BRICK, BOLTCUTTERS, OR FIRE, THIS IS THE DAWN OF LIBERATION.

THE ONLY THINGS SEPARATING LIFE FROM DEATH FOR THE MINK IN THESE DENS OF SUFFERING ARE A LATCH ON A CAGE AND YOUR OWN FEAR.

NOW IS THE TIME FOR ACTIVISTS WHO ARE UNWILLING TO RISK THEIR FREEDOM FOR THE ANIMALS TO QUESTION THEIR OWN DEDICATION AND CONVICTION.

- from the A.L.F. communique claiming responsibility for the release of 3,000 mink from the Isebrands Fur Farm; Jewell IA, August 21st 1998

THE FINAL NAIL

DESTROYING THE FUR INDUSTRY

NUMBER FOUR

SUMMER 2013

COMPLETE GUIDE TO LIBERATING FUR FARM PRISONI

And now, let's finish them off...

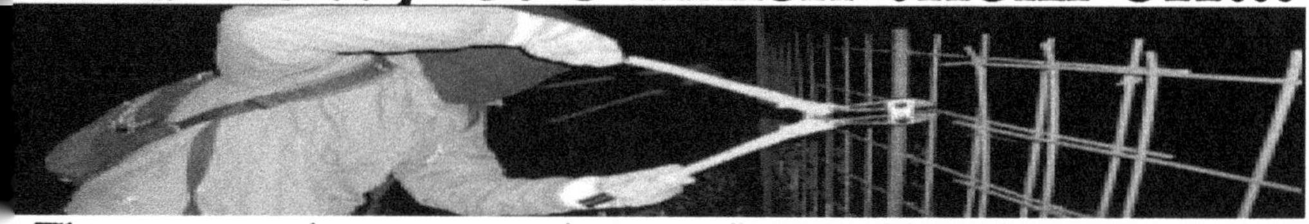

This represents the most comprehensive collection of fur industry addresses and tactical guidance on destroying the fur industry to date.

This is our attempt to bring accountability to those who shed the blood of the innocent every day.

Most importanly, this is for their victims.

ENDGAME: BACK TO DRIVE IN THE FINAL NAIL

n 1996, *The Final Nail #1*: Destroying the 'ur Industry circulated rapidly through he grassroots animal liberation move- nent. If offered the first comprehensive st of mink, fox, and lynx farms to date, evealing for the first time the exact physi- al location of fur farms across North merica. Prior to its release, there had een five fur farm liberations. In the 2.5 ears that followed, there were nearly 50.

'he following year, *The Final Nail #2* was eleased with updated info an many new arms. The ALF's fur farm campaign con- inued to accelerate, with larger and more requent raids. Despite *The Final Nail's* nassive impact, and the ALF continuing o raid dozens of farms, *The Final Nail* emained dormant for the next 11 years.

n the summer of 2008, *The Final Nail* was esurrected with the release of #3. The st had been massively updated, with over 00 previously unknown farms, and over 0 years of accumulated data on liberating ur farm prisoners. Fearing another surge n fur farm raids, the fur industry moved wiftly to have copies removed form he internet anywhere it appeared. It's irculation shifted to be largely limited to ard copy editions which were distributed erson-to-person and anonymously at onferences and gatherings.

Despite its limited circulation, *The Final Nail's* impact continued. Within 3 months f its release, 3 farms whose addresses vere first revealed in its pages were raided and nearly 9,000 mink released. *The Final Nail* was back.

The updated *Final Nail #4* comes 5 years later, in the summer of 2013, in what is perhaps the period of lowest activity since the ALF began it's fur farm campaign. The past year saw only a single release (13 foxes from a farm in Elkton, Virginia).

The Final Nail #4 offers these updates:

- Over 100 new fur farms since #3
- Specific details on fur farm layout (gathered from on-site investigations)
- Analysis of weak links in the industry

The spirit and function of *The Final Nail* is needed now more than ever. In a time when the climate in the movement has shifted from offensive to defensive, from a conversation on what we're going to do to stop them to what they're doing to stop us, from a time of ALF actions at a rate of one every two weeks to one of move- ment-wide paralysis inspired by rampant fear-mongering, *The Final Nail* represents a return to the essence of the ALF and the warrior model: the where, the how, and purpose that transcends all obstacles and fears.

To the rebirth of *The Final Nail*, and swift death of the fur industry.

The (anonymous) editors

From 2008 Until Today

A recent history of the ALF's fur farm campaign

Fur farm raids have seen a sharp decline since the last *Final Nail*, with just 13 fur farm actions occurring in the past 5 years.

Within two months of the release of *The Final Nail #3* in July 2008, 114 mink were released in an unreported raid of the Hunter Groves Mink Farm in South Jordan, Utah. This action was only made public in court documents after the arrest of two people for the raid that happened next...

On August 19th, 600 mink were liberated from the McMullin fur farm, also in South Jordan. The raid resulted in two arrests, after evidence such as cell phone records and a car key left at the scene linked two Utah activists to the raid.

Less than a month later, 150-200 mink were released from the S&N mink and fox farm in Scio, Oregon. The following year, the farm was reported to be empty, and is believed to be closed. The timing strongly indicates the ALF raid shut down this farm.

Less than two weeks later, the largest mink release since 2003 took place in Kayesville, Utah; with the liberation of 7,000 mink from the Lodder fur farm north of Salt Lake City.

The following month, another address first made public in The Final Nail was hit, with 1,500 mink liberated from the Ylipelto Fur Farm near Astoria, Oregon. A year later the farm was

Continued on Pg. 4

Complete list of U.S. fur farm raids: 1986 to 2013

93 raids.

Over 130,000 animals freed.

1986
Unnamed farm
Near Portland, Oregon
66 silver foxes liberated

August 13th, 1995
Davidson Fur Farm
Annendale, Minnesota
One coyote liberated

November 16th, 1995
Jordan Mink Ranch
Olympia, Washington
400 mink liberated
CLOSED

November 16th, 1995
Ma Ellis Fox Farm
Pleasant View, Tenessee
30 foxes liberated
CLOSED

January 15th, 1996
Zimbal Mink Ranch
Sheboygan, Wisconsin
400 mink liberated

April 4th, 1996
W. Bennet Fur Farm
Victor, New York
1,700 mink liberated

June, 1996
Brainard Fur Farm
Snohomish, Washington
80 mink liberated
CLOSED

June 7th, 1996
Fur Breeder's Agricultural Cooperative
Sandy, Utah
75 mink liberated

June 21st, 1996
Unknown fur farm
Riverton, Utah
1,000 mink liberated

July 4th, 1996
Latzig Mink Ranch
Howard Lake, Minnesota
1,000 mink liberated
NOW A FERRET FARM

July 17th, 1996
Holt Mink Ranch
South Jordan, Utah
3,000 mink liberated

August 9th, 1996
Carmel Mink Ranch
Hinsdale, Massachusettes
1,000 mink liberated
CLOSED

August 12th, 1996
Jorney Mink Ranch
Alliance, Ohio
2,500 mink liberated

September 28th, 1996
Jorney Mink Ranch
Alliance, Ohio
8,000 mink liberated

October 2nd, 1996
Paul Westwood Fur Farm
Salem, Utah
1,500 mink liberated

October 5th, 1996
Gauthier Fur Farm
Lindboro, New Hampshire
35 fox and 10 mink liberated

October 11th, 1996
Carmel Mink Ranch
Hinsdale, Massachusettes
75 mink liberated
CLOSED

October 23rd, 1996
Arnold Krohl Fur Farm
Lebaon, Oregon
2,000 mink liberated

October 25th, 1996
Reese Fur Farm
Coalville, Utah
2,000 mink and 200 fox liberated

October 29th, 1996
Bennett Fur Farm
Victor, New York
46 fox liberated

December 14th, 1996
Brainard Fur Farm
Snohomish, Washington
50 mink liberated
CLOSED

December 25th, 1996
Jack Brower Fur Farm
Bath, Michigan
150 mink liberated

April 9th, 1997
Kelly Fur Farm
DeBerry, Texas
10 chinchillas liberated

May 11th, 1997
Parson's Mink Ranch
Salisbury, Maryland
500 mink liberated
CLOSED

May 28th, 1997
Lou Masog Mink Farm
Lebanon, Oregon
80 mink liberated

May 30th, 1997
Arritola Mink Ranch
Mount Angel, Oregon
10,000 mink liberated

July 4th, 1997
David Smith Mink Farm
Cle Elum, Washington
4,000 mink liberated
CLOSED

July 8th, 1997
Tom Mohoric Mink Farm
Medina, Ohio
41 mink liberated

July, 1997
Jorney Mink Ranch
Alliance, Ohio
500 mink liberated

September 1st, 1997
Ides Mink Farm
Downers Grove, Illinois
3500 mink liberated
CLOSED

September 2nd, 1997
Adams Fox Farm
Anerson, Indiana
200 fox liberated

October 5th, 1997
Frye Mink Farm
Crystal Lake, Illinois
5,000 mink liberated

October 6th, 1997
Palmer Mink Farm
Preston, Idaho
5,000 mink liberated

October 17th, 1997
Turbak Mink Ranch
Watertown, South Dakota
3,000 mink liberated
CLOSED

October 19th, 1997
Circle K Farm
Sioux City, Iowa
5,000 mink, 100 fox liberated

October 21st, 1997
Fassett Fur Farm
Webster City, Iowa
1 mink liberated

)ctober 24th, 1997
meija Fur Farm
ndependence, Wisconsin
00 mink liberated

)ctober 24th, 1997
)tt Mink Ranch
omohawk, Wisconsin
00 mink liberated

)cotber 25th, 1997
ack Dittrich Minkery
Iedford, Wisconsin
,000 mink liberated
:LOSED

Jovember 5th, 1997
laine Leffers Fox Farm
'ort Wayne, Indiana
25 fox liberated

Jovember 28th, 1997
:armel Mink Ranch
Iinsdale, Massachusettes
mink liberated
:LOSED

ıly 3rd, 1998
nited Vaccines Research
:anch
Iiddleton, Wisconsin
10 mink liberated
:LOSED

ıly 29th, 1998
ur Breeder's Agricultural Co-op
andy, Utah
mink liberated

ıly 30th, 1998
ur Breeder's Agricultural
:o-op
andy, Utah
mink liberated

.ugust 18th, 1998
Iueller fur farm
:imball, Minnesota
,000 mink liberated
:LOSED

.ugust 20th, 1998
Iidden Valley Fur Farm
iuttenburg, Iowa
30 foxes liberated
:LOSED.
he farmer mentions two ac-
ons have occurred, only one
ction is known)

August 21st, 2008
Isebrand Fur Farm
Jewell, Iowa
3,000 mink liberated

August 27th, 1998
Brown Mink Farm
Beloit, Wisconsin
3,000 mink liberated

August 28th, 1998
Zumbro River Fur Farm
Rochester, MN
3000 mink liberated

October 26th, 1998
Pipkorn Inc
Powers, MI
5000 mink liberated

November 26th, 1998
Volo, Illinois
Empty fur farm sabotaged

December 2nd, 1998
Adams Fox Farm
Anderson, Indiana
150 fox liberated

February 13, 1999
Davidson Fur Farm
Annendale, Minnesota
6 fox liberated

February 17th, 1999
Nivison Mink Ranch
Richmond, Utah
9 mink liberated

February 23rd, 1999
Brainerd Fur Farm
Snohomish, Washington
150 mink liberated
CLOSED

August 3rd, 1999
Krieger Fur Farm
Bristol, Wisconsin
3000 mink liberated

August 8th, 1999
Gene Meyer Mink Farm
Plymouth, Wisconsin
2,500 mink liberated
(nearby United Feeds fur feed supplier burned down the same night)
CLOSED

August 14th, 1999
Frank Parsons Mink Ranch
Salisbury, Maryland
20 mink liberated
CLOSED

September 12th, 1999
Calvin Gunnink Fur Farm
Chandler, Minnesota
100 fox liberated

October 1st, 1999
Owl Creek Fox Farm
Montpelier, Indiana
30 fox painted with henna dye

October 25th, 1999
Calvin Gunnink Fur Farm
Chandler, Minnesota
5 lynx liberated

November 13th, 1999
Beckstead Mink Ranch
South Jordan, Utah
Hundreds of mink liberated

Janurary 29th, 2000
Brainerd Fur Farm
Snohomish, Washington
60 mink liberated
CLOSED

June 14th, 2000
Richard Gauthier Fur Farm
Lyndeborough, New Hampshire
500 mink liberated

September 7th, 2000
Drewelow & Sons Fur Farm
New Hampton, Iowa
14,000 mink liberated

October 1st, 2000
Indiana
30 fox painted with henna

April 19th, 2001
Brainerd's Fur Farm
Snohomish, Washington
200 mink liberated
CLOSED

October 16th, 2001
Scott Nelson Mink Ranch
Ellsworth, Iowa
2,000 mink liberated
CLOSED

October 20th, 2001
Scott Nelson Mink Ranch
Ellsworth, Iowa
1,600 mink liberated
CLOSED

May, 2002
Minkdek Brothers
Harborcreek, Pennsylvania
200 mink liberated

June, 2002
Lawrence Dana Fox Farm
Erie, Pennsylvania
All foxes liberated, breeding cards taken

August 18th, 2002
Misty Moonlight Mink Ranch
Waverly, Iowa
3,000 mink liberated

September, 2002
Minkdek Brothers
Harborcreek, Pennsylvania
50 minks liberated

September, 2002
Main Mink Ranch
Gerry, New York
Mink liberated and breeding cards taken
CLOSED

November 26th, 2002
Minkdek Brothers
Harborcreek, Pennsylvania
Fur feed storage building burned down

August 25th, 2003
Roessler Brother's Mink Farm
Sultan, Washington
10,000 mink liberated

April 1st, 2005
Kerry Littig's fox farm
Bluffs, Illinois
Dozens of fox liberated

August 14th, 2007
Carmel Mink Ranch
Hinsdale, Massachusettes
500 mink liberated
CLOSED

November 6th, 2008
Dale Marr's Mink Ranch
Deming, Washington
150-200 mink liberated

April 21st, 2008
Jefferson Fur Farm
Jefferson, Oregon
40 mink liberated

August, 2008 ("days before" mink release at McMullin Mink Farm)
Hunter Groves Mink Farm
South Jordan, Utah
114 mink liberated

August 19th, 2008
McMullin Mink Farm
South Jordan, Utah
600 mink liberated

September 8th, 2008
S&N Fur Farm
Scio, Oregon
150-200 mink liberated
REPORTED EMPTY 2009, MAY REOPEN

September 21st, 2008
Lodder's Mink Farm
Kaysville, Utah
7,000 mink liberated

October 17th, 2008
Ylipelto Fur Farm
Svensen, Oregon
1,500 mink liberated
CLOSED

October 4th, 2009
Ylipelto Fur Farm
Svensen, Oregon
300 mink liberated
CLOSED

November 18th, 2009
Lang's Mink Farm
Richmond, Minnesota
50 mink liberated

July 13th, 2010
Unnamed mink farm
Franklin, Idaho
30 mink liberated

July 27th, 2010
Ylipelto Fur Farm
Svensen, Oregon
Eight incendiary devices planted, buildings & vehicle burned
CLOSED

September 10th, 2010
Harvey Beck Mink Ranch
Granite Falls, Washington
400 mink liberated

September 24th, 2011
Western Star Fur Farm
Svensen, Oregon
300 mink liberated

October 10th, 2011
Palmer Erickson Mink Farm
Jewell, Iowa
1,200 mink liberated

October 12th, 2011
Miller's Mink Ranch
Gifford, Washington
1,000 mink liberated.

August 5th, 2012
D & S Fox Farm
Elkton, Virginia
13 foxes liberated

A Recent History of Fur Farm Raids (Cont'd...)

hit again (300 mink released). By the time the farm was visited a third time in 2010, with several vehicles and a building set on fire, the farm was believed to be closed. Again, the timing strongly indicates the ALF raids shut this farm down forever.

Two small, unreported mink releases occurred over the next year. The first took place in November 2009, where 50 mink were released from Lang's Mink Farm in Richmond, Minnesota. The next took place in July 2010, where 30 mink were released from an unnamed farm in Franklin, Idaho.

The Harvey Beck Mink Ranch near Seattle was next, with 400 mink released in September 2010. Activity remained non-existent for a year, until the Western Star Fur Farm in Astoria, Oregon was visited by the ALF and 300 mink released in 2011.

The next month saw three actions in just over 2 weeks. Rocky Mountain Fur and Fireworks, located on Interstate 80 in Heyburn, Idaho was set on fire. Damage was reported to be light. Soon after, 1,200 mink were released from the Palmer Erickson fur farm in Jewel, Iowa; and two days later 1,000 mink were released from Miller's Mink Ranch in Gifford, Washington.

The period between The Final Nail #3 and #4 closed out with the sole liberation in 2012: The release of 13 foxes from the D&S Fox Farm in Elkton, Virginia.

The fur industry is a weak link in the animal exploitation chain. The determined work of a caring few can finish it off forever.

Until victory.

Top 10 mink producing states as of 2007 (the latest year for which statistics are available), with the number of reported farms:

Wisconsin (71)
Utah (65)
Oregon (18)
Minnesota (23)
Idaho (24)
Iowa (17)
Washington (9)
South Dakota (3)
Ohio (9)
Illinois (7)

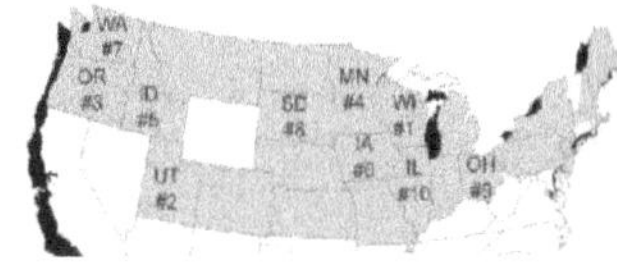

Weak Links

THE FASTEST WAY TO DESTROY THE FUR INDUSTRY

"Fight smarter, not harder."

Like any industry, fur has many layers, each feeding the one above it. At the top are the individual consumers. Below them, retail outlets the sell fur. Then wholesalers and manufacturers, and on downward. This article asks the question: What are the weakest links? What facets can be targeted by a few individuals that will weaken the entire industry and hasten it's collpase? And are there a few pillars that, if removed, would bring it down altogether?

Feed suppliers

Feed is the single biggest expense in raising mink. Even a small increase in feed costs would destroy many – if not most – fur farms. As an example, when the Fur Breeder's Agricultural Cooperative stopped delivering to a small town in Utah (forcing them to use another supplier or make their own), at least two fur farms there were forced to close.

UNITED FEEDS
BURNED DOWN BY THE ALF, 1999

Mink research

The Fur Commission USA spends a full 25% of its budget on mink farming research. Through research into feed, disease, pelt quality, and more, the US fur industry maintains a competitive edge over international markets.

Vaccine production

According to a Fur Commission USA poll, a disease outbreak is their second biggest fear as fur farmers (after attacks by animal rights activists). An aluetian disease outbreak can wipe out a mink farm in a matter of weeks. There are two companies producing vaccines: Merck (doing mink research at their suburban Omaha research farm) and United Vaccines (three locations around Madison, WI).

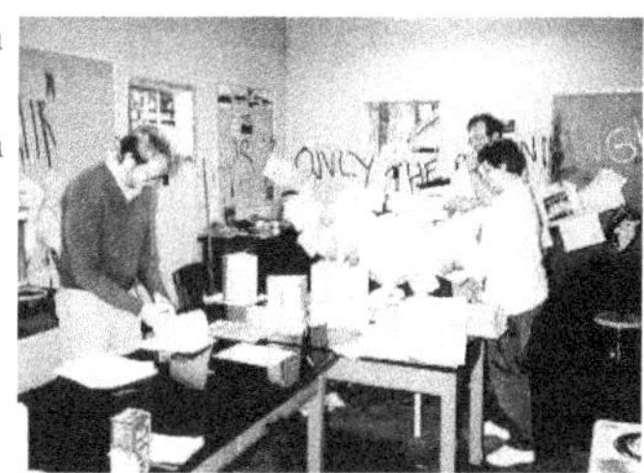

OREGON STATE UNIVERSITY
FUR LAB AFTER ALF RAID, 1991

Processing plants

Right now there is a severe shortage of facilities able to process raw animal skins. Currently, the only large-scale operation is the North American Fur Auctions processing plant in Stoughton, Wisconsin (near Madison). This plant has trouble handling current volume, and is an extremely significant lynchpin.

Melatonin implants

These implants can shorten the time it take to bring a pelt to market by six weeks. This brings the cost per pelt down significantly, and gives farms that use them a huge advantage. Currently there is one supplier of melatonin implants in the US: Neo-Dynamics, in Middleton, WI.

Auction Houses

Currently the Seattle Fur Exchange is the only auction house in the US for ranch-raised mink. Over 70% of all animals from US fur farms pass through this one building near Seattle.

SEATTLE FUR EXCHANGE
UNTOUCHED BY THE ALF... SO FAR

Industry Trends

The trend in the fur industry continues towards consolidation. The year of the first Animal Liberation Front mink release, 1995, there were 478 mink farms. In 2011, there were 268. Yet the number of animals killed has not decreased significantly (and is on the increase). Smaller farms are declining, while large farms are getting larger. The average mink farm in 1995 killed 5,864 mink (not including the breeders). In 2011, the average farm killed 11,529 mink. This means the average mink farm has doubled in size.

ANIMAL LIBERATION

Prisoners of War: A Brief History

Chatham Three

Action: ALF liberation of 1,542 mink from the Eberts Fur Farm in Blenheim , Ontario .

Arrested: Pat Dodson, 48; Hilma Ruby, 59; Gary Yourofsky, 26; Robyn Weiner, 25; Alan Hoffman, 47. All residents of Michigan.

Charges: Each charged with Breaking and Entering and Criminal Mischief. Dodson also was charged with Possession of Break-in Tools; Weiner and Hoffman were charged with Possession of Stolen Property Over $5,000. All were freed on $10,000 cash bail.

Outcome: Allan Hoffman and Robyn Weiner inform against the others, also implicating one person in release of 1,500 mink at the farm the week previous. Sentence: 6 months in jail.

Mass Four

Action: Release of 25 mink from Carmel Mink Ranch, Hindsdale MA on 11-28-96. Can of gasoline found near scene. Third mink release at the farm in three months.

Arrested: Alex Smolak, Warren Upson, Jamie Roth, Grant Upson

Charges: Breaking and entering in the night time with intent to commit a felony, trespass, larceny of property over $250 and malicious destruction of property over $250.

Outcome: $3,100 fine, three days jail, one year probation.

Seattle Five

Action: Daylight raid of 150 mink from Brainerd's Fur Farm, Snohomish WA; 2-12-99.

Arrested: Lindsey Parme, Kyle Salisbury, Geoff Kerns, Kim Berardi and Nicole Dawn Briggs.

Charges: Second-degree burglary and first-degree theft.

Outcome: Charges against all defendants were dropped when the prosecution was unwilling to reveal their informant in the case.

Utah case

Action: Release of 3,000 mink at Holt's mink ranch, South Jordan UT

Arrested: Clinton Colby Ellerman, Sean Gautschy, Brandon Mitchener, Trev Poulson, Alex Slack. Colby turned informant.

Outcome: Two years in prison.

Ohio Three

Action: Release of 100 mink from Jorney Mink Ranch, Alliance OH; 7-97

Arrested: Jesse V. Parsh, 19, Stephanie A. MacDougall, 18, and unknown third person.

Charges: Two counts of Vandalism, two counts of Breaking and Entering and one count of Possession of Criminal Tools. All felonies.

Outcome: Each plead guilty to five felonies.

Justin Samuel and Peter Young

Actions: Release of 3,000 mink from Turbak Mink Ranch, Watertown, SD; release of 5,000 minks and 100 fox from Circle K Farm, Sioux City, IA; release of one mink and destruction of breeding records from Fassett Fur Farm, Webster City, IA; release of 800 mink from Smeija Fur Farm, Independence, WI; release of 300 mink from Ott's Mink Ranch, Tomohawk, WI; release of 2,500 mink from Dittrich Minkery, Medford, WI.

Charges: Four counts of Disruption of Interstate Commerce Through Threats of Violence or Extortion, two counts of Animal Enterprise Terrorism.

Outcome: Justin Samuel turned states evidence and testified against Young. Both sentenced to two years

Bj Viehl & Alex Hall

Action: Release of 600 mink from McMullin & Sons fur farm, August 2010. Claimed by the ALF.

Charges: Animal Enterprise Terrorism.

Outcome: Sentenced to two years and two and a half years, respectively.

Victor VanOrden & Kellie Mashall

Action: Attempted raid of Circle K Fur Farm, Sioux City, IA, October 10th 2010.

Charges: Possession of burglar's tools (misdemeanor), second-degree criminal mischief.

Outcome: Served two months and one month, respectively.

Most Wanted List

National Feeds
Believed to be the largest feed supplier. Operates a production mill in New Holstein. For many years, operated a "research ranch" in Oshkosh, WI; yet the experimental fur farm is no longer at that location. It is possible the farm relocated, and if identified would be a significant target.

North American Fur Auctions plant
Currently a significant bottleneck point as the only large-scale pelt processor in the country, unable to handle current demand. Handles a large percentage of the raw pelts from US fur farms. In Stoughton, Wisconsin.

American Legend (Seattle Fur Exchange)
The only auction house in the US for ranch-raised mink. Over 70% of all pelts from US fur farms pass through one warehouse south of Seattle. Holds two auctions annually, where fur dealers and brokers from around the world converge to bid on the 3 million skins sold there each year. Also a pelt processor. This is the industry's most crucial choke-point.

Fraser Fur Farm
Largest and one of the only known wildcat farms in the country. There is evidence the farm no longer imprisons lynx, but does hold bobcats and other species. Located north of Missoula, Montana.

United Vaccines
Creates pharmaceuticals for fur farms. Operates a production facility in Fitchburg, WI (next to Madison), and there is evidence they operate a research facility in neighboring Verona.

Neo-Dynamics
The only manufacturer of melatonin implants in the US. Gives many farms an edge, without which they would go under. Located near United Vaccines in Middleton, WI.

University research
Three universities are believed to be actively doing research to benefit the fur industry: Washington State University, Idaho State University, and Michigan State University. Currently the US fur industry is only competitive on the global market through superior pelt quality made possibly be the industry's research apparatus's.

Strategy Sidebar

Feed Suppliers: The Weakest Link

In a letter to the to the FDA from Dale Lawson of Northwest Farm Food, he states that without inexpensive and specialized feed ensuring top pelt quality, the U.S. fur industry would collapse.

"The additional costs associated with [FDA proposal leading to increase in feed costs] would, in my opinion, totally eliminate the mink industry in the United States."

A farmer speaking this candidly about the critical role of feed is not uncommon. I have viewed other industry literature laying bare this reality of fur farming in the U.S.: With other countries now able to produce fur more cheaply than the U.S., the only way U.S. farmers can compete and the only edge they have in the global market is superior pelt quality. And along with breeding stock, the most crucial factor in pelt quality is specialized feed. In Utah, when the Fur Breeder's Agricultural Co-op stopped delivering to their town, several farms were forced to close.

Feed cost is the largest cost incurred by fur farms, representing 50-60 percent of the total cost of producing a pelt.

The current breakdown of known U.S. feed suppliers:

Central Fur Food (WI)
Medford Fur Food (WI)
Wisco Feed (unconfirmed if this company still manufactures feed) (WI)
United Feeds (WI)
National Fur Foods (WI)
Northwest Farm Food-Burlington (WA)
Northwest Farm Food-Astoria (OR)
Fur Breeder's Agricultural Co-op: Logan (UT)
Fur Breeder's Agricultural Co-op: Sandy (UT)
Rancher's Choice (NE)
Hawkeye Mink Cooperative
Heger Company (MN)

These are either uninvestigated, or believed to be smaller in size:

Alpine Clean Food (ID)
Midwest Ingredients (IL)
North Central Companies (MN)
Whalen Foods Inc. (MN)
Bob's Mink Ranch (MN)
Mazuri / Purina Mills (fox feed) (MO)
John & Peggy Smeal (NE)
Ormink, Mount Angel (OR)
Western Pennsylvania Fur Farmers Co-op (PA)
Shoreline Feeds, Lake Shore (UT)
LaBudde Group, Inc (WI)

How to Raid a Fur Farm

Animal Liberation in Eight Steps

Choose a Target

With this list as a starting point, use satellite images (from a public computer) to examine layout and parking options, then identify an appetizing target.

Gather equipment

Disposable dark clothing, facial coverings, wire cutters (come prepared with large and small pairs), gloves, and Maglight / small flashlights with red screen (less visible from a distance) and hands-free head strap (or headlamp).

Optional items include a digital camera (to document conditions and the raid itself), video camera (same), and radios (strongly recommended).

Park

Ideally, a parking spot will have been identified during daytime reconnaissance. However this is not required. Parking options included vacant lots, dirt paths that access corn fields / farms, nearby businesses such as grain elevators or unmanned animal farms, or just the side of the road. Use satellite images and pay special attention to parking options at neighboring properties behind the farm, which may be miles by road, but can offer quick access when used to approach on foot from the rear. Farms along rail road tracks allow for convenient parking, as tracks allow a path along which one can travel long distances unobstructed without encountering people or cars. Its possible to park a mile or more away, and use railroad tracks for a direct route to the farm.

Dismantle the fence

There is much variety among fences, and there are even those farms that have no fence at all. Every fence will be unique, and often that at first appears to be an impenetrable fence will have flaws which become apparent upon scrutiny. Very heavy fences are often kept in place only through attachment to fence posts. An entire fence can often be felled through a small number of calculated cuts at those points where the fence connects to the posts. If the entire fence cannot be brought down, many large holes should be cut giving the animals as many escape routes as possible. The fate to the compound should also be opened. Every bit of fence cut away can translate into more lives saved. Effectively dismantling the fence should be among the highest priorities.

Inspect for alarms

Although rare, do a quick sweep for photoelectric sensors in the corners of the compound and inside sheds, particularly at entrance points.

Destroy breeding records

While optional, this can be devastating to a fur farm and have tremendous economic impact. If there is time, a team should identify the sheds housing the breeders and destroy the records. These usually take the form of index cards on or above the cages. Maintaining a high-quality pelt though methodical breeding practices is essential to the operation of a fur farm. Time permitting, this should be the first stop in any fur farm action.

Open the cages

There are a wide range of cages and

latches, and this will often vary even within the same farm. In addition to simple latches, many cages will only be opened, or opened most effectively, through the removal of nesting boxes. These are large wooden boxes hooked to the front of the cages that can generally be lifted and set to the ground, allowing the animals to escape. Some cages may be individually wired shut, particularly for the breeding stock. Most often these are kept shut with a small o-ring that can be removed with one cut.

Fox cages can be found inside sheds or in outdoor pens, and vary greatly in latching mechanism and structure.

Post-raid work

Discard all tools and clothing far from the scene. See section on "Media Work" for guidance on disseminating the communique.

Alternate Actions

Releasing animals within the compound

in the rare cases where a fence proves unfellable, or weather conditions do not permit a release into the wild, the breeders and non-breeders can be released from their cages within the compound. The breeders and non-breeders will then mix, and the farmer will be unable to tell which is which. The farmer will be forced to pelt out his entire stock and start from scratch. This can be absolutely devastating to a fur farm. Breeding stock is most valuable aspect to an operation. In one recorded instance, the release of 800 breeding mink cost a fur farmer $240,000 ($3,000 per animal).

Dropping over the fence

An inefficient but in some cases necessary method of rescue. Animals can be placed over the fence manually. This can be useful in cases where dismantling the fence proves problematic, or the cages are too close to a house to risk the noise that follows a large mink release. There are no known cases of this tactic being employed in the US, yet a likely method would be to place animals individually in sacks and deliver them off site. Mink are very aggressive and heavy gloves are necessary when handling.

Dyes

Destroying the value of an animal's pelt can be accomplished with henna-based dye.

PRIVATE PROPERTY

NO TRESPASSING

A course of conduct involving criminal trespass is punishable under the ANIMAL ENTERPRISE TERRORISM ACT (PUBLIC LAW 109-347; 18 USC 43) with a fine and up to five years in prison

VIOLATORS WILL BE PROSECUTED UNDER THIS AND ALL OTHER APPLICABLE LOCAL AND FEDERAL STATUTES

Small Farm List

These farms are believed to imprison less than 5,000 mink, and are the smallest mink farms known.

Up to six micro-farms in downtown Franklin, ID
Bob Rodeghero, Morris, IL
North Star Fur Farm, Ollie, IA
Misty Moonlight Mink Ranch, Waverly, IA
Pelton Fur Farm, Rome, NY
Willes Fur Farm, Lehi, UT
D&B Fur Farm, Peoa, UT
Van Dyke Mink Farm, Springville, UT
North 40, Richmond, UT
Seth Dawson, Morgan, UT
J & G Mink Ranch, Highland, UT
Ovard Mink Farm, Wanship, UT
McMullin Fur Farm, South Jordan, UT
Samuel Schrock, Wautoma, WI

WITHOUT A TRACE
A Security Primer

Fingerprints
Wear gloves at all times. Never handle equipment that will be taken to the site – radio, flashlight, etc. – without wearing gloves. Be mindful of details such as prints on batteries inside flashlights.

Cameras
Video cameras at farms are not unheard of. Wear facial coverings at all times.

Cell phone tracking
BJ Viehl and Alex Hall were arrested for an ALF action at a Utah farm after being traced to the crime scene through cell phone records. Every cell phone is a tracking device. Turning a phone off is not sufficient, and time will tell whether removing the battery is in fact 100% effective. The safest practice is to leave cell phones at home.

Police agencies also have the ability to turn any cell phone into a microphone remotely, and monitor all conversations within earshot – even when the phone is turned off. Cell phones are a major liability in any clandestine activity and should be kept far away from the planning and execution of an action.

Tool marks.
Tool mark analysis linking wire cutters to fences at farms was the main evidence used against Justin Samuel and Peter Young. Tools should never be used at more than one location, and should be discarded a safe distance from the scene after use.

Clothing
Clothes will retain forensic evidence such as mink hair and organic matter after an action, and should be discarded. Shoes will leave unique prints, and should also be thrown away. Studying shoe tread patterns unique to each person is another investigative tactic, and new shoes should be used for each action. Covering shoes with socks is a second option. Keep nothing after an action – no tools, clothing, maps, or notes.

Other forensics
Humans leave a trail of hair everywhere they go. Masks must be worn to prevent against leaving hair containing DNA that can link someone to a crime scene. In Finland, saliva found at the scene of a fur farm raid was used to implicate an activist. Leave no DNA traces.

Clean the car thoroughly after an action.

Other traces

- Empty pockets of all debris before carrying out an action.
- Clean car thoroughly prior to an action to insure against miscellaneous debris falling out when exiting.
- Purchase nothing with a credit card. Purchase nothing used for an action anywhere nearby, even with cash.
- In in a small town, stop nowhere unless absolutely necessary. Small town residents are often very aware of outsiders.
- Be mindful of soft ground at the parking location that will leave tire tracks.
- Do not bring a GPS device or use a vehicle with one embedded.
- Do not park your vehicle in view of a surveillance camera, if parking in an area where cameras are a possibility.

Communiques
Great care should be given to post-raid media work. Only use a public computer where you can download TOR, which effectively anonymizes internet activity. Do all computer work, such as setting up email accounts and sending the communique, through the TOR network.

If the postal service is used for a communique or photograph/video distribution, assemble the package in a clean room with adequate gloves (single-layer latex gloves are no sufficient), and seal it with a sponge (not saliva). Tape is a magnet for traces of skin and hair – use cautiously. No handwriting. Burn all communique drafts, including the several layers of paper under the draft that will contain an imprint. Scrutinize any photo or video to be released for the visibility of revealing features such as tattoos or eyes. The FBI has measured the distance between eyes and pupils to match suspects to photos.

No one talks, everyone walks
We see through history the greatest threat to evading capture is the threat of talk. Ensure everyone in the cell is schooled in security culture. Never work with a braggart, drug addict, and person untested under pressure, or one who exhibits unstable behavior or heavily emotion-driven decision making. Never discuss an action after the fact – on the phone, over the computer, or in person. The Green Scare case has shown that allies can become enemies, and talking even in private can have disastrous consequences. Enact a strict code of silence.

Fur Farm Liberations: Myth Vs. Fact

Myth: Liberated mink will cause irreparable harm to the ecosystem.

Fact: This argument is usually preceded by the claim that the mink will starve to death because they haven't been taught to kill. If they don't know how to hunt, then they cannot kill wildlife. The truth is that mink kill out of instinct, much as does the domestic cat. No training or rehabilitation is necessary.

So do liberated mink kill wildlife? Of course they hunt wildlife. They are predators, and they help maintain the balance of nature by killing and eating prey animals. Yet they do not pose a threat to any particular species as a whole. Mink are not specialized predators. Certain predators, like lynx, will have a principal prey that they rely on. Lynx will usually only eat snowshoe hare, otter normally eat fish, etc. On the other hand, the mink will eat anything. Examination of mink scat shows they will eat mammals, fish, birds, reptiles and amphibians. They do not specialize, but rather eat whatever is most readily available. If liberated mink ate too many field mice, then it would be easier for them to then hunt nesting birds, fish, or even snakes. When the population of one food source grows low, mink will instinctively hunt what is more abundant, and therefore easier to find.

Furthermore, the mink is a solitary animal. The only time one will see mink together is when they are mating, or in the weeks immediately following their birth, when the mother is still caring for her kits. When released, mink go in search of their own habitat and will not tolerate the presence of other mink. Mink normally have a range of just under 3 square kilometers. Being so spaced apart, it is unrealistic to assume that the mink could have enough of an impact on any particular species to make a noticeable difference.

This doesn't have to be a hypothetical argument based on interpretations of scientific literature. Mink have been released in large numbers, so where is the damage? The fact is, there isn't any. We know they have survived. But yet we aren't seeing this ecological damage the fur trade has predicted. In fact, the A.L.F. has done the earth a favor by raiding these farms. In addition to stopping the mass accumulation of animal wastes by shutting these places down, they have re-introduced mink to areas where they had been nearly wiped out. For example, the A.L.F. freed 400 mink from a fur farm in Sheboygan, WI. At roughly the same time there was concern about the lack of mink along the Sheboygan River. The A.L.F. was the only relief that river has gotten, in regards to that particular problem. It is estimated that as few as 150 lynx may still exist in Montana, yet the state still allows a trapping season.

Montana is the home of several lynx fur farms, and there is likely more lynx in captivity than in the wild. The lynx is only a few short generations out of the wild and even the Forest Service has considered using ranch lynx for reintroduction. Imagine what direct action groups could do without all of the red tape and bureaucracy.

Until the last cage is empty......

Five Questions: Lightning Round

Why fur farms?

While no worse than any other factory farm, fur farms offer the Animal Liberation Front what is perhaps the greatest effort-to-yield ratio of any possible action, allowing a small number of people to save thousands of animals in very short time. Rescuing irreversibly domesticated animals brings the burden of having to home them, greatly limiting the number that can be saved. With the revelation in the 1990s that fur farmed animals can survive in the wild, the ALF had for the first time an option to save thousands of animals in one night. When combined with most people being within day's drive of a fur farm, and the industry's overall fragility, a fur farm raid is among the most high-impact options for the Animal Liberation Front.

How long does releasing mink take?

One source stated that in his experience, two people can release 1,000 mink every 15 minutes, or 4,000 mink an hour. By this formula, four people can release 2,000 mink every 15 minutes, or 8,000 an hour.

What does a fur farm look like?

The makeup is generally crude, with rows of sheds surrounded by a fence. A small processing and storage building is usually present. They are nearly always visible from the road. Generally a farmer's house will be on-site, but not always.

Are sheds ever locked? How do I get in?

Sheds are the most common structure used to house mink. Other structures include outdoor cages, and large canopy-style barns. Whatever the case, they are nearly always easily accessible. Because of the biology of mink, sheds usually must be porous and allow outside air to come in. In the rare event a shed door is locked (or even has a door), they can usually be accessed from the sides, which are generally only partially walled-off to allow outside air in.

What if I get caught?

The animals don't need excuses. And almost no one gets caught.

All actions against animal abuse industries are motivated by one goal: To save lives. Whether in the short term (mink liberation) or the long term (destruction of a feed supplier),

A look at the most commonly imprisoned animals on US fur farms:

Mink

By far the most common. Over 90% of the addresses here are for farms that only imprison mink. Over 3 million mink are killed on US fur farms annually (with the number rising due to a surge in demand from China).

Released mink will make a lot of noise in large numbers, and will fight each other. They will attack fingers / gloves through the cages, however seem to grow more "friendly" when released, and there have been no reports of mink attacking the feet / ankles of their liberators during a raid.

Fox

Because the industry is so small, there are no USDA statistics or other reliable figures on the number of foxes killed for fur. What is known is that fox farms are few and far between. Most fox farms are small backyard operations, with the largest known fox farm having close to 1,000 foxes (compared to the large mink farm, with over 120,000).

This niche of the fur industry is more difficult to track than mink, and it is possible only a small percentage of the actual number of fox farms is currently known.

Those we fight for
FUR FARM PRISONERS: A SPECIES OVERVIEW

Unlike mink, foxes are extremely timid and may not leave their cages immediately when released - if at all. Every effort should be made to coax them out, or physically remove them from the property if possible. The primary advantage to raiding a fox farm over a mink farm is that foxes are silent, and can be released without concern for awakening a fur farmer.

Miscellaneous species

Other species can be raised for fur, including coyotes, bobcats, and lynx. Information on lynx farms is very sparse. It was previously believed the largest (and one of the only) lynx farms in the country was the Fraser Fur Farm in Ronan, MT. New information indicates the farm may only imprison bobcats (which are nearly identical in appearance). The only farm confirmed to imprison lynx presently is the Schultz Fur Farm in Arnegard, North Dakota. Information on bobcat farms is nearly as scarce. Coalition Against Fur Farms has posted the addresses of dozens of bobcat farms, however the purpose of individual farms (fur or otherwise) isn't known.

One reason for the low number of lynx and bobcat fur farms, despite the high value of their pelts, is that they sell for a much higher amount when bred as pets. There are many large cat breeders across the country who breed domesticated bobcat and lynx, and some such farms that have been investigated have been found to be pet breeders.

EVASION AND CIRCUMVENTION

FUR FARM SECURITY: A SYNOPSIS

Since the tidal wave of mink releases in the 1990s, which saw dozens of farms raided and many farms shut down forever, fur farms have taken steps to increase security. But not as much as would be expected. With approximately 90 raids and 270 mink farms remaining, every farm that's left faces a very real threat of being hit by the ALF eventually. Yet one puzzling reality remains: Almost no fur farms have security. Why?

The reality is, fur farms operate on such a razor-thin profit margin that most simply cannot afford it. The rest arrogantly believe the ALF will never come to their farm, despite statistics that don't offer them the best odds.

Most fur farms are small family operations, and are either unaware of the threats or unable to afford to effectively prevent them. What this amounts to is that only a very small fraction of farms in the US utilize electronic or human security.

And when they do, the ALF has shown themselves to be capable of effectively circumventing it. Rick Aritolla of the Aritolla Mink Ranch reported his farm had a sophisticated motion-sensor security system in place before raiders released 10,000 mink there in 1997.

The best overview of fur farm security from the farmers perspective comes from a leaked document called *"Site Security and Protocols"*, published by the Fur Commission USA. This document was intended for distribution to fur farmers only, and reveals exactly what the largest fur farm trade group recommends farmers use to protect against the ALF (though almost none seem to heed their advice).

Fences
The most common deterrent, present at over 95% of all fur farms (yet there remain farms that do not even take this minimal precaution).

Each fence is unique, and a close look at the design should reveal the best approach to stripping it away. Remember the number of animals that escape is directly proportionate to the amount of fencing that is removed.

Fences charged with electricity are not uncommon. Generally only one or a small number of wires are charged and can be avoided.

Fencing alarms
There are no known reports of these being used, however the Fur Commission recommends them. These involve use of a wire which, if cut, activates the alarm system.

Photoelectric motion sensors. Advertising literature reads: "Create a fence you can't even see."

Photoelectric Sensors
These are invisible beams projected from small black boxes, usually positioned in the corners of the farm (inside the fence). These are extremely rare, however they have been reported at farms in the Northwest and at at least one farm in the Midwest. Some have reported success dropping to the ground and rolling under the beam. However other alarms appear to have a fan-shaped scope of coverage, where this would not be effective. As with any invisible-yet-potential threat, one can carry out the action that would trigger the alarm, then retreat to await a response. If there is no response, it can be presumed the alarm was bypassed.

Dogs
The occasional farm will have a dog loose among the sheds. Effective approaches for managing loud or threatening animals will vary by situation. Optimally, dogs can be tethered to the fence using an animal control-style emergency leash used for dangerous animals.

Cameras
Occasionally farms have video cameras. Farmers have also been advised by police to install still or video cameras triggers by motion. Note that the Fur Commission also advises the use of fake cameras for farms that can't afford real ones.

Security Guards
Another extremely rare form of security. There is evidence some larger farms have hired overnight security guards, particularly during pelting season. This is cost-prohibitive for all but the largest farms, yet sufficient reconnaissance should be employed before advancing on a larger farm to ensure no one is on site. Remember there is nothing that can't be circumvented with enough finesse.

A NOTE ON BREEDING SCHEDULES

ATTENTION MUST BE GIVEN TO BREEDING CYCLES IN THE LIBERATION OF FUR FARM PRISONERS. MINK AND FOX ARE KILLED IN NOVEMBER OR DECEMBER, AND ARE NOT WEANED UNTIL MAY OR JUNE. IT IS IMPORTANT TO BE MINDFUL THAT ANIMALS ARE NOT FIT TO BE RELEASED UNTIL THEY HAVE BEEN WEANED. THE MINK MUST BE AT A POINT WHERE THEY CAN BE SELF-SUFFICIENT IN THE WILD. THE WINDOW OF TIME ADVISABLE FOR FUR FARM LIBERATIONS IS JUNE TO OCTOBER. EARLIER AND THE ANIMALS MAY NOT BE IN A POSITION TO FEND FOR THEMSELVES, LATER AND IT MAY BE TOO LATE TO SAVE THEM.

	MINK	FOX	LYNX
Breeding	Feb./ March	Feb.- April	March
Gestation (in days)	40-75	52-53	
Birth	April	April/ May	May/ June
Weaned	May	June	April
Killed	Nov./Dec.		varying

GOING FOR THE THROAT

Highlights From The Frontlines

Drewelow & Sons Farm Raid
New Hampton, Iowa
September 7th, 2000
14,000 mink released

Largest animal release in North America to date. Days after the raid, the farmer reported 7,000 mink were still free.

Simultaneous Actions in Wisconsin
United Feeds arson
and
Release of 3,000 mink
Plymouth, WI
August 8th, 1999

As fire destroyed the cooperatively owned United Feeds mink feed operation, 3,000 mink were released from the nearby Gene Meyer Fur Farm. The simultaneous action saw the total destruction of the feed operation, jointly owned by over 20 mink farmers in a regioin with one of the highest concerntrations of fur farms in the country. Additionally, Gene Meyer announced in the wake of the action he could not survive the loss of profits and would be closing.

Scott Nelson fur farm double raid
Ellsworth, IA
October 16th, 2001
October 20th, 2001
Release of 2,000 mink
Subsequent release of 1,600 mink

The Animal Liberation Front took credit for the overnight release of every animal at the Scott Nelson mink farm. In the media the following day, Nelson announced most of the animals had been recaptured. The ALF returned 4 days later and re-liberated every animal. The following day, Scott Nelson announced the farm would be closing.

Operation Bite Back
Nationwide
June 1991 to October 1992

- Oregon State University Experimental Fur Farm
- Northwest Farm Foods
- Washington State University
- Malecky Mink Ranch
- Michigan State University
- USDA Predator Research Station
- Utah Fur Breeder's Cooperative
- Rocky Mountain Fur Company

Operation Bite Back was a campaign to destroy the fur industry, brought to five states over 16 months. Using arson, liberations, and theft and destruction of documents; 7 key points in the fur industry were targeted in an attempt to completely eradicate the fur industry's research apparatus. Rodney Coronado was indicted for his role in this campaign, and sentenced to 57 months in prison.

Media Work

Media coordination adds impact to an action. Releasing 5,000 animals brings immediate relief to those animals. National media attention brings to animal liberation message to millions, deals a public-relations blow to the fur industry, deters animal flesh or skin consumption among the public, and keeps the plight of animals a part of the public dialogue. This has the potential to indirectly save thousands or millions of more animals.

The following can be incorporated into an action to ensure maximum impact:

Photos

Documenting the conditions on a fur farm with photographs, and documenting the raid itself, can inspire activists and educate the public when the documentation is distributed to supportive above-ground groups and the media.

Video

When clandestine raiders released 2,000 mink from the Scott Nelson mink farm in Ellsworth, Iowa; they took video of the raid, released it to the media, and gave millions of people their first glimpse inside a fur farm. Video is only reasonable at farms so small that one person working a camera will not directly translate to few cages that will be opened - i.e. those farms guaranteed to be emptied even with one fewer hand.

Communiques

Issuing a communique detailing an action and the intentions behind it serve several functions. One, it gives those behind anonymous actions a voice. The media can and does broadcast content from communiques and incorporates them into their coverage, making your motivations clear, and countering the industry's inaccurate assertions of the ALF's motives being anything other than compassion. Two, they serve as an inspiration for others. Three, working information into communiques can be effective to disseminate valuable info to the activist community - info such as farm addresses and closures. (Anyone with new updates for our fur farm list is encouraged to distribute the info widely, preferably in the form of a communique claiming an action.)

Communiques can be distributed via email using the anonymizing service TOR, or by mail. (See the Without a Trace section for a list of precautions.) These can be sent to the media directly, or the Animal Liberation Press Office (who will take it from there).

Due to the research of a handful of dedicated individuals, we are closer to a complete list of US fur farms now than any point in history. However, there are farms that have so far flown under the radar.

DIY Research

A few tactics to discover new farms and supplement this list:

Follow feed supply trucks.
We are including a list of the known feed suppliers, whose trucks must regularly visit the majority of fur farms in the US – those farms known and unknown.

Media reports.
Recently, a new fur farm was learned of when an empty shed caught fire and the media made public it's location. Check news reports regularly.

Business entity searches.
Every state has a means by which individuals can review lists of licensed businesses in the state. Often these are available online.

Social engineering.
Sometimes the best way to learn something is to ask.

Satellite images.
Farms often cluster together. If you think there may be undiscovered mink farms in a particular area. Google satellite images should reveal their location. Mink sheds have a very telltale appearance which is generally obvious from above . One can aerially scan a large area for sheds in only a few minutes.

Ingenuity
Ask yourself who has the information you seek, and how you can get it. The best intelligence often comes out of the greatest ingenuity.

Hawkeye Mink Feed Cooperative, Jewel IA Broken Into, fur farm addresses taken 2002

THE FUR FARM LIST

A History

Hidden from public view is the secret (and rich) history of the fur farm list. Unlike other industries, whose addresses are compiled by industry and governments and readily available, fur farm addresses are heavily guarded. Fur farmers are instructed to never post their address online, to be weary of phone calls from anyone asking their address, and never reveal their locations even in insider trade journals. The industry is so small and decentralized, there may be less than a half dozen people – if any - who have the "master list."

Then how did activists obtain these addresses? From what little we know, it wasn't easy.

The first known lists of fur farms began to circulate in the early-1990s, released by Rod Coronado and his group **Coalition Against Fur Farms (CAFF)**. They enjoyed limited circulation, yet represented the first times addresses of fur farms and infrastructure targets had been made public. **The Coalition to Abolish the Fur Trade (CAFT)** and other groups distributed these lists over the next several years.

Then, in 1996, came *The Final Nail #1*. It was the first fur farm list distributed on a large scale, compiling the address of every known fur farm, feed supplier, fur industry researcher, and more. The results were instant and historic: in the 2.5 years that followed, there were over 50 raids of fur farms across the US. But where did the addresses come from?

It is widely speculated that the addresses in the original *Final Nail* (which form the foundation for the lists we have today), were derived from documents removed from fur industry research labs during Operation Bite Back (see *Going for the Throat – Highlights From the Frontlines*).

This is what we do know: *The Final Nail #1* and *#2* (released in 1997) were compiled by Darren Thurston, a former ALF prisoner form Canada. After another arrest for ALF actions in 20005, he admitted to the FBI that he created *The Final Nail.* Thurston turned informant and implicated others. After his release from prison he appears to have vanished from the animal liberation movement.

The Final Nail #3 was released in the summer of 2008. It offered the first (and largest) fur farm list update since 1996, with over 100 new fur farms. It is believed this windfall of new information

came from two sources: The combined notes of several ALF operatives over the previous 12 years of fur farm raids (the introduction stated "this information was pooled from... numerous individuals, none of whom will be revealed to protect those guilty of transgressing unjust laws"), and documents obtained from the break-in at the Hawkeye Mink Cooperative in Jewel, Iowa (2003).

Around this time, a new website, FinalNail.com (unrelated to the print version) launched, and continues to this day. The site is frequently updated with new fur farm addresses as they become known. The majority of new fur farm addresses from 2008 to 2013 have debuted on this site. One recent update included over 60 previously unknown mink farms.

In 2009, the **Fur Farm Intelligence Project** was launched, which sought to close the intelligence gaps and offer the largest and most detailed fur farm list ever compiled. The project added a road trip component, where over 200 fur farms were visited in person to confirm their "open" or "closed' status. This cleaned up the list significantly, with many farms that had lingered for years without having been confirmed were found to have been empty for years. Dozens of new farms were also uncovered, and hundreds of photos taken.

An anonymous group calling itself **The Fur Farm Intelligence Unit** issued communiques with new fur farm addresses, starting in 2009. In one from 2012, they released the addresses of over 90 (unconfirmed) fox farms. Within weeks, one of the farms that debuted on the list – the Scott Dean fox farm in Elkton, VA – was raided, with 13 foxes released.

In 2012, the publisher of the first fur farm lists, **Coalition Against Fur Farms**, was resurrected by all new volunteers. The groups continues where the previous incarnation left off, tracking the fur industry and regularly publishing new addresses on its website as they become known.

The editors of *The Final Nail #4* have brought together the work of everyone above to bring the most comprehensive and detailed fur farm list to date. Much of the how-to material from #3 was borrowed, with many updates added.

We release this volume in honor of the work, sacrifices, triumphs and losses of those who have at times risked everything to bring us the addresses contained herein. This is for them, and the animals we all fight for.

Ames Mink Farm
Tomahawk, WI

Mildbrand Mink Ranch
Medford, WI

Pagel Mink Ranch
Cambellsport, WI

Wiesman Mink Ranch
Caroline, WI

Geiger Mink Farm
Mosinee, WI

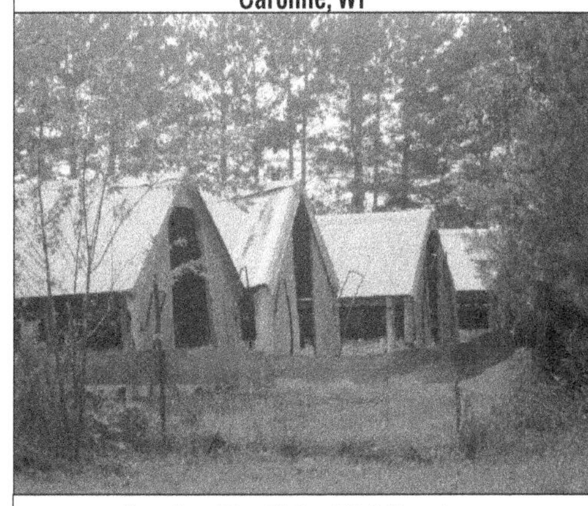

Gesslers Pine Ridge Mink Ranch
Tomahawk, WI

United Feeds
Plymouth, WI

National Feeds
New Holstein, WI

Central Mink Food
Medford, WI

Medford Fur Food
Medford, WI

Patrick Fur Farm
Westboro, WI

Albers Mink Ranch
Medford, WI

Washington State University
Department of veterinary medicine experimental fur farm
Pullman, WA

Anonymous report.

(Note: This anonymous 2009 report has two items of outdated information: It is believed this lab is no longer a USDA facility, and Dr. Gorham has died. His work is believed to be continued by David J. Prieur.)

"When the call went out soliciting the location of the USDA Fur Bearer Research Facility in Pullman, WA; we made the drive to locate the research farm ourselves.

It's been speculated the better part of the fur farm addresses we have today were confiscated from fur industry research labs raided during Operation Bite Back. One address that never surfaced was for one of the facilities raided, the USDA Fur Bearer Research Facility at Washington State University. To this day, John Gorham remains the second largest recipient of research grants from the Fur Commission USA, and holds the title of one of the world's foremost mink researchers. Gorham is still very much in business, and still a key figure in keeping the U.S. fur industry alive.

The A.L.F.-authored publication Memories of Freedom – an anonymous account of every (claimed) action in Operation Bite Back – offers the only published information giving clues on the research farm's whereabouts. Extracted from Chapter Four, we had only these crumbs of info to aid in our search:

- The farm was surrounded by barbed wire
- On the "outskirts" of campus
- Surrounded by grassland
- "...on a road to the local airport"

With little information to work with, we made the long drive to Pullman, WA to find the farm. We quickly narrowed the area that could potentially house the research farm to the various ag-research animal pens along Airport Road, on WSU's eastern edge. As described in M.O.F., along Airport Road we found pens of grizzly bears, sheep, goats, cows, and numerous other exotic and non-exotic species confined to small pens by WSU's expansive animal research machine.

At night, we explored the small labyrinth of dirt roads and paths along Airport Road on foot. In four hours, after inspecting numerous sheds, pens, and barns, we had narrowed potential sites for the farm to two locations:

- Two sheds of empty cages behind 1040 NE Airport Road.
- A fenced outdoor facility off a dirt road adjacent to Wilson Rd, housing various sheds and pens.

Evidence pointing to the former was its location close to the only known address associated with WSU mink research: "1040 NE Airport Rd". The sheds approximated the design of mink sheds, if bisected lengthwise. However the feeding devices on the cages appeared to more closely resemble those for birds than mink. And there was no grassy hill above the sheds, as described in M.O.F. Nothing else found near this address was likely to house mink. We took numerous photos of the two sheds for future review.

Our strongest suspicions fell on a heavily secured facility tucked a quarter mile from Airport Road. Binoculars failed to reveal what was inside, but certain large animal pens were visible, along with a large shed and barn. We left to do more research and return the following night for a closer look – and final answer.

The next morning we reviewed old campus maps in the library, and older archived satellite images. One thing stood out: images from the early-1990s show two long sheds in an area inspected the night before, where there was now a vacant field. Their long and narrow form would make it unlikely they housed anything other than mink.

Comparing new and old images revealed something further: While the sheds had been demolished, the fenced area under suspicion from the night before had been greatly expanded. Had the WSU consolidated its wildlife research into one secured facility after the 1992 A.L.F. raid?

The next night we made the hike back to this location. The site is hidden off a dark, unmarked dirt road (later learned to be called "Antelope Trail") branching east off Airport Road. Unlike every other animal facility off Airport Rd, this one was heavily secure, with a high barbed-wire fence, motionsensor spotlights, several video cameras, and heavy lighting. At the rear of the facility, we found numerous animal pens. When our eyes adjusted to the darkness, we found ourselves face to face with numerous deer, confined to small pens. We spent many minutes sharing the silence of the night with these animals, staring at us from behind two layers of fencing.

Beyond the deer pens, a large shed in the center had it's contents mostly obscured, and any animals that may be inside were not visible. On the north, elevated just above the compound and outside its fence, were three outdoor animal pens that were found empty. Inside the pens were red lights indicating alarms (or merely the appearance of them to serve as a deterrent).

We moved towards the most suspicious portion of the site: the low-lying sheds in the NE corner, where we suspected the mink were housed. The obscured siding told us whatever was inside was not domesticated enough to live in a totally enclosed structure, but was something the animals' captors wanted shielded from public view. We were within 20 feet of the pens when, from inside, a red flashlight began moving towards us. We vanished into the grasslands, just short of an answer as to what lay inside the sheds at 3055 Antelope Trail.

The following day we returned in daylight for photos, which are being submitted with this report.

Although inconclusive, evidence indicates that 3055 Antelope Trail is the most likely location for the mink imprisoned at W.S.U. A review of the evidence:

- Its level of security is commensurate with a facility fearing a(nother) break-in, and inconsistent with security at all other animal pens at WSU (where security is absent).

- A WSU building list puts the address as a "Wildlife Bio Animal Holding Facility"

- Allowing for the possibility this facility housed mink at the time of the A.L.F. raid; there are several animal pens (large enough for coyotes) on a hill just above this facility, consistent with the M.O.F. description (coyotes were released during the A.L.F. action from a "hill above the fur farm").

- WSU describes this address as housing deer "...and other wildlife species".

- The low-lying sheds in back are consistent with the general height of mink sheds, a height unique to structures housing mink (among commonly raised livestock).

- Barring the possibility the research farm has been moved to an entirely different part of campus since the A.L.F. raid, our extensive survey of the "road to the local airport" found these to be the only pens whose captives we could not confirm, and the only location found with the potential to house mink.

The combined evidence and photos make a strong but inconclusive case for 3055 Antelope Trail as being the location of the experimental fur farm.

Anonymous"

Possible location of Washington State University experimental fur farm Pullman, WA

Six mink, seven coytoes, ten mice rescued, 8-13-91

ALF communique
Malecky Mink Ranch, Yamhill, OR
Processing plant is set on fire. $125,000 in damages.
The farm closes.
VICTORY

"December 21 1991 – Western Wildlife Cell members of the Animal Liberation Front (A.L.F.) raided Malecky Mink Ranch in Yamhill, Oregon, and set an incendiary device that destroyed the processing plant of this farm near Salem.

Intelligence sources revealed that the fur farm was to be sold, with intentions to continue exploitation of fur animals. Malecky Mink Ranch was a recipient of information form Oregon State University's Experimental Fur Farm and had developed innovative methods of commercial exploitation of mink for the fur trade.

No mink or humans were injured in the A.L.F.'s fourth action against the United States Fur Farm industry. Fleshing machines, drying drums, skinning racks, feed mixers, freezers, and a workshop were all effectively destroyed in this economic attack against the tools of death and destruction.

This action was taken to avenge the lives of mink murdered on the ranch in the past and to prevent the further imprisonment of native wildlife in the future. 750,000 mink are slaughtered every winter in the Northwest for trade and four million nationwide on over (illegible –ed.) fur farms.

The Animal Liberation Front also announces a new campaign against the fur trade, one that directly targets the insensitive humans who wear fur garments. We will fight the fur-wearers in the streets. No longer shall the ecological arrogance of the public supporters of the fur trade go unchallenged. A.L.F. members shall arm themselves with battery acid and dye, and will inflict damage on the furs worn by humans. Fur is for four-leggeds, not two. The lives of fur animals will be avenged.

The fur industry is responsible for the demise of not only native north american wildlife, but the destruction of Native peoples' cultures as well. Over the last four hundred years this barbaric industry has waged a genocidal war against animals and humans. Through the introduction of social and physical disease, the fur trade has forced native people to participate in their bloody practice, or perish like so many animals in traps and cages.

It is time to eliminate this anthropocentric profit-centered beast before the last howl is heard. A.L.F. calls on all peoples to join in the battle against this ecologically destructive regime, and to defend the defenseless from the oppression of our own species.

We must destroy that which destroys the animals, earth, and ourselves. On behalf of the mink, fox, bobcat, lynx, and coyote nations.

A.L.F. shall wage non-violent war against the fur trade. Until the last fur farm is burned to the ground.

Animal Liberation Front, Western Wildlife Cell"

Dedicated to those left behind.

Economic Sabotage

1999

INTERVIEW WITH RONNIE LEE... P. 3

No Compromise!

The Militant, Direct Action Newspaper of Grassroots Animal Liberationists & Their Supporters

ALF Liberates 116 Animals from University of Minnesota

Whale Killed Despite Activists' Heroic Efforts

An overview of basic sabotage tactics.

WINDOWS

Windows are probably the easiest targets available and large display windows can cost hundreds of dollars, making them an ideal goal. In many highly active areas, popular targets have replaced their regular windows with extra thick, shatter-proof glass that's almost unbreakable under any amount of force. In these cases, etching fluid can still be effective in costing the animal abusers money.

Glass-etching fluid (hydrofluoric acid) can be readily found in arts and crafts stores. Available as liquid or cream, it eats through the surface of glass. The liquid can be poured into a squeeze bottle, a plastic lemon, for example. The cream version can be applied with a paintbrush, allowing slogans to be written on the window. Working quickly, you'll probably make a mess with the bottle, so bring a plastic bag to throw it into when finished. It's a quick and relatively safe way to cause some financial damage.

When possible, a less expensive—but much noisier—method is simply smashing windows. It is loud, so get ready to run.

Aside from throwing a brick or rock, a popular way to do this is with a slingshot, available in many sporting goods stores. The advantage of a slingshot is that you don't have to be directly next to the window to break it; slingshots can even be effective from moving cars. Try to fire symmetrical objects such as ball bearings or nuts, because with rocks or bolts, it will be hard to control the trajectory.

Whatever you shoot, be sure to remove all fingerprints first. It is always your responsibility to be certain there is nobody in or near the store who could get injured. Shooting from completely inside the car (as in, don't hang out the side) will make detection much harder.

Air guns (a.k.a. BB guns) are another option. They don't do as much damage to a window as a brick might, but they are very quick, can be used easily from inside a car and are relatively quiet. You can roll up to a store, stop in front for a second, roll down the window, take a shot and leave. Unless someone is standing right there, nobody will notice a thing.

Most of the time, a silver dollar-sized hole with a spider web crack will be left. Occasionally a window will completely shatter, though, so be ready for it.

There are generally two types of BB guns. One looks like a rifle and is powered manually. The second looks like a handgun and is powered by CO2 cartridges. The cartridges only cost about $2 each and will give you approximately 150 shots. The advantage of the CO2-style is that it is generally semi-automatic (meaning one shot is fired each time the trigger is pulled). Using such a device could take out more than a dozen windows in just a couple of seconds. It does look like a real gun, though, so if the police roll up, drop it immediately or risk getting shot.

Another option for breaking windows is a hammer. Tilers' hammers, found in most hardware stores, are best because of their pointed design. Windows, especially shatter-proof ones, are tougher than they seem, so use a hammer of some weight. The best time to do this technique is on a stormy night-the lack of visibility and the noise of the storm provide excellent cover. And, while you might naturally think to hit a window in the center, this is actually the strongest part. Always go for the comers, since they are the weak spots.

SHUTTERS

People in more urban areas are probably familiar with stores lowering metal accordion-like shutters over their windows while closed. After having windows smashed, a target store in a less urban area may do the same.

If you are dealing with the kind of shutters that are a grid of bars, etching fluid, slingshots, or BB guns will still work fine. It's also possible to simply lock any kind of object to the shutter, making it impossible to open. Sometimes store personnel won't use all of the holes for locks that are available on the shutter. If this is the case, put your own lock on the shutter. Make sure it's fingerprint-free first!

Try to fire symmetrical objects such as ball bearings or nuts, because with rocks or bolts, it will be hard to control the trajectory.

More difficult to work on are the full shutters without any holes. Hitting the shutter with a sledgehammer may be effective both in damaging the shutter and possibly breaking the window, if they are close enough together. A more subtle method of dealing with full shutters is gluing the shutter locks, (see "Gluing locks" section below). If store personnel have been dumb enough to put a shutter only over the main window, leaving a smaller one (such as on a door) uncovered, break the uncovered one, then reach in and break the main one.

VEHICLES

Vehicles are another easy target. There are a number of ways to damage them. When doing a battery of techniques to a vehicle, start with the quieter ones. There are two different approaches that can be taken with vehicles: destruction and sabotage. Destruction results in visibly damaged vehicles, while with sabotage, the action is not evident until the vehicle is run and mechanical problems are experienced.

There are many options with the destruction method. Slashing tires is quick and quiet. An ice pick, sharp knife or anything of that sort will work. Keep in mind, though, that tires, especially on trucks, are tougher than they seem, so use something thick and strong that won't break or bend.

Other methods include piercing the sidewall of the tires, making it impossible to repair; yanking out the stem (the thing you put air through) with a pair of pliers to flatten the tire; and punching holes in the radiator through the grill with a large screwdriver.

If you can get to the engine, you can cut wires and break various components. If the engine is not accessible, you can also cut what you can from underneath·. Bring something heavy-duty like small bolt cutters, since regular wire cutters won't be able to handle metal cables and such.

Both paint and paint stripper can damage the paint job. Break off windshield wipers, smash headlights and windshields or paint with etching cream, and glue locks. Since windshields are made to deflect rocks kicked up from the road, only more direct methods of breaking them, such as with a hammer, will work.

With the more subtle sabotage method, it is important to leave no signs you were there, so the vehicle is run and the damage is done. If dealing with trucks, look for levers on the side of the hood to release it and open it forward.

The stereotypic sabotage technique is pouring sugar in the gas tank. This will merely block the filter and do little damage. More effective fuel tank additives are sand or 10 to 15 mothballs. Be sure not to use sand from near home, as it can be traced. The best sabotage target is the lubricating system. If incapacitated, it will cause the engine to overheat, bind and generally destroy itself. Karo syrup in the oil filler hole is another classic that, in reality, only affects the filter. One option for major damage is to carefully remove the oil, either by punching a hole in the oil pan or removing the drain plug. Adding water to the oil is more effective, since it will not lubricate but will keep the oil pressure up, preventing the warning light from coming on.

Better than water is diesel or gasoline, as it will also break down existing oil. For maximum effect, consider adding abrasives to the lubricating system. The oil filler hole is not the only option here. All moving parts need lubrication, such as transmissions, differentials, and wheel hubs. Many lubrication points will have screw-on caps that can be removed with an adjustable wrench. Sand can be used for this as well. However, the top-of-the-line abrasive is the kind used to polish stones in tumblers, available in hobby and lapidary supply shops. A very fine powder grit mixed with a slightly coarser fine sand grit will have the best chance of getting throughout the whole engine and wrecking everything. A 400- and 600-grit sized mix works well. A mere half-pint of this will completely destroy an engine.

GLUING LOCKS

Gluing locks is one of the quickest, easiest, and safest forms of direct action and one of the most commonly used. The idea behind gluing locks is that time is money, and if you can keep an abuser's business closed, even for a short time, that's money lost and animals saved. Properly glued locks will require a pricey locksmith to fix.

To glue a lock, get a tube of glue, ideally the kind with a long, sharp tip or in the syringe. Approach your target, be it a store or vehicle, and put a small piece of wire, toothpick or similar object less than a fingernail's length, into the lock. Insert the glue tube into the lock and fill the lock with glue. Once the glue dries it will be practically impossible to open.

Some glues are effective, some aren't. Get some cheap locks and test them out for yourself until you find what works. In order for glue to work well, it must be thick enough not to run out of the lock and should dry solid, not rubbery.

Also consider drying time. Hardware stores have a wide selection of various glues, so try to find something with both of these properties.

PAINT

Paint is often a good way to get your message across and do some damage. Vehicles, billboards and buildings are all paintable. Spray paint is one option. Splashing paint out of a container, such as a plastic soda bottle, is another. To get more range, you can put a hole in the top, screw it back on, and then spray through it.

Paint bombs can be constructed by simply filling Christmas ornaments, light bulbs or even bell peppers with paint. Light bulbs take some work, but are easier to come by. Cut off the bottom part of the metal, below the glass. Very carefully break out the bottom part of the glass by the filament inside the remaining metal ring. Fill and carefully seal. You can use a screwdriver for that. The advantage of such paint bombs is that they are surprisingly quiet. Be positive they are print-free first, though. Always transport them in sealed plastic bags, in case one ruptures.

Balloons can be used, too, but they tend not to work as well. Paint can be inserted into these different containers via, ironically, a turkey baster. Always mix paint with equal amounts of water or paint thinner so it splatters better. Since paint on glass is easy to get off, try to get the paint on wood, metal or stone exteriors for greater effectiveness. Large markers can also work.

Super-soaker-type water guns filled with a paint/water mixture are useful as well. But, as they sometimes leak and drip, keep them in a plastic bag before and after a hit. It's impossible to wash all the paint out afterwards, making it strong, incriminating evidence against you if found and they can become clogged after a couple uses. Bearing this in mind, it may be a good idea to buy one, use it one night on a number of establishments, and dispose of it.

Just remember that paint is a messy business and has a tendency to gel everywhere, including all over you.

Paint stripper is another option, especially effective on vehicles. 3M Safest Strip or Extra Strength has the advantage of clinging to vertical surfaces. Dupli-Color makes ST 1000 Paint Stripper, available in auto parts stores. It comes in spray cans and can eat down to bare metal in just 30 minutes. Brake fluid is an effective paint stripper as well.

SECURITY CAMERAS

Places of exploitation that get hit a number of times may install security measures, such as cameras. Don't let this deter you. As long as your body is well covered, the best cameras can do is provide the general height of the people involved, which doesn't mean much. What they actually do for an establishment is the opposite of what they are intended for. Instead of protecting them, it gives you something else to break.

Security cameras are expensive and not all that hard to destroy. Aside from open cameras, look for boxes or spheres which sometimes house cameras. They are generally up high, so look up about ten feet. Avoid light systems are another thing you might see pop up. If you want to hit the place again but you're not too fond of all the light, try a slingshot to take them out of commission.

Remember that if they do install a security system, that means money out of their blood-soaked pockets, which is what you want anyway. It also means you're being effective, so keep it up. Just be careful-not to hit the same place too often or they'll be waiting for you.

STINK BOMBS

Various foul-smelling agents can serve a variety of purposes and be effective means of direct action. Some ideas include dropping stink bombs through mail slots or windows after being broken, inside trucks (especially if windows or doors are left open) and in places holding large fur sales or hunting conventions.

Numerous very weak acids have powerful and strong smells. Most well-known is butyric acid; two drops will clear a room and one ounce is enough for an entire building. Other options include caprylic acid, caproanic acid, isovaleric acid, proprionic acid, ethylamine, skatole, hydrogen sulfide, carbon disulfide and butyraldehyde. Many of these can be diluted 5 or 10 to 1 with water without losing much strength.

More commonly available options are the various lures used by hunters, such as deer urine. Any of these can be delivered using a medicine dropper or hypodermic needle.

GETTING THROUGH LOCKS

In some actions, particularly liberations, breaking in is an essential part of the action.

Locks can be dealt with in a number of ways. If you are attempting to get past a lock, you should take a close look at it, possibly when you check out the site your first time during the day or more likely your second time at night. Try to get the exact same kind of lock and see what works.

You can try to pry them open with a crowbar or cut them with bolt cutters. The other way through a lock is to use an electric powered drill and a new

1/8-inch high-speed drill bit. Depending on the hardness of the lock, it may take more than one bit. Never buy cheap drill bits—they'll let you down.

Most keyed locks are pin-tumbler types. In this kind of lock, a number of spring-loaded pins are pushed up when the key is inserted. When the tops of these pins are in perfect alignment with the "shear line," the "plug" into which the key is inserted can turn and the lock opens.

In many locks, parts are made of brass to prevent corrosion. Fortunately, brass is relatively soft and easily drilled. A drill can be used to destroy the pins along the shear line. Be careful not to drill too deeply, since this can damage the locking bar making it impossible to open. Drill only the depth of the key way, which is 3/4 of an inch in most padlocks, and 1 inch in most door locks. A "drill stop," available in most hardware stores, can be used to pre-set the depth required.

Once the lock has been drilled out, insert a pin (such as a nail) into the lock to press the remains of the pins above the shear line. You may have to insert the drill a few times to chew up bits of pins that are interfering with opening.

Finally, using a flat-head screwdriver, tum and open the lock. This operation takes practice, so get a few cheap locks and work on them first.

Books and tools for picking locks are not too difficult to come by. The other way to get past doors is to just go through them. Two ways are prying doors open with a crowbar and knocking them open with a sledgehammer. Another way is to cut a hole through the middle of the door just big enough to fit through A row of holes, drilled with a thick drill bit is one way to do this; portable power saws are another. The advantage of this method is that if the door is alarmed, going through the middle may not trigger the system.

Henna Raids

1999

A (very brief) guide to targeting fur farms with henna dye.

1. Henna raids - dyeing animals with henna, a reddish dye - are primarily done on fox farms for a number of reasons.

Foxes are slower to move away than mink; in fact, they usually don't move at all and don't have a nest box to hide in. Fox fur is usually lighter in color and fox pelts are more expensive than those of minks, making the dyeing more effective. And, minks also have a better chance at surviving when released.

2. The effectiveness of henna dye has been proven by studies in police laboratories in Finland. The farmers will still kill the animals, but won't make as much of a profit.

3. Henna dyeing does relatively more damage to fox farmers than just releasing the foxes from their cages. Most foxes are so apathetic that they won't even leave their cages if opened or move away if lifted out, and their chances of surviving in the wild are almost nil. Usually the farmer will recapture the majority, if not all, of the released foxes. From late autumn through the winter when there is snow on the ground in northern Scandinavia (where most of the fox farms are), many activists and experts consulted believe that the animals would have virtually no chance of survival. Life in the cage kills these noble animals mentally.

4. Henna raids are done in late autumn when the animals' fur has changed for the winter. At that time, the chances of survival in the wild have decreased drastically due to snow.

5. If the environment is appropriate and the timing is right (around October), nothing stops activists from both dyeing the animals and releasing them. As well, equipment and breeding information at the farm can always be destroyed. This has been done in many of these raids. It is with great regret, I believe, that activists walk (run!) away from a farm leaving the animals to certain death, but what can be done if the animal clearly has· no chance of survival whatsoever? At this point, the henna raids cause more economic damage than simply releasing the animals.

6. Most of the foxes on fur farms are Arctic foxes who do not naturally live in the area. Silver foxes are believed to survive better in the wild, but they are not as common on the farms.

7. The media reaction to henna raids has been relatively positive.

Don’t Get Caught

1999

How to not get caught.

Working With Others

Finding suitable partners to work with is one of the most important and potentially hazardous activities with which the beginner eco-warrior must contend. But, always remember that there is no rule that says you must have partners. If you simply cannot find anyone you trust or think is suitable for the type of work you want to do, consider working alone and setting your sights on jobs that can be completed by one person. Generally speaking, however, safely completing most jobs requires a driver and lookouts.

When considering potential partners, try to stick to people you have known for a long period of time. Look for stable, committed individuals who function well under stress. Unfortunately, there is no hard and fast system for finding reliable partners – simply use your best judgment. Avoid the faint-of-heart, the excessively paranoid, and the not-quite-thoroughly committed.

Avoid the casual acquaintance you only see at a protest rally, especially the ones who "talk tough." Such people may well be police spies or agents provocateurs. Government use of such infiltrators is widespread, both in the U.S. and abroad.

When evaluating partners, keep in mind that they are the people you will be trusting with your life and liberty. Try to imagine not only how they will act and perform in the field, but also how they will act and perform in the police station.

Talk only to those necessary for a particular job. There is no reason to put yourself in jeopardy by bringing in new faces if you already have enough people.

It can often be valuable to sit down with those you will be working with and pledge your dedication to the animals, as well as each other. Have everyone make a promise to the group to never grass or testify against another activist.

Not only does this build solidarity between activists, but it will also give everyone the chance to think about what they are doing and risking and give them the chance to change their minds.

Planning

Putting in the time to adequately plan your actions as well as preparing contingency plans for all likely outcomes will greatly increase the chances of things going smoothly, efficiently, and keeping activists out of jail. Every team member must fully understand the work to be done, individual assignments, timetables, radio frequencies and codes, routes to and from the scene, etc. Even the best of plans can be quickly disrupted by unforeseen events. Coping with and adapting to such problems is the ultimate test of one's monkey-wrenching abilities.

Before you begin planning your job, make sure everyone involved knows the type of security you expect. Do not talk over the phone or internet about the action! Do not talk in houses or cars! If you are saying anything in any of these places, assume that the FBI and police are also listening. When talking on the phone or in a house or car, do not use obvious codes or sound suspicious (it will just end up drawing attention to you and giving the feds reason to believe you might be up to no good).

The target you select should be reconnoitered in advance. When driving to and from meetings with other activists or to and from the target, always make sure you are not being followed. It can be extremely difficult to tell when you are under surveillance, so always be on the lookout. It is an excellent idea to carefully examine your vehicle for electronic listening or tracking devices REGULARLY.

Look at the target both during the day and night as different types of security measures may be employed at different times. Do not fool yourself into thinking a quick cursory glance is enough. Take the time to properly observe the target, noting the schedule of security guards or police who may patrol the area, lights that may go on and off at certain times, or various periods when the area suddenly becomes busy (cleaning crews, people leaving work, people arriving at neighboring buildings, etc.).

Use maps to familiarize yourself with the entire area surrounding the target. Excellent aerial and topographic maps are available from many public and school libraries. Know the location of all roads, trails, drainage ditches or anything else that may be of value should you have to make a quick retreat.

Decide ahead of time whether you will have someone drop you off and then return to pick you up, or if there is an appropriate place to leave a car. Make sure you will not be parked or driving in front of any security cameras that might record your license plate if you will be using your own car. Scout out areas to position your lookouts.

If you are being dropped off, figure out where to have them drop you and where they will pick you up. Decide how long you will give yourself to complete the job and pre-arrange back-up meeting times should you miss the pick-up. Always decide upon an emergency pick-up location slightly away from the target in case things go wrong and you need to leg it.

In planning out an action, simply sit down with your team and go over every single element. Create contingency plans for every foreseeable and unforeseeable circumstance that could affect the outcome of your action. Be prepared. Things that can go wrong often will go wrong. Staying out of jail will depend upon your ability to cope with unexpected circumstances.

Once you have picked your team, and selected and reconnoitered your target, it is time for the action itself. It is often an excellent idea to do a dry run the night before the action is to take place to test the waters, so to speak. Make sure that you don't trigger alarms, walk in front of cameras, or leave any footprints or other evidence that could alert the animal abusers or police to your presence.

On the night of the action, make sure everything is in order. Activists should be dressed in disposable clothing, shoes and masks, and wearing gloves. If you are going to be carrying light sources, apply red cellophane or nail polish to them to decrease the chances of someone spotting your lights, while not compromising your night vision.

Make sure activists who will be in the field have removed all jewelry, emptied their pockets of everything they will not need on the action, and covered all tattoos and other distinctive marks if applicable. It is a good idea for each person to have money on his or her body should fleeing become a necessity so everyone can get back home. You may also decide to carry pepper spray to be used for self-defense.

If you will be using scanners or radios, make sure everything is functioning properly (well charged and have spare batteries available) and that the scanners are programmed correctly.

Make sure that all tools, equipment and anything else that carries prints and will be taken into the field are wiped clean of fingerprints with a rag and rubbing alcohol. Items such as radios should be opened up, and their batteries and inside bits should be wiped clean as well.

Your vehicle should also be prepared for the action. If you will be transporting animals, make sure your vehicle is equipped to hold them. It is a good idea to put sheets down on the floor and seats of the vehicle to avoid leaving dirt or animal hair in the car that could connect it to the action. Having accessible, heavy-duty garbage bags as well as changes of shoes and clothing will help keep the car clean and expedite the removal of dirty clothing.

During the action make sure to keep your face covered and your gloves on. Do not let your skin touch anything. Fingers are not the only parts of the body that leave prints. And, if you are spraypainting, use block letters that contain no curvatures and keep in mind that investigators can tell a lot from the size of the letters (the length of your arm) and the height they are off the ground (your physical height).

After the action, all evidence should be disposed of promptly. Remember: even if you don't think you left footprints or picked up any fibers, dirt, or hairs that could connect you to the "crime," it is possible that you were caught on camera and could be identified by clothing. BE SAFE. Get rid of everything. It is often a good idea to dispose of tools as well, since many (such as bolt cutters, crowbars and wire cutters) can leave distinctive marks.

Clothing, shoes and tools should be disposed of many miles away from the site of the action if possible. Remember that police can link clothing to individuals in a variety of ways, including your own hair samples or those of companion animals that might have been left on your clothing. So make sure to dispose of your clothing, shoes, and tools in a place where they won't be discovered by law enforcement agents. They can be buried or thrown in a dumpster somewhere inconspicuous. Make sure to dispose of the sheets that were used to cover the floor and car seats as well. Take the car to be washed and vacuumed as soon as possible after the action.

One thing to keep in mind is that there are many factors (circumstantial evidence) that may not be grounds for a conviction in court but that can and probably will contribute to harassment from the cops which can impede your ability to participate in further actions for the animals.

In other words, you may be placed in an area on the night a slaughterhouse burns down and while that won't be enough to convict you in a trial, it will give investigators cause for suspicion and set them on a mission to find (or even plant) evidence against you. It's obviously best if there is no reason for the police to suspect you and/or target you for surveillance/ harassment.

Once the action is over, put it out of your head. It seems that the greatest threat to security that many activists face is their own mouths. Keep your mouth shut and talk to no one about the action. Loose lips sink ships!

If You Are Arrested

When volunteers join the IRA, they are promised nothing in return except for the likelihood of death or imprisonment. ALF activists should•be similarly prepared for the jail sentences that accompany a life of direct action. If you are arrested, remain calm and collected. What you say at this point may well make the difference between being freed and imprisoned. Never consent to a search of your person or vehicle if you have any say about it.

Most police officers are well aware of their power to intimidate. They know putting someone in handcuffs or driving them "downtown" is sometimes all it takes to make a suspect cooperate fully in incriminating himself or herself. The shock of arrest, isolation from friends and family, and well-practiced interrogation are all designed to force the suspect's cooperation, confession and the implication of others.

If you are arrested, do not talk to the police until you have talked with your lawyer. Do not be lulled into casual conversation; this is a standard method for lowering a suspect's defenses and causing a slip of the tongue. Your only safe answer to questioning is to politely tell the police that you have nothing to say until you have talked to a lawyer. Then say nothing, not even small talk. This measure alone may spare you from later conviction.

Also make sure not to say anything about the action (other than what the cops allege) on the phone or to other prisoners (including your co-accused). Calls are monitored, prisoners could well be undercover police officers and jail cells could very well be bugged.

Sending Communiques

Some activists may wish to disseminate communiques to publicize their actions. Try to keep your communiques simple and random, so that if you are arrested for one action you will not be tied to other actions by virtue of the similarity of your communiques. If you are sending them by mail, make sure you don't lick the stamp, envelope or leave any prints.

Letters can be typed on a public computer or typewriter. Do not use your own computer or typewriter (they can include identifying characteristics that could trace the document back to you)! If you decide to hand-write your communiques, be sure to use block letters, make a photocopy of the letter and destroy the original. Use a photocopier that cannot be traced to you in any way (i.e. one at your home, work, etc.). Copied communiques may be able to be linked to a certain copier by "trash" marks.

It is a good idea to drop the mail off at an out-of-town mailbox, since the postmark will tell the authorities from what city it was mailed. It is recommended that activists do not call in their actions using voice changers or by recording themselves and changing the speeds. Both of these methods can be unscrambled by the police and linked to your real voice.

Animal Liberations: Saving Lives Today

1999

A guide to live liberations.

Liberations are the quintessential direct action. Education and economic sabotage save animals' lives in the long run, but liberating animals from laboratories, factory farms or other places of abuse is the only way to save animals' lives here and now. Liberations are probably the most complex actions and some of the most risky. For both of these reasons, an incredible amount of planning and preparation are needed.

The first step in a liberation is research. You have to know all you can about the target. You have to know how many animals they have, what kind of animals, what they are doing to them and where they are located. Once these things are determined comes the most important part of a liberation: finding homes for the animals. Aside from the actual break-in group, another group of people may be needed for this aspect. NEVER liberate an animal for whom you have not found a good and loving home (unless he/she can successfully be released into the wild).

Liberated animals should be placed with people not associated with your group and hopefully not associated with the movement at all. Once animals are liberated, the police will be looking for them, so they must be placed somewhere that the police will not look.

Before being homed, an animal should be completely checked over by a trusted veterinarian. Again, before planning on how to get animals out of bad situations, be certain you have a good situation to put them in once they have been liberated. Special homes may be needed for some animals, considering you may be liberating animals not normally kept as companion animals or with special conditions inflicted upon them by the abusers. While caring for a dog taken from a laboratory breeder may not require special skill, the average person does not know how to care for a monkey with a hole cut in his or her skull and an electrode attached to his or her brain.

Liberations are often highly complex, requiring a number of people and a huge amount of planning. The people involved should each have an area of responsibility, a specialty. You will need people for the following: finding homes, researching and planning the raid, serving as look-outs, breaking in, carrying liberated animals out of the place of abuse, driving the animals away, as well as another person to coordinate the whole process.

If possible, the look-outs and break-in groups should arrive early so that the carriers and drivers are there for as short a time as possible. Of course, have a way for look-outs to notify everyone else if things go wrong, by audible signal or by walkie-talkies.

Many animals naturally make noise when disturbed or moved, and there's nothing you can do about it. All you can do is get in, get the animals and get out as quickly as possible. You need to have lookouts you can rely on so that you can concentrate on getting the job done and not have to worry about watching their backs. If things go wrong, get everyone together and leave quickly. Most people will be happy just scaring you off, so unless you're being shot at, don't leave anyone behind.

Parking vehicles near the site may be suspicious. It may be best to have the vehicles arrive early and park in nearby large parking lots or on side streets among other cars. Then, they can simply pull up, either at pre-appointed times or when notified (possibly by walkie talkie), get the animals and go. Always have the vehicle with the animals leave first. If the animals get caught, they face death; if you are caught you will only lose your freedom for a short time.

FUR FARM LIBERATIONS

Almost all animals raised on fur farms can be released safely into the wild. Police and fur farmers may disagree, saying they will starve or die in the wild, but wildlife officials confirm that this is a self-serving lie. Of course not all will survive the wild, but not all animals raised in the wild survive, either. Do animals on fur farms stand any better chances in cages facing certain death?

The survival rates make liberating animals from fur farms easier than those from laboratories. Fox, mink, wolf, bobcat, lynx, raccoon and coyote can all be safely released into the wild. The only animal commonly bred for fur who cannot survive the wild is the chinchilla.

Fur farms are also an easier target since they are more open and generally have less security, although with increasing fur farm liberations in the U.S., security measures are quickly on the rise. No huge ecological imbalance results from releasing these animals, even in massive quantities, into the wild. They all disperse quickly, with mink traveling 5 to 10 miles a day and foxes traveling 12. Fur farms are easily spotted: most use long sheds or rows of cages. Fur animals are kept as cold as possible, since this will thicken their coats. Therefore, cages are always open to the outside air, making liberation that much easier.

There are some points of safety for the animals that must be followed in a fur animal liberation. Animals are not old enough to be released until after they have been weaned. Also, they should never be released after late October, since by then winter has set in and they won't have time to learn to hunt since prey species will be more difficult to catch at this time.

The best method for releasing large amounts of animals is to cut holes in fences surrounding the compound, open the cages and let the animals find their own way out. Of course, some will not get out, but when releasing thousands of animals, it may be the only way. The more escape routes you can cut the better chances they will have (during some raids, fences have been pulled down entirely). With any release into the wild, some animals will be recaptured, but getting most or even some of the animals to freedom is still much better than all dying.

Chinchillas are small herbivores native to South America. They are generally not killed until spring. As was said earlier, chinchillas are the only fur-bearing animals not able to be released to the wild, so they should be found good homes with people who know how to care for them. An important thing to know is that they cannot tolerate temperatures over 80 degrees Fahrenheit. Books about their care are available at bookstores and libraries.

Even if a liberation is not possible, fur farms can still be disrupted. From October to December, the "pelting stock"— the animals about to be killed- and the "breeding stock" — those animals left to produce more animals-are the same size. By opening all the cages and releasing them into the compound they will be unable to tell which stock the animals came from. The breeding stock may be kept in just a few cages, so be sure to open them all or else you might miss the breeding stock and would have accomplished nothing.

You can also destroy the breeding cards, index card-sized slips which contain the genetic history (thus the value) of the stock, usually kept on the front of the cages. This action will not save the animals in the fur farm at that time; they will still be killed. In fact, they will probably kill all the animals and purchase new ones for breeding. But, such actions can cause a farm to shut down, thus saving countless animals in the long run. It's a question each individual must decide for him or herself.

Another method is to spray a non-toxic dye on each animal, rendering the pelt worthless. Again, they will still be killed, but possibly it will shut down the farm and save future generations.

Shadow Activist

1996 - 2005

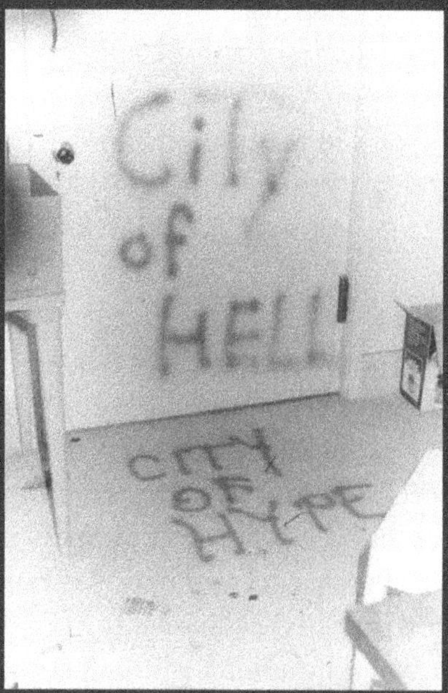

"Shadow Activist" was a long-running column in *No Compromise* magazine, where the anonymous Shadow Activist answered common questions about direct action and the A.L.F.

Compiled here are all 10 years of "Shadow Activist" columns.

How does one join the A.L.F.?

A person joins the A.L.F. simply by doing A.L.F. actions. There is no official membership. One simply becomes a member by taking action in accordance with the A.L.F. Guidelines:

- To liberate animals from places of abuse (i.e. laboratories, factory farms, fur farms, etc.) and place them in good homes where they may live out their natural lives, free from suffering.
- To inflict economic damage to those who profit from the misery and exploitation of animals.
- To reveal the horror and atrocities committed against animals behind locked doors, by performing non-violent direct actions and liberations.
- To take all necessary precautions against harming any animal, both human and non-human.

An A.L.F. activist typically begins an action by her (or his) self, or with a small core group of people who have been proven beyond a shadow of a doubt to be selflessly committed to animal liberation. Typically, they are also people the activist has known for several years. People who cannot keep quiet when the A.L.F. is discussed or who like to speculate about who may be doing actions ought to be avoided. On the rare occasion that A.L.F. members feel it is necessary to approach someone they haven't known for years already, it becomes vital that they spend extensive time alone with the person, discussing issues that are not related to animal rights, looking for indications of honesty, sincerity, and soft-spokenness. Most of all, they ought to look for a sign that the person has a serious understanding and a healthy concern for the legal consequences of illegal direct action, yet is not deterred by such concerns.

Do not ask the ALFSG to join the A.L.F. or any other group. This will only alert law enforcement who may be tapping phone lines or opening mail. The SG only becomes aware of A.L.F. activists' identities if and when they are arrested for committing an A.L.F. action and no longer deny their association.

Begin by yourself or with one or two people you have known for years or who have proven beyond a doubt to be selflessly committed to animal liberation. Avoid working with anyone who cannot keep quiet when the A.L.F. is discussed and blabber on about how they know who A.L.F. members are. Most likely, those who claim to know, know nothing. If you are considering approaching someone you haven't known for years, spend time alone with him or her, discussing issues not related to animal liberation and look for indications of honesty, sincerity, soft-spokenness and, most of all, a sign that he or she is not afraid of such personal consequences of strong-held beliefs such as imprisonment.

When you do discuss doing A.L.F. actions, primarily discuss security. Ask if he or she would consider no longer attending demonstrations or other events where police videotape attendants. Discuss any and all plans for A.L.F. actions only in person and never on the phone or computer or even in your own homes or cars. Go for a walk and avoid the cloak-and-dagger suspicious behavior you see in movies.

Make a pledge to each other, ceremonially if necessary, to prove your willingness to go to prison rather than inform on other A.L.F. members. Such words will reassure you when you or another are sitting in a cell wondering if your fellow A.L.F. cell members are talking.

With careful planning, meticulous reconnaissance and security precautions, you will reduce, to an absolute minimum, your risk of getting caught. Trust your intuition, avoid developing a pattern (like only striking on weekends), show respect to your fellow warriors on your path to empowerment, and remember that whatever you go through in a jail cell is nothing compared to the pain inflicted on animals.

I want to join the Animal Liberation Front. How do I find A.L.F volunteers in my area?

Obviously, the A.L.F. isn't like the P.T.A. or your local Elks Lodge; it's not an entity that one can just sign up for, pay the dues, and receive a monthly newsletter. And besides, if there were A.L.F. volunteers in your area you'd likely be unaware, as savvy nighttime warriors never work in their own backyard.

If you've contacted any of the groups listed in "In the Trenches" you most likely never received a reply... and for good reason. For everyone's security, there's no entity that can connect you with underground activists, and grassroots groups do NOT want to know who is looking and wanting to engage in illegal activity. A.L.F. volunteers have taken it upon themselves to get active and many began with nothing more than a desire, a can of spray paint and a couple of hefty rocks.

As one A.L.F. volunteer stated: Would anyone who put hundreds of hours into planning a covert, illegal direct action that could land them in prison for years risk asking a basic stranger for help simply because s/he was a vegetarian or belonged to the local animal rights group?! NO! (At least not if s/he wanted to stay out of jail)... Come up with your own plan! Really, it's not as hard as you think.

If the A.L.F.'s cause is so just, why don't they accept responsibility for their actions by turning themselves in and doing the jail time?

A.L.F. activists are not interested in self-aggrandizement or martyrdom — they are interested in being effective. Unlike many other direct action activists, the A.L.F. does not engage in symbolic actions designed to increase public awareness, but calculated attacks of sabotage meant to cripple, disrupt and eventually eradicate industries of exploitation. The A.L.F. does not disagree with the symbolic direct action activists, but they do recognize that different tactics are needed for different movements and in order for the A.L.F. to carry on their campaigns of compassion, they must remain free.

Furthermore, A.L.F. activists know they risk their freedom, and possibly their lives, on every mission they take — yet they accept those risks and are prepared to make those sacrifices if it will help save innocent animals from the hands of their tormentors.

If an A.L.F. cell is doing an action, and one of the members is caught by a fur farmer or police officer, what should the other cell members do?

One of the most important discussions to have with your A.L.F. cell, before an action, is what to do if caught. You should NEVER enter into illegal activity with anyone who has not ensured other cell members that they will support and take care of them should they be caught. No one can ever guarantee that you won't get caught and you should refrain from ever telling fellow activists that there is "no chance" of being apprehended. Such statements build a dangerous sense of false security, which almost always leads to getting caught.

Besides the promise of legal and moral support once caught, cell members should decide before doing an action, how to handle a confrontation with law enforcement or security forces. Cell members should assume these people will be armed and most likely have the law on their side, should they use violent force against you. Overpowering your confronter is usually impossible since most A.L.F. activists tend to be skinny vegans who are no challenge to Jim-Bob the 220 pound fur farmer. Even if versed in martial arts, anytime you initiate physical confrontation, the percentage risk of injury skyrockets. I've heard of some A.L.F. cells carrying pepper sprays and stun guns more for self-defense then offense of course.

In the 1940's the French Resistance to Nazi occupation was affectionately labeled by the Germans as "Noah's Ark" since captured resistance fighters could only identify each other through animal code names, even when tortured. They operated on a need-to-know basis, as should the A.L.F. Many times a French resistance fighter would be traveling to an undercover safe house in Nazi occupied territory only to see their fellow operatives being dragged away. At these times, the resistance fighters were taught not even to blink an eye but to keep walking as nothing could be gained in a fruitless effort to try and rescue them, except of course for another fighter to go down.

Strategically, it should be agreed that should one member be captured, the others will not risk their own capture to secure the release of the hostage. It's one thing if a member sprains an ankle and needs assistance to retreat, but if a cell member is being physically held or at gun-point, then damage control is needed to guarantee that other cell members get away.

Of course, here is where emotional thinking often overrides logical thought. When you witness someone you love in distress it is hard, if not impossible, and commendable to not want to help them. Here is where you must think of which is most important: going to prison with your comrades or proving your love and solidarity for them by continuing animal liberation actions in their honor.

Stay in good physical shape, carefully discuss a contingency plan should the unexpected take place, avoid being separated from your fellow warriors on an action and remember that the capture of a comrade isn't only a loss for you, but a loss for the animals.

Is using a list of "targets" sent to me from an above-ground group that I suspect is high on the FBI watch-list a dangerous thing to work from? Or am I just being paranoid?

Considering the FBI does monitor mail, it is probably best to not work from that list. Numerous other sources exist for generating targets that would be much safer. The phone book is always an excellent source of potential targets, as are the abuse industries' publications and journals or other publications like *The Final Nail* which are widely distributed.

Never confuse taking precautions and playing it safe with paranoia. It is better to be vigilant rather than take short-cuts that might compromise your freedom. Paranoia is only a problem if it scares you into inactivity—so just play it safe and stay active.

When activists say we are "militant," I envision war, fighting and bloodshed. But we are a non-violent movement, so what exactly does "militant" mean when applied to us?

I'll defer to Merriam-Webster (Dictionary) to answer this one. According to them, militant means "engaged in warfare or combat" which would explain why you associate violent images to the word. However, the second definition—and more appropriate one for us—is "aggressively active (as in a cause)." That's exactly what activists mean by calling themselves militant—they will not stand idle while atrocities against the animals and earth continue!

Should I do A.L.F. actions close to home?

Underground activists typically recognize the importance of not operating in areas where they may become a suspect simply because they are known activists. Engaging in actions outside of one's own state is often preferable. The first suspects in A.L.F. activity are always local animal rights activists with arrest records or connections to the militant animal liberation movement.

If an A.L.F. member lives in the city, s/he is most likely going to operate in a different city or out in the country. And s/he is certainly not going to visit other above-ground activists in the area s/he is operating in. Neither is s/he going to grab a bite to eat at the local vegetarian restaurant (no matter how good the food is)!

Avoid operating in any areas where you will already be a suspect simply because you are a known animal activist. Cross county lines or state lines, preferably. The first suspects in A.L.F. activity are always local animal rights activists with arrest records. If you live in the city, operate in another city or in the country. Do not visit people in your target area the same night you plan to strike there. Gas up well away from your target area and inspect your vehicle for broken lights or expired registration tags and remove any identifying stickers or decals. Although, D.A.R.E. stickers or "Support Your Local Sheriff" decals can't hurt. Also avoid the hours when bars or nightclubs are letting out as police will be looking for drunk drivers. If you must operate close to home, prepare an unsinkable alibi because, more than likely, you will be questioned if you are a known activist.

Is it true that criminal forensics investigators can identify you simply by finding a strand of hair, drop of blood or saliva?

Just because you got away from your last action doesn't mean they're not out to get you. Yes, the FBI and ATF can identify you through DNA testing-that is, if they can obtain a DNA sample through a subpoena or court order. Let's say you throw bricks through your local fur shop's window and paint slogans on its walls. On your way home, you throw your ski-mask out the window as you drive to drop off a press release to the local media. If you've cut yourself on glass at the store and dripped one drop of blood, you will have left enough DNA evidence for the FBI and ATF to identify you. If your ski-mask is found, the saliva or hair on it is even more evidence. If you licked the envelope in which you dropped off the press release or the stamp you mailed it with, then you had better get a lawyer. In an investigation with known suspects (possibly any or all local animal rights activists), police will use comparative studies to try to identify the culprit. From 1991 to 1993, activists were subpoenaed for hair, blood, saliva, fingerprint, and handwriting samples. So try not to slobber, bleed, or brush your hair when out on an action.

I've been experimenting with different types of paint bombs on billboards in my area, but I have yet to discover the perfect projectile. Christmas bulbs are fragile and hard to find out of season, bell peppers leak, and bottles are too hard to break. Can you help me?

Try light bulbs. Not only are they lightweight and inexpensive, but you can even recycle your old bulbs this way. Here's how you do it. First, take your burnt-out bulb and with a fine-toothed hacksaw, cut the aluminum base about 3/4 of an inch from the end, but leave it slightly connected. Next, bend open the cap at a 90 degree angle. Then, with a screwdriver, gently tap into the bulb to break off the filament from the body of the bulb. Be careful not to let the screwdriver fall through and break the bulb! Now empty out any loose fragments and pour in some oil-based red paint with a little paint thinner to make it nice and runny. Wipe off any excess paint and/or thinner from the rim of the bulb and fold back the cap. While holding the bulb end up, liberally affix duct tape around the cap until you are confident the bulb won't leak. Despite this, you should avoid carrying the bulb cap-side down. A cardboard six pack holder works for transport. So save those burnt-out bulbs and recycle!

Why do laboratory liberations?

Laboratory liberations are essential in the war against vivisection.

Education and economic sabotage save animals' lives in the long run, but liberating animals from laboratories or other places of abuse is the only way to save animals' lives now. Laboratory liberations are among the most complex and risky actions an activist may undertake. For these reasons, planning and preparation are the most important steps in this type of action.

How do you select a laboratory target?

There are a number of different criteria that a cell may use in selecting one target over another for a liberation or other action. The type of experiments going on, known security weaknesses, or homes arranged for a certain type of animal are all criteria that may influence an activist's decision. Because local law enforcement will always look into the local activist networks first when investigating a liberation it is a good idea to pick labs that are not in the same area where you live (especially if you're known in the community as an animal rights activist), or even in the same state or province.

How do you find out what kind of experiments (and on what species of animals) are going on inside the lab?

Research avenues are going to be different depending on what type of institution you are targeting. Some general rules for information searches do apply, though you will have to do some of your own research that is specific to your area and target.

Vivisectors themselves publish amazing amounts of information. Some places that you might go to find some of their information include: university libraries, published research sources such as scientific and medical journals, the world wide web, CRISP abstracts, annual reports, USDA inspection reports, Medline, APHIS databases, ICAR databases and media reports.

Another avenue for finding out information on government institutions, including universities, is through Freedom of Information requests. Legislation on the right to access information varies from state to state and province to province so you will have to find out what information you have the "right" to in your area. An important note: if you are going to use this information to plan a liberation, do not place the request in your own name or to your own address. Records of information requests are kept, and could be used to trace you to the action. Also be advised that F.O.I.A. requests can take several months to be processed.

What kind of preparation (reconnaissance) do you need to do before the action?

Because laboratory liberations are high-risk actions, the more preparation, the better.

After selecting your target, you must become as familiar with it as possible. Watch your target for many nights and days over a long period of time so that you can get a good idea of security on site: patrols and police response, staff and student activity, shift changes, other activity in the area, surrounding neighbors, and other factors. Keeping extensive written information of all of the above will help in the planning of the action.

It is preferable to have maps of the entire area, including road, topographical and aerial if possible. Maps can be obtained in university and city libraries. In addition, blueprints of the targeted building can sometimes be obtained in city or university libraries. Over the period that you do reconnaissance on the site, you should also draw your own maps including any features that you think are significant to your action including escape routes.

When drawing up a detailed action plan, leave nothing to chance. Figure out every step in the action and be certain that everyone in the cell is familiar and comfortable with the plan beforehand.

At least once before the action, your cell should go through a dry run that approximates the conditions you will face as closely as possible. This means that you should try to do the "rehearsal" on the same day of the week, at the same time that your action is planned for. This may include going right into the lab to copy documents, check types and number of animals, and to look for other features that may help or hinder the liberation.

Obviously, you should always have a contingency plan in place in case something goes wrong. It should be clear to everyone what the plan of action will be should you come into contact with security officers, police, students or staff on the scene. Know which way you will escape, if you will act as a group or alone, and where you will meet afterwards.

How do you get into a lab?

Obviously, there are many ways to enter a building, and which method you choose will depend upon the security of the building that you have targeted. Forcing doors, cutting through doors, picking and drilling locks, forcing or breaking windows, and accessing ventilation systems are all means by which you may enter the building. Roofs, and interior or exterior walls may also be cut or drilled through for entry.

What arrangements need to be made for the care of animals following the raid (short term and long term - vet care, safehouses, homes, and transportation)?

The most important part of a liberation is finding loving homes for the animals. Aside from the actual entry group, another set of people may be required for this task. NEVER liberate an animal that you have not found a good home for. Liberated animals should be placed in homes of people not associated with your group, and possibly not even associated with the movement at all. Once animals are taken, police will be looking for them, so they have to be placed somewhere police will not look, preferably well away from the area where the laboratory is located.

After being liberated, an animal should be completely checked over by a trusted veterinarian or other experienced animal caregiver. Special homes may be needed for some animals considering you may be liberating animals not normally kept as pets, or with special conditions inflicted upon them by the abusers. The majority of large lab animals are tattooed, may have implants, have organs or other body parts removed, or may be very ill and/or contagious.

As was said, liberations are often highly complex, requiring a number of people and a huge amount of planning. You will need people responsible for finding homes for animals, researching and planning the raid, lookouts, breaking in, carriers - people to get the animals out, and drivers, as well as someone to coordinate the whole thing.

How can one ensure they do maximum damage when destroying equipment?

Maximum damage to equipment and laboratory facilities can be done by a variety of means including use of paint, brute force, acid, water and/or fire. Your choice of method will depend on the facility itself, how much noise you will be able to make without being heard, whether there are animals being left behind, whether other humans in the building could be put at risk, and your own judgment of the situation.

Slogans may be spray painted on walls and other surfaces. Buckets of paint can be emptied anywhere inside the lab.

Brute force may include damage done using just the physical body as well as tools such as bolt cutters, hammers, crowbars, drills and other implements of destruction. Not all equipment is of high value - in order to choose your targets for maximum financial loss, familiarize yourself with equipment costs through vivisection industry magazines like Lab Animal and laboratory supply company catalogs.

Lots of easy damage can be done using water and water sources in the building. Running water while stopping up sinks, toilets and other drainage areas is a quick way to do extensive water damage to a building. In larger buildings, it is best to do this on the top floor so that damage is done to all floors below.

A lot of financial damage can be done quickly to equipment and paper files with the use of strong acid. Any strength of sulphuric acid will work (battery acid is weak sulphuric acid), muriatic acid will also work in a pinch.

Fire can also be an effective tool in destroying facilities. Your choice to use this tactic will depend on many things including the presence of animal and human life in the building, adjoining facilities that may be put at risk, environmental danger due to fire, and the comfort level of all cell members in setting the fire.

What kind of security measures need to be taken with regards to slogans and video, etc.?

Obviously, you don't want to "personalize" your action by leaving behind clues that could help investigators. When planning what to wear to an action, make sure that your clothes can be disposed of (including your shoes), and that hair and hands are covered throughout the action. You do not want to leave fingerprints or DNA in the form of hair strands or other organic matter at the scene of the liberation. When painting slogans, make sure that they are done in straight, block letters and that paint purchases cannot be traced back to you.

Make sure that as much of your body as possible is covered, especially the face and hand area in case of video surveillance. Wear a balaclava and gloves and make sure that all distinguishing marks such as tattoos are not exposed in any way. Be aware that video footage may reveal height, weight, sex and body shape.

What are some of the types of security concerns new A.L.F. activists need to think about?

First and foremost, any and all plans for A.L.F. actions are made in-person. They are never discussed over the phone, the computer, in one's own house, or in the homes of other activists. Instead, A.L.F. members take a walk when they want to discuss anything sketchy, and they are careful to avoid cloak-and-dagger suspicious behavior like what you'd see in the movies.

With careful planning, meticulous reconnaissance and security precautions, A.L.F. activists can reduce their risk of getting caught to an absolute minimum. The experienced activist recognizes the importance of trusting his own intuitive sense of danger, avoiding patterns (like only striking on weekends), showing respect to fellow warriors, and remembering that whatever activists go through in a jail cell is nothing compared to the pain inflicted on the animals.

First, I want to say I understand the importance of activist security. I never try to guess or gossip about who I think might be behind all of our local ALF actions, as rumors and innuendo is all it takes to convene a grand jury, and get someone, even an innocent person, in trouble. And, if I was an active ALF member, I certainly would not tell anyone about the hits I've been involved in, as that would put both my safety and the safety of the person I told at risk. Even if I was trying to start up a new ALF cell with people who I had known for a long time and trusted with my life, I would not tell them about my previous actions for the simple fact that they don't need to know. In these cases, it is always better to be safe than sorry. And, people who don't know anything can't talk now, can they?

However, sometimes people will start telling me about what they've done.

I know they shouldn't be saying these things, but what do I do? Sometimes they even say these things over the phone, email or other channels that could easily be monitored by police. How should I respond to "loose lips"?

This is a tricky situation, but not impossible to handle. As soon as you know that someone is going to be saying something they should not, interrupt them! If you are too shocked to say anything meaningful to interrupt them with eloquence and wit, then just belt out some noise to stop them and once you are more collected, explain activist security concerns to them.

An activist's involvement with the ALF should not be known to anyone except the other cell members that he or she works with. If other people are informed of their actions, those people become an "accessory after the fact," thereby putting their safety at risk. Many times if an ALF activist tells a "trusted friend" who tells their "trusted friend" who tells their "trusted friends," soon that activist's secret is no longer a secret, and your safety is highly compromised. It's the police and FBI's job to harass and intimidate information out of people... and their decades of experience have made them good at it. The less people who know who is doing what, when, the better. Activists should not have to find out which of their friends they can and cannot trust from behind bars... but they often do, unfortunately.

Even well-meaning friends can put them at risk. If they tell other friends, if they talk about it on the phone or email, channels which might be monitored by police, or if your friend accidentally tells an industry plant posing as an activist.

As we become more and more effective, we can expect more and more monitoring by the FBI, ATF and police. They often employ agents to gather information or just keep us paranoid. If rumors are floating around, they will be sure to pick that information up and get it back to headquarters. That is why activists should practice self-censorship and learn that they are the only person who they can trust 100%.

If you cannot stop that person before they finish telling you what they have done, say "Look, I know you haven't done those things, because if you had, you wouldn't tell me about it as that puts both your safety, and mine, at risk. Let's talk about activist security a little..." If you acknowledge the fact that they've been involved in an action, this makes you an accessory after the fact. By denying their action, you have negated that. By educating them about activist security, you can hopefully prevent this activist from telling the wrong people sometime.

Now, everyone makes mistakes. And, there may be some reason that people may need to know more than they should, but if you have repeatedly chastised a person for making these same mistakes over and over again, and they continue to commit these errors, you might start to get concerned that you have an informer or agent in your midst. They often pretend to be an ALF activist, or suggest "joining" the ALF in an attempt to find out who the ALF members are in the local area.

This is another reason why it is important to not let these errors go by without mentioning them. Activists who don't seem to learn after repeatedly explaining to them the importance of activist security, should have their actions scrutinized more closely. Frankly, they are either an informer—or an activist who for whatever reason, can't be quiet. In either case, they are very, very dangerous, and you and your friends should stay far away from them.

We, as activists, must be eternally vigilant in championing movement security because new activists are always coming into the movement unaware of the necessary security precautions. They need to be educated, and it is up to knowledgeable activists to do that.

How do you find out where fur farms are located?

The most valuable resource for locating fur farms is a booklet titled *The Final Nail.* It is a comprehensive list of known mink, fox and lynx farms, including addresses.

There is a huge gap between the number of farms listed in *The Final Nail* and the actual number of farms known to exist. This means the location of a large number of farms remains unknown. This is where detective work comes in. Often fur farmers will take out "help wanted" ads in local newspapers. Check the paper in rural areas where other fur farms are known to exist. An address can easily be obtained from a phone number using the internet.

College libraries often have extensive map collections, including agricultural survey maps pinpointing the locations of various types of "agriculture," including mink. Ask a university librarian. Search maps for "Mink Rd."; "Fur Farm Road"; or similar street names. These roads either host operating fur farms or did at one time.

Another method is to obtain the delivery lists of a region's fur feed co-op. Delivery lists are likely to be found in delivery trucks parked outside, and if not, inside the co-op's offices. Getting into the trucks and offices is up to you. Addresses of fur feed co-ops are in *The Final Nail.*

Libraries carry books listing all known publications, magazines, industry journals, etc. by title and subject. Obtain the addresses of industry publications such as *Fur Rancher* and write for a free sample copy or subscription. Farm addresses can be found in these magazines. CD ROMS such as "American Business Disc" contain lists of millions of businesses under hundreds of categories. Many farms not listed in *The Final Nail* can be found here. Also, search under "fur" in phone books of rural areas of states where fur farms are common.

(Editor's note: Replace "Terraserver" with "Google satellite images.") An often-overlooked method of finding fur farms is Terraserver. Terraserver catalogs thousands of satellite images of nearly every region in the country. You can visually search any town for which satellite images are available by zooming in and scanning closely for the rows of sheds characteristic to fur farms. Images are often indistinct, but when searching regions with high concentrations of fur farms, you can often pinpoint undiscovered farms. Remember, fur farms are often clustered together. This is also effective for finding farms in *The Final Nail* for which a town is known but only a "rural route" address is given.

What kind of reconnaissance needs to be done before hitting a fur farm?

One visit previous to the raid is usually sufficient. Look for favorable features (see below) and take note of every detail.

Remember, fur farms rarely (if ever) have overnight security or patrols, and as such extensive recon is usually not necessary.

What favorable features should one look for in choosing a target?

The most important feature to look for in choosing a fur farm target is the proximity of the farmer's house to the sheds. Once several hundred mink are released, they become extremely noisy. Choose a target in which the farmer's house is a safe distance away from the sheds if you are going to release mink.

Look closely for alarms as described below.

An easily-cut fence can make the difference between saving several hundred mink or several thousand. Cutting fences can take 15 minutes or several hours depending on the design. Determine in advance what is needed to remove the fence, or portions of it. Cutting the fence where it is attached to the fenceposts is the best method for removing large sections of fence quickly.

The best farms (other than those that have no fence at all) are those with a thin single layer wire fence fastened to fenceposts with staples or wire. By clipping around the staple with wire cutters or snipping the wire holding the fence down one can pull down large portions of fence without cutting the entire length of it. Another feature to look for is a safe, discreet place to park. Watch your tire tracks on site.

How does one gain access to a fur farm?

Simply cutting away the fence and bypassing possible alarms. The cages themselves can be opened a number of ways. Designs vary and how the cages of a particular farm open must be determined on site. Most have only a simple latch. Others require the nesting box to be lifted and removed. Some even have a wire ring on each cage, which must be snipped individually. Bring wire cutters.

When is the best time of year to release mink from their concentration camps?

Mink are releasable between May and December (though they are often killed in November so arrive before then if at all possible). Foxes are releasable between June and December and lynx between April and pelting time which varies.

Should mink be released even when you know some will be killed by cars or other animals, since they're all going to be killed anyhow?

All mink on fur farms will eventually be slaughtered, most in their first year of life. When mink are released from fur farms, even near roads, they at least have a fighting chance. But you can be sure the media will exploit the accidental deaths of any released mink in order to discredit the liberationists. It becomes undeniably part of the responsibility of the liberators to ensure that any released mink have the best chance of survival possible, unless your goal is simply to deny the fur farmer the money he'd make on the released mink's pelt.

Is there any chance that captive-bred mink will transmit disease to wild mink?

This is possible if mink are infected, but modern mink farmers are quick to isolate suspected disease carriers and are most likely to label them as such.

You should never release mink that are obviously separated from the majority of the herd. Outbreaks of disease on fur farms are known to wipe out an entire herd so it's vital for fur farmers to identify disease threats immediately and eliminate them.

Are mink dangerous to handle?

Yes. Mink are ferocious predators who will bite. Unfortunately, the only way to truly protect yourself if handling mink is necessary is with thick leather welding gloves purchased at a thrift store. Often heavy gloves are lying around the farm if you take the time to look.

How can one do maximum damage to the fur farm in addition to saving individual lives?

The destruction of breeding records is the single most damaging thing you can do to a farm. Breeding records are crucial for a farmer to breed the next year's stock and continue operation after pelting out every fall/winter. Most often breeder cards can be found clipped above the cages of the breeding stock. These should be torn up and scattered first thing, or kept and discarded off site after the raid.

Each fur farm has its prize breeder mink so it's always best to release or preferably remove those mink from the fur farm first. Breeders can be worth thousands of dollars and often are the product of years of selective breeding . Releasing the breeders mixes up the stock to where the farmer cannot determine which is which and must build another pelting stock from scratch. A farm in Tomahawk, WI visited by activists in October 1997 suffered a $200,000 loss despite having only 800 mink released. The mink were breeding stock.

When is it appropriate to use arson on a fur farm raid?

Only when it is guaranteed that no animal or human stands even the remotest chance of being injured. Never when wind is blowing towards non-target buildings or grass or other material is near that might carry the fire. Empty mink barns after pelting season in late Fall are good targets as are the pelting sheds and feed barns.

Large mink farms often dry their own pelts in large rooms with extractor fans to keep the humidity low. These areas make excellent targets when you know they are filled with pelts.

What kinds of security measures are likely to be found on fur farms and what can be done to bypass them?

Motion sensor alarms and infrared sensors are not uncommon. These are mostly seen in the high security farms of the Northwest and Utah. Moving more inland, many farms can be found which lack even fences. Video cameras are sometimes used but are of little concern to a masked activist. A farm with guard dogs can be hit by giving the dogs tranquilizers mixed into food. Just ask your vet for some saying you intend to take your large dog on a cross-country trip and want him to sleep most of the way. A barking dog is the most likely threat you will encounter rather than a biting dog.

Activists scouting some fur farms have reported encountering trip wires in the fields leading up to the actual sheds. These invisible wires are not actual alarms but can impede a speedy getaway.

The most common alarms can be identified as small boxes fixed on posts inside the fence near the comers. Most motion sensor and infrared alarms rely on a primitive wiring which can be taken advantage of to render them inoperable in under 30 seconds. If you can gain access to a farm during the daylight hours while the alarms are turned off, a simple manipulation of wires can disable them in such a way that they still appear to be functioning. Detailed "how-to" manuals on bypassing alarms are available from Loompanics and Paladin Press (specifically applicable is *How to Circumvent a Security Alarm in 10 Seconds or Less*).

A common alarm found on fur farms called an "Electronic Eye" emits a beam between two boxes fixed on posts. When the beam is crossed, the alarm is sounded. These are easily bypassed by dropping and rolling under the beam. Not all motion sensitive alarms emit this beam. Some emit an invisible motion sensitive fan-shaped area of coverage. These are more troublesome to avoid and distinguishing between the two can be difficult, but Electronic Eyes are identified as always having two adjacent boxes-one to emit the beam and one to receive it.

Individual sheds can also be alarmed. Cutting into the shed from the side can often circumvent these. Inspect the perimeter of farms closely as gaps in security often exist.

Before attempting any bypassing of alarms, it is important to visit the farm before the raid and do a dry run, entering the farm and retreating to wait for any possible response. Alarms are often silent. It all sounds tricky but keep in mind that alarmed fur farms are, at this point, the exception.

Remember, alarms can be bypassed. Do not be deterred by weak alarm systems, which rely more on visual intimidation than any actual protective features. One farm in Mt. Angel, Oregon has a one hundred thousand dollar alarm system, but this did not deter activists in 1997 from releasing 10,000 mink, the biggest mink raid in history.

Activists must not be deterred by alarms, they must circumvent them.

What equipment is needed to raid a mink farm raid?

Heavy gloves, disposable clothes, wire cutters, small bolt cutters, flashlights with red lenses, and scanner/radios (optional).

Many listings in *The Final Nail* give only a rural route. How can I determine the specific street address for these farms?

Rural routes exist for mailing purposes only and can be difficult to find. *The Final Nail* lists the owner of each farm, and a more specific address can often be found by looking up the farmer's name in the phone book of his town. This can also be done on the internet and phone book CD ROMS.

Phone numbers of farms are also given in *The Final Nail* and this is where a little social engineering can be useful. For example, call the farmer and pose as a phone or electric company representative. Ask about an "overdue bill," and when the farmer expresses confusion, ask him to verify some information, such as his name and, of course, his address. Write it down, apologize for the mix-up and hang up.

Keep in mind that if you call from a payphone, it might register "payphone" on their caller ID (if they have it) and tip off the farmer to be on the lookout for suspicious activity. Also, if the farmer thinks the call is suspicious, you should wait awhile before taking action.

What are the likely consequences should I be caught releasing mink from a fur farm?

If you've crossed state lines, federal criminal statutes can be used against you. Most states now have laws that specifically target A.L.F.-type actions. Also, the federal Animal Enterprise Protection Act is presently being used against Justin Samuel and Peter Young.

Still, as long as fire was not a tactic and you do not have a criminal record, mink releasing shouldn't net you the jail time that more serious actions like arson would. It is always best that you research the punishment for the crime you intend to commit and be prepared to do it.

I've seen video footage of A.L.F volunteers kicking down laboratory doors and read about cells scaling electrified fences; it all seems so physically demanding. How does the A.L.F physically prepare for such actions?

Two key aspects of nearly every successful action are stealth and speed. For both, one must be physically fit, and simply being vegan doesn't quite cut the mustard.

I'd suggest getting into a regular routine that, over time, escalates the degree of physical exertion. You might want to start with bicycle riding or jogging, in addition to push-ups and sit-ups in the morning. Combine cardiovascular exercise, like jogging, with muscle-building exercises, like weight lifting.

Of course, proper planning and stealth will reduce the possibility that one will have to run long distances through a field or sprint away from the police, but every action necessitates physical preparation, and scaling a wall or climbing a fence may not come naturally to everyone. I can remember one occasion where I narrowly escaped a startled fur farmer because I hopped a fence much faster than he could. It's safe to say that I had more experience at it than he did.

Practice makes perfect, and the physical preparation for nighttime activities begins long before the reconnaissance and planning phases of an action. Pick up a copy of *No Compromise* and read through the Diary of Actions to help you keep your "eye on the prize."

I've read about dozens of dogs being rescued in a single raid and hundreds upon hundreds of chickens being whisked away from factory farms... How do they transport so many animals at once, so quickly?

Different actions require different modes of transportation. Sometimes, it's possible to back a truck or van up to the building and just load the animals directly from there without having to travel too much distance. When rescuing a large number of animals it's the repetition—not the weight—of carrying them a great distance that starts to wear me out. The key is utilizing a mode of transportation that will temporarily house the animals safely and keep them properly confined so that one doesn't exert any more energy than necessary rounding up loose dogs or chicks jumping about.

Physical fitness is a particularly important factor when transporting animals over long distances, either through a field or from one end of a building to another. So before undertaking such an action, one had best be intimately familiar with pushups and those morning jogs. In terms of physical requirements, a well-planned action is one part brute force to four parts stamina/ endurance.

For chicks, something as simple as sturdy laundry baskets or large Tupperware bins with air holes cut out of the lid can do the trick. These allow for secure housing and comfortable handling. Use your imagination, but be sure not to pack chickens together too tightly or in a carrier that doesn't keep a solid shape.

For rabbits and puppies, large duffle bags are tried and true. These can get expensive, so one might have to do some bargain shopping for roomy, durable bags that have a secure closure (such as a locking draw string or zipper).

When rescuing rabbits and rambunctious puppies, one should take special care to minimize the stress to the animals. As rabbits and puppies often resist being picked up and shoved into a bag, it may be necessary to first put the bag over the animal's head and then body, and then carefully flip the bag over with her inside.

And remember to keep all tools free of fingerprints and DNA (hair fiber, skin particles, etc.) before and after procurement... This goes for laundry baskets and Tupperware bins as well as duffle bags (particularly nylon bags that may retain a fingerprint).

What's the best way to overcome obstacles like fences, walls, and barbed wire? Is it better to cut through a fence or just climb it?

It depends on the circumstances. Regardless, every single activist should know how to quickly scale a fence and wall. Climbing fences and walls requires a good deal of upper body strength, but true skill is being able to clear a shaky chain link fence with silent expertise. Most people, activists included, run with as much stealth as a herd of buffalo or jump a fence sounding as if a sack of soup cans has just been dropped from a five-story building. Being physically fit allows nighttime warriors to move slowly and deliberately—quietly descending a fence rather than just awkwardly tumbling over it and landing with a thud.

In the reconnaissance phase of an action, it is unwise to cut through a fence, as doing so will likely raise suspicion with anyone who later happens upon the evidence. Being able to silently scale a fence is crucial to conducting effective recon, and practice is necessary.

When dealing with barbed wire, one can simply throw a thick blanket or jacket over the barbs to safely and quickly eliminate the possibility of being cut or snagged.

For practice, find a random chain link fence somewhere isolated, and try climbing with speed (for fast getaways) and eventually with stealth (for recon missions). One might want to find a fence to routinely scale as part of those morning jogs. Or a construction site with a security guard who will give chase will do. This enables one to test one's level of stealth while at the same time feeling the rush of a chase should a security guard take notice.

In terms of cutting through a fence, every fence is different and the design of the cut depends upon the nature of the operation. Generally, with a minimal number of cuts running down the fence, perpendicular to the ground, one should be able to "peel" away a section of the fence. This is an ideal escape route or for taking animals through. To learn how to "peel" a fence, one might want to find a random fence far away from the target or obtain a sample of chain link from a hardware store or construction site and practice with hand-held wire cutters or a small set of boltcutters.

At the target site, a small, discreet opening is likely necessary to avoid detection by a security guard or passerby. A larger opening is more practical when the point of entry is isolated and can be used as an escape route or transfer point for animals during a liberation. In a fur farm raid, one needs to completely remove a substantial portion of the perimeter fence so as to provide multiple openings for the animals to find freedom. After the action, be sure to dispose of all tools. The markings left by boltcutters can be tied to the boltcutters themselves; so obviously, we don't want those lying around the house.

This may sound silly, but what is the best type of clothing to wear for a nighttime action?

Like they say on the E! Channel... Casual is in. And accessorize, accessorize, accessorize.

It all depends on the night's activities. For recon in an urban environment like a fur store or residential neighborhood, it might be best to begin recon in the daylight hours. Consider throwing on some jogging clothes or take a casual stroll with your dog. The key is to blend into your surroundings. If it's dark and rural, avoid any reflective or light-colored clothing. Wear black or camouflage.

Again, the key is to blend into the surroundings! One action at a fur store involved me wearing khakis and a cardigan. Of course, I accessorized with the balaclava when the mood was right.

- Don't wear nylon pants or clothes with zippers—they're noisy.
- Don't wear anything reflective (including shoes).
- Don't wear heavy fabrics, as your adrenaline alone will heat you up pretty fast (unless, of course, you'll be climbing razor wire or the potential of being bitten is high).
- Do wear comfortable, quiet shoes. (Depending on the action, you'll likely need to throw these away.)
- Do wear lightweight, comfortable pants and dark socks.
- Do wear long sleeves and ensure that your body's features will be obscured.
- Do wear a conspicuously-colored/logo t-shirt under your outer clothing in the unfortunate event that you need a quick change of appearance.
- Do pick up a pair of fabric gloves that will provide adequate protec-

tion for the job.

Remember to match form with function. Wear clothes that will keep you anonymous (from cameras or anyone who might catch a glimpse), inconspicuous (don't go creeping down Rodeo Drive decked out in military fatigues and a ski mask) and will increase productivity (lightweight, etc.).

I know how to complete the action. How do I avoid detection after the fact (i.e. DNA evidence, hair, fingerprints, video cameras, tools, etc.)?

You're not being paranoid, and you can never be too safe.

While this response isn't comprehensive, it covers the basics.

- Obtain your tools for the action out of town, at separate locations and pay with cash. Don't keep the receipt. Purchase the tools as far in advance as possible to rule out your image being preserved on video.
- Keep your tools and implements for destruction (rocks, bricks, water jugs, etc.) clean from the beginning. Never handle them with bare hands, as you may be unable or neglect to wipe off all of the prints. Always remember to wipe down your tools thoroughly before the action and don't forget to make sure to use fresh, clean batteries. Wipe things inside and out, even if you don't plan on leaving them behind (you may drop something). ALWAYS wear gloves.
- Always wear clothes that you plan on discarding. Don't leave your clothes lying on the floor at home (they'll pick up hair fibers) and don't brush your hair while wearing them. Make sure they're also free of companion animal hair. Wear clothing that keeps your body's features obscured (i.e.: shoes that are too big, a large sweatshirt that conceals your breasts, a mask and gloves that cover scars or indicating marks).
- Leave excess jewelry, clothing and everything else behind. Carry the absolute minimum.
- Don't lick any envelope or stamp if a communiqué is mailed out.
- Do not handwrite anything. Use an anonymous machine if possible.
- Make sure that you're not carrying any recon info en route to the action (unless absolutely necessary), don't retain anything connecting you to the action after the fact and destroy all evidence (clothing, tools, receipts, photo originals, etc.).
- Make sure that when destroying/ discarding evidence and tools that you are far away from the target and away from any video cameras or prying

eyes.

- If a rental car is used, make sure it's spotless when returned. If your own vehicle has been used for the action (tsk, tsk) make sure it is spotless thrice over. Be aware of hair and dirt fibers getting into upholstery so consider lining the vehicle with plastic or towels (and hope you don't get pulled over).
- Of course, never talk about the action after the fact and remember: No One Talks, Everyone Walks.

And make sure that you leave nothing behind but empty cages and maximum destruction.

How does the A.L.F. manage to get through fences? Barbed wire is one thing but what about razor wire?

The first hurdle to overcome when physically accessing your target is the fence. Fences may serve primarily as a deterrent, but there is no fence that can stop a determined cell.

Generally, you'll find fences at rural targets and not so much at urban or suburban facilities like laboratories, fur retailers, corporate offices and the like. In the urban/suburban environments you're more likely to find walls and iron fences, which are easy enough to climb, just keep in mind the likelihood of cameras once you scale the outer defenses.

You may recall in a previous issue of *No Compromise* (see Issue #23), where I talked about the importance of nighttime warriors being physically fit. Fences, especially the flimsy and loud chain link fence, require a fair amount of upper body and abdominal strength if you are to scale them with any stealth or efficiency. It is the older, less stable chain link fence that is more troublesome to climb, as it doesn't allow for a secure climb and makes quite a bit of noise. In such a case, find the supporting poles and climb the fence using them rather than throwing your weight on a fence that will give underneath you.

Barbed wire is a joke. You're more likely to find it, between waist and chest-high, being used to separate property lines in rural environments than as a security measure. Again, it is the poorly-maintained fence that can give you more trouble. Protect your hands with thick gloves and secure any loose clothing when stepping over, climbing, or squeezing in between such fences. A snagged crotch, tom shirt, or pricked hand leaves forensic evidence—so be aware!

Electrified fences, or "hot wire," are typically used to keep out predators rather than masked liberators—and they're not as scary as they sound. You can generally hear if a line is electrified, or "hot," before you even get to it. Electrified fences generally look like barbed wire fences, except the wire is not twisted with barbs along it. The wires resemble straightened wire coat hangers and typically run into a plastic box (often red and often situated at a fence post). If you can't access the box to open the circuit and kill the line, you can use thick rubber gloves (not dishwashing gloves) to navigate the fence. You should be fine stepping on the fence with rubber-soled shoes, or soles made of any material that, like rubber, don't conduct electricity.

Razor wire is something you've got to be very careful with, as it can easily tear you up. Depending upon the nature of your visit (reconnaissance vs. execution), you should consider removing the risk altogether. If the wire is atop a fence, consider cutting through the fence and avoiding the razor wire completely (which isn't exactly an option for recon operations). If you must scale the fence, slowly cut the razor wire with wire cutters and peel it away from the fence's support pole. This will leave you with a sturdier path to climb.

If physically altering or avoiding the razor wire isn't an option, consider procuring thick, heavy blankets (for forensic considerations, none that you've had on your bed, etc.) and placing them over the wire to serve as a shield as you scale the fence. Once the recon is done and the operation is complete, properly dispose of all blankets, tools, and clothing.

And remember, always leave yourself an out for a quick escape.

Safe navigating,

It would be useful to know how to send digital photos anonymously over the internet. As I understand it, if they are uploaded to a computer and sent with a newly-created email account used only for that purpose, there is still the chance of the photos being traced back to the specific computer that the e-mail account was accessed from (anonymized web browsers do not allow you to access e-mail accounts). And when the computer is identified, inquiring minds may ask the library or internet cafe workers about whom they may have seen, and they also could possibly get prints from the computer itself.

It's true that dummy email accounts can be traced back to their origin, internet cafes often have cameras, employees can have ridiculously good memories, and anonymous remailers are not always reliable—especially for something like photos.

There's no easy answer, but here are some options:

- Use a disposable camera. Make sure it's clean (no fingerprints or forensic evidence) and mail it to an aboveground group. But BEWARE: Disposable cameras don't take high-quality photos, you can't preview/edit the pictures before releasing them to the public (so make sure all identifiers are masked during the raid when the camera is out), they're not vegan, and if the film is intercepted or lost - that's it.
- The use of laser and color printers is very risky (you should never use your home computer or printer for editing, copying, printing, etc.—ever!!!) as laser printers, by default, create identifying numbers in the printed image to help law enforcement catch counterfeiters (and you).
- Similar to using a dummy email account, use a public computer to upload the photos to a website. Some websites offer free webpage hosting and other sites allow visitors to upload their photos for the public to view. Again, BEWARE: This carries the same risks as simply emailing the photos but allows law enforcement or the internet host to remove the images before supporters or the public can download them.
- Make digital copies of the photos and after previewing/editing them, put them on multiple disks and mail them to several aboveground, sympathetic organizations. BEWARE: It is believed that several models of digital cameras and editing software imprint an electronic 'fingerprint' or digital serial number into the image. Don't distribute first generation photos (another reason that high resolution originals are important).
- Using a clean laptop computer with a wireless card, tap into someone else's wireless network and do your work from there. Create a dummy account and send the images and communiqué with the laptop from someone else's non-secure network. Using your imagination, you're sure to find locations with easy access and anonymous web surfing—you don't even have to be in the same building. BEWARE: Law enforcement can still trace the email to its origin, so it is imperative that you do not simply log into your neighbor's network from your home computer. You must use a clean laptop—one that neither you nor anyone you know has used before or will use again—at a location far away from your home. The laptop must be ultimately disposed of, as it can directly link you to the photos, the communiqué and the action

itself.

Ideally, cells should have a clean computer and camera to edit and duplicate photos and video. Remember, the best technology is no technology. Generally, the more basic, the safer it is for you.

If you do use a public computer, keep in mind that emails and internet activity can be traced to the location and terminal, so don't leave any loose ends. Staff and employees are less likely to remember you if the place is busy, so make an effort to blend in. Cameras are less likely to identify you if you look nondescript and if you camouflage any distinguishing features (wear a hat, glasses, long sleeves and loose clothes). Computer terminals are less likely to reveal your identity if you leave without a trace. One way to avoid directly touching the keypad, mouse, or anything else is by wearing gloves (if it's cold outside), typing using pencil erasers or typing with tape over your fingers). Leave no finger or palm prints, keep no receipts and give no personal identifiers.

I keep reading about underground activists getting caught during and after their actions. Why are these people caught and how do more successful activists manage to evade capture?

Staying safe and free is a relatively simple task. It should be noted that most every person ever caught for night-time activities was discovered not through "good old-fashioned" police work," but by a snitch or by plain dumb luck.

Bear that in mind, but first realize that in order to stay safe and off law enforcement's suspect list, it's best to stay off the radar completely. This is not to say that one's career as a night-time warrior is over once observed at a protest or even if arrested, but being completely anonymous has numerous advantages in an age where "sneak and peaks" aren't so uncommon Aboveground activists are the first to be visited, and we appreciate their sacrifices, as law enforcement wastes time and energy harassing them. But there is little value—and much risk—in wearing two hats.

It cannot be overstated that it's through snitches and dumb luck that activists get nabbed... so cut those things out of the equation. One can never eliminate some random cop being in the right place at the right time or some other bad stroke of luck, but when we take all reasonable precautions, do our homework, and operate with deliberate care, that chance is reduced.

When we minimize to the greatest extent the factors listed below, we maximize our probability of staying safe, free and available for another night's work.

Routine

- Law enforcement is always looking for a pattern. Repetition gives the authorities the ability to predict future actions and lie in wait. It also gives them an easier case in proving past actions if a given number of actions all resemble one another in a distinct way.
- Vary the time of night and the night of the week for actions.
- Alternate targets and vary the tools used (timers, wires, bottles/ jugs, transportation, marbles, bolts, rocks, etc.).
- Don't use anything consistently or repeatedly.
- Don't use the same computer, email address, typewriter, notepad, mailbox, etc. when sending communiques.

Identifiers

- This is evidence, from the obvious to obscure. Don't leave finger-prints,
- DNA, tire tracks, or other forensic evidence.
- Cover the head, hands (don't use latex gloves), face and body.
- Wear clothes, including shoes, that are of a different fit and size in order to help obscure gender, height, body shape, and foot size in the event where photographs, video or footprints become available to investigators.
- Avoid unique equipment that is easily traced, like particular electronics and fuel/accelerants, for example.
- Leave no paper trail. Cell phone records, as well as ATM and credit card transactions tell authorities when and where a suspect has been.
- Keep nothing. That goes for anything such as receipts, computer files, notes, photos, video, maps, clothing and tools like bolt cutters and pry bars (they leave markings that are unique to the individual tool).
- Tone down the rhetoric in the communiques. The less you say, the better.
- Grammatical and spelling errors, typos, syntax and euphemisms all give investigators insight into the author's identity. If different claims of responsibility all have similar rhetoric or a similar style of writing, a pattern (evidence!) becomes available to investigators.
- Be anonymous. Besides empty cages and maximum destruction, leave nothing behind and keep nothing.

How do those within the underground stay safe, secure and active, es-

pecially now that the U.S. government considers A.L.F./ E.L.F.- related activity the "number one domestic terrorist threat"?

Essentially, they stay safe and secure the same way as always. With good security come good actions.

Typically, a cell must balance two priorities: security and its objectives. Without strong security, members of a cell are vulnerable to law enforcement, thus compromising the objective of animal/earth liberation. It's a fine balance where one part of the equation cannot overshadow the other, or a cell will inevitably fail. If a cell becomes myopic and lax with security, it will be destroyed from the outside. If a cell is overly cautious or paranoid to the point of inaction, it will fail from the inside.

There is no better time than now to do some "spring cleaning" and reassess one's limitations and priorities. The one thing worse than an absence of action is careless and foolhardy action that hands another victory to our opposition and reinforces the need for "a war on eco-terrorism."

Clean out that closet, toss out those old tools, and scrap those old notes left lying around the house. And activists must take the time to seriously ask themselves if the stakes have become too high. We hope the answer is a resounding "NO," but we must be honest with ourselves or others will suffer.

There are no guarantees in life, but the following tips have withstood the tests of time again and again. Trust us when we say that, typically, a secure and successful cell will:

- Choose friends wisely. Understanding that in the past, it has been these "friends" (lovers, roommates, etc.) who have put activists arrested on A.L.F./ E.L.F. charges behind bars.
- Refuse to work with couples who are romantically involved. Smart activists know that even though it may seem great at the time, it's an almost sure recipe for disaster.
- Never work with drug users or people who drink too much. Aside from unnecessarily risking arrest, such people are often unstable and typically prove a security risk.
- Never combine or mix cells. There's a good reason cells are anonymous, independent and autonomous.
- Trust no one completely, realizing that everyone has a breaking point,

especially under the threat of long prison time.

- Ensure that their members don't get in over their beads. If the line is drawn at arson, successful cell members respect that. They know their limits and how much jail time each member is willing to do. In fact, from the outset, they RESIGN themselves to spending a lot of time in jail.
- Never talk—even among fellow cell members—about past actions... especially arsons. They know that what's done is done, and nothing good can come out of ego-stroking conversation.
- Refrain from the lengthy, wordy and militant communiques.
- Operate on a "need-to-know" basis, with each cell member understanding that not every member needs to know about every detail of every action (i.e.: sources of funds, homes, safehouses, etc.)
- Never leave loose ends. Successful cells will expect that all possible leads will be followed up by law enforcement. The Feds now have the budget and resources to do so, thanks to the hysteria following Sept 11, 2001.
- Always remember: "Loose Lips Sink Ships."

Ultimately, a corrupt system of law enforcement can never stop our movement. Yet how we respond to their repression determines the extent to which they are able to hinder our struggle. Our "domestic terrorist" status only proves how serious the stakes really are. For active cells (and even dormant ones), it's lengthy jail time. For the animals and Earth, it's a death sentence.

FURTHER READING

DirectAction.info
FinalNail.com

At various times, Peter Young has been a fugitive, protester, author, prisoner, felon, spokesperson, entrepreneur, hobo, saboteur, publisher, speaker, and criminal of conscience.

By various federal agencies and trade groups, he has been called a terrorist, eco-terrorist, domestic terrorist, "special interest" terrorist, burglar, accessory after the fact, danger to the community, armed and dangerous, flight risk, escape risk, and unindicted co-conspirator.

Today he runs internet businesses and continues his lifelong, unbroken succession of conspiracies.

He can be contacted at:
peter@peteryoung.me

Also by Peter Young

Liberate

...and at least a dozen other books under fake names.

Photo credit: Melissa Schwartz @ Schwartz Studios